Praise for LAND OF PROMISE

"The book is rich with details. . . . Among the joys of Lind's book are small, little-known stories like the one about the Wright brothers that have clear relevance today." —*New York Times Book Review*

"[An] illuminating new book." —David Brooks, *New York Times*

"It would be difficult to find a book with more fascinating biographical details, statistical vignettes, and obscure but truly engaging, eye-opening details of U.S. economic history." —*Library Journal*

"Any good book of history tells a useful tale about the present as well as the past. And a great book of history looks into the future as well. Michael Lind has written such a book . . . [it] emerges as a fresh and bold challenge to the status quo." —*The American Conservative*

"An excellent book for history enthusiasts." —*Booklist*

"With dozens of short entries on the businessmen, financiers, inventors, and industrialists who helped transform the country and the political leaders and public servants responsible for handling the social consequences. . . . Lind memorably vivifies this constant churn of economic activity and political reconstruction. Timely, big-picture analysis that supplies vital context to our current economic and political movement." —*Kirkus Reviews*

"[It] makes a strong case that government can be, and often has been, a positive and even an essential force for technological change, economic nation-building, and social justice." —*Tulsa World*

ALSO BY MICHAEL LIND

Nonfiction

The Next American Nation

Up from Conservatism

Hamilton's Republic

Vietnam

Made in Texas

What Lincoln Believed

The American Way of Strategy

Fiction and Poetry

The Alamo

Powertown

When You Are Someone Else

Bluebonnet Girl

Parallel Lives: Poems

MICHAEL LIND

LAND OF PROMISE

AN ECONOMIC HISTORY OF THE UNITED STATES

HARPER

NEW YORK • LONDON • TORONTO • SYDNEY

HARPER

Grateful acknowledgment is made for permission to print the following: "The Grand Coulee Dam," words and music by Woody Guthrie; WGP/TRO-© Copyright 1958, 1963, 1976 (copyrights renewed) Woody Guthrie Publications, Inc. & Ludlow Music, Inc., New York, NY, administered by Ludlow Music, Inc. Used by permission.
"I Paid My Income Tax Today," by Irving Berlin. © Copyright 1942 by Henry Morgenthau, Jr., secretary of the treasury. © Copyright renewed and assigned to Irving Berlin. International copyright secured. All rights reserved. Reprinted by permission.

A hardcover edition of this book was published in 2012 by HarperCollins Publishers.

HarperCollins books may be purchased for educational, business, or sales promotional use. For information please write: Special Markets Department, Harper-Collins Publishers, 10 East 53rd Street, New York, NY 10022.

First Harper paperback published 2013.

Designed by Michael Correy

The Library of Congress has catalogued the hardcover edition as follows:
Lind, Michael, 1962–
Land of promise : an economic history of the United States / by Michael Lind.
p. cm.
ISBN 978-0-06-183480-6 (hardback) 1. United States—Economic conditions. I. Title.
HC103.L438 2012
330.973—dc23
2011047794

ISBN 978-0-06-183481-3 (pbk.)

13 14 15 16 17 OV/RRD 10 9 8 7 6 5 4 3 2 1

CONTENTS

COVER ART:
Achelous and Hercules, 1947 (detail) by Thomas Hart Benton.
Tempera and oil on canvas mounted on plywood; 67 ⁷/₈ x 264 ¹/₈ in. (159.6 x 671.0 cm)
Photograph courtesy of Smithsonian American Art Museum,
Washington, DC/Art Resource, NY
Art © Benton Testamentary Trusts/UMB Bank Trustee/Licensed by VAGA,
New York, NY

A LAND OF PROMISE

My first wish is to see this plague to mankind [war] banished from off the earth, and the sons and daughters of this world employed in more pleasing and innocent amusements, than in preparing implements and exercising them for the destruction of mankind. Rather than quarrel about territory, let the poor, the needy, and oppressed of the earth, and those who want land, resort to the fertile plains of our western coun-try, the second land of promise, *and there dwell in peace, fulfilling the first and great commandment.*

—George Washington, 1785[1]

From the beginning Americans have been anticipating and projecting a better future. From the beginning the Land of Democracy has been figured as the Land of Promise.

—Herbert Croly, 1909[2]

At the Great Falls of the Passaic River in New Jersey, two dozen miles from New York City, a torrent rushes over the rocks and plunges with a thunderous roar to the river seventy-seven feet below. Thirteen thousand years ago during the last Ice Age, the Passaic River followed a different course. When the glacier that had covered much of North America melted, it deposited a moraine of boulders that formed a dam, blocking the river's course. Diverted along the Watchung Moun-tains of New Jersey, the river gouged a new course, bursting through lay-ers of two-hundred-million-year-old basalt to create the largest waterfall in North America south of Niagara Falls.

It was here, on July 10, 1778, during the American War of Independence, that General George Washington of the Continental Army chose to rest and dine. Relaxing with him that day were the marquis de Lafayette, the aristocratic young French volunteer who would return home to fight for liberal constitutionalism in the French Revolution, Colonel William McHenry, later to be secretary of war of the United States, and Washington's young aide-de-camp, Alexander Hamilton.[3] The contents of the picnic are recorded by history—ham, tongue, and biscuits—but no record remains of the conversation.

It is certain, however, that Hamilton was impressed by the natural power of the falls. As the first Treasury secretary of the United States during the administration of President George Washington, Hamilton chose the Great Falls of the Passaic as the site for the Society for Establishing Useful Manufactures (SUM), an industrial corporation chartered in 1791 by the New Jersey legislature and Governor William Paterson, after whom the new factory town on the company's land would be named.[4] The creation of the SUM followed the Report on Manufactures delivered to Congress in 1791, in which Hamilton called for a variety of federal policies to promote industry in the young United States.

Hamilton's grandiose plans for the "National Manufactory" were not realized. But the SUM survived until 1945, when it sold its assets to the city of Paterson, by leasing its land to a number of increasingly sophisticated manufacturing concerns.[5] To create a system of raceways diverting water from the river through mills, the society hired the French engineer and urban planner Pierre L'Enfant, who later planned the city of Washington, DC, only to replace him with Peter Colt, who used a simpler plan.[6]

With the water-power infrastructure in place, Paterson became a flourishing center of industrial production. The township was soon the site of a cotton mill (1794), a candlewick mill (1800), and a paper mill (1804).[7] As the new railroads spread across the continent, Paterson became a center of steam-powered locomotive production, leading the industry by the 1850s.[8]

Hamilton, like Washington, was a champion of American manufacturing in part because of the difficulty experienced by the Continental Army during the American Revolution in obtaining adequate supplies. The tradition of US military support for the development of new technologies, including radio, atomic power, and computers, shaped the growth of Paterson from its earliest days. A deputy director of SUM, John Colt, perfected a nonmildewing cotton cloth that the navy used for the sails of all its ships in order to free itself from foreign suppliers.[9] When Samuel Colt, a relative of Peter and John Colt, invented the revolver, he opened his company in Paterson and found indispensable customers in the Texas Rangers and the US Army, whose procurement orders helped bankroll the development of the new technology. In the 1870s, an Irish American inventor in Paterson, John Philip Holland, experimented with submarine technology.[10] In 1890, the US Navy named its first commissioned submarine the USS *Holland* in his honor.[11]

By the end of the nineteenth century, when the town was the source of almost half of the silk in the United States, Paterson was known as "Silk City." A strike by Paterson silk workers in 1913 attracted worldwide attention and the support of bohemian intellectuals like the journalist John Reed and Mabel Dodge Luhan, who sponsored an avant-garde pageant at Madison Square Garden to publicize the strike.[12] The pageant was a success but the workers were crushed and Paterson and other northern textile centers lost out to competitors in the American South.

But once again, Paterson reinvented itself by taking advantage of technological innovation. Two of the transformative technologies of what historians call the second industrial revolution were electricity and aviation. In the 1900s, the SUM enlisted Thomas Edison and his company to design one of the world's first hydroelectric power plants.[13] The mills switched from old-fashioned waterpower to electricity from the plant, which opened in 1914 and still generates energy for Paterson today.

Soon the former Silk City became Aviation City, hosting the Wright Aeronautical Corporation, which was established by the inventors of the airplane, Orville and Wilbur Wright. Wright Aeronautical manufactured the custom-made engine that Charles Lindbergh used in his epochal solo flight across the Atlantic in 1927. The successor to Wright Aeronautical, the Curtiss-Wright Corporation, went on to play a major role in aircraft production during World War II, contributing to the Allied victory against the Axis powers in Europe and Asia.[14]

In the second half of the twentieth century, Paterson declined because of competition first from the low-wage American South and then from the state-sponsored industries of Asia and Europe. Symbolizing the rising importance of real estate and financial interests in the US economy, realtors sought to destroy much of the old industrial neighborhoods, which were plagued by dereliction and crime. The federal government, however, turned the Great Falls and their environs into a national park, reflecting another trend in deindustrializing America: nostalgic historic preservation. It remained to be seen whether the alternatives proposed for the once-great manufacturing city of Paterson, New Jersey—speculator-built condos and apartments or relic-filled museums of a lost industrial past?—represented local decline or a prophetic vision of a future American economy that had completely ceded high-value-added manufacturing to its military and economic rivals.

For generations, Paterson was what Detroit and Silicon Valley would be later: a dynamic center of enterprise and innovation that brought together investors, inventors, engineers, merchants, and a large and competent workforce. Hamilton's vision of an industrial city, after initial failures and delays, ultimately was realized. So was his vision of an industrial America. The opposition of the planter oligarchy of the South, which culminated in the Civil War, delayed but did not prevent the emergence of the United States as the greatest economic power of the world by the 1870s. Despite competition from Europe and East Asia, including newly industrializing China, the United States maintained its economic primacy into the early twenty-first century, with the third largest population in the world, an economy accounting for a quarter of global gross domestic product (GDP), and the privilege of having the dollar serve as the global reserve currency. In a little more than two centuries, a nation of four million people, mostly farmers and slaves, inhabiting a miscellany of former British colonies along the Atlantic rim of North America had grown into an economic and military colossus with a continental territory inhabited by a population that was predicted to grow to as much as half a billion by 2050.

INDUSTRIAL REVOLUTIONS AND AMERICAN REPUBLICS

Beginning with the Austrian American economist Joseph Schumpeter in the 1920s and 1930s, many students of economic history have argued that technological innovation comes in bursts of change, followed by long periods in which the implications of the latest innovations are worked out. Some economic historians have distinguished as many as five major waves of technological change since the industrial era began. Many identify three, based on radically new "general purpose technologies": the first industrial revolution of the late 1700s, based on the steam engine; the second industrial revolution of the late nineteenth century, based on electricity, automobiles, and science-based chemical industries; and the third industrial revolution of the mid- and late twentieth century, based on the computer.[15]

Students of American political history have argued that, despite the formal continuity of its political institutions, the United States has gone through two or three regimes or informal "republics." In earlier works, I have made the case for three American republics, each originating in a prolonged crisis—the American Revolution and its aftermath, the Civil War and Reconstruction, and the Great Depression and World War II.[16] It remains to be seen whether the global economic crisis that began in 2008 will mark the end of the Third American Republic and the gradual construction of a fourth republic by the 2020s or 2030s.

What is the connection, if any, between successive industrial revolutions and successive American republics? As many scholars have observed, there tends to be a time lag of a generation or two between the invention of a general-purpose technology and its widespread adoption in ways that revolutionize the economy and society. For example, the steam engine was developed in Britain roughly at the time of the American War of Independence of 1775 to 1783, but it was only in the 1830s that many American industries began using steam power and railroads and steamboats began reshaping society. Electricity, telephony, and the internal combustion engine were developed in the 1860s and 1870s, but these technologies of the second industrial revolution began to spread widely only in the early twentieth century and achieved their full potential only after 1945. Similarly, the groundwork for the information revolution was laid in the 1940s and 1950s, but widespread adoption of computer technology had to wait until the 1980s and 1990s and the full maturation of the information technology (IT) revolution may still be in the future.

This means that, while the invention phase of each industrial revolution has coincided roughly with the foundation of each American republic—in the 1770s and 1780s, the 1860s and 1870s, and the 1930s and 1940s, respectively—the disruptive deployment phase of the new technology has generally come midway through the seventy- to-eighty-year lifespan of each successive American republic. The result is a lag of several decades between technology-driven change in America's economy and society and the adaptation to the change of America's political and legal institutions.

To put it another way, each American republic has been destabilized by a wave of technology-driven change. The gap between a rapidly evolving society and an outmoded political order grows for several decades. Finally, during a war or depression or both, the outmoded political order crumbles and a new American republic is constructed, built on the ruins of its predecessor.

THE FIRST AMERICAN REPUBLIC

The First Republic of the United States was founded on water and undermined by steam. James Watt radically improved the steam engine around the time of the American Revolution, and delegates to the Constitutional

Convention in 1787 witnessed a demonstration by John Fitch of a steam-powered boat in the Delaware River. But there is often a gap of a generation or two between the invention of a new technology and its widespread diffusion and adoption. So it was with the steam engine. From the 1790s until the 1830s, the energy sources in the United States that augmented human and animal power were still water and wind. Sailing ships transported people and cargo more easily than overland forms of transportation like horses, carriages, and wagons. The population crowded along the Atlantic coastline and rivers, up to the north-south "fall line" beyond which ships powered by the wind could no longer sail. The first great achievements of US transportation infrastructure building were canals like the transformative Erie Canal that linked the Atlantic at New York City with that inland sea, the Great Lakes. The first factories in the United States were mills powered by waterwheels. Most towns were small and limited by the distance that people could walk, while counties were often defined by the distance that a horse could travel in a day.

It was only in the 1830s and the 1840s that the first industrial revolution began to change the nature of production, travel, and commerce in America. Steam engines began to replace waterwheels to provide the motive power of mills. The age of canal building came to an end and railroads sprang up, linking cities, regions, and then, just after the Civil War, the Atlantic and the Pacific edges of what by then was a continental nation. The first suburbs appeared, as the affluent began commuting from sylvan homes to urban businesses.

And in the South, the new technological power spawned a new political power that threatened to destroy the country. The cotton gin, along with the steamship, enabled southern slaveowners to switch from tobacco and rice and other crops and to specialize in producing cotton for the machine-powered textile mills of Britain. By the mid-nineteenth century, the cotton South was to industrial Britain what Saudi Arabia and the other oil-producing nations became in the late twentieth century to the industrial nations of the West and East Asia—the source of the key industrial raw material, ruled by an elite as reactionary as it was rich.

Appeased by the cotton-mill capitalists of New England, the southern planters used their domination of the federal government to thwart plans for the state-sponsored industrialization and modernization of the United States, preferring a regime with a weak center and powerful states.

Then the Kansas-Nebraska Act of 1854 created the possibility that slavery would be extended throughout the country and provoked the formation of a northern antislavery party, the Republicans. When the Republicans elected their first president in 1860, the planters pulled the southern states out of the Union. The cotton South had long been an informal economic colony of Britain, even though it was part of the United States. Now the planters sought to make the Confederate States of America into an independent country that would specialize in commodity exports to Britain as part of Britain's informal economic empire, like the postcolonial countries of Latin America in the nineteenth century. But the South's bid for independence depended on British intervention and, when that did not occur, it was inevitable that the forces of the Union, strengthened by modern industry and modern finance, would conquer a renegade region that had boasted of its rejection of both.

THE SECOND AMERICAN REPUBLIC

The reign of cotton gave way to the rule of rail. The Second Republic of the United States, forged by Lincoln and Congress during the Civil War and Reconstruction between 1861 and 1877, ensured that the United States would be a continental nation-state with an industrial economy, not a decentralized federation with an agrarian economy. The Republicans implemented a version of the American System that Henry Clay had promoted between the 1820s and the 1850s. After decades in which southerners and their northern allies blocked federal aid for internal improvements, Congress, liberated by the withdrawal of its southern members, lavished subsidies in the form of land and money on railroads, including the first transcontinental lines. Andrew Jackson had destroyed the second Bank of the United States, plunging the United States into monetary chaos; Abraham Lincoln signed the bill creating a national banking system. The southern planters had prevented the use of high tariffs to protect infant industries. Under Lincoln and his successors, the United States had the highest tariffs of any major nation in the world until World War II.

But even as America was being adapted to the demands of the first industrial era, a second industrial revolution was taking place in the mid- and late nineteenth century. On the basis of scientific research carried out chiefly in Britain, Germany, and other European countries, Thomas Edison, Nikola Tesla, and others on both sides of the Atlantic developed electrical technologies to power everything from appliances to cities. German researchers invented the gasoline-powered and diesel-powered engines, which, put into bicycle-like frames, produced the earliest automobiles and airplanes. German researchers also led the world in pharmaceuticals and innovative chemistry, including chemical fertilizers that transformed world agriculture. In the second industrial revolution, as in the first, Americans mostly adopted and adapted the innovations of others.

By the 1900s, the second industrial revolution was transforming the economy. Electric motors replaced steam engines, making factories far more productive. Exploiting the economies of scale made possible by America's continental protected market, giant manufacturing corporations like Ford and national retail chains like A&P emerged. Investment bankers, led by J. P. Morgan, specialized in corporate mergers and raising the vast amounts of capital needed by the behemoths that the mergers created.

Just as the first industrial-era economy strained and finally burst the First American Republic, so the second industrial economy grew increasingly misaligned with the Second American Republic that had been built during the Civil War and Reconstruction. A motor-age economy strained against steam-age government.

Two rival schools of reform emerged. Theodore Roosevelt and like-minded reformers who shared what Roosevelt called the New Nationalism thought that giant industrial and retail enterprises could be valuable if they were based on efficiency, but should be regulated by the federal government, not the states. The rival school of reform, led by the lawyer and later Supreme Court justice Louis Brandeis and called the New Freedom by Woodrow Wilson, was suspicious of big business and concentrated financial power. Their solution was to use antitrust policies to protect small and medium-size businesses, anti–chain-store laws to protect small stores, and anti–branch-banking laws to protect small banks.

THE THIRD AMERICAN REPUBLIC

The crisis of the Great Depression, followed by World War II, marked the collapse of the Second American Republic and the founding of the Third. Franklin Roosevelt's New Deal established the basic outlines, which were ratified by the three "Modern Republican" presidents: Dwight D. Eisenhower, Richard M. Nixon, and Gerald R. Ford. Under Roosevelt, rural electrification completed the continental electric grid. Under Eisenhower, the road grid was completed with the interstate highway system.

The Third Republic of the United States was a blend of institutions inspired by the New Nationalism and the New Freedom. The New Nationalism gave rise to the attempt of the National Industry Recovery Act (NIRA) to organize industry into self-governing associations that stabilized sectoral markets and provided for minimum wages. The Supreme Court struck down the NIRA as unconstitutional in 1935, but the equivalents of NIRA-code authorities were created in many sectors of the economy, from aviation to coal and oil production, and lasted until the late 1970s and 1980s. The quite different logic of the New Freedom inspired financial reforms that prevented the emergence in the United States of a few large, universal banks by maintaining anti–branch-banking laws and separating investment banking from commercial banking. The result in the 1950s and 1960s was a uniquely American version of the postwar settlements in other industrial democracies, characterized by a small number of giant corporations and thousands of tiny banks.

Even as the foundations of the Third American Republic were being laid, however, research funded by the US Defense Department during World War II and the early Cold War was inventing the technologies of the next industrial revolution, of which the most important for the economy was computer technology. Combined with the global physical infrastructure made possible by another military invention, the jet, and the container ship, the computer made possible the emergence of industrial production on a global scale. New global corporations, most of them former national corporations like Toyota and Boeing that began by dominating their home markets, coalesced in one industry after another. By the end of the twentieth century, nearly half of all international trade consisted of transfers within global corporations from one production site to another. At the same time, computerization and satellite-based communications transformed the nature of commerce and finance.

While the third industrial economy was slowly taking shape, the older economy of the second industrial era, based on mass production by national corporations, was reaching its limits. By the 1970s, automobile manufacturers had wrung as much innovation as possible out of the mature technologies invented nearly a century earlier. The slowing of technological innovation in the older industrial sectors and the global gluts in the same sectors produced by direct or indirect government backing of their "national champions" may have contributed both to the sharp slowdown of growth in the industrial economies that took place between the 1970s and the 1990s and the rise of inflation.

The New Deal in the United States and social democracy in Europe were erroneously accused of causing the slowdown by conservatives and libertarians, who came to power in one democracy after another, beginning in 1979 with Margaret Thatcher in Britain and in 1981 with Ronald Reagan—who followed Jimmy Carter, a conservative Democrat elected in 1976. Their program of checking inflation by crushing organized labor and radical deregulation failed to ignite a return to the high levels of productivity-driven economic growth. Instead, without intending to do so, the conservative reformers who came to be known as neoliberals triggered a series of debt-driven asset bubbles, causing ever bigger crashes, from the stock market crash of 1987 to the tech-bubble crash of 2001, ending in the catastrophic crash of 2008. The global economic collapse that began with the demise of Lehman Brothers in September 2008 brought to an end the Third Republic of the United States and inaugurated what in time may be seen as a prolonged and turbulent transition to a yet-undefined Fourth Republic.

"OPPOSED IN DEATH AS IN LIFE": HAMILTONIANS VERSUS JEFFERSONIANS

"Opposed in death as in life." With those words Thomas Jefferson explained why he placed a bust of his lifelong rival Alexander Hamilton opposite his own in his home, Monticello.[17] In the generations since, Americans in the Hamiltonian tradition, of right, left, and center, have continued to debate their Jeffersonian opponents, who come in liberal, centrist, and conservative versions as well.

The debates in America have been family squabbles. At issue was not the validity of the Lockean liberal ideals of the American Revolution—nearly everyone agreed on those—but rather the question of whether the United States would be a New Britain or an Anti-Britain.

Those who thought of America as a New Britain, like Hamilton, drew on the tradition of mercantilism, which dominated British practice before its unilateral adoption of free trade in the 1840s, when its industrial supremacy was secure. Beginning with Adam Smith, mercantilism has received a hostile press, although John Maynard Keynes tried to rehabilitate the reputation of mercantilist thinkers in *The General Theory of Employment, Interest, and Money* (1936).[18] Instead of being dismissed as a delusion of early-modern monarchs trying to maximize their gold supplies, mercantilism is properly viewed as an early-modern European variant of developmentalism, an approach to economics that continues to flourish not only in the industrial nations of East Asia and Europe but also to some degree in the contemporary United States.[19]

Developmental economics holds that the basic unit of the world economy is not the individual or the firm, but the polity—typically an empire or city-state in premodern times and a nation-state today. Competition or collaboration among countries, rather than among households or companies, is considered to be the central fact of economics. Developmental states, whether democratic or authoritarian, have usually encouraged private property and private enterprise. But they have viewed the private and public sectors as collaborators in a single national project of maximizing the military security and well-being of the community by means of technological modernization, while minimizing dependence on other political communities. The market is good to the extent that it helps necessary national industries and bad to the extent that it hurts them. The government is not the enemy of the private economy, but its sponsor and partner. Developmental capitalism looks at the economy from the point of view of the manufacturer and the engineer, rather than that of the merchant or banker.

A version of the developmental vision of economic growth as the result of a creative partnership among government, business, the nonprofit sector, and labor was set forth by Andrew Carnegie. In his 1889 essay "Wealth," Carnegie, without naming names, described an iron and steel magnate (himself), a railroad magnate (the Vanderbilts), a mining magnate (William Clark of Montana), and a meatpacking magnate (Gustavus Swift or Philip Armour).[20] Observing how they benefited from the creation of prosperous consumers in national and global markets made possible by railroads, Carnegie declared: "In the work and its profits the Nation was an essential partner and equally entitled with the individual to share in the dividends." Even the wealth of inventors—Carnegie mentioned "Graham Bell of the telephone, Edison of numerous inventions, Westinghouse of the air-brake"—was always "in great part dependent upon the community which uses his productions."[21]

THE PRODUCERIST VISION

The alternative in America to the Hamiltonian version of the developmental state is the antistatist tradition associated with Thomas Jefferson and his philosophical descendants. The term "liberal" is misleading, because developmental economics comes in liberal forms as well, so I will use a term that many historians use for the political economy of Jefferson and Smith: "producerism."

In this tradition, the implications of economic power for military power, which are central to developmental economics, are ignored. In the utopia of producerism, competition in free markets among great numbers of producers who lack the power to manipulate prices to their own benefit is assumed to minimize the cost of goods and services. The central role of government-sponsored technological innovation in reducing prices over time, even in monopolistic and oligopolistic markets, is ignored in producerist thought and its offspring, the academic school of neoclassical economics. Market-driven price reduction is equated with the interests of individuals as consumers. Other than a government with minimal defense and police functions, there is no public good or national interest distinct from the short-term interest of consumers in the lowest possible prices.

This vision of the economy translates into an adversarial vision of relations among governments and businesses. The purpose of the state is to remove barriers to free exchange among individuals and firms, and then, once those barriers have been removed, to limit its activities to enforcing the rules of competition, as a "nightwatchman" or "umpire." Cooperation by firms or their merger into large entities is viewed with suspicion and seen as a proper object of antitrust prosecutions. Producerist economics is hostile as well to collaboration between business and government.

Producerists have often been willing to sacrifice free markets, if by doing so they can protect small producers. In a producerist republic, government may protect small farms, small manufacturers, small retailers and distributors, and small banks from larger competitors, whose size, producerists suspect, is based on political favoritism and other forms of

corruption rather than on legitimate efficiencies resulting from economies of scale.

HAMILTONIAN PROGRESS AND
JEFFERSONIAN REGRESSION

In a spirit of philosophical bipartisanship, it would be pleasant to conclude
that each of these traditions of political economy has made its own valuable contribution to the success of the American economy and that the
vector created by these opposing forces has been more beneficial than the
complete victory of either would have been. But that would not be true.

What is good about the American economy is largely the result of the
Hamiltonian developmental tradition, and what is bad about it is largely
the result of the Jeffersonian producerist school. To the developmental
tradition of Hamilton, Washington and Roosevelt, Lincoln and Clay, we
owe the Internet and the national rail and highway and aviation systems,
the single continental market that allows increasing returns to scale to be
exploited by globally competitive corporations, the unmatched military
that defeated the Axis powers and the Soviet empire and has generated
one technological spin-off after another, and, not least, the federally enforced civil rights laws and minimum-wage laws that have eradicated the
slavery and serfdom that once existed in the South and elsewhere.

To the Jeffersonian tradition, even if it is exempted from blame for
slavery and segregation, the United States owes the balkanization of the
economy by states' rights and localism, underinvestment in infrastructure, irrational antitrust laws and anti–chain store laws designed to privilege small producers, exemptions from regulations and subsidies for small
businesses (defined for many purposes as those with fewer than five hundred employees), the neglect of manufacturing in favor of overinvestment
in single-family housing, and a panic-prone system of tiny, government-
protected small banks and savings and loans.

At key moments in American history, forces invoking the rhetoric of
producerist capitalism have defeated proponents of developmental capi-

talism. One turning point came in the 1830s, when Andrew Jackson and his followers thwarted Henry Clay's American System of national economic development based on protective tariffs for infant industries, national banking, and national infrastructure investment. Another less dramatic but equally significant turning point occurred in the late nineteenth century, when federal court interpretations of the Sherman Antitrust Act of 1890 prevented small and medium-size firms from collaborating in cartels. The unintended result was a wave of mergers before World War I that created a peculiarly American kind of giant, oligopolistic corporation that exists to this day, in place of cartels and cooperatives of small- and medium-size firms of the kind that exist in Germany and other nations.

Developmental capitalism in America suffered another blow in the early years of the New Deal in the 1930s, with the collapse and widespread repudiation of the National Recovery Administration—an experiment in business-labor-government collaboration of a kind practiced successfully in other industrial democracies. Yet another opportunity for developmental capitalism was missed in the 1980s and 1990s, when advocates of a manufacturing-centered, government-fostered American industrial policy were marginalized. Singing the praises of small entrepreneurs and free markets from the Jeffersonian hymnal, Republicans and Democrats alike complacently presided over the decline of American manufacturing and the inflation of the bubble economy that collapsed in 2008, bringing down the American and global economies in the worst economic crisis since the Great Depression.

There is a place in Hamiltonian developmentalism for state and local governments and small start-ups and suppliers. But unlike Jeffersonian producerism, the developmental school of economics identifies the wealth of nations not with small enterprises in lightly regulated markets, but with large-scale industrial production based on scientific and engineering breakthroughs that have usually originated directly or indirectly in government-sponsored research.

HISTORY IS NOT BUNK

In 1916, one of America's great innovators, Henry Ford, declared: "History is more or less bunk. It's tradition. We don't want tradition. We want to live in the present, and the only history that is worth a tinker's damn is the history that we make today."[22]

The purpose of this book is to prove him wrong. The history that we make today is illuminated by the history of our country and the world and the tradition of the values that we seek to preserve through time and change. Just as the American republic was not created as a perfect and unalterable system by a generation of demigods at the Founding, so the American economy is not a timeless and perfect market to be revealed in its natural splendor by stripping away distorting regulations. The American economy, like the American republic, exists to serve the American people, not vice versa. And economies and republics alike are created by human beings for human purposes.

From the generations of Americans who have struggled to master the tools of their time to create an economy worthy of the citizens of a democratic nation, those who continue that never-ceasing struggle in the United States and other lands have much to learn.

THE PREINDUSTRIAL ECONOMY

———◆———

THE ARGUMENT

In order first to win and then secure its independence from Britain, the early United States, under the leadership of gifted policymakers like Robert Morris and Alexander Hamilton, had to create a competent government with a dynamic capitalist economy. But no matter how efficient public and private institutions were, the growth and prosperity of the United States were constrained by the limits imposed on all preindustrial economies. The great fortunes in the early American republic, as in other premodern economies, were those of landowners like Stephen Van Rensselaer III and Robert Livingston or merchants like Stephen Girard and John Jacob Astor, who profited from long-distance trade in luxury items for the rich. Thomas Jefferson and other agrarian thinkers promoted the vision of a democratic republic that would limit the competition of parasitic landlords and rapacious merchants with family farmers for the small surplus produced by a premodern economy. In the context of an impoverished, largely static agrarian economy, Jefferson's vision made sense. But neither Jefferson nor Adam Smith and the early British economists foresaw the imminent liberation of humanity from Malthusian limits by industrial technology.

NATION 2 BUILDING

A people which had in 1787 been indifferent or hostile to roads, banks, funded debt, and nationality, had become in 1815 habituated to ideas and machinery of the sort on a grand scale.

—Henry Adams[1]

The time: Early evening, December 16, 1773. The place: Boston, Massachusetts. Two hundred men dressed as Indians board three British ships in Boston Harbor and dump their contents—tons of tea from the British East India Company—into the water. By doing so, these American Sons of Liberty do more than reject a particular tax to which they objected—the tax on tea, which had recently been lowered to mollify the American colonists. They also reject the asserted power of the British Parliament to levy any taxes on the colonies in North America without their consent.

"It was now evening," recalled George R. T. Hewes in 1833, "and I immediately dressed myself in the costume of an Indian, equipped with a small hatchet, which I and my associates denominated the tomahawk, with which, and a club, after having painted my face and hands with coal dust in the shop of a blacksmith, I repaired to Griffin's wharf, where the ships lay that contained the tea. When I first appeared in the street, after being thus disguised, I fell in with many who were dressed, equipped and painted as I was, and who fell in with me, and marched in order to the place of our destination." The protesters boarded the three ships and spent three hours smashing chests of tea and tossing them overboard. "We were surrounded by British armed ships," Hewes recollected, "but no attempt was made to resist us."[2]

The British government responded to the Boston Tea Party in 1774 with repressive measures, the Coercive or Intolerable Acts. When the British navy closed the port of Boston until the British East India Company was repaid, the colonists organized the Continental Congress. The conflict escalated until the first battles at Lexington and Concord near Boston on April 19, 1775, began the American War of Independence. As the citizens of the new United States would soon discover, political independence did not immediately translate into effective economic independence from Great Britain.

"IN SUBSERVIENCE TO THE COMMERCE OF GREAT BRITAIN"

In the beginning, there was no American economy, only the British imperial economy. The plantations, or colonies, in North America were intended to help the British Empire in its rivalry with the other major powers of Europe. In the centuries before it unilaterally began to adopt free trade in 1846, Britain, like other European states, practiced mercantilism, a policy that treated the economy as an instrument of state power. Mercantilist policies included subsidies and preferential tax treatment for favored industries and their raw material inputs, efforts to obtain surpluses in precious metals like gold and silver and in high-value-added exports, and the conquest or founding of colonies whose inhabitants would provide markets and raw materials for the mother country. In his 1684 treatise *England's Treasure by Foreign Trade*, the mercantilist theorist Thomas Mun wrote: "The ordinary means therefore to increase our wealth and treasure is by Foreign Trade, wherein we must ever observe this rule: to sell more to strangers yearly than we consume of theirs in value."[3] The king in 1721 told Parliament that "it is evident that nothing so much contributes to promote the public well-being as the exportation of manufactured goods and the importation of foreign raw material."[4]

No philosopher influenced the American Revolution more than the seventeenth-century English political thinker John Locke. Thomas Jefferson's Declaration of Independence is practically a paraphrase of Locke's writings on natural rights and liberty. In economics, Locke was a mercantilist, not a libertarian. In his *Letter Concerning Toleration*, Locke says that "the pravity of Mankind . . . obliges Men to enter into Society with one another, that by mutual Assistance, and joint Force, they may secure unto each other their Properties in the things that contribute to the Comfort and Happiness of this Life . . . But forasmuch as Men thus entering into Societies, . . . may nevertheless be deprived of them, either by the Rapine and Fraud of their Fellow-Citizens, or by the Hostile Violence of Foreigners; the remedy of this Evil consists in Arms, Riches, and Multitude of Citizens; the Remedy of the other in Laws."[5] For Locke, as for other early-modern mercantilists, military power, economic growth, and population growth were mutually reinforcing, and all three enhanced the ability of the state to defend its people in an anarchic world. In a journal entry in 1674, Locke wrote: "The chief end of trade is riches and power, which beget each other. Riches consists in plenty of moveables, that will yield a price to foreigners, and are not likely to be consumed at home, but especially in plenty of gold and silver. Power consists in numbers of men, and ability to maintain them. Trade conduces to both these by increasing your stock and your people, and they each other."[6]

The policy of mercantilism that Britain shared with other European empires included a division of labor in which British manufacturers sold finished products to a captive market of consumers in the American colonies, Ireland, and India, which in return exported raw materials and food to the British Isles. In 1721, the British Board of Trade told the king: "Having no manufactories of their own, their . . . situation will make them always dependent on Great Britain."[7] The British parliamentarian Edmund Burke, who sympathized with the American colonists, summarized the policy: "These colonies were evidently founded in subservience to the commerce of Great Britain . . . On the same idea it was contrived that they should send all their products to us raw, and in their first state;

and that they should take every thing from us in the last stage of manufacture."[8] Adam Smith made a similar observation in *The Wealth of Nations*, which was published in 1776, the same year in which the American colonies that would form the United States declared their independence: "The liberality of England, however, towards the trade of her colonies has been confined chiefly to what concerns the market for their produce, either in its rude state, or in what may be called the very first stage of manufacture. The more advanced or more refined manufactures even of the colony produce, the merchants and manufactures of Great Britain choose to reserve to themselves, and have prevailed upon the legislature to prevent their establishment in the colonies, sometimes by high duties, and sometimes by absolute prohibitions."

Beginning in the seventeenth century, England (which became Great Britain with the 1707 Act of Union with Scotland) sought to prevent the development of colonial manufacturing that might compete with British manufacturing by a variety of methods. The Navigation Acts, passed in 1651, 1660, and 1663, required all English trade to be carried in English ships with majority-English crews. All items in "enumerated" categories going to or from the American colonies had to be unloaded in Britain, taxed, and then reexported. The colonists were permitted to buy only British goods or goods that had been reexported from Britain.

The imperial government outlawed American exports that competed with British manufactured goods. For example, the 1699 Woolens Act forbade the sale of woolen cloth outside of the place where it was woven.[9] This destroyed the Irish woolen industry and prevented the emergence of one in the American colonies. In 1732, Britain similarly destroyed an emerging beaver-hat industry in the colonies by outlawing the export of hats to other colonies or foreign countries.[10] When Parliament lifted a ban on exports of pig iron and bar iron from the colonies in 1750, it outlawed further development of the industry. But the colonists ignored the prohibition and by 1775 the annual production of iron in the colonies, most of it for domestic consumption, was roughly the same as in Britain, despite the smaller colonial population.[11]

Even as it banned manufactured exports from the American colonies to Britain or other parts of the empire, the imperial government encouraged the export of raw materials from the colonies to Britain. Import duties on wood and hemp from the American colonies to Britain were abolished. The colonists also received bounties, or subsidies, for exporting raw materials. Timber from the abundant forests of North America was particularly important. The purpose of regulation was to create a buyer's market in raw materials and a seller's market in manufactured goods for British industry.[12]

Hindering the transfer of technology from Britain to America was another British mercantilist technique. In 1719, Britain banned the emigration of skilled workers in industries including steel, iron, brass, watchmaking, and wool. The law punished suborning, or recruitment, of skilled workers for employment abroad with fines or imprisonment. Skilled immigrants who did not return to Britain within six months of being warned by a British official faced the confiscation of their goods and property and the withdrawal of their citizenship.[13] Britain followed its ban on the emigration of skilled workers with a ban on the export of wool and silk technology in 1750. In 1781 and 1785, the act was enlarged into a comprehensive ban on machinery of all kinds. The ban on skilled emigrants was repealed only in 1825, while the ban on technology exports lasted until 1842.[14]

Evaluated in terms of its goal of fostering domestic manufacturing at the expense of other countries, Britain's mercantilist system was a great success. Between the reign of the Tudors and the nineteenth century, Britain's state-sponsored program of economic development turned the island nation first into a commercial and financial powerhouse and then into the first superpower of the machine age. But Britain's imperial trade laws thwarted American manufacturers and frustrated American merchants, who frequently smuggled goods from other colonies and countries. The government also antagonized the colonists after the Seven Years' War (French and Indian War) of 1756 to 1763, when it attempted to ban white settlement of large areas of the trans-Appalachian West, in order to avert conflict with the Indians. This enraged land-hungry Anglo-American frontiersmen as well as rich American colonials like George Washington who owned vast tracts of western land. These economic conflicts, along with struggles over power and status, helped to ignite the American War of Independence from 1775 to 1783.

FUNDING FATHERS

In the folklore of American patriotism, a collection of brave yeoman farmers along with a few urban tradesmen and gentry leaders like George Washington overthrew the mighty British Empire after the United States declared its independence on July 4, 1776. This story is doubly misleading. It is embarrassing for Americans to admit that the United States owed its independence to the intervention of France—in particular, to the French navy, which bottled up General Cornwallis's army at Yorktown, Virginia, permitting joint American and French forces to defeat it. It is even more embarrassing for Americans influenced by Jeffersonian populism to admit that the American cause might have failed, but for the skill of three financiers—an English immigrant, a Polish Jewish immigrant, and a rich American snob.

The English immigrant, Robert Morris, is unknown to most Americans, but his ability to muster and direct money was as critical as the military skills of General Washington and America's French allies. Born in Liverpool in 1734, Morris immigrated to the North American colonies with his father, an agent for a Liverpool tobacco importer. After his father was killed in 1750 in a freak cannon accident, Morris served as a clerk for Charles Willing in Philadelphia. Following Willing's death in 1754, Morris went into business with Willing's son Thomas. Their partnership, Willing and Morris, became the largest mercantile firm in Philadelphia and Morris grew rich from the West Indian trade.

As a member of the Continental Congress, Morris thought that the Declaration of Independence was premature but threw himself into supporting the war. Morris retired from Congress in 1778, then served in the

Pennsylvania Assembly in 1778–1779 and 1780–1781. He was appointed superintendent of finance in February 1781 and served until 1784, a year after Britain recognized America's independence.

Immediately after being appointed superintendent of finance, Morris created the Philadelphia-based Bank of North America, modeled on the Bank of England, headed by his partner, Thomas Willing, and chartered by Congress and also, because of doubts about congressional authority, by Pennsylvania. His proposal for a 5 percent tariff on imports to fund the government failed because of opposition from a single state, Rhode Island, which took advantage of the requirement of unanimity of states. Morris lent his own money to the government and used his own credit to raise other loans, issuing promissory notes which, depending on their terms, were known as "Long Bobs" or "Short Bobs."

Morris benefited from the assistance of Gouverneur Morris. Unrelated to Robert Morris, Gouverneur Morris was from a family of aristocratic New York landowners; his brother served in the British army and his mother was a Loyalist. He combined a caustic tongue with a habit of adulterous affairs, in one of which he is said to have lost his leg in the course of escaping from a tryst (officially the cause was a street accident). He thought little of ordinary people, whom he described as "reptiles," but served the cause of independence in Congress, where he mobilized for support for Washington's army at Valley Forge, and then as assistant to Robert Morris. After the war, he served at the Constitutional Convention, where he spoke more than any other delegate, wrote the Preamble, and edited the Constitution. Later he replaced Jefferson as America's minister to France, in time to witness the French Revolution, of which, unlike Jefferson, he disapproved.

As superintendent of finance, Robert Morris also drew on the talents of Haym Salomon, a Polish Jew fluent in eight languages who immigrated to the American colonies in the early 1770s. On behalf of the Patriot cause, Salomon spied on Hessian mercenaries while supplying them with goods. Arrested, he escaped, reportedly by bribing a Hessian guard. Having lost a small fortune in British-occupied New York, Salomon retained his international contacts and his reputation, which permitted him to sell $200,000 worth of government bonds on the basis of his personal credit. On behalf of Morris, Salomon arranged loans with the French government and also served as the paymaster for French forces in America. Afflicted with tuberculosis following his imprisonment by British forces, Salomon died in 1785. A statue of George Washington on Wacker Drive in Chicago is flanked by statues of Robert Morris and Haym Salomon, whose "genius and unselfish devotion" were praised in 1941 by President Franklin Delano Roosevelt.[15]

Morris argued for aligning the interests of the rich with those of the government, by means of institutions like the Bank of North America and a funded debt, because doing so would "give stability to government, by combining together the Interests of moneyed men for its support."[16] With respect to the creation of a new market in US public securities as a result of funding the debt, Morris wrote: "Even if it were possible to prevent Speculation, it is precisely the thing which ought not to be prevented; because he who wants money to commence, pursue, or extend his business, is more benefited by selling stock of any kind, than he could be by the rise of it at a future Period; Every man being able to judge better of his own business and situation, than the Government can for him."[17]

Morris practiced what he preached: "I shall continue to discharge my duty faithfully to the Public, and pursue my Private Fortune by all such honorable and fair means as the times will admit of."[18] Morris invested in a fleet of privateers that harassed British shipping and provided him with prizes that he could add to his wealth. A French envoy in Philadelphia observed in his diary that Morris "is, in fact, so accustomed to the success of his privateers, that when he is observed on a Sunday to be more serious than usual, the conclusion is, that no prize has arrived in the preceding week."[19] Morris wanted the nation's permanent capital to be located on the Delaware River at Trenton, New Jersey, where he owned land.[20]

In addition to the effect of the deeply rooted distrust of rich big-city bankers in American political culture, particularly those who are foreign-born, Morris's unhappy later career may explain his absence from the

American pantheon. Morris served as a Pennsylvania delegate to the Constitutional Convention and later as a US senator from Pennsylvania. In 1790, Morris bought two million acres in New York State and quickly sold it to a group of British investors, Pulteney Associates.[21] In another transaction, in December 1792, he sold 1.5 million acres in upstate New York and his son in Amsterdam, acting as his agent, sold another 1.8 million to a group of Dutch investors who formed the Holland Land Company.[22] Having invested in millions of acres of land in New York, Pennsylvania, Georgia, South Carolina, and Virginia, as well as the District of Columbia, Morris, unable to pay his debts, ended up in jail for three and a half years until the nation's first bankruptcy law came into effect. He died in 1806. Morris's longtime friend and business partner, Thomas Willing, outlived him and was nominated unsuccessfully to lead the second Bank of the United States.

BUILDING A NATIONAL ECONOMY

When Britain formally recognized the independence of the United States in 1783, the new country, under the Articles of Confederation, ratified by the states in 1781, was more of a loose alliance than a nation-state. The federal government lacked the power to raise revenue and depended on voluntary contributions from the state governments.

The War of Independence had left both the federal government and the state governments with large debts. There was no national currency and only a single bank, the small Bank of North America in Philadelphia, which began operations in 1782. Money took the form either of state-printed paper or specie, in the form of gold and silver, including foreign coins.

In addition to the debt of the US government, each state had debts from the war. Virginia and some other southern states paid down their debts. Rhode Island resorted to inflation. In 1786, when Massachusetts imposed taxes to pay for its debt, settlers in the western backcountry took up arms and rebelled. Several were killed and a thousand arrested by the time the so-called Regulators or Shaysites, who followed Daniel Shays and others, were defeated.

Shays's Rebellion underlined the weakness of the federal government under the Articles of Confederation. Congress had to approve the use of weapons in the Springfield, Massachusetts, armory, but it had been out of session when the crisis arose. The incident convinced many Americans that the United States needed a stronger government. Among them was George Washington, then living in retirement at his estate in Virginia, Mount Vernon. He wrote, "Let us have a government by which our lives, liberty and properties will be secured, or let us know the worst at once."[23]

In the summer of 1787, Washington presided over the Constitutional Convention at Philadelphia. After the new, stronger federal constitution was ratified by the states, Washington became the first president elected under the new system. To help in the consolidation of the nation's finances, he turned to Alexander Hamilton.

THE MASTERMIND

"The bastard brat of a Scotch peddler" was the description of Hamilton by his rival John Adams, the second president of the United States. Hamilton was born in 1757 on the British West Indian island of Nevis to Rachel Faucett Lavien and the son of a Scots laird, James Hamilton, who deserted his family when Hamilton was a boy. He was orphaned a few years later when his mother died. A merchant who noticed his abilities arranged for him to study at King's College (present-day Columbia University) in 1772. When the American Revolution began, he joined the New York militia and his abilities brought him to the notice of Washington, who made him one of his staff officers. Following the war, in which he distinguished himself not only by his logistical abilities but also by a raid on British forces at Yorktown, he married into the wealthy Schuyler family of New York and became a champion of a more centralized government, organizing and writing a majority of the *Federalist Papers*, which were used in the campaign for ratification of the new federal constitution.

In a 1780 letter to the New York revolutionary leader James Duane, the young Hamilton, then serving as an aide on General Washington's staff, proposed a constitutional convention to remedy the weaknesses of the existing confederation. His proposals included "complete sovereignty" of the federal government over the states, the authority of the federal government to tax citizens directly, a permanent military, a national bank, and "great officers of state—a secretary for foreign affairs—a President of War—a President of Marine—a Financier." Hamilton suggested that Morris would make an excellent "Financier."[24] Hamilton wrote to Morris, with his own plan for a bank. According to legend, when George Washington, on being elected president, asked Morris to serve as the first Treasury secretary of the United States, Morris declined and recommended Hamilton.

As the secretary of the Treasury, the largest and most important federal agency, Hamilton proved worthy of the responsibility. He submitted a series of great state papers, of which the most important were the Report on Public Credit (January 14, 1790), the report calling for the establishment of the Bank of the United States (December 14, 1790), the report calling for the establishment of a national mint and a bimetallic dollar standard (January 28, 1791), and the Report on Manufactures (December 5, 1791). Congress acted on most of his recommendations. In only a few years, he laid the solid foundation for America's future prosperity.

FROM COLBERT TO HAMILTON

Hamilton's self-education prepared him well for the task of building a nation out of a miscellany of former colonies. While serving during the Revolutionary War on Washington's staff, Hamilton studied what was then known as political economy rather than economics, reading David Hume and Adam Smith, among others. Scattered through his army pay book are notes quoting or summarizing a two-volume book by the British author Malachy Postlethwayt, published in London between 1751 and 1755:

The universal dictionary of trade and commerce; translated, from the
French of the celebrated Monsieur Savary, Inspector-General of the manufactures for the King, at the custom-house of Paris: with large improvements, incorporated throught the whole work; which more particularly
accommodated the same to the trade and navigation of the kingdoms,
and the laws, customs, and usages, to which all traders are subject.

Postlethwayt's book was a translation and adaptation of the *Diction-
naire universel de commerce*, written by Jacques Savary des Bruslons, completed by his brother Philemon-Louis Savary and published in Paris in
1723 before being translated into other languages. Jacques Savary was the
inspector general of the manufactures for the king at the Custom House
in Paris. He was the sixth son of Jacques Savary, a member of an elite
merchant family, who had been one of the architects of French economic
policy under the great French statesman Jean-Baptiste Colbert.

Colbert served as France's minister of finance from 1665 until his death
in 1683. A brilliant, hardworking public servant, Colbert presided over
a program to modernize the French economy and strengthen the state.
He created the French merchant marine, imposed quality standards on
French producers to make their products more attractive, and promoted
infrastructure projects like roads and canals, including the important Canal du Midi. Colbert used protective tariffs and other methods to promote
French infant industries. He fostered the French glass industry by banning Venetian glass imports. Another method was the use of state-owned
enterprises, like the royal Gobelin tapestry factories. Similar techniques
were employed by Britain before the 1840s, and would later be used by
the Americans and Germans in the nineteenth century and even later by
Japan and China.

At Colbert's request, Jacques Savary codified French commercial
practice in 1673, in what became known as the Code Savary. In addition,
Savary wrote a book called *The Perfect Merchant*, which was published
in 1675 and translated into German, Italian, Dutch, and English. The
universal dictionary of commerce that his two sons published, and that

Postlethwayt translated into English, built upon his work for Colbert. By way of the Savary family and Postlethwayt, the economic nation-building of Alexander Hamilton was influenced by the economic nation-building of Jean-Baptiste Colbert.

Britain as well as France provided Hamilton with a model for state-sponsored economic modernization. Such a system was established under British prime minister Robert Walpole in the early eighteenth century. In 1721, British commercial law was reformed to promote manufacturing by raising tariffs on foreign manufactured goods, eliminating export duties on most British manufactured goods, lowering or eliminating tariffs on raw materials used by British manufacturers, and providing subsidies to British export industries like silk and gunpowder.[25] The same era witnessed the founding of the Bank of England (1694), a model for the first Bank of the United States. Only after Britain over several centuries had successfully used protectionism, subsidies, and mercantilist trade policies to develop competitive industries did it take the risk of liberalizing trade.

FUNDING THE DEBT

One of Hamilton's first decisions as secretary of the Treasury was to ask Congress to establish America's creditworthiness in the eyes of American and foreign creditors by taking over the debt of the states. Opposition to Hamilton's funding plan was concentrated in the South. Virginia and several other southern states had paid their wartime debts and objected to being taxed to pay down the debts of other states. In addition, much of the debt had ended up in the hands of northeastern speculators, whose agents had traveled through rural areas buying debt instruments at a fraction of their face value.

James Madison's proposal to divide the payment between the original holders of the debt and those who had purchased it was unworkable. Hamilton was right to insist that a fluid market in securities meant that the government had to treat all holders of debt equally.

In June 1790, Hamilton was leaving George Washington's temporary home in New York when he encountered Thomas Jefferson, who had arrived for an appointment with the president. Jefferson later described the Treasury secretary as "somber, haggard and dejected beyond comparison." Jefferson invited Hamilton to dine with him and Madison at Jefferson's home on June 20. Legend has it that the Virginians promised Hamilton they would support his funding scheme if Hamilton delivered the support of northerners for a capital on the Potomac. The truth is more complicated. Such a deal had been in the works for some time, and Hamilton knew that Washington favored a site for the capital near his Mount Vernon plantation. In any event, a few days later Congress narrowly passed Hamilton's assumption system by a single vote. Congress subsequently chose the Potomac site for the federal capital and Jefferson was the first president to serve his full term there.

As Hamilton carried out his plan, the miscellany of federal and state securities were replaced by three new bond issues with a par value of $64 million. By law the debt was funded, that is, federal revenues were dedicated first to paying interest on the debt. Dutch bankers cooperated with Hamilton in managing the debt held by Europeans. Hamilton also increased a sinking fund. Justified by the need to pay down debt in the future, in fact this permitted him to perform what would later be called "open market operations" to stabilize the economy.

The *New York Gazette* on April 2, 1792, used nautical terminology to describe federal bonds:

> THE Six-per Cent, a first rate, belonging to the fleet commanded by Admiral HAMILTON, notwithstanding several hard contrary gales, and a strong lee current setting out of the Hudson and Delaware is still working to windward; and bids fair to gain her destined port.
>
> The Three per Cent, a frigate belonging to the above mentioned fleet, in sailing through Speculation Straights, received a land flaw, which threw her on her beam ends—She has, however, since righted, and is pursuing her voyage.[26]

Hamilton was confident that economic growth would permit the United States to pay down the consolidated federal and state debts. He told his friend and mentor Robert Morris: "Speaking within moderate bounds, our population will be doubled in thirty years; there will be a confluence of emigration from all parts of the world, our commerce will have a proportionate progress and of course our wealth and capacity for revenue. It will be a matter of choice if we are not out of debt in twenty years, without at all encumbering the people."[27]

FEDERAL TAXES

To pay for the debt and federal government operations, Congress followed Hamilton's advice and passed a general 9 percent tariff that President Washington signed into law on July 4, 1789. The government initially relied on loans until revenues from the tariff could be built up.

The tariff was supplemented by excise taxes, including a tax on whiskey passed by Congress in 1791. Resistance to its collection by frontier settlers in Pennsylvania escalated until 1794, when hundreds of armed men attacked the home of a federal tax inspector. Mobilizing the militia, President Washington mounted the saddle again, preparing to lead troops in person to suppress the rebellion. But in light of this show of force, the protests collapsed, and the small number of arrested men were pardoned.

While the excise tax was regressive, as a whole Hamilton's scheme for funding the state debts was more progressive than debt payments by the individual states would have been. For example, the state of Massachusetts alone had planned to pay its debt by raising more than $1 million a year in new taxes. In contrast, the interest on the consolidated national debt of $75.6 million required only $4.6 million from the entire United States, with another million going to the operating expenses of the federal government. And whereas states' repaying their debt would have relied heavily on property taxes or poll taxes, the federal government raised revenue mainly from tariffs paid primarily by the affluent. If the rich disproportionately benefited from federal assumption of state debt, they also disproportionately paid the costs and spared ordinary Americans the taxes that the states otherwise might have imposed.[28]

THE BANK OF THE UNITED STATES

On February 25, 1791, Congress chartered the Bank of the United States for twenty years. While Secretary of State Thomas Jefferson and Attorney General Edmund Randolph argued that the bank was unconstitutional, on the grounds that the Constitution did not give the federal government the power to charter corporations, Hamilton persuaded President Washington to sign the legislation with his argument that the Constitution implicitly gave the federal government the power to carry out its responsibilities.[29]

Hamilton viewed banking as a necessary utility: "Public utility is more truly the object of public banks than private profit."[30] Hamilton's models were the Dutch and British financial systems, the most sophisticated in the world.[31] The bank acted as the fiscal agent of the new federal government, making federal payments and holding federal revenues as deposits. The institution was designed so that the federal government owned 20 percent of the bank, while the other 80 percent was owned by investors. The bank's capital—$10 million in the form of 25,000 shares at $400 each—made it larger than all of the other American banks in 1791 combined.[32] With branches in several major cities, the bank helped to catalyze the formation of private banks throughout the country.[33] The sale of federal securities and shares of the bank created a stock market in the young United States. In New York and Philadelphia, individuals formed securities-trading clubs that developed over time into stock exchanges.

THE REPORT ON THE MINT

Another part of Hamilton's system was his January 28, 1791, report on the establishment of a mint and a bimetallic dollar standard. The goal of bimetallism was to encourage the use of paper money, convertible into gold and silver at fixed rates.

The division of currency by the decimal system as an alternative to Britain's confusing system of pounds, shillings, and pence, a reform suggested by Robert Morris, was endorsed by Jefferson in his Notes on the Establishment of a Money Unit, and of a Coinage for the United States.[34] In 1785, Congress ordained that the dollar would be the standard unit of currency. In 1786, Congress followed Jefferson's recommendations for fifty-cent, ten-cent (called a "dime," from Latin), five-cent, and one-cent coins, but instead of a twenty-cent coin authorized the quarter.

The term "dollar" was borrowed from Spain. In addition to using bills of credit, the colonists increased the amount of coin in circulation by obtaining Spanish dollars by means of trade, much of it illegal under the British Empire's laws, with the West Indies and Europe. In the sixteenth century, in what is now the Czech Republic, a count who owned silver mines near the town of Joachimsthal minted coins called "thalers," from "thal," the German word for "valley." The Hapsburg Empire, which then controlled the Spanish territories, turned gold and silver from Spain's mines in the New World into thalers, which became "dollars" in English. Spanish dollars were cut or "clipped" into halves, quarters, and eighths, also called "pieces of eight" or "bits." From that the slang phrase for a quarter is derived: "two bits."

During the colonial period, one method that the British government had used to discourage the growth of manufacturing in the colonies that might compete with British manufacturing had been to limit the supply of specie, or money in the form of coins. Britain's mercantilist policy was thwarted to some degree by colonists who used bills of credit as the primary medium of exchange. From this practice arises the term "dollar bill" as distinct from "pound note."[35]

THE REPORT ON MANUFACTURES

On January 15, 1790, the House asked the Treasury to report on plans for encouraging American manufactures. Hamilton delivered the Report on Manufactures to Congress on December 5, 1791.

To draft the report, Hamilton turned to an assistant at the Treasury, Tench Coxe. At the age of twenty in 1775, Coxe had joined the United Company of Philadelphia for Promoting American Manufactures, also known as the American Manufactory.[36] On May 11, three days before delegates began to deliberate on a new federal constitution in Philadelphia, Coxe had given a talk to some of the delegates at the home of Benjamin Franklin on the need for government to promote manufacturing in the United States.

After five drafts, the final Report on Manufactures weakened many of Coxe's recommendations, but still made a strong case for government promotion of industry in the United States. In the report, Hamilton rejected the view of Adam Smith and the French Physiocrats that "manufactures without the aid of government will grow up as soon and as fast, as the natural state of things and the interest of the community may require."[37] Hamilton dropped Coxe's proposal for tariffs to protect infant industries. A high-tariff regime would have threatened his plans for using revenues from British-American trade to fund the federal debt and federal government operations. In the final version, Hamilton argued for the superiority of bounties (subsidies) over tariffs. In *Federalist* 35, Hamilton had argued that protective tariffs "render other classes of the community tributary, in an improper degree, to the manufacturing classes, to whom they give a premature monopoly of the market."[38]

Hamilton also addressed the objection to the policy of promoting infant industry "from its supposed tendency to give a monopoly . . . to particular classes at the expense of the rest of the community, who, it is affirmed, would be able to procure the requisite supplies of manufactured articles on better terms from foreigners, than from our own Citizens." Acknowledging that prices could increase, Hamilton argued that in successful infant industries they would decline over time: "When a domestic manufacture has attained to perfection, and has engaged in the prosecution of a competent number of Persons, it invariably becomes cheaper. . . . The internal competition, which takes place, soon does away every thing like Monopoly, and by degrees reduces the price of the Article to the *minimum* of a reasonable profit on the Capital employed."[39]

KNOWLEDGE TRANSFER: SKILLED IMMIGRANTS AND INTELLECTUAL PROPERTY

Hamilton supported Coxe's proposals for encouraging skilled immigration, proposing that the federal government fund a board that would import both foreign workers and foreign technology. In 1787, in his capacity as secretary of the Pennsylvania Society for the Encouragement of Manufactures and the Useful Arts, Coxe had provided support for a British emigrant, Andrew Mitchell, to return to Britain and pirate textile technology, a scheme that failed when Mitchell was discovered and forced to flee to Copenhagen.[40] Thomas Digges smuggled nearly two dozen British textile workers to the United States, including some hired by Hamilton. In another case, an English weaver named George Parkinson was granted a US patent on textile technology in 1791; later he went on to work for the government-sponsored manufacturing center sponsored by Hamilton, the Society for Establishing Useful Manufactures (SUM). Secretary of State Thomas Jefferson, in charge of patent policy, arranged for the patent and helped arrange the emigration of Parkinson's family but did not help Parkinson directly in order to avoid violating British law.[41] Parkinson went into partnership with Coxe, then Hamilton's assistant at the Treasury, and Hamilton had the US Treasury subsidize Parkinson's living expenses.[42] Jefferson opposed Hamilton's policy of promoting skilled immigration, because of his prejudice against urban mechanics and factory workers. He wrote that such "ephemeral and pseudo-citizens" should be treated "as we do persons infected with disease."[43]

In addition to recommending policies to encourage manufacturing and the immigration of skilled labor, Hamilton sought to promote American industrialization directly. When he failed to persuade Congress to support the SUM, he and allies obtained a charter for the company from the state of New Jersey and founded the city of Paterson. As explained in chapter 1, following initial failures, Paterson became one of the most important centers of American manufacturing until the second half of the twentieth century.

The British government was alarmed by the Report on Manufactures and SUM. George Hammond, the British minister in Philadelphia, urged the British government "To prevent the emigration and exportation of machines necessary to the different branches of manufactures."[44] British agents in the newly independent United States worked to stymie American manufacturing development. In 1787, Phineas Bond, the British consul in Philadelphia, bought four carding and spinning machines that had been smuggled into the United States and sent them back to Britain.[45] Bond kept his superiors in London informed about American theft of British technology and called for enforcement of laws "against seducing manufacturers and conveying away implements of manufacturing."[46]

The contradiction between the promotion of theft of intellectual property from Britain and Europe and the patenting of technology, much of it stolen, by the US government bothered Secretary of State Thomas Jefferson and Attorney General Edmund Randolph. President Washington shared their concerns, opposing the establishment of a textile mill in Virginia that used stolen British technology because "it certainly would not carry an aspect very favorable to the dignity of the United States for the President in a clandestine manner to entice the subjects of another Nation to violate its Laws."[47]

While Hamilton did not challenge British restrictions on American commerce, in order to avoid jeopardizing the British-American trade on which the federal tariff depended, his manufacturing program directly challenged British industrial supremacy. Hamilton envisioned the United States not as a complementary resource-exporting economic colony of Britain but as a rival industrial nation—a "New England" indeed.

Hamilton was accused by many contemporaries and later historians of being an Anglophile. In fact, his complete program, if it had been carried out, would have used revenues from the federal tariff on British-American trade in order to subsidize American industries capable of catching up and competing with British industries. In the nineteenth century, US industrialization was accelerated by the protective tariffs that Coxe rather than Hamilton favored. But the result was similar. While tariffs kept out British manufactured imports, private British investors in American railroads and factories played a major role in financing the development of the American industrial base that eventually surpassed Britain's own.

WILLIAM DUER AND THE PANIC OF 1792

Hamilton's rational scheme for sound finance was undermined by speculative irrationality that gave rise to the panic of 1792. At the center of the crisis was William Duer, the British-born son of a West Indian planter who served in the Continental Congress, grew rich as a supplier during the Revolutionary War, and married into New York high society when he wed Catherine Alexander in a ceremony in which George Washington gave away the bride. Duer worked briefly for Hamilton in the new Treasury Department before quitting to trade on inside information, without Hamilton's knowledge or approval. He walked away unscathed from the Scioto scandal, a land scheme in the Ohio River valley that left a company bankrupt along with many of its investors, and secretly went into business with a land speculator named William Macomb and a number of rich New Yorkers. They formed the Six Percent Club, a group that sought to corner 6 percent federal bonds and other securities. Duer's group speculated in Bank of New York stock and announced the formation of a "Million Bank." Spreading rumors that it would merge with the Bank of the United States and the Bank of New York, in January 1791 the conspirators sold shares of the Million Bank at high prices, planning to cash out at the top of the market they had manipulated. But a rival faction of speculators led by the rich Livingston family, by driving down the price of Bank of New York stock, forced Duer into bankruptcy and, when he could not pay his many creditors, a run on the banks began.

On January 18, 1792, Hamilton wrote to the cashier of the Bank of New York, William Seton: "I have learnt with infinite pain the circumstance of a new Bank having started up in your City. Its effects cannot but be in every view pernicious. These extravagant sallies of speculation do injury to the Government and to the whole system of public Credit, by disgusting all sober Citizens and giving a wild air to everything. . . . I sincerely hope that the Bank of New York will listen to no coalition with this newly engendered Monster."[48] Interestingly, years later, Hamilton used the same phrase in noting that his enemy Aaron Burr, who would kill him in a duel in 1804, "by a trick established a *Bank*, a perfect monster in its principles; but a very convenient instrument of *profit* & *influence*."[49]

After Duer wrote a note informing him of his default, Hamilton replied on March 14: "Act with *fortitude* and *honor*."[50] Duer was thrown into a debtors' prison, which was surrounded by mobs of those whom he had defrauded. Hamilton obtained a temporary reprieve for him but Duer returned to prison and died there in disgrace. Hamilton's crisis management ended the panic by April, and there would not be another financial panic in the United States until 1819.

On May 17, 1792, two dozen brokers gathered under a buttonwood tree at 68 Wall Street in lower Manhattan to found an association to make and enforce rules to discourage unethical speculators like William Duer. Their club became the New York Stock Exchange.[51]

"WE ARE ALL FEDERALISTS, WE ARE ALL REPUBLICANS"

"We are all Federalists, we are all Republicans," Thomas Jefferson declared in his first inaugural address, after his election in "the revolution of 1800." Jefferson would serve two terms and be succeeded by James Madison, who also served two terms. During the Washington administration, Jefferson and Madison had opposed most of the elements of Hamilton's program for national economic development. Once they had to govern the country, they quickly learned how practical the Hamiltonian system was and reconsidered some of their Republican objections to the Federalist policies of Jefferson's predecessors, George Washington and John Adams.

For most of the period from 1800 to 1815, Britain and France were engaged in a world war that stretched from the steppes of Russia to North America. The weakness of the young American republic was demonstrated again and again. The British and French navies impressed, or drafted, American sailors, over the objections of the US government. Britain's orders in council, which established a blockade of French-dominated Europe, and Napoleon's Continental System, which sought to make his domain independent of Britain, disrupted American commerce. But when Jefferson and Congress sought to pressure the warring great powers with a US embargo on foreign trade, nicknamed the O-Grab-Me by its critics, the result was a disastrous contraction of the American economy, widespread smuggling, and sentiment for secession in mercantile New England. The War of 1812 that followed was an even greater disaster. The attempt by the United States to conquer British Canada failed. The British burned Washington, DC. Only the belated victory of Andrew Jackson at the Battle of New Orleans, which took place after peace negotiations had begun, prevented the war from being a completely humiliating experience.

American manufacturers had been helped, however, by the decline in trade during the embargo and the war. When a flood of British imports following the war, beginning in 1816, threatened to destroy many of the nascent manufacturing businesses, Congress passed the first truly protective tariffs—of 30 percent on iron and 25 percent on woolens and cotton. Because these were seen as reducing America's dependence on Britain, they were supported by Anglophobic southerners like John C. Calhoun and Andrew Jackson. In April 1810, Jefferson's Treasury secretary Albert Gallatin, influenced by Hamilton's former aide Tench Coxe, a political opportunist who never wavered in his support for American industry, published his own report on manufactures, recommending moderate increases in protective duties.[52] Ironically it was the Jeffersonians, out of hostility to Britain, who were more willing to use tariffs to protect industry than had been Hamilton, who had preferred bounties, or subsidies, in order not to disrupt British-American trade. Together with Gallatin's ambitious plan for a nationwide canal system and Jefferson's recommendation of a constitutional amendment to permit the federal government to fund internal improvements, Gallatin's report on manufactures showed that the Jeffersonians had accepted the major elements of Hamilton's program for state-sponsored national economic development.

In 1782, in *Notes on the State of Virginia*, Jefferson had written: "The political economists of Europe have established it as a principle that every state should endeavor to manufacture for itself; and this principle, like many others, we transfer to America, without calculating the difference of circumstance which should often produce a difference of result. In Europe the lands are either cultivated, or locked up against the cultivator. Manufacture must therefore be resorted to of necessity, not of choice, to support the surplus of their people. But we have an immensity of land courting the industry of the husbandman . . . while we have land to labor, then, let us never wish to see our citizens occupied at a workbench."[53] And in 1812 he set forth a vision of manufacturing limited to households on farms: "We have reduced the large and expensive machinery for most things to the compass of a private family, and every family of any size is now getting machines on a small scale for their household purposes."[54]

Jefferson's bias against the commercial Northeast endured. In 1816, from his retirement, he expressed his hope that the industrializing Northeast peacefully withdraw from the Union, leaving the states "which are for peace and agriculture." He wrote: "I have no hesitation in saying let us separate." The alternative, he thought, was the corruption of American society by "the mimicry of an Amsterdam, a Hamburgh, or a city of London."[55] But in the same year Jefferson told one correspondent: "You tell me I am quoted by those who wish to continue our dependence on England for manufactures. There was a time when I might have been so quoted with more candor, but within the thirty years which has since elapsed, how circumstances have changed! . . . He, therefore, who is now against domestic manufacture, must be for reducing either to dependence on that foreign nation [Britain], or to be clothed in skins, and to live like wild beasts in dens and caverns. I am not one of these; experience has taught me that manufactures are now as necessary to our independence as to our comfort."[56]

Madison, too, was won over to Hamiltonian infant-industry protectionism. During the debate about the "tariff of abominations" in 1828, the "Father of the Constitution" wrote several public letters insisting that the Constitution gave Congress the power to levy tariffs and defending the use of tariffs to protect American manufacturing against foreign competition and policies to encourage skilled immigration. Madison gave six reasons why the United States should pursue a policy of import-substitution protectionism: "1. The Theory of 'Let us alone,' supposes that all nations concur in a perfect freedom of commercial intercourse. . . . But this golden age of free trade has not yet arrived. . . . 2. The Theory supposes moreover a perpetual peace, not less chimerical, it is to be feared, than a universal freedom of commerce. . . . 3. It is an opinion in which all must agree, that no nation ought to be unnecessarily dependent on others for the munitions of public defence, or for the materials essential to a naval force, where the nation has a maritime frontier or a foreign commerce to protect. . . . 4. There are cases where a nation may be so far advanced in the pre-requisites for a particular branch of manufactures, that this, if once brought into existence, would support itself; and yet, unless aided in its nascent and infant state by public encouragement and a confidence in public protection, might remain, if not altogether, for a long time unattempted, or attempted without success. . . . 5. Should it happen, as has been suspected, to be an object, though not of a foreign Government itself, of its great manufacturing capitalists, to strangle in the cradle the infant manufactures of an extensive customer or an anticipated rival, it would surely, in such a case, be incumbent on the suffering party so far to make an exception to the 'let alone' policy as to parry the evil by opposite regulations of its foreign commerce. . . . 6. It is a common objection to the public encouragement of particular branches of industry, that it calls of labourers from other branches found to be more profitable, and the objection is, in general, a weighty one. But it loses that character in proportion to the effect of the encouragement in attracting skilful labourers from abroad."[57]

Earlier, in 1811, Jefferson had written to another friend, praising the tariff as a source of revenue as well as a stimulus to infant industries: "We are all the more reconciled to the tax on importations, because it falls exclusively on the rich, and with the equal partitions of intestate's estates, constitutes the best agrarian law. In fact, the poor man in this country who uses nothing but what is made within his own farm or family, or within the United States, pays not a farthing of tax to the general government, but on his salt; and should we go into that manufacture as we ought to do, he will not pay one cent. Our revenues once liberated by the discharge of the public debt, and its surplus applied to canals, roads, schools, etc., the farmer will see his government supported, his children educated, and the face of his country made a paradise by the contributions of the rich alone, without his being called on to spare a cent from his earnings."[58]

Federal support for internal improvements was another measure that Jefferson and his allies came to support, if only with qualifications. In 1803, Jefferson signed a law that permitted the federal government to use 2 percent of the money from the sale of federal land in Ohio on roads and other forms of transportation within Ohio or leading to it. The National Road grew out of this legislation. Then in his second inaugural address in 1805, Jefferson called for a constitutional amendment to allow any federal surplus once the debt was paid off to be divided "by a just partition among the states" and to "be applied, in time of peace, to rivers, canals, roads, arts, manufactures, education, and other great objects within each state." On April 6, 1808, Jefferson's Treasury secretary, Albert Gallatin, published a comprehensive report on roads and canals. While public construction was a possibility, Gallatin preferred government loans to private companies or government purchases of their stock.

Jefferson told the American diplomat Joel Barlow: "The time is fast approaching when the United States, if no foreign disputes should induce an extraordinary expenditure of money, will be out of debt. From that time forward, the greater part of their public revenue may, and probably will be, applied to public improvements of various kinds, such as facilitating the intercourse through all parts of their dominion by roads, bridges, and canals; such as making more exact surveys and forming maps and charts of the interior country, and of the coasts, bays, harbors, perfecting the system of lights, buoys, and other nautical aids; such as encouraging new branches of industry, so far as may be advantageous to the public, either by offering premiums for discoveries, or by purchasing from their proprietors such inventions as shall appear to be of immediate and general utility, and rendering them free to the citizens at large; such as exploring the remaining parts of the wilderness of our continent, both within and without our own jurisdiction."[59]

Even the Bank of the United States, which the Republican faction of Jefferson and Madison had denounced in the 1790s, came to be viewed as a necessity. The Jeffersonians who dominated Congress had refused to renew the bank's twenty-year charter when it expired in 1811. But the financial difficulties of the federal government during the War of 1812 convinced a number of War Hawks, including the young Henry Clay, that a national bank was necessary. Congress chartered a second Bank of the United States in 1816 and the law was signed by President Madison, who had opposed Hamilton's original proposal in 1791.

By the 1820s, a consensus on the need for infant-industry protection, internal improvements, and a national bank had coalesced. But the consensus would not survive. Soon Hamilton's vision of government-sponsored national economic development would be defeated, with results for the shape of the American economy that would last into the twenty-first century.

THE FIRST 3 AMERICAN ECONOMY

All for ourselves, and nothing for other people, seems, in every age of the world, to have been the vile maxim of the masters of mankind.

—Adam Smith, 1776[1]

Of the ten Americans whose wealth at their deaths was the greatest, as a percentage of the GDP of the United States, three died before 1850—the third wealthiest, John Jacob Astor (1763–1848), the fourth, Stephen Girard (1750–1831), and the tenth, Stephen Van Rensselaer III (1764–1839).[2] They owed their status not to the fact that they were particularly rich by modern standards, but to the fact that the American economy of their time was so small and poor.

It was not until the mid-nineteenth century that growth angled sharply upward in Britain, the United States, Western Europe, and other industrializing societies. Since the industrial era began, industrial countries have enjoyed average real growth of 1.5 to 2 percent a year, a growth rate roughly ten times greater than the negligible growth rate that existed in preindustrial societies.[3] The phenomenon of high, sustained economic growth is recent, following millennia of economic stagnation and, in some places, periods of regression. According to one calculation, the hourly wages of real construction workers in Britain were approximately the same from AD 1200 to the 1860s.[4]

In a premodern biomass economy, most energy came from firewood and human and animal muscle, supplemented sometimes by windmills and water mills. The majority of people in agrarian societies had to till the soil to feed themselves and the small upper classes. The self-sufficient village or plantation economies of the farm laborers who made up most of the population were divorced from interregional and international trade. Long-distance trade consisted almost entirely of trinkets and drugs that the landlords and courtiers of one country exchanged with the landlords and courtiers of another—gold and silver and silk, tobacco, coffee, opium, and tea. In the premodern economy, any growth in luxury trade meant greater exploitation of the peasant farmers who were taxed by the landlords to finance their purchases. Today's historians who write cheerfully about the "flourishing commerce" of Asia in the Middle Ages or early modern Europe and the Americas overlook the suffering of the exploited laborers who obtained or produced the mostly frivolous and unnecessary goods that were the objects of international trade: Chinese workers in porcelain and silk sweatshops, South American Indian silver miners, Bengali and Turkish poppy growers, and Indian and white fur trappers and traders in North America. Among these were the slaves of the Americas, North and South. Between 1700 and 1820, the number of Africans transported to the Western Hemisphere was roughly five times greater than the number of Europeans.

Manufacturing, too, was different in the preindustrial world. It did not mean the use of machinery to produce low-cost goods. The peasants and the poor were clothed, shod, and equipped with goods they made at home or purchased from village craftsmen. Premodern factories specialized in luxury goods that were consumed by the local aristocrats or sold to the foreign rich.

The workers in these sweatshops were among the most miserable of the poor. Frequently they were children of peasant or serf families who could not be supported by their starving parents in countries suffering from famine and overpopulation. Working seven days a week in dark premodern factories was almost as miserable as laboring in mines or galleys. In Britain, the acts of enclosure, which privatized land formerly held in common by village farmers, had contributed to the creation of an urban proletariat with no alternatives except destitution, which could be employed for subsistence wages in manufacturing.

The term "corporation" also had a different meaning in preindustrial Europe and America. Most corporations were government-chartered monopolies, created for a single purpose. Many of these were utilities, like bridges or canals or roads. Some were imperial agencies that functioned as quasi governments overseas, like the Dutch East India Company, the British East India Company, and the Virginia Company, which founded the first enduring British settlement in North America at Jamestown, Virginia, in 1607. The shareholders of these government-backed monopolies were usually well-connected aristocrats or wealthy businessmen who grew rich from tolls or other exactions.

The American Revolution promised freedom from the premodern institutions of monarchy and aristocracy to most Americans. But the promise of the liberation of most Americans from various forms of premodern economic subjugation, as a result of science and technological progress, would have to wait until the industrial revolution came to the New World from the Old.

AN ECONOMY BUILT ON WATER AND WIND

The first American economy was built on water and wind.

During the colonial period, most of the important cities and towns in the future United States had grown up along the fall line, where the rolling Piedmont plateau that stretches eastward from the foothills of the Appalachian Mountain chain drops down to the Atlantic coastal plain. Here, in the rivers that drained eastward from the mountains to the ocean, rapids or waterfalls prevented sailing ships from traveling farther upriver. Here cargo had to be unloaded for overland portage, and falls provided waterpower for mills. The cities of the fall line included Trenton, New Jersey; Philadelphia, Pennsylvania; Baltimore, Maryland; Georgetown, Maryland (later a part of Washington, DC); Richmond,

Virginia; Fayetteville, North Carolina; Columbia, South Carolina; and Augusta, Georgia.

Most of the US population was clustered near the seacoast. Coastal trade among the states was less expensive than overland trade. In order to create a US merchant marine that could be mobilized to support the navy in wartime, Congress protected the American shipbuilding and cabotage (intranational shipping) industry. The second law passed by Congress after the adoption of the federal constitution in 1789 required US flag ships to be built in American shipyards and imposed discriminatory duties on foreign ships in US ports. The Navigation Act of 1817 outlawed waterborne transportation of goods between two points in the United States by foreign vessels, reserving internal shipping for American ships. This protectionist measure had the support of no less an authority than Adam Smith, who in *The Wealth of Nations* endorsed the British Navigation Acts that required all trade to and from Britain to be carried in British ships: "The act of navigation is not favourable to foreign commerce, or to the growth of that opulence which can arise from it. . . . As defence, however, is of much more importance than opulence, the act of navigation is, perhaps, the wisest of all the commercial regulations of England."[5]

The Allegheny and Appalachian Mountains separated the Atlantic seaboard from the Northwest Territory that would be carved into Illinois, Indiana, Michigan, Ohio, Wisconsin, and part of Minnesota. The expense and hardships of overland travel made movement to the territory difficult for settlers and hindered the ability of the future Midwest to trade crops, timber, and minerals for goods from the East and overseas. Roads in the early American republic, including those built and operated by turnpike companies chartered by state governments, were crude and sometimes impassable. Before the evolution of steam-powered locomotives, the infrastructure projects that could best promote freight and passenger transportation were canals.

"LITTLE SHORT OF MADNESS"—THE ERIE CANAL

By far the most successful was the Erie Canal. In 1808, Jefferson told a New York assemblyman that the idea of a canal between the Hudson River and Lake Erie was "little short of madness."[6] New York City mayor and later New York governor DeWitt Clinton and Gouverneur Morris, who chaired the New York State board of canal commissioners, met with President Madison and obtained his and Treasury Secretary Gallatin's support for the Erie Canal. Gallatin even proposed to use money from a land grant in Indiana to pay for it.[7] But Congress rejected federal aid.

Undeterred, New York built the canal on its own. Alexander Hamilton's father-in-law, General Philip Schuyler, a New York senator, helped to create the Western Inland Lock Navigation Company to build a precursor to the canal and joined the lobbying effort to have the state build it. In 1817, Clinton persuaded the New York State legislature to authorize $7 million to build the canal. Half of the bonds for the Erie Canal were purchased by foreigners.[8]

The work was begun in 1817 and finished in only eight years. On October 26, 1825, Governor Clinton departed from Buffalo on a canal boat named the *Seneca Chief*. The *Seneca Chief* was accompanied by a canal boat called *Noah's Ark*, which carried, not two of each kind of animal, but symbols of the West: fish, birds including two eagles, a beaver, a bear, and two Seneca Indian boys. Cannons fired in a relay, bringing the news of Clinton's departure in two hours to New York City.

In Rochester, the captain of a boat called the *Young Lion of the West* took part with a member of the procession in a catechism:

"Who comes there?"

"Your brothers from the West on the waters of the Great Lakes."

"By what means have they been diverted so far from their natural course?"

"Through the channel of the great Erie Canal."

"By whose authority and by whom was a work of such magnitude accomplished?"

"By the authority and by the enterprise of the people of the State of New York."[9]

It took nine days for Clinton and his entourage to arrive at New York. Waiting there with the crowds were President John Quincy Adams, former presidents John Adams, Jefferson, Madison, and Monroe, and the marquis de Lafayette, who was visiting the United States.

Towed by eight steamboats, the canal boats arrived in New York Harbor on November 4, 1825. The steamboat *Washington* towed the *Seneca Chief* to Sandy Hook, where New York Harbor meets the Atlantic Ocean. Imitating the ceremonial marriage of Venice with the sea enacted by the doge, or elected chief magistrate, Clinton enacted the "marriage of the waters." He poured water from Lake Erie into the Atlantic, then mixed waters from eleven major foreign rivers, including the Rhine and the Amazon, with the mingled water of the Great Lakes and the Atlantic. In a subsequent ceremony on November 25, water from the Atlantic was poured into Lake Erie.

The 363-mile canal, with 83 locks and 18 aqueduct crossings over other bodies of water, ascended nearly six hundred feet from the Hudson River to Lake Erie. The Erie Canal facilitated passenger travel between the East Coast and the Great Lakes. Streams of pioneer families on canal boats traveled to new homes in the growing Midwest. It may be presumed they were less fastidious than the British visitors who wrote about the experience of canal-boat travel in America. Frances Trollope thought that American women settling into the confined spaces "look like hedgehogs, with every quill raised."[10] Another British traveler, Harriet Martineau, complained: "The heat and noise, the known vicinity of a compressed crowd, lying packed like herrings in a barrel, the bumping against the sides of the locks, and the hissing of water therein like an inundation, starting one from sleep; these things are disagreeable."[11]

The contribution of the Erie Canal to low-cost freight transportation was profound. By dramatically reducing the costs of long-distance shipping, the canal permitted farms in the Midwest to supply the Atlantic seaboard. Following the completion of the canal, the cost of shipping a ton of wheat from Buffalo to New York City dropped from one hundred dollars to ten dollars.[12] In 1829, 3,640 bushels of wheat traveled along the canal from Buffalo. In 1841, the number had grown to one million.[13] One consequence was the decline of wheat growing in New England under competitive pressure from the Midwest, to which many New Englanders migrated.

The Erie Canal enabled Manhattan to defeat its rivals Boston, New Orleans, and Baltimore for primacy as the leading American port. Beginning in 1790, when it had 33,000 inhabitants, New York increased its population by more than 50 percent each decade until 1860, when it had 800,000 residents. DeWitt Clinton's vision of the future of Manhattan was fulfilled: "The city will, in the course of time, become the granary of the world, the emporium of commerce, the seat of manufactures, the focus of great moneyed operations. And before the revolution of a century, the whole island of Manhattan, covered with inhabitants and replenished with a dense population, will constitute one vast city."[14]

CANAL MANIA

Even before construction began on the Erie Canal, Albert Gallatin, Jefferson's Treasury secretary, published an ambitious plan for a nationwide system of canals. Although the Gallatin plan was never enacted, many of the canals he proposed were built by individual state and local governments, in the era of canal building from 1815 to the 1840s.[15]

The success of the Erie Canal inspired other states to emulate New York in the 1820s and 1830s. Pennsylvania paid for its own "Portage and Canal System" from Philadelphia to Pittsburgh and the Miami Canal linked Cincinnati to Lake Erie. But the government of Virginia failed to complete the Chesapeake and Ohio (C&O) Canal, which ended at Cumberland in Maryland, and the James River Canal, which ended more than one hundred miles from the Ohio River.

Convict labor was sometimes used in canal construction and in the South some slaveowners rented out slaves. Much of the labor in every region was supplied by poor Irish immigrants, many of them indentured servants. Tools were primitive—wheelbarrows, shovels, and dangerous blasting powder. Irish laborers used the phrase "sprig of Shillelagh," a term for a club, to describe an endless screw machine that used a cable to snap trees so that they could be uprooted. As they built the Erie Canal, workers sang a ballad:

> I learned for to be very handy;
> To use both the shovel and spade;
> I learned the whole art of canalling;
> I think it an excellent trade.
> I learned for to be very handy,
> Although I was not very tall,
> I could handle the "sprig of Shillelagh"
> With the best man on the canal.

Accidents were common and disease even worse. The canal diggers spent much of their time partly immersed in water or in mud. They suffered from mosquito-borne illnesses, including malaria, typhus, and cholera. During the construction of the Erie Canal near Syracuse, a thousand workers suffered from typhoid fever, malaria, ague, and other diseases, and many died.

The combination of alcohol and exclusively male company led to frequent fights among the canal workers and between them and hostile locals. Workers frequently deserted projects like the C&O Canal. The *Maryland Chronicle* on February 22, 1786, warned local residents that "several servants who had been purchased to work on the Potowmack Navigation lately ran away, but being soon after apprehended, were sentenced to have their heads and eyebrows shaved, which operation was im-

mediately executed, and is to be continued every week during the time
of their servitude, or until their behavior evinces that they are brought
to a sense of their duty." The problem continued, however, forcing James
Rumsey, the manager who oversaw the project, to advertise on June 21,
1786: "Wm. Fee (Shaved,) James Nevin, Francis Cary, Arthur Mullin,
(shaved) Thos. Moore, James Munnay, Hugh Taylor, Rob't Meighan,
Taylor took a variety of clothes with him, among them a super fine green
cloth coat with bright buttons. £60 reward for all or £10 for each."[16]

SLAVERY AND THE TRAGEDY OF
GEORGE WASHINGTON

In the American South, the rhetoric of equal rights and democracy was
turned into a mockery by black slavery and a hierarchical social order, in
which a few rich white slaveowning families lorded it over their slaves and
poor whites. Thomas Jefferson tried to reconcile his vision of a nation of
humble white farmers and mechanics with his racist belief in black infe-
riority by proposing colonization, the voluntary emigration of freed slaves
to some other country. This doomed scheme was championed by members of the American Colonization Society, including such prominent
slaveholders as James Madison and Henry Clay. Clay's disciple Abraham
Lincoln championed colonization as well, abandoning it only reluctantly
during the Civil War.

Like Jefferson, Washington recognized the harm that slavery did to
his native region. Although Washington sought to appear nonpartisan,
he repeatedly sided with Hamilton and the emerging Federalist Party
against Jefferson, Madison, and the Republicans (who later became Democratic Republicans and then Democrats in the 1830s). In his political
and economic views, he had more in common with the merchants and
landowners of the North than with other southerners. Washington complained that his fellow Virginians had "the most malignant (and if one
may be allowed the expression, the most unwarrantable) disposition toward the new government."[17]

Washington believed in national and regional economic diversification. In 1774, he and other delegates in Williamsburg called on Virginians to reduce their imports from Britain and support "manufactures of all sorts." In his tour of New England as president in 1789, Washington was fascinated by its mills, ships, roads, and ports. In the same year, Washington wrote to Lafayette: "Equally certain it is, that no diminution of agriculture has taken place, at the time when greater and more substantial improvements in manufacturers were making, than were ever known before in America."[18]

Washington supported large-scale economic development for personal as well as patriotic reasons. Following the French and Indian War (1757–1763), he had obtained land in reward for his military service and added other purchases, in the amount of around thirty thousand acres in the Ohio River valley near present-day Pittsburgh. He was outraged when the British government, seeking peace with the Indians, banned settlement of the area with a royal proclamation in 1763. Following his retirement to Mount Vernon after the end of the War of Independence, Washington turned his energies to building his own economic empire. In 1784, he traveled to western Pennsylvania to visit some of the acreage he owned, and when he discovered that settlers had taken up residence and refused to leave, he successfully sued to have what he called this "grazing multitude" evicted.

In order to raise the value of both his western and eastern lands as well as to promote national commerce, Washington organized and became the first president of the Potomac Company, which sought to make the Potomac River navigable beyond Georgetown, where a series of falls, including the Great Falls of the Potomac, blocked ships from traveling farther upstream. Washington dreamed of making the neighborhood of Mount Vernon a center of national and global commerce. In his vision, goods from the Midwest would travel over a link between the Ohio River and the Potomac to meet with trade from Europe. An experiment with a steam engine in the Potomac inspired this reflection by Washington: "I consider Rumsey's discovery for working boats against the stream, by mechanical powers principally, as not only a very fortunate invention for these States in general, but as one of those circumstances, which have combined to render the present time favorable above all others for fixing, if we are disposed to avail ourselves of them, a large portion of the trade of the western country in the bosom of this State [Virginia] irrevocably."[19]

Washington envisioned a shift from a slave-based plantation economy in his home region to one based on economic diversification and free labor. In 1786, he wrote: "I never mean . . . to possess another slave by purchase; it being among my first wishes to see some plan adopted, by which slavery may be abolished by slow, sure and imperceptible degrees."[20] On his own estates he switched from tobacco for export to wheat and other crops. He proposed a national agency to promote scientific agriculture and supported the idea of a national university in the capital.

But all of Washington's grand schemes for the economic development of his part of Virginia were doomed to fail. Following his death in 1799, the Potomac Company was absorbed into the Chesapeake and Ohio Canal company, which completed a canal only to Cumberland, Maryland, in 1850. By that time the canal had been superseded by the Baltimore and Ohio Railroad. Long before, the Erie Canal had turned New York City into the dominant entrepôt of North America. Virginia fell further and further behind the commercial, industrial North. Not until the Lincoln administration was a US Department of Agriculture established, and Washington's gift in his will of fifty shares of Potomac Company stock to the never-founded National University in Washington, DC, was never used.

Washington had hoped to sell some of his western land to finance the purchase of the "dower slaves" at Mount Vernon that his wife, Martha, had inherited from her first husband, but he could not raise the money. In his will, he asked that his own slaves, who had intermarried with Martha's, be freed at her death, and that the younger should be educated while the elder should be cared for. But according to Abigail Adams, who visited Mount Vernon shortly after his death, his widow Martha "did not feel as tho' her Life was safe in their hands" and freed Washington's slaves to remove any incentive on their part to accelerate her demise in order to gain their freedom—a grim reflection on the nature of slavery. She did not free her own slaves in her life or in her will. And in the decades following Washington's death, the industrial revolution, by creating a lucrative market in Britain for slave-picked cotton, entrenched slavery in the Southern economy to the point that by the mid-nineteenth century many southerners viewed slavery not as an inherited evil but as a positive good.

LORDS OF THE MANOR

Outside of the South, the region with the most unequal patterns of land ownership and labor relations was the Hudson River valley of New York. In the seventeenth century, Dutch settlers called "patroons," or patrons, had been granted vast estates, which they populated with tenant farmers. When the British captured New Netherland from the Dutch in 1664 and made it part of the colony of New York, the British government kept and extended the system of patroonship for English settlers. Like other states, New York abolished primogeniture soon after the American Revolution, but for seventy years, until the 1840s, "lords of the manor" continued to lord it over their tenants along the Hudson.

A Pole who visited the region in the late 1790s wrote: "The word Patroun is pronounced by everyone with deference and a certain fear. [Stephen Van Rensselaer III] holds here the place held by the Radziwills in Lithuania. The Czartoryski family, that is the Livingstons, is large, wealthy and greatly honored."[21] The Van Rensselaers owned three-quarters of a million acres that stretched for twenty-four miles along the Hudson. In the late eighteenth century, the Livingston family owned 35 percent of the land in Columbia County, New York. Their holdings were divided between the Upper Manor, with about 600 tenant farms, and the Lower Manor, with around 120.[22]

Stephen Van Rensselaer III, who inherited the rights to the Manor of Rensselaerwyck, was the tenth richest American in US history to date, based on his personal fortune as a percentage of the national economy at the time of his death. Van Rensselaer's political ambitions were damaged when he proved to be a disastrous failure during the War of 1812. Elected to Congress, in 1825 he cast the deciding vote that put John Quincy Adams in the White House, even though he had received less of the popular vote than Andrew Jackson. A regent of the University of the State of New York, he founded Rensselaer Polytechnic Institute, which flourishes today. His marriage to Margarita Schuyler, daughter of the Revolutionary War general Henry Schuyler, made him an in-law of Alexander Hamilton, who married another of Schuyler's daughters, Elizabeth.

The contracts between patroons and their tenants were modeled on those between European aristocrats and their peasants. The leaseholders were required to provide payment in cash, kind, and personal service. For example, when James Van Deusen leased a 130-acre farm from Robert Livingston in 1785, the terms of his lease required him to bring, on "rent day" (January 1), thirty bushels of "good, clear, and merchantable Winter wheat," plus two fat hens. Two days a year, Van Deusen was required to provide unpaid labor or else pay a fine as a penalty. Van Deusen also had to pay 6 shillings a year to support the manor's own Protestant minister.[23] The tenants had to pay state taxes on the farms they leased, while the patroons themselves paid taxes only on farm and common land they controlled directly. The Van Rensselaers, Livingstons, and other manorial dynasties in New York also owned black slaves.

The Livingstons' manor house, Clermont, was described in 1813 by a New York newspaper as "among the largest and most commodious houses in the state. Its front on the river is 104 feet, depth 91, and it consists of a main body of 2 stories; and 4 pavilions. The south or garden-front is a greenhouse, with bathing-rooms and offices adjoining; over these is a large elegant breakfasting room, and 4 bedrooms. The second story is conveniently divided into rooms connected by a gallery. One of the pavilions contains a well chosen library of about 4000 volumes, in various languages."[24] Many of the tenants, however, lived in conditions little better than those of slaves in the South.

THE ANTI-RENT WARS

The manor of Rensselaerwyck had more than three thousand tenants. Before the American Revolution, there were tenant revolts against the patroons in 1755 and 1766.[25] Stephen Van Rensselaer III was known as the "good patroon" for his forebearance in collecting rents from struggling farmers among his roughly three thousand tenants. But when he died in 1839, his estate passed to his two sons, Stephen Van Rensselaer IV and William, who insisted that tenants repay all debts immediately.

After their protests failed, tenants organized a mass meeting on the symbolic date of July 4, 1839. When the sheriff's department served writs of ejectment against tenants, their allies organized vigilante groups whose members disguised themselves as "Injuns," wearing calico dresses, sheepskin hoods with holes for the eyes and mouth, and feathered headdresses. Led by men with code names like Bluebeard, Redjacket, Yellowjacket, Big Thunder, and Little Thunder, they vandalized property, burned farms and houses, and tarred and feathered sheriffs' agents. Their chief goal was destroying records of leaseholds.

On August 7, 1845, as he was confronting a mob of two hundred men in "Injun" costume and trying to confiscate cattle in repayment for a debt to the Van Rensselaers, Under-Sheriff Osman Steele was shot to death. Following the murder, hundreds of people were arrested. Around sixty were imprisoned and two were condemned to be hanged (their sentences were commuted later to life in prison).[26] Public opinion favored the tenants. The New York Constitution of 1846 abolished manorial leases, forcing the lords of the manor to sell most of their lands to former tenants or others.

FLOWERY FLAG DEVILS

The American Revolution had partly democratized the political order, but the economic structure of the new republic remained far from democratic, from the South, which was dominated by slave-owning planters like Washington, Jefferson, and Madison, to the Hudson River valley with its semifeudal patroons. In the first half of the nineteenth century, before the rise of a new class of rich industrialists, the nation's slavelords and landlords were joined by another wealthy elite, the merchants.

"I am sending some ships to China in order to encourage others in the adventurous pursuits of commerce," Robert Morris wrote in November 1783.[27] On February 22, 1784, the *Empress of China*, financed by Morris, set off from New York. Its major cargoes were ginseng, prized by Chinese as a medicine and aphrodisiac, and specie, or metal coin.

China traded with the outside world only through Canton (Guangzhou), where foreign trade was controlled by a guild of merchants, the Co-Hong. The most famous among them was Wu Ping-chien, known to British and American traders as Houqua ("qua" is a title like "mister"). Houqua was reputed to be the richest man in the world.[28]

After the arrival of the *Empress of China* at Canton on August 28, a crewmember wrote: "The Chinese had never heard of us, but we introduced ourselves as a new Nation, gave them our history, with a description of our Country, the importance and necessity of a trade here to the advantage to both which they appear perfectly to understand and wish." To distinguish the Americans from the other *fanqui* (foreign devils), the Chinese, mistaking the stars on the US flag for flowers, called them the "Flowery Flag Devils." Loaded with tea, silk, porcelain, and a buff-colored Chinese cotton cloth called "nankeen," the *Empress of China* returned to New York Harbor on May 11, 1785.[29]

Soon the China trade attracted Americans who dreamed of making a quick fortune and retiring to a rural estate or urban mansion. One of the wealthiest Americans in the early republic was Elias Hasket Derby, a shipowner in Salem, Massachusetts, who himself never went to sea. His ship *Light Horse* in 1784 was the first to trade with Russia. A pioneer of the China trade, he became known as "King" Derby because of the size of his fortune.

The race to beat other ships home inspired the evolution of the "clipper ship," from the word "to clip," meaning "to move quickly." One of the first clipper ships was named *Houqua*.[30]

Like other Western merchants, the Americans in the China trade had difficulty finding items that the self-sufficient Chinese needed or wanted. Officials in China prized sea otter fur, which they obtained at first from Russian traders in the Pacific Northwest. The American fur trade with China began in 1787, when five Boston merchants, including a son of Elias Derby, financed the *Columbia* and the *Lady Washington*. Their ships stopped on the Northwest Coast of North America, where their crews obtained animal pelts from the local Indians in return for blankets, beads, metal buttons, and fishhooks, among other items, then sailed to Canton and sold the fur. In addition to furs for the garments of affluent Chinese, they sought to sell ginseng and sandalwood, which was made into a paste and burned before Chinese religious images. American merchants even sold rice to China.

Then there was opium. While opium consumption dates back millennia in China, opium smoking is thought to have been introduced by seventeenth-century Dutch traders, who combined opium with tobacco in pipes. Although the Chinese government banned importation of the drug, the British East India Company made large profits by smuggling Indian opium to China. The firm of Jardine, Matheson originated as a British opium-smuggling operation. Britain's Indian opium was off-limits to American merchants, but in 1804 Benjamin Chew Wilcocks of Philadelphia found a substitute in Turkish opium. American ships bought opium from Smyrna, Turkey, either by sailing to the eastern Mediterranean or purchasing it at Gibraltar.

The leading American drug-smuggling operation in China was J. & T. H. Perkins Company, which brought in more Turkish opium than its rivals.[31] One of its principals, Thomas Handasyd Perkins, instructed a captain in 1791 that he had "best sell the furs down the River, to avoid [customs] charges."[32] On behalf of the *hong* merchants, Houqua warned the Americans: "Opium, the dirt used in smoking, has long been prohibited by an order received, it is not allowed to come to Canton."[33] The Americans, like the British, ignored the law. In 1817–1818, if silver coin is factored out, opium is estimated to have made up 10 to 30 percent of the value of

US commodities used to purchase Chinese merchandise, while Americans supplied between 10 percent and a third of the opium consumed in China.[34]

In 1823, Warren Delano II sailed to Canton and within seven years rose to be a senior partner in the Boston-based firm of Russell and Company. Having made his fortune, Delano retired in 1851 to Newburgh, New York. He wrote: "I do not pretend to justify the prosecution of the opium trade from a moral and philosophical point of view, but as a merchant I insist that it is a fair, honorable, and legitimate trade. I considered it right to follow the example of England, the East India Company, and the merchants to whom I had always been accustomed to look up to—the Perkins, the Peabodys, the Russells, and the Lowes." Delano's daughter Sara married James Roosevelt and gave birth to his grandson, Franklin Delano Roosevelt.[35]

In the Opium Wars of 1839–1842 and 1856–1860, the British, with assistance from the French, invaded China in response to the government's attempts to stamp out the foreign opium trade. Britain and other Western powers imposed "unequal treaties" that gave them commercial privileges on the Chinese. In 1844, the Treaty of Wang Hiya guaranteed Americans the same terms that were extorted by the British. Following the example of Britain, the United States imposed trade treaties on Japan beginning on July 8, 1853, when Commodore Matthew Perry's fleet steamed into Tokyo Bay.

From that point until the Chinese Revolution of 1911, China was a shattered state, riven by warlords and drenched with blood in the catastrophic Taiping Rebellion of 1850–1864. The historian John K. Fairbank called the opium trade in which American merchants took part "the most long continued and systematic international crime of modern times."[36]

STEPHEN GRASP-ALL

In January 1805, Stephen Girard wrote instructions to two of his agents in the Mediterranean: "I am very much in favor of investing heavily in opium. While the war lasts, opium will supply a good price in China."[37]

When Girard got out of the trading business around 1812, he invested much of the wealth he had made from trade in banking, real estate, Pennsylvania coal lands, and early railroads. He was one of the richest Americans of all time when, after suffering injuries in a street accident, he died in 1831.[38]

Born under the name of Étienne Girard into a family of merchants in Bordeaux, France, Girard sailed on trading trips to the West Indies. Fearing debtors' prison after losing money on goods he had purchased on credit, Girard moved to New York and became a mate or captain on ships trading with the West Indies and Louisiana. When war broke out in 1776, Girard brought his ship for safety to Philadelphia and settled there.

His marriage to his American wife produced no children and when she went insane she was confined for the last quarter century of her life to a hospital. When, during her confinement, she gave birth to a daughter, Girard claimed the child was not his; mother and daughter both soon died. Girard lived with several mistresses but never remarried.

The mature Girard whom his fellow Philadelphians came to know was a small, balding man with a blind, disfigured right eye. He spoke poor English with a French accent and made his home above his offices near the waterfront. Girard is still remembered in Philadelphia for his philanthropy. During a yellow-fever epidemic in 1793 that killed between four and five thousand people, Girard won the admiration of his neighbors by remaining in Philadelphia and organizing operations in Bush Hill Hospital.

Girard was the embodiment of the secular North Atlantic bourgeoisie in the age of the American and French Revolutions. He sided with the Francophile Jeffersonian Republicans against the Anglophile Hamiltonian Federalists. He named three of the ships in his merchant fleet the *Montesquieu*, the *Voltaire*, and the *Rousseau* and hired the painter and sculptor William Rush to fashion busts of the *philosophes* as their figureheads. All but $140,000 of the childless merchant's $7 million fortune went to Girard College for "white male orphans." In his will he stipulated that clerics would not be allowed in the school.

His enemies called the odd little French immigrant "Stephen Grasp-all." Girard bribed customs officials on three continents, forged ship man-ifests and other documents, and used young apprentices in order to avoid paying high wages for experienced sailors.[39] During a spell of exile in Philadelphia, Napoleon's brother Joseph, the former king of Spain, rented a house from Girard and wanted to buy an entire block. When Joseph Bonaparte proposed that he would pay the amount that resulted from covering the entire area with silver half-dollars, Girard is said to have re-plied, "I will take that offer, on condition that you stand them on edge."[40]

Girard got into the China trade in the 1790s. Much of his fortune was made in trade with the West Indies. Girard sent flour, rice, lard, ham, and other foodstuffs to be consumed mostly by slaves to the French sugar colony of Saint-Domingue (Santo Domingo), in return for sugar, molas-ses, coffee, and cocoa. On one occasion Girard instructed agents to give customhouse officers "a few portugaises to silence them."[41] He evaded customs duties and engaged in large-scale smuggling with the help of his brother, a resident of the island who threatened to blackmail the rival partner whom Girard chose after a quarrel.

When a massive slave rebellion broke out, following the revolutionary French Assembly's promise to grant rights to slaves, Girard suffered losses and helped refugees from the white French-speaking elite of the island in Philadelphia. He owned slaves, including a black woman named Hanna whom he freed and provided for in his will, as well as dozens of slaves who worked a Louisiana plantation he owned. Although historians dis-miss the rumor that he grew rich by stealing assets of refugees killed in the slave rebellion, Girard like many merchants and bankers of the time was deeply implicated in the institution of slavery. In 1906, the *New York Daily Tribune* reported: "The charge that Stephen Girard, philanthropist, was a slave dealer, is being forced upon the unwilling attention of the world by the recent discovery, in demolishing his old house at No. 22 North Water street, Philadelphia, of three tiers of underground cells that seem to have been used for the purpose of incarcerating human beings."[42] Wachovia Bank has officially apologized for the participation of one of its predecessors, the Bank of Stephen Girard, in the slave trade and the slave plantation system.

"NOW I WILL MAKE MY FORTUNE IN THE FUR TRADE"

Like Girard, John Jacob Astor was one of the richest Americans who ever lived, on the basis of the proportion between his wealth and that of the national economy. And like Girard, Astor made part of his fortune in the China trade, in part by selling opium but mainly by selling the furs of beavers, otters, and other North American mammals whose populations he did more than any other individual to decimate.

Astor was the son of a butcher, born in 1763 in Waldorf, Germany, near Heidelberg. Following the examples of his brother George in England and his brother Henry in New York, Astor emigrated, against the wishes of his father. Astor spent four years in London working with his brother George, before emigrating to join Henry in the United States in 1783, following the end of the war between Britain and its former colonies.

On his way to New York, Astor learned about opportunities in the fur trade from another German passenger on a ship. Soon he was working for a New York fur merchant, William Backhouse. Astor made arduous trips up the Hudson River to negotiate for furs from beaver, otter, muskrat, bear, and other mammals with members of the Iroquois and other tribes. He learned much of the business from a friend, Alexander Henry, an experienced employee of the British-Canadian Hudson Bay Company, which dominated the North American fur trade. From an early age he seems to have envisioned establishing a private monopoly that he would completely control to rival the Hudson Bay Company. When Jay's Treaty with Britain permitted both British subjects and American citizens to share in the jointly administered Northwest Territory, Astor exclaimed: "Now I will make my fortune in the fur trade."[43]

In 1800, Astor and fellow investors sent a ship called the *Severn* loaded with furs to Canton. On its return, Astor invested his profits in his own ship, which he named the *Beaver*, and soon began to invest in the Manhattan real estate that would further enrich him and his heirs. Following the Louisiana Purchase of 1803 and the Lewis and Clark Expedition of 1806, Astor saw an opportunity to expand his operations. He won the support of President Thomas Jefferson to establish a trading community called Astoria at the mouth of the Columbia River. The expeditions that he sent to Astoria ended in disaster, but Astor hired the celebrated writer Washington Irving to pen a romantic account of the debacle, portraying it as a success. *Astoria: Or Anecdotes of an Enterprise Beyond the Rocky Mountains* became a best seller.

In November 1807, a British order in council declared all ports in France and its allies blockaded. Neutral vessels were required to enter a British port and pay for a license. In retaliation, under the leadership of Jefferson in December 1807, the US adopted a self-imposed embargo—known by its critics as the "Dambargo" or "O-grab-me"—that outlawed all foreign trade, although American ships were permitted to engage in coastal trade in the United States. Instead of forcing Britain to change its policy, this ill-conceived measure merely crippled American commerce and inspired smuggling on a heroic scale. In 1809, Congress repealed the Embargo Act but maintained a prohibition on trade by US vessels with Britain, France, or ports they controlled.

When Jefferson's embargo banned American ships from engaging in international trade, Astor asked for an exemption from the law. First he pretended that he needed to bring back property he owned in Canton. After the Swiss-born Treasury secretary Albert Gallatin refused to grant an exception, the German-American merchant came up with another plan. Astor lobbied New York senator Samuel Latham Mitchell to write a letter to President Jefferson, explaining the desire of a Chinese merchant in the United States named "Punqua Wingchong" to return "to Canton, where the affairs of his family and particularly the funeral obsequies of his grandfather, require his solemn attention." A letter from the alleged mandarin followed. Jefferson told Gallatin: "I consider it a case of na-

tional comity . . . the departure of this individual may be the means of
our making our nation known advantageously at the source of power in
China to which it is otherwise difficult to convey information." Gallatin
obeyed, but complained to Jefferson: "Had I any discretion to the application itself I would have hesitated."

When news of Astor's ruse spread, other merchants protested. There
was speculation that Astor's "mandarin" was "a common Chinese dock
loafer" or an Indian "dressed up in Astor's silks and coached to play his
part."[44]

WHEN THE RICH BAILED OUT THE
GOVERNMENT

In modern America, the government sometimes is forced to bail out the
financial sector. In early America, the rich sometimes bailed out the government.

Stephen Girard bought shares in the first Bank of the United States,
which had been created by Alexander Hamilton, and lobbied for the renewal of the bank's charter in 1811. When Congress refused to renew
the charter, Girard bought not only most of the bank's assets but also the
buildings and hired much of the staff. He reopened the former Bank of
the United States under a new name: the Bank of Stephen Girard.

During the War of 1812, the federal government suffered from financial distress as well as humiliations such as the burning of Washington,
DC, by British forces and the defeat of the American attempt to conquer Canada. The Madison administration turned to Girard and Astor
for help. The two foreign-born financiers were joined by a third, David
Parish.

Parish was born in Germany into a trading dynasty founded by his
grandfather, a British merchant who moved to Hamburg. With the benefit of his family connections, Parish made a fortune in Antwerp during the wars of the French Revolution. In 1806, he went to Philadelphia
as the agent for a European syndicate involved in shipping silver from

Mexico to Napoleon and appears in that capacity in Hervey Allen's historical novel *Anthony Adverse* (1933). This made him even richer. He used his wealth to purchase two hundred thousand acres in upstate New York from Gouverneur Morris, developed the towns of Ogdensburg, Antwerp, and Parishville, and set up an ironworks after iron was discovered on land he owned at Rossie. After helping Gallatin, Girard, and Astor finance the War of 1812, Parish moved back to Europe to join a bank in Vienna. A financial crisis in 1825 led to ruin not only for him but also for his father and the following year Parish committed suicide by drowning himself in the Danube.

During the War of 1812, Girard teamed up with Astor and Parish to buy federal bonds and raise loans. In 1813, Girard, Astor, and Parish were the major subscribers to the government's Sixteen Millions Loan. In the spring of 1814, the three discreetly discussed plans to create a second Bank of the United States. When Gallatin took up his duties as peace commissioner at the end of the war, the Treasury was briefly in the hands of two native-born Americans, William Jones and George W. Campbell, who proved so incompetent that the post was once again given in the fall of 1814 to an immigrant who understood finance, Alexander Dallas, who was born in Jamaica and raised in Edinburgh and London. Dallas worked closely with Girard, Astor, and Parish to design the new bank.

The three financiers profited from the rise in the US bonds that they held following the new bank's charter. Girard and Astor also obtained seats on the bank's board of directors. Dissatisfied with its first president, William Jones, who proved to be as inept at the bank as he had been at the Treasury, Girard resigned. Girard was pleased by Jones's successors, Langdon Cheves and the even more capable Nicholas Biddle.

The domination of trade and finance in the early United States by immigrants from Europe or the West Indies—Albert Gallatin, Stephen Girard, John Jacob Astor, David Parish, and Alexander Hamilton—illustrates how provincial and undeveloped the United States was in this period. As a postcolonial, agrarian country, the early United States resembled the Central American "banana republics" of later times, with their inaccessible hinterlands, landed elites, and port cities where many of the merchants and bankers were expatriates.

As in Southeast Asia, where *guanxi* (connections) link overseas Chinese middlemen living in different countries, webs of kinship ties and personal relationships were critical to the success of most merchants and financiers in the preindustrial era. Girard, Astor, and Parish all worked with family members who lived abroad. This merely reinforced the assumption, among the agrarians who made up nine-tenths of the US population, that trade and finance were foreign and sinister.

ASTOR AND THE INDIAN FACTORIES

When Jay's Treaty with Britain restored commercial relations between the former colonies and the mother country in 1795, the Northwest was opened up to American fur traders. Astor bought cheap manufactured goods from Britain and sold them to Indians in return for furs, which he shipped to China in exchange for tea, silk, and chinaware. Astor created the Pacific Fur Company, headquartered in the town of Astoria on the Columbia River, to ship furs directly to China. His Southwest Fur Company bought out Canadian rivals in the Great Lakes region. Astor also made deals with the Russian government in then-Russian Alaska.

Following the War of 1812, one thing stood in the way of the fur trade monopoly of which Astor dreamed. The federal government had set up a system of trading posts, or "factories" (from the term "factor" for merchant), in Indian country, with the goals of winning Indian tribes away from Britain's influence while protecting them from unscrupulous private traders. However, the government licensed trading companies like Astor's to compete for trade with the government Indian factories.

In 1821, around the time that Astor was getting out of the opium trade in China, liquor became the American Fur Company's major item offered in exchange for animal pelts.[45] A federal agent wrote: "The traders that occupy the largest and most important space in the Indian country are the agents and engages of the American Fur Trade Company. They entertain, as I know to be the fact, no sort of respect for our citizens, agents, officers of the Government, or its laws and general policy. . . . The whisky is sold to the Indians in the face of the agents. Indians are made drunk, and of course, behave badly."[46]

Astor was the archetype of a "crony capitalist," buying political influence in order to plunder the public domain. Having opposed the creation of the Indian factories in 1796, Astor successfully appealed to President Jefferson to allow him to compete with the government trading posts. Following the War of 1812, Astor successfully lobbied for a protectionist bill that limited the ability of foreigners to trade with Indians on American soil without presidential permission. After he succeeded, he obtained permission to employ Canadian trappers from President James Monroe, who happened to owe Astor thousands of dollars for a loan.

During successive congressional sessions he sent his deputy, a Scots immigrant named Ramsay Crooks, to live in Washington in order to direct a lobbying campaign that included pseudonymous attacks in the press on the Indian factory system and its supervisor, a dedicated and idealistic civil servant named William McKenney. Among those on Astor's payroll was his legal representative in Saint Louis, Thomas Hart Benton, who happened to be the chair of the Senate Committee on Indian Affairs. On May 6, 1822, the law abolishing the nonprofit factory system went into effect. Crooks wrote Benton: "The result is the best possible proof of the value to the country of talents, intelligence, and perseverance, and you deserve the unqualified thanks of the country for destroying the pious monster."[47]

Once the federal factory system had been wrecked, Astor moved to monopolize the North American fur trade, with devastating results to Indian societies and the natural environment. Astor was now free to flood the Indian territories with smuggled alcohol, in violation of federal law. One contemporary observed: "So violent is the attachment of the Indian for it that he who gives most is sure to obtain the furs, while should any one attempt to trade without it he is sure of losing ground with his antagonist. No bargain is ever made without it."[48]

The Hudson's Bay Company of British North America (later Canada) was as ruthless as Astor and his associates, saturating Indian country with alcohol and even attempting to undercut its American rivals by decimating fur-bearing mammals east of the Rockies, in a kind of scorched-earth policy. In 1822, when Congress was debating an absolute prohibition of alcohol in Indian territory, Astor wrote the lieutenant governor of Missouri, William H. Ashley: "If the Hudson's Bay Company did not employ ardent spirits against us, we would not ask for a single drop. But without it, competition is hopeless."[49] What was called "Indian Whiskey" consisted of straight alcohol mixed with river water and other ingredients as various as red peppers, molasses, ginger, tobacco, gunpowder, and sometimes strychnine.[50]

Later generations romanticized the fur traders and scouts as mountain men, larger-than-life figures in deerskins and fur hats. The most famous was Kit Carson, a Kentucky-born frontiersman. Carson guided the early explorations of John C. Frémont, who went on to win fame in the United States–Mexican War of 1846–1848 and to be the antislavery Republican Party's first nominee for president in 1856 (the second was Abraham Lincoln in 1860). More than six feet tall, Virginia-born Jim Bridger was another archetypal mountain man. After his first two Indian wives died, he married a third. He identified Bridger's Pass for a route used by overland pioneers and later by the Union Pacific and interstate highway 80.

While some were free agents, most of the trappers and traders worked in brigades headed by a "boosway," a corruption of the French *bourgeois*. Most were white Americans and English Canadians, but their ranks included French Canadians, including part-Indian métis, Mexicans, and black Americans like Jim Beckwourth, the son of a Virginia slave by a British immigrant, Sir Jennings Beckwith. He was adopted by the Crow nation and blazed the Beckwourth Trail in Nevada and California. Following the decline of the fur trade, some traders served as scouts for the army or explorers, while others opened up trading posts, went into farming or ranching, or joined the Forty-niners in the California gold rush that began in 1848.

While he was poisoning Indians with alcohol and devastating the North American mammal population, Astor was exploiting the traders who worked for him. One of them, William Johnston, complained: "At these exorbitant charges, the traders were through necessity compelled to take the merchandise, the consequence was, and still is, that for them to pay for the goods, and barely to obtain a livelihood, they are in part compelled to use fraud and deceit towards the men they have in their employ."[51] Debt forced many of his employees to become, in effect, indentured servants.

In the 1830s, Astor pulled out of the fur trade and devoted his last years to real estate investments and founding a dynasty, which included one descendant who went down on the *Titanic*, another who bought his way into the British aristocracy, and Franklin Roosevelt's lifelong friend and confidant Vincent Astor. Legend has it that when asked if he had any regrets, John Jacob Astor said that he regretted not having bought every inch of Manhattan.

By 1834, when Astor sold his company, changes in fashion and the collapse of populations of fur-bearing mammals had doomed the ephemeral industry. A government Indian agent calculated that between 1815 and 1830 the fur trade on average sold $3,750,000 of furs, in the following quantities each year: 26,000 buffalo skins; 25,000 pounds of beaver skins; 4,000 otter skins; 12,000 raccoon skins; 150,000 pounds of deer skins; and 37,000 muskrat skins.[52]

Astor's company spread social and ecological blight beyond North America. Visiting Hawaii, his merchants discovered that Hawaiian sandalwood could sell for high prices in China. Hawaiian chiefs began to compete in harvesting the wood and quickly destroyed sandalwood forests. Suffering from disease and demoralization, the native Hawaiian population collapsed from more than a million in 1798 to fewer than a quarter of a million by the 1820s.

"THE CLEAREST AND MOST
BEAUTIFUL FLAME": THE WHALING INDUSTRY
IN THE EARLY AMERICAN REPUBLIC

The ecological effects of the American whaling industry were as destructive as those of the North American fur trade.

Two thousand nautical miles west of the coast of South America in the Pacific, on November 20, 1820, the American whaling ship *Essex* was attacking a pod of sperm whales when one whale fought back. The enraged creature rammed the ship and crushed its bow, causing it to sink. The captain and the surviving crew in lifeboats traveled thousands of miles across the open water for three months, surviving by cannibalizing the dead. The story of the *Essex*, along with legends about a white whale called Mocha Dick, because it was said to haunt the waters off the island of Mocha near Chile, inspired a young whaler named Herman Melville who later became a novelist to write his masterpiece, *Moby-Dick*.

The sailors aboard the doomed *Essex* were after whale oil, a term that included both oil made from the blubber of whales and sperm oil or spermaceti, a waxy substance found in the heads of sperm whales. In the days before kerosene and electric lighting, whale oil was coveted for its use in illumination. As America's minister to Britain following the War of Independence, John Adams, tried to persuade the British to lower their barriers to the import of American whale oil: "The fat of the spermaceti whale gives the clearest and most beautiful flame of any substance that is known in nature, and we are all surprised that you prefer darkness, and consequent robberies, burglaries, and murders in your streets, to the receiving, as a remittance, our spermaceti oil."[53]

When the industry peaked in 1847, nearly seven hundred American whaling ships operated on the oceans of the world. Whaling was the fifth largest industry in the United States, employing seventy thousand people and harvesting nearly eight thousand whales a year. The two largest whaling ports were Nantucket and New Bedford, Massachusetts. New

London, Connecticut, and Sag Harbor, New York, were important as well.

Whales like the right whale, the bowhead, the humpback, and the gray that remained near the shore were soon decimated in the Northern Hemisphere. Whalers began undertaking longer voyages into the South Atlantic and Pacific to target sperm whales. American whalers stopped in Hawaii for sex and alcohol, and San Francisco became a major port for them.

One whaler, Charles Melville Scammon, used "bomb lances" to decimate the nurseries of gray whales along the West Coast. Following his retirement from whaling, in 1874, Scammon published *The Marine Mammals of the North-Western Coast of North America*, writing without irony: "The mammoth bones of the California Gray lie bleaching on the shores of these silvery waters, and are scattered along the broken coasts, from Siberia to the Gulf of California; and ere long it may be questioned whether this mammal will not be numbered among the extinct species of the Pacific."[54]

By the 1840s, whale oil was being pushed out of the market by less expensive lard oil made from the fat of hogs, which were nicknamed "prairie whales."[55] Whale oil faced competition as well from camphene, distilled from alcohol and turpentine, and from "town gas," hydrogen derived from coal. Toward the end of the 1840s, a Canadian geologist named Abraham Gesner distilled kerosene from asphalt and bituminous tar. By the time the Civil War erupted in 1861, even before Edwin Drake successfully drilled for oil in Titusville, Pennsylvania, in 1859, Americans spent more on coal gas and kerosene than on whale oil.[56]

A shrunken American whaling industry survived for at time, supplying baleen (erroneously called "whale-bone"), a supple material used in women's corsets. But the development of pliant steel and plastics and changes in women's fashion eliminated the market for baleen as well. The American whaling fleet shrank from 735 ships at its height in 1854 to only 32 in 1914.[57] A cartoon in *Vanity Fair* in 1861 depicted a party in a ballroom filled with whales in fancy dress. Beneath festive banners that read

"Oils Well That Ends Well" and "We Wail No More For Our Blubber," the jubilant whales raised the glasses they held in their flippers in a toast. The cartoon's caption read: "Grand Ball Given by the Whales in Honor of the Discovery of the Oil Wells in Pennsylvania."[58]

THE AMERICAN REVOLUTION AND THE INDUSTRIAL REVOLUTION

The United States may have been the first modern republic, but it inherited a premodern economy. In the gap between the political revolution of 1776 and the industrial revolution, which only got under way on a large scale in the United States in the 1830s, negative views of large-scale capitalism took root in American culture and endured, even after premodern capitalism gave way to far more productive, less exploitative industrial capitalism.

The characteristics of premodern commerce, manufacturing, and corporations naturally led Jefferson, Madison, and other American agrarians to equate an industrial, urban economy with one in which a miserable, landless urban proletariat labored in sweatshops making trinkets for the rich, to the benefit of monopolists with government connections. In the zero-sum economy of the agrarian era, it was usually the case that the wealth of the elite and middlemen came at the expense of the majority. Like Adam Smith, who feared the crippling effects of premodern factory labor on the bodies and minds and souls of workers, Jefferson preferred a society in which as many people as possible were independent yeoman farmers.[59]

Adam Smith, David Ricardo, and other classical economists, including Thomas Malthus and J. S. Mill, did not expect industrial technology to produce radical improvements in the human condition. The measures that they advocated—eliminating parasitic government-sponsored monopolies, increasing the division of labor in labor-intensive production (as in Smith's famous pin factory), free trade, and specialization among countries along the lines of absolute advantage (Smith) or comparative advantage (Ricardo)—were intended to squeeze a little more efficiency out of an agrarian economy. In the twentieth century, the economist Joseph Schumpeter observed that Ricardo and Malthus "lived at the threshold of the most spectacular economic development ever witnessed . . . [yet] saw nothing but cramped economies, struggling with ever-decreasing success for their daily bread."[60] They believed that diminishing returns and declining profits were the norm in every industry. Ricardo predicted that in the long run landlords would prevail over both capitalists and starving workers. Malthus argued that any temporary improvements in human well-being caused by economic growth would be neutralized quickly by the breeding of the poor. The labor theory of value, which held that capitalists could grow rich only by stealing surplus labor value from workers, was combined with the pessimistic prediction of inevitably diminishing profits and opportunities for investment in the philosophy of Karl Marx, which, in spite of its idealization of the industrial worker, is a patchwork of preindustrial economic doctrines.

If there had been no industrial revolution, if the American and world economies had continued to be constrained by the amount of energy produced by firewood, wind, water, and human and animal muscle, the producerist political economy of Jefferson and the "system of natural liberty" of Smith would have remained relevant. By a striking coincidence, however, James Watt and his business partner Matthew Boulton produced their first commercial steam engine in 1776, the year in which *The Wealth of Nations* by Smith and the American Declaration of Independence drafted by Jefferson were both published. The industrial revolution begun by Watt quickly rendered the economics of Smith and the politics of Jefferson obsolete. But a lingering Jeffersonian distrust of large-scale enterprise, finance, and government would continue to shape American political culture, with sometimes damaging effects for America's industrializing, modern economy, from the nineteenth century to the twenty-first.

THE AGE
OF STEAM

———◆———

THE ARGUMENT

The first industrial revolution was based on the steam engine, which James Watt transformed into a revolutionary source of power that could be used in factories, locomotives, and steamships. During the first industrial era, knowledge and skills flowed from the modernizing British economy to the less developed United States and other countries that struggled to make the new technologies their own.

Like Alexander Hamilton, Henry Clay understood the potential of machine-based technology to transform the American economy. Clay's American System was a comprehensive plan by which the federal government would sponsor industrial capitalism in the United States, permitting the country to catch up with and surpass Britain, the first industrial nation. But Andrew Jackson and his allies, invoking the rhetoric of Jeffersonianism, thwarted Clay's plan for national development by destroying the Bank of the United States and blocking plans for federally financed infrastructure.

In the aftermath of Jackson's victory, the industrialization of the United States caused the North and the South to grow apart. The southern economy became a specialized adjunct of the British industrial economy, exporting cotton to the textile mills of the British Midlands. Threatened by the success of the antislavery Republican Party led by Abraham Lincoln, the southern slaveowner elite tried to form its own smaller union, the Confederate States of America. But when Britain did not intervene, both the South's bid for independence and the institution of slavery were doomed.

The period between the Civil War and Reconstruction and the 1890s witnessed the maturation of the steam-based technological system of the first industrial revolution. Until the end of the nineteenth century, the railroad companies dwarfed all other private businesses and rivaled the state and federal governments in their scale and revenues. The disruption of older ways of living and working by the railroads and steam-powered machinery inspired protests by farmers and strikes by industrial workers that were frequently and violently suppressed by the government.

But even as steam-age America took shape, it was doomed by new technologies—the electric motor and the internal combustion engine—that began emerging in the 1860s in the next wave of innovation in the laboratories of Britain, continental Europe, and the United States.

"THERE IS NOTHING THAT CANNOT BE PRODUCED BY MACHINERY": THE FIRST INDUSTRIAL REVOLUTION

Soon shall thy arm, UNCONQUER'D STEAM! afar
Drag the slow barge, or drive the rapid car . . .

—Erasmus Darwin, 1781[1]

America is the country of the future. It is a country of beginnings, of
projects, of vast designs and expectations.

—Ralph Waldo Emerson, 1844[2]

In 1851, the first world's fair, the Great Exhibition, opened in London. The industrial supremacy of Britain was demonstrated by the British products on display and symbolized by the Crystal Palace, a vast structure of cast iron and glass designed by the gardener and architect Joseph Paxton. Dominating global industry, leading the world in the transition from agrarian civilization to urban, industrial society, Victorian Britain was the center of the world economy. Other countries had the option of finding a place in an economic order centered on Britain—or competing with the first industrial nation on its own terms.

Developed at first in Britain by Thomas Newcomen and James Watt to pump water out of coal mines, steam power was soon applied to manufacturing and to transportation, in the form of steamboats and steamships and then locomotives. The steam engine marked a radical advance in civilization. No longer would societies be dependent in doing work on the muscle power of humans and animals or diffuse sources of energy like water, wind, or fires stoked by wood and other kinds of biomass. Machines powered by coal, oil, natural gas, and other fossil fuels, and later by nuclear energy, would free most human beings from farm labor to live in cities and suburbs and work in a proliferating variety of occupations that did not require constant, heavy labor.

The geographic and institutional scale of societies, too, would be transformed. Industrial transportation and communication infrastructures—first railroads and telegraph lines, then automobiles, planes, telephones, and radios, and then computer networks like the Internet, satellites, and massive container ships—would shatter old methods of production and enable the growth of vast enterprises in national and global markets. The struggles of societies to adapt to the forces unleashed by the new technologies would topple empires and dynasties in the Old World and contribute to civil war in the New.

The United Kingdom led the way, as the richest and most technologically advanced country in the world. The loss of its American colonies was more than compensated for by its status as the first industrialized nation. Britain led the world in the adoption of steam-powered manufacturing, railroads, and the shift of its population from agriculture to industry. In the early nineteenth century, British manufacturing equaled the combined output of Russia and France.[3]

Britain pioneered not only industrialization but also the productivity-driven shift of workers and jobs out of agriculture. In 1800, only 36 percent of the population of England was employed in agriculture, as a result of the industrial revolution. As late as 1815, according to the first census, 95 percent of Americans were rural, living on farms or in small towns. British industrial supremacy was reinforced by global naval supremacy and by the centrality of the City of London in global finance.

The story of American technology in the first industrial revolution was for the most part one of American adoption and adaptation of technologies invented in Britain and continental Europe.

INDUSTRIAL ESPIONAGE AND THE AMERICAN MILL INDUSTRY

Britain tried to preserve its lead in industry in the late eighteenth and early nineteenth centuries by banning the emigration of skilled mechanics and the transfer of intellectual property to other countries. Just as later-developing nations would pirate American intellectual property, the early United States built up its industrial capacity in part by encouraging skilled emigration in defiance of British law and the theft of British industrial designs.

The most important immigrant to bring British technology to the United States was Samuel Slater. Slater spent six years apprenticed to a British textile manufacturer, then emigrated to the United States in 1789. He went into business with two Rhode Island merchants, William Almy and Moses Brown, and, relying on his memory, constructed water frames in their factory in Pawtucket. He and his partners hired children between the ages of seven and twelve and provided jobs as construction workers and guards for their fathers, who considered factory work degrading. As his business expanded, Slater continued his paternalist approach, building cottages and churches for his employees.

By the early 1800s, Slater had his own firm, Samuel Slater and Company. He developed a number of small mill towns or "Arkwright Villages" at small waterpower sites, including one named Slatersville. At Amoskeag Falls on the Merrimac River, Slater established an integrated factory complex which grew into Manchester, New Hampshire, a leading manufacturing city named for Britain's major industrial center.[4]

During a visit to England in 1810, Francis Cabot Lowell, a thirty-six-year-old member of a Boston Brahman dynasty that would produce a Harvard University president, Abbott Lawrence Lowell, and a famous poet, Robert Lowell, arranged to be taken on a tour of a British textile mill. He memorized the details of the machinery and reproduced them back home in Waltham, Massachusetts. Lowell formed the Boston Manufacturing Company with other investors and hired a mechanic to build an imitation of the mill he had seen. The company made history with its adaptation of mechanized technology. The company also pioneered the practice of raising money by selling shares.

Lowell proved to be an astute, able political entrepreneur. Following the end of the War of 1812, his firm and others in the infant American textile industry were threatened by British imports. Textile manufacturers like Lowell wanted a protective tariff, but they knew that a high tariff would be opposed by southern planters who sold cotton to the mills of the British Midlands. Lowell's solution was ingenious. Because the primitive technology in his mill could only produce coarse cloth, there would be a higher tariff on coarse cotton goods, which Britain made with cotton from British India, and a lower tariff on finer cloth, much of it made from American cotton. Lowell himself drafted the relevant provisions of the Tariff of 1816.

At one stroke Lowell had appeased the South, sacrificing the high-end luxury market while monopolizing the low-end American textile market for American firms. In the twentieth century, Japan, the "Little Tigers" of East Asia, and China followed a similar strategy, using nontariff barriers or currency manipulation to protect low-end industries. Benefiting from a strategy of "learning by doing," with government backing the native firms would then gradually move up the chain of added value.[5]

Like Samuel Slater and his associates, Lowell experimented with a paternalistic form of welfare capitalism, employing young women in decent conditions. In time, as immigrants poured into the country from Ireland, Germany, and other countries, a low-wage workforce replaced children and young women. Following Lowell's death in 1817, the company purchased land along the Merrimack River. The new mill town of Lowell became one of the leading centers of large-scale manufacturing in the United States.

Only gradually did the steam engine displace the waterwheel in mechanized manufacturing in textile manufacturing and other industries. As late as 1869, water provided 48.2 percent of the overall energy and steam power only 51.8 percent.[6]

Technological innovations also spurred productivity in American agriculture. In 1834, Cyrus McCormick invented the McCormick reaper, a horse-drawn machine that radically reduced the time needed for harvesting.[7] In 1837, John Deere invented a steel plow that was stronger and more durable than cast-iron plows, founding a company that continues to flourish in the twenty-first century.[8]

STEAM NAVIGATION IN AMERICA

Some of the delegates to the Constitutional Convention held in Philadelphia in the summer of 1787 witnessed a demonstration of an early steamboat by John Fitch. The early history of this technology in the United States revolves around another inventor, Robert Fulton, and the investor Robert Livingston.

Livingston, known as Chancellor Livingston, was one of the rich patroons of the Hudson River valley. He held the highest judicial office in New York for a quarter of a century, and it was in that capacity that he administered the presidential oath of office to George Washington in 1789 in New York, then the temporary national capital. Livingston served his country as part of the five-member committee that drafted the Declaration of Independence, as secretary of foreign affairs under the Articles of Confederation, and as US minister to France, where on behalf of the Jefferson administration he negotiated the Louisiana Purchase of 1803.

When Livingston arrived in 1801 in France as US minister, he met the inventor Robert Fulton, who had been given a twenty-year monopoly on steamboat navigation on New York rivers by the state legislature, on condition that he provide working steamboats, versions of which already existed in Western Europe and the United States. Fulton's monopoly had expired, but after funding experiments on the Seine, Livingston went into business with Fulton. They renewed the monopoly on August 17, 1807, when Fulton's steamboat, later named the *Clermont*, traveled from New York City to Albany in around thirty hours and back in about the same amount of time.

In 1809 Fulton and Livingston, hoping to expand their monopoly over steamboat navigation in New York State to the continental interior, hired their fellow New Yorker Nicholas Roosevelt, the great-uncle of Theodore Roosevelt, to visit the Mississippi. When Roosevelt returned from a trip he undertook with his wife with encouraging reports, Fulton, Livingston, and other investors, including DeWitt Clinton, one of the champions of the Erie Canal, formed the Ohio-Steamboat Navigation Company. Roosevelt then supervised the construction of a steamboat called the *New Orleans* in Pittsburgh. With his pregnant wife on board, Roosevelt took the *New Orleans* down the Ohio River to Cincinnati and then from Louisville to New Orleans, where the party arrived on January 10, 1812. Their adventures included experiencing the effects of the 1811 earthquake in the vicinity of New Madrid, a Mississippi river town in what would later be Missouri. A wall of water covered the island to which the boat was moored and nearly sank it.

Their monopoly meant that steamboat operators anywhere in New York had to pay Livingston and Fulton for licenses. In 1811, Livingston and Fulton received a monopoly from the Louisiana legislature as well. They now controlled the access of the hinterlands to the ports of New York and New Orleans.

One of their licensees in New York, Aaron Ogden, sued a former business partner, Thomas Gibbons, who became a competitor in the ferry business between New York and New Jersey. Gibbons claimed that the Federal Coastal Licensing Act of 1793 trumped the New York statute that provided Livingston and Fulton and their licensees with a monopoly. Lower courts ruled against Gibbons, but the US Supreme Court sided with him in *Gibbons v. Ogden* (1824). Chief Justice John Marshall, who shared the nationalism of his cousin George Washington, argued that the Commerce Clause of the federal constitution gave Congress power to preempt state and local laws affecting interstate commerce. In the twentieth century, Congress and the courts relied on the Commerce Clause to justify federal regulation of the economy and federal enforcement of civil rights, in the interest of creating a national market without the kind of internal barriers imposed by would-be monopolists like Livingston.

Although Fulton and Livingston had been granted a monopoly of steamboat navigation by the Louisiana legislature, in the South as in New York, their privilege was successfully contested in the courts and soon a number of steamboat companies were competing for the traffic of the Mississippi. Their ability to travel upstream against the current permitted the extension of plantation agriculture much farther inland than had been possible in the days of keelboats and flatboats. The geographic extension of cotton agriculture westward into Texas accelerated the forcible dispossession of the Indians and, by increasing the demand for slaves, entrenched the "peculiar institution" even more deeply into the economy and society of the South.

In the Midwest and the South, steamboats became the main carriers of staple crops. The steamboat dramatically reduced costs on journeys up as well as down the Mississippi. The average steamboat freight rate for the upstream journey from New Orleans to Nashville plunged from five dollars before 1820 to twenty-five cents in 1850–1859. The downstream savings in the same period were less striking but still important—from one dollar to 32.5 cents.[9]

THE COMMODORE

One rags-to-riches tycoon of the first industrial era in America was Cornelius Vanderbilt. "Corneel" started out as a Staten Island ferryman. With his ally Thomas Collins, Vanderbilt battled the Fulton-Livingston steamboat monopoly on the Hudson. The battle anticipated later ones, with bribes to legislators, judges, and officials and appeals to public opinion. When the Supreme Court's decision in *Gibbons v. Ogden* in 1824

struck down the Livingston-Fulton monopoly, the race to dominate the
new steamboat industry began.

Vanderbilt and Collins flourished, dominating passenger transportation between New York City and Albany. Striking out on his own, Vanderbilt threatened the Hudson River Steamboat Association, America's largest, and received a handsome reward in greenmail, the purchase of his stock by his competitors.

Transatlantic steamboat travel was also initially organized in Britain as a government-chartered monopoly, by Canadian-born Samuel Cunard. Vanderbilt's former partner Collins persuaded Congress to subsidize his American alternative to the Cunard steamship line. Vanderbilt now declared war on Collins, creating his own transatlantic service. After Congress cut off the subsidies to Collins in 1858, Collins was bankrupted and Vanderbilt dominated American steamships.

In response to the California gold rush that began in 1848, Vanderbilt built his own canal through Nicaragua, to compete with a projected British-American canal across Panama under the Bulwer Treaty. His state-subsidized competitors in California paid Vanderbilt a fortune not to compete with them. Once again, he profited from greenmail.

When the Civil War began, Vanderbilt became the shipping agent for the War Department. He profited from the fact that he was both buyer and seller. Following the Civil War, Vanderbilt used the fortune he had made in shipping to invest in two other technologies: gas lighting and railroads.[10]

THE DAWN OF THE AGE OF RAIL IN AMERICA

In 1812, the American inventor Oliver Evans predicted: "The time will come when people will travel in stages moved by steam engines from one city to another almost as fast as birds fly—fifteen to twenty miles an hour. Passing through the air with such velocity—changing the scenes in rapid succession—will be the most exhilarating, delightful exercise. A carriage will set out from Washington in the morning, and the passengers will breakfast at Baltimore, dine at Philadelphia, and sup at New York the same day."[11]

Unfortunately, Evans would not live to see his prediction come true. Apprenticed to a wheelwright, Evans moved in 1791 from his native Delaware to Philadelphia, the new nation's temporary capital. His patent for an improved flour-milling machine was the third patent issued by the young federal government.

Along with Britain's Richard Trevithick, Evans developed high-pressure steam engines as alternatives to James Watt's low-pressure engines. In addition to building steam engines, Evans in 1804 provided the Philadelphia Board of Health with a device for dredging and cleaning the city's docks, which he called the Oruktor Amphibolos (Greek for "amphibious dredger"). His work on a "steam wagon" did not succeed and, in 1819, worn out by business failures and money troubles, he collapsed of a stroke and died after learning that his shop in Philadelphia had burned down.[12]

In Britain in 1804, Richard Trevithick built the first steam locomotive. The technology developed rapidly until 1829, when George Stephenson's *Rocket* won a widely publicized contest in Britain and inspired a railroad-building boom on both sides of the Atlantic. The United States imported locomotives from Britain before their domestic manufacture got under way in the 1830s. British imports also provided 80 percent of the iron rails used in American railroads before the Civil War.[13]

Among the American railroad pioneers were Colonel John Stevens and his sons. The elder Stevens was born into a wealthy landed New Jersey family with an interest in transportation; his father was a commissioner of the New Jersey turnpike system before the Revolutionary War and owned a merchant fleet. In 1826, with the assistance of his sons Robert Livingston Stevens, the mechanically adept member of the family, and Edwin Augustus Stevens, the colonel demonstrated a workable steam locomotive on a circular track on his wooded estate near Hoboken, New Jersey. In 1830, his sons founded the Camden and Amboy Railroad, which, together with a canal connecting the Delaware and Raritan Rivers, reduced travel time between New York and Philadelphia to a mere nine hours. The early railroads, like the canals, were built by cities competing with other cities to capture the trade of nearby areas.

Colonel Stevens wanted to develop his Hoboken property into a resort for Manhattanites. To serve as a ferry he completed a steamboat, the *Phoenix*, a year after Robert Fulton's *Clermont* was launched. But the monopoly on steamboat navigation that Fulton and his financial backer Robert Livingston had secured from the New York legislature forced Stevens to use his boat on the Delaware River. To arrive there by traveling along the Atlantic coast the *Phoenix* became the first oceangoing steamship.[14]

FROM WOOD TO COAL

Until after the Civil War, when prices began to rise because of logging-induced deforestation, the abundance of wood from America's forests delayed the transition in the United States from wood to coal that Britain had pioneered. For the same reason, the United States lagged behind Britain in shifting from the use of charcoal to that of coke in blast furnaces.

The earliest American trains burned wood rather than coal. This permitted them to be painted in gaudy colors instead of the black that became standard later when coal-burning engines emitted sooty smoke. Showers of sparks from the engines of early wood-burning trains burned holes in the clothes and luggage of passengers and ignited forests along the rail lines.

The commemoration of the Declaration of American Independence on July 4, 1828, was marked by similar ceremonies in Washington, DC, and nearby Baltimore, Maryland. In Washington, President John Quincy Adams struggled in the heat with a beribboned spade to mark a new beginning for the Chesapeake and Ohio Canal to which George Washington had devoted so much effort. Meanwhile, in Baltimore, an elderly founder, Charles Carroll, laid the first stone for the Baltimore and Ohio Railroad. The B&O ultimately doomed the C&O; the canal would eventually reach only Cumberland, Maryland, and then fall into disuse, having lost traffic to the railroads.

At first the B&O employed horse-drawn rail cars. Then in 1830, the inventor Peter Cooper's experimental locomotive *Tom Thumb* showed the company its future. The chief engineer of Charleston's South Carolina Canal and Railway Company, Horatio Allen, observed: "There is no reason to expect any material improvement in the breed of horses in the future, while, in my judgment, the man is not living who knows what the breed of locomotives is to command."[15]

Following the example of *Tom Thumb*, most locomotives switched from wood to coal. The American version of the locomotive developed its own distinctive features, including the cowcatcher. Collisions between early trains and livestock angered farmers, who sometimes pelted the outlandish vehicles with rocks or even shot at them.

By the beginning of the Civil War, US railroad mileage exceeded that of Britain, France, and the German states.[16] The railroad network was thickest in the Northeast and Midwest. In 1860, the South had only 29.2 percent of the nation's total railroad mileage.[17]

Unlike the British railroad industry, which used double tracks so that trains could pass one another, most American railroads used single tracking. This allowed much larger areas to be crossed sooner, but created dangers of collision that were ultimately reduced with the help of the telegraph.

WHAT HATH GOD WROUGHT

Like most technologies, the telegraph evolved incrementally, with a number of people working on the same problems and producing similar innovations at the same time. "Inventors" should really be called "improvers." While others preceded him in experimenting with using electricity to send messages, Samuel F. B. Morse, a painter and a professor at New York University, devised a system that used electric pulses along a wire to move a magnetic marker that wrote the symbols of Morse code on a strip of paper.

Much of the credit for the electric telegraph should go to Joseph Henry, the scientist who directed the Smithsonian Institution. In 1830, Henry caused a bell to ring by sending an electric current through a wire from a point a mile away. Building on Henry's work and that of others, and funded by his business partners Alfred Vail and Leonard Gale, Morse obtained funding by Congress for a telegraph line linking Washington, DC, with nearby Baltimore, Maryland.

On May 24, 1844, Morse sent a line selected by the daughter of a friend from Numbers 23:23, "What hath God wrought?" to Baltimore from the chambers of the Supreme Court, then located in the Capitol Building in Washington. A few weeks earlier, on May 1, Morse's business partner Alfred Vail had wired the news from Annapolis Junction, between Washington and Baltimore, of Henry Clay's nomination as president by the Whig Party at its Baltimore convention.[18]

Overland telegraphy was followed quickly by submarine telegraphy, when the first submarine cable connected Dover and Calais in 1851. In August 1858, a transatlantic cable permitted President James Buchanan and Queen Victoria to exchange messages.

"HELL WITH THE LID OFF"

The Pennsylvania coal seam spreads across an area of more than eleven thousand square miles under the Appalachians from Pennsylvania to Alabama. Most of the coal is soft or bituminous coal. Much of the world's supply of hard or anthracite coal, which burns more cleanly than soft coal and even wood, is concentrated in eastern Pennsylvania.

In the 1830s, skilled Welsh iron-goods makers, experienced in working with Welsh anthracite, were imported by coal-mine owners to transfer their skill in using anthracite in iron smelting. Improved iron-making technology led to dramatic decreases in the price of iron, enabling manufacturing enterprises using coal-fired steam engines and iron machines to flourish between the 1830s and the beginning of the Civil War. Among the earliest railroads in America were the rail lines that led out of the anthracite mines of Pennsylvania, where mules dragged carts of coal uphill along rails.

Coke is a compound of carbon and ash created by burning coal in controlled conditions to drive off gases. The British pioneered the use of coke made from soft coal to replace charcoal in making iron.

Eastern Pennsylvania was rich in anthracite coal that could only be used as a fuel in blast furnaces on a large scale after the "hot blast" method developed in Britain in the 1820s was adopted in the United States. Because coke had to be shipped by water or rail, Pittsburgh's proximity to anthracite and bituminous coal mines gave it an advantage over other manufacturing cities. Already before the Civil War, the smoke from its factories combined with its glowing, volcanic furnaces inspired a journalist to name Pittsburgh "Hell with the lid off."

THE AMERICAN SYSTEM OF MANUFACTURING

The federal government played a limited but important role in technological development before the Civil War. The US Army assigned some of its engineers and officers to conduct surveys for railroads. In the 1830s, the federal government gave Philadelphia's Franklin Institute a grant to study the causes of steamboat boiler explosions. The research produced innovations in the industry.[19]

The most important contribution of the federal government to early industrialization in America came from the army arsenals at Springfield, Massachusetts, and Harpers Ferry, Virginia. They were the incubators of the "armory system" that revolutionized manufacturing in the United States and the world. The phrase "the American System," used to describe Henry Clay's program for national economic modernization by means of tariff-based import substitution, a central bank, and infrastructure investments, is also used to describe the system of using interchangeable parts in manufacturing.

The American system of manufacturing ought to be called the French system, because it originated as "le système Gribeauval." Jean-Baptiste Gribeauval was a French general who proposed to rationalize French arms production by assembling standard weapons from standardized components. Gribeauval's idea was developed by Honoré Blanc. While serving as the US minister to France, Thomas Jefferson reported on his visit to Blanc's factory in a 1785 letter to Secretary of War Henry Knox: "Supposing it might be beneficial to the U.S., I went to the workman. He presented me with the parts of 50 [musket] locks taken to pieces and arranged in combination. I put several together myself taking pieces at hazard as they came to hand, and they fitted in the most perfect manner. The advantages of this, when arms need repair, are evident."[20]

Jefferson sent a copy of a pamphlet by Blanc to Knox. In 1793, a French military engineer who had served in the American War of Independence with Lafayette named Major Louis de Tousard fled the French Revolution and joined the US Corps of Artillerists and Engineers when it was formed in 1795. Tousard's 1798 proposal for a school of artillerists and engineers influenced the design of the US Military Academy at West Point, and in 1809 he published a three-volume treatise, the *American Artillerist's Companion*.[21]

The ideas of Gribeauval, Blanc, and Tousard were brought with them by the American military engineers who worked at the federal arsenals founded in 1794 at Springfield and at Harpers Ferry in 1798. The army negotiated contracts with private arms makers. Eli Whitney promoted the idea of mass-producing muskets, but failed to deliver. Simeon North was more successful, creating a milling machine that allowed quick creation of uniform parts to help him carry out a large contract for pistols.

The first head of the US Army Ordnance Department, Colonel Decius Wadsworth, who had served with Tousard in the Corps of Artillerists and Engineers, along with his assistant and eventual successor George Bomford, used his authority over the federal arsenals to work with private contractors to develop interchangeable-parts assembly. One contractor, Thomas Blanchard, invented the Blanchard lathe, which reproduced irregular shapes like musket stocks or ax handles in wood. A Maine craftsman, John H. Hall, developed a breech-loading rifle he had invented. (He was forced to share the royalties for his invention with William Thornton, the commissioner of patents, who insisted that he be named as coinventor.)

THE FIRST INDUSTRIAL REVOLUTION

By the 1830s, Hall at Hall's Rifle Works at Harpers Ferry and Simeon North in his Massachusetts factory were refining what became known as "the Armory practice." Between that period and the Civil War, the Springfield Armory under the leadership of its superintendent, Roswell Lee, led the way in developing advanced machine tools and training mechanics who diffused armory-practice techniques through emerging civilian industries.

One of those industries was civilian gun manufacturing. After failing in his first attempt to manufacture his patented revolver, Samuel Colt succeeded when he hired a former master armorer from Springfield named Thomas Warren. Lebbeus B. Miller, a veteran of a firearms company in Newark, introduced what was by now known as the American system of manufacturing to the sewing-machine industry, when he was hired in 1863 by Isaac Merritt Singer. Cyrus McCormick, the inventor of McCormick's reaper, struggled with the production of his product until he hired a veteran of Colt's company and other firearms companies named Lewis Wilkinson. When the British safety bicycle made bicycling popular in the United States, armory practice spread to that industry as well. George A. Fairfield, a former contractor at Colt's Hartford plant, became superintendent of the Weed Sewing Machine Company, which in spite of its name manufactured a variety of products, including the early bicycles of the leader in the industry, the Pope Manufacturing Company, and then early automobiles.[22]

The transfer of technology to the United States was made easier by the existence in the northern states of a population with a high level of basic literacy and mechanical skill.

In the first half of the nineteenth century, the United States lagged behind Britain and Western Europe in science and higher education. According to *Putnam's Magazine* in 1854, "The genius of this new country is necessarily mechanical. Our greatest thinkers are not in the library, not the capitol, but in the machine shop. . . . Our education is no genial culture of letters, but simply learning the use of tools."[23] In the Northeast and Midwest, a society of craftsmen and tinkerers formed, in part because of public schools. By 1830, the United States was second only to Germany in the proportion of its population in school. If southerners, white and black, were factored out, the antebellum United States might have been the most educated nation in the world.[24]

As early as 1851, Colt's firearm exhibit at the Great Exhibition in London impressed British observers with what became known as the American system of manufactures. The British government sent commissioners to study American manufacturing. Colt, who opened a factory in Britain, told a parliamentary committee: "There is nothing that cannot be produced by machinery."[25]

AMERICAN 5 SYSTEMS

Were the Americans, either by combination or by any other sort of violence, to stop the importation of European manufactures, and, by thus giving a monopoly to such of their own countrymen as could manufacture the like goods, divert any considerable part of their capital into this employment, they will retard instead of accelerating the further increase in the value of their annual produce, and would obstruct instead of promoting the progress of their country toward real wealth and greatness.

—Adam Smith, 1776[1]

Had our nation followed the lines of relative advantage advocated by free-traders, our country would be divided into three parallel belts, used for cotton, tobacco, and wheat.

—Simon Patten, 1890[2]

In 1846–1849, Britain was so confident in its industrial supremacy that it adopted free trade and began preaching it to other countries.[3] During its rise to industrial primacy, Britain had carefully protected and subsidized its own infant industries and its leaders knew that if agrarian societies renounced similar protective policies then Britain's own superior, inexpensive imports could kill the infant industries of its military and commercial rivals in the cradle. By the end of the Napoleonic Wars in 1815, Britain's promotion of its own industries, at the expense of those of its colonies in Ireland and India and its former American colonies, had succeeded in making it the world's leader in manufacturing. Britain sought to maintain its near-monopoly of steam-powered manufacturing by discouraging other countries from becoming its industrial competitors. In the colonial regions that it ruled directly or indirectly, such as Ireland, Canada, and the Indian subcontinent, it continued the mercantilist policies that it had imposed on its former North American colonies, destroying native industries that competed with British manufacturers and forcing the inhabitants to buy British goods while exporting raw materials to British factories and food to the British population.

Britain used diplomacy and even military force to compel many countries that were not formal colonies to accept a subordinate place in the global division of economic labor and to buy their manufactured goods from Britain. In return for British aid in gaining their independence from Spain, many Latin American republics became part of Britain's informal commercial empire by signing "unequal treaties." Among the other countries pressured by Britain into unequal treaties were Siam (Thailand), beginning in 1824, Persia (1836 and 1857), the Ottoman Empire (1838 and 1861), and Japan (between 1854 and 1911). Following the Opium Wars (1839–1842), in which Britain and France crippled the Chinese government, China was compelled by the British Empire to sign a number of unequal treaties, resulting in the appointment of a British official as the head of Chinese customs from 1863 to 1908.[4]

Lacking the power to impose unequal treaties on the United States, Britain used incentives to try to persuade its former colonies to specialize in the export of raw materials and food, while importing British manufactured products. British free traders argued that Britain should abolish its own tariffs on such items, such as its Corn Laws (British "corn" is wheat, not American maize). The parliamentarian Robert Cobden, one of the major British proponents of free trade, argued that the policy would discourage other countries from trying to industrialize, the way that the United States and Germany had begun to do: "The factory system would, in all probability, not have taken place in America and Germany. It most certainly could not have flourished, as it has done, both in these states, and in France, Belgium, and Switzerland, through the fostering bounties which the high-priced food of the British artisan has offered to the cheaper fed manufacturer of those countries."[5] British free trade advocates like Smith, Cobden, and others believed that global free trade would produce the same result as the British colonial legislation that condemned other countries to the role of resource colonies for British industry. In the nineteenth century, the British economist Stanley Jevons boasted: "Unfettered commerce . . . has made the several quarters of the globe our willing tributaries."[6]

In order to ensure that the United States would specialize in supplying commodities rather than compete with it for industrial markets, Britain did not limit itself to practicing and promoting free trade. It practiced economic warfare against the United States. American manufacturers had long suspected that British manufacturers engaged in "dumping," or selling below cost for a time, in order to destroy the fledgling American industries that had grown up in the period of reduced US trade with Britain and Europe during the Napoleonic Wars. John Adams wrote in 1819: "I am old enough to remember the war of 1745, and its end; the war of 1755, and its close; the war of 1775, and its termination; the war of 1812, and its pacification. . . . The British manufacturers, immediately after the peace, disgorged upon us all their stores of merchandise and manufactures, not only without profit, but at certain loss for a time, with the express purpose of annihilating all our manufacturers, and ruining all our manufactories."[7] The suspicions of Americans like Adams were vindicated in 1816, when Henry Brougham in a speech in Parliament observed that "it was well worthwhile to incur a glut upon the first exportation, in order, by the glut, to stifle, in the cradle, those rising manufactures in the United States, which the war had forced into existence, contrary to the natural course of things." Several decades later, a parliamentary report referred to the practice of voluntary losses by British employers during depressions and recessions "in order to destroy foreign competition and to gain and keep possession of foreign markets."[8]

THE SOUTH, NEW ENGLAND, AND FREE TRADE

Between the end of the Napoleonic Wars and the Civil War, the question of America's relationship to Britain underlay many seemingly unrelated disputes in American economic debates. Americans were divided between those who were content for the United States to be an agrarian resource colony in an international division of labor centered on industrial Britain, supplying raw materials to British factories and cheap food to British workers, and those who wanted the United States to catch up with and ultimately surpass Britain as an industrial power. Would the American economy complement the British industrial economy—or compete with it?

Then as now, academic economists and journalists tended to reflect the views of the economic elites in their cities and regions who subsidized their employment. In the antebellum years, there were two regional schools of free-market orthodoxy. One was in the export-oriented South and the other was centered in Boston and New England, where merchants opposed tariffs and where textile mill owners tended to identify their interests with those of their southern suppliers.

The planters opposed government-sponsored introduction of industrial capitalism into the United States for both economic and social reasons. If tariffs were used to keep out British and European manufactured goods, then agrarians would be forced either to pay tariffs on imports or to pay a higher price for American manufactured goods than they would have done, at least for a time, in the absence of tariffs. The same objection applied to other government efforts to promote American industries, such as bounties, or subsidies; these, like tariffs, would redistribute wealth from the agrarian sector to the manufacturing sector of the US economy. Because alternate ways of financing the federal government, such as federal income, wealth, or property taxes, were even less palatable to them, the southern oligarchs supported a tariff for revenue while opposing a tariff for protection—and were determined to keep both the tariff and the size of the federal government small.

An aversion to being taxed, directly or indirectly, to subsidize northern manufacturers was not the only reason that the southern planters opposed government-sponsored industrial capitalism in the United States. Neither the climate nor the population of the South was incompatible with an industrial society, as the industrialization of the Sun Belt in the twentieth century proved. But the hierarchical social order that the great slave-owning families had created in the South would be threatened by an urban, industrial economy based on free labor.

The southern planters and the professors whom they subsidized in southern universities cited the authority of the British classical economists who argued that the United States should specialize as a source of commodities for Britain's industrial economy. The favorite economist of America's agrarians, Adam Smith, in *The Wealth of Nations*, wrote: "It has been the principal cause of the rapid progress of our American colonies toward wealth and greatness that almost their whole capitals have hitherto been employed in agriculture. They have no manufactures, those household and coarser manufactures excepted which necessarily accompany the progress of agriculture, and which are the work of the women and children in every private family. The greater part both of the exportation and coasting trade of America is carried on by the capitals of merchants who reside in Great Britain. Even the stores and warehouses from which goods are retailed in some provinces, particularly in Virginia and Maryland, belong many of them to merchants who reside in the mother country, and afford one of the few instances of the retail trade of a society being carried on by the capitals of those who are not resident members of it. Were the Americans, either by combination or by any other sort of violence, to stop the importation of European manufactures, and, by thus giving a monopoly to such of their own countrymen as could manufacture the like goods, divert any considerable part of their capital into this employment, they would retard instead of accelerating the further increase in the value of their annual produce, and would obstruct instead of promoting the progress of their country towards real wealth and greatness."[9]

If Americans had paid attention to Adam Smith, the United States never would have become the world's greatest industrial economy—because it never would have become an industrial economy at all. Along with most countries in the Americas, Europe, Asia, and the Middle East, the United States, according to Adam Smith, should have forever remained a supplier of foodstuffs and raw materials to industrialized Britain.

THE AMERICAN SCHOOL

In every country during the steam era, manufacturing facilities were located near sources of coal and iron—the West Midlands in Britain, the Ruhr in Germany, and Appalachia in the United States. For this reason, the factory owners of Pennsylvania and other Midatlantic states became the chief advocates of high protective tariffs. With the support of its local industrialists, who viewed themselves as competitors of British industry, Pennsylvania became the center of the developmental, protectionist "American School" that contrasted itself with the "British School" of free trade and laissez-faire economics. According to the American School, the United States, having won its political independence from the British Empire, now needed to win its economic independence from the British System.

The rationale for import substitution, or infant-industry protection, in the United States was set out by Alexander Hamilton in his Report of the Secretary of the Treasury on the Subject of Manufactures (1791). In the report, Hamilton pointed out that "the United States cannot exchange with Europe on equal terms; and the want of reciprocity would render them the victim of a system, which should induce them to confine their views to Agriculture and refrain from Manufactures."[10] The leading writers of the American School were two Baltimore intellectuals, Hezekiah Niles and Daniel Raymond, the economists Francis Wayland and Mathew and Henry C. Carey of Philadelphia, and Friedrich List, a German American émigré.

The most important member of the American school of economic nationalism was Carey, author of *Principles of Political Economy* (1837) and many other books. Karl Marx and Ralph Waldo Emerson believed that Carey was the most important economist the United States had produced.[11] From his father, an Irish immigrant, Carey derived his Anglophobia and protectionism, along with a publishing empire closely allied with Pennsylvania iron and coal interests. Carey viewed free trade as the economic corollary of British imperialism: "By adopting the 'free trade,' or British, system we place ourselves side by side with the men who have ruined Ireland and India, and are now poisoning and enslaving the Chinese people."[12]

In the view of Carey and other American School thinkers and politicians, the industrializing North was opposed by a combination of the British Empire and its allies in the southern planter class, who shared an interest in a system in which the South would supply cheap cotton to British mills, in return for providing a market for British factory goods. Following the Civil War, Carey wrote in 1867: "Slavery did not make the rebellion. British free trade gave us sectionalism, and promoted the growth of slavery, and thus led to rebellion."[13]

HARRY OF THE WEST

In politics, the unlikely champion of the policy of American economic development on the basis of import substitution was a Virginia-born Kentucky slaveowner named Henry Clay. Over six feet tall, Clay became one of antebellum America's best-known orators, with the use of a broad mouth described by a historian in 1857: "In his old days, when the men crowded around him for a shake of his hand, and the women beset him for a kiss of his patriarchal lips it was remarked that his capacity of gratifying this latter demand was unlimited, for the ample dimensions of his kissing apparatus enabled him completely to *rest* one side of it, while the other side upon active duty."[14] Clay coined the phrase "self-made man" and considered himself one, though he owed his fortune not to business but to his marriage into the influential landholding family of his wife, Lucretia Hart, and lived at Ashland, a plantation worked by hundreds of slaves.

An unsuccessful candidate for the presidency five times, "Harry of the West" served in the cabinets of several presidents. As Speaker of the House and later as a leading senator, the "Great Compromiser" helped to avert southern secession and civil war by promoting the Second Missouri Compromise in 1821 and the Compromise of 1850. Clay began his political career as a Jeffersonian opponent of the Hamiltonian program of national banking and internal improvements. But his economic nationalism was a natural progression from the fear of British power that he manifested as a War Hawk during the War of 1812. Of Britain he wrote: "She sickens at your prosperity, and beholds, in your growth—your sails spread on every ocean, and your numerous seamen—the foundations of a power which, at no very distant day, is to make her tremble for her naval superiority."[15] Like Hamilton and Washington, Clay came to consider domestic manufacturing to be an essential element of US national security: "We should thus have our wants supplied, when foreign resources are cut off, and we should also lay the basis of a system of taxation, to be resorted to when the revenue from imports is stopped by war."[16]

"A GENUINE AMERICAN SYSTEM"

In a two-day oration in the House of Representatives on March 30 and 31, 1824, Speaker of the House Clay argued that the United States should have a machine-based economy of its own, in order to meet the challenge posed by the industrial supremacy of Britain: "But Britain is herself the most striking illustration of the immense power of machinery. . . . A statistical writer of that country, several years ago, estimated the total amount of the artificial or machine labor of the [British] nation to be equal to that of one hundred millions of able-bodied laborers. . . . In the creation of wealth, therefore, the power of Great Britain, compared to that of the United States, is as eleven to one."

Clay continued: "But there is a remedy, and that remedy consists in modifying our foreign policy, and in adopting a genuine AMERICAN SYSTEM." In support of a federal policy of protection and promotion of infant industries, Clay cited the policies "of the Edwards, of Henry the Great, of Elizabeth, of the Colberts, abroad; of our Franklin, Jefferson, Madison, Hamilton, at home." Then he quoted at length "the master spirit of the age"—Napoleon. "I at first confined myself merely to prohibiting the web," Clay quoted Napoleon as saying, "then I extended the prohibition to spin cotton; and we now possess, within ourselves, the three branches of the cotton manufacture, to the great benefit of our population, and the injury and regret of the English."[17] During the Napoleonic Wars, Napoleon had promoted the Continental System in France and French-occupied Europe, a program of government sponsorship of industries undertaken in response to Britain's blockade. Napoleon's Continental System and Clay's American System had the same geopolitical purpose: economic independence from Britain, the first industrial superpower.

Clay's American System had three major elements: infant industry tariffs, internal improvements, and a sound system of national finance.

Under the leadership of Clay, Congress revised the tariff in 1816 to protect American industries. Imports on all manufactured goods averaged 40 percent, while tariffs on imported agricultural products were also increased—in some cases amounting to 60 percent.[18]

Clay also promoted the use of funds from federal land sales to finance internal improvements like canals and railroads. Clay opposed proposals to allow settlers to buy federal lands at low prices, because that would reduce the funds for infrastructure projects. The federal government owned a vast amount of land, but land sales were never a major source of federal revenue. Tariffs provided 85 percent of the revenue for the federal government before 1860.[19] Federal land grants to railroads eventually fulfilled this part of Clay's program.

The third element of the Hamiltonian triad that made up Clay's American System was national finance. Although he opposed the renewal of the charter of the first Bank of the United States in 1811, he supported the creation of the second bank in 1816, and from 1822 to 1824, between stints in Congress, he was paid as the bank's general counsel. Critics pointed out that he profited in other ways from the policies he promoted, including tariffs on imports of hemp, a source of rope fibers, which he grew on his plantation.

OLD HICKORY

By the second decade of the nineteenth century, Jefferson, Madison, and Gallatin had reconciled themselves to aspects of the Hamiltonian system for national economic development such as the second Bank of the United States and some degree of federal support for manufacturing and internal improvements. But a new generation of southerners and their northern allies in the tradition of Jefferson proved to be more radical in their rejection of federal authority than Jefferson himself had been.

None was more influential than "Old Hickory"—Andrew Jackson, the hero of the Battle of New Orleans, who was elected twice to the presidency, in 1828 and 1832. Unlike the genteel and educated Virginians Jefferson, Madison, and James Monroe, Jackson, a Tennessean born in South Carolina, was a product of the Scots-Irish frontier culture with its machismo and suspicion of refinement. He first achieved renown as the hero of the Battle of New Orleans in 1814, a victory over the British won several weeks after peace had been negotiated, something that neither the American nor British combatants at New Orleans knew because of the primitive state of communications at the time. Jackson had won additional fame with his role in the bloody Creek Indian War of 1813. In 1819, Secretary of War John C. Calhoun recommended the censure of then-general Jackson for his actions during the Seminole War of the previous year, which included an unauthorized invasion of Spanish Florida and the execution of two British nationals. Clay's support for the censure motion, which Congress rejected, earned him Jackson's lifelong hatred.

Jackson's campaign for the presidency in 1824 had played on popular anti-intellectualism. The Harvard-educated northeastern patrician John Quincy Adams, the son of the second president of the United States, John Adams, was ridiculed for calling observatories "lighthouses of the skies," as though there could be such a thing. When the electoral college delivered the presidency to Adams, Jackson was furious and convinced that Clay had engaged in a "corrupt bargain" to deliver electoral votes to Adams in return for a place in Adams's cabinet as secretary of state. Jackson was finally elected president in 1828, but forgive and forget was not the code of the southern backcountry. Jackson was a man of violent hatreds who had a bullet lodged in his body from one of his many duels, in one of which he had killed his opponent. With Jackson's defeat of Clay, the Hamiltonian framework for the development of the American economy would be shattered.

THE TARIFF OF ABOMINATIONS AND THE NULLIFICATION CRISIS

In 1828 the tariff, last revised in 1824, was revised again, to protect American industries. Ironically, this measure was supported as a gambit by Jackson's running mate and vice president Martin Van Buren. Van Buren hoped to appeal to manufacturers in the North. He gambled that southern voters would acquiesce in the tariff.[20] Southerners and northern supporters of free trade denounced the 1828 tariff as the "Tariff of Abominations," and South Carolina threatened to "nullify" the law, by refusing to collect the duties at Charleston. When President Jackson threatened to use force to enforce the law, South Carolina backed down.

The crisis led to the Compromise Bill of 1832, brokered in part by Clay. The average tariff would be diminished from 40 percent to 20 percent over the decade to 1842.[21] The influence of the southern Democrats was seen in the Tariff of 1846, which imposed average duties on the major imports to 27 percent. This regime remained in place with few changes until 1861.

The Nullification Crisis divided Jackson from some of his fellow southerners. But on other issues he represented the views of the southern slaveowner elite, who were increasingly hostile to the federal government.

The tariff crisis had been about more than the tariff. At issue was the fear of southern slaveowners that federal power might be used to legislate the abolition of slavery. The conclusion that the protection of slavery in the South meant that federal power of any kind had to be crippled explains the transformation of South Carolina senator John C. Calhoun from a nationalist who shared Clay's support for federally sponsored internal improvements and the Bank of the United States into the leading philosopher of states' rights and the "concurrent majority," by which he meant a regional southern veto on all national action. In a letter of September 11, 1830, Calhoun explained: "I consider the tariff act as the occasion, rather than the real cause of the present unhappy state of things. The truth can no longer be disguised, that the peculiar domestic institution of the Southern States and the consequent direction which that and her soil have given to her industry, has placed them in regard to taxation and appropriations in opposite relation to the majority of the Union, against the danger of which, if there be no protective power in the reserved rights of the states they must in the end be forced to rebel, or, submit to have their paramount interests sacrificed, their domestic institutions subordinated by Colonization and other schemes, and themselves and children reduced to wretchedness."[22] The desire to cripple federal authority in order to protect slavery explains why, after Britain's abolition of slavery in 1830, the South's leaders became far more hostile to federal government activism than Jefferson, Madison, and Gallatin, who during and after the War of 1812 had accepted the need for many elements of the Hamiltonian program of national development such as support for internal improvements and domestic manufacturing.

THE MAYSVILLE ROAD VETO

In 1830 the National Road, begun in 1811, was still far from completion. President Jackson relished the chance to veto a bill to authorize federal funding of a turnpike between Maysville and Lexington, Kentucky, the home of his adversary Henry Clay. Jackson's vice president, Martin Van Buren, told a friend, "I had the most amusing scenes in my endeavors to prevent him from avowing his intentions before the bill passed the two houses."[23] In his veto message of May 27, 1830, Jackson argued that the Maysville Road, even though it was part of an interstate road, was a purely local project and declared that internal improvements, while important, should be left to the states and private enterprise.

In his veto message, Jackson made it clear that he did not object to state-sponsored internal improvements or truly national projects, however defined. But his veto of the Maysville Road had lasting consequences. In succeeding years, Congress would pass appropriations for small-scale road and "rivers and harbors" improvements. But not until the Federal Aid Road Act of 1916 would the federal government commit itself again to the project of building a national road system, a project that would culminate in the 1950s with the creation of the Interstate Highway System.

THE BANK WAR

The most important national economic institution to fall victim to Andrew Jackson was the second Bank of the United States (BUS). The bank, with twenty-nine branches by the 1830s, was the largest corporation in the United States and an inviting target for attacks based on economic interest or Jeffersonian ideology. The bank had been chartered in 1816 and its charter would be up for renewal in 1836. Its president was Nicholas Biddle, who could not have been more unlike Andrew Jackson.

Born into a patrician family in Philadelphia, Biddle was a child prodigy, nicknamed "Grammaticus" by his classmates. Biddle entered the University of Pennsylvania at the age of ten. When he was refused permission to graduate because of his age, he transferred to Princeton, graduating as the valedictorian of his class at the age of fifteen. As an unpaid clerk to an American envoy to France, the young Biddle toured Europe as far as Greece. On his return, he became an attorney, a member of the

Pennsylvania state legislature, and man of letters, editing the *Port Folio*, an important national literary journal. In 1819, after he was appointed a director of the second Bank of the United States, Biddle helped Langdon Cheves of South Carolina rescue the bank from insolvency. On becoming president of the bank in 1822, Biddle showed that he understood the functions of a central banker, regulating the money supply and keeping state banks in check. Under Biddle, the local branches of the bank also facilitated the transfer of credit and funds throughout the United States.[24]

In his first year as a banker, Biddle described his transition from man of letters to banker in verses he penned for a young lady's album:

> I prefer my last letter from Barings or Hope
> to the finest epistles of Pliny or Pope;
> my "much-esteemed favors" from Paris, to those
> which brought on poor Helen an Iliad of woes;
> one lot of good bills from Prime, Bell, or the Biddles,
> to whole volumes of epics or satires or idyls;
> nay, two lines of plain prose with a good name upon it
> to the tenderest fourteen ever squeezed in a sonnet.
> Why, I would not accept—not for Hebe's account—
> the very best draft from Helicon's fount,
> nor give—this it grieves me to say to their faces—
> more than three days of grace to all the three Graces.
> Then their music of spheres! can it thrill through the soul
> like kegs of new dollars as inward they roll?
> and Cecilia herself, though her lyre was divine,
> never gave to the world notes equal to mine.[25]

Although his sympathies lay with the Hamiltonian tradition identified with National Republicans like Adams and Clay, many of whom would move in 1843 into the new Whig Party, Biddle had voted in 1828 for Jackson. Jackson, however, shared the suspicion of government-chartered corporations expressed in 1825 by Thomas Cooper, the dean of the Jeffersonian school of political economy: "These institutions are founded on the right claimed by government, to confer privileges and immunities on one class of citizens, not only not enjoyed by the rest, but at the expense of the rest. . . . Generally in this country, it has glutted itself by incorporating banking companies, insurance companies, canal companies, and manufacturing companies of various descriptions. All these are increasing daily, the list of nuisances."[26]

Along with Jeffersonian and Jacksonian ideology, the jealousy of state banks inspired the campaign against the BUS. As early as July 1791, Hamilton's fellow Federalist Fisher Ames warned him: "I have had my fears that the state banks will become unfriendly to that of the United States. Causes of hatred and rivalry will abound."[27] Former president John Quincy Adams noted in 1832: "In every state in the Union there is a large capital . . . invested in stocks of multiplied state banks. Most of these are rivals in business with the Bank of the United States, and they have all boards of directors and most of them are colleague with newspapers, all eager for the destruction of the Bank of the United States—an institution doubly obnoxious to the system of Safety Fund Banks in the state of New York."[28]

As Adams noted, many in New York's financial community resented the fact that the federal revenues collected at the Port of New York, which were greater than those of all other ports combined, were deposited in the Wall Street office of the BUS, whose directors were primarily Philadelphians.[29] Jackson's vice president and successor was the New Yorker Martin Van Buren. In 1833, Biddle wrote: "It is a mere contest between Mr. Van Buren's [projected New York] government bank and the present institution—between Chestnut Street and Wall Street—between a Faro [gambling] bank and a National Bank."[30]

Alexander Hamilton's son James was a leader of the New York financial community. As acting secretary of state for a time, the younger Hamilton assisted Jackson in his crusade against the bank and recorded his surprise when Jackson showed his ignorance by saying that he admired Hamilton's father: "Colonel, your father was not in favor of the Bank

of the United States."[31] Hamilton's other son, Alexander, was an ally of
Biddle who warned the banker of the campaign against him.[32]

In his first two annual messages to Congress as president, Jackson denounced the bank. In 1832, Biddle sought to obtain the recharter of the
bank four years before it was scheduled to expire in 1836. Biddle reasoned
that the bank was popular among members of Congress, including some
who enjoyed its largesse, like Daniel Webster, a director of the Boston
branch. Rechartering the bank early gave Biddle's ally Henry Clay an issue in his campaign for the presidency against Jackson, who was running
for reelection.

"THE BANK IS TRYING TO KILL ME,
BUT I WILL KILL IT!"

Led by Clay and Webster, on July 3, 1832, Congress passed a law renew-
ing the charter of the bank. On July 10, President Jackson vetoed it.

Jackson asserted in his veto message that "the constitutionality and the
expediency of the law creating this Bank are well questioned by a large
portion of our fellow citizens." In fact, the constitutionality of the bank
could not be questioned. Although Jefferson and Madison had opposed
its creation, Jefferson accepted and used it and Madison favored the creation of the second bank. The Supreme Court upheld the bank's constitutionality in two cases.[33] The elderly Albert Gallatin, the former secretary
of the Treasury under Jefferson, opposed Jackson's policy and published a
defense of the bank in 1830. In 1841, he published a pamphlet arguing for
the creation of a third Bank of the United States.[34]

In addition to making constitutional arguments, Jackson posed as a
populist, declaring in his veto message that "when the laws undertake to
add to these natural and just advantages artificial distinctions, to grant
titles, gratuities, and exclusive privileges, to make the rich richer and the
potent more powerful, the humble members of society—the farmers, mechanics, and laborers—who have neither the time nor the means of securing like favors to themselves, have a right to complain of the injustice

of their Government." Jackson appealed to public xenophobia, arguing that foreign ownership of some of the bank's shares was "calculated to convert the Bank of the United States into a foreign bank, to impoverish our people in time of peace, to disseminate a foreign influence through every section of the Republic, and in war to endanger our independence." Amos Kendall, who wrote the first draft of Jackson's bank veto message, warned under his own name of a new nobility arising in America: "Its head is the Bank of the United States; its right arm, a protecting Tariff and Manufacturing Monopolies; its left, growing State debts and State incorporations."[35]

In his response to Jackson's veto message, Clay insisted that the bank was constitutional: "The power to establish a bank is deduced from that clause of the Constitution which confers on Congress all powers necessary and proper to carry into effect the enumerated powers." He dismissed the claim that foreign investors controlled it: "The assignable character of the stock is a quality conferred not for the benefit of foreigners, but for that of our own citizens. . . . The confidence of foreigners in our stocks is a proof of the solidity of our credit. Foreigners have no voice in the administration of this bank; and if they buy its stock, they are obliged to submit to citizens of the United States to manage it. . . . Will it not be a serious evil to be obliged to remit in specie to foreigners the eight millions which they now have in this bank, instead of retaining that capital within the country to stimulate its industry and enterprise?"

Although Jackson's veto of the bank's recharter created anger among his opponents in Congress, it was popular with the voters. Jackson easily won reelection, defeating Clay in the electoral college by a margin of 219 to 49. But trouble was only beginning. In September 1833, when Jackson ordered his Treasury secretary, William Duane, to put federal revenues in particular state banks he favored, rather than in the Bank of the United States, rather than carry out the order, Duane and his assistant resigned. Roger Taney was willing to obey the president, but the Senate refused to confirm him. On March 28, 1834, the Senate responded by a narrow vote that censured Jackson. The censure was expunged from the record in 1837.

Meanwhile, Biddle retaliated by contracting credit. Jackson exclaimed, "The bank is trying to kill me, but I will kill it!"

Jackson succeeded. When the House voted against a new charter, Biddle sought a charter for the Bank of the United States from the state of Pennsylvania. Hurt by unwise speculation on cotton futures, the bank closed its doors in 1841, a few years after Biddle retired in 1839. In 1844, he died, having lost much of his money along with his reputation. The center of gravity of American finance passed from the public-private hybrid BUS in Philadelphia first to Boston banking houses and then, by the 1850s, to the banking sector of New York. The United States would not have a national banking system again until the passage of the National Banking Act in 1863. Not until the Federal Reserve System was created in 1913 would the United States once again have a central bank.

In the aftermath of the bank's destruction, the states adopted a baffling variety of state-chartered bank forms, ranging from private or "free" banks to state bank monopolies, each issuing its own notes. Thomas Hart Benton, a Jacksonian Democratic senator from Missouri, complained in 1837 about the results of the bank's destruction: "I did not join in putting down the Bank of the United States to put up a wilderness of local banks. I did not join in putting down the paper currency of a national bank to put up a national paper currency of a thousand local banks."[36]

In 1836, in one of his last acts as president, Jackson issued the Specie Circular, which required payment in gold or silver, not banknotes, for federal land sales. The Panic of 1837 struck shortly after Jackson's ally and vice president Martin Van Buren was inaugurated as president. Historians disagree over whether to blame the financial crisis on the Jackson administration or on other factors, such as an increase in British interest rates or a price-lowering glut of cotton. Whatever the cause of the crisis, Van Buren reacted with yet more folly. In 1840, at his urging Congress created the independent treasury system, which ensured that federal money was locked up in subtreasuries where it could not help the banking system or the economy.

Clay's American System lay in ruins. Not until the 1860s would there be a move to strengthen the federal role in the banking system—and that would take place during a civil war among American sections that had practically become different nations.

That subsequent upheaval was foreshadowed by the strife of the Jacksonian era. The bank war led to more than rhetorical violence. In 1830, Nicholas Biddle's brother Thomas, a veteran of the War of 1812, was serving as a paymaster for the US Army in Saint Louis. After a local congressman, Spencer Pettis, denounced his brother Nicholas and the Bank of the United States, Thomas Biddle exchanged insulting letters with Pettis in a newspaper. Biddle then went to the hotel room in Saint Louis where Pettis was staying and proceeded to flog him with cowhide, a weapon chosen to show Biddle's disdain according to the code duello. Pettis challenged Biddle to a duel that took place on August 26, 1831, on Bloody Island in the Mississippi River. Each shot the other and within a few days both men died.

AN ERA OF STATE POWER

The defeat of the ambitious federal internal-improvements schemes envisioned by Jefferson and Gallatin as well as by Hamilton and Clay meant that financing roads, canals, and railroads was overwhelmingly the responsibility of the states before the Civil War. From 1790 to 1860, the federal government spent $54 million on transportation infrastructure; of this, $9 million was spent on roads. State and local governments spent roughly nine times as much—more than $450 million. State governments also provided as much as 40 percent of the funds for American railroads.[37] Surveying Jacksonian America, Jackson's rival John Quincy Adams complained that the nation was "palsied" in "an Era of State Power."[38]

The ambition of some of the state infrastructure projects can be inferred from the name of the Mammoth Bill of 1836 in Indiana. In promoting infrastructure without aid from the federal government, the state governments went deeply into debt. In 1841, of total government debt, the federal government accounted for only $5 million while the state debts totaled $193 million and local debt made up $25 million.[39] As a result of the Panic of 1837, many states defaulted on their debts. British financiers called on the federal government to assume the debts of the states, as it had done under Hamilton. But the federal government refused, and when it issued securities later in the year, the *Times* of London in 1842 declared that "the people of the United States may be fully persuaded that there is a certain class of securities to which no abundance of money, no matter how great, can give value; and that in this class their own securities stand pre-eminent."[40]

In Illinois, state-led internal improvements were opposed by many Jacksonian Democrats and supported chiefly by Whigs. One of the latter was a young Whig state legislator named Abraham Lincoln. In his bid for reelection in 1836, he declared: "Whether elected or not, I go for distributing the proceeds of the sales of the public lands to the several states, to enable our state, in common with others, to dig canals and construct railroads, without borrowing money and paying interest on it."[41]

During the Illinois legislative session of 1836–1837, Lincoln belonged to a group of Whigs called the "Long Nine" because all were at least six feet in height. The Long Nine gained enough allies among the Democrats to pass a bill authorizing construction of the Illinois-Michigan Canal and a state bond funding railroads and river improvements. Construction halted, however, during the Panic of 1837. Lincoln's law partner William Herndon later recalled that "every river and stream . . . was to be widened, deepened, and made navigable. A canal to connect the Illinois River and Lake Michigan was to be dug, . . . cities were to spring up everywhere, . . . people were to come swarming in by colonies, until . . . Illinois was to outstrip all others, and herself become the Empire State of the Union." However, "the internal improvement system, [in] the adoption of which Lincoln had played such a prominent part, had collapsed, with the result that Illinois was left with an enormous debt and an empty treasury."[42] Eventually Chicago grew into a major trade entrepôt and metropolis, thanks in part to the canal that linked the Illinois River with Lake Michigan.

Mixed-enterprise capitalism in the United States was a casualty of the canal and railroad bubbles of the 1830s. Following the Panic of 1837, corporations in which the federal or state governments owned shares along with private investors were denounced by Jacksonian populists. Like many other states, Illinois amended its constitution in 1848 to ban state subsidies to private corporations.

The public backlash against mixed enterprise inspired support for free or general incorporation—allowing corporations to form by registering with a state government, rather than depending on a special charter from a state legislature. This solved one problem—minimizing the incentive of businessmen to obtain corporate charters by bribing politicians—only to create another. The regulation of corporations that were chartered by legislatures or, as with the two Banks of the United States, by the federal government, posed no problems, because specific rules governing particular corporations could be spelled out in their individual charters. But when incorporation became easy in the second half of the nineteenth century, regulation had to be based on statutes, not on charters. The question of the authority of the state and federal governments to regulate corporations by statute created difficult issues that had not existed under the older system of mixed enterprise.

THE MODERNIZATION OF THE NORTHEAST

The collapse of the national development project in the 1830s meant that modernization by default became the project of state governments rather than the federal government. One consequence was the increasing divergence of different parts of the country. In the generation before the Civil War, the United States became three regional societies, each with its own distinctive economy.

New England was the most advanced, an industrializing nation within a nation. Of all the regions of the country, it was least affected by the financial chaos that followed the destruction of the second Bank of the United States. The Suffolk Bank of Boston performed some of the functions of a central bank for New England, stabilizing the financial environment to the benefit of merchants and manufacturers.[43]

By the 1830s, the United States had a third of the spinning capacity of Britain, most of it in New England.[44] The pioneering textile mills of Samuel Slater and Francis Cabot Lowell had given way to much more advanced factories. Waterwheels still provided almost all the power for American manufacturing, but the introduction of steam power was beginning.[45] If the antebellum North is thought of as a nation, then it was already quite industrialized, with a fifth of the workforce in manufacturing.[46]

JEFFERSON AND THE YEOMAN REPUBLIC

An agrarian America, not a commercial and industrial America, was the utopia of Thomas Jefferson and his allies and followers. It was the Midwest, not the South, that was to come closer than any other American region to fulfilling Jefferson's vision of a democratic republic of yeoman farmers. Influenced by Jefferson, the Northwest Ordinances of 1784, 1785, and 1787 sought to create the basis of an agrarian democracy in the states formed from the territory of the old Northwest (the present Midwest around the Great Lakes). The first two acts provided for the rapid transition from undemocratic territorial government to the status of self-governing states, which became Ohio, Indiana, Illinois, Michigan, and Wisconsin. And most consequential of all, in light of the long-term development of the United States, while the Northwest Ordinance of 1787 made provisions for a fugitive-slave law, it banned slavery from the states formed from the Northwest Territory.

Another policy of great importance for the evolution of a free society in the Midwest was the provision in the Northwest Ordinance that all government sales of land would be in fee simple. Yeoman farmers would own their land free and clear and would not suffer from the complex forms of "fee-tail," or encumbrances, which in British law were a relic of feudalism. The importance of fee simple is evident from a brief autobiography that Abraham Lincoln wrote during his 1860 campaign for the presidency. Lincoln explained that his family was forced to migrate from Kentucky to Indiana and Illinois "partly on account of slavery; but chiefly on account of the difficulty in land titles."[47] A British lawyer who met Lincoln in the White House in 1864 reported that the president "talked of the landed tenures of England, and said we had some 'queer things in the legal way' at home, of which he seemed to think 'quit rents' as queer as any. And then he told us how 'in the state of Kentucky, where he was raised, they used to be so troubled with the same mysterious relics of feudalism, and titles got into such an almighty mess with these pettifoggin' incumbrances turnin' up at evry fresh tradin' with the land, and no one knowin' how to get rid of 'em.'"[48]

The ban on slavery in what became the midwestern states prevented plantation agriculture from taking root in the region, making possible its characteristic family farms. In the slave states on the frontier, developers sold large tracts to planters who would bring in slave gangs to clear them for cotton and other crops. In the free states, land speculators had an incentive to divide land into small plots and supply them with infrastructure and public schools, in order to attract American and European immigrants. That was one reason that European immigration went disproportionately to the North. The two sections were roughly comparable in population in 1790, but by 1860 the free states outnumbered the slave states by nineteen million to twelve million.

In free Pennsylvania, most projects to promote infrastructure and industry were eventually adopted; in slave-based Virginia, most similar state programs failed to be enacted by the legislature.[49] In turn, transportation infrastructure, including the Erie Canal and a network of midwestern canals, by lowering transportation costs, created markets for midwestern farm products in the East.

A virtuous circle underlay midwestern development. The absence of slavery meant that farmers had to rely on wage labor, which was expensive. That gave them an incentive to invest in labor-saving technology, such as McCormick's reaper. Many farmers could afford such investments because of their success in raising cash crops for national and international markets. The family farmers of the Midwest also benefited from a supportive financial system, which allowed eastern bankers to finance midwestern farm mortgages.

Social equality reinforced the greater economic equality and mobility of the antebellum Midwest and North. In the early nineteenth century, American courts rejected the British inheritance of annual labor contracts, in favor of at-will employment, which could be terminated by either party, with wages paid to the point of termination.[50] Semantic changes accompanied legal reforms. American workers adopted the term "bosses," borrowed from *baas*, the word used for "master" by the Dutch in New York, because they did not like to call their employers their "masters," and both men and women preferred to be known as "help" rather than as "servants."

THE STEAM-AGE SOUTH

The third of the regional economies in the antebellum United States was that of the South. While northern reformers denounced its slavery-based social order as a relic of feudalism, the southern economy was quite modern, specializing in the supply of cotton, the essential raw material for the first mechanized global industry, the British textile industry. Cotton was to the global industrial economy of the nineteenth century what oil became to the machine civilization of the twentieth. In each case, reactionary oligarchs who controlled the indispensable material required by industry— the southern planters, the Saudis and other Arab monarchies—were able to enrich their class while holding off the forces of political and social modernization in the territories they controlled.

In 1784, customs officials at Liverpool seized eight bales of cotton brought from the United States. The officials took it for granted that the cotton was being smuggled from another source, because it was believed that cotton could not be grown in large quantities in Britain's former American mainland colonies.[51] In the mid-1780s only 0.2 percent of the cotton imported into Britain came from the United States, while cotton goods made up only 6 percent of British exports. By 1820, cotton surpassed tobacco as the major export of the South, and in that year 59 percent of the cotton destined for British mills came from the United States, while woven cotton goods accounted for almost an identical proportion, 60 percent, of Britain's exports.[52] By 1860, the percentage of Britain's cotton imported for its textile mills from the American South rose more than 90 percent.[53]

The specialization of southern planters in cotton is usually attributed to the cotton gin that Eli Whitney invented in 1794. His model was the product of a long line of development, and had to be perfected by others over time.[54]

Demand for southern cotton from the textile industries in Britain and the Northeast grew by 5 percent a year from 1800 to 1860.[55] Britain by 1860 was particularly dependent on Southern cotton.[56] In 1858, the South accounted for 66 percent of US exports.[57] Anticipating the industrial countries of later generations that would worry about their dependence on oil-exporting autocracies, in 1853, Britain's *Blackwood's Magazine* worried about "millions in every manufacturing country within the power of an oligarchy of planters."[58]

"Oligarchy" was the correct term. In 1860, the one-fourth of southern whites who owned slaves had among them slave "property" valued between $2.7 and $3.7 billion, a sum larger than the total of railroad and manufacturing capital in the United States.[59]

Most white southerners did not own slaves. Slaveowners on average owned five slaves, but slave ownership was highly concentrated, with 27 percent of slaveowners controlling 75 percent of the enslaved population.[60] In 1860, 70 percent of slaveowners owned fewer than ten slaves; one-quarter owned between ten and forty-nine; and only 3 percent owned fifty or more slaves.[61] Apart from those who owned slaves, southern whites were relatively poor. In 1860, the average white southerner was 80 percent wealthier than the average northerner, but the nonslave wealth of the South was 40 to 50 percent beneath the level in the North.[62]

The historian William Scarborough examined the 339 slaveowners who owned at least 250 slaves in 1850 or 1860, adding up to more than 100,000 slaves in all. Half of this elite within the southern elite lived in three states—Alabama, Mississippi, and Louisiana—while half of the rest lived in South Carolina. The richest was Nathaniel Heyward, a South Carolina rice planter, who owned an estate worth more than $2 million.

South Carolinians were overrepresented among the politicians who belonged to this exclusive slave society elite: five US senators, seventeen US representatives, fifteen governors or lieutenant governors, and seventy-three state legislators.[63] While hundreds of their slaves labored in the rice fields in the heat of a South Carolina summer, the Heyward family and their rich neighbors spent the months between April and November in the cool mountain air of exclusive resort villages like Flat Rock, North Carolina. The children of the planters went to resort village schools in the summer and played, hunted, and fished when the largely absentee landlord family returned to the plantation for a few months during the winter.[64]

When Heyward died in 1851, the inventory of his estate listed 1,648 slaves on fifteen plantations in South Carolina. To read their names is to wonder about the lives of so many people who were forced to labor so much so that a few could live in luxury. Clay Hall Plantation: Gabriel, Marcus, Neptune, Scipio, Ben, Judy, John, Leah, Maria. Lewisburg Plantation: July, Eve, Cudjoe, London, Di, Emanuel, Ben, Abbey, Sam. Middle House Plantation: Abram, Brutus, Joseph, Castle, Tim, William, Bess, Judy, Isaac, Sapho, Hannah.[65]

SLAVERY AND STAGNATION

Almost all of the five million immigrants who arrived between 1820 and 1860 went to the North. Because of its unattractiveness to immigrants, the South's share of the total US population declined from 45 percent of 7.2 million in 1810 to 35 percent of 31 million in 1860. In a seeming paradox, the high cost of slave labor used in manufacturing further hampered the industrialization of the South. Southern slaveowners charged high prices for renting their slaves to factory owners. J. S. Buckingham, a traveler in Athens, Georgia, recorded a conversation with a manufacturer in 1839: "The negroes here are found to be as easily taught to perform all the required duties of spinners and weavers as the whites, and are just as tractable when taught; but their labour is dearer than that of whites . . . and the hope expressed by the proprietor to me was that the progressive increase of white population by immigration would enable him to employ wholly their free labour, which, to him, would be more advantageous."[66]

In 1860, only one southern city was among the fifteen largest in the United States.[67] A European visitor, Friedrich Ratzel, described southern cities in 1874: "The general character of Southern cities [is] . . . very different from their Northern and Western counterparts. . . . [T]he commerce of this area is still not connected to any industrial activity to speak of. For that reason, besides the big merchants here there are no big industrialists, no skilled workers, nor a vigorous white working class of any size worth mentioning. The shopkeepers and handworkers cannot make up for the lack of these hearty classes that create civilization and wealth. Therefore, . . . this society has an incomplete, half-developed profile like that which one tends to associate with the industry-less large cities of predominantly agricultural countries. In this regard, New Orleans, Mobile, Savannah, and Charleston look more like Havana and Veracruz than, say, Boston or Portland."[68]

The journalist Hezekiah Niles, associated with the American School of economics of Henry Carey and Henry Clay, summed up the northern perception of the southern social order in 1829:

Free white labor is not honored;
The education of the poor is neglected;
A desire to excel is not stimulated;
Manufacturing establishments are not encouraged;
The mechanical class is degraded; and
Internal improvement is—LET ALONE[69]

FROM EXTORTION TO SECESSION

The southern slaveowners could count on allies in the Midwest, the Northeast, and New York City. Populated partly by Yankee migrants from New England and culturally similar Germans and Scandinavians, and partly by white southerners moving north, the Midwest held the key to domination of the federal government. For most of the period between the 1820s and the 1860s, the southern planters used the rhetoric of Jeffersonian and Jacksonian producerism to make the family farmers of the Midwest their political allies.

The alliance between the South and the Midwest had an economic rationale, as well. In his 1855 pamphlet *Cotton Is King; or, Slavery in the Light of Political Economy*, David Christy explained that one reason that the planters opposed the growth of an urban, industrial working class in the North was their concern that northern industrial workers would compete with their own slaves for the food grown in the Midwest, forcing the planters to recoup their costs by charging higher prices for cotton and making the US cotton industry less competitive compared to its rivals in Cuba and elsewhere: "The close proximity of the [food] provision and cotton-growing districts in the United States, gave its planters advantages over all other portions of the world. But they could not monopolize the [global] markets, unless they could obtain a cheap supply of food and clothing for their negroes, and raise their cotton at such reduced prices as to undersell their rivals. A manufacturing population, with its mechanical coadjutors [an urban working class], in the midst of the provision growers, on a scale such as the protective policy contemplated, it was conceived, would create a permanent market for their products [food], and enhance the price; whereas, as if this manufacturing could be prevented, and a system of free trade adopted, the South would constitute the principal provision market of the country, and the fertile lands of the North supply the cheap food demanded for its slaves."[70]

In 1860, the leading manufacturing industry in the United States was the northeastern cotton-textile industry, whose output was valued at $115 million, while wool and iron accounted for roughly $73 million apiece.[71] Although Boston was the center of abolitionist activity, most Massachusetts textile-mill owners did not want to antagonize their southern suppliers. They and their political representatives like Daniel Webster were denounced as craven "Cotton Whigs" by New England radicals.

Many of the fortunes in early industrial New England were based on processing cotton grown by southern slaves.[72] The merchants and financiers of New York City also had reason to appease the southern planters. New York was deeply involved in the cotton trade, as the third point on a triangle that connected the South with Liverpool, from which cotton moved to the steam-powered mills of the British West Midlands. In 1860, New York City voted against Lincoln. Its mayor, Fernando Wood, argued for the acceptance of southern secession and even suggested that New Yorkers should defend slavery even more ardently than southerners: "As commercial people it is to our interest to cherish and keep so good a customer. . . . Not only let us avoid making war upon her own peculiar system of labor but let us become even stronger defenders of the system than the South itself."[73] Early in 1861, as southern states seceded, Wood proposed that New York and several neighboring counties secede to form an independent commercial city-state. The prospect of losing the midwestern trade to the ports of a low-tariff Confederacy, however, persuaded many merchants in New York to support the Union.[74]

Counting on northern allies like these, in the decades preceding the Civil War the confident and aggressive southern planter class used the threat of secession to intimidate the rest of the country into submitting to its goals. Their strategy of extortion succeeded in producing the compromises of 1820 and 1850, which maintained the outnumbered South's equality in the US Senate, and in the compromise tariff of 1833.

As a result of the United States–Mexican War of 1846–1848, the territory of the United States increased by more than two-thirds, from 1.8 million square miles to 3 million. The geographic expansion of the Union threatened the balance among slave and free states in the Senate. In the last great effort of his life, Henry Clay became known as the "Great Compromiser" for brokering the Compromise of 1850.

But in 1854, the Kansas-Nebraska Act, as part of a plan to create a transcontinental railroad, repealed the Compromise of 1850. The possibility that the slave-plantation system could be universalized drove many midwestern Jacksonians together with former Whigs in the new Republican Party, which sought to prevent the extension of slavery beyond the South. Denouncing the Republicans as a purely sectional party, the southern slaveholders threatened secession when General John C. Frémont was nominated as the first Republican presidential candidate in 1856 and carried out their threat when Abraham Lincoln was elected president in the four-way race of 1860. The refusal of the federal government to recognize the new Confederacy made war inevitable, even before Confederate forces fired on Fort Sumter on April 12, 1861.

PLAIN MECHANIC POWER: THE CIVIL WAR AND THE SECOND REPUBLIC

Hail to victory without the gaud
Of glory; zeal that needs no fans
Of banners; plain mechanic power. . . .
No passion; all went on by crank,
Pivot, and screw,
And calculations of caloric.

—Herman Melville, 1866[1]

Who else would have declared a war against a power with 10 times
the area, 100 times the men, and 1,000 times the resources?

—William Faulkner, 1942[2]

In the early 1850s, the North and South were divided over the question of the location of a railroad that would connect the East with the West. With the intention of making Chicago the eastern terminus of a transcontinental railroad, Senator Stephen A. Douglas of Illinois sought to win southern support for his proposed northern route through the yet-unorganized Nebraska Territory. Because the Nebraska Territory was above the line of 36°30' latitude that divided the slave and free states as part of the Missouri Compromise, Douglas proposed to repeal that portion of the compromise and split the territory into two states, Kansas and Nebraska, whose inhabitants would choose whether the states were slave or free.

Douglas had hoped that allowing "popular sovereignty" to settle the question of slavery in the new states of Kansas and Nebraska would remove controversy. Instead, the northern public was alarmed by the passage of the Kansas-Nebraska Act, which was followed in 1857 by the Supreme Court's holding in a fugitive-slave case, *Dred Scott v. Sanford*, that the Missouri Compromise had been unconstitutional all along because Congress lacked the power to prohibit slavery in US territories. The debate over the extension of slavery shattered the older party system. From the wreckage emerged a new party, the Republican Party, composed of former Whigs, abolitionists, and antislavery Jacksonian Democrats, who feared that the "slave power" might obtain a permanent majority of states in the US Senate and bring slaves to the North and West to compete with free white farmers and workers. One of the leaders of the new Republican party was a former Whig from Illinois, Abraham Lincoln, who gained national prominence by debating his rival, Stephen A. Douglas, in an unsuccessful campaign for the Senate seat from the state. When Lincoln was elected president of the United States in 1860, in an election polarized along regional lines, first South Carolina and ultimately a total of eleven Southern states seceded to form the Confederate States of America.

Douglas, one of the losers of the 1860 presidential election, gave his full support to Lincoln and the Union during the war. He did not get the presidency, but the nation got the transcontinental railroad he wanted.

WHY THE CONFEDERACY LOST

The new constitution adopted by the Confederate States of America was poorly designed to enable the South to prevail in a long and costly war for independence. The Confederate Constitution was the US Constitution rewritten to reflect the anti-statism and anti-industrialism characteristic of extreme Jeffersonian and Jacksonian ideology. The differences between the two documents began with the preambles. The preamble to the US Constitution states: "We the people of the United States, in order to form a more perfect union, establish justice, insure domestic tranquility, provide for the common defense, promote the general welfare, and secure the blessings of liberty to ourselves and our posterity, do ordain and establish this Constitution for the United States of America." The preamble to the Confederate Constitution replaced "the people" with "the Confederate States," replaced "to form a more perfect union" with "to form a permanent federal government," and dropped the phrases "provide for the common defense" and "general welfare."

The provisions of the Confederate Constitution were carefully crafted to forestall the possibility that the new government would ever attempt anything like the programs of Alexander Hamilton and Henry Clay for national economic development. The constitution banned the Confederate Congress from appropriating money "for any internal improvement intended to facilitate commerce," with the exception of improvements for the waterborne commerce that the cotton oligarchs needed to ship their crops to foreign markets. The Confederate Constitution also outlawed government promotion of manufacturing, providing that "no bounties shall be granted from the Treasury; nor shall any duties on importation from foreign nations be laid to promote or foster any branch of industry."

Confederate senator W. S. Oldham of Texas in March 1862 described national defense itself as a tyrannical infringement on the rights of the states and the people: "The tendency to indoctrinate the people into the belief that there was no reliance in the State Government was the bane of the old republic, and would be, if not avoided, the bane of this. That government, from its commencement, gradually taught the people to centralize upon it, as the only reliance for their honour and welfare, and bought and bribed them not to rely upon the States themselves. The first measure was the establishment of a National Bank, the next the establishment of a Military Academy at West Point, and a Naval Academy at Annapolis, and so on."[3]

"A PECULIAR PEOPLE"

Even more important in the downfall of the Confederacy than the design of its political institutions was the structure of its economy. The underlying cause of the war was the economic specialization of the South in the export of cotton to the steam-powered textile mills of industrial Britain, and the hope of southern secessionists that the South could play the same role in the steam-era world economy as a sovereign nation rather than as part of the United States.

A few years earlier, Senator James Henry Hammond of South Carolina made the phrase "King Cotton" famous in a speech in the US Senate on March 4, 1858: "What would happen if no cotton was furnished for three years? . . . this is certain: England would topple headlong and carry the whole civilized world with her, save the South. No, you do not dare make war on cotton. No power on earth dares to make war upon it. Cotton is King."[4]

Hammond and other planters had reason to be confident. They counted on being supported by Britain. In 1860, more than eighty years after the beginning of the American War of Independence, the economy of the United States remained deeply integrated with that of Britain. America's largest trading partner by far, Britain received more than half of all American exports and provided 40 percent of American imports.[5] In 1860, America's industries were still in their infancy. Sixty-three percent of imports were finished and semifinished manufactured goods; only 16.3 percent of American exports fell in those categories. US exports were dominated by crude materials, including cotton (61.6 percent) and foodstuffs (22.1 percent).[6]

Once the Civil War broke out, the Confederacy placed an informal embargo on cotton, similar to Jefferson's ill-fated embargo of 1808. The purpose of the embargo was to force Britain and France to recognize their dependence on southern cotton and to intervene to help the South win its independence from the United States.

While the embargo as well as the Union blockade hurt the British textile industry, the damage was limited by supplies left over from the southern bumper crops of 1859 and 1860. The impact was further limited by imports of cotton from India and other sources. And British capital and labor found new uses, in building ships and arms for both sides in the American conflict. In 1864, the London *Times* observed, "We are as busy, as rich, and as fortunate in our trade as if the American war had never broken out and our trade with the states had never been disturbed. Cotton was no king."[7]

The failure of Britain to intervene to secure southern independence meant that the Confederacy was forced to mobilize its own resources. While the Union was able to muster the power of northern finance and industry, the Confederacy found itself handicapped by the undeveloped banking and manufacturing sectors of the South.

In 1861, former US senator from Texas Louis T. Wigfall told a British correspondent: "We are a peculiar people, sir! . . . We are an agricultural people; we are a primitive but a civilized people. We have no cities—we don't want them. We have no literature—we don't need any yet. . . . We want no manufactures; we desire no trading, no mechanical or manufacturing classes. . . . As long as we have our rice, our sugar, our tobacco, and our cotton, we can command wealth to purchase all we want from those nations with which we are in amity, and to lay up money besides."[8]

The journalist James B. D. Debow, writing before the Civil War, did not share Wigfall's complacency: "Our slaves work with Northern hoes, ploughs, and other implements. The slaveholder dresses in Northern goods, rides a Northern saddle . . . reads Northern books. . . . In Northern vessels his products are carried to market . . . and on Northern-made paper, with a Northern pen, with Northern ink, he resolves and re-resolves in regard to his rights."[9]

The southern states paid an enormous price for their specialization in export agriculture. At the beginning of the Civil War, the Union had a population of nineteen million, while the Confederacy had only nine million, one-third of whom were slaves. Northern industry produced ten times as much as industry in the South; the manufactured products of the entire Confederacy added up to less than one-fourth of New York State's manufacturing by value added.[10] The North had thirty-eight times as much coal, fifteen times as much iron, and ten times as much factory production.[11]

CONFEDERATE WAR SOCIALISM

Apart from the privately owned Tredegar Iron Works of Richmond, which were put under contract to the military, the Confederate states lacked the industry they needed to manufacture military supplies. The response was a crash program of state-guided industrialization from above that was more Hamiltonian than Hamilton. Among the government-owned factories of the Confederacy the most impressive was the Augusta Powder Works at Augusta, Georgia, created under the direction of Colonel George W. Rains on the basis of a pamphlet describing a British original.[12] In the absence of a native southern class of industrialists, military officers supervised the war socialism of the Confederacy, including, along with Colonel Rains, General Josiah Gorgas, who headed the Confederate Ordnance Bureau, and Colonel John W. Mallet, who supervised the production of explosives and ammunition.[13]

The Confederacy, like the Union, used a draft to fill its ranks. In both North and South, affluent men could pay for substitutes to serve on their behalf. Another exemption from draft service in the Confederacy for white men on plantations with twenty or more slaves inspired the bitter quip, "Rich man's war, poor man's fight."[14]

To finance the war effort, the Confederacy used produce loans (bonds paid for by promised crop shares). When this expedient was not sufficient, the government turned to tariffs and a progressive income tax. Out-of-control inflation in the final years of the war constituted an even more extreme form of taxation.[15]

TECHNOLOGICAL WARFARE

The Civil War was one of the first large-scale conflicts of the industrial era, foreshadowing the mechanized carnage of World War I. Both sides not only exploited existing technologies like the railroad and the telegraph but also sought to gain advantages by sponsoring technological innovations.

The North controlled twenty-two thousand miles of railroad compared to the South's nine thousand. Both sides used trains to move their troops rapidly from one region to another and to transfer supplies. And both sides destroyed the railroads of their enemies when they could.

The South had the advantage that it could use its railroads as internal lines of communication. Attempts by the Union forces to concentrate at one point could be met by Confederate troops, rushed by railroads to that location. General Ulysses S. Grant understood this, and promoted his "anaconda strategy" of squeezing the South all along its border, to prevent it from massing its forces. In his memoirs, he explained that those who could not skin could hold a leg. Grant created a huge railroad depot to supply his forces when they besieged Richmond and Petersburg, while William Tecumseh Sherman, during his march through the South, trained thousands of his troops to repair railroads that Confederate guerrillas had damaged so that they could be quickly used again.

The telegraph system helped to coordinate the war on both sides. To the discomfort of his generals, Lincoln used the telegraph to monitor events and pepper his subordinates with instructions. Telegraphy allowed far greater control over military operations by the president than had been possible in the past. Because the White House had no telegraph line, Lincoln spent much of his time in the War Department's telegraph office. It was there that he drafted the Emancipation Proclamation, between waiting for news and sending instructions.

MINIÉ BALLS AND IRONCLADS

More than two million Springfield model 1861 rifled muskets and similar British Enfield rifled muskets were used by both sides in the Civil
War. Named after a French inventor, Claude-Étienne Minié, the minié
ball—actually a conical bullet—was used in a musket whose rifled bore
imparted a spin to the projectile, giving it longer range, accuracy, and
deadliness. The US arsenals at Harpers Ferry, Virgina, and Springfield,
Massachusetts, developed the new technique.

Most of the guns used in the war were still muzzle loaded, with the
bullets inserted from the front. But in the Battle of Gettysburg, Union
forces successfully deployed Spencer repeating rifles, which were breach
loaded (side loaded) and could fire around fourteen shots per minute.

Experimental machine guns were developed during the war, but not
in time to play a role. President Lincoln tested one. During the Civil War,
Lincoln met with inventors and urged his military officers to test or adopt
new weapons, sometimes to their annoyance. He took part in tests of new
weapons in the Washington Navy Yard and on the White House lawn.
Lincoln's aide John Hay wrote: "He was particularly interested in the first
rude attempts at the afterwards famous mitrailleuses [machine guns]; on
one occasion he worked one with his own hands at the Arsenal, and sent
forth peals of Homeric laugh [*sic*] as the balls, which had not power to
penetrate the target set up at a little distance, came bounding back among
the shins of the bye-standers."[16] After watching the test-firing of a gun
that worked because gas was prevented from escaping, Lincoln turned
to a journalist and asked, "Now have any of you heard of any machine,
or invention, for preventing the escape of 'gas' from newspaper establishments?"[17] In his White House office, Lincoln had a model of a brass cannon that rested on land patents and a grenade that he used on his desk as
a paperweight.[18]

Lincoln's interest in innovative technology long preceded the Civil
War. With other modernizing Whigs and Republicans, Lincoln shared
a fascination with technology. His law partner wrote: "He would stop

in the street and analyze a machine. . . . Clocks, omnibuses, language, paddle-wheels, and idioms never escaped his observation and analysis."[19] While serving in the US House of Representatives, Lincoln patented "A Device for Buoying Vessels over Shoals" (patent number 6,469, May 22, 1849), which consisted of bellows that inflated beneath a ship's water line in order to help the ship rise in shallow water. He paid for a wooden model of the invention, which is now in the National Museum of American History of the Smithsonian Institution, but he never sold it. Lincoln envisioned other inventions. In 1859 he said in a speech in Milwaukee that he had given much thought to "a steam plough."[20] He hoped to make money as a public speaker by means of lectures such as his "Second Lecture on Discoveries and Inventions," written in February 1859.

The most striking wartime technological innovation was the ironclad. Both sides raced to create armored warships powered by steam. Low in the water and covered by iron plates, ironclads looked like something out of a Jules Verne science-fiction story.

On March 8, 1862, the Confederate ironclad CSS *Virginia*, formerly the USS *Merrimack*, attacked the Union ships that blockaded the Virginia port of Hampton Roads, smashing two combatant ships and several transports. If the Confederacy could use ironclads to break the Union blockade, it might be able to sustain its cause by importing weapons and supplies from Britain or France.

On March 9, 1862, a Union ironclad, the USS *Monitor*, in the Battle of Hampton Roads fought the *Virginia* to a draw before falling tides forced the *Virginia* to withdraw. Following the battle, both sides commissioned more ironclads, but the Union had proved that its blockade could not be broken.

The age of the wooden warship was over.

THE PRICE OF WAR

To pay for the war, the US federal government instituted income, inheritance, and excise taxes, and ran up a deficit of $2.5 billion. To cope with this, the Lincoln administration and its congressional allies created the

Bureau of Internal Revenue, later the Internal Revenue Service, within the Treasury Department, as part of legislation that Lincoln signed on July 1, 1862. The law also created the first US income tax, with a top rate of 10 percent on high incomes. After the first federal income tax was abolished in 1872, a federal income tax law was passed in 1894, only to be declared unconstitutional by the Supreme Court. In 1913, the Sixteenth Amendment, permitting federal taxation of incomes, was adopted. The income tax rate was initially no more than 7 percent on the highest incomes.

In August 1861, Secretary of State Salmon P. Chase, a former US senator and governor of Ohio, pressured northeastern bankers to provide a loan in return for Treasury bonds. When it became clear by 1862 that the war was going to be a long one, Congress authorized a combination of new bonds and "greenbacks" or dollars that were not backed by gold. The New York and New England banks bitterly disagreed with the Lincoln administration on whether bonds should be sold at or below par. The hostility of the northeastern financial community deepened after Chase and Congress decided to finance the war using fiat currency, or greenbacks that were not convertible into gold.

Chase turned to Jay Cooke, an Ohio-born Philadelphia banker who was a friend and political donor, along with his brother Henry, an aide to Chase at the Treasury who edited Ohio's main Republican newspaper. At the beginning of the war, Cooke successfully sold millions in bonds that raised money for the defense of the state of Pennsylvania. As agent for the federal government, Cooke carried out a brilliant campaign to sell federal bonds directly to the public, raising enormous sums for the Union cause from small-town bankers and businessmen and others. Cooke mobilized a national sales force of more than two thousand dealers, some of whom followed the Union army and tried to sell bonds to defeated southerners, and used the telegraph to coordinate bond sales. He persuaded Chase to issue the bonds in small denominations so that a majority of Americans would be capable of purchasing them. While Cooke made a modest amount of money from his one-sixteenth of 1 percent commission, he used the increased prominence of his firm and its power in the bond market to make a fortune, which he invested after the war in railroads before the crash of 1873 bankrupted his company.

The human costs of the Civil War were devastating: 600,000 soldiers killed and an equivalent number wounded. Some 250,000 Confederates died of wounds from battle or disease. If the Union forces had suffered proportional losses, instead of losing 360,000 men, they would have lost more than a million. The equivalent in World War II, in which the United States lost around 300,000 soldiers, would have been more than six million.[21] In addition to experiencing conquest and occupation, southerners experienced losses on a scale like that suffered by European nations in the world wars of the twentieth century. The defeated South spent $2 billion while the North ran up a debt of $3 billion. The abolition of slavery erased $2 billion of capital. Two-thirds of southern wealth vanished.

During the Civil War, the federal budget increased from $63 million in 1860 to $1.2 billion in 1865. After Lincoln's death, Mary Lincoln told Herndon that her husband had planned to take the family to Europe following his retirement from the presidency: "After his return from Europe, he intended to cross the Rocky Mountains and go to California, where the soldiers were to be digging out gold to pay the national debt."[22]

"AN OLD-LINE HENRY CLAY WHIG": THE POLITICAL ECONOMY OF ABRAHAM LINCOLN

When southern members withdrew from Congress on the eve of the Civil War, their ability to block the plans of the new Republican majority came to an end. Although the Republicans included some former Jacksonian Democrats who opposed the extension of slavery, most Republicans were heirs of the Whig party of Henry Clay.

The Civil War was, among other things, a battle between Jeffersonian and Hamiltonian conceptions of political economy. Not every northern

Unionist was a Hamiltonian; the prowar coalition united Hamiltonian Republicans with Jeffersonians in the North and Midwest inspired by Andrew Jackson's success in facing down the threats of South Carolina in the Nullification Crisis. And the South included a few Hamiltonians, including the vice president of the Confederacy, Alexander Stephens, an old friend and colleague of Lincoln and, like Lincoln, a former member of the nationalist Whig Party. Even so, the war pitted a Jeffersonian agrarian society, dedicated to the defense of states' rights, localism, and slavery, which troubled Jefferson but not the Confederate leaders, against a North that, while largely rural, was a rapidly industrializing society influenced by Hamilton's and Clay's vision of nationally sponsored technological and financial modernization.

The Hamiltonian tradition could not have found a better spokesman than Lincoln. Although his first political position—postmaster of New Salem, Illinois—was provided by the Jackson administration, Lincoln belonged to the Whig Party of Clay and Webster from the time it formed in the 1830s until divisions over the expansion of slavery destroyed it in the 1850s. In his first campaign manifesto, of 1832, the young Lincoln announced his dedication to Clay's American System: "My politics are short and sweet, like the old woman's dance. I am in favor of a national bank . . . in favor of the internal improvements system and a high protective tariff."[23] Lincoln called Clay his "beau ideal of a statesman." During Lincoln's presidency, one member of Congress observed that he "belongs to the old Whig party and will never belong to any other."[24] "I have always been an old-line Henry Clay Whig," Lincoln explained in 1861.[25]

Lincoln and his wife, Mary Todd Lincoln, were born in Henry Clay's adopted Kentucky. Some of his Todd in-laws knew Clay and belonged to the Whig circles in Springfield in which Lincoln moved. A relative, Lyman Beecher Todd, claimed in 1901: "I have seen him [Lincoln] when twice he visited Lexington, Kentucky,—on last occasion when he was the guest of Mr. Clay at Ashland."[26]

Two of Clay's sons fought for the Union while one fought for the Confederacy in the Civil War. In 1862, when John Clay sent Lincoln one of his father's snuffboxes together with best wishes from Clay's widow, Lincoln wrote, "Thanks for this memento of your great and patriotic father. Thanks also for the assurance that, in these days of dereliction, you remain true to his principles. In the concurrent sentiment of your venerable mother, so long the partner of his bosom and his honors, and lingering now, where he *was*, but for the call to rejoin him where he *is*, I recognize his voice, speaking as it ever spoke, for the Union, the Constitution, and the freedom of mankind."[27]

"A CENTRALIZATION OF POWER, SUCH AS HAMILTON MIGHT HAVE EULOGIZED"

Under the leadership of Lincoln, Clay's American System of national banking, internal improvements, and tariff-based import-substitution industrialization was finally enacted on a grand scale. Even before the war ended and the period of Reconstruction finally began, the remaking of the United States by northerners was well underway.

The Republican Party was divided in its attitudes toward banking. Former Whigs like Lincoln supported a national banking system. But many western Republican farmers who had earlier been Jacksonian Democrats had a populist suspicion of northeastern financiers and British finance. Their suspicions seemed to be confirmed when New York bankers refused to extend loans to the US government during the early part of the Civil War, when asked to do so by Treasury Secretary Salmon P. Chase.

The eastern banks also opposed key reforms of the American financial system that Chase proposed. One was the Legal Tender Act of 1862, which allowed the secretary of the Treasury to issue paper money based on federal government debt—"greenbacks."

When the Civil War began, the currency consisted exclusively of notes issued by banks chartered by the states and redeemable in gold or silver. The National Currency Acts of 1863 and 1864 created a new federal banking system. Under its provision, state banknotes were eliminated by a 10 percent tax on them, and a system of nationally chartered banks authorized to issue banknotes supplied by the Treasury was created. The Republicans did not create a third Bank of the United States, however. That occurred only in 1913 with the creation of the Federal Reserve. While the federal government drove state banknotes out of existence, many state-chartered banks chose not to seek federal charters. By prohibiting branch banking across state lines, the new national system itself reinforced state and local banks. Instead of withering away, state-chartered banks continued to exist alongside nationally chartered banks in a dual banking system.

The *New York Times* wrote on March 9, 1862: "The legal tender act and the national currency bill crystallized . . . a centralization of power, such as Hamilton might have eulogized as magnificent." The Democratic state committee of Indiana agreed, complaining in 1862 that President Lincoln had struck "down at one dash all the labor of Gen. Jackson for the last four years of his administration."[28]

INTERNAL IMPROVEMENTS

Internal improvements, or infrastructure projects, another part of Clay's Hamiltonian American System, were also established on a grand scale under Lincoln and his successors. The failure of the state internal improvements program in Illinois did not reduce Lincoln's commitment to the American System. During his first and only term in the US Congress, on June 20, 1848, Lincoln defended federal subsidies for internal improvements. Addressing the old claim by Jeffersonians that the constitution forbade federal aid to private enterprises, Lincoln argued: "The [question] of national power and state rights as a principle is no other than the principle of generality and locality. Whatever concerns the whole should be confided to the whole—to the general government; while whatever concerns only the state should be left exclusively to the state."

Lincoln himself owed much of his prosperity as a lawyer to the railroads. The Illinois Central Railroad was Lincoln's most important client.

He also obtained work as a lawyer from other railroad companies with Illinois interests, including the Ohio & Mississippi Railroad, the Alton & Sangamon Railroad, and the Tonica & Petersburg Railroad.[29]

Lincoln's most famous case was *Hurd v. Rock Island Bridge Company* (1857), which involved a clash of steam-age transportation technologies. In 1856, a steamboat struck a bridge across the Mississippi in Illinois that had been constructed by the Chicago, Rock Island and Pacific Railroad, called the Rock Island Railroad. Lincoln successfully defended the railroad in a case that helped to establish the right of railroads to cross rivers.

Remembered as "the rail-splitter," Lincoln would more accurately be remembered as "the rail-roader." He oversaw more land grants to railroads than any other president.

On September 20, 1850, one of Lincoln's predecessors in the White House, President Millard Fillmore, signed the first Federal Land-Grant Act. Guided through Congress by senators Stephen A. Douglas of Illinois and William King of Alabama, the act granted land that could be sold to finance the Illinois Central and the Mobile & Ohio line in Alabama and Mississippi. Until then, the only aid by the federal government to railroads had been a reduction on imported iron and rails from 1830 to 1843 and route surveys carried out on behalf of private railroads by US Army engineers.

Before 1860, no bill providing federal aid for the construction of a railroad from the East to the Pacific had ever passed in Congress.[30] In 1862, Congress passed legislation spending millions on a Pacific rail line to be built and operated by two companies, the Union Pacific and Central Pacific. Corrupt practices on the part of company officials, including allies of Lincoln, produced the Credit Mobilier scandal during the Grant administration, which will be discussed in the next chapter.[31] In spite of scandals and waste, the American railroad network grew between 1860 and 1870 from twenty-nine thousand miles to forty-nine thousand miles.[32] The United States had the highest proportion of railroad mileage to inhabitants in the world by 1868.[33]

THE TARIFF

The centerpiece of Henry Clay's plan for the industrialization of the United States had been a high protective tariff (Hamilton had preferred government subsidies to infant industries).

Lincoln told a correspondent in 1859, "I was an old Henry-Clay-Tariff Whig. In old times I made more speeches on that subject than any other. I have not since changed my views."[34] Throughout his political career, Lincoln seemed to illustrate the definition by a contemporary in protectionist Pennsylvania of man as "an animal that makes tariff speeches."[35] Early in his career, Lincoln had worn a suit of homespun jeans as a legislator, in emulation of George Washington's decision to dress in homespun for his inauguration, encouraging the spirit later manifested in "Buy American" campaigns. In arguing for a protective tariff, Lincoln followed Clay in identifying industrial Britain as America's economic rival, and claimed that those who purchased imported British goods were unpatriotic snobs: "Those whose pride, whose abundance of means, prompt them to spurn the manufactures of their own country, and to strut in British cloaks, and coats, and pantaloons, may have to pay a few cents more on the yard for the cloth that makes them. A terrible evil, surely, to the Illinois farmer, who never wore, nor never [sic] expects to wear, a single yard of British goods in his whole life."[36]

The tariff was part of the Republican Party platform of 1860, whose wording, the product of the efforts of Henry Carey among others, sought to please every constituency: "While providing revenue for the support of the general government by duties upon imports, sound policy requires such an adjustment of these imports as to encourage the development of the industrial interests of the country; and we recommend that policy of national exchanges, which secures to the working man liberal wages, to agriculture remunerative prices, to mechanics and manufacturers an adequate reward for their skill, labor, and enterprise, and to the nation commercial prosperity and independence."[37] One observer reported: "The Pennsylvania and New Jersey delegations were terrific in their applause over the tariff resolution, and their hilarity was contagious, finally pervading the whole vast auditorium."[38] The electoral votes of protectionist Pennsylvania and New Jersey were crucial in helping Lincoln and the Republicans win the White House in 1860. "Protection made Mr. Lincoln president," Carey said.[39]

After he had been nominated as the Republican presidential candidate in 1860, Lincoln took part in a parade in his hometown of Springfield, to which the contribution of the local woolen mill, according to one historian, was "an immense wagon containing a power loom driven by a steam engine. Several yards of jean cloth, from which a garment was fashioned for Lincoln, were made as part of a demonstration. The wagon bore the significant motto 'Protection to Home Industry.' "[40]

In May 1860, before the election, the House had passed the Morrill Tariff, which was passed by the Senate between Lincoln's election and his inauguration. Tariffs were raised again during the Civil War in 1862 and 1864. The administration of Abraham Lincoln inaugurated an era that lasted until World War II, in which the United States had the most protected home market in the world. Between 1867 and 1914, while many goods were admitted free from duties, the US tariff on dutiable imports, chiefly manufactured goods, hovered between 40 and 50 percent.[41]

From Ulysses S. Grant to Herbert Hoover, Lincoln's Republican successors shared his view that the government should protect and promote American manufacturing. President Grant pointed out that Britain had industrialized behind a wall of protective tariffs, turning to free trade only when its manufactured exports were superior to those of other countries: "After two centuries, England found it convenient to adopt free trade because it thinks that protection can no longer offer it anything. Very well, Gentlemen, my knowledge of our country leads me to believe that within 200 years, when America has gotten out of protection all that it can offer, it too will adopt free trade."[42]

William McKinley, who published a book on the tariff, succeeded Justin Morrill as the leading spokesman for protectionism in the Republican Party and gave his name to the 1890 McKinley Tariff. McKinley and his vice president and successor, Theodore Roosevelt, recognized the need for reciprocal trade liberalization in sectors where infant industry protection had successfully created mature American industries. But like other Republicans of their time, they remained committed economic nationalists. Roosevelt wrote in 1895: "Thank God I am not a free-trader. In this country pernicious indulgence in the doctrine of free trade seems inevitably to produce fatty degeneration of the moral fibre."[43]

The US model of import substitution became a model for other industrializing countries like Germany, Japan, Russia, and the British Dominions of Canada, Australia, and New Zealand. In the early twentieth century, the economist Frank W. Taussig, despite his commitment to free trade, conceded that without protectionism the development of American manufacturing might not have taken place as rapidly as it did.[44] Whether because of or in spite of protectionism, the US economy grew at 4.1 percent a year from 1870 to 1913, while free-trade Britain grew at only 1.9 percent a year.

THE WHARTON SCHOOL OF PROTECTIONISM

Before the Civil War, economics was taught as a part of moral philosophy, a subject that also included politics and ethics. University teachings on trade generally reflected the interests of the local business elites who served as university regents. Free-trade theory was taught in the cotton-exporting South and the commercial and financial Northeast. Pennsylvania, the center of American manufacturing, naturally became the center of protectionist economics.

Joseph Wharton was the patrician heir of a Philadelphia Quaker family that had made its fortune in real estate and trade. Wharton made a fortune of his own in mining and smelting industrial metals such as iron and later steel, lead, and zinc. He attended the economist Henry Carey's salon in Philadelphia and belonged to the Industrial League and the American Iron and Steel Association. Wharton viewed free trade as a "fungus . . . which healthy political organisms can hardly afford to tolerate."[45]

In 1881, in order to promote protectionism, Wharton founded the first business school in the United States. In his deed of gift to the Wharton School of Finance and Economy at the University of Pennsylvania, the industrialist specified that the school should teach "how by craft in commerce one nation may take the substance of a rival and maintain for itself virtual monopoly of the most profitable and civilizing industries; how by suitable tariff legislation a nation may thwart such designs."[46] He made his gift conditional: "the right and duty of national self-protection must be firmly asserted and demonstrated."[47]

A disciple of Carey named Robert Ellis Thompson, who became the first American professor of social science in 1874, helped to found the Wharton School. Thompson's book *Social Science and National Economy*, financed by Wharton, became the basis of instruction in economics.[48]

In 1883, leadership of the Wharton School was taken over by Edmund J. James, a German-trained scholar who was inspired by Germany's *Verein fur Sozialwissenschaft*, an organization that promoted policy-relevant research, to found the American Academy of Political and Social Science in 1889 and the National Municipal League in 1893. Another economist trained in the German historical school, Simon Patten, taught at Wharton and defended America's Hamiltonian import-substitution policy in *The Economic Basis of Protection*.[49]

By the early 1900s, many US industries no longer needed infant-industry protection, while German-trained academics were more interested in progressive and socialist causes. The result was the purging of progressive scholars by business-dominated boards of regents in the first decades of the twentieth century.

"THE CRIME OF 1873"—THE RETURN TO THE GOLD STANDARD

Manufacturers were only one constituency in the Republican Party. Republicans in finance and import businesses shared the traditional antipathy of those sectors to protectionism and put great value on the gold

standard, as it was adopted by most of America's trading partners in the
second half of the nineteenth century.

Following the conclusion of the Civil War, the New York financial
community, eager to resume its role as intermediary between the cotton
growers of the South and the British and European textile industries,
favored a lenient approach to Reconstruction that would facilitate the
resumption of cotton exports as quickly as possible. President Andrew
Johnson, who was dreaded and despised by the Radical Republicans
who later unsuccessfully impeached him, was lionized by the New York
elite when he visited the city in the summer of 1866. Earlier, in the
spring of 1865, the Chamber of Commerce of the State of New York
declared that Reconstruction should not "be condemned as needlessly
harsh or revengeful by the cool judgment of the humane and liberty-
loving in any part of the civilized world."[50] New York's financial community was appalled when, in his final annual message to Congress in
December 1868, Johnson reverted to his populist roots and proposed
to confiscate the interest owed to federal bondholders and use it to pay
down the federal debt.[51]

After many Democrats proposed repaying federal creditors in
inflation-depreciated greenbacks, it became a point of honor for Republicans to insist that holders of federal bonds be repaid in gold. In the Public
Credit Act of 1869, Congress declared its support of a gold-backed currency.

Within the Republican Party, however, greenbackers could be found.
Support for fiat money, like support for a powerful, activist federal government, was concentrated in iron-producing and manufacturing areas
like Pennsylvania and newly settled midwestern and western regions that
wanted government-sponsored infrastructure development.[52] Carey and
other members of the Pennsylvania protectionist wing of the Republican
Party favored greenbacks, because they had the effect of devaluing the US
currency, to the benefit of American exporters and the detriment of British and European manufacturers who sought to sell in the United States.[53]
For the same reason, William McKinley, who represented midwestern

manufacturers, preferred what was called "Buckeye Bimetallism" (after Ohio, the Buckeye State) to a pure gold standard during the presidential campaign of 1896, notwithstanding William Jennings Bryan's claim that McKinley and the Republicans sought to "crucify mankind upon a cross of gold."

THE HOMESTEAD ACT AND THE LAND-GRANT UNIVERSITY SYSTEM

Another important Republican constituency was made up of free farmers in the North. Many Republican agrarians had been Jeffersonian and Jacksonian Democrats, who joined the Republican Party out of fear that the expansion of slavery into the West and North would force them to compete with slaveowners for land or with slaves for jobs.

The Homestead Act, passed by Congress in 1859, was a concession to the former Jacksonian Democrats in the Republican Party. The law gave 160 acres to anyone who would live on the land and work it for five years. President James Buchanan, an ally of the southern slaveholding elite, vetoed the Homestead Act but it was passed again by Congress and signed by President Lincoln in 1862. The purpose of the act was thwarted to some degree by the success of railroads, other corporations, and rich investors in obtaining lands intended for settlers. Even so, more than half a million farmers received a homestead by 1900 (the act was repealed in 1977). The Morrill Land-Grant Act of 1862 provided every state with grants of federal land to pay for establishing state agricultural and mechanical colleges (A&Ms). Intended to provide a liberal education for rural Americans, the A&Ms were given a new and important role in scientific agricultural research by the Hatch Act of 1887, which established a network of agricultural experiment stations for America's oldest major economic sector.

THE SECOND REPUBLIC

The Civil War and Reconstruction replaced the First Republic of the United States, dominated for most of its existence by southern slaveowners, with a Second Republic dominated by the industrialists, financiers, and free farmers of the Northeast and Midwest. Alexander Hamilton's and Henry Clay's vision of developmental capitalism, not the adversarial, small-producer capitalism of Thomas Jefferson, shaped the economic policies of Abraham Lincoln and his allies.

The Lincoln Republicans saved the Union, freed the slaves—and freed the remarkable powers of industrial capitalism from subordination to an agrarian oligarchy, the southern planters. But like many newly industrializing countries, the United States after the Civil War sacrificed social justice and resource conservation to the imperative of economic growth. With harmful effects as well as good, the transformation of the American polity by the technologies of the first industrial revolution was under way.

THE IRON HORSE AND THE LIGHTNING

We have all heard of Young America. He is the most current youth of the age. Some think him conceited, and arrogant; but has he not reason to entertain a rather extensive opinion of himself? . . . The iron horse is panting, and impatient, to carry him everywhere, in no time; and the lightning stands ready harnessed to take and bring his tidings in a trifle less than no time. He owns a large part of the world, by right of possessing it; and all the rest by right of wanting it, and intending to have it.

—Abraham Lincoln, 1859[1]

Fifty-six miles west of Ogden, Utah, on May 10, 1869, the first of five transcontinental railroads was completed by a ceremonial golden spike that connected the Union Pacific and Central Pacific Railroads. Authorized by Congress in 1862 with the Pacific Railway Act, the transcontinental railroad linked the East and West. The North and South had already been riveted together in the Civil War of 1861–1865, with bullets and cannonballs.

As early as the 1830s, Americans discussed a transcontinental railroad. To facilitate a southern route, in 1853, a strip of land called the Gadsden Purchase was bought from Mexico and added to the former Mexican territories acquired by the United States after the United States–Mexican War. But rivalries between the North and South in Congress blocked agreement on a route.

The departure of southern representatives from the House and Senate during the secession of the southern states freed Congress and the Lincoln administration to charter two railroads with the Pacific Railroad Act that President Lincoln signed on July 1, 1862.

The bill chartered two companies, the Union Pacific and the Central Pacific, to connect Omaha and Sacramento. The Pacific Railroad Act authorized the Union Pacific to go west from Omaha, while the Central Pacific would go east from Sacramento. Each line was given twenty alternate sections of federal land for each mile built. The Union Pacific received twelve million acres of land and $27 million in government mortgage bonds, the Central Pacific nine million acres and $24 million in bonds. Later, the Texas Pacific received eighteen million acres and the Northern Pacific forty-four million acres. The two railroad companies raised additional private funds in the United States and Europe.

The Central Pacific broke ground in January 1863 in Sacramento, California. In December of the same year, the ground breaking of the Union Pacific took place in Omaha, Nebraska. The race to lay rails across the continent had begun.

Each railroad faced different kinds of obstacles. The Central Pacific had to grade and blast its way over the mountains. The Union Pacific, crossing the level Great Plains, was attacked by Sioux and Cheyenne Indians who were threatened by the invasion of their territory. At Plum Creek, Nebraska, Cheyenne warriors derailed and looted a freight train. Forts were established along the route and the workers were armed.

The workers who built the first transcontinental railroad included northern and southern veterans of the Civil War and freed slaves. The Union Pacific relied heavily on Irish immigrants, the Central Pacific on Chinese contract workers.

The tracks met in the Promontory Mountains in Utah. As delegates arrived to celebrate the project's completion, the target date of May 8, 1869, was missed. On May 9 the final twenty-five hundred feet of track were laid. On May 10, two trains, the Union Pacific's Number 119 and the Central Pacific's *Jupiter*, stood facing each other. A little after noon an official from each company used a silver sledgehammer to tap ceremonial gold spikes into the final tie. A signal flashed across telegraph wires to bring the news to the rest of the country: "Done."

In seven years the Union Pacific had built 1,086 miles of track, while the Central Pacific had built 690 miles. The Great Plains were opened to settlement, at the expense of the Plains Indians, who in the succeeding decades were confined to reservations. Before the transcontinental railroad, overland travel to the Pacific coast of the United States had taken months, as had the alternatives of sailing around the tip of South America or sailing to Central America, crossing the isthmus and boarding another ship. Now it was possible to travel from the East to the West Coast in less than a week for a fraction of the price.

RUINOUS COMPETITION

The railroad industry was America's first big business. Not until the late nineteenth century did giant corporations emerge in many manufacturing and retail industries. Until then, production and distribution tended to be carried out by relatively small shops and stores.

In 1896, the railroad industry accounted for 15 percent of gross national product, more than federal, state, and local governments combined.[2] The investment of $188 million in canals between 1815 and 1860 was dwarfed by the $1.1 billion invested in railroads between 1830 and 1859.[3] Until the end of the nineteenth century, railroad stocks and bonds dominated the American stock market. Around 1870, 50 percent of America's capital goods industries and 10 percent of its nonfarm labor were contributing to railroad construction.[4]

The railroad industry was afflicted by a problem that later injured a number of large-scale industries with increasing returns to scale—the problem caused by the gap between fixed costs (repayment of borrowing to build the physical structure) and variable or operating costs. The fixed-cost problem meant that the traditional answer to monopoly—increased competition—could not work and indeed would make matters worse.

If a railroad was challenged by a rival line, the resulting price war could doom both the incumbent and the challenger to bankruptcy.

In addition to fixed costs, the railroad industry was characterized by network effects. A railroad line between only two cities would suffer if the economy in one declined. In contrast, regional networks including many points were more stable than local systems, and national systems had the greatest stability of all.

Britain permitted railroads to engage in cartelization and prohibited mergers, in order to avoid consolidation while enjoying the benefits of co-ordination.[5] In France, with its tradition of administrative guidance of the economy, the government supervised management, regulated rates, and arranged mergers. Most European governments engaged in public rate setting, prohibited construction of competing lines, and enforced private cartels in the courts. By 1945, every major country in the world except for the United States, with the exception of the Wilson administration's nationalization of the rails during World War I, had nationalized its rail-ways.

In the United States, however, the Jeffersonian tradition of local-ism and laissez-faire dominated during the period of railroad con-struction between the Civil War and the 1890s. The result was massive overbuilding—by the 1880s the country had nearly twice as much track as it needed—and chronic bankruptcy: in the 1870s, nearly 40 percent of American railroad bonds were in default.[6] In 1895, one-fourth of Amer-ican railroads were in receivership as part of bankruptcy proceedings.[7] Waves of bankruptcy in turn resulted in the consolidation of the railroads into a few networks by the early twentieth century. William Vanderbilt, an heir to Cornelius Vanderbilt and a railroad owner, predicted accurately that the alternative to government-sanctioned pooling would be the ab-sorption of small firms by large railroads.[8]

Not until the early twentieth century did economists and public of-ficials acknowledge the inapplicability of competitive market econom-ics to railroads.[9] The Transportation Act of 1920 permitted pooling by railroads subject to regulation by the Interstate Commerce Commission.

Until 1980, the railroads were a consolidated, nationally regulated public utility. Following the deregulation of the railroads by the Staggers Act of 1980, the American railroads were quickly consolidated into a few private regional monopolies.

TRANSCONTINENTAL CORRUPTION

Ironically, the corruption associated with the construction of transcontinental railroads was the result of a system adopted in the hope of avoiding corruption. Direct federal construction of transcontinental railroads was rejected because, in the words of President James Buchanan in his annual message on December 6, 1858, government railroad construction "would increase the patronage of the Executive to a dangerous extent, and introduce a system of jobbing and corruption which no vigilance on the part of the Executive could either prevent or detect."[10] Another alternative, a private monopoly chartered by the federal government, was rejected in 1851 when the railroad promoter Asa Whitney asked Congress to provide him land grants for a railroad to the Pacific.[11]

In its final form, the Pacific Railroad Act that President Lincoln signed on July 1, 1862, was intended to minimize the possibility of corruption. The act provided that the railroads would receive federal lands only after the tracks were built; time limits were imposed; the railroads had to acquire sufficient private capital of their own, before using federal eminent-domain authority; and the twenty-member boards of the railroads included five government directors apiece.[12]

But greed found a way. In return for stock that they received in blatant violation of the bill itself, the government directors of the railroad companies looked the other way. While serving in Congress, Oakes Ames of Massachusetts, who with his brother owned one of the country's biggest shovel manufacturing companies, sat on the boards of the Union Pacific and its construction company, Credit Mobilier. Ames bribed many members of the House, Senate, and executive branch with company stock in return for their support of legislation favorable to the corporation, like an

1864 law that doubled the land that the Union Pacific received and made the federal loan guarantees more favorable.[13]

Credit Mobilier charged the Union Pacific two or three times the actual cost of construction. The Union Pacific also used other front companies, including the Wyoming Coal and Mining Company, which sold the coal to the railroad at three times the real cost. There was no similar scandal involving the Contract and Finance Company, the Central Pacific's equivalent of Credit Mobilier, because the financial records of the Central Pacific's construction company conveniently disappeared.

In the wake of these scandals, Congress refused to charter any more railroads, following its charter of the Texas and Pacific in 1871. The corruption associated with the transcontinental railroads that were supplied with federal land grants and other aids is often invoked by those who argue that government promotion of infrastructure and industry is inherently flawed. "Never heard of the Great Northern?" Bill Frezza of the Competitive Enterprise Institute wrote in *Forbes* in September 2011. "That's because they don't teach about it in government schools. That transcontinental railroad, completed in 1893, was the only one built entirely with private money on privately purchased land, by a self-made railroad tycoon, James J. Hill. . . . Many believe Ayn Rand got her inspiration for Taggart Transcontinental in her novel *Atlas Shrugged* from the Great Northern."[14]

In reality, Hill's Great Northern depended as much on government land grants as the other transcontinental railroads. When they purchased the St. Paul and Pacific Railroad, which had gone bankrupt in the panic of 1873, Hill and his partners purchased the assets, which included a 2.5 million-acre land grant from the state of Minnesota. Out of seventy-five land grants given to American railroads between 1850 and 1871, Hill's government land grant was the seventh largest.[15]

"THIRTEEN MILLION DOLLARS
IS ALSO SOMETHING"

The centrality of railroad issues on Wall Street quickly led to the emergence of a breed of speculators who were interested only in gaming railroad stocks to make quick money. The most celebrated stock market struggle of the period was what became known as the Erie War.

In 1868 "Commodore" Cornelius Vanderbilt, having moved from the steamship business into the railroad industry, sought to take over the Erie Railway Company, which was the main rival of his own New York Central Railroad. What was at stake was control of the railroad traffic between New York City and the west.

The Erie was run by the seventy-one-year-old Daniel Drew. In *Chapters of Erie*, Charles Francis Adams, the son of John Quincy Adams and a railroad president in his own right, wrote: "Drew sought to carry to a mean perfection the old system of operating successfully from the confidential position of director, neither knowing anything nor caring anything for the railroad system, except in its connection with the movements of the stock exchange, and he succeeded in his object."[16] Unlike the patrician Adams, and like his rival "Corneel" Vanderbilt, "Uncle Dan'l" was a self-made entrepreneur who observed: "Book learning is something, but thirteen million dollars is also something, and a mighty sight more."[17]

Drew's allies on the Erie board included James Fisk and Jay Gould, both in their early thirties. Fisk, plump and outgoing, was a former circus worker and peddler who had smuggled cotton from the Confederacy into the North during the Civil War. The thin and introverted Gould was a sickly individual from a family of poor farmers in New York who had become a master speculator. When Vanderbilt's agents tried to buy up controlling shares of Erie stock, the Commodore discovered that Drew, Gould, and Fisk secretly printed millions of dollars worth of new bonds in order to thwart the takeover bid. However, Vanderbilt arranged for a compliant New York judge named George Barnard, who belonged to the

Tweed Ring run by the notoriously corrupt William "Boss" Tweed, to rule that the Erie directors had violated an injunction. In response, Drew, Fisk, and Gould fled to New Jersey, where friendly judges would shield them, and made their refuge, Taylor's Hotel, into "Fort Taylor."

The battle then shifted to the New York State legislature in Albany, where each side battled to bribe lawmakers. When Fisk won over Boss Tweed, who was elected to the Erie board of directors, the balance of power shifted to the Erie group. Defeated, Vanderbilt dropped charges against Drew, Fisk, and Gould, in return for being paid by Erie for half of the shares he had bought. Vanderbilt said that the incident "has learned me it never pays to kick a skunk."[18]

Fisk and Gould went on to attempt to manipulate the gold market in 1869, with a scheme that implicated Abel Corwin, the brother-in-law of President Ulysses S. Grant. After being ejected as president of Erie in 1872, Gould captured the Union Pacific, assembled a railroad empire in the Southwest and West, took over Western Union for a time, and bought the *New York World*, which he sold to Joseph Pulitzer. He died at fifty-five in 1892. Fisk had died earlier, in 1872, at the age of thirty-six, shot by a former business partner who had taken up with his estranged mistress. He was memorialized in a folk song:

> We all know he loved both women and wine
>   But his heart it was right, I am sure.
> Though he lived like a prince in a palace so fine,
>   Yet he never went back on the poor.
>
> If a man was in trouble, Fisk helped him along
>   To drive the grim wolf from the door.
> He strove to do right, though he may have done wrong,
>   But he never went back on the poor.[19]

THE RISE OF WESTERN UNION

By creating a truly national market in a continental area, the railroads allowed other industries to reap the benefits of economies of scale. The first national industry to grow up along the railroads in the new national market they created was the telegraph industry.

Even though Congress had funded Samuel F. B. Morse's successful development of the telegraph, it refused his offer to sell the rights to the device to the federal government. In Britain, the government nationalized the telegraph system by the end of the nineteenth century. But in the United States, the telegraph industry, like the railroad system, was developed by private enterprise.

The telegraph and railroad industries grew up together, as telegraph companies helped railroads coordinate schedules and took advantage of railroad rights-of-way. The telegraph industry was similar to the railroad industry in the importance of fixed costs, and network effects, which made it a natural monopoly or oligopoly. Just as the railroad companies experimented with pools and cartels, so the six largest telegraph companies created a pooling arrangement called the Treaty of the Six Nations to coordinate competition, regulate prices, and exclude new entrants. Like informal pools and cartels in the railroad industry and other areas, this attempt failed because of the lack of effective sanctions on defectors. As an alternative, the three largest telegraph companies merged to form a single company named Western Union in 1855. Western Union built the first transcontinental telegraph in 1861 and by 1886, after it absorbed the Baltimore and Ohio Telegraph Company, Western Union's control of the telegraph industry was complete.[20]

In return for transmission of federal messages, the telegraph companies were given subsidies by the Pacific Telegraph Act of 1860. During the Civil War, the federal government took over and operated the telegraph system, and during the war it built thousands of miles of new lines. After the war the federal government gave them to the telegraph companies.

"EVERYTHING BUT THE SQUEAL"

Other industries expanded and adopted innovative reorganizations to take advantage of the continental markets created by the railroads. Many of the "tycoons" of the late nineteenth century made their fortunes during the Civil War.

Philip Armour was one. Plankton, Armour & Co., the firm that he founded with his partner John Plankton, became a major supplier of salt pork for the Union armies. Following the war, Armour moved his headquarters to Chicago, the center of the meatpacking industry, in order to be near the Union Stockyards, formed by a consortium of nine railroad companies. Armour pioneered innovations like the use of conveyor belts, airtight tin cans, and the slaughter and dressing of live animals at his meat-processing plants. He obtained lower rates from the railroad by operating his own rail cars. In 1874, Gustavus Swift's development of refrigerator cars expanded the business further, enabling the sale of meat at all seasons to customers in the United States and Europe. Armour recycled the offal of the slaughterhouses as glue, drugs, and other products, using "everything but the squeal," as he explained. Armour declared: "I like to turn bristles, blood, and the inside and outside of pigs and bullocks into great revenue."[21]

JOHN D. ROCKEFELLER AND THE RISE OF STANDARD OIL

Another American tycoon who owed his fortune to skillful exploitation of the commercial possibilities created by the railroads was John D. Rockefeller. The son of a scandalous patent-medicine salesman and bigamist, the devoutly pious and disciplined Rockefeller paid to be replaced by a substitute in the Civil War, and while other Americans his age, including his brother Frank, were fighting for the Union, he was making money. His confidence-man father had included "rock oil" in the patent medicines that he sold. The son found a better use for the substance.

On August 28, 1859, near Titusville, Pennsylvania, Edwin Drake struck oil. Rigs quickly sprang up around what came to be known as Oil Creek. Kerosene lamps soon replaced whale oil and expensive coal oil for illumination, in homes, offices, and factories. Petroleum also provided lubricants for machinery. The outbreak of the Civil War ensured that government procurement would help the infant industry.

With two partners, whom he later bought out, Rockefeller founded a company in Cleveland in 1863 to refine oil. With his subsequent partner Henry Flagler, he flourished, thanks to ruthless cost cutting and determination to buy out his competitors or drive them out of business. In 1870, Standard Oil was founded. "The Standard Oil Company will someday refine all the oil," a colleague heard him say.[22]

Following the conclusion of the war, Rockefeller secretly obtained discounts from rival railroads in return for his promises of large shipments. Then in the 1870s, he secretly connived with other big refiners and railroads to form a cartel, the South Improvement Company. When small producers learned about the cartel, the result was the "Oil War." Following the collapse of the South Improvement Company, Rockefeller focused on expanding Standard Oil's domination of the industry. He pioneered vertical integration, manufacturing railroad tanker cars, investing in pipelines, and buying up oil lands. By 1890, Standard was America's largest producer of oil as well as its largest refiner. Rockefeller's iron mines and fleet of ore boats, sold to J. P. Morgan, were the final ingredient of the United States Steel Corporation, which on its creation in 1901 surpassed Standard Oil as the largest corporation in the world. The development of electricity ended the age of kerosene lamps, but the new automobiles and aircraft needed gasoline, which had been treated as a useless by-product of the refining process. For a time Rockefeller was the richest man in the world. By 1904, Standard Oil controlled 85 percent of all sales and 90 percent of all US crude oil production. In 1911, the Supreme Court upheld an order to break Standard into more than two dozen companies, many of which, following multiple mergers, survive under different names today. For example, ExxonMobil, created in 1999, descends from two Rockefeller companies, Standard of New York (Socony), which merged with Vacuum Oil to become Mobil in 1966, and Esso, formerly Standard of New Jersey, which merged with Exxon in 1972.

"STEEL IS KING"

The railroads also made possible the success of the steelmaker Andrew Carnegie. Carnegie was born in a cottage in the Scottish town of Dumferline in 1835 into a family of weavers who worked in their home. When their business failed, they borrowed money from a neighbor and immigrated to Pennsylvania. While his father worked himself to an early grave and his mother took in washing, the teenage "Andra" worked at various jobs. His fortunes improved when an uncle helped him get a job with the Ohio Telegraph Company in Pittsburgh. By the age of fifteen, the messenger boy was a telegraph operator. In 1853, he joined the Pennsylvania Railroad as a clerk and secretary. Impressing Tom Scott, the president, Carnegie rose rapidly in rank.

By the age of twenty he was a capitalist, borrowing money to invest in the precursor to the Pullman railroad car company and oil land in Pennsylvania. At thirty he resigned from the Pennsylvania Railroad and invested in iron mills, selling iron from them to his own Keystone Bridge and Pittsburgh Locomotive Works. In 1868, he wrote a memorandum to himself: "Thirty three and an income of $50,000 per annum! Beyond this never earn—make no effort to increase fortune, but spend the surplus each year for benevolent purposes. . . . Amassing of wealth is one of the worst species of idolatry. . . . I will resign business at thirty-five."[23]

Carnegie, however, postponed his resignation from moneymaking. He gained control of the Edgar Thomson Steel Company and obtained the Mesabi iron ore lands along Lake Superior from John D. Rockefeller. A good judge of talent, Carnegie picked a Welsh immigrant, Captain William R. Jones, whom he paid the equivalent of the salary of the president of the United States. After Jones was killed when a vat of molten steel exploded, Carnegie replaced him with a young man named Charles Schwab.

Skeptical at first about the Bessemer process that rapidly turned iron into steel, Carnegie was converted, declaring, "The day of Iron has passed—Steel is King!" The tariff of 1870, imposed as Bessemer mills in America lowered steel costs, helped to strengthen the US steel industry against British competition. Even in the depressed years of the 1870s, the steel industry grew at 10 to 20 percent a year.[24] An absentee taskmaster, Carnegie bombarded his subordinates with notes urging them to cut costs from his Pittsburgh mansion, his New York office, and the Scottish castle he bought at Skibo.

One partner said: "Carnegie never wanted to know the profits. He always wanted to know the cost." By 1890, Carnegie was the victor in the iron and steel wars, producing a quarter of American steel. He wrote: "Two pounds of iron stone mined upon Lake Superior and transported nine hundred miles to Pittsburgh; one pound and one-half of coal mined and manufactured into coke, and transported to Pittsburgh; a small amount of manganese ore mined in Virginia and brought to Pittsburgh— and these four pounds of materials manufactured into one pound of steel, for which the consumer pays one cent."[25]

RAIL AND RETAIL

In distribution, as well as in production, the railroads created a national market that could be exploited by national firms. One was Sears, Roebuck.

In 1886, the railroads agreed to establish four time zones in the United States. The new precision of schedules led many passengers to rely on watches. In 1886, a railway agent at Redwood Falls, Minnesota, bought a shipment of watches after a local merchant refused them for fifty dollars and sold them to other railway employees and railroad passengers for five thousand dollars. Richard Warren Sears put the five thousand dollars in the R. W. Sears Watch Company and moved its headquarters from Minnesota to Chicago.

Needing a watch repairman, Sears brought on Alvah Curtis Roebuck from Indiana as a partner. In the 1890s, their mail-order catalog grew from one limited to watches and jewelry to a five-hundred-page compendium. When Roebuck retired, he sold his stake to two Chicago businessmen, Julius Rosenwald and his brother-in-law Aaron Nusbaum. Rosenwald took over Sears, Roebuck when Sears retired in 1908. The catalogs of Sears, Roebuck and Montgomery Ward became familiar fixtures in American homes. Legend has it that one child in a Sunday school class, when asked where the Ten Commandments came from, replied, "From the Sears, Roebuck catalog."[26]

YELLOW JOURNALISM AND PULP FICTION

American publishing was another industry that was transformed by combinations of steam-engine technology and telegraphy in the half century that followed the Civil War. The formation of a national market made possible the first versions of the mass media.

In 1810, Friedrich Koenig, a German inventor living in Britain, patented the first steam press. A New York inventor named Richard Hoe improved upon it in 1843, creating a steam-powered rotary press with cylinders through which papers were fed. The steam press lowered the costs of printing dramatically. The beneficiaries included publishers of "dime novels" and inexpensive magazines, which, because they were printed on cheap paper pulp, came to be known as "pulp fiction" and "pulp magazines." Low printing costs also led to the growth of mass-circulation newspapers that working-class readers could afford. The most important of these were Joseph Pulitzer's *New York World* and William Randolph Hearst's *New York Journal*. Their use of lurid headlines for sensational crimes and scandals inspired the dignified editor of the *New York Press*, Ervin Wardman, to dismiss them as "yellow kid journalism," after the Yellow Kid, a popular comic strip character created for Pulitzer by Richard Felton Outcault.

PANICS

The enlarged national and global markets made possible by the railroad, the steamship, and the telegraph made tremendous improvements in productivity possible. But the damage done by financial contagion and business cycles was worse in larger, more integrated industrial markets. Some historians speak of a long depression between the 1870s and the 1890s, punctuated by major and minor panics.

On the evening of September 17, 1873, Jay Cooke received a guest at his two-hundred-acre estate outside Philadelphia, President Ulysses S. Grant. With five hundred other elite guests, Grant had attended the housewarming party of Cooke's fifty-two-room mansion on its completion in 1865. The house, which Justice Salmon P. Chase called "Cooke's Castle," was named Ogontz after a local Sandusky Indian chief, who was immortalized in a bas-relief in the stairwell; other Indians were portrayed in stained glass windows.[27] The grounds included Italianate gardens with statues and fountains and the ruins of a castle imported from Europe.

Cooke had grown wealthy during the Civil War, when he had obtained a monopoly on the sale of government bonds in the United States. Following the war, he moved into railroad finance, investing in a new transcontinental railroad, the Northern Pacific. At breakfast the morning after the housewarming, the financier known as the Tycoon (a variant of the Japanese title "shogun") gave the president no indication of the distress he felt as he read alarming telegrams from his New York office of Jay Cooke & Co. Rushing to Philadelphia in his carriage, Cooke learned that the New York branch had closed. He ordered the closing of the Philadelphia headquarters and abruptly burst into tears.

The collapse of the largest bank in the United States led to a wave of bankruptcies of banks, railroads, and other companies. Mass unemployment produced civic unrest. In New York City, police beat hundreds of unemployed men and women in the Tompkins Square Riot of 1874. In 1875, a group of Irish coal miners, the Molly Maguires, went on strike, and in 1877 a nationwide railroad strike led to intervention by federal

troops and the arrest of its leader, Eugene Debs, who later became the
Socialist Party candidate for president.

Another panic in 1893 caused another recession, the original Great
Depression. More violence between employers and workers followed,
making the United States the Western country with the greatest amount
of labor violence at the time. The distress of southern and western farmers sparked the populist movement, which frightened elites and culminated in William Jennings Bryan's nomination for the presidency in 1896.

A PANIC-PRONE BANKING SYSTEM

Although the depressions of the late nineteenth century were global, the
particular form they took in the United States was influenced by America's peculiar banking system. Definitions of panics vary, but according
to one account there were nationwide bank panics in the United States
in 1819, 1837, 1839, 1857, 1861, 1873, 1884, 1890, 1893, 1896, and 1907, in
addition to three waves of bank failures between 1931 and 1933.[28] The
United States continued to suffer from banking panics at a time when the
problem was disappearing from other, similar countries. The explanation
is found in America's uniquely fragmented and brittle banking structure.

Banking panics have been relatively rare in countries whose banking systems are based on a small number of banks with many branches.
Unique among modern countries, the United States had thousands of
tiny banks, many of them "unit banks" with only a single office. These
unit banks served the interests of the local elites who owned them and
could loan themselves and their allies the money of their neighbors. The
Jeffersonian and Jacksonian defenders of small country banks protected
them from competition by big city banks by state laws and federal laws
not only limiting interstate branch banking but also, in some states, banning branch banking within the state. In states that allowed branching,
banks with branches were far less likely to fail than unit banks.[29]

National branch banking in nations like Canada and Australia that
permitted it, reduced the fragility of local banks by reducing their depen-

dence on fluctuations in the local or regional economy. While the United States had more than eight thousand independent banks in 1890, Canada at the same period had only about forty.[30] In Canada a few individual banks failed, but thanks to branching there were no national banking panics after the 1830s.[31] In Canada following World War I, there was only one major bank failure, in the 1920s, and no banks failed at all during the Great Depression. In Australia, where national branch banking was legal, there was only one national panic, in 1893, to interrupt a record otherwise free of them.[32] In contrast, bank failures were common in the United States in the 1920s and in the Depression the entire system collapsed.

America's fragmented system of tiny unit banks imposed other costs on the economy. Their greater riskiness meant that America's small unit banks had higher reserve ratios and lower loan ratios than Canada's larger, more stable branch banks.[33] Another cost of American unit banking was variations in interest rates among urban and rural banks and regions like the East, West, and South.

The decentralized, fragmented nature of the US banking system, characterized by thousands of small banks, meant that functions performed in more centralized banking systems had to be carried out by arm's-length transactions among separate institutions. One institution was the private clearinghouse system, which allowed banks to repay other banks with clearinghouse certificates based on bank assets. This freed up cash that the bank could pay out to depositors in panics like those of 1873, 1893, and 1907. In addition to private clearinghouse systems, there were private banks that acted as lenders of last resort, like the Suffolk Bank of Massachusetts, which played this role in New England during the Panic of 1837.

America's peculiar system of decentralized one-office banks also produced the "pyramid reserve" system, with small banks keeping some of their money with big urban money-center banks. The money-center banks then made call loans to stock-market investors. This invited trouble, because when distressed country banks recalled their reserves, the money-center banks would demand repayment of their call loans from investors, which might trigger a stock-market panic.

HUDDLED MASSES

In 1867–1868, the United States surpassed Britain in gross domestic product (GDP), becoming the world's largest economy.[34] The growth of the size of the American economy was driven by a combination of productivity growth with a rapid increase in population, driven by mass immigration from Europe between the 1840s and World War I.

The US population increased from forty million in 1870 to seventy-six million in 1900. Two-thirds of the growth was the result of natural increase, one-third the result of immigration.

Of the seventy-six million Americans in 1900, a third were either foreign born or the children of foreign-born parents. In 1910, the foreign-born and their first-generation children accounted for more than 70 percent of the population in New York, Chicago, Boston, Milwaukee, and Detroit.[35]

The Statue of Liberty was unveiled at a ceremony attended by President Grover Cleveland on October 28, 1886. The *New York Herald* described the scene: "Amid the uproar and excitement that succeeded the consecration of the statue, there glided through the Narrows a huge steamship crowded with European immigrants. From her decks the eyes of the strangers were fixed upon the wonderful drama in progress before them. The cannon smoke and vapor rolled up, and ringed in a huge, fire-fringed semicircle, they saw before them the mighty figure of Liberty. Imagination can only conceive of what to their tired eyes, weary with the hardships, the hopelessness and the cruelties of the Old World, this apparition must have conveyed."[36]

Although the purpose of the Statue of Liberty was to commemorate the French-American alliance during the American Revolution, it became an inspiring symbol to the millions of immigrants who passed it before arriving to be processed for entry to the United States at Ellis Island. The link between the statue and immigration was reinforced by "The New Colossus," the 1883 poem by Emma Lazarus engraved into the base:

Not like the brazen giant of Greek fame,
With conquering limbs astride from land to land;
Here at our sea-washed, sunset gates shall stand
A mighty woman with a torch, whose flame
Is the imprisoned lightning, and her name
Mother of Exiles. From her beacon-hand
Glows world-wide welcome; her mild eyes command
The air-bridged harbor that twin cities frame.
"Keep, ancient lands, your storied pomp!" cries she
With silent lips. "Give me your tired, your poor,
Your huddled masses yearning to breathe free,
The wretched refuse of your teeming shore.
Send these, the homeless, tempest-tost to me,
I lift my lamp beside the golden door!"

Immigrants sometimes mistook the torch held aloft by the goddess of Liberty for something else. One Hungarian thought that Lady Liberty was holding a broom. In his novel *Amerika* (1927), Franz Kafka, with appropriate surrealism, describes the Statue of Liberty's "arm with the sword."[37]

The difficulties of immigrants with English sometimes produced comic results. When an Ellis Island official, reading off a checklist, asked a woman if she approved of the overthrow of the United States government by subversion or violence, she hoped to give the right answer by replying, "Violence."[38]

In 1914, before World War I interfered with immigration, 878,052 of 1,218,480 immigrants to the United States entered through Ellis Island.[39] One of the new immigrants was Rocco Corresca, an orphan from Italy who ran a shoe-shine business in turn-of-the-century New York. "I and Francesco are to be Americans in three years," he told an interviewer. "The court gave us papers and said we must wait and we must be able to read some things and tell who the ruler of the country is."[40]

"Ach, it is just like what I see when I dream of heaven," a German girl said after she and a friend on a visit to a Coney Island amusement park had enjoyed the loop-the-loop, the razzle-dazzle, and the chute.[41] Other immigrants found pain and abuse in their new home, like the Greek pushcart peddler who reported: "I could not speak English and I did not know enough to pay the police. . . . Once a policeman struck me on the leg with his club so hard that I could not work for two weeks. That is wrong to strike like that a man who could not speak English."[42]

A Swede named Axel Jarlson followed his brother to America, after his uncle Olaf, a sailor, explained: "In America they give you good land for nothing, and in two years you could be a rich man; and no one had to go in the army unless he wanted to."[43] Jarlson, who settled a farm in Minnesota, told a journalist: "One thing I like about this country is that you do not have to be always taking off your hat to people. . . . Here any man of good character can have a vote after he has been a short time in the country, and people can elect him to any office. There are no aristocrats to push him down and say that he is not worthy because his father was poor."[44]

LABOR'S CAMPAIGN FOR
IMMIGRATION RESTRICTION

Most immigrants improved their lives by moving to the United States, in some cases dramatically. But their presence in the labor market drove down wages and permitted American employers to engage in divide-and-rule tactics. According to one estimate, in the absence of the immigration that took place after 1870, the US population in 1890 would have been 27 percent smaller in 1910 and the real wage would have been 9 percent higher.[45]

The 1911 US Immigration Commission concluded that "in many cases the conscious policy of the employers [is] mixing the races in certain departments and divisions . . . preventing concert of action on the part of the employees."[46] A manager of one of Carnegie's factories in Pittsburgh explained in 1875: "My experience has shown that Germans and Irish, Swedes, and what I denominate Buckwheats (young American country boys), judiciously mixed, make the most effective and tractable force you can find."[47]

In order to raise wages and bargaining power for workers, the labor movement campaigned for immigration restriction. Frequently it used racist arguments. In 1905, Samuel Gompers of the American Federation of Labor wrote that the "Caucasians are not going to let their standard of living be destroyed by Negroes, Chinamen, Japs, or any others."[48] Gompers coauthored a pamphlet in 1906 entitled *Meat vs. Rice: American Manhood Against Asiatic Coolieism. Which Shall Survive?*[49]

Between the 1880s and the early twentieth century, labor activists succeeded with a mixture of economic argumentation and racist rhetoric in prevailing on Congress to bring most immigration from Asia to a halt. The campaign by labor and old-stock nativists to restrict European immigration would not succeed until the 1920s, following the revival of immigration from Europe after World War I.

FROM THE KNIGHTS OF LABOR TO THE AFL

The American labor movement's campaigns to restrict immigration were among its few successes. In the decades after the Civil War, the battles fought by organized labor, many of them violent, usually ended in defeat. In the late 1870s and early 1880s, the United States had five times as many unionized workers as Germany, at a time when the two nations had similar populations.[50] There were more strikes in 1890—around twelve hundred—than in any other year in American history.

The National Labor Union, formed in 1866, became a third party and collapsed by 1872, bequeathing to posterity its campaign for the eight-hour day. Beginning in 1870 with nine members, the Knights of Labor had grown into a mass organization that numbered 728,000 by 1884 and admitted unskilled workers, blacks, and women. But it never recovered from the Haymarket riot.

In May 1886, during a strike against the McCormick Harvesting Company in Chicago, a police officer killed a striking worker. Anarchists called for a rally in Chicago's Haymarket Square. When police moved to disperse the rally, a bomb went off, killing seven police officers. Police fired into the crowd, killing four civilians. In trials that have been criticized as abuses of justice, seven anarchists were convicted. Four were hanged, three were pardoned by Illinois governor John Peter Altgeld, and one committed suicide. Although Terence Powderly, the head of the Knights of Labor, denounced the anarchist movement, the Knights were tainted by association in the public mind and the number of its members shrank to ninety-five thousand in 1892 and none in 1901.[51] In return for his support of the Republican Party in 1896, Powderly was appointed by President McKinley to be the second commissioner general of immigration. Serving from 1897 to 1902, Powderly used his prominence to campaign for protecting white American labor from Asian immigration.

The American Federation of Labor, led by British-born Samuel Gompers, who began as a worker in the cigar-making industry, presented itself as a moderate alternative to anticapitalist extremism. The AFL sought to organize only members of particular crafts, not all workers. Following its founding in 1886, the AFL grew to around 250,000 by 1892. Of these, 24,000 members belonged to its Amalgamated Association of Iron and Steel Workers. Gompers believed that the union movement should concentrate on obtaining higher wages for its members, not on broad political or social reform. Asked by a member of Congress what labor wanted, Gompers said: "More!"

Business and government were horrified by would-be industrial unions associated with radical politics, like the Industrial Workers of the World, the "Wobblies," particularly during the Red Scare in the United States that followed the communist takeover in Russia in October 1917. But the more conservative craft unions of Gompers's AFL were rejected by most American employers as well.

CLASS WARFARE

Labor violence was particularly intense in the railroad industry and in the new mass-production industries of the Steam Age.

In 1892, with the backing of Carnegie, who was vacationing in Britain, Henry Clay Frick locked out striking workers at the Homestead plant near Pittsburgh and fortified the steelworks, creating what some called "Fort Frick." When Frick brought in armed Pinkerton detectives to guard the steel mill, nine strikers and seven guards were killed in a twelve-hour battle. To escort replacement workers or "scabs" into the mills, the governor of Pennsylvania sent the state national guard. The strike collapsed, and the workers who were not purged worked for less pay, twelve hours a day, seven days a week. Carnegie's reputation was permanently stained by the incident. Frick, who was shot and wounded by an anarchist but recovered, eventually became his bitter enemy, passing along a message in his old age to his former partner Carnegie: "I'll see you in hell."[52]

In May 1894, thousands of workers for the Pullman Palace Car Company went on strike to protest wage cuts that followed the Panic of 1893. Led by Eugene V. Debs, the American Railway Union called on workers to refuse to work with trains that used Pullman cars. The attorney general of the United States, Richard Olney, who also happened to be general counsel for the Chicago, Milwaukee and St. Paul Railway, obtained an injunction against the strikers from a federal court, and President Cleveland ordered the US Army and US marshals to end the strike. By the time the conflict ended, thirteen strikers were dead and widespread damage to property had occurred. Radicalized by his arrest and imprisonment, Debs went on to run for president five times as the leader of the Socialist Party of America.[53]

Following the Civil War, there was a class war and the capitalists won. They won with the help of not only the national guard and the Pinkerton detective agency but also of the federal judiciary, which allowed the Sherman Act to be used to prosecute labor unions.[54] When Progressives in Congress enacted the Clayton Act of 1914 to exempt unions from antitrust laws as long as they engaged in nonviolent activity, federal judges interpreted the Clayton Act to permit even more injunctions to be used against labor unions than before.[55] By 1900, organized labor in any form was marginalized.

AMERICA'S INTERNAL EMPIRE:
THE SOUTH AND WEST

Other than replacing Britain as the informal hegemon of Central America and the Caribbean and acquiring some Pacific island bases that could serve as coaling stations for the US Navy and American trading vessels, the United States engaged in less imperialism than the other major powers. It did not need to. America had an internal empire. The people of the South, white and black alike, provided a captive consumer market for the manufactured goods of the factories in the Northeast and Midwest, and the mines of Appalachia and the sparsely settled West and later the oil fields of Texas and Oklahoma supplied the industry of the American industrial core region with cheap and abundant ore, coal, and oil. The integrated northeastern-midwestern industrial complex was a nation within a nation, the equivalent of Britain or Germany or France. The South and West were America's India and Africa and Central Asia.[56]

In the 1870s, the North abandoned its effort to restructure southern society. Federal troops were pulled out of the South following the Compromise of 1877. The desire of the northeastern bankers, the prewar allies of the South, for a rapid resumption of exports of cotton picked by a subservient labor force was fulfilled. The interests of most white and black southerners alike were sacrificed to a bargain between northern and southern elites, which granted the southern elite freedom to deal with its regional labor force as it pleased, in return for the South's position as an internal resource colony and market for northern industry.

The South's share of US wealth shrank from 30 percent to 12 percent between 1860 and 1870.[57] By 1880, the gap in per capita wealth between the North and South was comparable to that between Germany and Russia.[58] Many of the profits from southern agriculture, timber, and mining flowed out of the region to investors in the North and Britain. Southerners subsidized northerners by consumption of northern-made goods protected by high tariffs and by their taxes, which paid for pensions for Union war veterans from which Confederate veterans were excluded.

"I attended a funeral once in Pickens county in my State," wrote Henry Grady, a prominent Southern newspaper editor. "This funeral was peculiarly sad. It was a poor 'one gallus' fellow, whose breeches struck him under the armpits and hit him at the other end about the knee— he didn't believe in decollete clothes. They buried him in the midst of a marble quarry: they cut through solid marble to make his grave; and yet a little tombstone they put above him was from Vermont. They buried him in the heart of a pine forest, and yet the pine coffin was imported from Cincinnati. They buried him within touch of an iron mine, and yet the nails in his coffin and the iron in the shovel that dug his grave were imported from Pittsburg. They buried him by the side of the best sheep-grazing country on the earth, and yet the wool in the coffin bands and the coffin bands themselves were brought from the North. The South didn't furnish a thing on earth for that funeral but the corpse and the hole in the ground. There they put him away and the clods rattled down on his coffin, and they buried him in a New York coat and a Boston pair of shoes and a pair of breeches from Chicago and a shirt from Cincinnati, leaving him nothing to carry into the next world with him to remind him of the country in which he lived, and for which he fought for four years, but the chill of blood in his veins and the marrow in his bones."[59]

NEW FORMS OF SLAVERY

Immediately after the Civil War, southern states passed laws and constitutional amendments called "black codes," designed to re-create the equivalent of slavery. The black codes were abolished by the federal government during Reconstruction, but after federal occupation of the former slave states ended in 1877, the white southern elite used law and violence to reduce the freedmen to the status of a subjugated, disfranchised labor force. New forms of serfdom in the South were devised for black agricultural workers. In 1910, 93 percent of black Americans were living in the South; 60 percent of adult black men worked in farming.[60] Sharecropping and the crop-lien system forced poor whites and blacks alike into debt peonage. Another method of debt peonage took the form of the purchase by local oligarchs of the coerced labor of black men and women, by the method of paying their court fines for real crimes and trumped-up offenses alike.

In an exposé published in the North in 1904, an unidentified "Negro peon" told how he was tricked into debt peonage for a cotton planter known only as the Senator: "The next morning it was explained to us by the two guards appointed to watch us that, in the papers, we had signed the day before, we had not only made acknowledgment of our indebtedness, but that we had also agreed to work for the Senator until the debts were paid by hard labor."[61] The man ended up spending three years in the Senator's peon camp.[62]

The convict-lease system was another method by which the defiant South re-created slavery in all but name. Southern state governments and county sheriffs made profits by arresting blacks, often for minor offenses, and then leasing their labor to big farmers, capitalists, and corporations.[63] After Alabama established its convict-lease system in 1875, 20 percent died in the first year, 35 percent in the second, and 45 percent in the fourth.[64] Southern blacks were prevented from migrating to the North. Southern sheriffs harassed agents of northern companies who tried to recruit black workers, while the white working class in the North carried out violent pogroms against black migrants whom they viewed as competitors for jobs and neighborhoods. The Great Migration of blacks out of the South took place only after World War I, and subsequent immigration laws cut off the supply of European immigrant workers in the North. The federal government's indifference to de facto slavery in the South changed only when American racism became an embarrassment during America's crusades against the racist slave empires of Germany and Japan and America's Cold War competition with the Soveit Union to appeal to nonwhite populations in former European colonies.

THE WEST

In addition to the farms and timber plantations of the South, industrial America's internal resource colonies also included the mines of the mountain West and the ranches and farms of the prairie and the Great Plains.

The age of the great cattle drives following the Civil War was brief, although it lives on in Hollywood mythology. The heyday of the long-distance cattle drives to the markets of the Midwest and North came after the Civil War, from the 1860s to the 1880s, before railroads and refrigerator cars made them anachronistic.

Enormous amounts of range land had been opened up for grazing after the US Army had forced the remaining Plains Indians onto reservations. The cattle business in the Great Plains was dominated by large cattle companies owned by eastern and foreign investors, such as the London-chartered Spur Land and Cattle Company and the Scotland-based Matador Land and Cattle Company. The XIT Ranch in the Texas Panhandle was the largest fenced range in the world, at one point covering parts of ten counties in Texas. It originated when the Texas legislature conveyed three million acres of state-owned land in return for the construction of a new capitol building in Austin to Charles and John Farwell, two brothers who had made a fortune in the dry-goods business in Chicago. The Farwells created a London-based corporation, the Capitol Freehold Land and Investment Company, which sold bonds to British and American investors.

After harsh winters between 1884 and 1887 decimated many herds, a number of the cattle companies sold their land to small farmers. Conflict with ranchers who considered the grassland to be a common resource often broke out when the farmers fenced off sections with barbed wire, invented in 1874 by J. F. Glidden of Illinois. Aided by another new technology, the water-pumping metal windmill, farm families sometimes lived for a time in sod houses before putting up frame houses protected from the prairie winds by windbreaks of clustered trees and shrubs.

Putting up windbreaks was one method of obtaining land, under federal law. The original Homestead Act was followed by the Timber Culture Act of 1873, which granted 160 acres to settlers who planted 40 acres of trees. Because this proved to be unrealistic in the prairie and plains environments, in 1878, the law was amended to provide 10 acres in return for the construction of shelterbelts or windbreaks. The Desert Land Act of 1877 provided 640 acres to settlers who irrigated desert land; this challenge had few takers. Under the 1878 Timber and Stone Act, settlers were permitted to buy federal land unsuitable for farming at a discount if they cut timber or quarried stone on it.[65]

In 1890, the Census Bureau reported the closing of the western frontier. The symbolic closing of the frontier took place a few years later, on September 16, 1893, in Oklahoma. At the signal of a cannon's boom, a hundred thousand Americans, during one of the nation's worst depressions, raced each other on foot, horseback, or bicycles to claim parcels of land in the Cherokee Strip. Many of the "boomers" who had patiently waited for the boom of the cannon discovered that they had been preceded by "sooners" who gave Oklahoma its nickname, the Sooner State.

In the same year, 1893, at the World's Columbian Exposition in Chicago, the historian Frederick Jackson Turner delivered an influential paper to the American Historical Association entitled "The Significance of the Frontier in American History." Turner argued that the frontier had shaped American democracy and speculated about how American society would be affected by its disappearance in the essay and, no doubt, in the classes he taught at Columbia University, where one of his students was a young man named Franklin Delano Roosevelt.

DEFEAT OF THE WHEAT

The very success of railroads in creating national and international markets created economic problems for farmers on both sides of the Atlantic. As American grain and meat transported overland by rail and overseas by steamships poured into the markets of Britain and continental Europe, prices fell in both Central and Eastern Europe and the American Midwest. According to one British observer, the "revolution in the food supply of European countries" was caused by "the American railroad."[66] In Europe the prolonged distress of the agricultural sector led to mass immigration to the United States and other lands of European settlement. Peasant parties anticipated the fascist movements of the twentieth century by blaming economic problems on conspiracies by Jews and foreigners.

Similar distress afflicted many of America's farmers. As a result of the deflation produced by America's resumption of the gold standard, many farmers were affected by falling prices for wheat, cotton, and other commodities and rising payments for farm mortgages. They were also frustrated by railroad rates.

The Grange, an agrarian reform movement, set the stage for the People's Party, formed in 1887. The Populists' Omaha Platform in 1892 included a number of reforms that would later be realized, including direct election of senators, a progressive income tax, civil service reform, and an eight-hour day, and some that would not be, including the nationalization of railroads, telegraphs, and telephones. The Populist manifesto of 1892 painted a frightening picture: "The urban workmen are denied the right to organize for self-protection, imported pauperized labor beats down their wages, a hireling standing army, unrecognized by our laws, is established to shoot them down, and they are rapidly degenerating into European conditions. The fruits of the toil of millions are boldly stolen to build up colossal fortunes for a few, unprecedented in the history of mankind."[67]

Populists were instructed in the mysteries of finance by William H. "Coin" Harvey's bestselling book *Coin's Financial School* (1894), in which a fictional teenage boy in Chicago bests financiers in debate. The Populist movement included colorful characters like Mary Ellen Lease, known as "Mary Yellin" to her detractors, who moved on from populism to white supremacy, and Ignatius Donnelly, member of Congress, self-proclaimed expert on the lost continent of Atlantis, and author of *Caesar's Column*, a novel about the overthrow of American democracy by plutocracy.

The Populists were not the only group to enlist fiction in their cause. With his bestselling book *Progress and Poverty* (1879), Henry George founded an international movement to tax the "unearned increment" derived from the appreciation in land prices.

Edward Bellamy presented a socialist utopia in his bestselling novel *Looking Backward, 2000–1887* (1887). There were political novels defending contemporary American capitalism, as well. Using a pseudonym, John Hay, Lincoln's secretary and later secretary of state under McKinley and Theodore Roosevelt, published an antilabor novel, *The Breadwinners*, in 1884. Hay portrayed unions as criminal conspiracies against the public.

THE GREAT COMMONER

During the Depression of the 1890s, the hard-money policy and repression of railroad strikers carried out by Democratic president Grover Cleveland, a New Yorker, alienated many Democrats in the South and West, which remained the regional bases of the party. At the 1896 Democratic Convention in Chicago, populists captured the party. On the third day of the convention, William Jennings Bryan, their charismatic hero, declaring, "You shall not crucify mankind upon a cross of gold," mimed placing a crown of thorns on his head and stretched out his arms like the crucified Jesus Christ. According to the correspondent for the *Atlanta Constitution*, "Westerners shouted, waved handkerchiefs, hats, flags, canes, umbrellas and anything else conspicuous and portable. . . . Hundreds of umbrellas were opened by the apparently crazed people. Harmless missiles of paper and other things were hurled through the air on the delegates' heads."[68]

Appalled, like other northeastern patricians, Henry Adams wrote that "a capitalistic system had been adopted, and if it were to be run at all, it must be run by capital and by capitalistic methods; for nothing could surpass the nonsensity of trying to run so complex and concentrated a machine by Southern and Western farmers in grotesque alliance with city day-laborers."[69] To ensure a Republican victory, personal and corporate wealth were mobilized for a political campaign on a scale never before seen in the United States. Despite their efforts to reach out to northern industrial workers, the Democrats failed to expand beyond their southern and western agrarian base. In 1896, McKinley, campaigning on the slogan, "the full dinner pail," won an electoral college majority of 271 votes to Bryan's 176; in the popular vote, McKinley's 7,102,246 defeated Bryan's 6,502,925. A rematch between McKinley and Bryan in 1900 produced even larger margins for McKinley: 292 to 155 in the electoral college and 7,219,530 votes to 6,358,071.

The poet Vachel Lindsay recorded the agony that he shared with many others:

Election night at midnight:
Boy Bryan's defeat.
Defeat of the western silver.
Defeat of the wheat.
Victory of the Letterfiles
And plutocrats in miles
With dollar signs upon their coats,
Diamond watchchains on their vests
And spats on their feet.
Victory of the custodians,
Plymouth Rock,
And all that in-bred landlord stock.
Victory of the neat.
Defeat of the aspen groves of Colorado Valleys,
The blue bells of the Rockies,
And blue bonnets of old Texas,
By the Pittsburgh alleys.
Defeat of alfalfa and the Mariposa lily.
Defeat of the Pacific and the long Mississippi.
Defeat of the young by the old and silly.
Defeat of tornadoes by the poison vats supreme.
Defeat of my boyhood, defeat of my dream.[70]

Subsequent generations have debated whether Bryan was a precursor of twentieth-century liberalism or a provincial reactionary. The same Bryan who supported federal regulation of railroads and industry and the rights of organized labor later, in the final act of his life, prosecuted a Tennessee teacher for teaching Darwinism in the 1925 Scopes "Monkey Trial."

In 1896, Bryan was opposed by progressives including Robert La Follette, Louis Brandeis, and Woodrow Wilson. On becoming president, Wilson reached out to the populist wing of the party by making Bryan secretary of state, but complained to a friend that "the man has no brains. It is a great pity that a man with his power of leadership should have no mental rudder."[71] The socialist radical Jack London said he would vote for McKinley to stop Bryan.[72] Theodore Roosevelt, who became McKinley's second vice president in 1900 and his successor when McKinley was assassinated in 1901, warned that "if Bryan wins, we have before us some years of social misery, not markedly different from that of any South American republic."[73]

If anachronistic labels like "liberal" and "conservative" are dispensed with, in favor of the concepts of Hamiltonian developmentalism and Jeffersonian producerism, then Bryan's place in the American tradition is easily identified. Bryan declared: "What we need is an Andrew Jackson to stand as Jackson stood, against the encroachments of aggregated wealth."[74] Bryan was the last American presidential candidate to be an agrarian: "You come to us and tell us that the great cities are in favor of the gold standard. I tell you that the great cities rest upon these broad and fertile prairies. Burn down your cities and leave our farms and your cities will spring up again as if by magic. But destroy our farms and the grass will grow on the streets of any city in this country."[75]

Bryan led the Jeffersonian backlash against American developmental capitalism in the era of the first industrial revolution and the railroads. He followed Andrew Jackson, who led the Jeffersonian backlash against the American developmental state in the preceding era of canals and water mills. And Bryan preceded Barry Goldwater and Ronald Reagan, who led a later Jeffersonian backlash against the version of the American developmental state identified with Franklin Roosevelt's New Deal and Dwight Eisenhower's Modern Republicanism in the second industrial economy, based on electrification and the automobile.

Bryan's opponent William McKinley was the most important leader of the Hamiltonian tradition between Abraham Lincoln and Theodore Roosevelt. Having started out as an old-fashioned protectionist, McKinley had come to see that the success of America's protectionist import-substitution policies meant that major industries would benefit more from access to foreign markets than from continued protection. In the speech he delivered on the day he was fatally shot by an anarchist named Leon Czolgosz, McKinley emphasized the need for the United States to pursue reciprocal trade liberalization with trading partners.

Bryan shared the antiblack attitudes of most of his southern and western supporters and refused to criticize the Ku Klux Klan, for fear of creating divisions in the Democratic Party's base. In contrast, the Civil War veteran McKinley was fond of telling a story about a black flag bearer in Louisiana who died in battle during the Civil War: "Tell me that men made of that metal shall be deprived of their constitutional right! The fight will go on until every citizen will enjoy every right guaranteed by the constitution of the United States."[76] As governor of Ohio, McKinley used the national guard to protect black prisoners against lynch mobs. During a tour of the South in 1898, McKinley visited Booker T. Washington's Tuskegee Institute in Alabama and the black Georgia Agricultural and Mechanical College at Savannah.[77] His successor, Theodore Roosevelt, enraged white southerners by inviting Washington to dine at the White House.

Nor was McKinley the pawn of banking and business that generations of populists and progressives have caricatured. The heir to several generations of Scots-Irish manufacturers in the Midwest, McKinley, like many manufacturers, preferred bimetallism—in effect mild inflationism—to the deflationary gold standard preferred by creditors in the financial community. (In the slang of the time, this made him a "straddle bug" instead of a "gold bug.")

The quiet McKinley has been overshadowed by his rambunctious successor Roosevelt. But he was the major transitional figure between the old Hamiltonianism of Hamilton, Clay, and Lincoln, and the new Hamiltonianism of progressives like Theodore and Franklin Roosevelt.

THE MYTH OF THE ROBBER BARONS

The Steam Age was the first stage in the transformation from the agrarian to the industrial economy. In the preindustrial biomass economy, the wealth accumulated by merchants like Stephen Girard and John Jacob Astor came at the expense of exploited labor (Indian fur trappers, fur traders, and slaves on plantations) or the ecosystem (the beaver population that Astor decimated). The mines that produced oil for Rockefeller and ore for Carnegie might have scarred local areas, but they did not produce deforestation and mass extinctions. Standard Oil's kerosene helped to save the whales from extinction.

Americans have tended to judge industrial tycoons more harshly than landed plutocrats. The slaveholders of the Virginia dynasty like Washington and Jefferson, Madison and Monroe, are treated as noble statesmen, while the industrialists like Rockefeller and Carnegie and the politicians whom they supported and sometimes bribed are treated as villains. But even at their strike-breaking, influence-peddling, wealth-displaying worst, the northern railroad and industrial tycoons who dominated American politics and the economy in the second half of the nineteenth century represented a great improvement over the southern slaveowners who dominated the country in the first half of the century and then tried to destroy it. The northern industrialists may have repressed their workers, but at least they did not own them.

A plausible and dispassionate assessment of the period was provided by Franklin Delano Roosevelt in an address, drafted by Adolf Berle, that he delivered during his 1932 presidential campaign at the Commonwealth Club in San Francisco: "The history of the last half century is accordingly in large measure a history of a group of financial Titans, whose methods were not scrutinized with too much care, and who were honored in proportion as they produced the results, irrespective of the means they used. The financiers who pushed the railroads to the Pacific were always ruthless, we have them today. It has been estimated that the American investor paid for the American railway system more than three times over in the process; but despite that fact the net advantage was to the United States. As long as we had free land; as long as population was growing by leaps and bounds; as long as our industrial plants were insufficient to supply our needs, society chose to give the ambitious man free play and unlimited reward provided only that he produced the economic plant so much desired."[78]

THE MOTOR AGE

———————◆———————

THE ARGUMENT

The second industrial revolution of the mid- to late nineteenth century produced a dazzling variety of transformative technologies, of which the most important were the electric motor and the internal combustion engine. The Motor Age saw the rise of giant corporations and powerful investment banks. In response to the second industrial economy, some Americans sought to tame and use the new concentrations of industrial might and financial power, while others feared them and wanted to break them up. America's political institutions and policies grew increasingly misaligned.

Polity and economy were finally realigned during the cataclysm of the Great Depression and World War II by the New Deal. By the 1970s, however, the American economy faced growing foreign competition, slowing growth, and high inflation. The crises of the 1970s and 1980s inspired a Jeffersonian backlash against the Hamiltonian institutions of the New Deal: the Great Dismantling.

FRANKLIN'S BABY: ELECTRICITY, AUTOMOBILES, AND THE SECOND INDUSTRIAL REVOLUTION

The greatest invention of the nineteenth century was the invention of the method of invention.

—Alfred North Whitehead[1]

On a humid afternoon in Philadelphia in September 1752, Benjamin Franklin and his adult son William flew a kite made of silk, with a foot-long piece of wire sticking out of the frame. At the base was a string of hemp, a conductor, and a nonconducting ribbon of silk, with a metal key at their intersection. As rain fell, the Franklins took shelter in a barn. What happened next was described by British correspondent and colleague Joseph Priestley in 1767: "When, at length, just as he was beginning to despair of his contrivance, he observed some loose threads of the hempen string to stand erect, and to avoid one another . . . he immediately presented his knuckle to the key, and (let the reader judge of the exquisite pleasure he must have felt at that moment) the discovery was complete. He perceived a very evident electric spark."[2]

If lightning had actually struck the kite, Franklin might have been killed. As it was, he had been knocked out during an earlier attempt to electrocute a turkey.[3] In 1753, a Swedish scientist in Saint Petersburg,

Russia, was killed by lightning when he repeated Franklin's experiment.

Franklin built on the work of many predecessors. Otto van Guericke in 1670 devised a mechanism capable of producing an electric charge, and a generation later Charles-François de Cisternay du Fay demonstrated the difference between negative and positive charges. In 1745, the Leyden jar, an early version of the condenser, was invented.

More breakthroughs followed Franklin's successful experiment, thanks to Priestley, who in 1766 showed that the force between charges varies inversely with their distance, and Charles-Augustin de Coulomb, who in 1777 invented a device to measure electric charges. After Hans Christian Oersted proved in 1819 that electrical currents generate magnetic fields, Michael Faraday demonstrated that an electric current in one wire could induce a current in another. James Clerk Maxwell, building on Faraday's work, set out the formal mathematics of electromagnetism in 1873 in his *Treatise on Electricity and Magnetism.*

Technology built on science. Already in 1800, Alessandro Volta had invented the first battery. Then in the 1840s, James Prescott Joule showed that a magneto could convert mechanical energy into electrical energy. In 1867, dynamos that used magnets to turn rotary motion into electrical power were invented in parallel by Werner Siemens in Germany and Charles Wheatstone in Britain.[4] As early as the 1870s, Siemens adapted electromagnetic dynamos to create electric arc furnaces for smelting metals.

The American historian Henry Adams, writing about himself in the third person, described his response to the dynamo he encountered at the Paris Exposition of 1900: "As he grew accustomed to the great gallery of machines, he began to feel the forty-foot dynamos as a moral force, much as the early Christians felt the Cross. The planet itself seemed less impressive, in its old-fashioned, deliberate, annual or daily revolution, than this huge wheel, revolving within arm's-length at some vertiginous speed, and barely murmuring,—scarcely humming an audible warning to stand a hair's-breadth further for respect of power,—while it would not wake the baby lying close against its frame. Before the end, one began to pray to it; inherited instinct taught the natural expression of man before silent and infinite force. Among the thousand symbols of ultimate energy the dynamo was not so human as some, but it was the most expressive."[5]

Adams thought that the dynamo "would not wake the baby lying close against its frame." Earlier a baby had been used as a metaphor for electrical technology itself.

Franklin may or may not have asked, in connection with electricity, "What is the use of a newborn baby?" (Some accounts have him asking the same question after witnessing a balloon ascension in France.)[6] And the great British scientist Michael Faraday may or may not have quoted Franklin in the context of electricity, although he certainly did so in the context of the discovery of new elements in an 1816 lecture: "Before leaving this substance, chlorine, I will point out its history as an answer to those who are in the habit of saying to every new fact, 'What is its use?' Dr. Franklin says to such, 'What is the use of an infant?'"[7]

FROM LONE INVENTOR TO CORPORATE LABORATORY

With each succeeding wave of technological innovation, the individual inventor has become less important than teams of scientists and engineers, informed by the latest scientific advances and working in laboratories supported by financiers, corporations, and, increasingly, by governments, the only entities capable of funding basic research on a massive scale. The first industrial revolution had largely been the result of individual inventors like James Watt and Robert Fulton, relying on trial and error. In the words of the historian Joel Mokyr, "It created a chemical industry with no chemistry, an iron industry without metallurgy, power machinery without thermodynamics."[8] Increasingly, invention depended on science. The European inventors, including Gottlieb Daimler and Karl Benz, who invented the automobile with a gas-fueled internal combustion engine, enjoyed the benefits of state-sponsored science in Germany, the country which, along with France, initially led automobile development before Americans like Henry Ford naturalized the technology and exploited the economies of scale provided by America's enormous market.

The industrialization of research and development (R&D) and invention became a defining feature of twentieth-century industrial capitalism. In 1901, General Electric established the first corporate research laboratory in the United States. Other corporations that established their own research facilities included DuPont (1902) and Eastman Kodak (1913). The most famous was Bell Labs, established by the American Telephone and Telegraph Company (AT&T) in 1925. Between 1920 and the 1980s, the number of employees of corporate research labs rose from six thousand to nearly a million.[9]

Even more important in the long run was the contribution of the federal government to innovation. Beginning with the Morrill land-grant college acts in the late nineteenth century, the federal government created a sophisticated technological innovation system in agriculture, in which federally funded regional and state laboratories worked on problems and disseminated solutions by way of county extension services to American farmers. Attempts to construct an equivalent system for American manufacturing repeatedly failed. But a large-scale federal role in research and invention became permanent during the third industrial revolution during and after World War II, with the establishment of the National Science Foundation and the National Institutes of Health and military-related contracts to industrial firms and academic researchers who developed the first few generations of computers and created the Internet.

THOMAS EDISON AND THE RISE OF R&D

Thomas Edison provides an example. Dirty, disheveled, and dressed in workman's clothes in many of the photographs he posed for, Edison played the archetype of the folksy American genius as successfully as Franklin had played the role of backwoods sage in a coonskin cap. When Nikola Tesla, a brilliant Serbian engineer who had worked in Paris, successfully applied for a job with Edison in the United States, the dapper European recalled: "I was thrilled to the marrow by meeting Edison, who began my American education right then and there. I wanted to have my shoes shined, something I considered beneath my dignity. Edison said, 'You will shine the shoes yourself and like it.' He impressed me tremendously. I shined the shoes myself and liked it."[10]

In reality, Edison was less an individual than the director and public face of an institution. Born in Ohio, Edison was raised in Michigan, where he struggled to make money in his teen years by selling newspapers and candy on trains. When he saved a three-year-old boy from being hit by a train, the boy's grateful father, a station agent, taught Edison to be a telegraph operator. Telegraph technology inspired Edison's early inventions, including a stock ticker and a vote counter.

While Edison was a brilliant inventor himself, most of the products for which he is given credit, from the incandescent lightbulb to the phonograph and motion picture technology, were the work of the engineers he organized into teams in a succession of laboratories. No lone genius, he was the director of his own research lab and was funded throughout his career by corporations like Western Union and by financiers like Jay Cooke and J. P. Morgan.

He established a small workshop in Newark and then, in 1876, he created a large laboratory in Menlo Park, New Jersey. Menlo Park consisted of a six-building complex on thirty-four acres that Edison had purchased in 1875, because of its combination of rural quiet and proximity to New York investors. His team at Menlo Park patented around four hundred inventions, including the lightbulb and the phonograph, before moving in 1882 to a larger laboratory in West Orange, New Jersey.

Called the "Wizard of Menlo Park" by a journalist, Edison drew on the talents of a research team with members from many countries, including his English chief mechanic, Charles Batchelor, his German glassblower, Ludwig Boehm, and his Swiss clockmaker, John Kruesi. While mathematicians, machinists, and carpenters in his team of two dozen worked on new devices, the business side of Edison's "invention factory" was handled by bookkeepers, secretaries, and draftsmen who created drawings for the patent office, and his lawyer and agent, Grosvenor Lowery. His research staff included a number of individuals who went on to illustrious subsequent careers, including Johann Shukert, who would found what became Siemens in Germany, and John Kreusi, who became chief engineer at General Electric.[11]

SUBDIVIDING ELECTRICITY

Everyone knows that Thomas Edison invented the lightbulb, and he did—almost.

Others had experimented with incandescent lighting. The first form of electric illumination was the arc lamp, devised by a Russian, Paul N. Jablochkoff, and improved by an American, Charles F. Brush. In the 1870s and 1880s, arc lighting began to replace gas lights in public places like streets and railway stations, but it could not be used in residences and offices.

As early as 1859, Moses Farmer lit his home in Salem, Massachusetts, with glowing platinum wires. Joseph Swan, a British scientist, patented the first incandescent lightbulb in 1878. After making his home the first to be lit by electric bulbs, Swan turned a lecture hall in Newcastle into the first public building to be lit by bulbs in 1880 and then, in 1881, made the Savoy Theatre in London the first theater to be lit completely by electricity.

When he founded his Menlo Park, New Jersey, laboratory in 1876, Edison focused on electricity. In 1879, after testing six thousand plant fibers, Edison's team in New Jersey, like Swan, chose carbonized cotton for the filament. The bulb owed its design to the earlier work of two Canadian inventors, Henry Woodward and Matthew Evans.

Swan sued Edison for patent infringement. The British courts forced Edison to make Swan a partner in his British company, which became Ediswan. In 1882, Edison sold the US patent rights to the Brush Electric Company. In 1883, the US Patent Office had declared that Edison's pat-

ents were invalid because they were based on the designs of William Saw-
yer. But Edison was a master of self-promotion and to this day receives
credit for the invention of the incandescent bulb.

Edison's most important contribution was to create an entire system of
electric lighting, from the generator through the wires to the incandescent
bulb in the electric lamp. Edison announced that his goal was to make
electricity "subdivided so that it could be brought into private homes."

A DYNAMO NAMED JUMBO

At 3 p.m. on September 4, 1882, Thomas Edison activated a switch and
the age of electricity began.

Power in the form of direct current (DC) surged from the Pearl Street
Station at 255–257 Pearl Street, several blocks away. Complete with an
early version of an electric meter to monitor usage by customers, the
Pearl Street Station was the first modern electrical-power network in the
United States; another station designed by Edison had begun operating
in Holborn Viaduct in London on January 12, 1882. A steam dynamo
called "Jumbo" sent electricity through wires in tubes that at Edison's
insistence had been buried deep underground. The Pearl Street Station at
its inception provided electricity to 110 customers in Lower Manhattan.
One of the early customers was the *New York Times*, which published a
description of the light from the fifty-two incandescent lightbulbs that lit
up that afternoon as "soft, mellow and graceful to the eye . . . without a
particle of flicker to make the head ache."

Just as significant as the technology that Edison introduced to the
world was the place that he chose for the introduction. Edison flipped
a switch and turned on hundreds of lightbulbs in the offices of Drexel,
Morgan, in the presence of J. P. Morgan, the preeminent financier in the
United States. Beginning in 1878, Morgan and his partners, along with
the Vanderbilt family, had financed Edison, helping him incorporate the
Edison Electric Illuminating Company in December 1880. In 1892, Morgan would arrange the merger of Edison Electric, based in Schenectady,

New York, and Thomson-Houston Company, based in Lynn, Massachusetts, to create General Electric, one of the first twelve companies to be
included in the Dow Jones Industrial Average. As his reward, Morgan got
not only one of the first offices but also the first home in New York to be
lit by Edison's invention.

The alliance of Edison and Morgan symbolized a new era for the
American economy. Between 1880 and 1900, electric lightbulbs became
twice as efficient and only one-fifth as expensive. Fluorescent lighting was
used for offices and large buildings because of its energy efficiency.[12] Along
with the automobile, electricity was the most important technology of the
second industrial revolution that rendered the steam-based technology of
the first industrial revolution obsolete. And the entrepreneurial capitalism
represented by the individualistic railroad barons of the Steam Age was
rapidly giving way to the new finance capitalism symbolized by Morgan,
described in the next chapter.

THE ELECTRIC GRID AND THE
BATTLE OF THE SYSTEMS

When first cities and then regions began to build electric grids, a decision
had to be made whether to use direct current or alternating current. On
the side of DC were Thomas Edison and Edison Electric; the champions
of AC were Tesla and Westinghouse.

The "battle of the systems" was fought in multiple arenas: legislatures,
courthouses, and the court of public opinion. Harold Brown, a New York
engineer with a knack for publicity, was hired by Edison to lead the crusade against AC.

At Columbia University in 1888, Brown claimed to demonstrate the
danger of AC by using it to electrocute a dog that he first tortured with
DC, to the disgust of his audience. He had practiced for the demonstration by using dogs for which he had paid New Jersey children. Undeterred, Brown carried out other public electrocutions of dogs as well as
calves and a horse. When George Westinghouse scoffed at these specta-

cles, Brown publicly challenged him to an electrical duel: "I challenge Mr. Westinghouse to meet me in the presence of competent electrical experts and take through his body the alternating current while I take through mine a continuous current."[13]

When the state of New York, with Edison's advice, carried out the first execution in an electric chair, the criminal, William Kemmler, did not die at first, but squirmed in agony; successive doses of electricity killed him only by cooking him, to the horror of the witnesses. Edison tried to promote "Westinghousing" as a synonym for "electrocution."

The war was won by AC. After J. P. Morgan eased Edison out, Edison General Electric merged with Thomson-Houston General Electric (later General Electric) and cooperated with Westinghouse to build a Niagara power station that supplied electricity to a local industrial complex and the city of Buffalo, New York. The electric utility industry adopted a synthesis of DC and AC that remains standard today.

The battle of the currents had a gruesome coda. In 1903, her owners decided to put down Topsy, an elephant at a Coney Island amusement park who had killed three people, including a trainer who tried to force a burning cigarette into her mouth. After it was decided that hanging an elephant was impractical, the owners settled on electrocution, and in front of a crowd on January 4, 1903, festooned with electrodes, Topsy collapsed as more than six thousand volts of electricity coursed through her massive body. Edison distributed a motion picture entitled *Electrocuting an Elephant*.

THE ELECTRIC MOTOR

Electricity transformed industrial production by permitting the factory to be located far from the ultimate source of power. Equally important was the adoption by industry of the electric motor.

In 1824, the British scientist and inventor Michael Faraday demonstrated that electromagnetic induction could convert electrical current into rotary motion. Faraday invented the electric motor in 1821 and the dynamo in 1831. Edison made small DC motors in the 1880s, but the industry was soon dominated by the three-phase (polyphase) AC motors that Westinghouse began to sell in 1892.

Electric motors transformed industrial production. In steam-powered factories, steam engines transmitted their motion to the machinery by way of shafts that turned belts and pulleys. Within the factory, small electric motors could now power separate machines. This allowed factories to spread out horizontally on a single story and opened up space overhead for electric lighting or natural light admitted through sawtooth windows. By the 1940s, four-fifths of the power in American factories was supplied by electric motors.[14] Electric motors transformed the household as well as the factory. Small electric motors powered refrigerators, washing machines, driers, gramophones, radios, televisions, videocassette recorders, and personal computers.

THE STEAM TURBINE

Most of the world's electricity in the early twenty-first century comes from steam turbines that use heat generated by coal, oil, natural gas, or nuclear energy to turn water into steam. The steam spins the blades of a turbine fan; the mechanical energy is then converted to electricity in a turbogenerator.

While Thomas Edison is a household name, few have heard of Charles Parsons. And yet he was one of the founders of the modern electrical industry. The son of a famous astronomer, William Parsons, third earl of Rosse in Ireland, Parsons graduated from Cambridge with a first-class honors degree in mathematics. He made an unusual choice for someone of his background and became an engineer. In 1884, he was the head of the electrical equipment division of Clarke, Chapman and Co., which manufactured ship engines near Newcastle in Yorkshire. Parsons developed a steam turbine that made electricity both abundant and cheap. In 1888, he installed steam turbines at a Newcastle power station. In 1889, he founded his own company to equip military and civilian ships with turbines. In 1897, he demonstrated the *Turbinia*, an experimental ship that was the fastest in the world. Parsons licensed his turbine technology to Westinghouse in the United States. Parsons's steam turbine cost only a third as much as early steam engines, had an eighth of the weight, and occupied only a tenth of the space.[15] Water turbines provide roughly a fifth of global electricity today.[16]

The age of electricity might just as well have been called the age of coal. Americans obtained twice as much energy from wood as from coal in 1876. But in 1900, coal provided 71 percent of America's energy supply, wood 21 percent, and oil, natural gas, and hydropower less than 3 percent each.[17] At the beginning of the twenty-first century, coal still provided by far the majority of the energy used to generate electricity in American power plants.

THE INTERNAL COMBUSTION ENGINE

After electricity, the most important transformative technology of the second industrial revolution was the internal combustion engine.

Internal combustion engines come in two varieties, both invented in Germany in the nineteenth century: the Otto engine and the Diesel engine. In the 1860s, numerous inventors experimented with engines driven by explosive mixtures of gas or oil and air. After a Belgian inventor, Jean-Étienne Lenoir, developed a gas engine between 1859 and 1876, the German inventor Nikolaus August Otto developed the four-stroke engine. In 1878, Otto patented an engine that used coal gas as a fuel. In 1885, Gottlieb Daimler and Wilhelm Maybach adapted Otto's engine to use gasoline. Early electric cars and steam-powered cars could not compete with the performance of cars with gasoline engines. In the same year, 1885, Karl Benz built the first automobile, powered by a gasoline engine of his own design.

Rudolf Diesel's engine, patented in 1892, was based on a different approach. High pressure caused the fuel to ignite spontaneously. Diesel engines are more efficient, with energy conversion ratios of 40 percent, compared to 30 percent for the best gasoline engines. Cheaper but heavier, they were quickly used for trucking, rail, and shipping, but not aviation, in which lighter kerosene was employed. Because of high gasoline taxes in Europe, nearly half of passenger automobiles ran on diesel fuel by the beginning of the twenty-first century.

In 1891, Émile Lavassor established what remains the basic design of the automobile, down to the electrical ignition and the carburetor. The automobile industry benefited from the earlier development of the bicycle industry. Widespread use of bicycles followed the development of the safety bicycle by a British inventor, John K. Starley, in 1885. In 1888, an inventive veterinarian in Ireland, J. B. Dunlop, put the first pneumatic tires on the wheels of his son's tricycle. First the spread of bicycling and then the use of automobiles produced a demand for modern roads and highways.

Internal combustion engines were soon used not only for automobiles but also for planes, boats, tractors, and small devices like lawn mowers. During World War I diesel engines were used in ships and submarines and became the basis of global shipping.

MAGICAL MATERIALS

Many other technologies were part of the second industrial revolution in the late nineteenth and early twentieth centuries. Often they served the most important technologies, as rubber served the electric industry and the oil industry served the automobile industry.

In 1859, Colonel Edwin Drake drilled a petroleum well in Pennsylvania; his original goal was to substitute kerosene for costly whale oil in lamps. As the oil fields of Pennsylvania were depleted, new fields were discovered in Texas and California and abroad, in Dutch Indonesia, the Baku fields on the Caspian Sea, Romania, Mexico, Venezuela, Trinidad, and Iran. After World War II, new oilfields were developed in the Middle East, Nigeria, Siberia, and Alaska. By 1960, oil surpassed coal as the primary fossil fuel in the world.[18]

When electric lighting replaced kerosene lamps, oil found a new use, as a fuel for cars, trucks, tractors, planes, and ships. Natural gas (methane), at first considered a worthless by-product of crude oil, began to be used for heating and transportation.

Rubber was another key technology of the second industrial revolution, important for electrical insulation as well as for its use in automobile tires. In the 1840s, the American inventor Charles Goodyear succeeded in using a blend of sulfur, latex, and white lead to create "vulcanized" rubber. In 1852, when Goodyear sued a rival in Trenton, New Jersey, for infringement of his patent, he was represented by Daniel Webster, while another great American lawyer, Rufus Choate, represented his opponent. Webster brought all his oratorical gifts to bear in describing the new substance: "It is hard like metal and as elastic as pure original gum elastic. Why, that is as great and momentous a phenomenon occurring to men in the progress of their knowledge, as it would be for a man to show that iron and gold could remain iron and gold and yet become elastic like India Rubber." Webster contrasted Goodyear's vulcanized rubber with the older kind, which tended to melt in heat and grew rigid with cold: "A friend in New York sent me a very fine cloak of India Rubber, and a hat of the same material. I did not succeed very well with them. I took the cloak one day and set it out in the cold. It stood very well by itself. I surmounted it with the hat, and many persons passing by supposed they saw, standing by the porch, the Farmer of Marshfield."[19] Goodyear won his case but thanks to further patent litigation he died in debt.

In 1842, Goodyear gave some samples of his product to Stephen Moulton, a British businessman, and they made their way to the Scottish manufacturer Charles Macintosh, who had independently created the waterproof garment that bore his name. But it was in the late nineteenth century that the rubber industry grew rapidly, to supply tires first for bicycles and then for cars.

Goodyear Tire and Rubber Company, founded in 1893, became the largest rubber manufacturer in the United States and the world. The Firestone tire business was founded by Harvey Firestone, a mechanic who worked in Akron, Ohio, at his cousin's factory, putting rubber tires on horse-drawn carriages. Henry Ford visited in 1895 and adopted Firestone's solid rubber tires for the rims of the metal wheels of his cars. In later years, Ford, Firestone, and Edison vacationed together. Benjamin Franklin Goodrich, the founder of B. F. Goodrich, adapted the pneumatic tires devised by Michelin in France to American automobiles.

Until the early twentieth century, rubber continued to be derived from rubber trees. Seeking to avoid dependence on the British rubber plantations in Indonesia and Malaya, Firestone established his own rubber plantations in Liberia while Ford tried but failed to do the same in Amazonia in Brazil. Between World War I and World War II, American and German chemists learned how to make artificial rubber. This allowed the United States to make a million tons of rubber a year during World War II, even after Japan had conquered Southeast Asia.

Although steel was superior to wrought iron, in premodern times its cost limited its use to valuable implements like swords and plowshares. In 1856, Henry Bessemer discovered a method to make steel cheap. The Bessemer converter, followed by other innovations, radically reduced the cost of steel, benefiting existing industries like railroads and making possible entirely new uses for steel—in the framework of skyscrapers, for example.

Germany, with its superior system of state-funded research universities, led the world in the development of scientific chemistry and the chemical industry. German scientists and industrialists learned to create synthetic substitutes for natural dyes like indigo. Fritz Haber, Carl Bosch, and Alwin Mittasch devised the Haber-Bosch process for creating artificial ammonia used in fertilizers and explosives, including dynamite, which was developed by the Swedish chemist and engineer Alfred Nobel, who used his fortune to endow the Nobel prizes. The Germans also learned to create artificial potash or potassium, an ingredient of fertilizers, as a substitute for the variety derived from plants. The use of fertilizers produced by the chemical industry rather than nature made possible a revolution in agricultural productivity, as did the falling costs of steel farm implements and the development of tractors and other machines using internal combustion engines.

Plastics were another transformative technology spawned by the chemicals industry. John Wesley Hyatt, an American, devised celluloid, the first plastic, in 1869, and Leo Baekeland, a Belgian immigrant in the United States, discovered Bakelite in 1907.[20] Applied chemistry also transformed medicine, by supplying disinfectants, anesthetics, and aspirin (discovered by Felix Hoffman and manufactured by the German firm Bayer AG—thus Bayer Aspirin).[21]

Canned food first became important during the Civil War and later allowed growing urban populations to eat preserved meat, vegetables, and fruit. As early as 1870, refrigerated beef was shipped from the United States to Britain, and in 1876 Charles Tellier, a French engineer, devised the first refrigerated ship, the *Frigorifique*.[22] The development of small-scale refrigerators for the home helped to revolutionize domestic life.

HOW GOVERNMENT MODERNIZED AMERICAN AGRICULTURE

The modernization of the American economy between the 1890s and the 1930s was not solely the work of the private sector. In agriculture, radio, and aviation, the federal government acted as inventor, entrepreneur, and investor, in a return to the mixed-enterprise tradition of the early American republic.

In the 1790s, George Washington had lobbied unsuccessfully for a national agricultural university devoted to improving American agriculture. His vision of federal support for agricultural research was realized during the Civil War. The Morrill Act of 1862 used federal lands to subsidize land-grant agricultural and mechanical (A&M) colleges in the states. American agricultural reformers were inspired by the success of Germany in applying government-sponsored research to agriculture. The 1887 Hatch Act provided each state with federal funds on the condition that it establish at least one central experiment station "to conduct original researches or verify experiments . . . bearing directly on the agricultural industry of the United States."[23] Subsequent acts—the Adams Act (1906), the Smith-Lever Act (1914), the Purnell Act (1925), and the Bankhead-Jones Act (1935)—also provided money for research.

By the early twentieth century, a sophisticated industrial policy had developed in American agriculture. State land-grant colleges and regional experiment stations worked on the problems of American farmers. New techniques were disseminated by extension agents, who by 1914 numbered more than two thousand and were found in three-fourths of the agricultural counties of the United States.[24] County agents initiated the formation in 1919 of the American Farm Bureau, a private trade association that became the most important farm lobby in the nation.

THE FEDERAL GOVERNMENT
AND AMERICAN AVIATION

The US government played a key role in the development of manned flight, although initially it backed the wrong inventor. Samuel Pierpont Langley was a brilliant astrophysicist, the director of the Smithsonian Institution, and a friend of Alexander Graham Bell, who witnessed the successful flight of Langley's unmanned, steam-powered glider above the Potomac River near Washington on May 6, 1896. In 1898, the War Department commissioned Langley to produce a manned military aircraft, giving him a grant of fifty thousand dollars—roughly $1.3 million in 2010 dollars. But in test flights over the Potomac on October 7 and December 8, 1903, the manned version of Langley's glider, now powered by a gas engine, crashed and the pilot barely escaped each time. A little more than a week after the second attempt failed, on December 17, 1903, Orville and Wilbur Wright made the first successful flights of a manned heavier-than-air craft on the beach at Kitty Hawk, North Carolina. Humiliated and ridiculed, Langley died in 1906.

But the United States quickly lost the lead in aviation, as the great powers of Europe developed the new technology for military purposes. Between 1908 and 1913, the US government spent only $435,000 on aviation, compared to the $28 million spent by Germany, the $22 million spent by France, and the $12 million spent by Russia.[25]

As World War I approached, however, the government played a greater part. Between World War I and World War II, the federal government promoted the development of the American aviation industry by three methods: military procurement, public R&D in aeronautics, and airmail subsidies.

Although it had bet on the wrong inventors, the US government was quick to get into the airplane business. The military was the first client for the company that the Wright brothers set up.

Patent wars among early aircraft companies ended with the advent of World War I, when the aircraft manufacturers established the Manufacturers' Aircraft Association to coordinate wartime aircraft manufacturing in the United States and formed a patent pool with the approval of the US government. All patent litigation ceased automatically. Royalties were reduced to 1 percent and free exchange of inventions and ideas took place among all the airframe builders. The government-encouraged pooling of patents set a precedent for similar enlightened technology-sharing arrangements that the military and civilian agencies later imposed on contractors and federal grantees.

The federal government also promoted American aviation by means of a system of publicly funded R&D that resembled the American system of agricultural experiment stations. In 1915, as the possibility of US intervention in World War I increased, Congress used a naval appropriations bill to establish the National Advisory Committee on Aeronautics (NACA), the ancestor of the National Aeronautics and Space Administration (NASA). In the 1920s, NACA performed R&D at its Langley Field facility in Virginia. This was joined in the 1930s by other research centers, including one at Moffett Field near Sunnyvale, California, close to aircraft manufacturing, and a NACA center established in 1940 in the center of aircraft engine manufacturing, Cleveland, Ohio, in order to research improvements in aircraft engines. Thanks in part to public R&D, the 8 percent annual productivity growth in US aviation outstripped that in other industries between the 1920s and the 1960s.[26]

In 1958, NACA was merged with the newly founded NASA, which was charged with the most spectacular state capitalist project in American history: the US space program, which culminated with the 1969 landing of the first astronauts on the moon.

Beginning in 1918, the federal government used the airmail program to subsidize the infant American aviation industry. The use of contract carriers for airmail encouraged the growth of aviation companies. The McNary-Watres Act of 1930 indirectly subsidized passenger flights, by replacing payment by weight of airmail with a fixed price for airmail per mile, no matter how much space was used for passengers.

President Herbert Hoover's postmaster general, Walter Folger Brown, used his power to award airmail contracts to compel mergers that created a few large carriers. As a result, from the early 1930s until after World War II, the US airline industry was dominated by four airlines: American, TWA, Eastern, and United.[27]

The federal government's investment in aviation paid off. By the time World War II broke out, the United States had the largest commercial airline system and the most advanced commercial airliner, the Douglas DC-3, which continued in service until the 1960s.[28]

THE FEDERAL GOVERNMENT AND THE CREATION OF AMERICAN RADIO AND TELEVISION

The federal government also shaped the radio industry, which later pioneered television. The US Navy was wary of Britain's domination of global communications by means of its global underwater cable system. While taking part in postwar negotiations at Versailles in 1919, President Woodrow Wilson identified three areas of economic rivalry with military implications between the United States and Britain: oil production, merchant shipping, and global telecommunications. The United States had a lead in oil production, but the British Empire led in merchant shipping, and the British lead in global telecommunications threatened to increase because the Marconi company was based in London.

Frustrated by the need to rely on the British government because of Guglielmo Marconi's British patents, in 1919 the navy, led by Assistant Secretary of the Navy Franklin Delano Roosevelt, persuaded General Electric, Westinghouse, AT&T, and other companies to pool their radio-related patents and form the Radio Corporation of America (RCA), to ensure that interlocking American corporations controlled radio development in the US. GE bought out the patents of the American subsidiary of Marconi and gave its patents to RCA.[29]

The initial purpose of RCA was military and commercial, and large-scale radio broadcasting was delayed by the lack of a business model, since anyone could listen without paying. One proposal, a government station paid for by licenses for radio owners, was suggested by David Sarnoff and taken up as the funding model for the British Broadcasting Corporation (BBC). In 1922, AT&T solved the problem differently by selling advertising and linking several New York stations together in a network. Threatened by AT&T, Westinghouse, GE, and the others in 1926 forced AT&T to sell its stations and agree to lease its long-distance lines to a new network, the National Broadcasting Corporation (NBC). In 1931, anti-trust judgments separated Westinghouse and GE from NBC, and RCA was forced by subsequent orders to sell its Blue network, which became the American Broadcasting Company (ABC), in 1943.[30]

The modern age of television in the United States began on April 30, 1939, when antennas atop the Empire State Building in Manhattan broadcast live images of President Roosevelt at the opening ceremonies of the New York World's Fair. On the same day, RCA's affiliate NBC began regular US television broadcasts, which were limited at first to New York and other big cities in the Northeast.

RCA had delayed the evolution of American television by engaging in patent litigation with Philo T. Farnsworth, a brilliant Mormon from Utah who began dreaming of broadcasting images while studying at Brigham Young University in Provo, Utah. Helped by research engineers at the California Institute of Technology and investors after he moved to San Francisco, Farnsworth established the Farnsworth Television and

Radio Company and obtained a patent in 1927. RCA, backing television research by Vladimir Zworykin, a Russian émigré engineer, fought Farnsworth over the patent in the courts. The nascent British television industry licensed Farnsworth's technology and began regularly scheduled programming for a limited audience in 1936. The 1936 Berlin Olympics were the first to be televised. Only after World War II, however, did television transform society by reaching mass audiences.

THE TRANSFORMATION OF THE LANDSCAPE BY THE SECOND INDUSTRIAL REVOLUTION

The second industrial revolution created a distinctive pattern of production, work, and entertainment, based on the automobile and the electric grid. In the pedestrian city, the walkable area was about three square miles, with the edge of town limited to a mile from the center. Although mass transit is frequently advocated as an alternative to automobile-created suburbanization, the earliest suburban sprawl was created in the nineteenth century by mass transit. Taking advantage of the fact that horses could pull greater weights along rails, New York in the 1830s, followed by other American cities, adopted horsecar omnibus lines. The horsecar lines permitted the distance of the edge from the center of town to increase to 2.5 miles, producing an increase in area of twenty square miles. The horsecar began the process of migration of middle-class and working-class Americans to less crowded and less expensive housing on the urban periphery.[31]

Because of the noise and pollution they produced, steam locomotives were opposed as a method of urban transportation. Electricity provided an alternative. Following many experiments, the first genuine electrical streetcar system was created in the 1880s by Charles Van Depoele in Montgomery, Alabama. Frank Sprague, a former member of Edison's Menlo Park team, created the Richmond, Virginia, electric streetcar system. Sprague's streetcars used an overhead electric wire that "trolled" along other wires, thus the name, "trolley." Sprague's version became the standard when Henry Whitney adopted it to replace the world's largest horsecar rail system, the West End Railway of Boston.[32] The Boston trolley system pioneered the use of a flat fare for any length of ride, which further encouraged the working class to disperse to suburban lodgings. Electric trolley systems were soon joined by electric interurbans. The difficulty of creating new overland routes through existing neighborhoods led Boston, New York, and other cities to invest in subway systems.

By World War I, middle-class and working-class suburbs were growing up on the edges of cities. Industrial plants followed them, to take advantage of lower rents and more space. Polluting industries were nudged out by means of zoning, a form of urban regulation that spread rapidly in the early twentieth century.

As the central city was emptied of residents and manufacturing, it evolved into the downtown, a district that specialized in retail businesses, including department stores that served entire metropolitan areas, like Macy's and Gimbel's in New York and Filene's in Boston. The new downtowns were characterized by a distinctive skyline created by tall office buildings. In the preindustrial era, large buildings had generally been limited to five or six stories accessed by stairs. The elevator allowed buildings to grow. The earliest elevators were cargo-hoisting machines employed in warehouses of a kind that would have been familiar to medieval and ancient engineers. Elisha Graves Otis, the founder of Otis Elevator, devised a cable-drawn elevator. In 1857, the first safe passenger elevator was installed in the H. V. Haughwort Store in New York.[33]

While the elevator had solved the problem of vertical transportation, the height of buildings was still limited by the nature of masonry construction, which required greater and greater thickness at the base as the height increased. This problem was solved first by cage construction and later by curtain-wall construction. A wrought iron cage was used as the skeleton of the seven-story Harper's Building in 1854 by the architect James Broadus. The first true skyscraper, however, was the Equitable Insurance Building in New York, built between 1868 and 1870. It was an office building that combined an iron cage with an elevator.[34]

But it was Chicago, not New York, that would develop the skyscraper. Architect William Le Baron Jenney's ten-story Home Insurance Building used a steel cage that permitted more light and larger windows, producing a distinctive Chicago skyscraper style. New Yorkers were so wary of heights that the architect of the eleven-story Tower Building at 50 Broadway in 1889 put his own office in the top floor to persuade Manhattanites of its safety.[35]

The offices in the new downtown buildings were filled with the clatter of adding machines and typewriters. The product of a long evolution, the familiar mechanical typewriter was first produced in 1874 by Philo Remington, a New York manufacturer of sewing machines and other devices, on the basis of a design patented in 1867 by a retired newspaper editor named Christopher Latham Sholes. Samuel Langhorne Clemens, who was better known under his nom de plume Mark Twain, wrote a testimonial:

Gentlemen:

Please do not use my name in any way. Please do not even divulge the fact that I own a machine. I have entirely stopped using the Type-Writer, for the reason that I never could write a letter with it to anybody without receiving a request by return mail that I would not only describe the machine but state what progress I had made in the use of it, etc, etc. I don't like to write letters, and so I don't want people to know that I own this curiosity breeding little joker.

Yours truly,
Saml. L. Clemens[36]

By the 1920s, electricity and the automobile were reshaping the geography of American production, distribution, consumption, and residence. Thanks to electrical power, factories no longer needed to be located near

coal mines or waterways that carried the coal that powered steam engines. Railroads were eclipsed by long-distance trucking, as canals earlier
had been eclipsed by railroads. And the migration of Americans from the
farms to the cities gave way to the migration from the cities to the suburbs.

While the visible transformation of the American landscape by the
second industrial revolution was dramatic, the transformation of the
landscape of American business and politics would prove to be even more
consequential.

THE DAY
OF COMBINATION

Once admitted that the machine must be efficient, society might dis-
pute in what social interest it should be run, but in any case it must
work concentration.

—Henry Adams, 1905[1]

The day of combination is here to stay. Individualism has gone, never
to return.

—John D. Rockefeller, 1880[2]

Repeatedly in American history, waves of technological innovation have led to the reorganization of business and markets, before the political order could catch up. By the first years of the twentieth century, the second industrial revolution of the late nineteenth century, based on the new technologies of electricity and automobility, was already outgrowing the structures of American economic life that had been inherited from the last wave of reform in the United States during the Civil War and Reconstruction.

In 1901, the economist John Bates Clark wrote: "If the carboniferous age were to return and the earth were to repeople itself with dinosaurs, the change that would be made in animal life would scarcely seem greater than that which had been made in business life by these monster-like corporations."[3] By 1932, according to Adolf A. Berle and Gardiner C. Means in *The Modern Corporation and Private Property*, half of the assets of non-financial corporations in the United States were controlled by only two hundred firms.[4] "The day of combination is here to stay," John D. Rockefeller declared. "Individualism has gone, never to return."[5]

The second industrial era that began in the 1870s and 1880s was an age of giantism in production as well as invention. By 1890 the assets of US manufacturing, at $6.5 billion, were approaching those of US railroads, at $10 billion, although while each of the ten largest railroads had assets of $100 million each, few manufacturing corporations were worth more than $10 million.[6] The "great merger wave" of 1895–1904 created giant corporations in industries ranging from steel to tobacco.

The new industrial leviathans existed in a country whose political institutions, despite the reforms of the Civil War and Reconstruction, were still those of a decentralized, agrarian society. The misalignment between the emerging technological and economic order and the archaic political system was a challenge that different groups of reformers sought to meet in different ways.

ANTITRUST AND THE SUPREME COURT

One historian observes that around 1900 "a big majority of the economists conceded that the combination movement was to be expected, that high fixed costs made larger scale enterprise economical, that rivalry under these circumstances frequently resulted in cutthroat competition, that agreements among producers were a natural consequence, and the stability of prices usually brought more benefit than harm to the society."[7] A number of American economists argued that older notions of laissez-faire were irrelevant in an economy transformed by the use of steam power in transportation and manufacturing. For example, Richard T. Ely wrote that "owing to discoveries and inventions, especially the application of steam to industry and transportation, it became necessary to prosecute enterprises of great magnitude."[8] In 1889, another leading American economist, David Ames Wells, argued that the application of steam engines to manufacturing made possible "excessive competition" and losses that could only be avoided if firms combined to limit output.[9] As a result, he declared: "Society has practically abandoned—and from the very necessity of the case has got to abandon, unless it proposes to war against progress and civilization—the prohibition of concentrations and combinations."[10] John Bates Clark wrote that large industrial combinations "are the result of an evolution, and the happy outcome of a competition so abnormal that the continuance of it would have meant widespread ruin. A successful attempt to suppress them by law would involve the reversion of industrial systems to a cast-off type, the renewal of abuses from which society has escaped by a step in development."[11]

In addition to recognizing the legitimacy of large corporations in industries with increasing returns to scale, by the 1890s, many otherwise conservative economists argued for the reality of "ruinous competition" in railroads and other industries with high fixed costs and variable operating costs. According to this argument, too many firms competing in a capital-intensive industry could drive prices below the minimum prices needed to recoup long-term, fixed investments in railroads or factories. As a result, most or all of the competing firms could be plunged into bankruptcy. Traditional free-market competition could not work in such industries, it was argued. What was needed instead was either cartelization among firms that agreed upon minimum prices or consolidation of entire industries by monopoly or oligopoly.

Both methods were tried by entrepreneurs and financiers in the railroads and other industries. Informal price-fixing cartels, known as "pools," tended to fail, because there was no penalty to prevent one or more firms from undercutting the agreed-upon minimum prices. In other countries, including Britain, Germany, and Japan, cartels were tolerated or legal and allowed to enforce price agreements upon all firms in an industry. But in its interpretations of the vague language of the Sherman Antitrust Act of 1890, which prohibited combinations to create monopolies, the Supreme Court, clinging to preindustrial economic theory, ruled repeatedly in the late nineteenth and early twentieth centuries that avoiding ruinous competition was not a defense of price-fixing or other forms of collaboration among firms in the same industry.

THE GREAT MERGER MOVEMENT

Even as it forbade firms in the same industry to collaborate, the Supreme Court permitted mergers that created firms that could dominate particular industries. The court inadvertently reshaped the industrial landscape of the United States, as companies responded to its rulings by abandoning attempts at cartelization and taking part in what has been called "the great merger wave." The merger wave of the 1890s and 1900s was followed by a second in the 1920s and a third in the period of conglomerate-building in the 1950s and 1960s.

Most companies in the early republic were created by "special incorporation," specific charters issued by the legislature that detailed their powers and responsibilities. The Supreme Court struck a blow to the practice of chartering corporations as monopolies in 1837 in the *Charles River Bridge* case, in which it held that a corporate charter did not imply a monopoly in that industry. Hostility to special incorporation was part of the ideology of Jacksonian populists, for whom it was a source of political corruption and a violation of the principle, "Equal rights for all, special privileges for none." The revulsion against special incorporation by state governments increased when state fiscal crises followed canal and railroad bubbles in the 1830s and 1840s. By the mid-nineteenth century, most states had enacted general incorporation laws that no longer required special action by the state legislature.

Even so, corporations usually were not allowed to own stock in other corporations. In 1889, in order to encourage companies to incorporate in the state, the New Jersey legislature passed a law that allowed any corporation chartered in New Jersey to own stock in the corporations of any other state. This permitted enormous corporations to be created as holding companies. In 1901, for example, J. P. Morgan incorporated US Steel as a New Jersey holding company. New Jersey was succeeded by

Delaware, which still has the leading position among states as a home for American companies.

The combination of the outlawing of cartels and new corporate laws like that of New Jersey resulted in the great merger movement of 1895–1904. In that brief period, eighteen hundred firms were combined into 157 companies, most of them in manufacturing. New Jersey's 1888 general incorporation law for holding companies of national businesses stimulated a wave of consolidations that grew from four in 1895 and six in 1897 to sixteen in 1898. The wave peaked in 1899, with sixty-three consolidations, followed by twenty-one in 1901, seventeen in 1902, and three in 1904.[12]

Of ninety-three consolidations studied by the historian Naomi Lamoreaux, seventy-two created companies that controlled at least 40 percent of their industries and forty-two controlled at least 70 percent.[13] Among the corporations that dominated 40 percent or more of their industries were the familiar (Eastman Kodak; Otis Elevator; United Steel; National Biscuit, now known as Nabisco) and the forgotten (National Candy, United States Envelope, and American Stogie).[14] The new giants included General Electric, which was formed from eight firms and controlled 90 percent of its market; International Harvester, formed from four companies and controlling 70 percent of its market; DuPont, formed from sixty-four firms and controlling 65 to 75 percent of its market; and American Tobacco, which controlled 90 percent of its market after forming from the merger of 162 firms.[15]

The Wall Street publisher John Moody, founder of Moody's ratings service, a defender of industrial concentration, claimed that the US economy in the first years of the twentieth century was dominated by seven "Great Industrial Trusts": United States Steel, Amalgamated Copper, American Smelting and Refining, American Sugar Refining, Consolidated Tobacco, International Mercantile Marine, and Standard Oil.[16] In 1894, three-fourths of the output of the entire US steel industry came from Carnegie Steel and Illinois Steel.[17] In the chronically troubled railroad industry, consolidation around 1900 resulted in the ownership of 62 percent of the US railway network by seven corporations.[18] The period also witnessed the emergence of giant firms in extractive industries like lumber. Economies of scale that permitted upgrades in milling technology were costly and led to the replacement of small operators by large companies like those of Frederick Weyerhaeuser, Charles Stimson, and D. A. Blodgett.

MORGANIZATION

The great merger wave produced enormous firms that confronted a fragmented system of nearly thirty thousand unit banks in the early 1900s. In Germany, large universal banks were able to help a firm throughout its life cycle, by making loans in its early years, underwriting shares as it expanded, and policing and monitoring the firm in its maturity, as a proxy for the firm's shareholders. The growing importance of the stock market in financing large corporations was the result in part of the inability of America's mostly small unit banks to grow in scale along with businesses, because of state and federal anti–branch-banking laws. Until the 1890s, railroads dominated the stock and bond markets. Then companies representing the industries of the second industrial revolution, like General Electric and US Steel, became important.

As the new corporate leviathans turned to other sources of financing, banks increasingly made loans to small local businesses. The share of corporate debt in the form of bank loans plunged from 32.1 percent in 1920 to 23.3 percent in 1929. America's small unit banks also lost out in consumer lending to specialized consumer lenders and corporate vendor financing, like that of the General Motors Acceptance Corporation. Many banks were forbidden by law to branch even within their home states.[19]

Investment banks in the United States performed the functions of underwriting and monitoring large corporations by the same method of corporate board memberships that was used in Germany by large universal banks. Investment banking costs were high, however, in the United States, compared to Germany, with its universal banks. Restrictions on the size and resources of banks raised the costs of underwriting securities and bank lending to industrial corporations.[20]

The need for giant corporations to raise enormous sums increased the importance of investment bankers as intermediaries between the shareholding public and individual companies. In 1912, five American banks—J. P. Morgan and Company, First National Bank, National City Bank, Guaranty Trust Company, and Bankers' Trust—had representatives on the boards of sixty-eight corporations whose combined assets added up to more than half of US gross national product.[21]

The dominant figure in American investment banking around 1900 was John Pierpont Morgan, a Europe-educated patrician from a wealthy American banking dynasty. A dedicated art collector, a pillar of the Episcopal Church, an adulterer who supported Anthony Comstock's Society for the Suppression of Vice, with a nose discolored by the skin disease rosacea and an impressive stature and girth, Morgan was a larger-than-life figure. Morgan's grandfather Joseph was a founding investor in the Hartford and Aetna insurance companies. His father, Junius, worked in business in Hartford and Boston for a few years before joining the merchant bank of George Peabody, a Baltimore expatriate living in London. On Peabody's retirement, Junius changed the name of the firm to J. S. Morgan & Co.

Morgan was born to Junius and his wife in 1837 in Hartford, Connecticut. A sickly youth, Morgan grew into an unhealthy adult who never exercised, saying, when his son began to play squash every morning before work, "Rather he than I."[22] Educated in Boston, Switzerland, and Germany, and with a degree in art history from the University of Göttingen in Germany, Morgan turned down an offer to stay as an assistant to a mathematics professor at the University of Göttingen and moved to New York, where he worked for a Wall Street firm, Duncan, Sherman & Co., surprising them when, during a trip to New Orleans, he bought a shipload of coffee and sold it for a profit on the firm's account, without asking permission. His first wife, Amelia "Memie" Sturges, was suffering from tuberculosis when he wed her; too weak to stand during their wedding, she died four months later in Nice, leaving Morgan a widower at twenty-four. Toward the end of the Civil War he married his second wife, Frances Tracy, with whom he had three daughters and a son, Jack Morgan Jr., who inherited the leadership of J. P. Morgan and Company.

In 1860, he became the American agent for his father's firm and made his first fortune on commissions for selling US bonds in Europe during the Civil War. Like many upper-class Americans, Morgan avoided service in the Civil War by paying three hundred dollars for a substitute. Later he inherited his father's firm and formed his own partnerships, first Dabney, Morgan & Co. and then Drexel, Morgan and Co. He formed a syndicate that successfully challenged Jay Cooke's monopoly of government finance.

Morgan's eminence grew in 1879, when he sold British investors 150,000 shares of the New York Central Railroad that William H. Vanderbilt, Cornelius's son, wanted to divest himself of in order to diversify his holdings. By holding the proxies of the British investors, Morgan got a place on the New York Central's board and a foothold in the railroad industry. With Vanderbilt's approval, Morgan sought to end a war between the New York Central and the Pennsylvania Railroad by persuading their directors to work out a truce aboard his yacht on the Hudson River. Morgan frequently invited quarreling railroad chiefs to settle their differences at his dinner table, in his library, or on his yacht, named the *Corsair*, in keeping with his piratical reputation.

Morgan transferred the technique of consolidation from the railroad industry to other industries. Morgan created General Electric, American Telegraph and Telephone (AT&T), the Pullman Company, National Biscuit (Nabisco), and International Harvester. Morgan's most famous consolidation was the 1901 merger that produced US Steel, the world's first billion-dollar company. He paid $480 million for Carnegie Steel, making Carnegie the richest person in the world. The initial capitalization of US Steel—a billion dollars—was twice the US federal budget.

The process by which the House of Morgan acquired, consolidated, and reorganized railroads and other companies and controlled them by placing Morgan partners on their boards of directors came to be known as "Morganization." Morganization was popular with shareholders and entrepreneurs who believed that Morgan's reputation helped the companies attract investment. Charles S. Mellen, the president of the New York, New Haven and Hartford Railroad, declared, "I wear the Morgan collar, and I am proud of it."[23] When a railroad executive spoke about his railroad, Morgan exploded: "*Your* railroad? Your railroad belongs to my clients."

By 1900, Morgan and his partners had a place on the boards of directors of companies that accounted for over a quarter of the wealth of the United States. Did Morganization produce criminal monopolies or efficient firms that benefited from technological and commercial economies of scale? The historian of business Alfred D. Chandler Jr. noted that many of the largest US firms in industries such as petroleum, transportation equipment, rubber, chemicals, and food products were the same in 1973 as in 1917. These market-dominating "center firms" tended to be more capital-intensive and technologically advanced than small, labor-intensive "peripheral firms" in the same industry. Chandler found a similar pattern among the center firms of Britain, Germany, France, and Japan, which suggests that the formation of large manufacturing corporations in the second industrial era could only be explained in terms of efficiency, not local conspiracies against the public good. Building on Chandler's work, Thomas K. McCraw concluded that these international comparisons discredit polemical accounts of the rise of nefarious "trusts."[24] The economist Bradford DeLong has concluded that Morganization did produce value for its beneficiaries.[25]

HOW J. P. MORGAN BAILED OUT
THE UNITED STATES

Morgan was so powerful that it was necessary for him to intervene to help rescue the federal government from financial crises in 1895 and 1907. In 1895, after the Panic of 1893 had caused a depletion of the US Treasury's gold reserves, Morgan visited Democratic president Grover Cleveland in the White House and promised help. On returning to New York, he locked a number of leading financiers in the ornately decorated library of his lavish mansion and refused to allow them to leave until they had agreed to contribute money to a syndicate that would bail out the federal government by supplying the Treasury with gold in return for federal bonds. The plan worked, but outrage among populist Democrats contributed to the party's nomination of William Jennings Bryan in 1896 and 1900, when Morgan and other American financiers and industrialists, mobilized by Mark Hanna, contributed record-breaking sums of money to defeat Bryan and elect McKinley twice.

Again in 1907, Morgan was reluctantly called upon by President Theodore Roosevelt to help avert a financial crisis. On the evening of Thursday, October 24, 1907, most of the leading bankers in New York were summoned to Morgan's library. Morgan ordered them to figure out a way to restore public confidence in the banks, then retired to his office to play solitaire. The plan the bankers worked out was to allow banks to settle their accounts among themselves in New York Clearing House notes, freeing them to lend out their clearing-house balances in the form of cash to depositors. The system had been used successfully in earlier panics. In addition, Morgan raised $13 million in call money for the stock exchange, while John D. Rockefeller contributed $10 million to the national banks in addition to $10 million from the US Treasury.

Shocked by the dependence of the federal government on the private power of the House of Morgan in 1895 and 1907, Congress decided to create an American central bank. On December 1913, eight months after J. P. Morgan died in Rome, President Woodrow Wilson signed the Federal Reserve Act into law. The legislation was based on a 1912 report by the National Monetary Commission, headed by the powerful chair of the Senate Finance Committee, Rhode Island senator Nelson W. Aldrich. Several members of the commission—Aldrich, Paul M. Warburg, Henry P. Davison, Frank A. Vanderlip, A. Piatt Andrew, and Benjamin Strong, a vice president at Bankers Trust, who later became the highly capable first governor of the New York Federal Reserve—had secretly traveled to the Millionaire's Club at Jekyll Island, Georgia. They told journalists they were going duck hunting, and Davison and Vanderlip in the earshot of train personnel and other passengers called each other Orville and Wilbur.

The Aldrich plan that emerged from these discussions combined a central board of private bankers with regional reserve banks. The Democratic majority in Congress reduced the influence of private bankers by adding a presidentially appointed governing board in Washington. At the insistence of southerners and westerners who feared the domination of central banking by the New York financial community, a decentralized system of regional Federal Reserve banks was created, in what ultimately proved to be the vain hope that this would limit the influence on the Federal Reserve of the New York financial community.

PROGRESSIVISM IN AMERICA

In response to the challenges posed by giant industrial corporations, some Americans advocated doing nothing at all. Herbert Spencer's laissez-faire doctrine was championed in the United States by William Graham Sumner of Yale and Edward Livingston Youmans, the editor of *Popular Science Monthly*, founded in 1872. Asked by the champion of land reform, Henry George, what he would do about social problems, Youmans replied: "Nothing! You and I can do nothing at all. It's all a matter of evolution. We can only wait for evolution. Perhaps in four or five thousand years evolution may have carried men beyond this state of things. But we can do nothing."[26]

Other Americans were not willing to wait four or five thousand years for social progress. Many American academics had studied in Imperial Germany and had been impressed by the social reforms and economic regulation that Chancellor Otto von Bismarck's regime had undertaken since the founding of the united Reich in 1871. In the late nineteenth century, even as the authoritarian government of Imperial Germany outlawed unions and the Social Democratic Party, it passed reforms: health insurance (1883), accident insurance (1884), and old age and disability pensions (1889). By World War I Britain under David Lloyd George had adopted many similar reforms. Admirers of these reforms in America adopted the name "progressive" for themselves by translating the German word *Fortschrittliche*. Their counterparts in Britain called themselves the New Liberals, and by the 1930s "liberal" came to be preferred to "progressive" by Americans like Franklin Roosevelt, who described himself as "slightly left of center."

The American progressives were influenced by the German historical school of economics, which dismissed classical liberal economics in the tradition of Adam Smith and David Ricardo as superficial "Manchester liberalism." According to the historical school, political economy was a form of statecraft, not a science modeled on physics that could identify "laws" of economics that would be valid in all societies and all times. The historical school was influenced by Friedrich List, who had argued that Germany should model itself on the United States by creating a large internal market and using a protective tariff to promote its infant industries; in addition, List dreamed of American-style democracy for Germany, not Bismarckian authoritarianism. List had been an evangelist for the American school of developmental capitalism associated in the first half of the nineteenth century with Hamilton, Clay, Raymond, Carey, and others. The American progressives of the 1900s who imported German historical school ideas were thus, in a sense, reimporting the modified themes of the earlier American school of political economy. They went on to found the institutional school of American economics, which had a profound influence on American reform in the first half of the twentieth century, even though it was marginalized in the American academy after World War II by excessively abstract, unrealistic approaches to economics. Similar themes are found in the "evolutionary economics" of the late twentieth and early twenty-first centuries that drew inspiration from the economist Joseph Schumpeter's vision of technology-driven "creative destruction."[27]

In the early twentieth century, the radical left was marginal, especially after World War I brought about the collapse of the Socialist Party, followed by the postwar Red Scare. The major debate was between champions of neo-Hamiltonian developmental capitalism and neo-Jeffersonian producerists, who idealized small producers. The former school can be called by Theodore Roosevelt's term, the New Nationalism; the latter, by Woodrow Wilson's phrase, the New Freedom. New Nationalists favored economies of scale, but within the context of stakeholder capitalism. Their idea of reform was increasing partnership among large, efficient corporations, a strengthened federal government, and (for some) national labor unions. The neo-Jeffersonian producerists of the New Freedom school sought to use federal and state laws to tilt the playing field toward small businesses, small distributors, and small banks. Both schools opportunistically denounced their adversaries for interfering with the market, but each school favored government intervention in the economy in order to promote its vision of the future of American society.

THE NEW NATIONALISM

In his influential book *Relation of the State to Industrial Action* (1887), the economist Henry Carter Adams distinguished industries with increasing returns from those with constant or diminishing returns. In industries with increasing returns to scale, the greater efficiency of large units meant that the largest firm would be likely to drive its rivals out of existence and become a monopoly. Adams argued that an industry with increasing returns to scale would tend to be either an "irresponsible, extralegal monopoly, or a monopoly established by law and managed in the interest of the public."[28]

In his 1909 manifesto *The Promise of American Life*, the progressive journalist Herbert Croly, the founding editor of the *New Republic*, wrote: "The constructive idea behind a policy of the recognition of the semi-monopolistic corporations is, of course, the idea that they can be converted into economic agents . . . unequivocally for the national economic interest."[29] The trade-union leader Samuel Gompers favored the formations of industrial trusts capable of negotiating with labor unions. At J. P. Morgan's death, a socialist is supposed to have said: "We grieve that he could not live longer, to further organize the productive forces of the world, because he proved in practice what we hold in theory, that competition is not essential to trade and development."[30]

This progressive version of America's tradition of Hamiltonian developmental capitalism found a champion in Theodore Roosevelt. Roosevelt condemned "malefactors of great wealth." He wrote: "Of all forms of tyranny the least attractive and the most vulgar is the tyranny of mere wealth, the tyranny of a plutocracy."[31]

But TR did not believe that breaking up large corporations could restore a golden age of equality among small farmers and small shopkeepers. He complained: "Much of the legislation not only proposed but enacted against trusts is not one whit more intelligent than the medieval bull against the comet, and has not been one particle more effective." In his annual address to Congress in 1902, he wrote: "These big aggregations are an inevitable development of modern industrialism, and the effort to destroy them would be futile. The line of demarcation we draw must always be on conduct, not on wealth; our objection to any given corporation must be, not that it is big, but that it behaves badly."[32] In his "New Nationalism" speech at Osawatomie, Kansas, in 1910, Roosevelt observed: "The effort at prohibiting all combination has substantially failed. The way out lies, not in attempting to prevent such combinations, but in completely controlling them in the interest of the public welfare."[33]

Critics noted that when Roosevelt distinguished "good trusts" from "bad trusts," the good trusts were often organized by J. P. Morgan, who funded his campaigns. For example, although his Justice Department successfully brought an antitrust suit against the Morgan-backed Northern Securities railroad trust, TR saw US Steel as a good trust, and when a lawsuit against it was brought under the Sherman Act, a federal district court agreed, throwing out the suit in a 1915 decision upheld by the Supreme Court in 1920. The satirist Finley Peter Dunne, in Irish dialect, restated Roosevelt's distinction between good and bad trusts: " 'The trusts,' says [Roosevelt], 'are heejous monsthers built up be th'inlightened intherprise iv th' men that have done so much to advance progress in our beloved country,' he says. 'On wan hand I wud stamp thim undher fut; on th'other hand not so fast.' "[34]

When in 1902, Roosevelt ordered Attorney General Philander Knox to prosecute Morgan's Northern Securities Corporation for violating the Sherman Antitrust Act, Morgan visited the White House and told the president, "If we have done anything wrong, send your man to my man and they can fix it up." After Morgan departed, TR told Knox: "Mr. Morgan could not help regarding me as a big rival operator, who either intended to ruin all his interests or else could be induced to come to an agreement to ruin none." Their clashes did not prevent Morgan along with other major financiers and industrialists from contributing money to Roosevelt's 1904 election campaign, on the grounds that the agrarian populist Democrats were a greater threat than the patrician progressive. But Morgan never forgave Roosevelt. When he learned that the recently retired president had gone to Africa on a hunting expedition, Morgan told friends: "I hope the first lion he meets does his duty."[35]

As an alternative to the blunt instrument of antitrust, TR supported a federal incorporation law. Representative William P. Hepburn of Iowa in 1908 introduced a bill inspired by a 1907 report of the National Civic Federation. Founded in 1900 by a Chicago Republican editor named Ralph Montgomery Easley, the National Civic Federation brought together leaders from the realms of business, labor, politics, the academy, the clergy, and journalism who shared a common interest in moderate reform that avoided the extremes of radicalism and reaction. Mark Hanna was the first president and Samuel Gompers the first vice president. Andrew Carnegie and August Belmont belonged to the NCF, as did John R. Commons of the University of Wisconsin, one of the most important of the progressive economic reformers.

The Hepburn bill proposed federal incorporation of firms engaged in interstate commerce and exempted not only unions but also farms and business combinations "in the public interest." A commissioner of corporations in the Commerce Department, rather than lawyers in the Justice Department, would have supervised corporate behavior. Jeffersonian paranoia doomed this sensible Hamiltonian reform. The Senate Judiciary Committee denounced the proposed registration of companies engaged in interstate commerce with the commissioner of corporations: "Shall we confer power upon the mere head of a bureau that the Parliament of England were unwilling to accord the King, and which they regarded as a menace to their liberties?"[36]

WILSON, BRANDEIS, AND THE NEW FREEDOM

Like Theodore Roosevelt, Woodrow Wilson recognized that there could be no return to an American economy dominated entirely by small enterprises. In 1900, he complained about populists like William Jennings Bryan: "Most of our reformers are retro-reformers. They want to hale us back to an old chrysalis which we have broken; they want us to resume a shape which we have outgrown."[37] In 1908, Wilson told the National Democratic Club: "No one now advocates the old *laissez faire*."[38] In 1912, at the Democratic Party's annual Jefferson Day banquet, Wilson dismissed the relevance of Jeffersonian political economy, arguing that the United States "is not the simple, homogeneous, rural nation that she was in Jefferson's time." He concluded: "We live in a new and strange age and reckon with new affairs alike in economics and politics of which Jefferson knew nothing."[39] In 1912, Wilson declared: "Nobody can fail to see, no matter how clearly you perceive the evils that have come upon the country by the use of them—nobody can fail to see that modern business is going to be done by corporations. *The old time of individual competitiveness is probably gone by*. . . . We will do business henceforth when we do it on a great and successful scale, by means of corporations" (emphasis in original).[40] On accepting the presidential nomination of the Democratic Party in the same year, Wilson emphasized, "I daresay we shall never return to the old order of individual competition, and that the organization of business upon a great scale of co-operation is, up to a certain point, itself normal and inevitable."[41]

Nevertheless, Wilson had misgivings about centralized power, which he shared with another southern-born Progressive, Louis Brandeis. The first Jewish justice of the Supreme Court, appointed by Wilson in 1916, the Kentucky-born Brandeis campaigned all his life against what he called "the curse of bigness," inspiring a school of influential Brandeisian liberals including Felix Frankfurter and Benjamin Cardozo.

Brandeis denied the very existence of increasing returns to scale in technology-based industries: "I am so firmly convinced that the large unit is not as efficient—I mean the very large unit—is not as efficient as the smaller unit, that I believe that if it were possible today to make corporations act in accordance with what doubtless all of us agree should be the rules of trade no huge corporations would be created, or if created, would be successful."[42] He attributed the large size of modern industrial and infrastructure corporations not to economies of scale but to a conspiracy of New York bankers: "There is the consolidation of railroads into huge systems, the large combinations of public service corporations and the formation of industrial trusts, which, by making businesses so 'big' that locally independent banking concerns cannot alone supply the necessary funds, has created dependence upon the associated New York bankers."[43] He did not explain why large enterprises in manufacturing were common in other industrial countries beyond the reach of New York bankers. Brandeis would have resolved the emergent contradiction between large corporations and small unit banks—"locally independent banking concerns"—by cutting companies down to the scale of unit banks. Brandeis's neo-Jeffersonian alternative to industrial corporate capitalism was a vague vision of a social order based upon small enterprises and cooperatives, of a kind that has not existed in any modern industrial country since the nineteenth century.

The Brandeisian wing of progressivism stoked Jeffersonian and Jacksonian dread of "the trusts," a pejorative term for large enterprise that continued to be used long after New Jersey's incorporation law permitted companies to abandon the unwieldy form of trusts in order to expand. Charles Francis Adams complained that every plan to coordinate railroads was immediately "characterized in the papers as a vast 'trust'—in these days, everything is a 'trust'—and denounced as a conspiracy."[44] The journalist Ida Tarbell, who had written a bestselling attack on John D. Rockefeller and Standard Oil, wrote in her autobiography that the public was wrong to believe "that the inevitable result of corporate industrial management was exploitation, neglect, bullying, crushing of labor, that the only hope was in destroying the system."[45]

Many Brandeisians believed mistakenly that large corporations survived only because of high tariffs. They hoped that the Underwood Tariff Act of 1913, by slashing tariff rates, might cause industrial trusts to crumble under new competition. In fact, the most successful industrial corporations no longer needed the tariff and favored a policy of reciprocal trade liberalization so that they could export more to foreign markets, especially Europe. When the United States adopted low tariffs after World War II, most of the Morgan-created behemoths, instead of crumbling, as Brandeisian theory predicted they would, dominated the global market as well as the American market.

For critics of the trusts like Brandeis, the real purpose of antitrust was not to protect consumers, who often benefited when economies of scale permitted lower prices, but rather to protect small, inefficient producers who sought to use the state to compensate for their own lack of competitiveness. Anti–chain-store legislation similarly sought to protect small stores from competition by national retailers.

While the New Nationalists in the Hamiltonian tradition sought to remove economic governance from the adversarial environment of judges and juries to the realm of federal public administration, the neo-Jeffersonian advocates of the New Freedom sought to strengthen the prosecutorial antitrust system. In 1914, the Clayton Act backed by the Wilson administration sought to make the Sherman Antitrust Act even harsher by specifying monopoly practices. The Federal Trade Commission, created in 1914, was empowered to police restraints of trade, in addition to the courts.

Another progressive reform directed at the new elite of industrial and financial millionaires was the federal income tax. The Constitution provided that any federal direct tax be apportioned on the basis of the population of a state rather than its wealth. This meant that if New York had 30 percent of income but only 10 percent of the population, only 10 percent of an income tax's revenue could come from New York. This provision did not prevent Congress from passing a federal income tax during the Civil War. It expired in 1872, but in 1895, Congress passed a law taxing all personal and corporate income. In a narrow five-to-four decision, the Supreme Court ruled that the income tax was unconstitutional because it was not apportioned among the states by population. Congress responded by approving the Sixteenth Amendment in 1909, and the amendment became part of the Constitution in 1913 after three-fourths of the states ratified it. In the same year, the Revenue Act imposed rates from 1 to 6 percent on incomes and a 1 percent rate on corporate incomes. Rates were raised in World War I but cut again in the 1920s, when Treasury Secretary Andrew Mellon argued that reducing taxes on the rich would stimulate economic growth, an argument revived in the form of "supply-side economics" during the Reagan era that began in 1981.

THE MONEY TRUST

As governor of New Jersey, Wilson argued in 1911: "The great monopoly in this country is the money monopoly." This was an absurd statement, given the existence of thousands of legally privileged and protected unit banks, but one that appealed to the Jeffersonian and Jacksonian prejudices of the largely southern and western Democratic Party of his time.

A southern Democrat, Louisiana congressman Arsène Pujo, used his subcommittee of the House Banking and Currency Committee to investigate Wall Street's role in American finance. In December 1912, Morgan was forced to testify before the Pujo Committee. With the aid of committee counsel Samuel Untermyer, a progressive lawyer, the Pujo Committee issued its report on February 28, 1913. According to the report, American industry and finance were dominated by associates of J. P. Morgan, including the investment banking firms Kidder, Peabody; Lee, Higginson; National City Bank; and First National Bank.

Brandeis drew on the Pujo Committee hearings in a series of essays in *Harper's Weekly* and a book, *Other People's Money: And How the Bankers Use It* (1914). Brandeis argued that the leaders of three banks—J. P. Morgan, George F. Baker at First National, and James Stillman at National City Bank—were at the center of a "money trust" that had captured the American economy. Brandeis complained that members of J. P. Morgan and Co. had seventy-two directorships in forty-seven of America's largest corporations, while Baker and his First National colleagues served on forty-nine boards, and Stillman and his colleagues at National City served on forty-eight. George F. Baker, a Morgan partner who was also head of First National Bank, sat on the boards of six railroads that owned 90 percent of Pennsylvania anthracite coal. Membership by bankers on corporate boards has been commonplace and uncontroversial in other countries, including the democratic Federal Republic of Germany after 1945. But Brandeis insisted: "The practice of interlocking directorates is the root of many evils. It offends laws human and divine. It is the most potent instrument of the Money Trust."[46]

BETWEEN THE NEW NATIONALISM AND THE NEW FREEDOM

Veering between the poles of the New Nationalism and the New Freedom, federal antitrust policy set by courts and executive branch officials produced an incoherent pattern, producing uncertainty for American businesses and investors. Supreme Court rulings in *E. C. Knight* (1895) and *Addyston Pipe and Steel* (1898) suggested that the Sherman Act would not be used by the federal judiciary to block mergers. However, the Supreme Court created confusion in 1904 by ordering the dissolution of Northern Securities—a holding company created with the help of J. P. Morgan to merge the Great Northern and Northern Pacific railroads. The court found an intent to restrain trade and forced a breakup.

The Supreme Court ordered that American Tobacco and Standard Oil be broken up as well. The penalty against Standard Oil was the equivalent of half the money coined by the US government in a year. Mark Twain responded to news of the fine by quoting the bride on the morning after her wedding night: "I expected it but didn't suppose it would be so big."[47] Then in 1920, the court decided in favor of US Steel, even though its president, Elbert Gary, had made no secret of his company's cooperation with other firms in stabilizing prices in the industry, at meetings known as "Gary dinners."

The Supreme Court announced a "rule of reason," but from the beginning US antitrust policy has lacked rhyme and reason. The fact that the United States was the only leading industrial nation that repeatedly harassed and sought to destroy many of its successful industrial enterprises merely on account of their scale can be explained only by the lingering residues of preindustrial Jeffersonian ideology in the radically different circumstances of industrial America.

As the second decade of the twentieth century began, both the New Nationalism and the New Freedom could claim victories in the struggle to shape the emerging American economy based on the technologies of the second industrial revolution. US entry into World War I would shift the balance of power in favor of the New Nationalism, leaving a legacy that would shape American institutions for generations.

THE NEW ERA

We are passing from a period of extremely individualistic action into a period of associational activities.

—Herbert Hoover, 1924[1]

Addressing a special session of Congress on April 2, 1917, President Woodrow Wilson called on Congress to declare war on Germany: "With a profound sense of the solemn and even tragical character of the step I am taking and of the grave responsibilities which it involves, but in unhesitating obedience to what I deem my constitutional duty, I advise that the Congress declare the recent course of the Imperial German Government to be in fact nothing less than war against the Government and people of the United States; that it formally accept the status of belligerent which has thus been thrust upon it, and that it take immediate steps not only to put the country in a more thorough state of defense but also to exert all its power and employ all its resources to bring the Government of the German Empire to terms and end the war."

On April 6, Congress voted for war. American participation in World War I was brief, lasting only between April 1917 and the armistice declared on November 11, 1918, but it was decisive in bringing about the defeat of Germany and its allies.

After the imposition of a draft on May 18, 1917, the US Army of 200,000 rapidly expanded. Ultimately a total of nearly five million Americans served in uniform during the war. Two million American troops were sent to Europe. Of those, 53,400 were killed, a fraction of the thirteen million lost by the other powers combined.

US industrial production tipped the balance in World War I, as it did in World War II. In 1914, US gross domestic produce (GDP) was greater than the combined GDP of Germany, Britain, and France. The US accounted for 32 percent of global manufacturing, Germany for 14 percent. When the war began in 1914, Britain, France, and the other Allied powers had 28 percent of the world's manufacturing capacity, compared to 19 percent for Germany and its allies, the Central Powers. When the United States joined the war in April 1917 on the side of the Allies, the Allied share rose to 52 percent of the global total.[2]

Around a quarter of America's workforce, 9.4 million out of 37 million, took part in production for war.[3] All Americans were affected by the lasting changes produced by the wartime mobilization of America's industrial resources and financial sector. As a result of the war, the progressive income tax became a permanent pillar of federal taxation.

An even more important legacy of World War I was the wartime partnership between the federal government and self-regulating trade associations in many industries. This experience of public-private collaboration inspired the associationalist movement led by Secretary of Commerce Herbert Hoover during the 1920s. The institutions and methods of World War I also inspired the responses to the Great Depression undertaken by both Hoover and Franklin Roosevelt in the 1930s. The spirit of the War Industries Board, the War Finance Committee, and other agencies of World War I would be reincarnated in multiple forms from the 1920s until the late twentieth century. The organization of the American economy during World War I is a key to understanding the reorganization of the American economy in the generations that followed.[4]

GERMAN-AMERICAN RIVALRY: PRELUDE TO WAR

Few subjects in American history are more contested than the US entry into World War I. For generations, some have denounced the American effort as a tragic and unnecessary war, engineered by Wall Street financiers to make sure that their loans to Britain, France, and other combatants would be paid. Others have dismissed material factors and explained American participation in the conflict as a tragic mistake caused by Woodrow Wilson's utopian vision of a liberal international order.

But geopolitical strategy, not corruption or idealism, motivated America's participation. The entry of the United States into the war in April 1917 was the culmination of a deepening rivalry between the United States and Imperial Germany that dated back to the 1880s.

When the German states outside of the Hapsburg monarchy were unified under Prussia's Hohenzollern dynasty by Otto von Bismarck in 1871, the newly united Germany immediately became the most populous and powerful state in Europe. Worried about provoking the antagonism of Germany's neighbors, Bismarck favored a cautious foreign policy. But he was dismissed in 1890 by the young Kaiser William II, who wanted Germany to be not just first among several European powers but a "world power." Even before 1900, Germany was viewed as a threat by the powers that would form an alliance twice in the twentieth century to defeat it—Russia, Britain, France, and the United States.

The American naval imperialism of the late 1800s and early 1900s was in part a response to Germany's drive to obtain naval bases in the Caribbean, Mexico and Central America, and the Pacific. The United States clashed with Germany over Samoa, and one motivation for the Spanish-American War of 1898, which led to US domination of Cuba, and annexation of Puerto Rico and the Philippines, along with Hawaii, was to deny potential island bases to the German navy.

In 1902, Germany, Britain, and Italy blockaded Venezuela to punish the country for not paying creditors among their citizens. In his 1904 annual address to Congress, Theodore Roosevelt announced the Roosevelt Corollary to the Monroe Doctrine—the United States would intervene in the region on behalf of extrahemispheric parties, when necessary. Although presented as a public service to other countries, the purpose of the Roosevelt Corollary was to deny Germany the ability to use controversies involving its citizens and businesses as a pretext for military intervention near US borders. The United States intervened in the Dominican Republic (1916–1924), Haiti (1915–1934), and Nicaragua (1912–1933). In 1917, the United States purchased the Virgin Islands from Denmark.

To impress the other great powers with America's new blue-water power-projection capabilities, President Theodore Roosevelt sent a US battle fleet, the "great white fleet," around the world from 1907 to 1909. Roosevelt also fulfilled the generations-old dream of a Central American canal, which would allow the US fleet to move forces more easily from the Atlantic to the Pacific, in the event of future overseas wars, with Germany and Japan regarded as the most likely opponents. A French attempt to build a canal through the Panama region of Colombia had begun in 1880 but had been abandoned because of the difficulties and the high mortality rate among workers caused by yellow fever and malaria. In 1902, with the help of the US Navy, rebels in Panama backed by the Roosevelt administration won their independence from Colombia and negotiated a treaty with the US. Chief Engineer Colonel George Washington Goethals of the US Army Corps of Engineers directed construction of the canal. More than five thousand workers died of disease, but the numbers were a fraction of those who had died during the earlier French attempt, thanks to Dr. Walter Reed's promotion of screening, sanitation, and other programs to combat mosquito-borne diseases. Begun in 1904, the "big ditch" was completed two years ahead of schedule in 1914—the year that World War I began.

The Mexican Revolution that erupted in 1911 turned into a proxy war between the United States and Imperial Germany. In order to minimize the United States as a factor in future conflicts in Europe or Asia, Germany sought to tie American forces down on the southwestern border. Germany armed General Victoriano Huerta, one of the rival Mexican leaders. To prevent a German arms shipment to Huerta's forces from arriving, the Wilson administration occupied Veracruz in April 1914. Huerta died in a jail in El Paso, Texas, in 1916, having been arrested for violating US neutrality laws by negotiating with German agents in New York.

American neutrality in the first years of World War I was little more than a pretense. The United States accepted the British blockade of

German-controlled Europe, but denounced German submarine warfare for interrupting the supplies streaming to Britain and France from the "neutral" United States. After German submarines sank the *Lusitania* in 1915 and the *Sussex* in 1916, killing American citizens aboard, President Wilson in 1916 threatened to sever diplomatic relations with Germany. To forestall direct US intervention, Germany ended submarine warfare for a time.

President Wilson hoped that the United States, as a neutral, could use its good offices to broker a peace acceptable to all sides, along the lines of Wilson's Fourteen Points, a visionary plan for a peaceful postwar world. Wilson was reelected in November 1916 in part because "he kept us out of war." But in 1917, Germany resumed submarine warfare to cut off American aid to Britain. In the hope of tying down the United States along the border, the German ambassador to Mexico, Arthur Zimmerman, encouraged Mexico to attack the United States. The Zimmerman telegram, intercepted and decoded by Britain and publicized in the American press, outraged the American public, which supported Congress's declaration of war against Germany on April 6, 1917.

THE HOUSE OF MORGAN GOES TO WAR

Between January 1915 and April 1917, when the United States entered the war, J. P. Morgan and Company acted as the exclusive purchasing agent in the United States for the governments of Britain and France.[5] To carry out its procurement duties, the House of Morgan created an export department that purchased and shipped arms and supplies. The department was headed by Edward R. Stettinius, formerly the president of the Diamond Match Company. Stettinius went on to work for General Motors and US Steel, to administer the lend-lease program during World War II, and to serve as secretary of state for presidents Franklin D. Roosevelt and Harry S. Truman from 1944 to 1945.

During the war, US trade with the Allies expanded rapidly, growing from $825 million in 1914 to $3.2 billion in 1916, while trade with Germany and Austria-Hungary collapsed from $169.3 million to $1.16 million.[6] As American exports to the Allies boomed, J. P. Morgan accounted for a large share—84 percent of American exports of war materials and munitions and 21 percent of overall US exports.[7] The House of Morgan also arranged for private loans to Britain and France. In total, between January 1915 and April 1917, the Allies borrowed $2.6 billion, of which $2.1 billion went to Britain and France, while Canada and Australia received $405 million, and Russia and Italy $75 million.[8]

A member of the firm observed that the functions carried out by J. P. Morgan "assumed in many of their aspects a governmental rather than a commercial character."[9] When the United States formally entered the war in April 1917, the Wilson administration spurned offers of help by the Morgan leadership and public lending by the federal government replaced private lending.

In the 1920s and 1930s, isolationists like North Dakota senator Gerald P. Nye accused J. P. Morgan and other "merchants of death" of dragging the United States into an unnecessary war in order to assure the repayment of their loans. War profiteering presumably explained the fortune of the wealthy guardian of the popular cartoon character Little Orphan Annie. His name was Daddy Warbucks.

PAYING FOR WAR

In all the United States spent $38 billion in World War I. The government paid for the war by a combination of borrowing (61.4 percent), taxation (24.5 percent), and the creation of new money (14.1 percent).[10]

Secretary of the Treasury William Gibbs McAdoo sponsored rallies across the country featuring actors and other celebrities to encourage Americans to buy bonds. Between May 1917 and April 1919, the US government, replacing J. P. Morgan and other private lenders, provided the Allies with four Liberty Loans and a postwar Victory Loan, with a total amount of $9.6 billion.

The contribution of taxes in paying for World War I was lower than in the Civil War but higher than in World War II.[11] As a percentage of

US GNP, wartime spending peaked in the last quarter of 1918 at 28.6 percent.[12] As in World War II a generation later, tax revenues came primarily from progressive income taxes and corporate income and excess profits taxes.

To pay for the war, the government taxed the rich heavily. The Emergency Revenue Act of 1916 increased the income tax. The highest personal income tax rate, levied on incomes greater than $1 million, rose from 10.3 percent in 1916 to 70.3 percent in 1918. On top of this was added a surcharge on incomes over $20,000 with a maximum of 13 percent, raising the effective income tax of the richest Americans to 15 percent. Other taxes on the wealthy took the form of increased estate taxes and corporate income taxes.[13]

THE WAR INDUSTRIES BOARD

One participant in the mobilization effort, Howard E. Coffin, vice president of the Hudson Motor Car Company, explained, "Twentieth century warfare demands that the blood of the soldier must be mingled with from three to five parts of the sweat of the man in the factories, mills, mines, and fields of the nation in arms."[14]

Following America's entry into the war, in July 1917, the National Defense Advisory Committee, created in August 1916, was replaced by the War Industries Board (WIB). Initially the mandate of the WIB was not clear, and the War Department and other government agencies continued with their own independent procurement policies. The chaos that resulted threatened the war effort by the winter of 1917–1918. In March 1918, President Wilson empowered the WIB to direct the mobilization of the economy as a whole.

To head the WIB, President Wilson turned to Bernard Mannes Baruch. Born in Camden, New Jersey, in 1870, Baruch was the son of a German immigrant who attended South Carolina Medical College and Richmond's Medical College of Virginia and became a Confederate Army surgeon on the staff of Robert E. Lee. His mother was a proud

Confederate and Baruch, whose Southern accent formed before his family moved to New York when he was ten, kept in touch with his southern roots by buying a huge estate in South Carolina, called Hobscaw Barony.

After graduating from the City College of New York in 1889, Baruch worked as a runner for Wall Street firms and worked his way up from broker to partner in A. A. Housman and Company, becoming a millionaire by his thirtieth birthday. He and his brother Hartwig formed Baruch Brothers and bought a commodity firm, Hentz and Company, with New York, Paris, London, and Berlin offices. Baruch left Baruch Brothers to become an independent speculator. As an adviser to Wilson, Franklin D. Roosevelt, Truman, and other presidents, Baruch became known as the "park bench statesman" after a favorite park bench in Lafayette Park across from the White House in Washington, DC.

To mobilize the wartime economy, the WIB under Baruch organized fifty-seven commodity sections to deal with particular industries. The government's commodity sections worked with around three hundred semiofficial war service committees organized by businesses and certified by the US Chamber of Commerce.[15]

While the commodity sections worked with particular industries, the Priority Division of the WIB sought to overcome shortages. The WIB's Price Fixing Committee set the prices of critical materials such as iron, steel, rubber, and coke. The Conservation Division sought to eliminate waste by, among other things, reducing the varieties of products that American factories produced. The Conservation Division directed the automobile industry to reduce the number of styles of tires from 287 to 9 in two years.[16]

The WIB and its commodity sections tended to be staffed by executives from the relevant industries, many of them "dollar-a-year men" who volunteered for no pay. For example, the Automotive Products Section was headed by the treasurer of the Studebaker automobile company, Charles C. Hanch, while the Agricultural Implements and Wood Products Section was directed by Edward E. Parsonage, the manager of the John Deere Wagon Company.[17] The president of First National City

Bank, Frank A. Vanderlip, ran the War Savings Stamp campaign, while Charles M. Schwab of Bethlehem Steel ran the Emergency Fleet Corporation.

The blurring of lines between the government and corporate sectors by these dollar-a-year men aroused the wrath of Jeffersonian populists and leftists in World War I and again in World War II. But in the absence of an enormous, permanent, experienced federal bureaucracy capable of performing the task, the United States had little choice but to rely on corporate executives in its mobilization efforts.

MOBILIZING THE ECONOMY FOR WAR

In addition to the WIB, a number of other agencies were established to mobilize the US economy for war. The War Finance Corporation was established in March 1918 by the same law that created the Capital Issues Committee. The War Finance Corporation funded industries, while the Capital Issues Committee reviewed the issuance of new securities.

The US Fuel Administration, created in August 1917, sought to conserve energy by means of "heatless Mondays" and "gasless Sundays." One of the Fuel Administration's energy-saving measures became a permanent part of American life: daylight savings time.[18]

In September 1916, the US Shipping Board was created to supervise a crash program of ship acquisition. Its head, Edward Hurley, a retired businessman, appointed Schwab to run the Emergency Fleet Corporation, which created an enormous American fleet from practically nothing by the end of the war, albeit at the price of great waste and enormous delays. In the winter of 1917–1918, the railroads were nationalized under the US Railroad Administration, headed by Treasury Secretary McAdoo.

Before World War I, German firms dominated the production of synthetic organic chemicals such as dyes and related pharmaceuticals. When the war halted the supply of German chemicals to the United States, key American policymakers, manufacturers, and chemists sought to build a domestic industry, and to that end German chemical patents were confiscated by the Office of Alien Property.

To prevent labor strife from crippling the war effort, Congress and the Wilson administration created the National War Labor Board in April 1918, cochaired by Frank P. Walsh, the former chairman of the Commission on Industrial Relations, and former president William Howard Taft. Strikes were punished by federal raids of union offices and arrests of labor leaders. In general, however, organized labor benefited from wartime arrangements. Between 1916 and 1918 union membership grew from three million to four million and real wages in 1918 were 4 percent higher than they had been in 1914.[19]

HOOVERIZING

President Wilson appointed Herbert Hoover as the head of the US Food Administration. The future commerce secretary and president of the United States had already become an international celebrity before the United States entered the war.

Born into a Quaker family in Iowa in 1874, Hoover lost both of his parents by the age of ten and was raised by relatives in Oregon. He was part of the inaugural class of Stanford University, where he met his wife, Lou. Hoover grew rich from the mining business in China and Australia. He was living and working in London when World War I began. To aid the famine-stricken Belgians, Hoover used his own business organization, winning the right for his relief ships to pass through the British blockade without being sunk by German submarines.

Hoover was a hero on both sides of the Atlantic when Wilson appointed him to head agricultural production in the United States after the United States entered the war in 1917. Hoover sought to work through state and private organizations to minimize waste and maximize production. He led a nationwide propaganda campaign for the "wheatless kitchen," encouraging the use of wheat substitutes like potato flour and oatmeal.[20] Food conservation was called "Hooverizing," a phrase later used to mock then-president Hoover during the early years of the Great Depression.

When the war ended, Hoover's Food Administration fed millions in Europe, among the defeated nations as well as the victors. Despite his opposition to communism, he saved millions of Soviet citizens from starving, declaring, "Twenty million people are starving. Whatever their politics, they will be fed."[21]

A LEGACY OF COOPERATION

Following the armistice declared on November 11, 1918, the Wilson administration and Congress moved to rapidly demobilize the economy. An attempt to create a peacetime version of the WIB, the Industrial Board, collapsed because of opposition by the public and the Wilson administration by spring of 1919.[22] The War Finance Corporation existed on a small scale in the 1920s, with a new mission of financing exports.[23]

In his book *American Industry in the War*, Bernard Baruch held forth the cooperative economy of World War I as a model for the future: "We have been gradually compelled to drift away from the old doctrine of Anglo-American law, that the sphere of Government should be limited to preventing breach of contract, fraud, physical injury, and injury to property, and that the Government should exercise protection only over non-competent persons. The modern industrial processes have been rendering it increasingly necessary for the Government to reach out its arm to protect competent individuals against the discriminating practices of mass industrial power."[24]

To maximize cooperation in industry, antitrust standards were relaxed during the war, marking the achievement of a longtime goal of many conservative business executives and progressive nationalists alike. Experience under the War Industries Board had made not only the big companies that dominated the Chamber of Commerce but also the small firms of the National Association of Manufacturers enthusiastic about extending the relaxation of antitrust laws into peacetime.[25]

In the words of the historian Eric Goldman, "Many of the dollar-a-year men went back to their fifty-thousand-dollar-a-year jobs with an idea buzzing in their heads. . . . Why not give up the talk about competition and draw firms together in trade associations, which would standardize products, pool information, advertising, insurance, traffic, and purchases, and draw up codes of proper practices?"[26] Between 1919 and 1929, the number of national trade associations grew from around seven hundred to more than two thousand.

THE MODEL T

Although the electric motor, the internal combustion engine, and other transformative technologies of the second industrial revolution had been invented decades before, it was only in the 1920s that the second industrial era reached maturity. Its symbol was Henry Ford's mass-produced automobile, the Model T.

Most of the early cars in the United States were propelled by electric batteries or steam engines. Among the latter were the Stanley Steamers produced by the Stanley Motor Carriage Company from 1902 to 1924, when it went out of business after warning in advertisements against "the internal explosion engine." Gasoline, previously a waste product produced by refining oil for illumination, prevailed as the source of energy for cars because of the light weight and versatility of gasoline-fueled engines. Gasoline surpassed kerosene as the leading oil product sold in 1911.[27] Initially, gasoline sold in cans in general stores or grocery stores. The first service station or filling station opened in 1907 in Saint Louis.

The earliest American automobiles were manufactured chiefly in New England. But the Midwest became the center of US automobile production, in part because it had an abundance of engineers who had begun in the bicycle industry.

One of them was Henry Ford. Born on a farm in Detroit, Ford began his career by working as a machinist for companies including Westinghouse and the Edison Illuminating Company, where he rose to the rank of chief engineer in 1893. When Thomas Edison died, Ford urged one of those at his deathbed to catch his dying breath in a test tube. Long before that moment, however, the breath of inspiration had passed from Edison to Ford.

Ford built his first car, the Ford Quadricycle, in 1896. Encouraged by Edison, Ford improved the vehicle and formed a company with a local Michigan capitalist, William H. Murphy. Disagreements led to Ford's resignation from the company, which was renamed the Cadillac Automobile Company, and his founding of Ford Motor Company in 1903, with the backing of John and Horace Dodge and a coal dealer named Alexander Malcolmson.

With the Model T, a simple, versatile, standardized car, Ford created the first car for the masses in 1908. The first Model T was offered for sale on October 1, 1908. Standardization reduced its cost. Because black paint dried quickly, Ford is alleged to have said that customers could have a Model T in any color, as long as it was black (in fact, Model Ts came in different colors).

The United States surpassed France in automobile production in 1906 and by 1910 produced more cars than the rest of the world combined.[28] Between 1909 and 1925, the price of a Ford Model T dropped from $950 to $250.[29] The number of automobiles in the United States rose from a few thousand in 1900 to millions in the 1920s. In 1915, there had been one car for every two hundred Americans; by 1920, there was one for every ten.[30] By the end of the 1920s, there was one car for every five Americans.[31] In 1920, half of the world's automobiles were Model Ts.[32]

THE RISE OF DETROIT

The success of one major technology of the second industrial era, the internal combustion engine, depended on the development of another: electricity. The automobile industry was the most important industry to be transformed by electric power.

Henry Ford became the leading capitalist of his age because of his process as well as his product. In 1913, Ford and his colleagues perfected the moving assembly line, putting cars together on electric conveyor belts in enormous factories. In 1925, Ford's spokesman William J. Cameron drafted an article on mass production for the *Encyclopaedia Britannica* that was published under Ford's name, although Cameron said later that he "should be very surprised to learn that [Ford] had read it."[33] According to the entry, "Mass production is not merely quantity production, for this may be had with none of the requisites of mass production. Nor is it merely machine production, which also may exist without any resemblance to mass production. Mass production is the focusing upon a manufacturing project of the principles of power, accuracy, system, continuity, and speed."[34]

The automobile created enormous demand for the products of other industries, such as petroleum, steel, rubber, glass, felt, and paint, and produced entirely new service industries, ranging from gas stations to motels. As Rockefeller had done in oil and Carnegie in steel, Ford used vertical integration to control every aspect of production from raw materials to finished products, substituting administration within a giant corporation for market transactions among suppliers of goods and services. Built on two thousand acres of land at the conjunction of the Rouge River and the Detroit River, Ford's River Rouge plant fed coke, steel, and iron furnaces and assembly buildings with raw materials from the iron mines, coal mines, forests, and rubber plantations owned by the company and shipped by Ford's own fleet of freighters to the docks, where they were transferred throughout the complex along the hundreds of miles of an internal railroad system and road system. Ford sought to control all stages of input, all the way to rubber plantations in Latin America. His River Rouge plant had its own hospital and fire department—as well as its own police force, the notorious Service Department that was deployed in conflicts with striking workers.

Before World War I, Ford had subsidiaries in Canada and Britain. After the war the Ford Motor Company made automobiles in continental Europe, India, and the Soviet Union. Among other things, Ford pioneered the multinational corporation.

Like other innovative industries, the young automobile industry was populated by many startups; fifty new companies went into the business in a single year in 1902.[35] The automobile industry soon evolved into an oligopoly.

The reign of the Model T lasted less than a decade. In the 1920s, General Motors surpassed Ford as America's major carmaker. Formed from the merger of Oldsmobile, Buick, Pontiac, Chevrolet, and Cadillac, which became divisions of the new company, General Motors was headed by Alfred P. Sloan, who served as CEO from 1923 to 1946. Sloan sought to differentiate the market by providing different models for different income groups and advertising new models each year to encourage frequent replacement. The result was another American commercial innovation— "planned obsolescence."

THE HOUSE OF INSULL

The creator of the major commercial electrical-transmission empire, Samuel Insull, like Henry Ford, was a protégé of Thomas Edison. After Insull went to work for one of Edison's agents in Britain, Edison noticed him and hired him to be his secretary in 1881 at the age of twenty-two. By 1889, Insull was vice president of Edison General Electric in Schenectady, New York, and in 1892, when J. P. Morgan took control of the Edison companies, Insull was assigned to head Chicago Edison.

Originally customers of electrical utilities in the United States were charged by the number of bulbs that they used in homes or businesses. During a trip to his native Britain in 1894, Insull was surprised to find the coastal resort town of Brighton lit up at night, and discovered that the local power plant had invented a meter to measure how much each home or business used. Returning to Chicago, Insull introduced the meter to the US electrical industry.[36]

Surviving shakedowns by Chicago's famously felonious political class, Insull flourished. By 1910, Commonwealth Edison Company, formed from the merger of nearly two dozen private utilities, was the world's leading utility company. Insull took control of Chicago's electric trolley lines, consolidating them into the Chicago Rapid Transit Company (CRT) or "L" (for elevated). Insull's Middle West Utility Corporation grew by absorbing hundreds of electric-transit companies and electric utilities that became known as the House of Insull.

Insull's empire was based on holding companies that evaded state regulations, at a time when there was no federal regulation. The holding companies were highly leveraged. They would prove vulnerable to downturns in the stock market and Insull would lose his business, his fortune, and his reputation in the Depression. But in the 1920s, the private electric-utility industry flourished, evolving into an oligopoly in which, by 1932, the eight biggest utility holding companies controlled 73 percent of the private electrical power industry. By the mid-1920s, the House of Insull, with 600,000 shareholders, controlled one-eighth of the electricity and natural gas used in the United States.[37]

MA BELL

While the automobile and electric power industries evolved into mature oligopolies, another industry based on a technology of the second industrial revolution, the telephone industry, became an outright monopoly in the United States. Here, too, J. P. Morgan played a critical role.

Appropriately enough, Theodore Vail, the mastermind of telephone monopoly, spent much of his early career as a bureaucrat in Washington, where he rose to be general superintendent of Railway Mail Service. Appointed general manager of Bell Telephone in 1878, he retired in 1888, after he was passed over for president of American Bell. In 1907, when J. P. Morgan obtained control of the board of directors of AT&T, Vail was brought back from retirement. With Morgan's backing, Vail set about realizing his ambitious vision of "One system, one policy and universal service."

Although Vail retired in 1919 and died the following year, his vision of AT&T as a public utility became the basis of the American telephone system until the 1980s. The Bell System was divided into a long-distance service and regional companies. Small telephone companies continued to exist, mostly in rural areas, but for all practical purposes the company that tried to endear itself to the public as "Ma Bell" was *the* telephone company for Americans for most of the twentieth century. Along with US Steel and General Electric, Ma Bell was one of the corporate leviathans that arose from the technologies of the second industrial revolution and the finance capitalism of J. P. Morgan.

EDISON AND THE MOVIE TRUST

Not all of the consolidated enterprises in industries based on the new technologies of the second industrial revolution could be justified by the efficiencies provided by increasing returns to scale or network effects. Some were old-fashioned predatory monopolies. That was the case with Thomas Edison's movie trust.

Motion picture technology was developed simultaneously by a number of inventors on both sides of the Atlantic. William Kennedy Laurie Dickson and others on Edison's laboratory staff developed a motion picture camera, the Kinetograph, and the Kinetoscope, a viewer with a peephole that evolved into the nickelodeon, a popular attraction at carnivals and fairgrounds. In addition to manufacturing the equipment, the Edison Manufacturing Company began to produce films, most of them short features showing celebrities, news events, disasters, and curiosities. Movie producers soon began to produce more ambitious, longer films, such as *The Great Train Robbery* in 1904.

In 1908, Edison created the Motion Picture Patents Company (MPPC), a cartel uniting Eastman Kodak, the major supplier of film, and the distributor George Kleine, with eight motion picture companies in addition to Edison's own. Unlike railroads, steel, oil, or other mass-production industries in which cartelization could be defended, the motion picture industry was an industry with low fixed costs and low barriers to entry in which monopolies and cartels were likely to be predatory. Independent filmmakers, many of them Jewish immigrants who had started in the nickelodeon business, were harassed when they refused to pay licensing fees to the motion picture trust. In order to escape adverse court judgments in New Jersey, many of the independents moved to California, where the legal climate as well as the weather for filming was more favorable, and founded Hollywood. In 1915, a federal court ruled that the MPPC violated federal antitrust law. In Hollywood, some of the independents, including Karl Laemmle, Adolf Zukor, and Louis B. Mayer, became "movie moguls" whose studio oligopoly proved to be as hostile to independent filmmakers as Edison's movie trust had been.

FROM PIGGLY WIGGLY TO A&P

In the late nineteenth century, the railroad and the telegraph had created new kinds of distributors, including mail-order companies like Sears, Roebuck. In the early twentieth century, technology-driven commercial change produced dramatic innovations in how goods were bought and sold.

One innovation was self-service. In 1916, Clarence Saunders of Memphis, Tennessee, founded a chain of innovative grocery stores in which customers, instead of asking clerks for items kept behind the counter, would use baskets to pick up items marked with prices from the shelves directly. By reducing staff costs, the Piggly Wiggly chain allowed savings to be passed on to customers.

Another innovation was the department store. Some, including Macy's and Bloomingdale's in New York, began as small retail shops that grew, while others, such as Marshall Field and Company in Chicago, were the retail branches of companies that did most of their business in wholesale.

Then there were the chain stores. The greatest of these was A&P, founded by George F. Gilman as the Great American Tea Company. With his partner George Hartford, Gilman had established more than a hundred stores by 1880. The name was later changed to the Great Atlantic and Pacific Tea Company. Expanding into groceries, A&P created the "economy store," with no home delivery, in 1913. Following Gilman's retirement, George and John Hartford took over. By 1929, A&P had fifteen thousand stores and made more money than Sears, Montgomery Ward, and J. C. Penney combined.[38]

The first "dime store," in which nothing cost more than a dime—which went considerably further in those days, to be sure—was established by Frank W. Woolworth in Lancaster, Pennsylvania, in 1879. Woolworth's grew into another national chain.

The older mail-order businesses that survived were forced to adapt to the new world of car-based suburbs that was appearing even before World War II. Robert Wood Johnson, a former army general who worked for Montgomery Ward, argued that urbanization meant that the company should shift its focus from mail-order catalogs to retail outlets. For his prescience he was fired by Montgomery Ward, but he was hired by Sears, Roebuck, which he persuaded to buy large areas of land on the outskirts of cities for stores and parking lots.

The enormous cash flows of mail-order stores, department stores, and chain stores made it unnecessary for them to raise large sums by issuing stock. Unlike in the large industrial companies of the time, control tended to remain in the hands of the founding families such as the Hartfords of A&P, the Woolworths, the Wanamakers, and the Gimbels.

Small-town distributors were threatened by the innovative national retailers. As the largest retailer in the United States, A&P drew hostility similar to that directed at Walmart nearly a century later. Representative Wright Patman of Texas, a Jeffersonian populist, sought to destroy it with the Robinson-Patman Act, which tried to prevent chains from getting lower prices from manufacturers in order to charge less to consumers. When Patman next tried to pass a law imposing a federal tax on chain stores, he failed. A&P successfully defended itself by allowing the unionization of its workforce in 1938, thereby gaining organized labor as a constituency, and by skillfully wooing consumer groups and cooperatives.

FROM PRODUCERS TO CONSUMERS

In the new era of mass consumer demand for mass-produced goods, a new industry evolved in the United States: advertising. Appropriately, the American advertising industry was pioneered by Edward Bernays, a nephew of Sigmund Freud who applied his uncle's insights into psychology to commercial advertising. Supported by advertising, radio became the first of the mass media, bringing a common popular culture into homes otherwise divided by region and class. The "consumer," a type hardly heard of a generation before, began to replace the small producer as the symbol of middle-class America.

Consumer durables, of which the automobile was the most important, made up four-fifths of the growth in GNP in the decade between 1919 and 1929.[39] Consumer credit was another innovation that spread rapidly in the 1920s. A. P. Giannini, the son of Italian immigrants in California, pioneered installment loans, thereby turning his tiny Bank of Italy into what at his death was the nation's largest bank, the Bank of America. Many of America's small one-office unit banks, however, lost much of the business of consumer lending to specialized consumer lenders and companies that financed customer purchases.

BIG BUSINESS, MANAGEMENT, AND WALL STREET

Partly in response to antitrust laws, many industrial corporations adopted "vertical integration," solving the problem of coordination by bringing a variety of activities and every stage of the production process into a single, complex, hierarchical institution. Because such bureaucratic behemoths could not be run by a single entrepreneur, a new class of professional managers and a new discipline of scientific management developed in the late nineteenth and early twentieth centuries.

While ceding control over day-to-day operations to professional managers, the founders of industrial empires like Rockefeller and Carnegie found themselves relying on the developing stock market. The separation of ownership and control evolved as a result of the decision of large firms to become publicly traded corporations, a decision that created a market for their securities in addition to railroad bonds and stocks. During the merger wave of the late 1890s and early 1900s, only 6 percent of industrial stocks were sold to the public. Forty-nine percent was exchanged for the stock of other firms in mergers and 45 percent was issued by corporations to their own shareholders.[40]

In the 1920s, the stock market expanded as companies sold stock to employees and customers. The number of stockholders increased from 4.4 million in 1900 to 18 million in 1928.[41] Already by the early 1900s, the ratings agencies Standard and Poor's and Moody's were performing the function of rating stocks for investors.

Frequently swindled, middle-class shareholders contributed to the rapid evolution of the stock market in the years before 1929.

WONDER BOY

Following the election of Herbert Hoover to the presidency in 1928, President Calvin Coolidge, asked to make a decision, reportedly replied, "We'll leave that to the Wonder Boy."

Wonder Boy was one nickname for Hoover. The Great Engineer was another. Vannevar Bush, the MIT engineer who more than anyone else created the post–World War II system of federally funded research, admired Hoover and called him the Chief.

When President Warren G. Harding offered Hoover a post in his administration, Hoover chose the Department of Commerce, converting what had been a small and poorly funded agency into a powerful central directorate of several administrations and the economy as a whole. His Commerce Department absorbed the Bureau of Customs Statistics from the Treasury Department, the statistical programs for the farm machinery, meatpacking, naval stores, and woolen industries from the Department of Agriculture, and the Bureau of Mines and the Patent Office from the Department of the Interior.[42] He also extended his influence over transportation, power and waterway development, and construction.[43] Hoover was described by one contemporary as "Secretary of Commerce and Under-Secretary of all other departments."[44]

"The only trouble with capitalism is capitalists. They're too damn greedy," Hoover observed.[45] During his first week in the White House, he complained that "excessive fortunes are a menace to true liberty."[46] In his 1922 book *American Individualism*, Hoover called for a "progressive individualism." "In our individualism we have long since abandoned the laissez faire of the 18th Century—the notion that it is 'every man for himself and the devil take the hindmost.'" According to Hoover, "We have learned that the impulse to production can be maintained at a high pitch only if there is a fair division of the product. We have also learned that fair division can only be obtained by certain restrictions on the strong and the dominant." Hoover wrote that progressive regulation in the early twentieth century was necessary because "we were threatened with a form of autocracy of economic power. Our mass of regulation of public utilities and trade is the monument to our intent to preserve an equality of opportunity. This regulation is itself proof that we have gone a long way toward the abandonment of the 'capitalism' of Adam Smith."[47]

Hoover overshadowed the secretaries of labor in the administrations in which he served. As secretary of commerce, Hoover was a convert to the "new economics" of wage-driven growth. In his memoirs, he wrote that "not so many years ago—the employer considered it was in his interest to use the opportunities of unemployment and immigration to lower wages irrespective of other considerations. . . . But we are a long way on the road to new conceptions. The very essence of great production is high wages and low prices, because it depends upon a widening . . . consumption, only to be obtained from the purchasing-power of high real wages and increased standards of living."[48]

Animated by a vision of a harmonious, high-wage capitalism, Hoover sought to persuade the railroad and coal companies to cooperate with labor and recommended private programs of unemployment insurance.[49] Hoover pressured Harding into meeting with American steel company presidents and urging them to drop the twelve-hour day for the eight-hour day.[50]

In the Hamiltonian tradition, Hoover championed American infrastructure and infant industries. He successfully campaigned for the Air Commerce Act to promote the infant American aviation industry, devised the system of regulation that would govern radio, and worked to stabilize the oil and coal industries. The Roosevelt administration later built on his efforts to promote an ambitious inland-waterway plan and the construction of hydroelectric dams. One was Boulder Dam or Boulder Canyon Dam, which Secretary of the Interior Ray Lyman Wilbur named Hoover Dam in 1930. Following Hoover's departure from office, Franklin Roosevelt's secretary of the interior, Harold Ickes, changed the name to Boulder Dam again. In 1947, the Republican Congress changed the name back to Hoover Dam.

Hoover's approach to public dams illustrates his idiosyncratic sense of the line between the public and the private. He supported public construction of dams and yet denounced the idea of sales of electrical power from publicly owned companies to the public as "fascism." True American individualism, according to Hoover, required that the power be sold to private middlemen, who would then resell the power to the public, after taking their cut.

ASSOCIATIONALISM

The term "associationalism" has been used by historians to describe what Hoover himself called "progressive democracy," the "Cooperative Committee and Conference System" and "the American System" (not to be confused with Henry Clay's nineteenth-century American System of import substitution, infrastructure investment, and national banking, or the nineteenth-century American system of manufacturing based on interchangeable parts).[51]

Associationalist ideas predated World War I. In his 1912 book *The New Competition*, Arthur Jerome Eddy inspired the open-price association movement, which encouraged firms in a particular business to publicize their prices and costs. This was regarded with suspicion by many as a way to circumvent laws against price-fixing.

As secretary of commerce, Hoover was sympathetic to the movement, but the Justice Department viewed open-price associations as attempts to fix prices in defiance of antitrust laws. When Attorney General Harry Daugherty was forced to resign in 1924 because of the Teapot Dome scandal, Hoover's relaxed approach to antitrust law prevailed.

Although they would become rivals for the presidency and bitter enemies, in the 1920s Hoover and Franklin Roosevelt were amicable veterans of the wartime Wilson administration. The two organized the American Construction Council, with Roosevelt as its president. Funded by 250 trade associations, the council under FDR favored standardization, planning by the industry, and moratoriums on building during speculative booms to smooth out boom-bust cycles. The council held annual conferences and published reports, including "Elimination of Construction Peaks and Depressions."

The Webb-Pomerene Act of 1918 allowed US companies to take part in cartels without fear of antitrust prosecution, as long as they did so only abroad. In the 1930s, nearly 19 percent of American exports originated with export associations organized under the Webb-Pomerene Act.[52] Four-fifths of Webb-Pomerene cartels fixed prices or allocated foreign markets among their members.[53]

Corporations had numerous motives for joining global cartels, in addition to stabilizing industries by fixing prices. One motive was sharing the overhead costs of marketing. Three out of five Webb-Pomerene cartels created a common sales agency to handle shipping, billing, and the taking of orders.[54] Joint marketing organizations were of particular benefit to small and medium-size businesses. In industries like canned milk, dried fruit, metal laths, milled rice, and paperboard, cartels helped American exports by allowing many American exporters to pool their efforts and reduce the costs of marketing by as much as 50 percent.[55] In high-tech industries like electricity and petrochemicals, cartels permitted competitors to share technological patents without mergers or duplication of expensive research.

In the years after World War I, Gerard Swope organized International General Electric (IGE) on behalf of General Electric to coordinate the company's foreign operations. In 1924, IGE and other companies formed the Phoebus cartel in the electric-lamp market. Each company that belonged to the cartel was assigned quotas in its home market and quotas for exports; members of the cartel that exceeded their quotas were fined. A Swiss corporation named Phoebus, after Apollo, the Greek god of light, monitored compliance.[56] Because General Electric and the Phoebus cartel began to substitute brighter and more energy-efficient but less long-lived bulbs for older ones, the cartel became the subject of an enduring conspiracy theory that it suppressed an "eternal light bulb."

THE GREAT MIGRATION

In 1921, supported by organized labor and an ethnic coalition of Anglo-Americans and the "old immigrants," German and Irish Americans, Congress enacted a national origins quota system. The system, made permanent in 1924, used the 1890 census, the last before the flood of "new immigrants" from Southern and Eastern Europe, in order to inflate the numbers of German and Irish as well as British immigrants who would be allowed in the United States. The United States would admit immigrants up to 2 percent of the number of people from a country who lived in the United States in 1890. Also in 1924, the shutdown of Asian immigration to the United States was completed. Under the national quota system that lasted, with modifications, until the Kennedy and Johnson administrations, immigrants from Northern and Western Europe received 82 percent of the annual quotas; immigrants from Southern and Eastern Europe, 14 percent; and immigrants from the rest of the world outside the Western Hemisphere received 4 percent.[57]

Wages rose in the tighter labor markets that immigration restriction produced. In 1938, looking back at the earlier era of mass immigration, economists Harry Millis and Royal Montgomery concluded that the leaders of organized labor had been correct to argue that "as labor markets were flooded, the labor supply was made more redundant, and wages were undermined."[58] In 1964, Stanley Lebergott concurred: "It [is] most unlikely that the rate of productivity advance or the nature of productivity advance changed so [much in the 1920s] as to explain [the spurt in real wage growth]. Instead we find that halting the flow of millions of migrants . . . offers a much more reasonable explanation."[59]

Black Americans benefited the most from the end of mass immigration, which opened up jobs that previously had gone to European immigrants. In the Great Migration, 1.6 million black Americans moved out of the South between 1910 and 1930 and another 5 million left in the period of low immigration between the 1940s and the 1970s. When the mass immigration of unskilled immigrants resumed in the 1970s, low-income black Americans in particular suffered from lowered wages and job competition.

FORDISM

The tight labor markets created by the restriction of mass immigration forced many employers to treat their workers better. Before World War I, corporate management relied on the brutal "drive" system, which assumed that workers had to be coerced. Foremen were charged with carrying out the system. The result had been frequent violence and high rates of turnover.

In the 1920s, progressive companies replaced the drive system with policies to boost morale among the workforce. Personnel managers were hired, to deal with grievances. Companies like General Electric experimented with "welfare capitalist" programs like employer-provided benefits to employees.

The smaller companies that made up the majority of American businesses, however, remained hostile to organized labor. Their representative, the National Association of Manufacturers, sponsored the American Plan, which successfully marginalized labor unions during the 1920s.

More than any other company, Ford was identified with a new era of high-wage capitalism. At a time when common laborers earned around $2.50 a day, Ford announced that he would share the profits of his company by paying the majority of his workers $5 a day. Although Ford's primary motive had been to reduce turnover in the workforce, what came to be known as "Fordism" was hailed around the world as a method of ensuring that mass demand kept up with mass production.

Despite his image as an enlightened employer, Ford viewed welfare capitalism as a way to avoid unionization. He provided company hospitals, newspapers, and even part-time farms for employees—and combined them with his notorious Service Department, headed by a former navy boxer named Harry Bennett, which spied on workers and harassed union members and organizers.

Around the world, Fordism became a symbol of the mass society, embraced by some, feared by others, and parodied by Aldous Huxley in his novel *Brave New World*, in which people in the future have replaced AD with AF (after Ford). Ford inspired Charlie Chaplin's movie *Modern Times* and Adolf Hitler's People's Car, or Volkswagen. Lenin and Stalin admired Ford's methods and sought to adopt them to a communist economy. For his part Ford, who hated bankers, was an anti-Semite who arranged the publication of anti-Semitic conspiracy theories in the company newspaper, the *Dearborn Independent*. His acceptance of a medal from the Nazi regime became an embarrassment and during World War II, Ford, a bitter opponent of the New Deal, helped the federal government mobilize American industry to defeat the Axis powers.

THE LIMITS OF FORDISM

Even with consumer credit innovations, the new consumer durables were unaffordable for as many as half of the households in the United States.[60] Like workers, consumers failed to share in the gains of rapid productivity growth. Despite productivity gains, American business as a whole did not practice Fordism in the 1920s. The reality was not mass consumption, but "class consumption." The market for the new consumer durables of the second industrial revolution was the most affluent Americans.

The electrification of American industry produced remarkable gains in productivity. In the early twentieth century, American industries quickly replaced steam engines with electric motors. Between 1914 and 1929, the use of electricity in industry rose from 30 to 70 percent.[61] In 1899, only 4 percent of machinery derived its power from electricity; in 1929, the figure had risen to 75 percent.[62] In the 1920s, horsepower per industrial worker grew by 50 percent.[63]

But while productivity increased 32 percent between 1923 and 1929, wages increased only 8 percent.[64] During the 1920s, productivity permitted a major expansion of manufacturing output without an increase in manufacturing employment. Manufacturing employed the same number of workers in 1929 as it had a decade earlier, in 1919.[65] Between 1923 and 1929, labor's share of income in manufacturing, mining, transportation, and utilities declined from 77.9 percent to 72.9 percent, while the share going to capital rose from 19.6 percent to 25.5 percent.[66] In the same period, the share of income received by the top 1 percent grew by 35 percent, from 13 percent of the total in 1923 to 19 percent in 1929. Overall, between 1923 and 1929, profits increased by 62 percent but wages increased only 11 percent.[67] The wages of unskilled workers underwent absolute decline.[68] Meanwhile, during most of the 1920s, the lower 95 percent of the nonfarm population experienced a slight decline in per capita income.[69] Only 8 percent of the population owned stocks and most stocks financed the expansion of holding companies rather than new capital formation.[70]

GLOBAL IMBALANCES

The maldistribution of income in the United States was accompanied by global imbalances that resulted in large part from the contradiction between America's post–World War I role as the world's major creditor and its inherited system of protectionism, which was retained long after it had succeeded in nurturing successful infant industries.

As early as the 1870s, the United States overtook Britain as the world's largest economy. In 1913, the United States had 35.8 percent of global manufacturing capacity: by 1926–1929, that had risen to 42.2 percent, outstripping Germany (11.6 percent), Britain (9.4 percent), France (6.6 percent), the Soviet Union (4.3 percent), and Japan (2.5 percent).[71]

By the 1900s, the high-tariff infant-industry policy adopted by the United States during its period of catch-up industrialization had served its purpose. As a mature industrial nation, the United States should have moved toward reciprocal trade liberalization through negotiations with other industrial countries. On September 5, 1901, the day before he was assassinated, President William McKinley in a speech at the Pan-American Exposition in Buffalo, New York, called for a shift in American economic strategy toward greater trade liberalization. Warning that "we must not repose in fancied security that we can forever sell everything and buy nothing," McKinley said, "We should take from our customers such of their products as we can use without harm to our industries and labor." His successor, Theodore Roosevelt, also favored a new policy of "reciprocity without injury."[72] However, the political power of protected industries ensured that between the 1880s and 1910, US import duties averaged 20 to 30 percent of the value of all imports and 40 to 50 percent of the value of all dutiable imports.

From 1866 to 1875, the United States ran trade deficits; from 1876 to 1940, the United States ran consistent trade surpluses. During World War I, the United States became the world's leading creditor nation as well as the world's leading exporter, fulfilling a prophecy made in 1902, at a eulogy for the assassinated President McKinley, by his secretary of state, John Hay, who had served Lincoln as a top aide: "The 'debtor nation' has become the chief creditor nation. The financial center of the world, which required thousands of years to journey from the Euphrates to the Thames and the Seine, seems passing to the Hudson between daybreak and dark."[73]

Following World War I, Britain owed the United States $4.7 billion and France owed $4 billion (France also owed Britain $3 billion). Other European countries owed the United States $3.2 billion; they owed Britain $8.1 billion and France $3.5 billion. At the same time, Germany owed enormous reparations to Britain and France, whose own economies had been weakened by war. Germany could not pay for those war debts by exporting goods to the United States, because of high American tariffs and superior American productivity in industry and agriculture. Like Germany, primary-product exporters such as Britain's dominions and the countries of Latin America owed huge debts. And like Germany, to service their debts these commodity-exporting countries needed either to run large trade surpluses with creditor nations or to attract new lending. But at a time when Europe and Latin America needed to export more to the United States, imports as a share of American GDP fell.[74] Instead of accepting more imports, the United States ran chronic trade surpluses with the rest of the world.

The United States reconciled its two roles as the world's leading exporter and the world's leading creditor by recycling some of the money it earned from trade surpluses in the form of private loans and investments abroad. Because isolationist pressure prevented the federal government from acting to help stabilize postwar European finances, representatives of the US banking community closely associated with the House of Morgan devised the Dawes Plan in 1924 and helped create the Bank of International Settlements (BIS) in 1929. The Dawes Plan was negotiated by the Chicago banker Charles G. Dawes and Owen D. Young, chairman of the board of General Electric, which had been created by J. P. Morgan, while the BIS was negotiated by Young and Morgan's son J. P. "Jack" Morgan Jr. and his alternate, Morgan partner Thomas Lamont. The Dawes Plan arranged for US private loans to Germany to help it pay its reparations to Britain and France. To promote it, J. P. Morgan managed $110 million of a $200 million loan.

The Dawes Plan led to a $100 million loan by the US government to Germany, followed between 1924 and 1929 by $6.4 billion in loans, 75 percent of which went to governments. Around half of American lending went to Europe, a quarter to Latin America, and a sixth to Canada. The scale was comparable to the post-1945 Marshall Plan; indeed, US private and public lending exceeded America's current-account surplus in the 1920s.[75]

Together with America's new role as the world's leading lender, the establishment of foreign subsidiaries by major US corporations created an alliance of economic elites in favor of a more internationalist foreign policy. In 1900, American foreign direct investment had chiefly funded agriculture in the Caribbean and Central America and foreign raw materials extraction. By 1929, over half of US overseas investment was carried out by the financial community, especially the House of Morgan and other New York banking interests, and the emerging oligopolistic corporations that dominated automobiles, electrical appliances, chemicals, and rubber.[76]

The New York financier Otto Kahn observed: "Having become a creditor nation, we have got now to fit ourselves into the role of a creditor nation. We shall have to make up our minds to be more hospitable to imports."[77] Owen Young complained to Commerce Secretary Herbert Hoover in 1926, "I am sincerely troubled by our national program, which is demanding amounts from our debtors up to the breaking point, and at the same time excluding their goods from our American markets, except for those few raw materials which we must have."[78]

But the majority of businesses in the United States, including much of the manufacturing sector, were small enterprises that feared import competition, particularly if their labor-intensive strategies might be undercut by cheaper foreign labor. Following World War I, the Republican majority in Congress and the Republican administrations of Harding, Coolidge, and Hoover prevented the United States from taking part in the League of Nations and from signing a treaty with Britain to protect France against future attacks by Germany. They increased protection with the Emergency Tariff Act of 1921 and the Fordney-McCumber Tariff of 1922, which the French Finance Ministry denounced as "the first heavy blow directed against any hope of effectively restoring a world trading system."[79] President Calvin Coolidge declared: "Those who wish to benefit foreign producers are much more likely to secure that result by continuing the present enormous purchasing power which comes from our prosperity that has increased our imports over 70 percent in four years than from any advantages that are likely to accrue from a general tariff reduction."[80]

FROM THE NEW ERA TO THE NEW DEAL

Just before the 1929 crash, the American banker and diplomat Norman Davis wrote in alarm: "History teaches us that whenever a newly-arisen, asset-rich nation refuses to open its markets to other countries or fails to effectively channel its financial resources to the development of the world economy, the result is growing conflict between the old order and the new. In the past, these conflicts have led to war, and to the division of the world economy into blocks demarcated by protectionism. Today's intensifying international economic frictions and the mounting protectionism in the United States are both warning signs that the world is once again faced with such a crisis."[81]

In the "New Era" of the 1920s, the United States resembled the China of the 2000s. Both the United States in the early twentieth century and China in the early twenty-first were only partly industrialized. In each country, a huge gap existed between the industrial regions and the agricultural hinterland. In each country, rapidly growing profits for the industrial sector were accompanied by the suppression of the wages of industrial workers and growing inequality. Each country followed a mercantilist strategy in international trade, maintaining trade surpluses in manufactured goods and accumulating hoards of foreign reserves—gold in the case of the United States and dollar-denominated financial assets in the case of China. In both cases, the combination of limited imports with inadequate domestic demand, resulting from low wages for labor and agrarian poverty, created a mismatch between overbuilt manufacturing capacity and national and global consumer demand.

In each case, domestic and global imbalances contributed to a global economic crisis—the Great Depression of the 1930s and the Great Recession that began in 2008. During the Great Recession of the twenty-first century, many economists argued that China needed to shift from a beggar-thy-neighbor export-oriented development strategy to a new economic model based on trade liberalization, higher domestic consumption resulting from higher wages for urban workers and state-sponsored rural development, and social-insurance programs that would reduce the need for individual Chinese to hoard savings for retirement and medical treatment.

There was a historical precedent for such a dramatic shift in economic strategy for a giant, newly industrialized economy. It was America's New Deal. But to go from the New Era to the New Deal, the United States had to endure the ordeal of the Great Depression.

A NEW DEAL
FOR AMERICA

The true conservative seeks to protect the system of private property and free enterprise by correcting such injustices and inequalities as arise from it. . . . I am that kind of conservative because I am that kind of liberal.

—Franklin Delano Roosevelt, 1936[1]

By eleven o'clock on Thursday, October 24, 1929, there was frantic selling in the New York stock market. "Black Tuesday" followed on October 29. The Dow Jones Industrial Average plunged by nearly 13 percent, as sell orders paralyzed the ticker tape system of Wall Street. The collapse of the stock market left individual stocks by mid-November at half of their earlier price.

The stock market declines in the fall of 1929 resulted from attempts by the Federal Reserve to prick a dangerous stock bubble by raising the discount rate (the interest rate at which banks borrow from the Fed) in a series of steps, from 3.5 to 4 percent in February to 6 percent in August. The last rate increase was followed by "Black Thursday."

At first many assumed that the Depression was an ordinary cyclical recession. In May 1930, President Herbert Hoover said: "I am convinced we have now faced the worst." But at the end of 1930, a wave of bank failures swept through the United States. In 1931–1932, more than five thousand American banks failed.

On May 11, 1931, the failure of Austria's largest bank, Creditanstalt, triggered a wave of financial crisis throughout Germany and Central Europe. Many US banks had much of their capital in German securities and were affected by the rippling collapse of the German financial system. In order to provide Germany with temporary relief from the burden of reparations payments imposed on it by the victors of World War I, Hoover ordered a one-year moratorium on debts to the United States by America's World War I allies. But this was too little and too late to prevent the German banking system from toppling, to the benefit of Adolf Hitler's National Socialist Party.

By the time the stock market hit bottom in July 1932, the Dow had lost almost 90 percent of the value of its high point in September 1929. From 1929 to 1931, 15 percent of American banks went out of business. At the beginning of 1933, US employment in industrial production had dropped to half of its 1929 level. National income dropped from $83.3 billion to $40 billion between 1929 and 1932. By the time Hoover left office in March 1933, unemployment had increased to 24.9 percent. In the ultimate sign of the failure of American capitalism, 100,000 Americans applied for six thousand job openings in the Soviet Union.[2]

The Depression discredited the Republican Party, which had dominated American politics since the Civil War, and brought to power a new coalition of Democrats and progressive Republicans led by America's only four-term president, Franklin Delano Roosevelt (the Constitution was amended, in 1951, after his death to limit presidents to two terms). Just as the Civil War and Reconstruction had been the Second American Revolution, so the New Deal and World War II were a Third American Revolution. In the course of a decade and a half, the New Deal modernized America's political and economic institutions to better realize the potential prosperity made possible by the second industrial revolution based on electricity and the internal combustion engine. On the foundations laid by New Deal liberals from Roosevelt to Lyndon Johnson, the American middle class experienced its greatest expansion in numbers and growth in prosperity.

WHAT CAUSED THE GREAT DEPRESSION?

What caused the Great Depression? Following earlier recessions and depressions, there had been rapid recoveries. The persistence of the Depression has been blamed on both short-term policy mistakes and long-term structural weaknesses in the American and global economies.

The Depression is sometimes blamed on the passage of the Hawley-Smoot Tariff, which was signed into law by Hoover on June 17, 1930. In a televised debate about the North American Free Trade Agreement (NAFTA) in 1993 with the former independent presidential candidate Ross Perot, Vice President Al Gore displayed a photograph of Senator Reed Smoot and Representative Willis Hawley and blamed the Depression on the tariff that bore their names. According to Jude Wanniski, a proponent of conservative "supply-side economics" in the Carter and Reagan years: "The stock market Crash of 1929 and the Great Depression ensued because of the passage of the Smoot-Hawley Tariff Act of 1930."[3] Richard Cooper, who served as undersecretary of state in the Carter administration, wrote: "The seeds of the Second World War, both in the Far East and in Europe, were sown by Hoover's signing of the Hawley-Smoot tariff."[4]

The Hawley-Smoot Tariff became law in June 1930, with the support of farmers and labor but over the objections of financiers and 1,028 academic economists who signed a petition against it. The bill had been moving through Congress in the summer of 1929 before the crash of the stock market and it was not a response to the Depression, just as it was not a cause.

The tariff became the highest in American history only because duties were set in terms of dollars, not shares of a product's price, so that when prices of imports collapsed during the Depression, the tariffs rose to levels that the bill's drafters had not intended, to a peak rate of 59.14 percent on dutiable imports. Had prices remained at 1929 levels, the average tariff on dutiable imports would have been 41.6 percent, a level exceeded by US tariffs for 51 years out of 94 between 1821 and 1914.[5]

While there was some foreign retaliation against the tariff, this did not cause global trade to collapse. US exports were no more than 7 percent of GNP in 1929. Between 1929 and 1931, US exports fell by 1.5 percent of GNP, while US GNP declined by 15 percent.[6] The volume of world trade shrank by two-thirds from the last quarter in 1929 to the first quarter in 1933. The global collapse in trade that came after the passage of the tariff was the result of a sudden, universal drop in demand, not of retaliation against American protectionism. A similar collapse in trade occurred in 2008–2009 at the beginning of the Great Recession, in the absence of tariff wars.

Economists from Milton Friedman on the right to Paul Krugman on the liberal left have dismissed the idea that the Hawley-Smoot Tariff caused or worsened the Depression.[7] If the tariff had any effect on the US economy, it was probably a slightly positive one, by substituting domestic for foreign production.[8] The demonization of the Hawley-Smoot Tariff persists as a cliché in American discourse because of the fear of American internationalists that the United States will revert to its pre-World War II isolationism and protectionism. In the same way that "Munich"—British prime minister Neville Chamberlain's agreement with Hitler in 1938—was invoked by the American foreign policy elite as a symbol of appeasement, so "Hawley-Smoot" became a symbol of the protectionist economic strategy that the now-hegemonic United States repudiated following World War II.

Other explanations of the Depression are taken more seriously by scholars. In the 1960s, Milton Friedman argued that the Great Depression was purely the result of the failure of the Federal Reserve to loosen the money supply.[9] Others emphasize the decision of the United States to remain on the gold standard after Britain and other countries had abandoned it, a decision that limited America's flexibility in monetary policy. Yet other economists and historians have criticized explanations of the Depression in terms of mistakes by Federal Reserve or Treasury technocrats because those explanations neglect real factors such as the trade and income imbalances emphasized by many thinkers of the time.[10]

Theories that attributed the severity as well as the triggering cause to mistakes by government policymakers gained in appeal among academic economists after the revival in the late twentieth century of free-market conservatism. By putting the blame for the prolongation of the Great Depression entirely on mistakes by technocratic policymakers, these theories implied that there had been nothing wrong with the structure of American capitalism in 1929.

That complacent late-twentieth-century consensus is more difficult to defend, however, following the crash of 2008 and the Great Recession that followed. The decades preceding both the Great Depression and the Great Recession were characterized by extreme global trade and currency imbalances—chronic American current account and capital account surpluses before 1929, chronic Chinese current account and capital account surpluses before 2008. And before each crash, there was a dramatic increase in income inequality, with many of the gains to the rich from their disproportionate share of growth being used to engage in speculation that inflated bubbles in stocks, real estate, and other assets.

In the years preceding the crash of 1929, a growing number of thinkers and reformers were concerned about the implications of the maldistribution of income for the functioning of the new mass-production economy. Before John Maynard Keynes made the idea of government spending to maintain aggregate demand academically respectable, William Trufant Foster and Waddill Catchings, in a series of influential books in the 1920s, popularized the idea of using relief or public works programs to get purchasing power into the hands of consumers.[11] Edward Filene, the founder of the Century Foundation and Filene's department store, with its Automatic Bargain Basement (later Filene's Basement), argued that the translation of business profits into stock speculation rather than consumption by workers damaged the economy: "At a time when more buying was the need of the hour, [capitalists] were still calling upon the masses to refrain from buying goods, and to invest their savings in more production; and when industries languished from want of customers, they advised reducing wages, a process which must result in a further falling off of sales."[12]

This analysis was shared by Marriner Eccles, the Utah banker whom Franklin Roosevelt appointed as chairman of the Federal Reserve, a post he held from 1934 to 1948. In his memoirs, Eccles argued that insufficient purchasing power by middle- and low-income Americans was the underlying cause of the Depression: "As mass production has to be accompanied by mass consumption, mass consumption, in turn, implies a distribution of wealth—not of existing wealth, but of wealth as it is currently produced—to provide men with buying power equal to the amount of goods and services offered by the nation's economic machinery. Instead of achieving that kind of distribution, a giant suction pump had by 1929–30 drawn into a few hands an increasing portion of currently produced wealth. This served them as capital accumulations. But by taking purchasing power out of the hands of mass consumers, the savers denied to themselves the kind of effective demand for their products that would justify a reinvestment of their capital accumulations in new plants. . . . Had there been a better distribution of income from the national product—in other words, had there been less savings by business and the higher-income groups and more income in the lower groups—we should have had far greater stability in our economy. Had the $6 billion, for instance, that were loaned by corporations and wealthy individuals for stock-market speculation been distributed to the public as lower prices or higher wages and with less profits to the corporations and the well-to-do, it would have prevented or greatly moderated the economic collapse that began at the end of 1929."[13]

Employee compensation as a percentage of net income in manufacturing was 77.6 percent in 1923 and 75.3 percent in 1929; as a share of the economy in general, employee compensation was 77.9 percent in 1923 and 72 percent in 1929.[14] Because the employee share of compensation did not dramatically decline in the 1920s, some have dismissed theories based on underconsumption and maldistribution. But those theories rested on the claim that, from the beginning of the industrial era several generations earlier, the maldistribution of wealth had contributed to destabilizing cycles of boom and bust, which might have been moderated by greater consumption by the many and less saving and speculation by the few.

A historical event as cataclysmic as the Great Depression need not have had a single cause. An event or trend can trigger an economic collapse that is ultimately caused or prolonged by underlying structural defects of the economy.

"THE MOST GIGANTIC PROGRAM OF ECONOMIC DEFENSE AND COUNTERATTACK"

In his 1932 campaign for reelection, President Hoover declared that "we might have done nothing. That would have been utter ruin. Instead we met the situation with proposals to private business and to Congress of the most gigantic program of economic defense and counterattack ever evolved in the history of the Republic. We put it into action."[15] The journalist Walter Lippmann agreed: "The policy initiated by President Hoover in the autumn of 1929 was something utterly unprecedented in American history. The national government undertook to make the whole economic order operate prosperously. . . . [T]he Roosevelt measures are a continuous evolution of the Hoover measures."[16]

Partisan Democratic propaganda convinced later generations that Hoover had been a believer in laissez-faire who did nothing while the economy crumbled. In fact, Hoover believed that government had a duty to intervene in economic downturns. In 1929, Hoover supported and Congress passed a stimulative tax cut, justified in Hoover's view by an anticipated federal surplus.[17] He supported reductions in interest rates by the Federal Reserve. In November 1930, Hoover sent state governors, including New York governor Franklin Roosevelt, a telegram with an exhortation to "energetic, yet prudent, pursuit of public works." He called on federal agencies to expedite public work projects and sought an additional $423 million from Congress for the Federal Public Building Program.[18] Under Hoover the Commerce Department created a Division of Public Construction that increased ship-construction subsidies and asked Congress for additional public-works appropriations.[19]

In April 1930, he signed a bill that provided $575 million for new roads and asked Congress for an additional $28 million for building bridges.[20] Among the public works projects that were launched were the San Francisco Bay Bridge, the Los Angeles Aqueduct, Boulder Dam (later Hoover Dam), and the Grand Coulee Dam on the Columbia River, which the Roosevelt administration later completed. Hoover negotiated with Canada to create the Saint Lawrence Seaway, but construction did not begin until World War II as a war measure.

At the same time, he addressed the problems of mortgage debt and labor market conditions. Hoover called for reforming bankruptcy laws to prevent bankruptcies.[21] In 1930, he sought to tighten the labor market by reducing immigration, accelerating deportation of "undesirable" aliens, and urging young people to leave the labor market for school.[22]

Nor did Hoover neglect the depressed farm sector. His panacea for the depressed agricultural sector was cooperative marketing associations. As president, he signed into law the Agricultural Marketing Act, which created the Federal Farm Board. The FFB sought to hold up prices by persuading cooperatives to keep wheat off the market—indirectly at first, by loans to the cooperatives, and then by buying surplus wheat directly, through the FFB's National Grain Corporation, later the Grain Stabilization Corporation. The FFB undertook similar programs in the cotton, wool, livestock, dairy, and tobacco industries. These had the perverse effect of encouraging overproduction, and the Roosevelt administration combated price deflation with the opposite policy of encouraging the removal of land from production and the plowing under of crops and slaughtering of livestock.

When the Depression deepened in 1931 and 1932, Hoover departed even further from laissez-faire economic orthodoxy. In international policy, as noted earlier, Hoover declared a moratorium on debt repayments from Britain and France, which was intended to help Germany in its economic troubles. In October 1931, Hoover backed the creation of the National Credit Corporation, funded by banks to help other banks in distress. New York bankers agreed to contribute $500 million to the National Credit Corporation only if Hoover agreed to ask Congress to create something along the lines of the War Finance Corporation of World War I to recapitalize troubled banks.[23] The first chairman of the new Reconstruction Finance Corporation (RFC) was Eugene Meyer, the former chairman of the Federal Reserve and a member of the War Industries Board during World War I. By the time that Roosevelt was inaugurated in March 1933, the RFC had issued more than $2.9 billion in loans. More than a billion went to banks, while agricultural credit corporations received nearly $500 million, with $453 million going to state and local governments and $360 million going to the railroads.[24]

Increasing liquidity, the objective of the establishment of the RFC, was also the purpose behind the creation of the Federal Home Loan Bank Act of July 1932. This created a system of twelve regional home-loan banks to help struggling homeowners and to revive the stricken housing industry by rediscounting home loans. The Hoover administration and Congress also expanded the Federal Farm Loan Bank System, which had been created in 1916.

This kind of large-scale state capitalism, which Hoover only reluctantly supported, marked a departure from his associationalist ideal of self-help by business and banking with moral support from government. What Hoover called the "new individualism" could go up to the edge of an invisible line that only he perceived; if it crossed the line, then in his opinion it became "socialism" or "fascism." An example of this phenomenon was his reaction to the Swope Plan, a 1931 proposal by Gerard Swope of General Electric for a combination of government-enforced cartelization of industries with mandatory company-based employee-benefit programs like those of GE. The plan was modeled on the War Industries Board of World War I, when Swope had worked with the head of the WIB, Bernard Baruch. The Chamber of Commerce put forth a plan with a similar combination of antitrust revision under government supervision. The liberal writer Stuart Chase, who coined the term "new deal," called for a Peace Industries Board modeled on the War Industries Board.[25] But the addition of an element of compulsion made this version of associationalism intolerable to Hoover, who denounced the Swope plan as "the most gigantic proposal of monopoly ever made in history."[26]

HERBERT HOOVER AND "THE BITTER-END LIQUIDATIONISTS"

A central part of Hoover's program for combating the Depression was to persuade employers not to cut wages. To this end he held conferences with business leaders and barraged them with pleas to maintain wage rates. He boasted, "For the first time in the history of depression, dividends, profits, and the cost of living, have been reduced before wages have suffered. . . . They were maintained until the cost of living had decreased and the profits had practically vanished. They are now the highest wages in the world."[27] The British economist John Maynard Keynes approved of the Hoover administration's policy of defending wage rates.[28]

Then and later, the naive idea that a policy of allowing wages as well as prices to fall will cure a depression appealed to many who failed to understand that Depression was caused by a collapse of aggregate demand.[29] A downward deflationary spiral would reduce wages and prices even further. As wages fell, demand would shrink, leading businesses to cut prices further, while cutting wages further. The reductio ad absurdum of this panacea is an economy in which everyone is employed, nobody is paid, and everything is free. In the real world, long before the cycle of wage and price cuts had gone very far, there would be riots in the streets or the government would be overthrown.

Hoover understood this. In his memoirs, he claimed that Treasury Secretary Andrew Mellon prescribed harsh medicine in November 1929: "Liquidate labor, liquidate stocks, liquidate the farmers, liquidate real estate. It will purge the rottenness out of the system. High costs of living and high living will come down. People will work harder, live a more moral life. Values will be adjusted, and enterprising people will pick up from less competent people."[30] Whether Mellon actually said this or not is not clear. In public, Mellon repeated the administration's philosophy in

May 1931: "In this country, there has been a concerted effort on the part of both government and business not only to prevent any reduction in wages but to keep the maximum number of men employed, and thereby to increase consumption."[31]

Hoover rejected the liquidationist school: "Some of the reactionary economists urged that we should allow the liquidation to take its course until we had found bottom. . . . We determined that we would not follow the advice of the bitter-end liquidationists and see the whole body of debtors of the United States brought to bankruptcy and the savings of our people brought to destruction."[32] In light of the tendency of free-market libertarians, at the time and during the Great Recession, to argue that deflation should be allowed to run its course in a depression, it is interesting to note that the influential libertarian economist Friedrich Hayek, in a 1979 interview, agreed that deflation must be stopped by government action: "I agree with Milton Friedman that once the Crash had occurred, the Federal Reserve System pursued a silly deflationary policy. I am not only against inflation but I am also against deflation. So, once again, a badly programmed monetary policy prolonged the depression."[33]

HOOVER'S POLICY MISTAKES

Hoover anticipated many of the policies of the Roosevelt administration, such as support for maintaining wages, and worked with Congress, sometimes reluctantly, to create some of the institutions that played a central role in the New Deal, such as the Reconstruction Finance Corporation. Hoover wrote that "after coming to the Presidency, almost the whole of Roosevelt's credit supports were built upon our measures."[34] In 1948, the economist Henry Simons of the University of Chicago wrote: "The N.R.A. [National Recovery Adminsitration] is merely Mr. Hoover's trust policy and wage policy writ large. The agricultural measures and many other planning proposals are the logical counterpoint and the natural extension of Republican protectionism."[35] Rexford Tugwell, a member of Roosevelt's brain trust, later said: "We didn't admit it at the time, but practically the whole New Deal was extrapolated from programs that Hoover started."[36]

This does not mean, however, that the New Deal was merely a continuation of Hoover's policies. Hoover was right to try to fight deflation, an effort that Roosevelt continued. But Hoover made several basic mistakes that Roosevelt corrected. His most important mistakes were supporting the gold standard and raising taxes dramatically in an ill-timed attempt to balance the budget in 1932.

The gold standard required a country's central banks to raise interest rates, with contractionary effects on the economy, to prevent the outflow of gold, which served as the basis for the nation's bank reserves. Following a run on the dollar in 1931, the Federal Reserve, instead of ignoring the gold standard and acting as a lender of last resort to failing banks, worsened the crisis by making credit scarce, in order to prevent an outflow of gold. Eventually, in the spring of 1932, the Fed injected a billion dollars of new money into the economy, after Congress had passed the first Glass-Steagall Act, which lowered the amount of gold the Fed needed to hold to back the dollar. While this helped, it was too little and too late. Only the abandonment of the gold standard by the Roosevelt administration in 1933 gave the government the freedom of action it needed. Britain, which abandoned the gold standard in 1931, suffered less than the United States during the Depression.

Another mistake was Hoover's support for the Revenue Act of 1932, the most dramatic increase in taxes in peacetime in American history. In his December 1930 address to Congress, Hoover said: "Prosperity cannot be restored by raids upon the Public Treasury." Hoover supported a mild stimulus in 1929 only because the federal budget was then in surplus. During a depression caused by a collapse of aggregate demand, premature attempts to balance government budgets only contract demand further, by raising taxes and cutting spending. In Hoover's defense, it should be pointed out that Roosevelt denounced him during the 1932 campaign for doing too little to balance the budget. Although Roosevelt recognized the need to run deficits during his first few years in office, his fiscal conservatism led him to support a premature attempt to balance the budget in 1937, which tipped the United States back into recession.

HOOVERVILLE

Hoover's greatest failure was not of policy, but of leadership. He had many of the virtues of a great leader but lacked the mysterious quality of charisma. Introverted and reserved, he was incapable of inspiring the American people at a time when hope was most needed.

Federal relief programs might not have cured the Depression, but they would have convinced citizens that the leaders in Washington cared about the millions of unemployed and suffering Americans. Early in the Depression, on February 3, 1930, after rebuking the request of the Conference of Governors for a billion-dollar federal appropriation, Hoover said: "I am willing to pledge myself that if the time should ever come that the voluntary agencies of the country, together with the local and state governments, are unable to find resources with which to prevent hunger and suffering in my country I will ask the aid of every resource of the Federal Government."[37] But even when roughly one in five Americans was unemployed, Hoover rejected more than minimal intervention in the economy by the federal government: "It is not the function of the government to relieve individuals of their responsibilities to their neighbors, or to relieve private institutions of their responsibilities to the public."[38]

Hoover continued to insist that relief was a matter for voluntary charities and state and local governments. Only reluctantly did Hoover choose not to wield the veto when Congress, which had been captured by the Democrats in 1930, passed the first federal relief legislation, the Emergency Relief and Construction Act, in July 1932. The act allowed the RFC to provide $300 million in loans to the states that could be used for relief. The act also provided for more public works spending and the creation of regional agricultural credit corporations to lend money to farm cooperatives.

Ironically, Hoover had become a celebrity for his role in administering relief in Belgium during World War I. This "volunteer effort" in fact derived four-fifths of its money from the governments of Britain and France, until the United States declared war in April 1917 and provided all the funding.

Hoover's attempts to minimize the severity of the Depression were intended to boost business and consumer confidence, but they seemed callous. Homeless men called "hoboes" traveled on freight cars from place to place in search of work or charity. Hoover remarked: "The hoboes . . . are better fed than they have ever been. One hobo in New York got ten meals in one day."[39]

Public contempt for the president was expressed in satire. Freight cars were renamed "Hoover Pullmans" and shantytowns for the homeless became "Hoovervilles," while lesser game animals eaten reluctantly by the hungry, including armadillos and opposums, were "Hoover hogs." A "Hoover purse" was an empty, turned-out pocket.

A parody of the Twenty-third Psalm was widely circulated:

Hoover is our shepherd
We are in want
He maketh us to lie
Down on the park benches
He leadeth us beside the still factories
He disturbeth our soul
He leadeth us in the path of destruction for his party's sake
Yea, though we walk through the valley of depression
We anticipate no recovery for those who are with us
Thy politicians and diplomats frighten us
Thou preparest a reduction of our salary in the presence of our enemies

Our expenses runneth over
Surely poverty and unemployment will follow us
And we will dwell in mortgaged homes forever[40]

In the winter of 1931–1932, several marches took place in Washington, including more than a thousand national hunger marchers and another group of fifteen thousand led by Father James Cox. Democrats and progressive Republicans called for direct federal relief programs or greatly expanded public-works spending, only to meet Hoover's opposition.

In the spring of 1932, when veterans of World War I called the "Bonus Army" marched on Washington to demand the payment of promised bonuses immediately instead of in 1945 or to their families upon their deaths, Hoover ordered the US Army under General Douglas MacArthur to destroy their camp near the Capitol. Although stories that soldiers had butchered infants and children were false, the nation was shocked by the use of bayonets and tear gas against the unemployed in the nation's capital. In his memoirs, Hoover wrote: "As abundantly proved later on, the march was in considerable part organized and promoted by the Communists and included a large number of hoodlums and ex-convicts determined to raise a public disturbance."[41]

THE NEW DEAL COALITION

By 1932, the American people were ready for a "new deal." The New Deal was not primarily a movement of the Left. It was an alliance of several groups—international bankers and international businesses, workers in the industrial core, farmers, and local champions of economic development in the southern and western periphery.[42] (A fifth interest group, the consumer movement, was vocal but not politically significant until the end of the New Deal era in the 1960s and 1970s.)

Each of these groups that coalesced in support of Franklin Roosevelt's Democratic Party during the Depression had its own reason to oppose the Lincoln-to-Hoover Republican coalition that dominated the federal government between the Civil War and the Depression. The international bankers and multinational businessmen wanted the United States to move away from protectionism toward free trade. The industrial workers wanted to share more of the profits of American industry, by means of higher wages, benefits, and shorter hours. The farmers wanted to rig agricultural markets to reduce volatility and increase their incomes.

The local economic elites in the South and West, resenting the treatment of their states as resource colonies by northeastern bankers and absentee capitalists, wanted the federal government, acting as state capitalist, to guide credit and manufacturing industries to their parts of the country. Among the members of this faction were a number of powerful Texans who surrounded Roosevelt. His vice president, John Nance Garner, known as "Cactus Jack," was a conservative who turned against him and was dropped from the vice presidential spot on the ticket in 1940 in favor of the more liberal Henry Wallace. Garner famously described the vice presidency as not "worth a pitcher of warm spit." Roosevelt worked closely with Sam Rayburn, an East Texas populist who served as majority leader in the House from 1937 to 1941 and as the longest-serving Speaker of the House in history, 1941 to 1961, with interruptions during brief periods of Republican control in 1947–1949 and 1953–1955. Roosevelt and Rayburn promoted the career of a dynamic young Texan politician named Lyndon Johnson.

The most powerful Texan of all during the New Deal years was Jesse Jones. A rich banker, Jones had helped to make Houston a leading port city, investing in some of the city's first skyscrapers. Having turned down Woodrow Wilson's offer to be secretary of commerce, Jones agreed to direct the American Red Cross during World War I. From 1933 to 1945, he ran the Reconstruction Finance Corporation and, from 1940 to 1945, served as commerce secretary. Because of his position at the center of New Deal state capitalism, he was given the title "The Emperor Jones," a reference to a play by Eugene O'Neill. Under Jones, the RFC, originally created during the Hoover years to recapitalize banks, funded both New Deal agencies such as the Works Progress Adminstration (WPA; renamed the Works Projects Administration in 1939) and industrial-mobilization projects during World War II.

The New Deal was a social revolution as well as an economic revolution. Just as it united the "outs" of economic policy, so it empowered ambitious Americans from ethnic groups or regions who were despised and marginalized by the elite white Anglo-Saxon Protestants (WASPs) of the Northeast and Midwest. By discrediting the old WASP oligarchy, the Depression made possible a more meritocratic society, even if racial integration had to wait until the civil rights revolution a generation later. Jewish Americans including Benjamin Cohen, Jerome Frank, and David Lilienthal, Irish Americans like FDR's political fixer Tommy "the Cork" Corcoran and Joseph Kennedy, the father of the future president, businessmen from the future Sun Belt like George and Herman Brown of Texas—whose Brown and Root construction firm became Halliburton— the Italian American banker A. P. Giannini and the Mormon banker Marriner Eccles: all these outsiders broke into citadels of power from which people with their backgrounds had been excluded.

A diverse and discontented crowd was waiting in the wings of American politics. The failure of Herbert Hoover would give them their chance onstage.

A DISCIPLINED ATTACK UPON
OUR COMMON PROBLEMS

In 1930, the Democrats captured the House. In 1932, they captured the Senate and the presidency.

"With this pledge taken," Franklin Roosevelt vowed in his first inaugural address on March 4, 1933, "I assume unhesitatingly the leadership of this great army of our people dedicated to a disciplined attack upon our common problems."[43] On becoming president, Roosevelt broke with the policy of Hoover in a number of areas and took bold measures which, in the view of many historians, ended the downward spiral of deflation and set the US economy on the road to recovery.

In April 1933, Roosevelt invoked emergency powers to ban the private holding of gold and remove the United States from the gold standard. Immediately after his inauguration, on March 6, Roosevelt shut down the national banking system by proclaiming a federal bank holiday (earlier some states had declared similar holidays). On March 9, Congress passed the Emergency Banking Act, which allowed the Federal Reserve in effect to insure bank deposits. In his first fireside chat by radio on March 12, Roosevelt explained the system to the American people. When the banks opened again the next day, depositors who had been hoarding cash stood in line to return it. In the next two weeks, half of the hoarded cash in the country was deposited in the banks.[44]

The temporary insurance of bank deposits became permanent with the Glass-Steagall Act of 1933, which also reorganized the Federal Reserve, separated commercial and investment banking, and created deposit insurance by establishing the Federal Deposit Insurance Corporation (FDIC). An old Jeffersonian panacea favored by southern and western politicians that enabled small one-unit banks to hold smaller capital reserves, deposit-insurance schemes at the state level had failed, both before the Civil War and in the early twentieth century, with every recent effort collapsing in the 1920s.[45]

Roosevelt thought that deposit insurance was a crackpot idea. So did Senator Carter Glass, who lent his name to the Glass-Steagall Act and who preferred liberalized interstate branch banking along with higher reserve requirements and the government as lender of last resort. The provision for deposit insurance was not introduced until late in the bill's evolution, on April 4, 1933, at the insistence of Glass's counterpart in the House, Representative Henry B. Steagall of Alabama. In spite of Roosevelt's misgivings, deposit insurance eliminated bank panics.

The inclusion of deposit insurance made it necessary to separate commercial banks, which would be insured by the government, from investment banks, which would not be. Brandeis and his allies had long supported the separation of commercial and investment banking, on the basis of their hostility to investment bankers like the late J. P. Morgan Sr. The Rockefeller interests supported the measure, which happened to cripple their rival, the House of Morgan, by forcing J. P. Morgan and Company to turn itself into two entities—a commercial bank that kept the name of J. P. Morgan and Co. and an investment bank, Morgan Stanley. The

Democrats also exploited popular anger at bankers to pass the Securities Exchange Act of 1934.

Abandoning his campaign pledge to balance the budget, Roosevelt engaged in deficit spending. In the introduction to the first volume of his presidential papers, FDR wrote: "To balance our budget in 1933 or 1934 or 1935 would have been a crime against the American people. To do so we should have had to make a capital levy that would have been confiscatory, or we would have had to set our face against human suffering with callous indifference."[46] Deficit spending continued until 1937, when Roosevelt and Congress repeated Hoover's mistake by prematurely trying to balance the budget, throwing the country back into recession.

While Hoover as president had vetoed federal relief programs, Roosevelt as governor of New York had presided over the first state relief program funded by bonds, the New York Temporary Emergency Relief Administration (TERA). Its head, the social worker Harry Hopkins, went on to lead the Federal Emergency Relief Administration (FERA) that was created in the spring of 1933. Roosevelt's fiscal policy, though on a much larger scale than under Hoover, was still far short of what was needed. But taken together, his policies arrested and reversed the death spiral of the economy.

Whatever the merits of particular elements of the Roosevelt program, the result was dramatic: the decline of the American economy reversed around the time of Roosevelt's "Hundred Days" of decisive activity. What followed between 1933 and 1937 was the most rapid peacetime growth in American history. Although his program fell short of what was needed to eliminate lingering unemployment, Roosevelt was far more successful than Hoover.

THE BLUE EAGLE

When Roosevelt was elected, there were a number of competing alternatives for a recovery program: massive public-works spending; wage-and-hours laws to increase purchasing power; increasing output through relaxation of antitrust laws; loans to industry or guarantees against losses; and even antitrust measures (some argued that monopoly had caused the Depression). Roosevelt was spurred to action when the Senate passed the Thirty-Hour Bill of Senator Hugo Black of Alabama, a law that sought to promote work sharing by mandating a thirty-hour workweek. Roosevelt thought that the Black bill was too radical, but rather than oppose it directly he preferred to sideline it by setting forth his own recovery plan.

What became the National Industrial Recovery Act (NIRA) was cobbled together from the efforts of two groups: one led by General Hugh Johnson, a veteran of the WIB, and supported by brain trust member Raymond Moley, budget director Lewis Douglas, and Donald Richberg. The other team included New York senator Robert Wagner, labor secretary Frances Perkins, undersecretary of commerce John Dickinson, and Jerome Frank.[47] The NIRA drew on several alternatives to please several constituencies. It provided antitrust relief to industries, fostered minimum wages and hours to be determined by trade associations and labor representatives, and included a modest public works program in the form of the Public Works Administration (PWA).

Much nonsense has been written by conservative and libertarian critics of the New Deal about the alleged origins of the NIRA in Italian Fascism. When FDR pushed General Hugh Johnson, its first head, out of the leadership of the National Recovery Administration, the erratic general invoked the "shining name" of Benito Mussolini.[48] Roosevelt, who despised Hitler, described the Italian dictator at one point as "that admirable Italian gentleman." Mussolini's invasion of Ethiopia and alliance with Nazi Germany embarrassed a number of people, including the composer and songwriter Cole Porter, who changed the lyrics to his song "You're the Top!" to leave out the line "You're the top! You're Mussolini!"[49]

Among Mussolini's earlier admirers was Winston Churchill, who praised "Fascismo's triumphant struggle against the bestial appetites and passions of Leninism."[50] In his book *Liberalism*, published in 1927 after Mussolini had seized power in Italy, one of the heroes of modern libertarian critics of Roosevelt and the New Deal, Ludwig von Mises, wrote: "It cannot be denied that [Italian] Fascism and similar movements aimed at the establishment of dictatorships are full of the best intentions and that their intervention has for the moment saved European civilization. The merit that Fascism has thereby won for itself will live on eternally in history."[51]

None of this is relevant, because the actual origins of the NIRA lay in the Wilson administration, not the Mussolini regime. The NIRA revived the WIB of World War I under a new name. The trade associations that were supposed to write industry-wide codes under government supervision were a version of the commodity sections and war-service committees of the WIB. The denial of the Blue Eagle emblem to uncooperative firms was merely a revival of the technique of shaming companies into compliance that had been used by the WIB during World War I. Hugh Johnson was the former deputy of Bernard Baruch at the WIB.

Roosevelt declared in his inaugural address: "It is high time to admit with courage that we are in the midst of an emergency at least equal to that of war." He invoked World War I associationalism as the model for recovery on April 7, 1932, when he called "for plans like those of 1917 that build from the bottom up not from the top down, that put their faith once more in the forgotten man at the bottom of the economic pyramid."[52] Like the Reconstruction Finance Corporation (RFC), a reincarnation of the War Finance Corporation of World War I, and the Home Ownership Loan Corporation, the major programs of the New Deal were inspired by wartime agencies. Jesse Jones, whom Roosevelt appointed to head the RFC, was a veteran of the WIB, as was George Nelson Peek, who directed the agricultural equivalent of the NIRA, the Agricultural Adjustment Administration (AAA). The Securities and Exchange Commission (SEC) was based on the Capital Issues Committee during World War I.

In addition to the WIB, the precedents for the NRA included the Swope Plan of General Electric's Gerard Swope. While Hoover had denounced the Swope Plan for government-sponsored cartelization, Roosevelt began consulting with Swope while he was still governor of New York. The trade associations that Hoover had sponsored as secretary of commerce were another inspiration. Rooseveltian "corporatism" was Hooverian associationalism with teeth.

One foreign precedent that influenced American New Dealers of the 1930s was the trade board or wages council, an institution that had been adopted in other English-speaking democracies a generation before the Depression. In 1896, the Australian state of Victoria established wage boards to set wages in industries with impoverished and exploited workers. By 1911, all the Australian states except for West Australia had adopted the system. Similar reforms were undertaken in New Zealand. Following a study of the Australian and New Zealand systems by the British Parliament, Winston Churchill, then a member of Parliament in the Liberal Party and the president of the Board of Trade, introduced the Trade Boards Act of 1909 that created boards made up of representatives of employers, workers, and the general public to set wages and standards in "sweated" professions employing chiefly poor women, such as lace making and box making. In the form of "wage councils," the trade board system was expanded to cover other industries in Britain. Under Churchill's law, the wage rates suggested by the tripartite boards became compulsory when approved by the president of the Board of Trade. The similarity to the NRA codes, which became compulsory when approved by the president of the United States, was pointed out in the *Atlantic* in February 1934 by the British political theorist Harold J. Laski, who observed: "In principle, they [the codes] are nothing more than the British system of trade boards against sweating in industry; and the wonder is that men can still be found to inspect their well-tried habits in a mood of panic."[53]

In promoting the NIRA, Franklin Delano Roosevelt was following in the footsteps, not of Benito Mussolini, but of Woodrow Wilson, Bernard Baruch, Gerard Swope, Herbert Hoover, and Winston Churchill.

DID THE NIRA IMPEDE RECOVERY?

The NIRA offered industries a relaxation of antitrust policy in return for their agreement to provide minimum wages to workers. Roosevelt hoped that trade-association codes would eliminate businesses that relied on inadequate wages: "No business which depends for existence on paying less than living wages to its workers has any right to continue in this country."[54] Henry Harriman, head of the Chamber of Commerce, agreed: "We must take out of competition the right to cut wages to a point which will not sustain an American standard of living, and we must recognize that capital is entitled to a fair and reasonable return."[55]

The claim that the NIRA retarded recovery by imposing minimum wages in different industries is not taken seriously, except by those whom Hoover derided as "die-hard liquidationists." If labor unions cause unemployment, by raising the cost of labor, then the 1930s should have been prosperous, because unions were weak and included few workers, and the 1950s, when a third of the workforce was unionized, should have suffered from a depression.

John Maynard Keynes made a more subtle and persuasive argument against the NIRA. Roosevelt had expressed the hope that the NIRA codes, by raising aggregate demand, might promote short-term recovery in a July 24, 1933, radio broadcast: "If all employers in each competitive group agree to pay their workers the same wages—reasonable wages—and require the same hours—reasonable hours—then high wages and shorter hours will hurt no employer. Moreover [it] makes more buyers for his product."[56]

Keynes politely demurred, in an open letter to the president in 1933, published in the *New York Times*: "You are engaged on a double task, Recovery and Reform;—recovery from the slump and the passage of those business and social reforms which are long overdue." He warned that "even wise and necessary Reform may, in some respects, impede and complicate Recovery. For it will upset the confidence of the business world and weaken their existing motives to action, before you have had time to put other motives in their place." The NIRA, he suggested, was a distraction: "That is my first reflection—that N.I.R.A., which is essentially Reform and probably impedes Recovery, has been put across too hastily, in the false guise of being part of the technique of Recovery." Keynes wrote: "I do not mean to impugn the social justice and social expediency of the redistribution of incomes aimed at by N.I.R.A. and by the various schemes for agricultural restriction. The latter, in particular, I should strongly support in principle."

The alternative favored by Keynes was deficit-financed public expenditure on a scale comparable to that of wartime: "But in a slump governmental Loan expenditure is the only sure means of securing quickly a rising output at rising prices. That is why a war has always caused intense industrial activity. In the past orthodox finance has regarded a war as the only legitimate excuse for creating employment by governmental expenditure. You, Mr President, having cast off such fetters, are free to engage in the interests of peace and prosperity the technique which hitherto has only been allowed to serve the purposes of war and destruction." He suggested projects "which can be made to mature quickly on a large scale, as for example the rehabilitation of the physical condition of the railroads. . . . Could not the energy and enthusiasm, which launched the N.I.R.A. in its early days, be put behind a campaign for accelerating capital expenditures, as wisely chosen as the pressure of circumstances permits? You can at least feel sure that the country will be better enriched by such projects than by the involuntary idleness of millions."[57]

While praising him in public, Keynes privately said that Roosevelt "had about as much idea of where he would land as a pre-war pilot."[58] In hindsight, Keynes was right that the NIRA was a measure of long-term reform that distracted the energy and attention of the Roosevelt administration and Congress from more urgent recovery measures. Roosevelt, though, had not been impressed with Keynes in his meetings with him and, until the late 1930s, he was not persuaded by the British economist's argument for large-scale deficit spending during a depression. In his "forgotten man" speech in April 1932, candidate Roosevelt rejected proposals for massive government deficit spending: "People suggest that a huge expenditure of public funds by the Federal Government and by State and local governments will completely solve the unemployment problem. But it is clear that even if we could raise many billions of dollars and find definitely useful public works to spend these billions on, even all that money would not give employment to the seven million or ten million people who are out of work. Let us admit frankly that it would only be a stop-gap. A real economic cure must go to the killing of the bacteria in the system rather than to the treatment of external symptoms."[59]

THE BLUE EAGLE FALLS TO EARTH

The NIRA did not last long enough to do much good or harm. Hugh Johnson's erratic personality and flamboyant style made him a poor choice to head a controversial program. When he was appointed to head the NIRA agency, Johnson told friends: "It will be red fire at first and dead cats afterward. This is just like mounting the guillotine on the infinitesimal gamble that the axe won't work."[60] The general described the NIRA as a "Holy Thing . . . The Greatest Social Advance Since Jesus Christ." He removed "I" from the National Industrial Recovery Administration to make the acronym NRA, following a *Business Week* article that mocked NIRA as "Neera, My God To Thee."[61]

On May 27, 1935, the Supreme Court ruled in the case of *A. L. A. Schechter Poultry Corp. v. United States* that the NIRA was unconstitutional on two grounds: Congress lacked the power to regulate intrastate commerce and had sought to delegate too much discretion to the president. The occasion for the ruling was a suit brought by the Schechter family poultry business in Brooklyn, New York, which had been accused of selling diseased meat. The NRA's Blue Eagle, it was said, had been defeated by the "sick chicken."[62] In January 1936, the Supreme Court struck down the Agricultural Adjustment Act (AAA), the equivalent of the NIRA in agriculture; in 1938 Congress re-created it in a second bill that passed constitutional muster.

In May 1935, after the Supreme Court struck down the NIRA as unconstitutional, Justice Louis Brandeis told FDR's aide Thomas Corcoran: "You go back and tell your President that this Court has told him it is not going to permit the centralization of power. . . . Furthermore, . . . I warn you to send back to the states all those bright young men you have brought to Washington. It is in the states where they are needed."[63] Roosevelt denounced the decision as a "horse and buggy" interpretation of federal economic power. The decision inspired Roosevelt's unsuccessful and unpopular "court-packing" plan to enlarge the Supreme Court's membership in order to dilute the influence of the reactionary justices.

Within a few years, the *Schechter* opinion was effectively reversed. Its attempted ban on delegations of congressional power to the executive was ignored by later courts, which tolerated significant grants of discretion to presidents and executive-branch agencies by Congress. And its prohibition of federal minimum wage laws in "intrastate" commerce was overruled in *United States v. Darby* (1941), which upheld the minimum wage created by the National Labor Relations Act of 1935. Far from saving America from statism, the *Schechter* decision was a last gasp of reactionary nineteenth-century Jeffersonian ideology in the federal judiciary.

In her anti–New Deal polemic *The Forgotten Man*, the conservative journalist Amity Shlaes tried to turn the case into a libertarian melodrama, portraying the Schechters as poor, struggling immigrants victimized by a tyrannical federal government.[64] In reality, A. L. A. Schechter was not a struggling small business, but the largest of the firms in Brooklyn's kosher slaughterhouse industry, making more than a million dollars a year, in part by using low wages to undercut its rivals. Nor were the Schechters victims of Gentile anti-Semites in the federal bureaucracy, as some conservatives have claimed. Orthodox rabbis helped to draft the NRA poultry code and the critics of the Schechters included groups that represented their rivals, including the Official Orthodox Slaughterers of America.

Notwithstanding their collision with the NRA, the Schechters, like most Jewish Americans in the 1930s, were ardent supporters of FDR. In 1936, a *New York Times* headline read: "ARCH-FOES OF NRA VOTE FOR NEW DEAL; ALL 16 BALLOTS IN THE SCHECHTER FAMILY WENT TO PRESIDENT, POULTRY MAN REVEALS." The *Times* quoted Joe Schechter: "I wonder if it would be possible to congratulate President Roosevelt through the newspapers and tell him that sixteen votes in our family were cast in his favor."[65]

FROM THE WRECKAGE OF THE NIRA

While many historians have distinguished a second New Deal from the first New Deal, this ignores the continuity between the NIRA and subsequent programs. Much of the New Deal's lasting legacy consisted of pieces of the shattered NIRA, which were pried from the wreckage and re-created as separate programs. A number of the industry-wide code authorities of the NIRA, for example, were re-created in the form of commissions that oversaw regulated industries, from bituminous coal and oil to aviation and trucking. These will be discussed in chapter 13.

The collapse of the NIRA led the Roosevelt administration to seek the goals of union recognition, minimum wages, and social insurance directly, by means of government regulation and provision, rather than indirectly, by means of trade-association agreements. The Wagner Act of 1935, a free-standing equivalent of section 7(a) of the NIRA, gave unions the right to engage in collective bargaining. The Fair Labor Standards Act (FLSA) of 1938 created a national minimum wage and instituted the eight-hour day. Conservative Democrats in the South exempted the occupations in which most black Americans worked, such as agricultural work and domestic work, but they were gradually added later in successive revisions of the act.

The Wagner Act and the statutory minimum wage created by the FLSA in 1938 were poor substitutes for a more flexible and adaptable system that might have evolved over time in the United States, if the NIRA had survived. In Britain, Germany, and other European countries, statutory minimum wages for a long time were limited to a few sweatshop industries, like those supervised by Churchill's trade boards. France was one of a few European democracies to adopt a national minimum wage from an early period, for the same reason that the United States did—the proportion of workers who belong to unions has always been much lower in France than in Central and Northern Europe.[66]

The weakness of unions in the United States is often blamed on the Taft-Hartley Act of 1947, which weakened the Wagner Act, or the failure to organize the American South, or hostile attitudes toward unions by courts and government agencies, beginning with the presidency of Ronald Reagan and his Republican successors. But in every other modern democracy where substantial portions of the private sector workforce are unionized, NIRA-style employers associations, called "peak associations," bargain at the national or regional level with labor representatives. Most of the democratic countries with such tripartite government-business-labor sectoral wage-setting systems have seen their productivity increase at roughly the US rate over the last half century. There is, however, one difference—thanks in large part to higher levels of unionization, the distribution of income in those countries is far less unequal and there is greater upward economic and social mobility than in the United States.

"NO DAMN POLITICIAN CAN EVER SCRAP MY SOCIAL SECURITY PROGRAM"

The Social Security Act of 1935 created a comprehensive system of shared federal-state responsibility for unemployment insurance, means-tested welfare for the poor, and—in a radical break with tradition—a purely federal public pension for the elderly. Corporate opposition was muted because Social Security, a contributory program in which higher earners enjoyed higher benefits, was far more conservative than populist alternatives like the Townsend Plan, which would have given every retiree two hundred dollars on the condition that he or she spend it within the month. The first Social Security check, check number 00–000–001, was issued in the amount of $22.54 on January 31, 1940, to Ida May Fuller, a retired schoolteacher and legal secretary in Brattleboro, Vermont, who had gone to high school in Rutland, Vermont, with Calvin Coolidge.

Roosevelt insisted on paying for old-age pensions with a payroll tax, rather than general revenues or another dedicated tax, because that would destroy the "relief attitude." He explained to his adviser Luther Gulick, who doubted that payroll taxes alone could sustain Social Security in the long run, "I guess you're right on the economics. They are politics all the way through. We put those pay roll contributions there so as to give the contributors a legal, moral, and political right to collect their pensions and their unemployment benefits. With those taxes in there, no damn politician can ever scrap my social security program. Those taxes aren't a matter of economics, they're straight politics."[67]

PRESIDENT ROOSEVELT WANTS YOU TO JOIN THE UNION

By the time of his second presidential race in 1936, Roosevelt, who believed he was saving American capitalism, was baffled and embittered by the hostility of most of the American business community to the New Deal. The rift between Roosevelt and business grew deeper as American labor grew more militant.

In 2006, a retired coal miner named Jack McReynolds told a reporter: "I have three pictures side by side in my house: John L. Lewis, Franklin Delano Roosevelt and Jesus. . . . I draw Social Security on account of FDR. I draw a pension on account of John L. Lewis, and I'm going to Heaven because of Jesus."[68]

The members of this Trinity did not necessarily get along. Roosevelt, like other patrician progressives, was not a wholehearted champion of unions.[69] Many of his allies shared the view of his secretary of labor, Frances Perkins, who said she would rather pass a law than organize a union.[70] For his part, Lewis, the flamboyant president of the United Mine Workers, turned against Roosevelt because of the US entry into World War II and wartime labor policy.

But in the mid-1930s Lewis distributed signs that read: "President Roosevelt Wants You to Join the Union!" Across the country, prounion

workers clashed with employers and their security forces. In 1935, there
was the largest wave of strikes since the early 1920s, involving more than
a million workers and more than two thousand work stoppages.[71]

At the American Federation of Labor (AFL) convention in Atlantic
City in 1935, Lewis, frustrated with the organization's commitment to
craft unionism instead of industrial unionism, punched one of his opponents, William Hutcheson of the Carpenters Union. At a meeting in
November in Washington, DC, Lewis, Sidney Hillman of the Amalgamated Clothing Workers, and David Dubinsky of the International Ladies'
Garment Workers Union formed a new organization, the Committee for
Industrial Organization, which broke away from the AFL in 1938 to become the Congress of Industrial Organizations (CIO). The competition
of the two federations, which would be reconciled and merge in 1955,
accelerated the campaign for unionization.

Union organizers employed a new and powerful technique, the sit-
down strike. Without giving any warning, employees who wanted to join
a union stayed inside the factory or store and simply stopped working, to
paralyze the business.

> When they tie the can to a union man,
>   Sit down! Sit down!
> When they give him the sack, they'll take him back,
>   Sit down! Sit down!
> When the speed-up comes, just twiddle your thumbs,
>   Sit down! Sit down!
> When the boss won't talk, don't take a walk,
>   Sit down! Sit down![72]

The climax of the struggle came in January 1937, when sit-down strikers took control of the General Motors plant at Flint, Michigan, as well as
others in Cleveland, Atlanta, and elsewhere. Although GM chairman Alfred Sloan bitterly opposed negotiating with the union, behind-the-scenes
pressure by President Roosevelt led GM president William Knudsen to

recognize the United Auto Workers (UAW) on the forty-fourth day of the strike, February 11, 1937. US Steel signed a union contract with the Steel Workers Organizing Committee (SWOC) later that year, but several of the smaller firms called "Little Steel" held out until 1942. Only the urging of his wife Clara led Henry Ford, a bitter foe of organized labor, to allow Ford to be unionized in 1941.

FROM BRAINS TRUSTERS TO TRUST BUSTERS

In his first few years in office, Roosevelt had been influenced by his brains trust advisers Adolf Berle and Rexford Tugwell, whose vision of central-ized government-business cooperation was closer to Theodore Roosevelt's New Nationalism than to the decentralist New Freedom of Wilson and Brandeis. Following the collapse of his plan for a national unity program based on harmony among business, labor, and government, Franklin D. Roosevelt fell under the influence of the Brandeisian wing of the New Deal Democrats such as Thurman Arnold, Thomas Corcoran, Robert Jackson, and Benjamin Cardozo. Many of them were protégés not only of Brandeis but also of the influential Harvard law professor Felix Frank-furter, whom Roosevelt appointed to the Supreme Court in 1938. Their critics called the disciples of Frankfurter "the Happy Hot Dogs."

Dismissing the Keynesian analysis that held that a lack of demand was the problem, they claimed that business was prolonging the crisis by hoarding cash. Their proposed cures for the Depression were a tax on retained earnings to force business to disgorge its savings and a vigorous application of antitrust policy.

Angry at the opposition of business leaders to the New Deal, the presi-dent lashed out at "economic royalists" in his 1936 speech to the Democratic National Convention. "The real truth of the matter is, as you and I know," Roosevelt wrote Wilson's former adviser Colonel Edward Mandell House, "that a financial element in the larger centers has owned the Government ever since the days of Andrew Jackson—and I am not wholly excepting the Administration of W.W. [Woodrow Wilson]. The country is going through a repetition of Jackson's fight with the Bank of the United States—only on a far bigger and broader basis."[73] Repudiating his earlier support for business-government collaboration, he sided with liberal critics of monopoly. He welcomed exposés of industrial concentration by the Temporary National Economic Committee (TNEC), established by Congress in 1938.

The Brandeisian faction influenced FDR's claim in a speech to Congress in 1938 that the cause of the recession that started in 1937 was not contractionary federal policy but monopoly: "Among us today a concentration of private power without equal in history is growing. This concentration is seriously impairing the economic effectiveness of private enterprise as a way of providing employment for labor and capital and as a way of assuring a more equitable distribution of income and earnings among the people of the Nation itself."[74]

Roosevelt appointed Arnold to the Justice Department, where he began a vigorous series of antitrust prosecutions. In his five years at the Justice Department's Antitrust Division, Arnold was responsible for half of the antitrust lawsuits filed since the Sherman Act was passed in 1890.[75] Arnold was from Laramie, Wyoming, and his antitrust team at the Justice Department was dominated by other westerners—Tom Clark from Texas, later attorney general and a Supreme Court justice, Wendell Berge of Nebraska, and Corwin Edwards of Nevada.[76] Arnold blamed eastern monopolies for the underdevelopment of his native West. In 1941, he wrote: "For the past twenty years the economy of the South and West has been developing along colonial lines. The industrial East has been the Mother Country. . . . The colonies have furnished the Mother Country with raw material. The Mother Country has been exploiting the colonies by selling them manufactured necessities at artificially controlled prices."[77]

THE MISTAKE OF 1937 AND THE ROOSEVELT RECESSION

In 1937, repeating the mistake made by Hoover when he sought to balance the budget in 1932, President Roosevelt joined his treasury secretary,

Henry Morgenthau, in supporting legislation in Congress to balance the budget by cutting spending and raising taxes. Roosevelt told Congress in his annual address on January 6, 1937: "Your task and mine is not ending with the end of the depression." On April 2, Roosevelt said at a press conference: "I am concerned—we are all concerned—over the price rise in certain markets." The next day the *Wall Street Journal* reported "a change in the trend of the government's recovery measures away from the emphasis which has been placed upon stimulation of industrial activity and the recovery of prices."[78]

Marriner Eccles, the chairman of the Federal Reserve, decided to double bank reserve requirements between August 1936 and May 1937. The contractionary effect of tighter fiscal and monetary policies was worsened by the Treasury's program of sterilizing gold inflows (that is, preventing them from becoming part of the monetary base and expanding it).[79] Finally, in 1936, Congress passed a large bonus for veterans, overriding the veto of President Roosevelt, as it had earlier, in 1930, overridden the veto of President Hoover. The first part of the veterans' bonus was distributed in June 1936; then half that amount was distributed in June 1937, after which this form of stimulus ceased. The result of these measures was a second sharp recession, the Roosevelt Recession, that erased many of the gains of the previous Roosevelt Recovery.

In this troubled period of his presidency, Roosevelt came to believe that a group of powerful capitalists was deliberately sabotaging the economy—a belief that the role of the Du Ponts and other rich families in funding the anti–New Deal Liberty League made plausible. As labor organizers battled company police forces and local police at plants throughout the country, Alfred Sloan of General Motors and other leading executives resigned from the NRA's Business Advisory Council (BAC) and joined the American Liberty League. Founded by major corporations, the Liberty League brought Republicans and conservative Democrats like Roosevelt's former New York ally Al Smith together in a campaign to discredit the New Deal as "socialistic" and "fascistic." Smith, in a 1936 address to the Liberty League, said, "It's all right with me if they want to disguise themselves as . . . Karl Marx, or Lenin, or any of the rest of that bunch, but what I won't stand for is allowing them to march under the banner of Jefferson, Jackson, or Cleveland!"

Roosevelt blamed the recession on a conspiracy by American capitalists, rather than on premature budget balancing. Then-chairman of the SEC William O. Douglas recounted his conversation with FDR during the "Roosevelt recession":

> "What about this market?" he asked.
>
> "Markets are two-way streets," I replied.
>
> "But this one is going down as a result of a conspiracy."
>
> "Whose conspiracy?"
>
> "Business and Wall Street against yours truly."
>
> "Mr. President," I replied, "You are dead wrong. The market is going down because you cut spending."[80]

In an attempt to win Roosevelt back from the Brandeisian trustbusters, Adolf Berle teamed up with Morgan partner Thomas Lamont to form a committee that included Owen Young, Rexford Tugwell, and Charles Taussig of the Roosevelt administration, John L. Lewis of the CIO, and Philip Murray of the steelworkers' union. After the group met at the Century Association in New York, Lamont had an encouraging meeting with Roosevelt, but the Brandeisians killed the initiative by arranging for bad press about the meeting.[81]

Finally Roosevelt was persuaded by his allies to overcome his initial suspicion of the novel theories of the British economist John Maynard Keynes, who argued that large-scale spending by government was necessary to overcome deficiencies in aggregate demand. Keynesianism influenced the Works Financing Bill or "Spend-Lend" Bill. Introduced in 1939 by Senator Alben Barkley of Kentucky, the bill was backed by Federal Reserve chairman Eccles and shaped by his deputy Lauchlin Currie, who drew on a report by John Kenneth Galbraith and Griff Johnson.[82] In his memoirs Currie wrote: "The real importance of the bill, however, was in giving the Government a permanent means, *outside the budget* [emphasis in original], of varying highly desirable expenditures to compensate for excessive variations in private expenditures—another built-in stabilizer. It is almost impossible to conduct proper compensatory policy in timing and volume through the regular routine of new legislation and appropriations."[83] But the conservative backlash against the New Deal was well under way and the Works Financing Bill was the first major spending bill backed by Roosevelt that went down to defeat.

THE SUCCESS AND FAILURE OF THE NEW DEAL

In the United States, the Depression consisted of two recessions—the first from 1929 to 1933, followed by a recovery and then a second recession in 1937–1938. The period from FDR's inauguration in 1933 until 1937 was one of rapid recovery, in which the economy grew at 8 percent a year. Between 1938 and 1941, the economy grew at more than 10 percent a year.[84]

The four-year period between 1934 and 1937 saw economic growth at a rapid pace with no parallel in US history, outside of wartime. The 25 percent deflation from 1929 to 1933 was followed by 11 percent inflation from 1933 to 1937.[85] When Americans employed in work-relief programs are included among the employed, unemployment plunged under the New Deal from 21 percent when FDR took office in 1933 to 9 percent in 1937. If work-relief program employees are counted as unemployed, the numbers are slightly higher but the dramatic improvement remains the same. The ill-advised attempt to balance the budget created the Roosevelt Recession, boosting unemployment to 13 percent.[86] Even with the setback of the 1937–1938 recession, unemployment was down to 11.3 percent in 1939.

When the unprecedented speed of the recovery between 1933 and 1937 is considered along with the rapid decline in unemployment, it is impossible to argue that the New Deal made the Depression worse. On the contrary, even before the disastrous attempt in 1937 to balance the budget prematurely, the federal government in the 1930s spent too little to combat the Depression, not too much.

The title of the January 1937 *Life* two-page photo-spread told the story: "What President Roosevelt Did to the Map of the U.S. in Four Years with $6,500,000,000." The map depicted the Los Angeles aqueduct and the Grand Coulee, Fort Peck, and Norris dams, the Triborough Bridge and Midtown Tunnel in New York City, a public school in Fort Worth, Texas, and Dinosaur Park and the spectacular Trans-Mountain Highway in Glacier National Park in northwestern Montana.[87]

The WPA alone between 1935 and 1943 was responsible for 572,000 miles of rural roads; 67,000 miles of urban streets; 31,000 miles of sidewalks; 122,000 bridges; 1,000 tunnels; 1,050 airports; 1,500 sewage treatment plants; 500 water treatment plants; 24,000 miles of sewers; 19,700 miles of water mains; 3,300 stadiums; 5,000 athletic fields; 12,800 playgrounds; 36,900 schools; 1,000 public libraries; 2,552 hospitals; 2,700 firehouses; 900 armories; 19,400 state and local government buildings; 416 fish hatcheries; and 7,000 miles of firebreaks.[88] In his autobiography, *An American Life*, Ronald Reagan wrote: "The WPA was one of the most productive of FDR's alphabet soup agencies because it put people to work building roads, bridges and other projects."[89] The National Youth Administration (NYA) provided assistance to four and a half million young Americans, ranging from work relief to work-study programs, benefiting poor black Americans in particular in spite of political concessions to white racism. The Civilian Conservation Corps (CCC) put unemployed men to work in conservationist projects like reforestation.

All of this, however, fell short of what was needed to provide a stimulus for the American economy commensurate with its problems. Federal credit programs like the RFC and federal employment programs like the WPA and CCC were helpful but inadequate. In a 1940 study for the government, Galbraith concluded that 13 to 15 percent of the total number of unemployed workers were employed by federal public-works programs, with another 18 to 21 percent engaged in work-relief construction jobs.[90] Even worse, the federal government's expansionary fiscal policies failed to offset the contractionary effects of state and local budget cuts and tax increases in all but two of the seven years beginning in 1933.[91] The states responded to the revenue shortfalls caused by the Depression by raising sales and excise taxes, including gasoline taxes, and personal and corporate income taxes.[92]

In 1956 the economist E. Carey Brown concluded: "Fiscal policy, then, seems to have been an unsuccessful recovery device in the 'thirties—not because it didn't work, but because it was not tried."[93]

While the New Deal failed to pull the US economy completely out of the Depression before World War II, Roosevelt succeeded in rescuing American capitalism by reforming it. Although the New York patrician did his best to identify himself with Jefferson and Jackson, the heroes of the Democratic Party of his day, Franklin Roosevelt, like his cousin Theodore, arguably was a progressive nationalist in the tradition of Hamilton, Clay, and Lincoln. Roosevelt's speechwriter Robert Sherwood suggested that the New Deal "was, in fact, as Roosevelt conceived it and conducted it, a revolution of the Right, rising up to fight its own defense."[94]

Whether he was an enlightened conservative or a pragmatic liberal, Roosevelt excelled in evoking the hatred of the privileged and the admiration of ordinary Americans. During the Depression, a North Carolina farmer declared, in all sincerity, "I'm proud of our United States and every time I hear the 'Star-Spangled Banner' I feel a lump in my throat. There ain't no other nation in the world that would have sense enough to think of WPA and all the other A's."[95] "Dear President," a furniture maker in Paris, Texas, wrote in 1936. "Know you are the one & only President that ever helped a Working Class of People."[96] A North Carolina millworker was more pungent in his praise: "Mr. Roosevelt is the only man we ever had in the White House who would understand that my boss is a son-of-a-bitch."[97]

A more eloquent tribute came from Roosevelt's most important protégé and successor, Lyndon Johnson. In October 1964 in South Gate, California, President Johnson, recalling FDR's 1933 inaugural address, explained why Roosevelt's leadership had been so important:

I remember the first President I ever saw, and the greatest President I ever knew. I saw him stand up one day in his braces, with pain in his legs, and anguish in his face, but vision in his head and hope in his eyes. I saw him talk to almost this many people, maybe more. It was a rainy, cold day in March 1933. The banks were popping in the country just like popcorn, just like firecrackers going off at Christmastime. They were closing.

The railroad men had come running down to Washington and the insurance companies and all these captains of finance, all these smart conservatives, and the roof had caved in. People were burning their corn. Cotton was selling for 5 cents. You couldn't find a job and relief lines were longer than from here to that airport I landed at, and that is 15 miles away.

But this man stood up in that time when things weren't near as good as they are today, with the braces on his legs, out of his wheelchair, and he grabbed that microphone, and he stuck his chin up, and his jaw out, and he said, "The only thing we have to fear is fear itself," and he electrified a nation, and he saved a republic.[98]

ARSENAL OF DEMOCRACY

The United States is like a giant boiler. Once the fire is lighted under it there is no limit to the power it can generate.
—British Foreign Secretary Sir Edward Grey to Winston Churchill[1]

Winning the war is a matter of oil, bullets and beans.
—Admiral Chester Nimitz[2]

In 1940 in the *New Republic*, John Maynard Keynes wrote: "It seems politically impossible for a capitalistic democracy to organize expenditures on the scale necessary to make the grand experiment which would prove my case—except in war conditions."[3] That grand experiment took place in the United States, following the Japanese attack on Pearl Harbor on December 7, 1941, and the formal entry of the United States into World War II.

In December 1943, President Franklin D. Roosevelt told journalists that "Dr. New Deal" had given way to "Dr. Win the War." Earlier, on December 29, 1940, almost a year before the Japanese attack on Pearl Harbor brought the United States directly into the war, Roosevelt in a radio address to the American people called for the United States to mobilize its industrial power to aid the British and other victims of Axis imperialism: "American industrial genius, unmatched throughout all the world in the solution of production problems, has been called upon to bring its resources and its talents into action. Manufacturers of watches, of farm implements, of Linotypes and cash registers and automobiles, and sewing machines and lawn mowers and locomotives, are now making fuses and bomb packing crates and telescope mounts and shells and pistols and tanks."

The president continued: "But all of our present efforts are not enough. We must have more ships, more guns, more planes—more of everything. ... I want to make it clear that it is the purpose of the nation to build now with all possible speed every machine, every arsenal, every factory that we need to manufacture our defense material. . . . We must be the great arsenal of democracy."[4]

PREPAREDNESS

Even before the United States entered the war, the country rapidly expanded and reoriented the economy toward war production. In June 1939, Congress passed the Strategic Materials Act, to stockpile critical materials. In August, the War Resources Board was created.

In September 1939, Britain and France declared war on Germany following the joint German-Soviet invasion of Poland. At the time, unemployment in the United States averaged 17 percent and only 1.4 percent of GNP was devoted to military expenditure.[5] Late in 1939, Congress amended the Neutrality Acts to permit the shipment of arms and other aid to Britain and France. Roosevelt asked Congress for a two-ocean navy and billions more for national defense.

Defense spending increased again following Germany's invasion of France in May 1940. In June 1940, as Hitler's armies overran France, the federal government drew up a National Roster of Scientific and Specialized Personnel, many of whom worked on the Manhattan Project, which will be described in chapter 15. In August 1940, the Defense Plant Corporation, funded by the Reconstruction Finance Corporation (RFC), was created to build defense factories and other facilities. In September 1940, Congress created the first peacetime draft in American history with the Selective Service Act. Also in September 1940, the destroyers-for-bases agreement provided Britain with fifty obsolete US destroyers, in return for ninety-nine-year leases by the United States of specified British military bases around the world.

The Roosevelt administration hoped that the Axis powers of Germany, Japan, and Italy could be defeated without direct US participation in the war by a combination of American aid and economic warfare. On March 11, 1941, Congress passed the Lend-Lease Act, which permitted the president to send arms or supplies to aid in the defense of any country that he deemed was "vital to the defense of the United States." Under the lend-lease program, the United States provided $50 billion in aid, much of it in the form of weapons, tanks, locomotives, and other supplies, to its allies Britain, the Soviet Union, France, and China. Two-thirds of lend-lease aid went to Britain and its empire.

Another form of economic aid took the form of international cartels sponsored by the US government. During World War II, the United States engaged in dozens of commodity agreements in industries like coffee, sugar, and wheat, designed to stabilize prices. Most of these were with commodity-exporting Latin American nations whom the United States wanted as allies. In the words of one scholar, "By 1945, much of U.S. foreign trade ran through what were in effect government-controlled cartels."[6]

By the final quarter of 1941, 16 percent of US GNP was being spent on defense—the equivalent of the highest levels during the Cold War conflicts in Korea and Vietnam.[7] The United States hoped to thwart Japan's attempt to consolidate its empire in China without war by starving Japan of crucial war matériel. On October 16, 1940, Roosevelt imposed an embargo on scrap iron and steel exports to countries other than Britain and nations in the Western Hemisphere. This was followed on July 26, 1941, by a US embargo, joined by Britain and the Netherlands, on oil exports to Japan.

Japan faced a choice between abandoning its imperialism or attempting to seize oil and other resources in the British and Dutch colonies in Southeast Asia and neighboring countries. Choosing to persist, Japan hoped to buy time to consolidate its position in Asia by crippling as much of the US Navy as it could, as it had done in May 1904, when it destroyed much of the Russian fleet in the Russo-Japanese War.

On December 7, 1941, Japan attacked the US fleet at Pearl Harbor, Hawaii. On December 11, Germany declared war on the United States.

DRAFTING THE ECONOMY

When World War II began in 1939, the United States was unprepared, with an army of 200,000, a navy of 125,000 and a Marine Corps of 20,000. In 1939 and 1940, American soldiers used trucks to simulate tanks and broomsticks to imitate rifles.[8]

Because of failures of mobilization during World War I, the United States had been forced to rely on munitions supplied by Britain and France. General John J. Pershing complained: "It seems, 'odd' that with American genius for manufacturing from iron and steel, we should find ourselves after a year and a half of war almost without these mechanical contrivances which had exercised such a great influence on the western front in reducing infantry losses."[9] Following World War I, Congress charged the military with responsibility for ensuring that such a debacle did not occur again. As World War II approached, however, mobilization plans were abandoned and the Roosevelt administration improvised. After several abortive efforts, the administration settled on the Office of War Mobilization in May 1943. Donald Nelson, formerly the chief merchandising executive of Sears, the world's biggest distribution firm at the time, was appointed by FDR as chairman of the War Production Board in January 1942.

To the disappointment of many on the political Left who wanted a socialized defense sector, the Roosevelt administration chose to mobilize private corporations to produce war matériel, as the Wilson administration had done during World War I. Before the war, the United States had produced 78 percent of the world's cars and 64 percent of the world's trucks and buses.[10] After Pearl Harbor, civilian automobile production halted and automobile factories were modified to produce tanks, planes, jeeps, and other vehicles. The Ford Motor Company, for example, made bombers at its eighty-acre Willow Run site outside Detroit as well as tanks instead of cars. Charles Lindbergh described Willow Run as the "Grand Canyon of the mechanized world."[11]

Academic American economists played a role in shaping American strategy during the war. In 1942, American policymakers engaged in a secret debate about the feasibility of a US-British invasion of German-occupied Europe in 1943. In a classified report for the War Production Board, two economists, Robert Nathan and Simon Kuznets, concluded that it would not be possible to produce the necessary matériel until 1944 at the earliest. The army's chief military supply officer, General Brehon Somervell, was furious. He denounced "this board of 'economists and statisticians' . . . without any responsibility or knowledge of production." He called for the suppression of the report, which should "be carefully hidden from the eyes of all thoughtful men." But the argument of Nathan and Kuznets prevailed, and D-Day was a success in 1944 instead of a disaster in 1943.[12]

STATE CAPITALISM

The United States used state capitalism as well as private capitalism to mobilize the economy for war. The federal government expanded manufacturing capacity both directly, by building factories and war housing, and indirectly, by means of loans and tax breaks to private companies.

The purpose of the Reconstruction Finance Corporation (RFC), which itself had been modeled on the War Finance Corporation of World War I, changed from recapitalizing banks and businesses and funding public works projects to funding the expansion of industry for military purposes. The RFC created and funded a number of wartime agencies, including the Defense Supplies Corporation, the Defense Plant Corporation, the Metals Reserve Company, the Petroleum Reserve Corporation, the Rubber Development Corporation, the Rubber Reserve Company, and the US Commercial Company.

The government invested heavily in aluminum production. Before the war, Alcoa had been the only major producer of aluminum, which was used in airplanes. The federal government built new plants and brought Reynolds Metals Company into the industry. The Bonneville and Grand Coulee Dams generated electricity used to make aluminum for aircraft production and other military uses.

When the war ended, the federal government owned more than half of the country's aluminum-production capacity. The government turned some of its facilities over to Alcoa's competitors Kaiser Aluminum and Chemical Corporation and Reynolds Metal Company.

SYNTHETIC RUBBER

After the Manhattan Project, to be described in chapter 15, the greatest crash program undertaken by the federal government during World War II was the effort to produce synthetic rubber. In 1942, Japan's conquest of much of Southeast Asia cut the United States off from its major suppliers of natural rubber, leaving it with an eighteen-month supply. Without rubber, the United States could not run its civilian economy, much less mount a successful global war effort.

At the beginning of 1942, only one small synthetic rubber plant existed in the United States and only 540,000 tons had been stockpiled. In September 1942, a committee headed by Bernard Baruch declared the existence of a synthetic-rubber shortage emergency.

The federal government rapidly built synthetic-rubber factories, which were leased to private operators by the Defense Plant Corporation. The factories generated 8,383 long tons in 1941; 22,434 in 1942; 231,722 in 1942; and 753,111 in 1944.[13]

Three-fourths of the synthetic rubber manufactured in the United States during World War II was buna rubber, which derived its name from the chemicals in its makeup: *bu* from butadiene and *na* from natrium (sodium). Buna rubber was first synthesized in Germany in the 1930s. The circumstances by which the United States obtained it gave rise to a conspiracy theory about the alleged collaboration between Rockefeller oil interests and Hitler which, like other conspiracy theories, refuses to die.

In 1929, IG Farben, one of Germany's industrial firms, developed a process to create oil from coal. In order to obtain access to the patents for this process and other innovations, Standard Oil of New Jersey created two joint ventures with IG Farben, called the Standard/IG Company and the Joint American Study Company (Jasco), in which Standard owned 80 percent of the stock and IG Farben 20 percent. Jasco ended up owning the patent rights to the process for artificial synthesis of buna rubber.

Between the outbreak of World War II in 1939 and the US entry in 1941 following Pearl Harbor, Standard and a number of other American firms with similar joint ventures, foreign subsidiaries, or membership in international cartels in particular industries found themselves in a difficult situation. The US government was officially neutral and could not abrogate the contracts without in effect declaring war on Germany, something it was unwilling to do, while it was difficult for the companies to disentangle themselves. The Japanese attack on Pearl Harbor, followed by Germany's declaration of war against the United States on December 11, solved the problem. The US Alien Property Custodian seized the American assets of IG Farben, including not only its stock in Jasco but also IG Farben's two important American subsidiaries, General Aniline and its marketing company General Dyestuffs, which controlled 40 percent of the American dyestuffs market.

IG Farben's buna rubber was easier to make than neoprene, another kind of synthetic rubber developed by DuPont. Immediately following the Pearl Harbor attack, Standard Oil in December 1941 put its buna rubber technology patents into a pool to help American rubber production.

The matter should have ended there. But Thurman Arnold, the Justice Department's chief antitrust lawyer, chose this moment to sue Standard for its ties to IG Farben. Protesting its innocence, Standard reluctantly settled with the Justice Department, only to find itself subjected to trial in public opinion. Before Senator Harry Truman's committee overseeing wartime mobilization, Arnold blamed Standard Oil for the rubber shortage in the United States: "We believe that the cartel arrangements with Germany . . . are the principal cause of the present shortage of synthetic rubber."[14] Arnold's charges, recycled by journalists and historians, became the basis of enduring conspiracy theories about sinister ties between Hitler's Germany and Standard Oil, which had long been demonized in the press by Ida Tarbell and others.

The truth was quite different. From 1939 onward, Standard had sought to develop synthetic rubber, but the quality was low and the price was high, compared to natural rubber. In 1940, before the United States entered the war, Standard Oil appealed to the government to build synthetic-rubber plants. The Roosevelt administration rejected the idea, on the assumption that there would be uninterrupted access to the natural rubber supplies of Asia.

The shortage of artificial rubber in the United States was the fault of the government, not of private industry. On coming to power in Germany in 1933, Hitler ordered a four-year plan to make Germany self-sufficient in food and chemicals, in preparation for the war of conquest he already planned. The Nazi regime forced German industry to use artificial rubber, despite its cost and low quality. As a result the German military machine was well supplied with artificial rubber when Hitler launched his war.

Wearying of Arnold's antibusiness crusade in the middle of a world war in which American success depended on government-business collaboration, President Roosevelt removed him from the Justice Department by "kicking him upstairs" to the US Court of Appeals for the District of Columbia Circuit. After two years Arnold resigned to found the Washington law firm known today as Arnold and Porter.

INNOVATION FOR VICTORY

In 1947, twice as many Americans worked in industrial-research centers as in 1940.[15] Among the breakthroughs that resulted from wartime research, in addition to nuclear energy, were jet engines, radar, computers, synthetic rubber, and a range of new drugs: penicillin, synthetic quinine, and sulfa drugs.

A massive government R&D and production effort was devoted to penicillin. In 1928, Alexander Fleming had discovered that penicillin could kill bacteria. During World War II, the US government coordinated efforts by universities, the Department of Agriculture, and nearly two dozen pharmaceutical companies to devise technologies for the mass production of the drug.[16]

Catalytic cracking is the process of creating high-octane fuel from petroleum feedstocks. During the war, the oil industry drew on the research into catalytic cracking of Eugene Houdry, a French engineer who immigrated to the United States in 1930 and patented the catalytic converter that is used in most automobiles today. At Baton Rouge, Standard Oil built the first full-scale operational catalytic cracking plant in 1942, a web of pipes containing tanks. Soon "cat crackers" were springing up in refineries across the country.

WARTIME INFRASTRUCTURE PROJECTS

In its capacity as state capitalist, the government also engaged in massive domestic infrastructure projects that bolstered the war effort. One was the Alaska Highway, connecting the United States with Alaska through Canada, which was authorized by Congress in 1942 and remarkably was completed by the end of the year. Another was the Saint Lawrence Seaway, connecting the Atlantic Ocean with the Great Lakes. Backed by Herbert Hoover, the proposal for the seaway was stalled until December 1940, when Roosevelt declared that "the United States needs the St. Lawrence Seaway for defense." In 1941, the United States and Canada negotiated an agreement. The project was finally completed in 1959, when President Dwight Eisenhower and Queen Elizabeth presided at a ceremony in Montreal.

One consequence of the destroyers-for-bases transfer of ships to Britain was a shortage of tankers to transport oil within the United States. In May 1941, executives from eight major oil companies met in New York to discuss the problem. Their proposed solution was a twenty-four-inch pipeline from Texas to the East Coast. The government rejected the idea, but following Pearl Harbor the proposal was revived and approved. A corporation called War Emergency Pipelines, Inc., was formed and funded by the RFC.

Through mountains and swamps and over bridges, the Big Inch snaked from Longview, Texas, to Phoenixville, Pennsylvania, where it split into two segments, one terminating at Philadelphia and the other at Linden, New Jersey. Only 350 days after construction began, the Big Inch was complete. Each day it carried five times as much oil as had ever been carried in a pipeline before to the refineries of the East Coast.

The Big Inch was soon joined by the Little Big Inch, a pipeline that stretched 1,475 miles from Beaumont, Texas, to Linden, New Jersey. While the Big Inch carried crude oil, the Little Big Inch transported gasoline, diesel, fuel oil, and aviation fuel.[17] Six of the seven billion barrels of oil used by the Allies in World War II came from the United States.[18]

FROM GUN BELT TO SUN BELT

The New Deal Democrats were supported by southern and western interests like the Brown brothers of Texas, whose Brown and Root evolved into Halliburton; Henry J. Kaiser of Kaiser Aluminum; and independent oil producers like Sid Richardson, who challenged the Rockefellers and Pews of the northeastern oil industry. Members of Congress and administration officials from the South and West used the military emergency to create defense plants in their regions as the nuclei of postwar economic development, achieving the goal of industrial decentralization.

The importance of World War II in the industrial transformation of the United States cannot be exaggerated. Between 1940 and 1945, nearly half of the previous total investment in all US industry was made in war production by the federal government. Before Pearl Harbor, the only states in which a third or more of the workforce was in the manufacturing sector were New Jersey, Pennsylvania, Ohio, Michigan, and the states of New England. Between 1950 and 1970, the share of traditional manufacturing activity in the northeastern core declined by 3 percent and grew in the Sunbelt by 56 percent.[19] During the war, the South was the site of two-thirds of military training camps, 47.7 percent of federally financed chemical, coal, and petroleum production, 36.5 percent of total awards for military facilities in the continental United States, and 23 percent of the new plants built for the war.[20]

Between the Japanese attack on Pearl Harbor on December 7, 1941, and V-J Day on September 2, 1945, the landscape and economy of Texas were transformed by military-led modernization in a revolution far more profound, and with more lasting effects, than Reconstruction or the New Deal. In addition to increasing oil and gas production, the federal government made Texas the site of factories that produced rubber from petroleum, to replace natural rubber supplies from Japanese-occupied Asia and from Brazil, and also magnesium and aluminum. The government expanded and upgraded existing shipyards and created a Texas shipbuilding industry from nothing. The draining of the rural population into military service and factory work accelerated the mechanization of Texas agriculture, increasing its efficiency.

The Houston construction firm of Brown and Root, a longtime backer of Lyndon Johnson, grew rich from government contracts during World War II and the Cold War. In California, similar beneficiaries of military state capitalism were Kaiser Steel and Bechtel Corporation, which provided many of the members of Ronald Reagan's cabinet (Reagan voted four times for Roosevelt for president, so his alliance with a corporate client of the Rooseveltian state was only appropriate).

Texas Instruments began before the war as Geophysical Services, Inc., building electronics to help oil companies find oil. During World War II, the company built instruments to help the navy search for enemy submarines. It specialized as a defense contractor providing electronics to the US military by the time it changed its name to Texas Instruments in 1951. TI later produced the first commercial silicon transistors, integrated circuits, and handheld calculators. The history of TI symbolized the birth of a high-tech economy from the oil-patch economy of Texas, midwifed by the US military.

KAISER'S LIBERTY SHIPS

Another beneficiary of wartime industrial development was California. World War II produced a massive expansion of the aircraft production industry around Los Angeles. The region continued to be home to prominent defense contractors for half a century until the end of the Cold War.

Henry J. Kaiser was a master builder who thought in grandiose terms. After moving in 1906 to California, the native of Sprout Brook, New York, founded a road construction company. In the 1930s, the firm took part in the construction of the Hoover, Grand Coulee, and Bonneville Dams. Although he had never built a ship, his record helped Kaiser win a grant from the government in World War II to build shipyards in Los Angeles, Portland, Houston, and elsewhere. Inspired by Henry Ford's assembly line, Kaiser perfected the mass production of cargo-carrying Liberty Ships, building one in only four days. Kaiser built a steel plant in California and created Kaiser Aluminum.

In addition to being an innovator in shipbuilding, Kaiser was a welfare capitalist in the tradition of Gerard Swope and Owen Young of GE. During the war, Kaiser's employees were offered prepaid medical plans and, in 1945, Kaiser joined with Dr. Sidney Garfield, who ran the hospital for the Kaiser Shipyards and had first worked with Kaiser during the construction of Grand Coulee Dam, to found the Kaiser Permanente health management organization (HMO). In 1948, he founded the

Henry J. Kaiser Foundation, which focuses on health care. Proving that no good deed goes unpunished, Kaiser and his nonprofits were attacked by the for-profit medical industry. Today Kaiser Permanente, a nonprofit organization, is the largest managed-health-care plan in the United States.

"THE MAN WHO WON THE WAR FOR US"

Dwight D. Eisenhower described him as "the man who won the war for us" and Hitler grumbled that he was the "new Noah" after 156,000 Allied soldiers landed on the shores of Normandy on D-Day, June 6, 1944, in craft designed and built by Andrew Jackson Higgins. Higgins began his business career as the proprietor of A. O. Higgins Lumber and Export Company, a New Orleans firm that built its own fleet in a small boatyard to transport its products. Higgins supervised twenty thousand workers who completed seven hundred boats a month, of two kinds—fast PT boats like the one commanded by the young John F. Kennedy in the Pacific and landing craft like those used on D-Day. His motto was "The Hell I Can't."

After Higgins died in 1952, the subsequent history of his Michoud facility illustrated the continuing role of government procurement in the development of the postwar South. It was part of what had been a 1763 grant by the French royal government of 34,500 acres to a New Orleans merchant named Gilbert Antoine de St. Maxent. Part of that property was acquired by Antoine Michoud, the son of Napoleon's administrator of domains, who turned it into a sugar plantation and refinery after arriving in New Orleans in 1827. Following his death in 1863, the property was kept intact by his heirs until it was incorporated into a factory facility for Higgins Industries.

The Michoud facility found a new use during the Korean War, when Chrysler used it to manufacture engines for tanks that never went into production. The inactive facility was employed again as the space race intensified. NASA took over the plant and assigned it to Chrysler and Boeing to make stages of Saturn I and Saturn V rockets that could be transported by water to Cape Canaveral (later Cape Kennedy). After the Apollo program ran its course, Martin Marietta used the property to make tanks for the space shuttle in the 1980s.[21]

THE END OF UNEMPLOYMENT

Unemployment fell from 17.2 percent in 1939 to 1.2 percent in 1944. Mass unemployment came to an end, as millions of unemployed men were drafted or drawn into the military or the defense-industrial workforce. At the end of 1940, five million Americans were still unemployed; by the end of 1941, there were two million in the army and navy.[22] The US Army expanded from 167,767 in 1940 to 8,266,373, with 5 million overseas, in 1945.[23] At the peak of World War II, more than sixteen million men and women were in the US armed forces and the merchant marine. Millions of women as well served in the military or worked in defense plants. No longer needed, the WPA and other emergency public-employment programs were dissolved.

Between 1940 and 1945, seventeen million Americans found jobs—ten million in the armed forces, two million working for the military and other government agencies, and five million in the civilian sector, producing both military and civilian goods. Of these seventeen million, seven million had formerly been unemployed; ten million were new entrants to the labor market, about half of them women, with other new entrants provided by former farmers.[24] The farm population shrank by a fifth during the war.[25]

ORGANIZED LABOR

Tight wartime labor markets increased the bargaining power both of white unionized workers and African Americans. By executive order on March 19, 1941, President Roosevelt created the National Defense Mediation Board (NDMB), a tripartite arbitration board with representatives of management, labor, and the public. The membership of the AFL increased by 63 percent between 1940 and 1945, while the CIO made even greater gains, with a 66 percent increase in membership.[26]

But relations between government and organized labor were strained by wartime strikes. John L. Lewis had broken with Roosevelt over US involvement in World War II and became a bitter critic of the president. He led the United Mine Workers on a strike in the bituminous coal industry. Enraged, FDR called for a national-service law to ban strikes and compel able-bodied adults to be assigned to productive work. He did not get it, but he rescinded draft exemptions for striking miners under the age of forty-five.[27]

During a strike in May 1941, the US Army took over the North American Aviation factory in Los Angeles. In all the government seized industrial facilities during labor disputes a total of sixty-three times.[28]

ROSIE THE RIVETER

In 2010, Geraldine Hoff Doyle died, survived by five children, eighteen grandchildren, and twenty-five great-grandchildren. Few Americans would have recognized her name, but many would have recognized the name that made her face famous: Rosie the Riveter.

In 1942, at the age of seventeen, Geraldine Hoff, then unmarried, was working as a metal presser in the American Broach and Machine Company in Ann Arbor, Michigan, when her picture was taken by the photographer J. Howard Miller. An image of her looking determined, with her sleeves rolled up and her hair wrapped in a scarf, was used in a morale-boosting poster used in Westinghouse plants, with the slogan "We Can Do It!" The poster did not identify her by name, and it was only in the late twentieth century that the Westinghouse poster became identified with the mythical Rosie the Riveter, who symbolized American women working to defeat the Axis in the factories on the home front.

Rosie the Riveter got her name from a 1942 hit song by Redd Evans and John Jacob Loeb.

All the day long,
Whether rain or shine
She's part of the assembly line.
She's making history,
Working for victory
Rosie the Riveter[29]

The inspiration for the song was Rosalind Palmer Walter, who worked as a riveter during the night shift on the marine fighter airplane, the Corsair. Far from being proletarian, this Rosie came from a patrician family, married the chairman and CEO of International Flavors and Fragrances, and became a major philanthropist, funding, among other institutions, Long Island University, the American Museum of Natural History, and public television.

There were other Rosies, too. Kentucky-born Rose Will Monroe, the daughter of a carpenter, was working at Henry Ford's enormous Willow Run Aircraft Factory in Ypsilanti, Michigan, when she was spotted by the actor Walter Pidgeon and cast as Rosie the Riveter in a series of wartime films. Another Rosie was Mary Keefe, a dental hygienist. She posed as Rosie the Riveter for a painting by Norman Rockwell for the cover of the *Saturday Evening Post*, taking a break to eat a sandwich with her feet propped up on Hitler's *Mein Kampf*.

The "real Rosie" who came closest to the archetypal character, perhaps, was Rose Bonaventura, whose parents had immigrated to the United States from Italy. President Roosevelt sent her a letter of commendation after she and her partner set a record drilling holes and driving rivets into a bomber during one overnight shift in 1943.[30]

There were millions of Rosies. By 1944, women were 40 percent of the workers in the aircraft industry, 34.2 percent of all ammunition workers, 10.6 percent of all steel workers, 10 percent of all workers in shipping, and 8 percent of railroad workers.[31]

The mass entry of American women into the industrial workforce created a crisis in child care. In 1934–1935, the WPA had created 1,900 emergency nursery schools as part of its work relief program. During the war the government increased their number to 3,102 for 128,357 children.[32]

By 1944, female participation in the workforce rose to 36.3 percent, with 71 percent remaining outside. However, the mobilization of women was far more limited in the United States than in Britain and the Soviet Union, where only 30 percent of women remained outside of the workforce during World War II.[33]

The United States never mobilized its workforce or its economy as much as the other participants in the war did. The sheer size of its economy and the safety from attack provided by its geographic distance from the centers of conflict permitted American leaders to ask for far less sacrifice than the leaders of other nations on both sides demanded. Indeed, in the United States, unlike in Britain or other Allied countries, personal consumption actually grew during the war.

BATTLING RACISM ON THE HOME FRONT

Almost a million black Americans moved from the rural South to industrial jobs in the North and West. Those who remained behind benefited from a tighter labor market.

In the summer of 1941, A. Philip Randolph, the president of the Brotherhood of Sleeping Car Porters, threatened to lead a march on Washington, DC, to demand equal opportunity for blacks in defense jobs. Secretary of War Henry L. Stimson wrote in his diary on January 24, 1942: "What these foolish leaders of the colored race are seeking is at the bottom social equality."[34]

After Randolph refused to back down following a meeting with the president and other officials, Roosevelt signed Executive Order 8802, which banned racial discrimination in defense industries. This not only marked the first time that the federal government had intervened on behalf of black rights since the end of Reconstruction after the Civil War, but it also laid the groundwork for the postwar civil rights movement led by Martin Luther King Jr., whose 1963 march on Washington was inspired by Randolph's idea.

While the federal government took the first tentative steps toward dismantling segregation in the workforce, it also carried out one of the worst acts of official racism in American history. Between 1942 and 1945, 110,000 Americans of Japanese descent, the majority of them Nisei, or US citizens, were forcibly relocated to ten internment camps. Decades later, the federal government compensated survivors with only $38 million, a fraction of the $200 million in property that they had lost.

Even as their relatives were interned in the United States, Japanese American soldiers fought from Asia to Europe. Daniel Inouye, who had planned to become a doctor, lost an arm while fighting the Germans in Italy; he later became the first Japanese American senator. The 100th Infantry Battalion earned the name "Purple Heart Battalion" because so many of its members were injured in combat. The 100th, along with the 442nd Regimental Combat Team that followed it, rescued a besieged battalion of Texans in the Vosges Mountains in France in the depths of winter in 1944. When its size and length of service are considered, the 100th Infantry Battalion/442nd Regimental Combat Team was the most decorated military unit in American history.[35]

Latinos suffered from racism and economic exploitation during the war, as well. In 1943, white sailors and marines stationed in Los Angeles took part in violence in the "zoot suit riots," named for the zoot suits worn by Mexican American youth. The labor shortage in agribusiness along the Southwestern border was addressed by the Bracero Program, a system of indentured servitude for Mexican nationals that was so exploitative it was abolished during the civil rights era of the 1960s.

Although the United States remained a deeply racist society, World War II had a liberalizing and integrating effect. The fact that the United States was fighting totalitarian and racist regimes allowed reformers to identify antiracism and support for civil liberties with the American way of life. The military-based economic development of rural areas shocked much of the country into modernity. Old-stock Americans and first- and second-generation immigrants, whites, blacks, Latinos, and Asians, mingled in factories at home and in military units around the world. The integrated platoon, with Italian Americans, Jews, Texas cowboys, and black Americans, provided Hollywood with a symbol of a postracist America.

PAYING FOR THE WAR

The US government paid for its World War II effort by a combination of taxes and borrowing. The national debt swelled from 43 percent of GNP in 1940 to 129 percent in 1946. Thanks to a combination of economic growth and inflation, as a percentage of GNP the war-swollen national debt declined from two-thirds in 1955 to 47 percent in 1965 and 34 percent in 1981.

Although the government relied chiefly on borrowing, taxes were still high—about 45 percent of all war expenditures, a higher percentage than in World War I or the Civil War.[36] Rejecting a general sales tax to pay for the war, the government imposed the personal income tax on 60 percent of households by the end of the war. During the war the practice of withholding taxes from biweekly wage payments, now a fixture of American life, was first instituted. The personal income tax surpassed the corporate income tax as a source of federal revenue, and by the late twentieth century three-fourths of federal revenues came from personal income taxes and payroll taxes.

During World War II, millions of middle-class and working-class Americans for the first time paid income taxes, which previously had fallen on the affluent. The Office of War Information commissioned the composer and songwriter Irving Berlin to write "I Paid My Income Tax Today," which was performed by the actor and comedian Danny Kaye:

I said to my Uncle Sam,
"Old Man Taxes, here I am."
And he was glad to see me,

Mister Small Fry, yes indeed—
Lower brackets, that's my speed,
But he was glad to see me.

I paid my income tax today
I never felt so proud before
To be right there with the millions more
Who paid their income tax today.
I'm squared up with the U.S.A.
See those bombers in the sky?
Rockefeller helped to build them; so did I—
I paid my income tax today.

I paid my income tax today.
A thousand planes to bomb Berlin,
They'll all be paid for and I chipped in;
That certainly makes me feel okay—
Ten thousand more and that ain't hay!
We must pay for this war somehow;
Uncle Sam was worried but he isn't now—
I paid my income tax today.

In addition to paying income taxes, ordinary Americans had to endure the rigors of wartime rationing. "General Max" was not a soldier, but a policy: the General Maximum Price Regulation policy of the Office of Price Administration (OPA). The mission of the OPA was to use rationing to avert inflation.

Because they were not permitted to raise wages, US employers competing for workers in the tight labor market began offering fringe benefits, like employer-provided health insurance. Minor at first, this fringe benefit ballooned into the major method by which Americans received health care by the late twentieth century, after the defeat of postwar plans for government-provided universal health care.

"OIL, BULLETS AND BEANS"

In 1944, the United States completed one plane every five minutes, launched fifty merchant ships a day, and finished eight aircraft carriers a month.[37] Mobilized for war, the US economy grew as rapidly during World War II as it declined in the early years of the Depression. US GDP doubled between 1938 and 1944.[38] While in 1938 capacity use in the steel industry had been only 40 percent, in 1943 US Steel and other firms in the industry were operating at 98 percent capacity.[39] The extent to which capacity had lain unused during the 1930s was illustrated by the fact that, between 1939 and 1944, US gross national product grew in real terms by 52 percent.[40] By 1944, the United States was producing as many munitions as its allies and enemies combined.[41] Between 1938 and 1948, US national income rose from the equivalent of that of Germany, Britain, France, and the Benelux countries combined to twice as much, and from three times the size of the economy of the Soviet Union to six times.[42]

America's converted factories produced 88,410 tanks and self-propelled guns; 257,390 artillery pieces; 105,054 mortars; 2,679,840 machine guns; 2,282,311 trucks; and 324,750 aircraft.[43] The number of aircraft manufactured in America grew thirty-fold between 1937 and 1944.[44] Aircraft production peaked at more than 96,000 in 1944.

The United States also undertook a prodigious shipbuilding effort, constructing 141 aircraft carriers, including escort carriers, 8 battleships, 48 cruisers, 349 destroyers, and 33,993 gross tons of merchant shipping.[45] The United States also produced most of the energy and raw materials that fueled the victory of the Allies over the Axis powers: 2,129.7 million metric tons of coal, 833.2 million metric tons of crude oil, 369.9 million metric tons of iron ore, 334.5 million metric tons of steel, and 4.12 million metric tons of aluminum.[46] On D-Day, June 6, 1944, the Germans could deploy only 319 aircraft. The United States and its allies deployed 12,837.[47]

According to the historian Alan Milward, "The war was decided by the weight of armaments production."[48] The combination of American state capitalism and large-scale corporate industrial capitalism, with the help of organized labor, women, and nonwhite Americans, helped to defeat Hitler and his allies. Admiral Chester Nimitz, commander of the US Pacific fleet, put it best: "Winning the war is a matter of oil, bullets and beans."[49]

THE GLORIOUS
THIRTY YEARS

*The 1929 crash, the slow recovery of 1930, and the ensuing spiral
descent into an abyss of unemployment, bank failures, and commercial
paralysis was not corrected by market processes. . . . Out of the crisis
was born the American economic republic as we know it today.*

—Adolf A. Berle, 1963[1]

In Germany, the period was called the *Wirtschaftswunder*, the economic
miracle. In 1958, John Kenneth Galbraith coined the phrase "the affluent society."[2] Looking back, Americans today often call it the Golden
Age. In a 1979 book, the French demographer Jean Fourastie called the
era from 1946 to 1975 *les trente glorieuses*, the glorious thirty, a reference
that evoked the *Trois Glorieuses*, or glorious three days of revolution in
France of July 27–29, 1830.

During the thirty glorious years, the Western democracies experienced similar combinations of high growth and rapid expansion of
mass middle classes, underpinned by high labor-union membership,
middle-class welfare states, and highly regulated economies. By the
1950s, all the democratic societies of the North Atlantic world had "settlements" or "new deals" that were similar in combining various forms
of social insurance with increased government regulation of or ownership of banking and industry. The term "mixed economy" was sometimes used for an economy that blended private enterprise with public

regulation, redistribution, and in some cases public ownership. Shared prosperity gave electorates in America and other white-majority democracies the confidence to eliminate the racial-caste systems that had long made a mockery of their ideals.

The restructuring of the economy after World War II in the United States and other nations coincided with the maturation of the technologies of the second industrial revolution, electricity and the internal combustion engine. In the 1950s and 1960s, the United States completed its electrical grid system and put it under the dull but safe management of local utilities that replaced rival corporate empires. The United States also undertook one of the greatest works of civil engineering in history—the construction of the interstate highway system. Together, the two grids transformed the landscape and the American way of life, by permitting the decentralization of production, work, shopping, and homes.

While the electric grid and the highway grid were visible manifestations of the second industrial order, the unseen motors hidden in household appliances were just as revolutionary. The industrialization of the household with the help of labor-saving appliances like refrigerators, washing machines, and dishwashers allowed the members of America's new mass middle class to spend time formerly devoted to household chores on other activities, including listening to the radio, watching television shows, and going to the movies.

Other countries caught up rapidly, as they rebuilt themselves after the devastation of the second global war in a generation. All the industrial democracies, from Japan to North America to Western Europe, created mass middle classes by using the technologies of the second industrial era for liberal and democratic ends. But it was in the United States that the promise of the liberating technologies of the second industrial revolution was first fulfilled.

THE PAX AMERICANA AND THE COLD WAR

In their planning for the postwar world, the Roosevelt and Truman administrations assumed a rapid demobilization by the United States. The US military sought to possess new island bases around the world on the assumption that there would be no permanent US military garrisons in Asia and Europe once the occupations of the defeated Axis powers came to an end. These assumptions were slowly abandoned, as hopes for postwar cooperation between the Soviet Union and the United States were thwarted by the tensions of the Cold War.

Although it included proxy wars in Korea, Indochina, Afghanistan, Latin America, Africa, and the Middle East, arms races, espionage, sabotage, and propaganda, the Cold War waged by the United States was essentially a war of economic attrition. The United States sought to cripple the Soviet economy by two methods. The first was an embargo of advanced dual-use, or civilian-military, technology, under the direction of the Coordinating Committee for Multilateral Export (CoCom), which was established in 1949 and which governed allied trade with the communist bloc until it was dissolved in 1994. The second was preventing the Soviets from controlling or intimidating West Germany and Japan and other industrial nations.

From the American perspective, the central assets at stake in the Cold War were the factories of defeated Germany and conquered Japan. As the American diplomat George Kennan pointed out, the strategy of the United States was to deny the Soviet Union control of or influence over the other centers of military-industrial power in the world, which at the time were located in Germany/Europe, Japan, Britain, and North America. If the United States directly or indirectly controlled all the centers of manufacturing outside of Soviet borders, then its internal resources alone would not allow the Soviet Union to mount a military challenge to the United States without risking bankruptcy.

During World War II, the Roosevelt administration considered a proposal by Secretary of the Treasury Henry Morgenthau to permanently "pastoralize" or deindustrialize Germany. But in early 1947, Herbert Hoover, sent to Germany on a fact-finding mission by President Harry S. Truman, was shocked by the hunger that he found. Hoover's argument that European economic recovery depended on Germany's economic recovery prevailed. In June 1947, at a Harvard commencement address, secretary of state George Marshall outlined what became known as the Marshall Plan, an offer of substantial amounts of aid to the countries of Europe, including the Soviet Union.

Stalin rejected Marshall Plan aid and denied it to the Eastern European countries under the control of the Red Army. As East-West tensions rose, the American, British, and French zones of occupied Germany were merged into the Federal Republic of Germany, leaving the eastern section of Germany to become a separate country, the German Democratic Republic. The two Germanies would be reunited only after the Cold War ended, in 1990.

The ultimate solution to "the German problem" was integration—the integration of German industry into multinational systems, first the European Coal and Steel Community in 1951 and then the European Economic Community, and the integration of a rehabilitated German military into the North Atlantic Treaty Organization (NATO) alliance in 1955. The extension of multinational control over Germany's coal and steel resources ensured that they would not be enlisted again in the service of military aggression.

West Germany and Japan rearmed, but they remained semisovereign states, subordinate to the United States and, in the case of Germany, to the other members of the European community and NATO. Having ceased to be independent military powers, these great powers devoted their energy to running up manufacturing export surpluses. By the end of the twentieth century, their new specialization would produce problems for the world economy, but in the 1950s Americans were glad to encourage their former enemies to devote their efforts to making cameras and cars instead of Zeros and Panzers.

America's economic superiority allowed it and its allies to prevail in the

Cold War, as in the world wars. The United States was able to bankrupt the Soviet Union, which spent between a third and a half of its smaller economy on the military, while spending no more than an average of 7.5 percent of GDP on defense between 1948 and 1989.[3]

THE GLOBAL OIL CARTEL

Among the global public goods that the United States, as the hegemonic power, supplied to its allies and protectorates was secure access to cheap and abundant petroleum, which was essential to the second industrial economy. In seeking to secure energy supplies for itself and its friends, the United States sacrificed its support of free markets and democracy to the imperatives of geopolitical strategy.

A global oil cartel dated back to the 1920s. After new production in Texas and Oklahoma caused prices to collapse, a cartel was organized by the three largest global oil companies, Standard Oil of New Jersey, Royal Dutch Shell, and Anglo-Iranian Oil (British Petroleum). At a meeting in Scotland, the companies negotiated the "As Is" agreement. The accord provided that, outside of the United States, where antitrust laws applied, the companies would preserve their proportional shares of the global oil market.

This was followed in 1932 by an agreement to fix quotas, enforced by fines and rebates set by a central organization in London. The cartel now included Gulf Oil, Texaco, and Standard Oil of New York (Socony/Mobil). When Standard Oil of California (Socal/Chevron) developed oil fields in Bahrain, it was pressured into joining the cartel and using the marketing organization of the existing cartel member, Texaco.[4]

The global oil cartel might not have survived without regulation of production in the United States, which was the world's leading producer during World War II and for some time afterward. The greatest danger was that many small operators would lack the money and technology to cap wells, leading to the waste of a precious natural resource. The problem was illustrated on January 1, 1901, when a well drilled into the salt dome called Spindletop under Beaumont, Texas, blew. By the time the well was capped on January 19, the well had spouted a two-hundred-foot column of oil into the air, wasting seventy thousand barrels a day.

The danger of waste was apparent to Herbert Hoover, who proposed a federal regulatory commission to supervise oil production. In the fall of 1930, an independent oil operator or "wildcatter," seventy-one-year-old C. M. "Dad" Joiner, discovered the largest oil field yet known in Rusk County in East Texas; he sold out to H. L. Hunt, later one of the biggest and most reactionary Texas oil tycoons. What followed was anarchy.

Texas politicians were painfully aware of a crisis of waste, overproduction, and prices too low to encourage investment. The Texas Railroad Commission (TRC), founded in 1891 to regulate railroads in Texas, was given responsibility to regulate Texas oil and gas in 1919. By the 1930s, Texas produced half of the crude oil in the world. In 1931, the TRC began to engage in "prorationing," that is, issuing production quotas. To enforce the railroad commission's orders, Governor Ross Sterling, a former president of Humble Oil Company, ordered the Texas National Guard to impose martial law on East Texas oil fields.

When the smuggling of "hot oil" produced in violation of the quotas became a problem, the Roosevelt administration sought to coordinate oil production under the oil and gas sections of the NIRA. Influential Texans in Washington, including Roosevelt's first vice president, John Nance Garner, Senator Tom Connally, and Congressman Sam Rayburn, fought back. The Connally Hot Oil Act gave the federal government the power to enforce directives of the TRC in interstate commerce. State governments and oil companies formed a public-private cartel, the Interstate Oil Compact (IOC). The US Bureau of Mines in the Department of the Interior and the American Petroleum Institute, a trade association, collected data about the industry. This awkward, jury-rigged system succeeded from the 1930s until the 1970s; it was critical to the success of the Allied forces in World War II and became an integral part of the US-dominated global oil system in the early Cold War.

THE POWER POLITICS OF ENERGY

During World War II in 1943, a leading American geologist, Everette Lee DeGolyer, was sent to evaluate the oil-producing potential of the Persian Gulf. Previously, there had been discoveries of oil in Iran (1908), Iraq (1927), and Bahrain (1932). In 1938, Anglo-Persian and Gulf Oil had discovered oil in Kuwait, while Chevron and Texaco in the same year found oil in Saudi Arabia. DeGolyer told the Roosevelt administration, "The center of gravity of world oil production is shifting from the Gulf-Caribbean area to the Middle East—the Persian Gulf area."[5]

Britain considered the Middle East to be its sphere of influence, and competed with the United States to win the favor of the Saudi monarch Ibn Saud. In 1944, the United States and Britain negotiated a petroleum agreement, which the leader of the British delegation called "a monster cartel," while the American government used the euphemism "commodity agreement." The agreement was withdrawn from submission to the Senate for approval because of intense opposition from independent oil producers and liberal antimonopolists.[6]

In 1953, the United States and Britain sponsored a coup in Iran to overthrow its democratically elected prime minister, Mohammad Mossadegh, before he could nationalize the Anglo-Iranian Oil Company. Installed as ruler of Iran until he was overthrown in the revolution of 1979, Muhammad Reza Shah Pahlavi presided over a system in which the country's petroleum industry, nominally owned by Iran, was managed and developed by a consortium of Western oil companies.[7] The major oil companies similarly collaborated in developing Saudi oil through the Arab-American Oil Company (Aramco).

In the generation that followed World War II, the global oil industry was dominated by Texaco, Gulf, Standard Oil of New Jersey (Exxon), Royal Dutch Shell, British Anglo-Persian Oil Company (British Petroleum or BP), Standard Oil of New York (Mobil), and Standard Oil of California (Chevron). They were called *le sette sorelle*, the Seven Sisters, by an Italian oil man, Enrico Mattei.

According to the Federal Trade Commission, in 1952 the Seven Sisters controlled 88 percent of global oil reserves outside of the United States and the USSR.[8] In 1960, the seven controlled 60 percent of global oil.[9] When the Justice Department's Antitrust Division planned a criminal suit against the Seven Sisters, President Truman ordered the investigation to be suspended. His successor, Dwight D. Eisenhower, also suppressed the litigation, although the investigation survived until it was abandoned in 1968.[10]

Texas alone provided more than a third of the oil used by the United States until the 1970s. The Organization of Petroleum Exporting Countries (OPEC) was founded in Baghdad in 1960 and by the early 1970s power had shifted to OPEC from the TRC. In 1973, during the Arab-Israeli war, OPEC demonstrated its power by imposing an oil embargo on the United States and other allies of Israel.

GIANT POWER

The construction by the United States of a stable global oil infrastructure was accompanied by the completion of the second industrial revolution at home. While Lincoln's Second Republic of the United States was built on railroads, Franklin Roosevelt's Third Republic was built on electric grids and interstate highways. The two grids of the second industrial era permitted the decentralization of factories and people, within regions and across the continent.

In the 1920s, three-quarters of the electric-utility sector was controlled by eight holding companies, including Samuel Insull's. The holding companies eluded state-level regulation and used layer on layer of complexity to baffle regulators and investors alike. Many were as highly leveraged as the House of Insull, which controlled $500 million in assets with only $27 million in equity. Gifford Pinchot, the progressive Republican governor of Pennsylvania, campaigned for Giant Power, a scheme that would replace commercial electric power empires with public utilities. The power companies promoted their private alternative, Super Power.

When the Depression struck, the fragile, overleveraged structures of holding-company systems like Insull's came tumbling down. Insull lost his fortune, while many of the 600,000 investors in his utility empire lost their life savings. Roosevelt campaigned for the presidency in 1932 denouncing "the lone wolf, the unethical competitor, the Ishmael or Insull whose hand is against every man's."

Insull's fall from grace was swift and dramatic. Shunned in Chicago, Insull and his wife fled to Europe. When Cook County indicted him for embezzlement, larceny, and other offenses, Insull was in Greece. The Greek government refused to extradite him to the United States, but it refused to renew his visa, forcing him to board a steamer to Romania, which turned him away. The Turkish government jailed him and extradited him to the United States, where, after all his travails, he was finally acquitted after standing trial. His health and spirits broken, he moved with his wife to Paris, where he died after collapsing in a Paris metro station. As a final indignity, a Parisian thief took his wallet from his corpse.[11]

Following Roosevelt's election, the federal government revolutionized the electric utility business. Responding to the abuse of holding companies as a method of escaping state utility regulation, the Public Utility Holding Company Act of 1935 put the new Securities and Exchange Commission (SEC) in charge of regulating utility holding companies, while the Federal Power Act of 1935 subjected utilities engaged in interstate activities to the jurisdiction of the Federal Power Commission (FPC).[12]

Rural electrification was another priority of the Roosevelt administration. The Rural Electrification Administration (REA), created in 1936, provided financial assistance to rural electric cooperatives. The number of farm homes with electricity tripled between 1932 and 1941. Thanks in large part to the rural-electrification efforts of the New Deal, the number of farm households with access to electricity and electric appliances like electric lighting, refrigerators, and radios increased from 10 percent at the beginning of the 1930s to 90 percent by 1950.[13]

The federal government also went into the electrical-power-generation business itself. The best-known example is the Tennessee Valley Authority (TVA), which constructed a series of dams to bring electricity to a depressed rural region as large as Western Europe. Roosevelt adapted as his own a proposal by Nebraska senator George Norris to create a public agency responsible for using hydroelectric power to catalyze the development of the depressed Tennessee Valley region.

The TVA was an independent public agency modeled on the Panama Canal Commission.[14] Its second director, David Lilienthal, helped to create the Electric Home and Farm Authority to provide low-interest loans for manufacturing and purchasing electric appliances like waffle irons. With forty-two dams and reservoirs, the TVA lowered the price of electricity, improved freight transportation, controlled flooding, and provided irrigation and fertilizers for the farms in the river valley. In World War II, the TVA provided the power for the Oak Ridge laboratory that helped to develop the first atomic bombs as part of the Manhattan Project. The Lower Colorado River Authority (LCRA), sponsored by Franklin Roosevelt's dynamic young protégé, Texas congressman Lyndon Johnson, was a similar success in bringing cheap energy and economic development to the impoverished Hill Country of central Texas.

Like the South, the American West was transformed by federally sponsored hydroelectric power. In the middle of the 1930s, all five of the biggest structures in the world were dams that were being built in the United States—the Hoover Dam (Colorado River), the Grand Coulee (Columbia River), the Bonneville (Columbia River), the Shasta Dam (Sacramento River), and the Fort Peck Dam (Missouri River). Another massive water project in the West was the Central Valley Water Project, which diverted water supplied by the Shasta Dam on the Sacramento River and the Friant Dam on the San Joaquin River by way of a series of canals to farms in California's Central Valley.

The Grand Coulee Dam—more than 550 feet tall and four-fifths of a mile in width—was the largest structure ever built.[15] The dam held the record for size until it was surpassed by the Itaipu Dam along the Brazil-Paraguay border in 1982, which in turn was surpassed by China's Three Gorges Dam in 2006. In World War II, the electricity generated by the dam powered aluminum plants for aircraft. The Bonneville Power Authority hired the folk singer Woody Guthrie to celebrate the Columbia River projects with a collection of songs, including "Roll on, Columbia" and "The Grand Coulee Dam":

Well the world has seven wonders that the trav'lers always tell,
Some gardens and some towers, I guess you know them well,
But now the greatest wonder is in Uncle Sam's fair land,
It's the big Columbia River and the big Grand Coulee Dam. . . .

Uncle Sam took up the challenge in the year of thirty-three,
For the farmer and the factory and all of you and me,
He said, "Roll along Columbia, you can ramble to the sea,
But river, while you're rambling, you can do some work for me."

Now in Washington and Oregon you can hear the factories hum,
Making chrome and making manganese and light aluminum,
And there roars the flying fortress now to fight for Uncle Sam,
Spawned upon the King Columbia by the big Grand Coulee Dam.

As impressive as they were, the dams of the New Deal era contributed only a fraction of the energy consumed by industries and homeowners in the boom years that followed World War II. Coal-powered utilities provided the majority of electricity. As an icon of modernity, the hydropower dam was soon overtaken by the nuclear power plant. The Atomic Energy Commission (AEC) worked with the private sector in the 1950s to promote the peaceful use of atomic power. In 1957, the first commercial nuclear power plant opened in Shippington, Pennsylvania. To keep up with growing demand, utilities ordered more nuclear plants in the following decades. Following the accident at Three Mile Island in 1979, public opinion turned against nuclear energy. Even so, by 2000 there were more than a hundred nuclear power plants in the United States, which provided nearly a fifth of the nation's electricity.

THE INTERSTATE HIGHWAY SYSTEM

In 1915, the wealthy socialite Emily Post wanted to take a trip by automobile across the United States. When she asked a friend who had made several cross-country trips by car what the best route would be, she was told, "The Union Pacific."[16]

But change was coming. As early as 1893, the Post Office Rural Free Delivery Act helped to create a constituency for good roads by permitting farmers to shop using mail-order catalogs like the Sears, Roebuck catalog. (In order to prevent postmasters from telling local merchants what they were doing, mail-order customers sometimes asked for the catalogs to be delivered in plain wrappers.) In the early 1900s, farmers, bicyclists, and early automobile-club members had united in a campaign for better roads, whose first success was the Federal Aid Road Act of 1916, which provided matching federal grants to states for road construction.

The American highway system found a champion in Thomas Harris MacDonald, known as the "Chief," who headed the Bureau of Public Roads from 1918 until 1953, when he was eased out by the Eisenhower administration. Born in Leadville, Colorado, MacDonald grew up in Iowa, where he saw his father, a lumber and grain dealer, forced to pay a "mud tax" because of poor road conditions. MacDonald's greatest legacy would be the interstate highway system, for which the Eisenhower administration, which fired him, gets the credit. It was MacDonald's opposition to toll roads that ensured that the federal highway system would be paid for by gasoline taxes.

Although what became the interstate highway system began under Franklin Roosevelt, Eisenhower supported the legislation that completed it. In 1919, a US Army convoy made an arduous trip that began in Washington, DC, and ended sixty-two days later in Oakland, California, having traveled chiefly on dirt roads west of Kansas City. The lesson was not lost on Eisenhower, one of the young soldiers. Later he was impressed by the German autobahn system. So intense, however, was the resistance to a modern highway infrastructure in the antistatist United States that the

legislation was only passed in 1956 when it was named the National Interstate and Defense Highways Act and backed by the prestige of the former
commander of America's armies in Europe in World War II.

DECENTRALIZING POPULATION AND INDUSTRY

Like many progressives of his time, including his uncle Frederic Delano
of the Regional Planning Association and his own National Resources
Planning Board, Roosevelt favored the decentralization of population and
industry. In January 1933, Roosevelt had said that it was necessary to "get
[the unemployed] out of the big centers of population, so that they will
not be dependent on home relief."[17] Harry Hopkins, director of the Federal Emergency Relief Administration (FERA), observed, "It would be
a good thing for America if large cities disappeared and their industries
were scattered in a thousand small communities."[18] In September 1933, a
TVA publication advocated the dispersion of small industries to "smaller
communities" in order to "avoid the unfortunate social consequences of
excessive urbanization."[19]

The two key technologies of the second industrial revolution, electricity and the internal combustion engine, permitted decentralization to
be carried out. The dream of mass-producing low-cost homes had been
shared by many liberals, including Roosevelt, as head of Secretary of
Commerce Hoover's American Construction Council in the 1920s. With
the help of the Truman administration, the Lustron Corporation sought
to mass-produce stainless steel houses. But that experiment ended in failure and scandal. Instead of Lustron, Levittown became the symbol of
postwar suburban housing, thanks to the success of the Levitt brothers
of Long Island in modeling the construction of housing developments on
mass-production techniques in the auto industry.

The combination of Federal Housing Administration (FHA) loans
and the GI Bill created the postwar suburbs that sprang up alongside new
federal and state highways. Before the New Deal, only around 40 percent
of the American population lived in a single-family home. Typical down

payments were 30 to 35 percent, interest rates were often around 8 percent, and loans had to be repaid in five to ten years. Following the creation of the Home Owners' Loan Corporation in 1933 and subsequent housing measures, the federal government standardized the thirty-year loan with down payments of 10 percent and interest no higher than 5 percent.[20] In 1990, 46 percent of the US population lived in the suburbs.

The golden arches of McDonald's became the international symbol of America's postwar suburban middle-class lifestyle. The restaurant chain was founded in the 1930s by two brothers, Dick and Maurice "Mac" McDonald, who created a glass-walled drive-through restaurant that made hamburgers by assembly-line methods. A former milk shake salesman from Chicago, Ray Kroc, and a financial genius, Harry Sonneborn, turned McDonald's into the largest owner of retail real estate on the planet by the 1980s—and even opened a Hamburger University. "The french fry would become almost sacrosanct for me, its preparation a ritual to be followed religiously," Kroc explained in his autobiography.[21]

The conspiracy theory that automobile companies deliberately destroyed mass transit in order to force Americans to rely on cars has no basis in fact and has been debunked repeatedly by scholars.[22] Mass-transit ridership peaked in 1919 and began its rapid decline as millions of Americans bought cars.[23] Cities began to switch to buses because rail transit was losing ridership and buses were more flexible than fixed-rail lines. A similar shift has taken place in other industrial countries. As automobile ownership spread in Europe and Japan, mass-transit ridership declined as well, although it is still at higher levels than in the United States, which was the first nation with mass automobile ownership.[24]

The new automobile-centered culture was derided by American intellectuals, many of whom were downwardly mobile children of affluent parents who could afford to live and play in expensive bohemias in New York, San Francisco, and other big cities. By the late twentieth century, the American intelligentsia was all but united in its snobbish disdain for America's working-class and middle-class suburbs, claiming that "sprawl" deadened the spirit and threatened the environment.

FROM DIXIE TO THE SUN BELT

The greatest triumph of government-sponsored decentralization of production during the thirty glorious years was the incorporation of the South into the American mainstream. Before the New Deal the United States had been two countries—a developed or developing industrial core in the Northeast and Midwest, and a poor and primitive periphery in the South and West that served as a resource colony for the manufacturing region. The federally sponsored infrastructural and agricultural modernization of the South and West, followed by the civil rights revolution, turned these two economies into a single national economy for the first time. From Texas to California to Florida, the formerly impoverished hinterland gave way to the booming new Sun Belt. Immigrants, businesses, and investors poured into parts of the South and West that their predecessors in earlier generations had avoided. One southerner quipped, "Cotton is going West, Cattle are coming East, Negroes are going North, and Yankees are coming South."[25]

In 1938, President Roosevelt explained to an audience in Fort Worth, Texas, one of the purposes of the Fair Labor Standards Act in creating a national minimum wage: "You need more industries in Texas, but I know you know the importance of not trying to get industries by the route of cheap wages for industrial workers."[26] Federal minimum wages, by making labor more expensive, forced southern planters to mechanize farming, while the farm-price-support system and federal aid to farmers helped them to carry out long-term investments in productivity. Many of the black and white farm laborers and tenants displaced by mechanization made their way to cities in the South and other parts of the country, where many found better lives even as some were trapped in urban poverty. In 1910, 89 percent of black Americans lived in the South; by 1960, that number dropped to 53 percent, with 39.5 percent in the North and 7.5 percent in the West.[27]

In 1920, nine of the ten largest cities were in the Northeast or Midwest. In 1990, six of the ten largest—Los Angeles, Houston, Dallas, Phoenix, San

Diego, and San Antonio—were in the Southwest.[28] A new technology, air-conditioning, accelerated the migration of Americans from the Northeast and Midwest to the booming states of the new Sun Belt like California, Texas, and Florida. But climate was less important as a factor than federal public investment. During World War II and the Cold War, the federal government built great numbers of army bases, air bases, naval facilities, and defense-production plants in the South and West. The Sun Belt was also the Gun Belt.

New Deal liberalism succeeded in its goals of raising the incomes of farmers and industrial workers and raising the wage and living standards of the South. Between 1919 and 1940, the income of workers in agriculture was only 47 percent of the national average; by 1950–1955 it had nearly doubled, to 76 percent.[29] In 1930, per capita income in the South was only 55 percent of the national average; by 1960, it had risen to 78 percent of the national average.[30]

THE MOTORIZED HOUSEHOLD

While the electric grid, the interstate highway system, and the pattern of suburban development that they enabled provided striking icons of the second industrial era, the motorized appliances that colonized the postwar American household had an equally transformative effect on how Americans lived. The aesthetic conservatism of most Americans ensured that postwar houses would be built in styles that evoked one or another historical tradition—colonial, Tudor, or ranch style, the last based loosely on the hacienda architecture of Old California. But while most Americans chose not to live in futuristic metal domes like the Dymaxion house designed by the engineer R. Buckminster Fuller, behind the traditional facade the new American house had utility systems and devices that would have been found only in science fiction a few decades earlier.

Nothing changed life more than the convenience of indoor plumbing. At the beginning of the twentieth century, water had to be lugged into most homes from wells or creeks, at the risk of spreading typhoid or cholera. Ninety-eight percent of white households and 92 percent of black households in 1970 had running water in the home, compared to only 24 percent in 1890 (the disparity among blacks and whites in 1970 was the result of black rural poverty).[31]

The self-cleaning oven and then the microwave, along with the dishwasher, the washing machine, and the drier, eliminated much of the drudgery of daily life. Between 1900 and 1975, the average time per week spent on meals and cleaning dropped from forty-four hours to ten, while the hours devoted to laundry fell from seven to one.[32]

In 1900, most families had to load stoves with wood or coal and lamps burned kerosene or coal oil. By 1950, more than 95 percent of households had electric lighting and central heating.[33] Sixty-three percent of households had air-conditioning by 1987.[34]

Servants became as rare and anachronistic as vaudevillians and country peddlers. Thanks to labor-saving appliances, minimum-wage laws, and the restriction of mass immigration before its resumption in the 1960s, domestic servants became rare in the United States. In 1910, there were twenty million households and two million domestic servants. By 1970, only 1 percent of forty-six million households had a live-in servant.[35]

Postwar Americans enjoyed more personal space. In 1970, fewer than 8 percent of households had more than one person per room, compared to more than half in 1900.[36] And they enjoyed more personal time. From an average work schedule for nonfarm workers of ten hours a day, six days a week, the workweek had declined to forty hours, thanks to greater productivity and New Deal labor laws.[37]

From the global level to the interior of the household, the second industrial revolution was reaching its maturity. Inhabiting a new structure built on the foundations of electricity and oil, ordinary Americans experienced a generation of unprecedented progress and prosperity.

THE VIRTUAL NIRA

The institutional as well as the physical underpinnings of the American economy were rebuilt in the New Deal era between the 1930s and the

1970s. According to conventional histories of the New Deal and the post-war era, the associationalist arrangements of the NIRA were forgotten following the Supreme Court's destruction of the NIRA and AAA in the midthirties. Liberals, it is said, reconciled themselves to a combination of free enterprise and Keynesian demand management.

Nothing could be further from the truth. Keynesian demand-management policies were pursued inconsistently under presidents Truman, John F. Kennedy, and Johnson and hardly at all under Eisenhower. Nor was the postwar economy based on free markets, as those are usually defined. The major sectors of the economy were either organized as government-backed cartels or dominated by a few oligopolistic corporations. Unions were concentrated in the same sectors.

Following the demise of the NIRA in 1935 and the AAA in 1936, the Roosevelt administration and Congress quickly created a number of "mini-NIRAs" and "mini-AAAs" in a number of sectors of the American economy. As we saw in the previous chapter, an NIRA-like cartel was set up in the oil industry. Another miniature NIRA was created in the bituminous coal industry by the Bituminous Coal Conservation Act (the Gaffey Act) of 1937, which created an NIRA-like commission to supervise labor standards and prices. The Agricultural Adjustment Act (AAA) was ruled unconstitutional by the Supreme Court in *United States v. Butler* (1936), a year after the Court struck down the NIRA. But aspects of the AAA were reincarnated with the help of the Soil Conservation and Domestic Allotment Act of 1936, the Agricultural Marketing Act of 1937, and the Agricultural Adjustment Act of 1938.

With the exception of bituminous coal, oil, and agriculture, which was highly regulated and subsidized, most of the government-sponsored cartels were found in essential infrastructure industries where price volatility and ruinous competition could not be tolerated. As we have seen, the Public Utility Holding Company Act of 1935 replaced private electric-power consortiums with regional, publicly regulated utility companies. The Civil Aeronautics Act of 1938 created a price-and-entry cartel, labor standards, and a supervisory commission, the Civil Aeronautics Board

(CAB). The Interstate Commerce Commission (ICC) cartelized the trucking industry with price-and-entry regulation. In telecommunications, the seven-member Federal Communications Commission (FCC) allocated radio and later license facilities, regulated rates, and oversaw the regulated monopoly of AT&T. Following World War II, 15 percent of the US economy was regulated by these agencies and others, including the Securities and Exchange Commission (banking and finance), the Federal Power Commission (natural gas, hydro dams, and nuclear energy); the Department of Agriculture's Farm Bureau (agribusiness); and the Federal Maritime Commission (shipping).[38]

Far from being an embarrassing aberration, the NIRA was the unacknowledged blueprint for the prosperity of the Golden Age between World War II and the 1970s. Resurrected in the wages and hours laws of the NLRA, the price supports and subsidies of the agricultural sector, the infrastructure industries with price-and-entry regulations, and the oligopolies of the industrial sector with de facto tripartite bargaining among business, labor, and government, together created what might be called a "Virtual NIRA" structured much of the American economy after World War II until it was partially dismantled between the 1970s and 1990s.

THE AGE OF OLIGOPOLY

In concentrated manufacturing sectors like automobiles, steel, and rubber, employer-union agreements and the power of the dominant oligopolies to set prices made formal mini-NIRAs unnecessary. As in the depressions of the nineteenth century, the Great Depression produced greater concentration of industry as surviving companies devoured victims. Between 1947 and 1968, the share of value added in manufacturing of the two hundred largest industrial corporations in the United States rose from 30 percent to 41 percent, while their share of total corporate manufacturing assets increased from 47.2 percent to 60.9 percent.[39] In 1976, the combined gross income of the three biggest industrial corporations—Exxon, General Motors, and Ford—exceeded the total income of all US farms, including government subsidies.[40] In the same year, two companies—AT&T and General Motors—employed 2 percent of the US civilian labor force.[41]

Television was dominated by the Big Three (CBS, NBC, and ABC) and the automobile industry by another Big Three (General Motors, Ford, and Chrysler). In steel, there were United States Steel, Republic, and Bethlehem; in chemicals, DuPont, Allied Chemical, and Union Carbide; in food processing, General Foods, General Mills, and Quaker Oats; and in jet engines only two major companies, General Electric and Pratt & Whitney. Observing the scene at the time, Adolf Berle and John Kenneth Galbraith agreed that most of the midcentury American economy was largely planned, by the public sector in the regulated industries and by private management in the industries dominated by corporate oligopolies.[42]

Many firms in the industrial sector benefited from large-scale privatization of government property after World War II. A significant portion of America's postwar 1945 industry consisted of privatized government factories. During the war, the Defense Plant Corporation, a branch of the RFC, funded the construction of numerous industrial plants.[43] At the time it was dissolved on June 30, 1945, the corporation owned 10 to 12 percent of US industrial capacity. This included 96 percent of the capacity of the American synthetic rubber industry, 90 percent of capacity in the magnesium industry, and 58 percent of capacity in the aluminum industry, as well as significant portions of the capacity in the iron and steel, gasoline, machine tool, and radio industries.[44] The War Assets Administration, succeeded by the General Services Administration, oversaw the sale of these assets to the private sector at a fraction of their actual cost, providing a massive transfer of public resources to private industry. Among the beneficiaries of the government sell-off was the rubber industry. During the war, the federal government spent $700 million building fifty-one factories to produce the ingredients for synthetic rubber. These government factories were sold to private industry by the middle of the 1950s.[45]

America's oligopolistic corporations were both stable and prosperous. Between 1954 and 1976, fewer than five of the one hundred largest industrial corporations lost money, with the exception of a two-year period.[46]

Private R&D in the United States was dominated by a small number of large, oligopolistic companies. In 1974, three-fourths of all industrial R&D was performed by 126 companies with more than twenty-five thousand employees. The four companies with the largest R&D efforts were responsible for 19 percent of all industrial R&D.[47]

The Brandeisian strain of liberalism did not die out completely. During World War II, the need for government-business cooperation prevailed but, following the war, the Truman administration adopted a vigorous antitrust policy. By 1949, nearly half of the one hundred largest industrial companies, including Alcoa, DuPont, and US Rubber, were confronted with antitrust prosecutions.[48]

The Celler-Kefauver Act of 1950 ordained that, to avoid antitrust prosecution, businesses could not engage in horizontal mergers with firms in related businesses. The consequences of this law for American business and the American economy will be discussed in the next chapter. Here it is enough to observe that trust-busting provided a minor counterpoint to the main theme of big business and industrial concentration in the 1950s and 1960s.

FROM FINANCE CAPITALISM TO MANAGERIAL CAPITALISM

The Glass-Steagall Act and the creation of the Securities and Exchange Commission (SEC) brought an end to the era of American finance capitalism symbolized by J. P. Morgan. Investment bankers were separated from commercial bankers and forbidden to be on the boards of directors of corporations.

The dominance of productive industry over finance during this period is shown by the reduced dependence of corporations on Wall Street. According to a congressional report in 1962, following World War II, industry was financed primarily from within. Borrowing from banks and issuing securities accounted for only a quarter of capital: "As compared with the 1920s, corporate financing in recent years featured a higher reliance on internally generated funds, a modest rise in the importance of long-term borrowing, and a sharp reduction in stock flotations."[49] The post-1945 boom, by allowing many firms to finance themselves to a greater degree from retained earnings, reduced the influence of the financial sector over corporate America even more.

Freedom from autocratic founders and financiers provided the managers of big companies with stability of tenure. In 1952, three-quarters of eight hundred senior executives in three hundred industrial, railroad, and utility companies had been with the same corporations for more than twenty years.[50] There was no market for executives, of the kind that developed at the end of the twentieth century. In the concentrated sectors, lifetime employment was the norm for managers and employees alike. Promotion was typically from within the company. Because executive salaries were restrained, the perquisites of office—the key to the executive bathroom or the corner office—were the goals of competition. On retirement, managers and many if not all employees of large companies could look forward to a defined-benefit pension plan.

Many of the executives who worked their way up to the top of companies began as engineers. In the early 1900s, Thorstein Veblen had called for a "soviet of engineers." James Burnham, Leon Trotsky's deputy in the United States and later a founder of the conservative movement, argued that in all industrial societies a "managerial elite" was displacing capitalists. In 1932, in *The Modern Corporation and Private Property*, Adolf Berle and Gardiner Means had called for managers to become a "neutral technocracy." In his 1964 book *The American Economic Republic*, Berle argued that most economic power was now exercised by corporate managers, the managers of pensions and mutual funds, government officials, and scientific experts.[51] In his 1966 Reith Lectures for the BBC, which became his book *The New Industrial State*, John Kenneth Galbraith made a similar argument that a "technostructure" of managerial firms had replaced the market with private planning in the concentrated, capital-intensive sectors of the economy.[52]

"WHAT WAS GOOD FOR OUR COUNTRY WAS GOOD FOR GENERAL MOTORS"

When President Eisenhower nominated Charles Erwin "Engine Charlie" Wilson, the president of GM, to be secretary of defense in 1953, Wilson was asked at a Senate confirmation hearing about conflicts of interest. Wilson replied: "I cannot conceive of one because for years I thought what was good for our country was good for General Motors, and vice versa. The difference did not exist. Our company is too big. It goes with the welfare of the country."[53] In the popular press and history books, Wilson was often accused of having said something different: "What is good for General Motors is good for America." But in his actual statement he put the good of the country first.

Wilson was Veblen's engineer and Burnham's manager rolled into one. An electrical engineer by training, he worked for Westinghouse and then General Motors, where he became president in January 1941. Wilson's career symbolizes the collaboration of the military and the private sector in promoting technological innovation in the twentieth century. During World War I, Wilson helped Westinghouse develop radio generators and electric motors for the US military. During World War II, as head of General Motors, he directed the company's war production.

Wilson was typical of the "organization men" who dominated the American economy during the Golden Age of high growth and widely shared prosperity from 1945 to 1973. What has come to be known as the "stakeholder" conception of the corporation was widely shared during the Golden Age. In 1951, the chairman of Standard Oil of New Jersey explained: "The job of management is to maintain an equitable and working balance among the claims of the various directly affected interest groups . . . stockholders, employees, customers, and the public at large. Business managers are gaining professional status partly because they see in their work the basic responsibilities that other professional men have long recognized in theirs."[54] Thomas Murphy of GM explained: "The UAW may have introduced the sit-down strike to America, but in its relationship with GM management it has also helped introduce . . . mutually beneficial cooperation. . . . What comes to my mind is the progress we have made, by working together, in such directions as providing greater safety and health protection, in decreasing alcoholism and drug addiction, in improving the quality of life."[55]

Founded in 1942, the Committee for Economic Development (CED) was a spin-off of the Business Advisory Council of the Department of Commerce. Dominated by representatives of large and medium-size firms, the CED carried on a version of the associationalist tradition, in opposition to the hard-edged antistatism of the National Association of Manufacturers and its small-business constituency. William Benton, the founder and vice president, explained: "The historic attitude of business has been to use government if it could, and abuse it if it couldn't. Philosophically, business was committed to the doctrine that, 'that government is best which governs least.'" The CED attitude was that "government has a positive and permanent role in achieving the common objectives of high employment and production and high and rising standards of living for people in all walks of life. . . . This is our present answer to the European brands of socialism. Long may it thrive."[56]

The role of government in the era of American stakeholder capitalism was not limited to serving as an umpire enforcing neutral rules of competition and transparency in a free market. The government was part of a tripartite system that also included management and labor, which, if less formal than the aborted NIRA system of the 1930s, was similar in spirit. Unofficial and fragmented as it was, interest-group pluralism was the successor to NIRA corporatism and the equivalent of more formal tripartite government-business-labor bargaining systems in other Western democracies. What Galbraith later called "countervailing power" was described by the journalist John Chamberlain as the essence of the "broker state" created by the New Deal: "The labor union, the consumers' or producers' co-operative, the 'institute,' the syndicate—these are the important things in a democracy. If their power is evenly spread, if there are economic checks and balances to parallel the political checks and balances, then society will be democratic. For democracy is what results when you have a state of tension in society that permits no one group to dare to bid for total power."[57]

THE TREATY OF DETROIT

Following World War II, the uneasy peace between government and business was joined by a shaky rapprochement between business and organized labor. During the New Deal era, organized labor reached a degree of influence that it did not possess before or afterward. After the Supreme Court struck down the NIRA, some of the prolabor provisions that it contained were included in the National Labor Relations Act, signed in June 1935 by Roosevelt, and the 1938 Fair Labor Standards Act. The Taft-Hartley Act of 1947 shifted the balance of power back toward management, while leaving the structure of labor relations created during the Roosevelt years intact.

In 1950, Walter Reuther's United Auto Workers (UAW) signed a five-year agreement with the Big Three automobile makers of Detroit—Ford, GM, and Chrysler. The UAW agreed to forgo strike activity in return for inflation-adjusted salaries, health and retirement packages, and other benefits. The five-year contract that GM signed with the UAW in 1950 that provided generous benefits to auto workers became known as "the Treaty of Detroit." Ford and Chrysler signed identical agreements and many lesser companies followed their lead.

Even in the absence of the sector-wide bargaining that the NIRA-code authorities had sought to promote, contracts in the concentrated industrial sector served as informal models for wage-and-benefit policies in other industries until the 1970s. The percentage of Americans who belonged to labor unions, only 2.7 percent in 1900, had risen to 12.1 percent in 1920, only to fall to 7.4 percent in 1930. By the mid-1950s, roughly one in three American workers belonged to a union.

Because US economic growth slowed in the late twentieth century, pensions, health insurance, and other company-based benefits imposed crippling costs on America's automakers and other companies. For this reason, it is often argued that unions crippled US manufacturing industries. But the corporations, not the unions, preferred employer-based benefits systems. They spurned UAW leader Walter Reuther's proposal that the car companies "go down to Washington to fight with us" for universal federal health care and retirement benefits. In the 1950s and 1960s, the Big Three and other corporations were confident that they could always pass on the cost of benefits to consumers. In addition, they preferred to increase benefits rather than wages. For example, in 1961, GM was able to raise wages by only 2.5 percent by increasing pension obligations in the future by 12 percent.[58]

BANKING AS A PUBLIC UTILITY

The revolutionary changes in the economy and society that occurred during and after World War II were accompanied by a degree of stability in the financial sector without precedent in American history. In the mature New Deal order between the 1940s and the 1970s, finance went from being the master of American industry to being its servant. The Glass-Steagall Act and other New Deal–era reforms made commercial banking a boring, safe sector dominated by small banks serving local and state businesses. A scaled-down investment-banking sector played an essential but limited role in raising capital for large corporations.

Investment banks were partnerships, not the corporations with limited liability that they became at the end of the century (before they metamorphosed into "bank holding companies" in order to be rescued by the Federal Reserve following the crash of 2008). Before the 1970s, the SEC required investment banks to be partnerships, so that the prospect of personal liability for firm losses would encourage the partners to be risk averse and prudent.

Between World War II and the 1980s, American banking was safe and dull. Commercial banks took deposits and made loans. Commercial banks were also the main source of credit to most companies except for the largest, which could raise money in the bond market. Savings and loans (S&Ls) facilitated mortgage lending.

Another reform intended to steer finance away from speculation into productive investment was Regulation Q, passed as part of the Glass-Steagall Act of 1933 and reaffirmed by the Banking Act of 1935. Regulation Q banned the provision of interest payments on checking accounts at commercial banks. It also allowed the Federal Reserve to set interest-rate ceilings on savings accounts and time deposits such as certificates of deposit. Like the other elements of the New Deal system, the regulation sought to limit competition among banks for customers that might drive banks into risky practices. Another goal of Regulation Q was to encourage community banks to lend to productive local businesses and enterprises, rather than hold large balances with big metropolitan banks that might use the money for unproductive speculation.[59] Ruinous competition among banks was also checked by the 1927 McFadden Act, which preceded the New Deal and imposed restraints on interstate and intrastate branch banking. Banks were stable, protected public utilities, not dynamic firms in a competitive marketplace. Banking had become a boring business, symbolized by the "3–6–3" rule that summed up the banker's job: "Borrow at 3 percent, lend at 6 percent, golf at 3 p.m."

In addition to regulating finance, the federal government acted as a banker in its own right. Although the Reconstruction Finance Corporation was effectively abolished in 1953, its offspring continued to provide the country with public-investment banks for particular purposes. The Farm Credit System; the Federal Home Loan Banks, Fannie Mae and FHA; the Export-Import Bank; and other public-development banks helped to provide inexpensive credit on fair terms to farmers, small businesses, and the new home-owning majority.

DEMOGRAPHIC CHANGE

The 1920 census was the first in which urban Americans outnumbered rural Americans. By 1950, two-thirds of native-born white Americans lived in urban areas, whereas two-thirds had lived in rural areas in 1900.[60]

In 1950, 88.7 percent of whites worked in nonfarm occupations, compared to only 11.3 percent on farms. The white workforce was divided between blue-collar manual jobs (46.2 percent) and white-collar jobs, including sales and clerical jobs along with managerial and professional jobs (45 percent).

Only 8.8 percent of whites worked as domestic servants or in other menial services. Blacks, however, were heavily represented in those services (17.1 percent), farms (18.8 percent), and manual labor (52.1 percent), and were underrepresented in white collar jobs (11.9 percent).[61] Jobs remained highly segregated by gender, with women largely limited to the occupations of secretary, teacher, and nurse. Clerical jobs accounted for three-tenths of the nonfarm jobs for women in 1950.[62]

Mid-twentieth-century Americans were more educated than previous generations had been. Before 1910, the average white American had only an elementary school education. As a result of the establishment of high schools, which occurred along with the prohibition of child labor, by 1950, both native-born and second-generation white men who were twenty-five or older had an identical 9.8 years of education, while blacks had 6.4 years.[63]

Medical advances in combating polio, influenza, typhoid fever, and tuberculosis led to reductions in mortality. In 1950, black life expectancy was eight years less than that of whites.[64]

What came to be known as "the Pill" was the new medical technology with the greatest impact on society. Fertility was affected both by reductions in child mortality and by access to contraception and abortion. The combination of falling fertility and restricted immigration produced a slowdown in population growth from a level of 2 percent a year in 1905–1910 to a low of 0.7 percent in the 1930s.[65] The baby boom that followed World War II was a temporary blip in the long decline of native fertility, which fell below replacement levels among native-born whites in the United States, as in Europe.

THE CIVIL RIGHTS REVOLUTION

By the 1950s, the United States was no longer a nation of immigrants, but rather a largely closed economy with relatively little trade or immigration and whose population was overwhelmingly native born. The reduction in European immigration caused by World War I, and then by legal restrictions in 1921 and 1924, reduced the average annual rate of immigration to the United States between 1915 and 1950 to only one-fifth of its earlier rate.[66] The foreign-born declined as a percentage of the US population from 13.4 percent in 1900 to only 6.7 percent in 1950.[67]

In the sixth edition of his famous *Economics* textbook, Paul Samuelson wrote: "After World War I, laws were passed severely limiting immigration. Only a trickle of immigrants has been admitted since then. . . . By keeping labor supply down, immigration policy tends to keep wages high."[68] It is doubtful that organized labor could have enjoyed as much success in the mid-twentieth century without the low levels of immigration that existed following the restriction of European immigration in the 1920s.[69]

In 1950 the nonwhite population, at 10 percent, was lower than in 1900, when it had been 11.6 percent, and was overwhelmingly made up of black Americans, with only 0.5 percent of the population composed of members of the "other" category—chiefly Chinese, Japanese, and American Indians.[70] The fact that the new, postethnic white population felt secure in its majority may have contributed to the acceptance by most white Americans of the dismantling of America's version of white supremacy.

Led by Martin Luther King Jr. and his allies, the civil rights movement reached completion with the passage of the Civil Rights Act of 1964, the Voting Rights Act of 1965, the antiracist immigration reform of 1965, and the Fair Housing Act of 1968. During the civil rights era, Latinos as well as blacks struggled for economic rights. The battlefields were literal fields. Cesar Chavez, the leader of the United Farm Workers, used nonviolent protest tactics and boycotts like those of black civil rights champions to pressure California into outlawing *el cortito*, or *el brazo Diablo*, "the devil's arm," a short-handled hoe that inflicted pain on farmworkers and symbolized their oppression. In the thirty-five years after the short-handled hoe was banned, back injuries among California's farmworkers declined by 34 percent, according to the California Rural Legal Assistance program (CRL).[71]

Another target of reform in the civil rights era was the exploitative Bracero ("arm worker") program. Begun in 1942 to supply US farmers with migrant Mexican workers during the wartime labor shortage, the program had turned into a system of indentured servitude, permitting American agribusiness to use foreign nationals in serflike conditions rather than to hire Americans and legal immigrants to work in decent conditions for decent wages. At the time of the Bracero program's creation, a Texas farmer said: "We used to own slaves, but now we rent them from the government."[72] Lee G. Williams, a Labor Department officer who supervised it, described the Bracero program as "legalized slavery."[73] Chavez explained: "The jobs belonged to local workers. . . . Braceros didn't make any money, and they were exploited viciously, forced to work under conditions the local people would not tolerate."[74] Chavez and Dolores Huerta, the cofounder of the United Farm Workers, joined with labor and liberals to persuade Congress to abolish this form of indentured servitude in 1964. In testimony against other agricultural guest-worker programs before the US Senate on April 16, 1969, Chavez observed: "In abolishing the bracero program, Congress has but scotched the snake, not killed it. The program lives on in the annual parade of illegal and green carders across the United States-Mexico border to work in the fields."[75]

THE WAR ON POVERTY

Ronald Reagan quipped that Lyndon Johnson declared war on poverty and poverty won. Conservatives succeeded in portraying the War on Poverty as a dismal failure. But the evidence indicates otherwise. Between the presidencies of Lyndon Johnson and George W. Bush, black poverty declined from a little more than 40 percent to 22 to 24 percent. More than half of that reduction came between 1966 and 1969 alone, when black poverty plummeted from 40.9 percent to 30.9 percent. Poverty among non-Hispanic whites dropped from 14.7 percent in 1962 to 6.1 percent in 2006.[76] The overall poverty rate would have been even lower in the early twenty-first century if not for the mass immigration that followed the 1965 immigration reforms. Because US immigration was dominated by poor people from Mexico and Latin America, Latinos accounted for all the growth in poverty after 1990.[77]

In 1978, the economist Martin Anderson, who became a leading adviser in the Reagan administration, conceded that, despite problems with fraud and inefficiency, welfare programs had eliminated most poverty in the United States: "The 'dismal failure' of welfare is a myth. . . . But if we step back and judge the vast array of welfare programs, on which we spend billions of dollars every year, by two basic criteria—the completeness of coverage for those who really need help, and the adequacy of help they do receive—the picture changes dramatically. Judged by these standards our welfare system has been a brilliant success. The war on poverty is over for all practical purposes."[78]

Like his mentor Roosevelt, LBJ preferred work to welfare and sought to combat poverty by means of training programs and jobs programs like the Job Corps and Volunteers in Service to America (VISTA). Describing the Economic Opportunity Act of 1964, which promoted jobs and training for the poor, Johnson said: "This is not in any sense a cynical proposal to exploit the poor with a promise of a handout or a dole. We know—we learned long ago—that answer is no answer. . . . We are not content to accept the endless growth of relief rolls or welfare rolls." When the bill was being drafted, Johnson ordered one aide, Lester Thurow, to remove any cash-support programs and told another aide, Bill Moyers, "You tell [Sargent] Shriver, no doles."[79]

UTILITY CAPITALISM AND
THE MASS MIDDLE CLASS

On November 8, 1954, in a letter to his brother Edgar, President Dwight Eisenhower reacted angrily to the criticism that his administration was continuing the policies of his immediate predecessors Franklin Roosevelt and Harry Truman: "Now it is true that I believe this country is following a dangerous trend when it permits too great a degree of centralization of governmental functions. I oppose this—in some instances the fight is a rather desperate one. But to attain any success it is quite clear that the Federal government cannot avoid or escape responsibilities which the mass of the people firmly believe should be undertaken by it. . . . Should any political party attempt to abolish social security, unemployment insurance, and eliminate labor laws and farm programs, you would not hear of that party again in our political history. There is a tiny splinter group, of course, that believes you can do these things. Among them are H. L. Hunt (you possibly know his background), a few other Texas oil millionaires, and an occasional politician or business man from other areas. Their number is negligible and they are stupid."[80]

At the beginning of the Depression, the federal government played almost no role in protecting Americans from economic hardship; by the 1950s, the federal program of Social Security and the federal-state unemployment and welfare programs had created a modern safety net for an urban, industrial society. Before the Depression, corporations had all but extinguished unionization in the United States; in the mid-1950s, following the New Deal, one in three American workers was unionized. When the stock market crashed in 1929, many American companies were controlled by powerful investment banks; following World War II, managers were powerful and the once-powerful financial sector was reduced to the status of a tightly regulated utility. The "class market" for automobiles, radios, refrigerators, and other inventions of the second industrial revolution became the mass market of the Eisenhower era.

The New Deal liberal system of trickle-up, demand-side economics succeeded in creating a mass middle class that was also a mass market for the products of American factories and farms. Thanks to the New Deal, working Americans were guaranteed a minimum income by minimum-wage laws and unemployment insurance, while retirees were guaranteed a minimum income in old age by Social Security. Union membership added an additional wage premium for Americans in organized industries. These income guarantees benefited American businesses in two ways. By removing the possibility that competitors would use starvation wages to their advantage, they permitted all businesses to compete on the basis of price and quality rather than success in exploiting labor. And they solved the pre–New Deal problem of the maldistribution of income and underconsumption by enabling sufficient levels of mass consumption by adequately paid workers and retirees.

The American economy between the 1940s and the 1970s was a version of the associationalist economy envisioned by the progressives of the 1900s, and embodied successively in the economic mobilization agencies of World War I, the voluntary associationalism promoted by Herbert Hoover as commerce secretary in the 1920s, and Franklin Roosevelt's NIRA and the little NIRAs that re-created it piecemeal. The historians Jonathan Hughes and Louis P. Cain emphasize the extent to which the New Deal re-created the institutions of World War I: "The WIB would reappear in 1933 as the National Recovery Administration (NRA). The United States Grain Corporation would resurface in the 1930s as the Commodity Credit Corporation. The planning activities of the Food Administration would reappear in the two Agricultural Adjustment Acts. The Emergency Fleet Corporation came back as the National Maritime Administration. The Federal Housing Administration of the 1930s had been born first as the wartime United States Housing Corporation. The Fuel Administration under the Lever Act reemerged in the 1930s as the Bituminous Coal Division in the Interior Department."[81] Thus there is a direct line of descent from the economic mobilization of World War I to the NIRA and beyond to the highly regulated and cartelized economy of the United States in the mid-twentieth-century Golden Age of American capitalism.[82]

In the *Schechter* case of 1935 in which the Supreme Court struck down the NIRA, the "sick chicken" killed the Blue Eagle. But the Blue Eagle was reborn from the ashes like a phoenix. Before the deregulation efforts of Jimmy Carter and the union-busting campaign of Reagan in the 1970s and 1980s, the United States was governed by a virtual NIRA system characterized by oligopoly and unionization in major mass-production industries and regulated cartels in major energy, transportation, and utility industries. The vision of Fordism was realized, as high wages for workers translated into high aggregate demand for the products of American factories in a national economy little affected by foreign trade or investment. The New Deal turned a number of major industries including finance into regulated utilities.

Beginning in the 1990s, neoliberal Democrats and Republicans reversed this process. Correlation does not prove causation, but the historical record is suggestive. The American middle class enjoyed its zenith under a system of highly regulated, partly cartelized capitalism, and suffered under the less regulated capitalism that preceded it and followed it.

THE GREAT
DISMANTLING

In the present crisis, government is not the solution to our problem;
government is the problem.

—Ronald Reagan, 1981[1]

On June 3, 2003, the Treasury Department's James Gilleran brought a chainsaw to a photo op. While speaking to reporters, he promised to cut up piles of paper representing regulations of the financial sector. Joining him were representatives of four other US regulatory agencies in charge of overseeing finance, armed with less formidable (but still sharp) gardening shears. The message was clear: The Bush administration was tearing down the final pieces of the New Deal regulatory wall.[2]

With the financial panics and stock manias of previous decades in mind, the architects of the New Deal created a regulated financial system in the United States that established a firewall between investment bankers on the one hand and savings banks and savings and loans on the other. For five decades, the United States was free from the bank panics that had plagued the economy before the New Deal. By the 1970s, however, the lessons of the 1920s had been forgotten. Influenced by contributions from the financial industry, the US Congress under Democratic and Republican presidents alike dismantled the system the New Deal had built to stabilize American finance. The result was predictable—larceny and

losses on a colossal scale. The savings and loan meltdown in the 1980s was
followed by the subprime mortgage crisis of the 2000s, another result of
excessive financial deregulation.

The destruction of the New Deal order was not limited to the financial sector. Managerial capitalism gave way to a new financial-market
capitalism. Corporate raiders successfully challenged the autonomy of
American corporate managers, whose personal interests were increasingly aligned with the short-term interests of investors by means of the
stock options that played an ever increasing role in their compensation.
At the insistence of Wall Street investors, vertically integrated industrial
corporations were dismantled into pieces. Former brand-name corporations became mere "brands," slapped onto products assembled in East
Asia and other regions that nurtured rather than neglected their manufacturers. Squeezed by foreign competition, companies sought to raise
their profit margins by ending the postwar truce with organized labor
and smashing unions. By 2000, private-sector union membership in the
United States had fallen to the lows of the early 1900s. A flood of unskilled immigration, legal and illegal, put additional downward pressure
on the wages of the nonunionized workforce. A new category unique to
the United States among industrial nations was discovered—the "working poor," millions of full-time workers who could not subsist on a minimum wage that the federal government had allowed inflation to turn
into a starvation wage.

The dismantling of the big corporations brought with it the dismantling of the always-inadequate employer-based benefit system that
complemented government insurance programs like Social Security and
Medicare. Some companies could not afford to pay their pensions, while
others shifted the risks of retirement investment to employees by replacing
defined-benefit with defined-contribution pension plans.

Utility regulations, too, were dismantled. In the areas of transportation
and trucking, deregulation caused a return of the ills that had prompted
regulation in the first place, like chronic industry-wide bankruptcies in
the airline industry and volatile prices for electricity. The Golden Age of

infrastructure spending between the 1930s and the 1960s gave way to an era of crumbling bridges and barge-canal locks and traffic and freight congestion, as spending on infrastructure declined.

The era between the 1970s and the bubble economy that followed the end of the Cold War has yet to find a name. The most appropriate is the Great Dismantling.

THE MANAGERIAL ELITE: FROM ENGINEERS TO FINANCIAL OFFICERS

The prosperity of the US economy following World War II disguised a hidden rot in the culture of American management. While other industrial nations relentlessly developed their capacity to catch up with and challenge America's industrial leadership, as the United States had done in its race to catch up with industrial Britain in the nineteenth century, the nature of management in America's major corporations changed for the worse.

As we saw in the last chapter, following the breakdown of the NIRA experiment in business-government collaboration, in the late 1930s, Roosevelt sided with liberals in the Brandeisian antitrust tradition who were hostile to corporate concentration. This led to a flurry of antitrust suits in the late 1930s and again in the late 1940s, interrupted only by the war. In 1950, Congress passed the Celler-Kefauver Act, also known as the Anti-Merger Act. Intended to close loopholes in the Clayton Antitrust Act, the Celler-Kefauver Act made it more difficult for corporations to buy their rivals or suppliers in the same industry. However, it was relatively easy for corporations in different industries to merge.

What followed, in the late 1950s and 1960s, was one of the oddest episodes in the history of the American economy: the conglomerate movement. Just as the outlawing of cartels but not mergers prompted the great merger wave of the 1900s and 1920s, so the Celler-Kefauver Act had a surprising and harmful effect on US industrial organization that was not anticipated by its backers. Forbidden to grow by absorbing firms in their own fields, many American corporations expanded by annexing companies in completely unrelated lines of business. Unlike the merger waves of the 1890s to the 1900s and the 1920s, which concentrated ownership in particular fields, the merger wave of the 1950s and 1960s produced conglomerates made up of units in entirely different lines of business. Between 1950 and 1978, Beatrice Foods made 290 acquisitions, W. R. Grace 186, and International Telephone and Telegraph (IT&T) 163.[3] W. R. Grace, which began as a chemical company, went into western wear, banking, lumber and timber, fire extinguishers, Mexican restaurants, chemicals and sports teams, battlefield radar, and, last but not least, Hostess Twinkies snack cakes.[4]

Not since Supreme Court decisions in the late nineteenth century inadvertently set off the great merger wave, by outlawing industry-wide cartels while tolerating industry-dominating mergers, had legal factors inadvertently altered the very structure of American industry on such a dramatic scale.

The share of all corporate assets owned by the 200 largest manufacturing companies increased from 47 percent in 1947 to 59 percent in 1967. Between 1948 and 1955 only 10 percent of acquired assets resulted from cross-industry conglomeration; by 1972–1979 that figure had risen to 46 percent. Among the 148 corporations that made the list of the top 200 leading corporations in both 1950 and 1975, the mean number of lines of business controlled by the corporation grew from 5.2 to 9.7.[5]

The architects of the conglomerates unwittingly blazed the trail for later "takeover artists." By taking over a company with a low price-earnings ratio, a conglomerate could get a one-time boost in its reported earnings. Conglomerate-building corporations financed their takeovers first with cash, then with stock, and then, by the 1970s, increasingly with debt. The debt-to-equity ratio in manufacturing rose from 0.48 to 0.72 between 1965 and 1970.[6]

The harm done by the conglomerate movement in the wake of Celler-Kefauver was compounded by the change in corporate culture that it produced. Many of the CEOs of the great industrial corporations of the mid-twentieth century, like Alfred Sloan and Charles Wilson, had engineering degrees. In the new conglomerates, corporate leadership increasingly passed to chief financial officers (CFOs) and CEOs with backgrounds in finance who did not know anything about any particular product or industry. "Companies do not make money," the influential management theorist Peter Drucker insisted. "Companies make shoes." That might have been the motto of the triumphal managerial capitalism of the middle decades of the twentieth century. But in the second half of the century, more and more managers as well as investors disagreed. It did not necessarily matter what a company made as long as it made money.

Even as Japan, South Korea, Taiwan, Germany, and other industrial countries focused on developing world-class manufacturing, the leaders of many American manufacturing companies neglected the making of superior products in order to pursue short-term gains from mergers and financial manipulation. Beginning in the 1970s, these trend lines would converge and the American economy would pay a heavy price.

THE 1970S: DECADE OF CRISIS

The Golden Age of postwar capitalism ended in the 1970s. The decade was a time of geopolitical and economic disasters that shook the faith of Americans in the New Deal order constructed by Roosevelt and Truman, ratified by Eisenhower, and expanded by Kennedy and Johnson. The United States abandoned its allies in Indochina and withdrew from Vietnam and the global market experienced oil shocks following the Arab-Israeli War of 1973 and the Iranian Revolution of 1979.

The postwar settlement in the world and at home was clearly falling apart. In the United States and other Western democracies, the post-1945 truce between labor, business, and government was threatened by inflation. The rate of economic growth in every industrial democracy slowed abruptly in the 1970s, reviving only in the late 1990s. At the same time, the demands of organized labor for higher wages added "wage-push inflation" to the causes of inflation. Inflation reached a peak of 18 percent in the last years of the Carter administration.

Assuming that high levels of economic growth would continue forever, Americans in the 1960s were entranced by technological optimism when thinking about the future, envisioning futuristic cities and colonies on the moon and Mars in the near future. But America's temporary monopoly of world trade came to an end, with the revival of Japan and Western Europe. From 1973 to 1996, American economic growth fell dramatically, compared to the previous two decades. All the industrial economies suffered a productivity slowdown around the same time, perhaps as a result of the maturity of second-industrial-revolution technologies like electricity and automobiles. Whatever the reason, the result was stagflation—a toxic combination of declining corporate profit margins and spiraling wage-price inflation.

AMERICA'S EMBATTLED MANUFACTURERS

The prosperity of postwar America rested on foundations that grew weaker over time. One was the assumption that free trade was unproblematic. The unchallenged supremacy of the US economy in the world could last only until America's industrial rivals recovered from the devastation of World War II—in large part because of generous American help.

Recognizing that the policy of import-substitution protectionism was no longer necessary, now that the US was the dominant global economy, Congress passed and President Roosevelt signed the Reciprocal Trade Agreements Act (RTAP) in 1934. While Roosevelt did not share the utopian belief in peace through free trade, he favored an integrated global trading system that would ensure all nations access to markets and raw materials without the need for war or colonialism. During World War II, the United States led the way in creating the World Bank, the International Monetary Fund (IMF), and other institutions of what came to be known as the Bretton Woods system, after the hotel in New Hampshire

where many of the negotiations took place. To get the shattered economies of Europe going again, the United States provided Europe with financial aid under the Marshall Plan.

The postwar global trading system, however, never functioned as designed. With the outbreak of the Cold War, the Soviet Union and its satellites formed their own economic bloc. During the Cold War and after it,
the United States subordinated its preference for a liberal global trading
system to the imperatives of keeping its European and Asian allies within
the American-led alliance, even if that meant sacrificing the interests of
particular American industries.

The United States made one-way trade concessions in order to secure
the cooperation of other countries needed as allies, first in the struggle
against the Axis powers and then against the Soviet bloc during the Cold
War. Between 1939 and 1943, the United States offered unbalanced trade
concessions to Iceland, a number of Latin American countries, and Turkey, in order to lure them away from Nazi Germany and its allies.[7]

Following World War II, the United States provided $33 billion in
nonmilitary aid between 1946 and 1953.[8] Because of the limits to foreign
aid imposed by American public opinion, American foreign-policy makers suggested what the historian Alfred E. Eckes calls a policy of "trade,
not aid."[9] In an unpublished page for his memoirs, President Harry Truman wrote: "American labor now produces so much more than low-
priced foreign labor in a given day's work that our workingmen need no
longer feel, as they were justified in feeling in the past, the competition of
foreign forces."[10] In December 1946, the State Department instructed its
officials to help the countries in which they were stationed to export to the
United States: "In general, a Foreign Service officer should give the same
attention to serving United States importers as he would give to United
States exporters."[11] A commission on trade headed by Daniel W. Bell, the
former budget director of the Roosevelt administration, proposed to increase exports of manufactured goods even if that led to unemployment
for an estimated sixty thousand to ninety thousand American workers:
"In cases where choice must be made between injury to the national inter-

est and hardship to an industry, the industry [should] be helped to make adjustments by means other than excluding imports—such as through extension of unemployment insurance, assistance in retraining workers, diversification of production, and conversion to other lines."[12] President Eisenhower argued that measures "which tend to drive away an ally as dependable as Great Britain . . . do much more harm in the long run to our security than would be done by permitting a US industry to suffer from British competition."[13]

Not content to sacrifice American industries to help Cold War allies prosper, the United States in the 1960s sought to use access to the American market to drive development in the postcolonial world. In 1963, President Kennedy called on the United States and its allies to open "our markets to the developing countries of Africa, Asia and Latin America."[14] Kennedy warned an AFL-CIO convention in Dallas that protection of US industry risked "driving potential trading partners into the arms of the Soviets."[15] In March 1964, a Johnson administration task force on foreign economic policy called for a "war on poverty—worldwide. . . . The whole country would be the gainer if, over time, we could shift resources away from textiles, shoes and other unsophisticated manufactures into more advanced items where we have a comparative advantage . . . [such as] capital, scientific and technological research, skilled and educated labor."[16]

One of the few government officials who dissented from the prevailing orthodoxy was George Humphrey, Eisenhower's secretary of the Treasury. A veteran of the mining industry, Humphrey declared at a 1954 cabinet meeting, according to another participant, that "we were protectionists by history and had been living under a greatly lowered schedule of tariffs in a false sense of security because the world was not in competition. That has changed now and the great wave of competition from plants we had built for other nations was going to bring vast unemployment to our country."[17]

By the 1970s, America's policy of tolerating foreign mercantilism was harming American industry. US manufacturers like Detroit's Big Three automakers were being battered by imports from Europe and especially from Japan, which had devised a superior just-in-time (JIT) system of assembly-line production. America's embattled automakers claimed correctly that they were excluded from the Japanese automobile market by various subtle forms of Japanese protectionism. But Japan's discrimination against foreign imports was not the only reason for its success. Another reason that the US automakers suffered in competition with Japanese firms was a lack of scale. Even though they were smaller than the big American carmakers, the leading Japanese car companies made cars in plants that were much larger. In the mid-1980s, the average plant for GM and Ford produced 182,000 cars per year, while the average plant of one of the four largest Japanese car companies produced around 460,000 cars per year.[18]

American industry had contributed to its own problems. While the Japanese improved production processes like JIT manufacturing, and while the Germans continued their tradition of fine craftsmanship, American manufacturers had rolled out shoddy (and, in the case of cars, dangerous and polluting) products and relied on advertising to inspire American consumers to buy the latest models. High oil prices following the OPEC embargo in 1973 damaged the US automobile industry by creating a market in the United States for fuel-efficient Japanese compact cars. The bitterly adversarial tradition of US labor-management relations made it hard for the United States to compete against Japanese companies with their paternalistic labor relations and against German companies in which codetermination by managers and workers was part of the law. An even more significant cost of increased foreign rivalry was the inability of business to pass on the costs of higher wages for workers to consumers, now that its profits were constrained by international competition.

The major industrial countries—the United States, the European Economic Community (EEC), and Japan, as well as Canada, Australia, Switzerland, Sweden, Norway, Austria, and Finland—grew at a rate of 4.9 percent a year from 1950 to 1970, compared to 2.6 percent a year from 1870 to 1913 and only 1.9 percent a year between 1913 and 1950.[19] In part because they were more advanced, the United States (3.5 percent) and Britain (2.8 percent) grew much more slowly than France and Finland (5 percent) and the former Axis countries Italy (5.6 percent), Germany (6.3 percent), and Japan (9.8 percent).[20] In the 1980s, this inspired the rueful quip, "The Cold War is over, and Germany and Japan won."

EAST ASIAN MERCANTILISM:
THE JAPANESE MIRACLE

Japan was the most important beneficiary of the US policy of tolerating mercantilist trade policies carried out by America's Cold War protectorates. Without asymmetric trade between the United States and Japan, there would have been no Japanese economic miracle between the 1960s and 1980s. The average Japanese growth rate of 10 percent in the 1960s dropped to 5 percent in the 1970s and 4 percent in the 1980s, before plunging to 1.5 percent in the "lost decade" of the 1990s.

During US-Japanese trade negotiations in 1955, a Japanese negotiator remarked that "if the theory of international trade were pursued to its ultimate conclusions, the United States would specialize in the production of automobiles and Japan in the production of tuna; . . . such a division of labor does not take place . . . because each government encourages and protects those industries which it believes important for reasons of national policy."[21] Following those negotiations, the United States granted $37.2 million in trade concessions and received only $6.4 million from Japan. While Japan, following classic mercantilist strategy, reduced its duties on raw materials and foodstuffs, the United States reduced its duties on Japanese manufactured imports like electrical products, apparel, and glassware.[22] In addition to making its own trade concessions to Japan, the United States offered access to the US market for other countries if they opened their own markets to Japanese exports.[23]

Following the end of the US occupation in 1950, Japan carried out a long-term industrial policy, using methods such as direct subsidies, preferential tax policies and off-budget finance, channeled credit to targeted industries, controls on foreign exchange and imports, encouragement of domestic cartels, and informal bureaucratic guidance.[24] In agriculture and strategic manufacturing, Japan used tariffs, quotas, and informal barriers to limit imports. Money was funneled from Japanese consumers to Japanese corporations by markups over the world price for many items. In the 1990s, it was estimated that Japanese paid more than 600 percent of the world price for radios and televisions.[25] Credit allocation was another key element of Japanese mercantilist industrial policy. The Postal Savings Bank offered consumers poor returns on savings, while steering their deposits to Japanese manufacturing and infrastructure companies.

The Japanese government in 1960 declared that computing was a strategic industry. The Ministry of Trade and Industry (MITI) ordained that the role that the Pentagon played in the United States in procuring and promoting a computer industry would be played by Japan's National Telegraph and Telephone Company (NTT), a government monopoly. The Japanese government pressured International Business Machines (IBM) into licensing all its technology to Japanese producers, and compelled IBM's Japanese subsidiary to agree to export 60 percent of its production and to submit new models for approval to the government. In addition, the Japanese government imposed a 25 percent tariff on imported computers that included IBM computers produced inside Japan.[26]

As a result of these mercantilist policies, Japan's merchandise trade surpluses with the United States and other countries ballooned. Between 1980 and 1989, Japan accounted for 38 percent of the US current account deficit.[27] In 1975, the United States absorbed 12 percent of the world's manufactured exports; by 1987 that had grown to 22 percent. Japan's economy was half the size of the US economy, and yet Japan admitted to its protected national market only 2 percent of the world's manufactured exports in 1975 and merely 4 percent in 1987.[28]

One Japanese CEO explained: "We don't export because it's profitable. We export because it is national policy."[29]

EAST ASIAN MERCANTILISM:
THE LITTLE TIGERS

The so-called Little Tigers—South Korea, Taiwan, and Singapore—
employed variations of mercantilism as part of their own export-oriented
strategies of national economic development. Emulating Japan, they exploited their importance to the United States in its Cold War competition
with the Soviet Union and China in order to gain access to American
consumer markets and American technology, while protecting their domestic markets and carrying out state-guided industrial policies.

The Korean "miracle" of the 1960s through the 1980s was an example
of modern mercantilism in action. Like Japan, South Korea relied on
one-way access to US consumer markets and technology transfer by US
corporations. The US Agency for International Development (USAID)
provided financial and technical assistance for transferring US technology to the newly created Chungju Fertilizer Company, created in 1960.
When the first South Korean oil refinery was established in 1967 by the
Korea Oil Corporation (KOCO), Dow Chemical, as part of a joint venture, agreed to share its technology, train Korean engineers, and use them
to replace American engineers as soon as possible. All the American engineers were replaced by 1976, and then in the 1980s Dow sold off its
interests in South Korea.[30]

Like Japan, South Korea quickly moved up the value chain from garments to high-value-added industries like electronics and automobiles.
South Korea became even more mercantilist following the ascension of
the military dictator General Park Chung-hee in the 1960s. In the 1970s,
South Korea reversed financial liberalization, so that its government-
controlled banking sector could make "policy loans" to targeted strategic
industries. The military government controlled foreign exchange, to the
point of mandating the death penalty for foreign-exchange violation.[31]

In addition to using the state-controlled financial sector to steer credit
toward strategic industries, the South Korean government also used state-
owned enterprises (SOEs) such as the nationalized steelmaker, POSCO.

In South Korea, the equivalents of Japan's *keiretsu* were the *chaebol*, or business families, several dozen large groups of companies. Before the 1997 Asian financial crisis, government-*chaebol* collaboration was central to South Korean industrial policy.

Taiwan, another former Japanese colony, also emulated Japanese mercantilism. Taiwan used tariffs, nontariff barriers, and channeled credit to promote targeted manufacturing sectors. Like other Asian mercantilist countries, Taiwan relied on a state-controlled credit system and lax intellectual-property protection.

As city-states, Singapore and Hong Kong were necessarily more open, lacking hinterlands and large internal markets of their own. They pursued different but equally mercantilist policies of export-driven economic development.

NIXONIAN *REALPOLITIK*: THE ROAD NOT TAKEN

Richard Nixon is often thought of as a precursor of Ronald Reagan, but that honor belongs to Jimmy Carter, whose administration first adopted economic neoliberalism and began the large-scale dismantling of the New Deal system. Nixon was the last New Deal president. The policies of the Nixon administration can be understood as an attempt to deal with the problems caused by the contradiction between the New Deal order at home and the global economy by sacrificing America's post-1945 hegemonic grand strategy in favor of a more overtly nationalistic US foreign military and economic policy.

Nixon inherited a global system in which the bills were coming due for the obligations undertaken by his postwar predecessors. In his inaugural address, Kennedy had glibly declared: "Let every nation know, whether it wishes us well or ill, that we shall pay any price, bear any burden, meet any hardship, support any friend, oppose any foe, in order to assure the survival and the success of liberty."[32] Nixon, presiding over the disengagement of the United States from the involvement in Vietnam that Kennedy had begun and Johnson had escalated, declared that in the future America's allies would be expected to rely chiefly on themselves for their defense—the Nixon Doctrine. Nixon and his national security adviser, Henry Kissinger, argued that the bipolar world had been replaced by a multipolar world, in which the United States should pursue realist policies to maximize its own strategic interests.

Nixon's foreign economic policy was a form of nationalistic Realpolitik. He found a like-minded ally in Treasury secretary John Connally, who once confided in his deputy Pete Peterson, "The foreigners are out to screw us."[33] Unable to reconcile America's role as global economic hegemon with its national interests, Nixon and Connally abandoned that role for American self-help.

In 1971, the United States experienced its first current-account deficit, earning less on the value of its exports than it owed on the value of its imports. Nixon retaliated against Japanese mercantilism by slapping a tariff on Japanese imports, an act remembered in Japan as the "Nixon shock." Lacking enough gold to pay foreign claims, the Nixon administration suspended the convertibility of the dollar to gold, at first temporarily and then permanently in 1973. Freed from the gold standard, the United States devalued the dollar.

Like Franklin Roosevelt, who dismissed the gold standard as one of a number of "fetishes of international bankers," Nixon was less interested in the global system than in American national interests.

Had Nixonian nationalism prevailed, the New Deal order might have been saved by a tailoring of America's military and trade policies to domestic objectives. But beginning with Jimmy Carter and Ronald Reagan, the United States took a different path. Instead of modifying New Deal regulations, neoliberal Democrats and conservative Republicans alike dismantled them and replaced them in many cases with no regulations at all.

THE COUNTERREVOLUTION AGAINST NEW DEAL LIBERALISM

In the 1970s, the public's loss of faith in authority included a growing hostility to big business. The Harris polling agency found that the percentage of Americans who expressed "a great deal of confidence" in the heads of large corporations dropped from 55 percent in 1966 to 15 percent in 1975. In a July 1975 Gallup poll of public confidence in institutions, business came in last at 34 percent, below organized labor at 38 percent, and Congress at 40 percent.[34]

For its part, American business in the 1970s glared back at American society and did not like what it saw. "The have-nots are gaining steadily more political power to distribute the wealth downward," one executive complained at a meeting in a series hosted by the Conference Board in 1974 and 1975. "The masses have turned to a larger government."[35] Another participant complained: "Our enemies want cradle-to-grave security for everyone."[36] One business executive lashed out at democracy itself: "One man, one vote will result in the failure of democracy as we know it."[37]

Conservative American business elites had long demonized American liberalism by comparing it to German National Socialism or Soviet Communism and, when those canards seemed excessive, accusing American liberalism of being French was sure to win applause. The postwar stagnation of Britain provided the American Right with another nightmare. "We are following England to disaster, trying to beat them where they are going," one businessman complained at a Conference Board meeting. Another warned: "England is our future over the next decade. First, they got the dole, then we got our relief. First, they had socialized medicine, then we got Medicaid and Medicare. First, they had nationalized industry, now our institutions are in danger of being taken over by the government."[38]

American companies increasingly offshored production to countries where wages were low, workers were nonunionized and sometimes repressed, and where governments offered subsidies and other incentives for foreign direct investment. By 1980, more than 80 percent of semiconductors were produced by US multinationals in foreign countries including Singapore, South Korea, Taiwan, and Mexico.[39]

The business and financial sectors also poured funding into the conservative intellectual movement and conservative media outlets.

From the 1940s to the 1960s, a conservative and increasingly mathematical and unworldly version of Keynesianism, described by the
British economist Joan Robinson as "bastard Keynesianism," came to
dominate US economics departments. Mathematical economists in the
tradition of Paul Samuelson, author of the leading textbook in the
field, pushed out institutional economists in the tradition of John Kenneth Galbraith, who were more interested in studying the real world
than in devising pseudoscientific models. The increasingly arcane interests of the academic Keynesians left them disarmed against a coun-
teroffensive by free-market conservatives, who spread their ideas in the
mass media as well as in academic seminars.

The leader of the free-market Chicago School was Milton Friedman,
whose Nobel Prize for economics in 1976 marked the rightward shift of
economic thinking. With *Free to Choose*, a bestselling book that became
a television series, Friedman and his wife, Rose, popularized libertarian
economic ideas that had been marginalized in the United States and other industrial countries for a generation after the Depression. Conservative
and libertarian think tanks, funded by rich donors and business interests,
and the business press, most notably the *Wall Street Journal*, spread the
message: economic problems are almost always the fault of the government, not the market. President Ronald Reagan gave voice to this dogma
in his first inaugural address, when he declared that "government is not
the solution to our problem; government is the problem."[40]

Reagan and other conservatives adopted what became known as
"supply-side economics," based on the erroneous belief that, by increasing
the rewards to effort, tax cuts would generate more than enough revenue
through growth to compensate for the cuts. Supply-siders were fond of
pointing to the Kennedy-Johnson administration's use of a tax cut in 1964
to stimulate the economy. Galbraith presciently told the Joint Economic
Committee of Congress in 1965 of his misgivings about the tax cut of
1964: "I was never as enthusiastic as many of my fellow economists over
the tax reduction of last year. The case for it as an isolated action was
undoubtedly good. But there was danger that conservatives, once intro-

duced to the delights of tax reduction, would like it too much. Tax reduction would then become a substitute for increased outlays on urgent social
needs. We would have a new and reactionary form of Keynesianism with
which to contend."[41]

While besieged by a newly confident and aggressive free-market
Right, New Deal liberalism was attacked from the Left by Marxists and
environmentalists. Marxist scholars denounced "corporate liberalism,"
declaring that New Deal liberals like Roosevelt and Johnson were pawns
of the capitalist class and rewriting history to make industrial regulation
a conspiracy by the industries themselves.

Even more influential was the increasingly powerful environmentalist movement. Franklin Roosevelt, like his cousin Theodore, belonged
to the conservationist tradition, which favored the "wise use" of natural
resources for purposes of economic growth and re-creation. Liberal con-
servationism was eclipsed in the 1970s and 1980s by radical environmen-
talism, which drew on nineteenth-century romanticism. For radical environmentalists, the dams and highways that symbolized the New Deal
were unnatural abominations that desecrated nature. Influenced by the
British writer E. F. Schumacher, author of *Small Is Beautiful*, environmentalists on the Left condemned automobiles, electrical grids, suburbs,
mass consumption, and industrialized agriculture and industry, and fan-
tasized about a postindustrial utopia of locally grown food and "soft energy" sources like solar power and wind energy.

The Limits to Growth, a report published by the Club of Rome in
1972, convinced many Americans of the existence of an imminent crisis
of resource depletion. When resource exhaustion turned out not to be a
problem, the apocalyptic imagination of the environmentalist movement
invoked other threats—peak oil and global warming—to justify its cri-
tique of industrial society and consumerism. In 1982, Hugh G. Parris,
manager of power for the TVA, gave a speech entitled "The New TVA:
Managing in a No-Growth Environment." The TVA began to emphasize energy conservation as well as energy production. In a move that
would have appalled Roosevelt and Lilienthal, the TVA offered more

than a thousand poor households in East Tennessee and East Georgia a premodern technology: wood stoves.[42]

By the 1960s and 1970s, New Deal policies were being criticized from across the political spectrum. The stage was set for the Great Dismantling.

JIMMY CARTER: THE FIRST NEOLIBERAL

The Great Dismantling began during the administration of Jimmy Carter, not Ronald Reagan. Richard Nixon, a veteran of the Office of Price Administration who expanded government and fought inflation by imposing price controls, was a Modern Republican like Dwight Eisenhower who did not challenge the basic assumptions of the New Deal. If Nixon was the last New Dealer, Carter was the first neoliberal in the White House.

In 1980, the Carter administration showed a belated interest in strategic national economic policy as an alternative to the free-market ideology that became known as neoliberalism. The Treasury Department undertook a study of the Reconstruction Finance Corporation, while the State Department commissioned studies of industrial policy in Japan, Germany, France, and Sweden. In August 1980, Carter announced an economic revitalization plan, complete with a national development bank, an Economic Revitalization Board, targeted policies for particular sectors, and tripartite committees for major industries.[43] Bold on the surface, Carter's plan represented the most comprehensive vision of American developmental capitalism since the New Deal. But the plan was hastily drawn up to appease liberal and labor critics of the administration and it was forgotten after Carter was defeated by Reagan in 1980.

Many otherwise liberal Democrats viewed deregulation as a way to combat runaway inflation. From around 1 percent in 1960, inflation rose to 12 to 14 percent in 1979–1980. To this day, nobody is quite sure why. One factor may have been the refusal of the Johnson and Nixon administrations to raise taxes to pay for the Vietnam War and expanded domestic spending.

The oil shocks of the 1970s provided an additional source of trauma as well as of inflation. Until the 1970s, the Texas Railroad Commission, by regulating the output of Texas oil wells, had been able to control the world price of oil. The embargo imposed by OPEC on the United States and other allies of Israel following the Arab-Israeli War of 1973 demonstrated that control of the global oil price had passed to other oil-producing countries. Saudi Arabia, America's ally since the 1940s, nationalized the holdings of American oil companies. Increasingly the United States seemed to be, in the words of Richard Nixon, "a pitiful, helpless giant." Another oil shock followed in 1979 with the Iranian revolution.

Inflation became endemic as part of the wage-price spiral, as unionized workers anticipating further inflation won wage increases from employers, who passed them on to consumers via higher prices, with accommodating central banks like the Federal Reserve under Arthur Burns printing money. Nixon had failed to stop inflation with wage-and-price controls and Gerald Ford had been ridiculed for asking Americans to wear buttons with the motto "WIN (Whip Inflation Now)."

By the time that Jimmy Carter was inaugurated in 1977, many economists and policymakers hoped that free-market competition in infrastructure industries such as transportation and energy could lower the cost of goods and reduce inflation. The Carter administration treated deregulation as part of its inflation-fighting efforts. The April 1977 anti-inflation program of the administration combined a two-year extension of Nixon's Council on Wage and Price Stability, which oversaw wage-and-price controls, with a call for deregulation of communications, trucking, and other industries that had been regulated since the New Deal.[44]

THE GREAT DISMANTLING

The result, in the years from Carter to Clinton, was the rapid dismantling of most of the system governing the US economy erected during Roosevelt's presidency. The Carter administration supported the deregulation of airlines (1978), rail (1980), and trucking (1980); the bus industry was deregulated in 1982. Telecommunications was partly deregulated in 1996; in 1999 came the Gramm-Leach-Bliley Act, repealing the separation of commercial from investment banking established by the Glass-Steagall Act of 1933.

Deregulation decimated labor unions in airlines, trucking, and tele-communications—a result that was welcomed by many of the proponents of deregulation, who blamed inflation on unions whose wage costs were passed along by businesses in the form of higher prices. In 1979, 8.6 percent of the private workforce was found in the highly regulated, highly unionized transporation and utility sectors.[45] As a percentage of the private-sector workforce, unionized labor fell from 20 percent in 1980 to 10 percent in 1990 to less than 7 percent in 2010.

In some industries, a case could be made for deregulation. The regulated utility system of the New Deal era sometimes slowed the diffusion of new technologies and preserved archaic distinctions among industries. The organization of the telephone industry dominated by AT&T made sense as long as wire-based telephony created natural regional and continental monopolies. But the case for monopoly was undermined by technological advance in the area of radio communications. Like so many technological innovations, this emerged from the US military. During World War II, the US Army Signal Corps, seeking an alternative to wire or cable telephony, developed microwave transmission. This technology diffused to the private sector and, in the 1960s, Microwave Communications Inc., which became MCI, sought to compete with AT&T for long-distance service. In 1974, the Justice Department filed an antitrust suit against AT&T. AT&T was found guilty, among other things, of allegedly limiting competition by cross-subsidizing its state units. But state regulators had long insisted on low local-service rates, which could only be delivered by a policy of cross-subsidies. In other words, the federal government punished Ma Bell for doing what state governments forced her to do.[46] Under a consent decree in 1982, the company divested itself of its local operating companies—the Baby Bells—and retained only its long-distance, manufacturing, and research components. In succeeding years, cell phones rapidly replaced land lines and continuing technological innovation blurred the boundaries among telephone, cable, satellite radio, and Internet providers.

In other cases, such as airlines and electricity, deregulation turned healthy industries back into the "sick industries" that regulation had been designed to cure. The Civil Aeronautics Act of 1938 had turned the US airline industry into a regulated utility under the Civil Aeronautics Board (CAB). Like other regulated industries, the airline industry was exempt from antitrust laws so that airlines could set rates together. Among the enlightened regulations of the CAB were prohibitions on charging more for short flights than long ones and rate floors to prevent "fare wars." But by the 1970s, the example of independent local airlines like Southwest in Texas persuaded many analysts that airlines could not only increase routes but also combat inflation by lowering fares. The Carter administration supported the Airline Deregulation Act of 1978, which eliminated federal controls over entry, routes, schedules, financing, and fares. In 1984, the CAB itself was abolished.

The result of airline deregulation has been a chronically sick industry. Other than Southwest, few new entrants to the market have survived the Darwinian struggle. No airline went bankrupt in the era of regulation; since deregulation, more than 160 airlines have gone out of business, including Pan Am, TWA, Braniff, and Eastern. Only one of 58 airline companies created between 1978 and 1990 survived past 2000.[47]

As a result of mergers and alliances between particular cities and particular airlines that turned airports into "fortress hubs," competition diminished. By 2000, there were a dozen "dominated" hubs, where one airline had more than 50 percent of local passengers or two airlines had more than 60 percent.[48] Evidence of predatory monopoly behavior was abundant. The Government Accounting Office (GAO) found that fares were higher at dominated hubs.[49]

In 1981, Paul Stephen Dempsey accurately predicted three phases in the future of the US airline industry following deregulation: "In the first, price and service competition are increased, carriers become innovative and imaginative in the types of price and service combinations they offer, and consumers thereby enjoy lower priced transportation." In the second stage, "the intensive competition they are forced to endure under deregulation will force many carriers to float 'belly up' in bankruptcy."

The final outcome, Dempsey predicted, would be worse than the pre-regulation system: "Stage three of deregulation will constitute the ultimate transportation system with which the nation is left. A monopolistic or oligopolistic market structure will result in high prices, poor service, and little innovation or efficiency. . . . Small communities will receive poorer service and/or higher rates than they enjoyed under regulation. . . . In the end, the industry structure created by the free market may be much less desirable than that which was established by federal economic regulation."[50]

Another deregulatory disaster occurred in the electrical utility business. Because electrical utilities are so widely considered to be natural geographic monopolies, free-market libertarians saw them as the ultimate challenge—if electricity can be deregulated, anything can. Libertarians proposed that power providers other than utilities should be allowed to sell electricity on utility lines.

Allowing wholesale prices to be set by the market while limiting consumer-price increases created opportunities for market manipulation that were quickly exploited by Enron, a Houston-based energy company. A modern-day Samuel Insull, Ken Lay, the CEO of Enron, died in prison after his manipulative energy empire crumbled, exposing a shocking variety of criminal practices. According to one government report, Enron used market-manipulation scams with secret internal names like Black Widow, Get Shorty, Big Foot, Ricochet, and Death Star. The Death Star scam involved tricking state utilities into believing that there was congestion, forcing the state governments to pay "congestion fees" to Enron. The result was a series of "rolling blackouts" in California in 2000 and 2001.[51] In testimony to the US Senate in 2002, the chair of the California Power Authority, S. David Freeman, explained: "There is one fundamental lesson we must learn from this experience: electricity is really different from everything else. . . . And a market approach for electricity is inherently gameable."[52]

FINANCE AND THE GREAT DISMANTLING

Dismantling New Deal–era regulations had even more dramatic effects in the area of finance. As we have seen, the New Deal regulatory system continued the Jeffersonian tradition of protecting small "country banks," but it had the beneficial, if incidental, side effect of averting "ruinous competition" among banks and other financial institutions that might lead to reckless practices capable of endangering the economy. Thanks to Glass-Steagall and federal and state restrictions on interstate and intrastate branch banking, the US banking system was dominated by small local and regional banks. Between 1945 and 1970, the number of commercial banks dropped only slightly from 14,126 to 13,690; as late as 1991, there were nearly 12,000 banks.[53] From the late 1930s until deregulation began in the 1980s, the failure rate of banks and other financial institutions was extraordinarily low.

In the 1970s, money-market funds began to compete for customers with banks. Between 1977 and 1989, the share of American households with savings accounts shrank from 77 percent to 44 percent, while the bank share of household financial assets dropped from 30 percent in 1989 to only 17 percent in 2004.[54] In response, commercial banks panicked by falling profits lobbied Congress to repeal restrictions on their activities. In a short period of time, the walls between commercial banking, investment banking, thrifts and savings and loans, and insurance companies were torn down. In 1978, the Supreme Court in *Marquette National Bank v. First Omaha Service Company* struck down a South Dakota state usury law. Rapidly, limits on interest rates disappeared nationwide.

In 1980, the Depository Institutions Deregulation and Monetary Control Act began the process of elimination of Regulation Q (established by the Glass-Steagall Act; see chapter 13) and state-imposed usury limits. The Garn–St. Germain Depository Institutions Act of 1982 authorized money-market accounts. The Competitive Equality Banking Act of 1987, by limiting the ability of nonbanks to expand, gave them an incentive to become bank holding companies. The Financial Institutions Reform, Recovery and Enforcement Act of 1989 dealt with savings and loans. In 1994, the Riegle-Neal Act repealed the prohibition on interstate banking of the 1927 McFadden Act. Following the technically illegal merger of Citicorp and Travelers Insurance in 1998, the repeal of the Glass-Steagall ban on the combination of investment banks and commercial banks took place in 1999.

The result was a wave of mergers among banks and other financial institutions. Between 1990 and 2007, the number of FDIC-insured commercial banks dropped from more than twelve thousand to around seventy-five hundred. In 2007, the ten largest banks had 51 percent of banking industry assets and 40 percent of US domestic deposits.[55]

THE VOLCKER RECESSION

In 1943, the Polish economist Michal Kalecki predicted that attempts by governments to promote full employment would lead to inflation and provoke a backlash by business and investors: "The assumption that a government will maintain full employment in a capitalist economy if it knows how to do it is fallacious. . . . The workers would get out of hand and the 'captains of industry' would be anxious to 'teach them a lesson.' . . . A powerful bloc is likely to be formed between big business and *rentier* interests, and they would probably find more than one economist to declare that the situation was manifestly unsound."[56]

Sir Alan Budd, chief economic adviser to British prime minister Margaret Thatcher, wrote: "The Thatcher government never believed for a moment that [monetarism] was the correct way to bring down inflation. They did, however, see that this would be a very good way to raise unemployment. And raising unemployment was an extremely desirable way of reducing the strength of the working classes. . . . What was engineered—in Marxist terms—was a crisis of capitalism which re-created the reserve army of labour, and has allowed the capitalists to make high profits ever since."[57]

Three months after Thatcher became prime minister of the United Kingdom, Paul Volcker was appointed as chairman of the Federal Reserve by Carter in 1979 and reappointed by Reagan. He served until 1987. Volcker was a former executive of Chase Manhattan Bank. As Carter's domestic policy adviser Stuart E. Eizenstat explained, "Volcker was selected because he was the candidate of Wall Street. This was their price, in effect. What was known about him? That he was able and bright and it was also known that he was conservative. What wasn't known was that he was going to impose some very dramatic changes."[58]

Volcker's Fed raised short-term interest rates 7 percent over the rate of inflation to 19 percent. The result was two sharp recessions in three years. To the surprise of most policymakers, foreign money poured into the United States to take advantage of the high interest rates. The dollar rose 40 percent against other currencies in the four years after 1981. The sharp increase in the value of the dollar against other currencies priced American exporters out of many foreign markets.

America's manufacturing base was devastated. By late 1982, unemployment reached 10.8 percent. Factories were idle and neighborhoods and cities turned into wastelands. Volcker did more than anyone else to turn America's manufacturing region into the derelict Rust Belt. The chairman of Atlantic Richfield Oil Company, Robert O. Anderson, a Republican himself, complained about Volcker and Reagan that "they've done more to dismantle American industry than any other group in history. And yet they go around saying everything is great. It's like the Wizard of Oz."[59]

By 1984, inflation was no more than 4 percent and remained at low levels thereafter. Was Volcker's artificial recession really necessary to defeat inflation? Subsequent history suggests that a period of low inflation was about to begin anyway. As a factor in wage-price inflation, the bargaining power of workers was already diminishing rapidly, thanks to dwindling union membership. The contraction of the manufacturing sector as a result of productivity growth and offshoring, and the growth of employment in the nonunion service sector was already under way. Another structural factor might have moderated inflation without an artificial near-depression by the mid-1980s. The oil shocks of the 1970s were followed by an oil glut in the 1980s. The real price of crude fell from its high in 1980 to low levels for a generation. If the structural underpinnings of long-term low inflation were already in place before Paul Volcker took office, the damage that the Volcker recession inflicted on millions of Americans and critical US industries might have been a tragic and avoidable mistake.

THE BIRTH OF THE BUBBLE ECONOMY

Although they had no intention of doing so, Volcker, Reagan, and other policymakers of the 1980s accidentally laid the foundation for the US bubble economy of 1980–2008. What the financier George Soros has called a "super-bubble" created an illusion of prosperity, based on the underpinnings of debt that became unsustainable and led to the collapse of 2008. In the wake of the Volcker recession, policymakers and economists in the United States and other countries learned the wrong lesson. As governments vigilantly focused on the slightest threat of inflation, they pursued policies of low interest rates and credit-market deregulation that spawned the inflation of assets like stocks and real estates. The Volcker recession inspired shocked investors to shift from inflation-proof assets like gold and land to financial assets like stocks and bonds. The bubble economy was born.

The troubles of American manufacturing were compounded by a strong dollar that hurt American exporters even as it helped East Asian mercantilist nations and American consumers. Hoping that a higher yen would reduce Japan's chronic trade surplus, Reagan's Treasury secretary, James Baker—a Texan realist in the tradition of Nixon's Treasury chief,

John Connally—in 1985 negotiated a deal with the finance ministers and central-bank heads of the Group of Five or G5 (France, Germany, Japan, the United Kingdom, and the United States). Called the Plaza Accord after the New York hotel where the group met, the agreement devalued the dollar relative to the yen, whose value the Japanese had suppressed to help their exports. The policy failed to balance US-Japanese trade, however, because the Japanese government continued to pursue an export-oriented industrial policy by other methods. One was to lower domestic interest rates. This encouraged Japan's export industries to invest in even more overcapacity. By making speculation cheap, the low-interest-rate policy also encouraged speculation that led to bubbles in real estate and stocks. The funds from Japan's enormous trade surpluses permitted easy credit creation by Japanese banks, which led to a real-estate bubble in Japan. Prices rose far out of relation to fundamental values. At one point, the Imperial Palace grounds were said to be worth more than Tokyo. The collapse of the Japanese real-estate and stock-market bubbles produced decades of slow growth in Japan, beginning in the 1990s.

The policy of devaluing the dollar came to an end in 1987 with the Louvre Accord. From that point until the crisis of 2008, the United States followed a strong-dollar policy, to the benefit of Wall Street and to the detriment of productive export industries in the United States.

To the surprise of supply-siders, fiscal conservatives, and Keynesians alike, the Reagan deficits were easy to finance because of the inflow of foreign money, much of it from Japan. Dollars spent on Japanese imports were recycled in Japan to finance America's public and private deficits.

Unwilling to raise taxes much higher or to engage in painful cuts in military and domestic spending, the Reagan administration learned to live with twin fiscal and trade deficits. According to R. Taggart Murphy, "The real causes of the imbalances were twofold: first, the U.S. federal deficit, which the Reagan administration had structurally embedded into the U.S. body politic, and secondly, the Japanese 'developmental state' system of national leverage, centralized credit allocation, and credit risk socialization . . . which required exports to close the economic circle."[60]

The paradoxes involved in the interaction of free-market America and mercantilist Japan were marked by observers. The financial analyst David Hale wrote: "Future historians will probably note with more than ironic delight that at the end of the 1980s it was graduates of the Ministry of Tokyo Law School presiding over the Finance Ministry of the industrial world's least deregulated economy who helped to rescue the Reagan administration and the international economic system from currency misalignments, trade imbalances, and financial crises produced by the fiscal and monetary policies of economics graduates of the University of Chicago."[61]

The United States was now the world's largest debtor and Japan was the world's largest creditor. The Japanese central bank bought huge quantities of US government bonds to keep the yen artificially low, thereby subsidizing Japanese exports while hurting American exports. The same mercantilist technique would be adopted on a much larger scale by China a few decades later, with disastrous results for the economy of the United States and the world.

THE END OF THE NEW DEAL

The New Deal era came to an end in 1976, not 1980. The Age of Reagan should be called the Age of Carter.

Carter, not Reagan, pioneered the role of the fiscally conservative governor who runs against the mess in Washington, promising to shrink the bureaucracy and balance the budget. Early in his administration, Carter was praised by some on the Right for his economic conservatism. Reagan even wrote a newspaper column entitled "Give Carter a Chance." The most conservative Democrat in the White House since Grover Cleveland, Carter fought most of his battles with Democratic liberals, not Republican conservatives.

Today's Democrats would like to forget that supply-side economics was embraced by many members of their own party during the Carter years, while it was resisted by many old-fashioned fiscal conservatives in the GOP. As the economist Bruce Bartlett points out in a history of supply-side economics, "By 1980, the JEC [Joint Economic Committee of Congress] was a full-blown advocate of supply-side economics, despite having a majority of liberal Democrats, such as Senators Edward Kennedy (D-MA) and George McGovern (D-SD). Its annual report that year was entitled, 'Plugging in the Supply Side.' "[62]

In defense spending, as in supply-side economics, Reagan continued what his predecessor in the White House had begun. The reversal in the post-Vietnam decline of American military spending began under Carter, following the shock of the Iranian revolution and the Soviet invasion of Afghanistan. Carter called for raising defense spending from a starting point of 4.7 percent of GDP to 5.2 percent of GDP in his final budget for fiscal year 1981. The Carter administration called for defense spending to rise even further by 1987 to 5.7 percent of GDP—only a little below the 6.2 percent at which it peaked in 1986.[63]

In hindsight, the neoliberal cure was far worse than the New Deal liberal disease. The maturity of the New Deal's system of regulated, managerial capitalism coincided with the post–World War II boom and the greatest expansion of the middle class in American history. Consumer advocates, however, blamed it for stifling diversity, libertarians and conservatives claimed it choked off economic progress, and political scientists denounced it for spawning "interest-group liberalism."

To the applause of liberal Democrats and conservative Republicans alike, the New Deal system of regulation was dismantled in one sector of the economy after another in the late 1970s and 1980s. The result was not the flourishing diversity hoped for by liberal consumer activists nor the solid, sustainable economic growth promised by free-market ideologues. Instead, the result was the collapse of unions, the decline of private R&D, three decades of wage stagnation, and an economy driven by financialization, speculation, and rising debt rather than by productive industry and rising wages.

THE INFORMATION AGE

———————◆———————

THE ARGUMENT

The Information Age began to transform daily life toward the end of the twentieth century. But the technologies that produced the personal computer and the World Wide Web originated in the mid-twentieth century.

Most of the transformative technologies of the third industrial revolution were products of research backed by the US government. R&D funded by the military, during World War II and the early Cold War, led to nuclear energy, computers, and the Internet.

Combined with a new global infrastructure based on container ships, cargo jets, and satellite communications, computer technology made possible the emergence of global corporations engaged in production in many countries and several continents. The first attempt at an information-age global economy, however, was profoundly flawed. China, Japan, Germany, and other export-oriented nations sought to maintain permanent manufacturing trade surpluses, while American consumers, supplementing stagnant wages with unsustainable levels of debt, provided the engine of growth for the world economy. Mediated by an ever more reckless financial industry and swollen by the flow of the gains from growth to the gambling few rather than the consuming many, global imbalances built up as they had in the 1920s until the world economy crashed in 2008.

AS WE MAY THINK: THE THIRD INDUSTRIAL REVOLUTION

Today, it is truer than ever that basic research is the pacemaker of technological progress. In the nineteenth century, Yankee mechanical ingenuity, building largely upon the basic discoveries of European scientists, could greatly advance the technical arts. Now the situation is different. A nation which depends upon others for its new basic scientific knowledge will be slow in its industrial progress and weak in its competitive position in world trade, regardless of its mechanical skill.

—Vannevar Bush, 1945[1]

Beneath a concrete marker in Flushing, New York, is a message to the people of the year AD 6939. Designed by Westinghouse as part of its exhibit at the New York World's Fair of 1939, the time capsule was buried on the autumnal equinox, September 23, 1939. In addition to the Bible and "The Book of the Record of the Time Capsule," which contains messages on special paper in nonfading ink from Albert Einstein among others, the buried cache contains an electric lamp socket and electric wall switch, pieces of industrial machinery, samples of alloys, Portland cement, a newsreel, a watch, an alarm clock, a camera, a safety razor, fountain pen, swatches of cloth and asbestos, a lady's hat, coins and a dollar bill, and a Mickey Mouse cup.

At one of the darkest moments in history in 1939, the introduction to "The Book of the Record of the Time Capsule" was defiant in its optimism: "In our time many believe that the human race has reached the ultimate in material and social development; others that humanity shall march onward to achievements splendid beyond the imagination of this day, to new worlds of human wealth, power, life and happiness. We choose, with the latter, to believe that men will solve the problems of the world, that the human race will triumph over its limitations and its adversities, that the future will be glorious."

In the three decades that followed World War II, that optimism was vindicated, at least in the United States and its Western European and East Asian allies. The Westinghouse Corporation buried another time capsule nearby during the 1964 World's Fair. The later time capsule contained items that had not existed at the time of its predecessor, including graphite from the world's first nuclear reactor under Stagg Field at the University of Chicago in 1942, a reentry heat shield from the Mercury Aurora 7 spacecraft, the synthetic fibers Orlon, Dacron, and Lycra, a plastic heart valve, a laser rod, a transistor radio, parts of a satellite, and credit cards. And while there was also a Bible, the inclusion of the Beatles single "A Hard Day's Night," a bikini, and birth control pills suggested the social changes that had taken place. The technological advances of the mid-twentieth century amounted to a third industrial revolution.[2]

VANNEVAR BUSH

Thirteen miles from ground zero, Vannevar Bush lay on a tarpaulin thrown over the desert sand in the darkness of the early morning. The fifty-five-year-old director of the Office of Scientific Research and Development (OSRD) waited expectantly, next to his deputy, James Conant. They listened to the countdown by the physicist Saul Allison: "Three . . . two . . . one . . . zero." At 5:29:45 Mountain War Time on July 16, 1945, civilization changed forever.

The flash lit the distant desert mountains. Through a piece of dark glass, Bush looked at the fireball rising above the New Mexico desert. The Trinity test was a success. The United States had exploded the first atomic bomb. Returning to the gate of the nearby base, Bush waited for the physicist J. Robert Oppenheimer, the chief scientist in the project, to drive past on his way to a vacation. Bush tipped his hat. Oppenheimer wrote later: "We knew the world would not be the same. A few people laughed, a few people cried, most people were silent. I remembered the line from the Hindu scripture, the Bhagavad-Gita. Vishnu is trying to persuade the Prince that he should do his duty and to impress him takes on his multi-armed form and says, 'Now, I am become Death, the destroyer of worlds.'"[3]

On August 6, the United States dropped an atomic bomb on Hiroshima, Japan, killing 100,000 of its inhabitants. On August 9, a second bomb incinerated Nagasaki. On August 15, Emperor Hirohito announced the surrender of Japan. Earlier, on May 7, following the suicide of Adolf Hitler on April 30, the German government had formally surrendered. World War II was over. And the third industrial revolution was under way.

Many individuals contributed to the third industrial revolution of the mid-twentieth century, which engendered nuclear energy and information technology, as the second industrial revolution had produced electric power generation and the internal combustion engine and the first had given rise to the steam engine and the telegraph. But even when he was playing only a supporting role, Bush was present at key moments in the early years of the third industrial era, with personal connections to everything from the Manhattan Project and the computer to microwave ovens.

Thomas Edison was similarly ubiquitous during the second industrial revolution, inventing or contributing to the development of transformative technologies including electric-power generation, the incandescent lightbulb, the phonograph, and the motion picture. Edison was a folk hero in his day and his fame endures. In contrast, Bush is little known, except to historians of information technology. What explains Edison's continuing celebrity and Bush's relative obscurity?

One reason is publicity. Partly in order to raise funds from private investors, Edison did everything in a blaze of self-generated publicity, often making promises of imminent breakthroughs that he could not keep. In contrast, the wartime work of Bush and the Office of Scientific Research and Development was classified.

Another reason for the failure of Bush to find a place in the imagination of later generations has to do with the changing nature of technological innovation. Already by Edison's time, corporate and government laboratories and university research institutes in Germany, Britain, and the United States were displacing the individual inventor, even as enormous, consolidated managerial companies were succeeding small firms owned and operated by their founders. By World War II, the personnel and resource requirements of basic scientific research were so immense that only governments like the US federal government could organize and fund them.

As an engineer and scientist in his own right, Bush made many contributions to the evolution of technology and inspired countless others. But his most lasting contribution may be not any particular technology but the institutional structure that generates technological breakthroughs. In his report and later book *Science, the Endless Frontier*, commissioned by President Roosevelt, and his work with Congress in establishing the National Science Foundation, Bush helped to lay the foundation for the creative collaboration among government, the academy, and industry from which most transformative innovations in recent generations have emerged.

"AS WE MAY THINK"

In July 1945, as Bush was overseeing the Trinity test, the *Atlantic* published his essay "As We May Think," in which he speculated about the possibilities for technological augmentation of the human mind.[4] Among the new technologies that Bush correctly predicted in "As We May Think" were a "thinking machine" (the calculator), a "vocoder" which would type in response to dictation (voice-activated software), and a "cyclops camera" worn on the forehead (this has yet to arrive, although cell phones with digital photography are close approximations).

The most important of the imaginary devices that Bush described in his 1945 essay was the memex, a version of the personal computer that became a universal appliance in developed societies by 2000. He got the mechanism wrong, speculating that the combination of pictures and text would be embodied in microtape. But his vision of a desk and a screen inspired the engineers who developed the monitor and the mouse. And his speculations about a universal network with a library that could be accessed through "trails" mimicking the associative nature of human thought anticipated the Internet, online dictionaries like Wikipedia, and hyperlinks.

The impact of "As We May Think" was magnified by media interest in the article. After its initial publication in the *Atlantic*, the essay was popularized on July 23, 1945, in *Time* under the title "A Machine That Thinks" and on September 10, 1945, *Life* magazine published an illustrated condensation: "A top U.S. scientist foresees a possible future world in which man-made machines will start to think."[5]

What prevented "As We May Think" from being a catalog of gadgets was Bush's discussion of how information technology could be used to augment human intelligence. Popularization of his work notwithstanding, he was more interested in a machine to help thinking than in a thinking machine. Because human thought is based to a large degree on associations among ideas and images, Bush believed that there was a need for "associative indexing, the basic idea of which is a provision whereby any item may be caused at will to select immediately and automatically another. This is the essential feature of the memex. The process of tying two items together is the important thing."

Bush's memex would tie together items by means of "trails." He provided an example: "The owner of the memex, let us say, is interested in the origin and properties of the bow and arrow. Specifically he is studying why the short Turkish bow was apparently superior to the English long bow in the skirmishes of the Crusades. He has dozens of possibly pertinent books and articles in his memex. First he runs through an encyclopedia, finds an interesting but sketchy article, leaves it projected [on the screen]. Next, in a history, he finds another pertinent item, and ties the two together. Thus he goes, building a trail of many items. Occasionally he inserts a comment of his own, either linking it into the main trail or joining it by a side trail to a particular item."

In addition to main trails and side trails, there would be the "skip trail which stops only on the salient items." Individuals would save their information trails and share them with friends and colleagues. Bush predicted: "Wholly new forms of encyclopedia will appear, ready made with a mesh of associative trails running through them, ready to be dropped into the memex and there amplified."

In tribute to Bush, this chapter will be organized as though it were a series of associative trails on an imaginary memex. By following them, we discover that Bush is celebrated as a pioneer of virtually every aspect of today's computer technology, from its physical form to hyperlinks and the Internet.

MISTER SCIENCE

Let us begin with the main trail of Bush's biography. "It is interesting that Mister Science looks so much like Mr. America," *Coronet* magazine reported in a profile of Bush published in 1952. "He reminds you of somebody—Will Rogers? Uncle Sam? Anyway, you've seen this face before, and it belonged to a man you liked."[6]

Bush was the quintessential New England Yankee inventor, born the son of a Universalist minister in Everett, Massachusetts, in 1890. Earning degrees from Tufts, Harvard, and MIT, he worked for the navy during World War I on the problem of detecting submarines and then became a professor at MIT. While working on a "network analyzer" that simulated electrical networks, Bush and his MIT team developed the differential analyzer. The differential analyzer was an early computer that used electromechanical gears and spinning disks to do calculations, a version of the "difference engine" of which the Victorian British scientist Charles Babbage had dreamed. Bush continued to improve the analyzer after being appointed vice president of MIT and dean of its School of Engineering.

In 1938, as the world moved toward the second global war in a generation, Bush's appointment as president of the Carnegie Institute brought him to Washington, DC. In June 1940, Bush met with President Roosevelt and argued that there was a need for an organization that could coordinate research in military technology. With Roosevelt's backing, Bush became chairman of the new National Defense Resource Committee (NDRC). In his memoirs Bush wrote: "There were those who protested that the action of setting up NDRC was an end run, a grab by which a small company of scientists and engineers, acting outside established channels, got hold of the authority and money for the program of developing new weapons. That, in fact, is exactly what it was."[7]

In June 1941, the NDRC was superseded by the OSRD. As its director, Bush reported directly to the president. He presided over the greatest R&D organization of all time. With inexhaustible military resources at his command and teams made up of great scientists who had fled Hitler, such as Leo Szilard, Enrico Fermi, and Niels Bohr, as well as brilliant Americans, Bush supervised one breakthrough after another, in fields as different as radar and nuclear energy, jet engines, and early computers. Science was now organized, marshaled, and mobilized in the service of the war against Hitler and his allies. The press called Bush "the general of science."

Bush found the perfect patron and partner in Roosevelt. All his life FDR was entranced by visions of abundance and freedom made possible by technological advances. Following World War I, in his role as assistant secretary of the navy, Roosevelt promoted the infant American radio industry by creating the public-private Radio Corporation of America (RCA). In the only book he ever published, *Whither Bound?,* a 1926 lecture at the Milton Academy prep school, Roosevelt praised "the scientist people, and economists, and industrialists, and wild-eyed progressives" who were "bringing so many new things into everyday life." He foresaw the day "when by the twist of a knob or the push of a button you see and talk with some true friend half the world away. . . . Cheaper power, canned power, compressed into light weight and small bulk, will make our present flying abilities childish within our own lives. So, too, with transportation by land."[8]

As the war drew to a close, FDR and his chief scientist pondered what was to become of the federally funded research system that had produced so many innovations. Bush recollected: "Roosevelt called me into his office and said, 'What's going to happen to science after the war?' I said, 'It's going to fall flat on its face.' He said, 'What are we going to do about it?' And I told him, 'We better do something damn quick.'"[9]

The president commissioned Bush to write a report on the future of science in America. Roosevelt was dead in 1945 when Bush presented the report to his successor, Harry Truman.[10] Published as *Science, the Endless Frontier*, the book became a best seller. Bush proposed a national research foundation that would provide contracts for research and scholarships to young scientists. Populists in Congress like Representative Harley Kilgore of West Virginia opposed Bush's vision of federal grants to top-ranking research universities as elitist, preferring a decentralized system of government laboratories modeled on the highly successful federal agricultural research stations. When it was finally created in 1950, the National Science Foundation (NSF) was more modest than Bush had hoped but in the years that followed the system of federal support for science and technology developed largely along the lines he had sketched out.

THE MANHATTAN PROJECT

From this main trail of information about Bush, our imaginary memex permits us to move at any time to side trails linking Bush to specific topics relevant to the third industrial revolution. One is the link between Bush and the development of the atomic bomb.

In December 1938, the success of German scientists in splitting the atom alarmed the physicists Leo Szilard and Eugene Wingner. They persuaded Albert Einstein to write a letter to President Roosevelt warning him of the possibility that Hitler's Germany might create atomic bombs. In October 1939, a month after Germany invaded Poland, the letter was delivered to FDR by a friend of his, Alexander Sachs. Concerned about the slow speed of research in the United States under the Uranium Committee supervised by Lyman Briggs, the physicists, under Einstein's signature, wrote FDR again in March and April 1940. But it was not until Britain's MAUD (military application of uranium technology) committee concluded that an atomic bomb could be made in the next few years that the American government began to move quickly. In fall 1940, the British government sent two leaders of its wartime science effort, Sir Henry Tizard and Sir John Cockcroft, to Washington to share the results of their research into the creation of two fissile materials.

Bush's involvement with the atomic bomb began in 1940, when he extended the jurisdiction of the newly created NDRC over the Uranium Committee. Under the auspices of the OSRD, organized in June 1941 under Bush, teams at the University of Chicago, Columbia, the University of California, and Princeton worked on the secret atomic project. In spring 1942, California's Ernest Lawrence made a breakthrough in plutonium production.

On March 9, 1942, Bush wrote FDR: "Present opinion indicates that successful use is possible, and that this would be very important and might be determining in the war effort. It is also true that if the enemy arrived at results first it would be an exceedingly serious matter." He estimated that bombs could be produced in 1944. Roosevelt answered two days later: "I think the whole thing should be pushed not only in regard to development, but also with due regard to time. This is very much of the essence."[11]

In 1942, Bush arranged for what came to be called the Manhattan Project to be turned over to the Army Corps of Engineers under the leadership of General Leslie Groves, but he continued to supervise the work as chair of the Military Policy Committee, which advised the president. The cultures of the US military and American corporate engineers and executives frequently clashed with that of immigrant atomic scientists, many of whom were political leftists suspicious of business and the military.

The secret project had practically unlimited resources. The federal government spent more than $2 billion between 1939 and 1945 on atomic research. In December 1942, a team that included the Italian physicist Enrico Fermi produced the first self-sustaining chain reaction in the first nuclear reactor, located under the bleachers of Stagg Field on the University of Chicago campus. The team leader, Arthur Compton, reported the result to Washington: "The Italian navigator [Fermi] has just landed in the new world."

Plutonium and uranium were produced in factories in Hartford, Washington, and Oak Ridge, Tennessee—the latter powered by Roosevelt's Tennessee Valley Authority hydropower dams. The first atomic bombs were assembled at Los Alamos, New Mexico, by a scientific and engineering team led by J. Robert Oppenheimer. And so we return to Bush at ground zero on July 16, 1945, where we began.

THE INVENTION OF THE JET

Following another side link, we find that Bush played an administrative role in the development of the jet engine. Alarmed by intelligence reports about German advances in turbojet technology, in February 1941, General H. H. "Hap" Arnold of the army air corps asked Bush to form a committee on jet propulsion. Bush organized a Special Committee on Jet Propulsion, headed by W. F. Durand, that brought together representatives of GE, Westinghouse, and Allis-Chalmers. GE was selected to develop the turbojet engine designed by Britain's Frank Whittle.

As often occurs in the history of invention, two inventors—Whittle in Britain and Hans von Ohain in Germany—came up with the idea of gas turbine engines to power aircraft around the same time. A gas turbine engine compresses air to raise its temperature, then forces it through a combustion chamber. The hot air spins the turbine and provides thrust as it escapes through an exhaust nozzle.

In 1928, Whittle's thesis for the RAF College suggested that piston engines and propellers were inadequate for fast flight at high altitudes. In 1929, he suggested that gas turbines be used, and he obtained a patent in 1932. While serving as an RAF officer, Whittle founded a company, Power Jets, in 1935, to build an engine for a high-altitude, fast-mail plan.[12]

Meanwhile, Ohain, ignorant of Whittle's work, obtained the backing of industrialist Ernst Heinkel, along with Herbert Wagner of Junkers and Helmut Schelp of the German Air Ministry.[13] Ohain's engine was tested by the experimental Heinkel-178 on August 27, 1938. Whittle's engine was tested by the experimental Gloster on May 15, 1941.

Under Bush's supervision, GE developed Whittle's engine for the United States. With two GE engines, the Bell XP-59A became the first American jet aircraft to fly, on October 1, 1942.[14]

Jets went into military service only in the summer of 1944. After 1945, the Allies studied captured German aeronautical research. German swept-wing designs inspired Boeing to put swept wings on the B-47 jet bomber of 1947.[15]

Britain led the world into the jet age with the DeHavilland Comet. After three Comets disintegrated in midair in 1953 and 1954, all Comet flights stopped, resuming only in 1958. The vacuum was filled by the United States with the Boeing 707 and the Soviet Union with its Tupolev Tu-104. Boeing followed up the 707 with the 727, which could use shorter runways. The global jet era started in 1958, when Boeing 707s began regular commercial flights across the Atlantic. Boeing's 737 and its jumbo jet, the 747, used a turbofan rather than a turbojet engine. Turbofans maximized their peak thrust at lower speed, making wide-bodied passenger jets and cargo jets possible.[16]

THE SPACE AGE

In October 1957, the Soviets launched Sputnik, the first artificial satellite. Americans were shocked to find that they had fallen behind in what became known as "the space race." In response, in 1958 the Defense Department created the Advanced Research Projects Agency (ARPA) and the National Advisory Committee on Aeronautics (NACA) was turned into the National Aeronautics and Space Administration (NASA).

The development of missile and rocket technology for both military purposes and the exploration of space has been an important part of the third industrial revolution. In consulting the memex, we learn that Bush's main role in this area was that of naysayer. For example, Bush predicted that the ballistic missile "would never stand the test of cost analysis. If we employed it in quantity, we would be economically exhausted long before the enemy."[17]

In 1960, Bush told Congress: "Putting a man in space is a stunt: the man can do no more than an instrument, in fact can do less. There are far more serious things to do than indulge in stunts. . . . [T]he present hullabaloo on the propaganda aspects of the program leaves me entirely cool."[18] Bush's opinion eventually was shared by the American government, which abandoned the Apollo program in the 1970s and then, in the 2010s, shut down the space shuttle without having any other method of sending astronauts to space except for reliance on, ironically, Russian rockets.

Along with exploration of the planets by robotic probes, the most important products of the space program have been satellites, used for military purposes, environmental monitoring, and communications. The United States created the US-dominated Communications Satellite Corporation (Comsat) in 1962, and the International Telecommunications Satellite Organization (Intelsat) in 1964, a multigovernment consortium that was privatized in 2001. The United States controlled 61 percent of Intelsat's original ownership, compared to 30.5 percent for Western Europe and 8.5 percent for Canada, Australia, and Japan. In order to be less dependent on the United States, the Europeans eventually founded the European Space Agency in 1971.[19]

As the basis of global communication, submarine cables were eclipsed by communications satellites in the years following Sputnik. By 2000, the majority of international telephony took place by means of satellites.

THE EVOLUTION OF THE COMPUTER

One trail leads us back to Bush's differential analyzer, from which we follow another trail to the earliest origins of the computer. The US federal government bore paternal responsibility for the infant computer industry. In 1886, Herman Hollerith, an employee of the US Census Office, invented an electrical punch-card reader that could be used to process census information and other data. The company that Hollerith formed in 1896, the Tabulating Machine Company, evolved by 1924 into International Business Machines (IBM). In 1911, another Census Office employee, James Powers, devised an automatic card-punching machine and founded the Powers Tabulating Machine Company which, in 1927, merged with Remington Rand. In the decades that followed, Remington Rand and IBM dominated much of the private-sector development of information technology.

At MIT, Bush advanced the technology of computing with his electromechanical device. An early model of the analyzer inspired a front-page headline in the *New York Times* in 1930: "'Thinking Machine' Does Higher Mathematics; Solves Equations That Take Humans Months."[20] Inspired by Bush, others built differential analyzers at Aberdeen Proving Ground, General Electric, and the universities of Pennsylvania, Texas, California, and Cambridge. Other analyzers were constructed in Germany, Russia, Norway, and Ireland. Beginning in 1935, the Rockefeller Foundation invested in the analyzer's development.[21]

But the future of the computer would be electronic and digital, not electromechanical. In 1939, IBM funded Howard Aiken, a graduate student at Harvard, on the basis of a memo that Aiken had written about digital computing. By 1944, IBM had developed the automatic sequence controlled calculator.

Bush's analog approach to computing would be superseded by the far more efficient binary approach. Here, too, there is a link. One of Bush's graduate students at MIT, Claude Shannon, in his master's thesis, explored the idea of using electrical circuits to replace the clumsy mechanical components of Bush's differential analyzer. Shannon proposed using a binary system based on Boolean algebra. When he went to work for Bell Labs, he influenced the evolution of telephone technology. His 1948 work, "A Mathematical Theory of Communication," developed his binary system, which became the basis of modern telecommunications and computing. It has been called the Magna Carta of the information age.

During World War II, Bush turned down an application to the NDRC for funding a project on digital computers from Norbert Wiener, a leading mathematician at MIT, for fear that it would divert resources from the war effort for a long-term project. For the same reason, Bush also refused to fund the electric numerical integrator and calculator (ENIAC), which was funded instead by the army.

The role of the US military in nurturing information technology began in the 1930s, when the army needed a computer capable of calculating artillery-firing tables. The Army's Aberdeen Ballistics Research Laboratory provided funding for a team at Pennsylvania's Moore School of Electrical Engineering led by John W. Mauchly and J. Presper Eckert. Inspired by theoretical work done earlier by Iowa State's John V. Atanasoff, the Pennsylvania team in 1946 built the first all-purpose electronic computer, ENIAC. The army was joined in its sponsorship of the computer industry by the Office of Naval Research, NACA, and the Census Bureau, with its perennial interest in rapid data processing.[22]

The initiative then shifted back to Remington Rand and IBM. In 1950, Remington Rand acquired the Eckert-Mauchly Computer Corporation, along with its contract with the US Census Bureau. Then, in 1952, Remington Rand acquired another company, Engineering Associates, formed by veterans of work done for the navy on the use of computers in cryptology.

Meanwhile, in 1950, the head of IBM, Thomas Watson Sr., boasted that a single IBM computer on display in New York could "solve all the important scientific problems in the world involving scientific calculations."[23] Work done by IBM for the attempt of the US and Canadian governments to build a Semi-Automatic Ground Environment (SAGE) air defense against Soviet missiles for North America led to major breakthroughs. By the mid-1950s, IBM was responsible for two-thirds of all computer sales and, after it introduced its System 360 in 1960, it dominated the mainframe computer industry for a generation.

IBM is so important in the history of modern computer technology that we decide to follow a trail to learn more about the company.

"NOTHING IN THE WORLD WILL EVER STOP IT": THE RISE OF IBM

In January 1926, Thomas Watson Sr., the founding president of IBM, predicted to the star salesmen at his One Hundred Percent Club convention: "This business has a future for your sons and grandsons and your great-grandsons, because it is going on forever. Nothing in the world will ever stop it. The IBM is not merely an organization of men; it is an institution that will go on forever."[24] To date his prediction has been borne out.

In its centennial year of 2011, IBM ranked eighteenth on *Fortune*'s list of America's biggest companies and the seventh most profitable, and fifty-second on the list of the Fortune Global 500. IBM was ranked number one in information technology services. In the same year, IBM ranked twelfth out of fifty on a list of the world's most admired companies, and number one in information technology (IT) services.[25] The previous year, the company had filed eighteen thousand patents—more than any company in the world—and spent $24 billion on R&D. Among its projects were Smart Planet, a program to use computer networking to ease traffic and help power grids.

In 1997, an IBM computer, Deep Blue, defeated the chess champion Garry Kasparov at chess. In February 2011, Ken Jennings, the record-holding champion, and another contestant, Brad Rutter, battled Watson on the American television quiz show *Jeopardy*. Watson was a computer capable of understanding questions in natural language and developed by

IBM's DeepQA project, headed by David Ferrucci. Watson defeated its human rivals, to win the prize of $1 million. In his final *Jeopardy* response, Jennings, alluding to a line in an episode of the TV cartoon show *The Simpsons*, wrote: "I, for one, welcome our new computer overlords." IBM had influenced popular culture before. The company's name is thought to have inspired the intelligent computer in Stanley Kubrick's and Arthur C. Clarke's 1968 science fiction movie *2001: A Space Odyssey*, each letter of whose name is one letter removed from IBM: HAL.

Watson was named after IBM's founder, Thomas J. Watson Sr. The son of a farmer and lumber dealer in upstate New York, Watson began his career peddling pianos, organs, and sewing machines. He discovered his talents as a salesman as a protégé of John H. Patterson, the dynamic and eccentric president of National Cash Register (NCR). Along with Patterson and other NCR managers, Watson was accused by the government of violating antitrust laws as part of a scheme to dominate the used cash register market. Like Patterson, Watson was cleared, but six months later the temperamental Patterson fired him for disagreeing with him in public.

In 1914, Watson became head of the Computer Tabulating Recording Corporation (CTR), whose name he changed to International Business Machines in 1924. Founded a few years before his arrival, in 1911, CTR was the product of mergers of several other companies. The most important was the Tabulating Machine Company, whose founder, as we saw earlier, was the inventor and former Census Bureau official Herman Hollerith.

Watson was a rare combination of technological visionary, marketing genius, and supersalesman. In the late twentieth century, the stereotypical tech company founder in the popular mind was a brilliant bohemian from the San Francisco Bay area who favored informality and a casual approach to organization. Watson could not have been further from that archetype.

A strict Methodist, Watson insisted that his male employees wear only white shirts and dark suits and avoid embarrassing themselves with alcohol. Influenced by Patterson's methods, Watson created a revival-like atmosphere to inspire his sales force at meetings and the conventions of his One Hundred Percent Club. Alleged to have influenced Japanese and other East Asian managers, Watson motivated employees with inspirational slogans like the Five C's—Conception, Consistency, Cooperation, Courage, and Confidence—and hymnlike songs, including this, from his days at CTR:

> Mr. Watson is the man we're working for
> He's the leader of the CTR
> He's the fairest, squarest man we know.[26]

One of his mottoes was: "IBM products are not bought; they are sold." His most famous slogan became a fixture in IBM offices and advertisements:

T-H-I-N-K.

In 1929, Watson funded a statistical laboratory at Columbia University, where Wallace J. Eckert worked closely with IBM. At Harvard in 1936, Howard Aiken, a graduate student in physics, proposed the creation of a massive computer, inspired by the work of the nineteenth-century British theorist of computing, Charles Babbage. IBM's chief engineer, James Bryce, brought the idea to the attention of Watson, who funded the project and assigned engineers to assist Aiken. The result was the five-ton Harvard Mark I, completed in 1943. Furious that Aiken neglected to mention IBM's support at the press conference, Watson got his revenge by establishing the Watson Computer Laboratory at Columbia in 1945. Led by Wallace Eckert, the Columbia laboratory developed the selective sequence electronic calculator, which overshadowed Harvard's Mark I when it debuted in 1948. Displayed on the ground floor of IBM's headquarters in New York City, the computer became a sensation.

FROM SAGE TO SABRE

According to legend, a myopic Watson stated after World War II that there was only a market for a dozen or so computers in the world. In reality, IBM was working on numerous computer projects at the time. When the Korean War began in June 1950, IBM won a government contract to develop a "defense calculator."

IBM's most important military contract of the 1950s was the Semi-Automatic Ground Environment (SAGE) program. The ancestry of the SAGE project can be traced to a memo written by Jay Forrester in 1948, outlining a computerized national air-defense system inspired by radar defenses in World War II for North American defenses against Soviet bomber (and later missile) attacks. Forrester had been working since 1944 at MIT on Project Whirlwind, a digital air-combat-information program. When IBM received a contract to work on SAGE, it received the Whirlwind technology. In addition to IBM, contractors on the SAGE project included MIT's Lincoln Laboratories, Western Electric, the SDC branch of RAND, and the Burroughs Company. The Computer System Division of Lincoln Laboratories in 1958 became the MITRE Corporation, which worked on software and systems integration.

When complete, the SAGE system consisted of twenty-three concrete bunkers in the United States and one in Canada. Each of the direction centers contained an IBM AN/FSQ-7 computer, along with a standby. Each AN/FSQ-7 weighed 250 tons, and contained forty-nine thousand vacuum tubes. The installations were designed for the simultaneous analysis of vast amounts of data coming in from radar on the ground and mounted on ships and planes.

The most ambitious computer project in history to date, the SAGE system was completed in 1963 and remained operational until it was decommissioned in 1983. Although it was technologically obsolete almost as soon as it was finished, the system helped to inspire later innovations. The linkages between the nodes in the SAGE system helped to inspire J. C.

Licklider's musings, which in turn led to the development of ARPANET and the Internet.

For its part, IBM drew on its experience in the SAGE project in the early 1960s when it received a contract from American Airlines to devise a computerized airline reservation system entitled SABRE (Semi-Automatic Business Research Environment—even the name was modeled on SAGE). SABRE became the basis of modern airline reservations.

THE COMPUTER THAT IBM MADE, THAT MADE IBM

But it was in civilian office computing that IBM would make its greatest mark. Earlier in 1947, J. Presper Eckert and John Mauchly had incorporated the Eckert-Mauchly Computer Corporation to make the UNIVAC and other computers. Their commercial difficulties led the two to visit Watson and his son and eventual successor as head of IBM, Thomas Watson Jr. Perhaps remembering his earlier brush with antitrust law at NCR, the senior Watson had checked with IBM's lawyers and told the inventors that the Justice Department probably would not allow IBM to absorb their company because of antitrust considerations. Instead, the rights to UNIVAC were sold to James Rand, the president of Remington Rand, making the company a leading computer manufacturer. (In 1955, Remington Rand merged with the Sperry Corporation to become Rand, later Sperry; a merger between Sperry and Burroughs in 1986 produced Unisys.) On live television on election eve 1952, a UNIVAC computer correctly predicted a landslide for Republican presidential candidate Dwight Eisenhower (the computer's operators thought at first the computer must have been mistaken).

Motivated by competition with Remington Rand, IBM in 1953 brought out its inexpensive model 650, which used magnetic tape instead of punched cards. Thomas Watson Jr. observed that "the 650 became computing's 'Model T.' "[27]

In the early 1960s, IBM took on the challenge of providing office computers that used compatible software. In secrecy, the company sponsored one of the greatest corporate research programs in history, code-named the New Product Line. Thousands of programmers and engineers labored urgently in multiple laboratories and IBM began to manufacture more semiconductors than any other company in the world. Finally in April 1964, IBM unveiled its System/360 product line of software-compatible mainframe computers. The System/360 was described as "the computer that IBM made, that made IBM."

FROM VACUUM TUBE TO SILICON CHIP

Early computers were hobbled by reliance on vacuum tubes that took up space and generated heat. At AT&T's Bell Laboratories, the physicist William Shockley led a research group that developed solid-state transistors between 1947 and 1950. By the mid-1950s, Texas Instruments led in the manufacture of silicon transistors. The next step, propelled by US military demands for smaller computers, was the combination of transistors on a single circuit board. Working independently of each other, Robert Noyce at Fairchild Semiconductor and Gordon Moore at Intel invented the silicon "chip," a single "integrated circuit" that combined transistors and capacitors. Moore's law, named after Gordon Moore, was based on the fact that the number of transistors per microchip doubled roughly every seventeen months after 1972, when the Intel 8008 chip had 2,500 transistors, to 2000, when the Pentium 4 processor had forty-two million transistors.

Soon there were three kinds of integrated circuits: memory chips, microprocessors, developed by Intel, and microcapacitors. Raytheon and the optical equipment manufacturer Perkin-Elmer developed a method of photolithography fabrication that made possible the mass production of silicon chips.

SIDE TRAIL: RAYTHEON AND THE RADARANGE

Let us follow a side trail on the imaginary memex to learn more about Raytheon. It brings us to the microwave oven, the first major innovation in cooking since primitive hominids began to cook with fire.

Percy Spencer, an engineer working at Raytheon, was startled one day in 1946 when a candy bar in his pocket melted as he was working on a new vacuum tube called a magnetron. Realizing that the magnetron was the cause, Spencer successfully popped popcorn kernels by placing them nearby and then cooked an egg, which exploded in his face. By spring 1946, Spencer and a colleague, P. R. "Roly" Hanson, were working on a project given the secret code name Speedy Weenie. Their work led to Raytheon's 1946 patent for the microwave oven. In 1947, a contest among employees to name the device produced a winner: "Radarange." By 1976, more American households owned a microwave oven than owned a dishwasher.[28]

At the time that it invented the microwave, Raytheon was a leading manufacturer of vacuum tubes, having acquired or merged with other companies in the field including Acme-Delta and Q.R.S. Company. In 1928, it had chosen the name Raytheon Manufacturing Company to replace its previous name, the American Appliance Company, because of the visibility of one of its products called the Raytheon ("light of the gods"), an electron tube used in a "battery eliminator" that converted the alternating current in household wiring to direct current that could be used in radios, as an alternative to batteries.

The Raytheon electron tube was the invention of Charles G. Smith, who had founded the American Appliance Company in Cambridge, Massachusetts, in 1922, with two partners. One was an engineer named Laurence K. Marshall. The other founder of the company to be known as Raytheon was Marshall's engineering school classmate and college roommate at Tufts University, the thirty-two-year-old Vannevar Bush.

THE ORIGINS OF SILICON VALLEY

Using a skip trail on the memex, we return to the main trail and Bush. Was there any connection between Bush and Silicon Valley? Under the label "Silicon Valley" we find an interesting side trail.

We learn that Professor Bush's first graduate student at MIT was named Frederick Terman. After taking a job as a professor of electrical engineering at Stanford University, Terman was disappointed by the lack of employment opportunities for graduates of his department in Northern California. With his encouragement, two of his students, Bill Hewlett and Dave Packard, founded an electronics company named Hewlett-Packard in Packard's garage. Some myths are true; the garage is now a historical landmark in Palo Alto.

After working during the war at Harvard to develop the technology of radar, Terman resumed his post at Stanford and joined others in an attempt to make that university a center of high technology in collaboration with business and government. The railroad baron Leland Stanford, one of the captains of industry of early industrial America, bequeathed his eight-thousand-acre ranch to the university that bore his son's name. Terman and his colleagues leased out Stanford's acreage, now called the Stanford Industrial Park, to select high-technology firms including General Electric and Eastman Kodak. One of Terman's biggest prizes was William Shockley. Shockley joined the faculty at Stanford and directed the Shockley Laboratory of Beckman Instruments.

Several of his protégés, nicknamed "the Traitorous Eight," quit to form Fairchild Semiconductor. Its veterans in turn went on to found dozens of companies like Intel in what became Silicon Valley, an area that included Palo Alto and—here is a link to the second industrial revolution—Menlo Park, named after Thomas Edison's famous research laboratory in New Jersey.

Meanwhile, Hewlett-Packard had grown into a substantial electronics firm that moved into the computer market. The earliest documented use of the term "personal computer" has been found in the October 4, 1968, issue of *Science* magazine, in an ad for Hewlett-Packard's HP 9100: "The new Hewlett-Packard 9100A personal computer is ready, willing, and able . . . to relieve you of waiting to get on the big computer."[29] At forty pounds and costing nearly five thousand dollars, the HP 9100A could be improved upon. And it was—by, among others, Steve Wozniak, who worked for HP before teaming up with Steve Jobs to found Apple Computer.

In another garage, the garage of Jobs's parents' house, Wozniak and Jobs experimented with assembling small personal computers. Wozniak's boss at Hewlett-Packard reportedly told him, "HP doesn't want to be in that kind of market."[30] Jobs and Wozniak founded Apple Computer, Inc., which in 1977 brought out the first successful personal computer (PC), the Apple II.

Jobs went on to have one of the most remarkable careers in the history of American business. Apple developed a cultlike following with its Apple Macintosh PC. But Jobs was forced out of the company by its board of directors. In 1985, he founded another company, NeXt. When NeXt was bought by Apple, Jobs returned as CEO from 1997 to 2011, overseeing the release of the innovative iPod, iPhone, and Apple Tablet.

Two other hobbyists, Bill Gates and Paul Allen, wrote beginners all-purpose symbolic instruction code (BASIC) to be used by Atari fans. They went on to found Microsoft, which began as a small Seattle company with only a few dozen employees.

Having decided to enter the personal computer market, IBM decided that it needed skilled outsiders to provide software. First it approached Gary Kildall of Data Research. For reasons that remain disputed, IBM instead chose Microsoft, run by Allen and the twenty-nine-year-old Gates. Microsoft bought software from a local firm, Seattle Computer Products, and developed it into the operating system MS-DOS. IBM brought out its personal computer, the IBM PC, in August 1981. Bundled with most IBM PCs and compatible machines, MS-DOS became the industry standard after IBM chose to buy its operating software from Microsoft—making Gates for a time the richest person in the world—and its microprocessors from Intel.

VENTURE CAPITAL

The term "venture capital" is frequently found in the memex discussion of Silicon Valley, so we follow a side trail to a treatment of that topic that begins with George Doriot.

Doriot is often identified as the founder of the American venture capital sector. This son of a founder of France's Peugeot car company moved to the United States after World War I and became first a student and then a professor at Harvard Business School, where he taught for more than four decades.

During World War II, Doriot went to work for the US Army's quartermaster corps as head of research and development, overseeing the creation of the portable meals known as K-rations and water-repellent boots and clothes, and taking part in the crash program to develop synthetic rubber. Plastic armor capable of resisting bullets was named Doron after him.

Following the war, Doriot, who had been promoted to general, went back to Harvard Business School. He founded American Research and Development (ARD), a pioneering venture capital company that commercialized new technologies, many of them devised at MIT. One of the companies that ARD invested in was Zapata Off-Shore, founded by the son of Connecticut senator Prescott Bush, the young George Herbert Walker Bush.[31]

At Harvard Business School, General Doriot taught a popular class called Managing. Doriot tried to interest one of his students, Tom Perkins, into succeeding him at ARD. Instead, Perkins teamed up with an Austrian Jewish refugee from the Nazis, Eugene Kleiner, to form Kleiner Perkins in 1972. Kleiner Perkins and other venture capital firms played an integral role in the development of the tech industry in Silicon Valley and elsewhere.

OF MICE AND HYPERTEXTS

Returning to Vannevar Bush, we follow another trail on the imaginary memex that connects him with Douglass Engelbart. In 1962, Engelbart, then an engineer at Stanford Research Institution, wrote Bush: "I rediscovered your article about three years ago, and was rather startled to realize how much I had aligned my sights along the vector you had described."[32]

Engelbart was in the navy, working as an electronics technician, when he read "As We May Think" at the time of its publication in 1945. Influenced by Bush's description of the memex, he came up with the idea of a display like that of a radar set capable of interaction with users. He labored for years developing his ideas for an NLS (oNLine system) at Stanford University, before unveiling the finished product in San Francisco's Brooks Hall on December 9, 1968. In what has been described as "the mother of all demos," Engelbart demonstrated the use of the computer mouse to control symbols on a screen, along with texts and graphics sharing a screen, videoconferencing, and hyperlinks.[33]

Using "hyperlink" as the key phrase, our imaginary memex allows us to follow a "skip trail" to Theodore H. "Ted" Nelson. "Bush was right," Nelson declared in a 1972 paper entitled "As We Will Think."[34] Nelson coined the term "hypertext" for the two types of trails that Bush imagined for his memex: side trails and step trails. Tim Berners-Lee incorporated Nelson's term into "hypertext transfer protocol," or "http." Berners-Lee also named the World Wide Web, the source of the Internet address www.

THE INTERGALACTIC COMPUTER NETWORK

On the imaginary memex, we return to "As We May Think" and read: "Wholly new forms of encyclopedias will appear, ready made with a mesh of associative trails running through them, ready to be dropped into the memex and there amplified." In his 1965 book *Libraries of the Future*,

J. C. R. Licklider described "As We May Think" as the "main external influence on his ideas."[35]

Licklider, a psychologist and computer scientist, worked for the Advanced Research Projects Agency (ARPA), created in order to achieve an American lead in technology following the shock of the successful launching of the first satellite, Sputnik, by the Soviet Union in October 1957. ARPA was renamed the Defense Advanced Research Projects Agency (DARPA) in 1972. Renamed ARPA in 1993, it became DARPA again in 1996 so that it could be shielded against conservative opposition to government spending on science and technology that is not defense related.

Licklider proposed a computer network allowing researchers working on defense contracts to communicate with each other. His 1962 memo about an "Intergalactic Computer Network" laid out a vision of the Internet, the first element of which was created by ARPA and MIT in the form of ARPANET, the world's first packet-switching network. Contrary to folklore, the purpose of ARPANET was to allow researchers working on projects for ARPA to communicate with each other, not to create a communications system to survive nuclear war. In 1986, ARPANET was connected to NSFNET, a network created by the National Science Foundation (NSF) to allow researchers funded by its grants to communicate with each other. NSFNET was opened first to all academics and then to businesses and the general public, evolving into today's Internet, which is global if not yet intergalactic.

A side trail leads us from NSFNET to Vannevar Bush's brainchild, the NSF, from which another side trail goes to a discussion of the Digital Library Initiative (DLI). Among the graduate students funded by the DLI project were Larry Page and Sergey Brin, who was also supported by an NSF graduate student fellowship. Their research led them to create a superior search engine and in 1998—with an initial office in a garage, of course—they incorporated Google, Inc. With the help of Eric Schmidt as CEO, Page and Brin defeated competitors like Inktomi and Dogpile and built Google into the world's dominant search engine.

Google's search engine results were closer than anything yet to the trails on the imaginary memex. Searching for any number of topics involved in the third industrial revolution would lead to articles and books mentioning Vannevar Bush and "As We May Think."

Right back where we began.

THE BUBBLE 16 ECONOMY

*The nineteenth-century pattern of boom and slump, culminating in
the World Depression of 1931, promises not to repeat itself since most
governments have learnt the importance of preventing the collapse of
their financial systems.*
    —James Foreman-Peck, *A History of the World Economy* (1983)[1]

In the early decades of the computer era following World War II, visions of the impact of information technology on American society in what was quaintly called "the year 2000" ranged from the utopian to the dystopian. Optimists envisioned an egalitarian future in which a universal middle class was freed from onerous labor by robots and computers. Pessimists worried about technological unemployment or the regimentation of society under the surveilliance of an omniscient Central Computer.

Nobody in the 1950s or 1960s could have guessed that average Americans in 2000 would be working longer hours or that their incomes, in real, inflation-adjusted terms, would not have risen in a generation, while a few rich Americans would have collected most of the gains from thirty years of economic growth. Americans during the glorious thirty years of capitalism after World War II would have reacted with shocked disbelief if they had been told that leading American companies would shut down their factories in the United States in order to exploit poor, unfree labor in China, an authoritarian state whose economy combined many of the most oppressive features of communism and capitalism. And they would have concluded that the visitor from the future who told them that the big winners in the computer age would be bankers—*bankers?*—was a complete lunatic.

THE INFRASTRUCTURE OF GLOBALIZATION

In earlier eras, transportation technologies such as canals, railroads, and interstate highways and communication technologies such as telegraphy and telephony had enlarged markets and transformed business models. The economic globalization of the late twentieth and early twenty-first centuries similarly rested on technologies that included jets, container ships, computers, and satellites.

The jet made air travel affordable to ordinary people around the world. It also revolutionized business. Diminishing air-flight times permitted increasingly centralized management of multinational corporations, by allowing managers from the home country to visit subsidiaries and allies. In the 1920s, Ford's British division was a largely independent company. By the 1960s, thanks to jet travel and improved communications, it was completely controlled by the headquarters in Detroit.[2]

In addition to making centralized global corporations possible, jets transformed global supply chains. Wide-bodied jets were used by the commercial cargo fleets of FedEx and UPS. In ton-kilometers, global air cargo rose from 750 million in 1950 to 140 billion in 2005—a 200-fold expansion.[3]

Along with the jet, the most important part of the new global infrastructure of commerce that evolved during the third industrial era was the container ship. The age of container shipping began on April 26, 1956, when Malcolm Purcell McLean, owner of a North Carolina trucking company, sent a World War II T-2 tanker named *Ideal X* with fifty-eight large containers on deck from Port Newark, New Jersey, to Houston, Texas. The scale grew from the first specialized container ship built in 1960, with a capacity of 610 TEU (twenty-foot equivalent units), the *Emma Maersk*, which in 2006 had a capacity of 11,000 TEU.[4]

Modern freight shipping is dominated by two kinds of ships—tankers and dry-bulk carriers, on the one hand, and container ships on the other. In 2005, there were forty-eight hundred ships in the global tanker fleet. Nearly half carried crude oil, while sixty-five hundred dry-bulk carriers hauled other cargoes.[5] The leading dry-bulk commodities were coal, iron ore, and grain.[6]

Container-ship technology transformed ports as well. The off-loading of ships, once a prolonged, laborious process, became swift and mechanized. Cranes lifted cargo containers directly from ship to dock, truck, or train. Modern cargo ships are off-loaded twenty times faster than their predecessors were in 1950.[7]

WALMART AND THE GLOBALIZATION OF RETAIL

In the nineteenth and early twentieth centuries, the linking of local markets into a single national market first by railroads and then by highways permitted the emergence of national distributors like Sears, Roebuck and A&P. In the same way, the development of a global commercial infrastructure based on container ships and cargo jets, along with computerized business management, allowed national retailers to become global giants. Walmart was the biggest. In 2005, Walmart was not only the world's largest retailer but also the world's largest profit-making corporation.

Walmart was founded in Bentonville, Arkansas, by Sam and Bud Walton. They took advantage of road construction in the 1950s to replace small crossroads stores with Walmarts at highway intersections, first in the rural South and then throughout the nation.

Walmart embodied the reactionary southern version of American capitalism that survived the New Deal and the civil rights revolution below the Mason-Dixon Line. Fordism was the system in which well-paid production workers provided a mass market for the products that they made. Walmart represented anti-Fordism. Its low wages and lack of benefits for most workers resulted in a workforce dominated by teenagers, retirees, and female workers. In the mid-twentieth century, factory supervisors at GM earned five times as much as the average production employee. Half a century later, Walmart district store managers earned ten times as much. In 1950, GM president Charles E. Wilson earned 140 times as much as each assembly worker. H. Lee Scott, Walmart CEO, in 2003 earned 1,500 times as much as a full-time Walmart employee.[8] The heirs of the founders of Walmart together were as rich as the family of Bill Gates.

Another part of Walmart's anti-Fordist version of American capitalism was the fact that the goods it sold were made elsewhere, chiefly in China. In 2006, Walmart sourced 80 percent of worldwide sales from China.[9] Many goods came from Shenzhen, the center of Chinese manufacturing for export. In Fordist America, high wages permitted American workers to buy goods produced by other well-paid American workers. In post-Fordist America, low prices for Chinese imports permitted low-wage American service workers to buy goods produced by poorly paid Chinese workers.

FROM INTERNATIONAL TRADE TO TRANSNATIONAL PRODUCTION

The most important economic effect of the third industrial revolution on the world economy was the replacement of traditional global trade by global production.[10] Information technology, satellite technology, and efficient, inexpensive container-freight transport allowed the establishment of corporations and industrial production networks on a regional or global scale. Between 1974 and 2000, world trade grew faster, at a rate of 5 percent a year, than overall world GDP, which grew at an annual rate of only 2.9 percent.[11] By the early years of the twenty-first century, between a third and a half of what was labeled as global "trade" was intrafirm trade—that is, the transfer of components within a single multinational enterprise located in several countries.

Between the end of the Cold War and the crash of 2008, globalization resulted in the organization of one global industry after another as an oligopoly, with most of the transnational enterprises headquartered in the United States, Europe, or Japan. A similar pattern of consolidation was evident among both final-assembly, or "system-integrator," firms and their suppliers.

Two companies, US-based Boeing and Europe's Airbus, had 100 percent of the global market share in large jet airliners. Among their suppliers, the global market for jet engines was divided among three firms: GE, Pratt and Whitney, and Rolls-Royce. Microsoft enjoyed 90 percent of the global market share for PC operating systems. Four firms divided 55 percent of the PC market among themselves, while three companies shared 65 percent of the market for mobile handset phones. Three firms dominated the world market in agricultural equipment (69 percent) and ten companies dominated the global pharmaceutical market (69 percent).[12] Ninety-five percent of microprocessors (chips) were made by four companies—Intel, Advanced Micro Devices, NEC, and Motorola. Four automobile companies—GM, Ford, Toyota-Daihatsu, and DaimlerChrysler—manufactured 50 percent of all cars, while three firms—Bridgestone, Goodyear, and Michelin—made 60 percent of the tires. Owens-Illinois and Saint Gobin made two-thirds of all the glass bottles in the world.[13] Concentration in global finance was accelerated by US deregulation, which allowed the emergence of a small number of US-based megabanks, some of which grew even more during the Great Recession when, with the support of the US government, they absorbed failing banks, as Bank of America took over Merrill Lynch and JPMorgan Chase acquired Washington Mutual (WaMu).

In addition to being dominated by oligopolies, the emerging world economy was highly regionalized and still connected to the nation-state. The hundred largest multinationals in 2008 had 57 percent of their total assets and 58 percent of their total employment abroad, and foreign sales made up 61 percent of their total sales.[14] As this demonstrates, the typical multinational still had a distinct national identity, with around half of its assets, employment, and sales within its home market. Few multinational corporations did an overwhelming majority of their business outside their home countries. Those that did, such as Nestle and Ikea, tended to be based in small countries, so their markets were largely foreign. More typical were the large automobile companies, each of which assembled and sold a majority of its products in its home region, with a minority of its sales in other regions.

The domination of global commerce by corporations based in the United States, Japan, and Germany—the three most populous industrial democracies—showed the continuing importance of a large domestic market as a base for multinational sales and operations. Despite the celebration of global corporations by libertarians and their denunciation by leftists and populists, global companies turned out to have national identities after all during the crisis that began in 2008, when major banks and automobile companies turned to their home country governments for bailouts.

THE CURRENCY WARS

Far from being created abruptly by the end of Communism or the rise of the Internet, the global economy of the 1990s and 2000s represented an extension of the America-centered "free world" economy of the Cold War era to former Communist countries like China and former neutral third world countries like India that had practiced import substitution during the Cold War. Following World War II, the United States had offered its defeated great power rivals Germany (in the form of West Germany) and Japan a deal. If they accepted the status of semisovereign, largely demilitarized powers in world politics, the United States would protect their interests, including access to resources like Middle Eastern oil. In return for giving up the ambition to be independent military powers again, the Germans and the Japanese also would be informally guaranteed access to American consumer markets for their exports and to American investments and technology. West Germany and Japan accepted the offer and specialized as civilian trading states. They made cars, not wars.

Following the collapse of its bubble economy, the Japanese government asked the Clinton administration to allow Japan to try to export its way out of its problems with the help of a devalued yen. The administration agreed, and in 1996 the "Reverse Plaza Accord" ended a decade of US policy and lowered the value of the yen to the dollar by 60 percent.

The strong-dollar policy benefited Wall Street. But it was a catastrophe for American exporters. And the Reverse Plaza Accord had even more disastrous effects on Japan's rivals in East Asia. In the decade since the original Plaza Accord, many developing countries in Asia had pegged their currencies to the weak dollar in order to compete more effectively with the Japanese for export markets in the United States and elsewhere. The Reverse Plaza Accord abruptly made their exports more expensive, even as Japan's became cheaper.

The US government and the IMF had pressured developing countries to open up their financial markets to foreign investors—yet another policy that benefited Wall Street. As growth slowed in many Asian countries, however, foreign investors became nervous and troubles in Thailand inspired an irrational rush of foreign capital out of many Asian countries in a short time. The Asian financial crisis that began in 1997 crippled many of the nations in the region, hitting Thailand, Indonesia, and South Korea particularly hard. China and Malaysia, which had resisted American pressure to liberalize their financial systems, proved to be less vulnerable and suffered less.

The Asian financial crisis was only the first of a series of unforeseen disasters that went off like a string of firecrackers following the Reverse Plaza Accord. The collapse of the preceding boom in Asia led to a decline in oil prices, which in turn triggered the Russian financial crisis of 1998. The Russian crisis led to the collapse of an American hedge fund, Long-Term Capital Management, foreshadowing greater crises to come.

BRETTON WOODS II

In the 1990s and 2000s, China grew rapidly to surpass Japan in the size of its economy. The Chinese economic model was a variant of the mercantilist system used by Japan and the Little Tigers, with distinctive Chinese characteristics.

Like Japan, China intervened in currency markets to undervalue its currency, the renminbi, in order to help Chinese exports and cripple American exports. If the exporters of a nation with trade surpluses are allowed to turn their dollar earnings into buying domestic cash, such as Chinese yuan or Japanese yen, then the surplus country's money supply will increase and the currency will appreciate relative to other currencies, making its exports less competitive. In order to prevent the currency from appreciating, the surplus country must purchase and hold foreign exchange. Beginning in 2003, China, followed by other East Asian governments, engaged in currency intervention on a massive scale to keep the US dollar high, Chinese exports strong, and American exports weak. To facilitate its mercantilist industrial policy, China forbade its companies to sell or buy debt or stocks in transactions with foreigners without government approval. Using different methods, Japan pursued a similar currency manipulation strategy of imposing "currency tariffs" on American exports.

The strategy of relying on undervalued currencies to promote export-led industrialization required China, Japan, and other governments to accumulate either dollars or dollar-denominated assets like US federal debt and the debt of government-backed entities like Fannie Mae and Freddie Mac, thereby keeping the US dollar high and crippling rival American export industries. The massive purchases of US federal debt by the Chinese and Japanese central banks, in return, allowed the US Treasury, and, through it, American banks and other financial institutions, to keep interest rates low.

Exporters of manufactured goods like the East Asian countries and Germany were not the only countries to run chronic surpluses with the United States. In the first decade of the twenty-first century, American oil imports accounted for about half of the American trade deficit. Like the mercantilist manufacturing exporters, the petrostates helped to enable America's debt-led consumption by recycling their earnings into US

Treasury securities and dollar-based assets, permitting lower interest rates and more borrowing in the United States.

Some economists claimed that the system of currency manipulations and global imbalances was stable, sustainable, and beneficial for all sides; they dubbed it "Bretton Woods II" after the Bretton Woods system of exchange rates that had existed from the late 1940s until the 1970s.[15] It should have been clear that Bretton Woods II was a Ponzi scheme, in which excessive borrowing by American consumers permitted overinvestment in manufacturing and infrastructure by East Asian mercantilist economies, doomed to end when American consumers hesitated to borrow and spend.

WORKSHOP OF THE WORLD

By the early twenty-first century, China was the workshop of the world economy. In 2005, the world's leading container ports of origin were Singapore, Hong Kong, Shanghai, and Shenzhen. The leading receiving ports were Rotterdam, Los Angeles, Long Beach, and Hamburg.[16]

There was far more to China's successful mercantilist program of crash industrialization than currency manipulation. In addition to manipulating their currencies to help their export industries, East Asian mercantilist regimes steered credit toward targeted industries on the basis of national goals rather than market logic. The East Asian mercantilist model is usually described as export-oriented growth; it can also be described as "investment-driven growth."[17]

Following the death of Mao Zedong, China's government abandoned Communist economic policy, even though the one-party Communist dictatorship remained. In the 1980s, Deng Xiaoping's reforms helped township and village enterprises (TVEs), to the benefit of the entire country and rural China in particular. But in the 1990s, the emphasis shifted toward a version of the export-led development model focused on exports to the US consumer market like the strategies of of Japan, South Korea, Taiwan, and Singapore. Export-processing zones in coastal areas used young, low-wage workers from the rural hinterland to produce goods for multinational corporations that would be sold in foreign markets— primarily the American market.

Following the 1997 Asian financial crisis, the older hub-and-spoke system of Pacific trade, in which Japan and the Little Tigers individually targeted the US consumer economy, was replaced by a new, China-centered system. In the new system, Japan, South Korea, Taiwan, Hong Kong, Singapore, and other regional countries exported components to Chinese production facilities, which then incorporated them into goods for export to the United States and elsewhere. While high-value-added components from industrial countries flowed into China's factories, commodity-exporting countries from Australia, Chile, and Brazil to African countries supplied China with raw materials and food. Chinese workers mostly assembled components imported from Japan, Singapore, Taiwan, South Korea, and other, more advanced countries. In 2003, China, including Hong Kong, had trade deficits with Japan, South Korea, and Taiwan, even as it enjoyed a growing surplus with the United States.

A major feature of the early-twenty-first-century Chinese model was state capitalism, or state ownership of major banks and businesses. All major Chinese financial institutions were state controlled, so that lending tended to reflect government priorities, not market logic. By the second decade of the twenty-first century, three of the world's four largest banks by market value were Chinese.[18] In 2010, forty-one Chinese state-owned enterprises (SOEs) were among the world's five hundred largest companies; three were among the top one hundred.[19] In 2008 one SOE, China Mobile, the state-controlled wireless phone company, was the world's fourth largest company by market value.[20]

As China used currency manipulation, credit steering, subsidies, wage suppression, and other mercantilist techniques at the expense of its trading partners and rivals, its economy grew at the rate of 10 percent a year from 2003 to 2005, 11.6 percent in 2006, and 13 percent in 2007. China's current-account surplus swelled from 3.6 percent of GDP in 2004 to 7.2

percent in 2005 to an unsustainable 11 percent in 2007.[21] In 2010, China surpassed Japan as the world's second largest economy.

AMERICA'S CHRONIC TRADE DEFICITS

In 1971, America was shocked by its first trade deficit of the twentieth century, of $1.5 billion. From 1989 to 1997, the US current-account deficit hovered below 2 percent of GDP. Following the East Asian financial crisis of 1997, the deficit rose in 1998 to 2.4 percent of GDP. In 2006, just before the crash that began the Great Recession, the US current-account deficit had grown to 6 percent of US GDP and nearly 2 percent of global GDP.[22] The US trade deficit between 1976 and 2010 added up to more than $7 trillion; of that, more than 70 percent was accumulated after 2000.[23]

Between 1998 and 2008, the US merchandise trade deficit with China alone rose 375 percent. The top US sales to East Asia were semiconductors, aircraft parts, waste and scrap metal, basic organic chemicals, and soybeans.[24] Other than "waste and scrap metal" and "organic chemicals," the major American exports to China were from industries that relied on US government support—the Defense Department, in the case of aircraft parts, and federal farm subsidies, in the case of soybeans.

Between the early 1980s and 2006, the US economy grew by a factor of 12 and the current-account deficit grew by a factor of 158.[25] Because of the artificial strength of the dollar that resulted from foreign-currency manipulation, as well as other mercantilist techniques used by foreign governments to promote their industries, US exports lost one-fifth of global market share in the first decade of the twenty-first century.[26] The deindustrialization of the United States accelerated. In 1980, manufacturing accounted for 21 percent of US GDP and finance for only 14 percent. By 2002, the proportions were reversed, with 14 percent of GDP accounted for by manufacturing and 21 percent devoted to finance.[27] While manufacturing as a share of employment declined in all Organization for Economic Cooperation and Development (OECD) countries, from around a quarter in 1970 to an average of 15 percent in 2008, it declined least in countries with export trade surpluses like Germany (19 percent) and most in countries running large merchandise trade deficits like the United States (9.5 percent in 2008).[28] Meanwhile, the share of total corporate profits accounted for by the financial sector exploded from 18 percent in 1980–1990 to 36 percent in 2001–2006.[29]

RISE OF THE MEGABANKS

By the early twenty-first century, three banks—Citibank, JPMorgan Chase, and Bank of America—dominated the American commercial-banking sector. Citibank grew by turning itself into a conglomerate with commercial banking, investment banking, and other services. JPMorgan Chase was the product of mergers by Chase Manhattan, Manufacturers Hanover, JP Morgan, Chemical Bank, First Chicago, and National Bank of Detroit. North Carolina National Bank, based in Charlotte, North Carolina, took the name of A. P. Giannini's old California-based Bank of America in the course of an acquisition spree beginning in the 1980s. By 2007, shortly before the Great Recession began, Bank of America's assets were the equivalent of 16.4 percent of US GDP, JPMorgan Chase's were 14.7 percent, and Citigroup's were 12.9 percent. To put this into perspective, in 1983 Citibank, then America's largest, had controlled assets amounting to only 3.2 percent of US GDP.[30] The Big Three grew even more as a result of the global financial crisis, as Bank of America absorbed the investment bank Merrill Lynch and America's largest mortgage lender, Countrywide, while JPMorgan Chase swallowed up America's largest savings and loan, Washington Mutual, and the investment bank Bear Stearns.[31] From 1980 to 2000, the financial assets of commercial banks and securities firms swelled from 55 percent to 95 percent of GDP.[32]

In the decades of the bubble economy, the culture of investment banking changed. Brokers had worked on fixed commissions. The inflation of the 1970s resulted in a bear market and low securities yields. Pension funds and other institutional investors lobbied to end fixed commissions on trading, so that they could negotiate discounts with brokers. The abolition of fixed commissions in 1975 shifted the business of Wall Street from traditional investment banking to securities trading, with traders motivated to rake in commissions by frequent "churning" of investment portfolios. In 1968, volume discounts were authorized; then commissions were deregulated in 1975. As a percentage of industry revenues, brokerage commissions declined from 53.8 percent in 1972 to 17.3 percent in 1991.[33]

Before 1970, the New York Stock Exchange (NYSE) required that member firms be partnerships, on the grounds that partners would take fewer risks than managers of corporations enjoying the shield of limited liability. Over the objections of the NYSE, a brokerage firm called Donaldson, Lufkin & Jenrette became a publicly traded corporation in 1970 and by 1999 all the major investment banks had become public corporations. Within investment banks, there was a shift away from members of the social elite who could fraternize with old-school CEOs toward "quants" who could maximize revenue for the investment bank with ever more complex computer programs.

In a 2009 interview with the London *Times*, Goldman Sachs CEO Lloyd Blankfein, who was awarded a $9 million bonus that year, explained that Goldman "does God's work" by helping "companies to grow by helping them to raise capital."[34] But in 2007, the year before the crash, the activity of helping companies by underwriting stock for them accounted for only 3 percent of Goldman's revenues. Sixty-eight percent of its revenues came from trading and principal investments.[35]

The New Deal financial order had been almost completely dismantled by the time Glass-Steagall was repealed in 1999. No adequate new system of financial regulations replaced those that had been torn down. Taking advantage of "regulatory arbitrage," the increasingly large, rich, powerful firms engaged in activities that were poorly supervised by a miscellany of agencies, from the Securities and Exchange Commission (SEC) to the Commodity Futures Trading Commission (CFTC), not to mention state agencies. Many of the regulators looked forward to jobs in the firms that they regulated.

Free-market ideology led government officials to resist new regulations and enforce existing regulations lightly or not at all in what became known as "the shadow banking system." For example, Fed chairman Alan Greenspan rejected calls for regulating over-the-counter (OTC) derivatives: "In the case of the institutional off-exchange derivatives market, it seems abundantly clear that private market regulation is quite effectively and efficiently achieving what have been identified as the public policy objectives of government regulation."[36]

FROM MANAGERIAL CAPITALISM TO FINANCIAL-MARKET CAPITALISM

The rise of a few universal banks from the wreckage of the New Deal financial system was only part of a larger story: the replacement of managerial capitalism by a new system that can be described as "financial-market capitalism." Even as traditional banking activities shrank to a portion of the activities of financial markets—some regulated, some part of the unregulated shadow banking system—pressures emanating from Wall Street were reshaping the American corporation.

Wall Street investment bankers and free-market theorists shared a hostility to midcentury America's corporate oligopolies with their bureaucratic managers. Some of the debt incurred by conglomerates in takeovers, or in fending off hostile takeovers, was rated as junk bonds that were below investment grade. Michael Milken, then working for Drexel Burnham, began selling these high-risk but high-yield junk bonds to institutional investors. Milken and other corporate raiders borrowed money to take over conglomerates in leveraged buyouts and then sold off various parts, repaying lenders while pocketing profits.

Sometimes the takeover artists made companies more efficient, refocusing companies on single lines of business. In many cases, however, the raiders simply broke up corporations in order to sell their assets, raising short-term shareholder returns at the expense of America's long-term productivity base. Jack Welch, the CEO of General Electric, sold off Bell

Labs to a French company, Lucent. Many once-great corporations were reduced to brands, euphemistically known as "original equipment manufacturers" (OEMs), that were attached to products made largely by other firms (outsourcing) or foreign manufacturers (offshoring). The chairman of Ford, William Clay Ford Jr., remarked: "It's easy to build a car. It's harder to build a brand."[37]

The dismantling of the vertically integrated, oligopolistic industrial behemoths that had formed in the merger waves of the 1890s and early 1900s and the 1920s and had survived the decades of the New Deal era until the 1970s was evident from the statistics. The same companies were in the list of the four top American corporate employers in both 1960 and 1980: GM, AT&T, Ford, and GE (1960) and AT&T, GM, Ford, and GE (1980). In 2007, the top four employers were Walmart, UPS, McDonald's, and IBM. AT&T had been broken up as a result of a federal antitrust suit in the 1980s, and GM and Ford had dropped out of the list not only of the top four employers but also of the top ten. In 2007, only GE remained among the top ten employers, below the four listed above and Citigroup, Target, and Sears Holdings.[38]

The growth of financial-market control over corporations probably would not have occurred but for the growth of institutional investors seeking high yields. As late as 1952, households—mostly rich families— held 90.4 percent of all corporate stock. By 1994, households owned only 48 percent. Meanwhile, in the same period, the pension fund share of corporate stock ownership grew to 25 percent and that of mutual funds increased to 10 percent.[39] The share of corporate equities owned by public and private pension funds grew from 6 percent in 1965 to 23 percent in 2007, while the share owned by mutual funds increased from 5 percent in 1985 to 26 percent in 2007.[40] The shift from defined-benefit plans to defined-contribution plans like 401(k)s and individual retirement accounts (IRAs) further swelled the assets under institutional management. IRA savings invested in mutual funds expanded from 17 percent in 1985 to 49 percent in 1999.[41] By 2008, the brokerage firm Fidelity was the largest shareholder in approximately one in ten publicly traded corporations listed on Nasdaq and the NYSE, exercising potential power far beyond that of J. P. Morgan in the days of interlocking directorates.[42]

This phenomenon in turn was driven by a peculiarity of America's midcentury social contract: the role of employer-provided defined-benefit pension plans and, later, tax-favored defined-contribution plans like IRAs and 401(k)s. Social Security's low rate of preretirement income replacement made a growing number of Americans desperate to see high rates of return from the retirement savings they or their employers had entrusted to mutual funds. By 2005, institutional investors like mutual funds accounted for three-fourths of the ownership of the typical large corporation.[43]

The rapid expansion of stock ownership on the part of mutual funds increased the pressure on corporations to maximize their short-term earnings, at the expense if necessary of long-term investment and growth. In 2005, 80 percent of more than four hundred chief financial officers responded to a survey by saying that "they would decrease discretionary spending on such areas as research and development, advertising, maintenance, and hiring in order to meet short-term earnings targets."[44] Short-termism was reflected in the fact that institutional investors and others moved away from long-term investments in companies. The annualized turnover of all stocks on the NYSE rose from 36 percent in 1980 to 118 percent in 2006.[45]

In the new age of financial-market capitalism, as in the era of finance capitalism in the early 1900s, American industry was subordinate to finance. But there was a profound difference. Finance capitalists like J. P. Morgan were long-term investors who sought to profit over many years from the industrial corporations and utilities that they owned. The new financial-market capitalism, by contrast, was marked by short-term ownership of stocks by the agents of millions of anonymous investors, most of whom had no idea what company stocks were being bought and sold on their behalf.

While some corporate managers lobbied state legislatures to create laws protecting their companies against takeovers, most CEOs in the

United States were reconciled to financial-market capitalism by means of stock options. In 1993, Congress changed the tax code to encourage corporations to reward their executives with stock options. By the beginning of the twenty-first century, more than half of the compensation of the average *Fortune* 500 executive took the form of stock options.[46]

Federal Reserve chairman Alan Greenspan observed that large stock options "perversely created incentives to artificially inflate reported earnings in order to keep stock prices high and rising."[47] The goal was no longer to build a productive company that would make useful products and last for generations, but to maximize short-term profits in time for the next quarterly earnings report. "Wall Street can wipe you out," the CEO of Sara Lee observed. "They are the rule-setters. They do have their fads, but to a large extent there is an evolution in how they judge companies, and they have decided to give premiums to companies that harbor the most profits for the least assets. I can't argue with that."[48]

MASTERS OF THE UNIVERSE

Stock options created fortunes for many CEOs—particularly when their companies drove up the price by buying back stock. In the 1990s, stock buybacks became the major method of distributing corporate revenues to shareholders, even as they increased the wealth of corporate executives who were compensated in stock options. Even so, rising CEO compensation could not keep up with the fortunes being made in the swelling American financial sector. From 1948 to 1980, pay in finance was comparable to that in other lines of business; from 1980 onward, financial-industry compensation on average was twice the pay in other American industries.[49] Beginning in the 1980s, compensation in banking rose much faster than compensation in the rest of the private sector. By 2007, the average financial-sector employee earned twice as much money as the average worker in the rest of the private sector.[50] In 2004, the top twenty-five hedge-fund managers made more money than all the CEOs in the corporations of the S&P 500 put together.[51]

Prestige followed wealth and power. In an article in *Harper's* in 1949, the management theorist Peter Drucker observed: "Where only twenty years ago the bright graduate of the Harvard Business School aimed at a job with a New York Stock Exchange house, he now seeks employment with a steel, oil, or automobile company."[52] Richard Fisher, the chairman of Morgan Stanley from 1991 to 1997, recollected that after he graduated in the 1960s from Harvard Business School "investment banking was about the worst-paying job available to us. I started at Morgan Stanley at $5,800 a year. It was the lowest offer I had. . . . I'm sure my classmates who went to Procter & Gamble started at $9,000 a year."[53] By the end of the twentieth century, business students who preferred Procter & Gamble to Morgan Stanley would have been ridiculed. Between 1950 and 1980, graduates of Harvard who went into finance were paid no more than those who went into law, engineering, and medicine. By the 2000s, those who worked in finance made nearly twice as much as their colleagues in other professions.[54]

Between 1980 and 2007, the financial sector's share of US GDP grew from around 10 percent to a peak of around 40 percent. In Britain, where a similar process of financialization produced cancerous growth of the City of London's financial industry, finance's share of GDP grew by more than 10 points from 1990 to 2006. In the same period, finance expanded its share of the economies of Germany and France by no more than 6 percent.[55]

FROM THE GREAT COMPRESSION TO
THE GREAT REGRESSION

Between the 1970s and the early twenty-first century, what some scholars have called "the Great Compression" of incomes in the United States was reversed. Between 1913 and the beginning of the New Deal in 1932, the share of income in the US going to the top 10 percent was between 40 and 45 percent, only to plunge and level off at between 31 and 32 percent from World War II until the 1970s. Beginning in the Reagan years, inequality began to grow until it neared its pre-1929 level before the crash of 2008.

In fact, not one but two forms of inequality revived—earnings inequality and asset inequality. As the economist James K. Galbraith demonstrated, wealth inequality was accounted for largely by the disproportionate gains to investors and the stock options received by Silicon Valley entrepreneurs during the tech bubble of the 1990s.[56]

Attributing rising inequality within the United States to allegedly unstoppable forces of globalization or technology appealed to the American elite by implying that their disproportionate gains had nothing to do with the power of some economic classes relative to others. But the most plausible explanations for late-twentieth-century and early-twenty-first-century inequality in the United States attribute it to changes in the bargaining power of capital, labor, and professionals, not to long-run forces beyond human control.

The ability of the working-class majority in the United States to bargain for higher wages was undermined after the 1960s by several purely domestic phenomena: the declining real value of the minimum wage as a result of inflation, low-end labor markets flooded with unskilled, low-wage immigrants, and the decline of labor unions.

REVOKING THE SOCIAL CONTRACT

While wages stagnated in the neoliberal era, economic security declined for many American workers. The welfare-state components of America's New Deal social contract such as Social Security and Medicare remained robust, despite long-run challenges to their funding. But the welfare-capitalist elements, such as company pensions and employer-provided health care, crumbled rapidly in the late twentieth century. Bankruptcies in the airline, automobile, and other industries forced the Pension Benefit Guarantee Corporation to take over many corporate pensions.[57] Some companies, including Ford and GM, replaced health coverage of retired workers with health retirement accounts.[58] Between 1981 and 2003, the number of employees with corporate pension plans who had defined-benefit (DB) plans declined from 81 percent to 38 percent.[59] Under pressure to cut costs, employers increasingly replaced DB pension plans with defined-contribution (DC) plans like 401(k)s for the minority of Americans who had any pensions at all.

Conservatives and libertarians sought to replace the post–New Deal hybrid of welfare capitalism and welfare statism with tax-favored private accounts. Another welfare-market technique was using tax credits rather than direct public spending to achieve social goals. In the last decades of the twentieth century, the tax code was riddled with new tax subsidies for individuals—the child tax credit and the child-care tax credit among them—joining older ones like the home-mortgage-interest deduction. While the child tax credit was refundable—that is, paid to individuals who made too little income to pay federal income taxes—most federal income-tax credits were not available to the bottom half of American wage earners, who had been effectively removed from the federal income tax rolls by 2000. This meant that what the social scientist Christopher Howard called "the hidden welfare state" consisted largely of means-tested subsidies of a novel kind—subsidies available only to the affluent, not the poor.[60] The oligarchic nature of the evolving American political system was symbolized by the lack of protest that greeted the "child-care tax credit," which in essence was a subsidy by Americans who could not afford nannies or other private child care to the affluent minority who could.

AN AMERICAN PLUTONOMY?

In the late nineteenth century, the American elite was identified with the Four Hundred—the number of guests who could be accommodated in Mrs. Astor's ballroom in New York. From 1992 to 2007, the ratio between the income of the median household and the top four hundred households grew from 1,124 to 1 to 6,900 to 1.[61] For the top four hundred households, pretax income, adjusted for inflation, ballooned by 409 percent between 1992 and 2007, while for the median American family of four it increased by only 13.2 percent.[62] The top four hundred households in the United States enjoyed a decline in their effective tax rates (the percentage of income paid in taxes) from 26.4 percent in 1992 to 16.6 percent in 2007.[63] Hedge-fund managers benefited from a tax provision that allowed the income they were paid for managing their hedge funds to be taxed at a low capital gains rate rather than the highest income tax rate.

While conservatives and libertarians promoted visions of "the ownership society" in which every American would be an investor, capital income grew much more concentrated. In 1979, the top 10 percent of Americans by income received 67 percent of the income from capital, while 33 percent went to the bottom 90 percent. In 2006, the share of capital income that went to the top 10 percent of Americans had increased to 81.3 percent while that of the bottom 90 percent had declined to 18.7 percent.[64] The percentage of the increase in disposable income that went to the top 1 percent of US households fell from 22–23 percent in 1929 to a low of 8–9 percent in the 1970s, before rising to a remarkable 73 percent during the two terms of George W. Bush.[65] Because capital gains were taxed at lower rates than income from labor, Warren Buffett observed that he and other billionaires were taxed at lower rates than their secretaries.

In 2005, three Citigroup analysts—Ajay Kapur, Niall MacLeod, and Narendra Singh—described the United States as a "plutonomy." They explained, "Plutonomies have occurred before in sixteenth century Spain, in seventeenth century Holland, the Gilded Age and the Roaring Twenties in the U.S. What are the common drivers of Plutonomy? Disruptive technology-driven productivity gains, creative financial innovation, capitalist-friendly cooperative governments, an international dimension of immigrants and overseas conquests invigorating wealth creation, the rule of law, and patenting inventions. Often these wealth waves involve great complexity, exploited best by the rich and educated of the time." In a plutonomy, the economy is driven by the consumption of the classes, not the masses: "In a plutonomy there is no such animal as 'the U.S. consumer' or 'the UK consumer,' or indeed the 'Russian consumer.' There are rich consumers, few in number, but disproportionate in the gigantic slice of income and consumption they take. There are the rest, the 'non-rich,' the multitudinous many, but only accounting for surprisingly small bites of the national pie." The Citigroup analysts speculated that a plutonomic world economy could be driven by the spending of the world's rich minority, whose ranks are "swelling from globalized enclaves in the emerging world."[66]

According to Moody's, the top 10 percent of American earners accounted for 22 percent of all spending and the top 25 percent for 45 percent of all consumer spending. The bottom 50 percent of Americans accounted for only 29 percent of all American consumer spending. At the same time, however, the top 10 percent of earners received 50 percent of all income, while they accounted for only 22 percent of spending. Where did the rest of their money go?

Much of the money of the American rich went into speculation in the two waves of the bubble economy between the late 1990s and 2008. Had more of that money been in the hands of the bottom 50 percent, more of it would have been spent on consumer goods, including manufactured products, and far less would have gone to gambling on condos in Manhattan and Miami and trendy stocks.[67] Just as a ship with a broad base is more stable than a top-heavy boat, so an economy in which well-paid workers create mass markets for goods and services is more stable than a top-heavy plutonomy.

SECURITIZATION: THE WEAK LINK IN THE GLOBAL ECONOMY

Securitization proved to be the weak link in the global economy. This innovative financial practice originated in the 1970s, when the Government National Mortgage Association (GNMA, or Ginnie Mae), began bundling mortgages together and selling them to investors. The larger US quasi-public mortgage agencies, Fannie Mae and Freddie Mac, quickly adopted the practice. With the help of increasingly sophisticated computer programs, the financial industry devised ever more ingenious methods for packaging and selling debt-based securities of various kinds.

Securitization revolutionized the way that banks did business. In the past, banks had been limited in how much they could lend by the debts that they were owed. By permitting them to clear the books, securitization permitted them to engage in a much greater volume of lending. They could not have done so had there not been a market for structured debt products. But China and other countries had an insatiable appetite for dollar-denominated debt, where they could park dollars earned from trade surpluses which, if released into the markets, would have led their currencies to appreciate at the expense of the export industries on which their growth strategies depended.

In these conditions, the business model of American banks and other lenders changed for the worse. The old practice of buy-and-hold was replaced by originate-and-distribute. Because banks and other lenders made a profit on every mortgage, they had less of an incentive to monitor the creditworthiness of borrowers. If the borrower could not repay the loan in the future, that would be somebody else's problem. In the meantime, they would have collected their fees.

In their search for profits, banks and other lenders offered loans that required low down payments or no down payments at all. People described as NINJAs (no income, no job, no assets) found it easier to take out mortgages. Paperwork suffered, as lenders hired employees known as "robosigners" to approve loan applications as quickly as possible. Confused paper trails would cause problems later, when banks sought to foreclose on properties.

In theory, bundling a number of risky mortgages or other loans into one structured security would lower the risk of default, because all of the borrowers were not likely to default at the same time. That was the theory of the ratings agencies that provided high ratings for increasingly complex structured-debt products, which central banks and other financial institutions bought, believing them to be safe assets.

The flaw in the theory was revealed beginning in 2007, when, as a result of recession in the United States, many American homeowners began to default. In the old days, the losses would have been borne by the lenders who held the mortgages. But now that the mortgages were packaged and distributed widely, nobody could be certain which mortgages were valuable and which were toxic. Paralyzed by uncertainty, the global financial system suffered the equivalent of cardiac arrest.

THE BUBBLE BURSTS

At the beginning of the twenty-first century, global imbalances and skyrocketing inequality in the United States were strikingly similar to trends in the 1920s. Would they be followed by a global economic decline on the scale of the Great Depression? In 2007, the views of the mainstream neoclassical economics profession were summed up by the Nobel Prize–winning economist Robert Lucas, in his presidential address to the American Economic Association: "The problem of depression prevention has been solved."

Faith in the post–New Deal American model of capitalism was shaken to its foundations when, in August and September 2008, the Federal Reserve and the Treasury mounted the greatest economic rescue effort in world history. Fannie Mae and Freddie Mac, the government-backed corporations that underwrote a majority of America's home mortgages, were effectively nationalized. Most of the great investment banks on Wall Street, including Bear Stearns, Lehman Brothers, and Merrill Lynch, victims of bad gambles on home-mortgage debt, either vanished or were absorbed by or converted into large commercial banks. In a desperate effort to stop the contagion of bad debt and avert a credit freeze that could cause a new depression, the US government promised a bailout of the financial sector of more than a trillion dollars.

The crisis began the previous year. Home prices rapidly declined as the bubble collapsed. In 2007, the recession led to fear that inability by homeowners to make their payments would trigger defaults throughout the complex tranches of mortgage-based securities. To forestall trouble, in

September 2007, the Fed lowered the federal funds interest rate from 6.25 percent to 5.75 percent; by December it had lowered the rate to 5.25 percent. The Fed dropped the rate by a dramatic 0.75 percent on January 22, 2008, and again by another 50 basis points a little more than a week later, for a total reduction of 2.25 percentage points in only three months.[68]

When the investment bank Bear Stearns, with a capital-to-assets ratio leveraged by 35 to 1, found itself in crisis, the government provided emergency financing so that JPMorgan Chase could purchase Bear Stearns in March 2008. In June, Bank of America took over Countrywide, which had been responsible for a fifth of American mortgages. Concern about the value of the more than $5 trillion in mortgage-backed securities held by Fannie Mae and Freddie Mac led Treasury secretary Henry Paulson to ask Congress for authority to inject billions into the two government-sponsored enterprises (GSEs). Congress passed the American Housing Rescue and Foreclosure Prevention Act in July.

In September, Bank of America absorbed Merrill Lynch, while Treasury and the Fed unsuccessfully tried to find a buyer for Lehman Brothers. Lehman filed for bankruptcy on Monday, September 15, 2008, sending shock waves through the global financial system. On the evening of September 16, the Fed announced a bailout of the American International Group (AIG), fearing that its collapse so quickly after Lehman's would be devastating. The chair of the House Financial Services Committee, Massachusetts Democrat Barney Frank, joked that September 15 should be called Free Market Day: "The national commitment to the free market lasted one day. It was Monday."[69]

The financial system was now in a death spiral. On the evening of September 18, Paulson, Ben Bernanke, chairman of the Federal Reserve, and Christopher Cox, the chairman of the SEC, met with members of Congress, warning that the country faced what Bernanke called "Depression 2.0." They asked for $700 billion for the Troubled Assets Relief Program (TARP). Their pleas were rejected on September 29, when the House voted down the Emergency Economic Stabilization Act. But the continuing economic collapse led to another vote and on October 3, 2008, a modified version of the act was passed by Congress and signed into law by President Bush. In December 2008, the federal government also allocated more than $17 billion to rescue GM and Chrysler.

To prevent what came to be called the Great Recession from turning into a second Great Depression, both monetary policy (interest rates) and fiscal policy (spending and taxation) were required. By December 16, 2008, the Fed had set the federal funds rate at 0 to 0.25 percent.

The United States was now in the "liquidity trap" described by Keynes, in which normal monetary policy cannot function and expansionary fiscal policy is needed. The economist Dean Baker has calculated that government spending of $1.5 trillion a year beginning in 2009 would have been required to offset the demand lost in the residential housing sector ($600 billion), lost consumption demand ($500 billion), lost demand in nonresidential construction ($250 billion), and lost demand caused by states and local governments that cut spending to balance their budgets ($150 billion). Instead, the stimulus in 2009 and 2010 amounted only to around $300 billion a year.[70]

Christina Romer, one of President Barack Obama's economic advisers, argued that to counteract the contraction of the economy the federal government should undertake a $1.2 trillion fiscal stimulus. Instead, Obama proposed a package half that size. On February 13, 2009, Congress passed the American Recovery and Reinvestment Act (ARRA), which spent only $787 billion over several years until September 30, 2011.

In addition to being too small, the stimulus was limited in its effects by the economic contraction imposed by state governments whose constitutions required them to balance their budgets, even in a near-depression, by slashing expenditures, firing employees, and raising taxes. Two economists, Mark Zandi and Alan Blinder, concluded that the ARRA had reduced unemployment only by 1.5 percentage points and created only 2.7 million jobs.[71] Meanwhile, the stingy and fragmentary nature of America's social safety net, in the form of "automatic stabilizers" like unemployment insurance and Social Security, meant that the United States suffered greater unemployment and economic contraction than European democracies with more generous systems of social insurance. Unemployment was far more severe for less educated workers. In 2011, unemployment among college-educated Americans was 4.3 percent, while it was 14.3 percent among workers lacking a high school diploma.[72]

Having passed an inadequate Keynesian stimulus, the Obama administration and the Democratic majority in Congress turned their attention away from the economic crisis to focus on measures of long-term reform: the Patient Protection and Affordable Care Act of 2010 that sought to provide universal health-insurance coverage, the Dodd-Frank Wall Street Reform and Consumer Protection Act passed in July 2010, and a controversial and ultimately failed attempt to create a cap-and-trade system to reduce greenhouse gas emissions that contribute to global warming. The diversion of attention and energy away from the immediate unemployment crisis that accompanied these other projects brought to mind the warning of Keynes to the Roosevelt administration in its first term that "even wise and necessary Reform may, in some respects, impede and complicate Recovery."

In the November 2010 midterm elections, the Republicans regained the House. The activists of the conservative Tea Party movement were reminiscent of the anti–New Deal Liberty League in their denunciations of the supposed "fascism" and "socialism" of the Obama administration. As it had done since the Reagan years, the Republican Party asserted without evidence that further tax cuts for the rich and corporations were the solution to all problems. On the left, the Occupy Wall Street movement, spreading from downtown Manhattan to cities throughout the nation in the fall of 2011, gave voice to the frustration of many Americans with the financial industry.

Having originated in America, the crisis dragged the entire global economy down. The major industrial countries protected their own banks and industries and responded according to their national traditions and interests. China shoveled more state-controlled credit at its overbuilt export sector and infrastructure. "Euroland," the European area that shared the euro as a common currency, was crippled by disputes between Germany and debtor nations like Greece.

THE PREDATORS BALL

Even before the Great Recession began in the crash of September 2008, the first decade of the twenty-first century was a Japanese-style "lost decade" in the United States. Compared to the 24 percent overall growth of the 1990s, the US economy grew by only 6 percent in the 2000s.[73]

What little growth there was went to a tiny plutocratic minority. During the Bush years, two-thirds of the income growth in the United States went to the top 1 percent of the US population.[74] Over a longer period, 82 percent of all gains in US wealth between 1983 and 2009 went to the richest 5 percent of American households.[75] By the early twenty-first century, the Gini coefficient, a measurement of economic inequality, showed that the United States was radically different from other developed nations and resembled other highly unequal nations including Rwanda, Ecuador, and the Philippines.

In 1985, junk-bond king Michael Milken threw a party he called "the Predators Ball." By the second decade of the twenty-first century, it was clear that the party was over.

THE NEXT AMERICAN ECONOMY

The history of the productive apparatus is a history of revolutions. So is the history of transportation from the mailcoach to the airplane. . . . This process of Creative Destruction is the essential fact about capitalism.

—Joseph A. Schumpeter, 1942[1]

We believe that this country will not be a permanently good place for any of us to live in unless we make it a reasonably good place for all of us to live in.

—Theodore Roosevelt, 1912[2]

In the early twenty-first century, Paterson, New Jersey, is a troubled city in a troubled country. The city that traces its origins back to Alexander Hamilton's Society for Establishing Useful Manufactures (SUM) has lost most of its manufacturing businesses to other countries. Like other cities in America's deindustrialized Rust Belt, Paterson has been plagued for decades by poverty, crime, and urban decay. Like other northern industrial cities, Paterson became a home of black migrants from the South just as many manufacturing jobs that provided ladders to middle-class status were disappearing. National shifts in demography are reflected in Paterson, where a majority in the city now consists of Latino immigrants and their descendants. Immigration has helped to revitalize the city, to some degree. But levels of poverty, illiteracy, and illegitimacy are high.

About twenty miles south of Paterson in Elizabeth, New Jersey, is something called Foreign Trade Zone 49. FTZ 49, established in 1979, is one of hundreds of special business districts created in recent years in the United States that provide special customs treatment for companies engaged in international trade. Operated by the Port Authority of New York and New Jersey, FTZ 49 is one of the largest contiguous foreign trade zones in the country. Its 3,587 acres include 2,075 acres in the Port Newark/Elizabeth Port Authority Marine Terminal; 41-acre Global Marine Terminal and 145-acre Port Authority Auto Marine Terminal, both in Jersey City/Bayonne; 125-acre Industrial Park at Elizabeth; 53-acre Greenville Industrial Park in Jersey City; a 23-acre site in Bayonne; a 40-acre tank farm and fuel-distribution system at Newark Liberty International Airport; a 407-acre industrial site in South Kearny; 316 acres in Port Reading Business Park in Woodbridge and Carteret; 115 acres in the I-Port 12 industrial park in Carteret; 72 acres in Port Elizabeth Business Park in Elizabeth; and 176 acres in the I-Port 440 industrial park in Perth Amboy.

FTZ 49 sponsors industries involved in manufacturing, pharmaceuticals, petroleum products, and special chemicals and hosts companies that include motor-vehicle importers and an importer of frozen-orange-juice concentrate. The industrial park is connected to world commerce by Newark Liberty International Airport and the ExpressRail Intermodal Rail System, with dedicated facilities at major container terminals in Elizabeth and Staten Island. Nearly ten thousand workers are directly employed at FTZ 49, while the multiplier effects of its economic activity create a far greater amount of indirect employment in the area and the nation.[3]

FTZ 49 is Alexander Hamilton's SUM reborn. Power is provided by electricity rather than by water, and the products include many that did not exist when the United States was founded. Ingredients are brought in and products taken out by trucks, trains, and planes, not by boats and wagons. The purpose of American economic policy in the twenty-first century is no longer to catch up with industrial Britain, but to allow the United States to participate in high-value-added global supply chains in a world of transnational production, without sacrificing strategic industries. But the project of creative collaboration between government and private enterprise to ensure that America remains a land of promise is no different today than it was on that fateful day of July 10, 1778, when General Washington and Colonel Hamilton, enjoying a respite from war, admired the thundering falls of the Passaic and imagined what America might be.

The story of the American economy that has been told in this book can be summarized in a paragraph. When the United States won its independence and organized its Constitution, the world's economy was still the preindustrial economy that had existed for millennia since the invention of agriculture—an economy in which human and animal muscle provided most of the power, supplemented where possible by the force of windmills and water mills, in which the burning of wood and other biomass provided heat and light, and in which passengers and freight were most efficiently moved by water. Within decades of the Founding, America began to be transformed by the industrial revolution, which has radiated outward from workshops and laboratories in three waves—the first industrial revolution based on steam and telegraphy, the second industrial revolution based on electric and oil motors, and the third industrial revolution based on computers. Each wave of technological innovation has destabilized existing economic, social, and political arrangements, forcing Americans to adapt by creating, in effect, a series of new republics while keeping, for the sake of continuity, the old name of the United States of America and the old federal Constitution of 1787, with formal and much more important informal amendments.

American history shows a recurrent pattern: a thirty- to forty-year time lag between technology-driven economic change and the modernization of political and legal structures to deal with its consequences. During this period of misalignment, such as the 1830s through the 1860s, the 1890s through the 1930s, and the 1970s through the 2000s, the institutions of the economy and the polity drift further and further apart. Nostalgic Jeffersonian politicians like Andrew Jackson, William Jennings Bryan, and Ronald Reagan who idealize a smaller-scale past often win wide support in these eras of drift and stagnation. Finally, after three or four decades of misalignment between economy and polity, there is a crisis—the Civil War, the Great Depression, the Great Recession. The crisis provides an opportunity for reformers to reconstruct the economy and political system in an attempt to realize perennial American democratic and liberal ideals in forms adapted to the new technological era. The Hamiltonian tradition enjoys a revival, in light of the urgent need for large-scale, ambitious programs of national development based on collaboration rather than conflict between government and private enterprise.

If American history is any guide, the cycle of Jeffersonian nostalgia and partial regression that began with Carter and Reagan will give way at some point to a neo-Hamiltonian era of nation building—or, to be more precise, nation rebuilding. Eventually, however, the next political-economic order will be obsolete. As long as technological progress continues to transform the way we work and live, the economy and the polity inevitably will become misaligned again, challenging new generations of reformers.

THE GREAT RECESSION AND BEYOND

The Great Recession that followed the global financial crisis of 2008 is best thought of as a depression whose worst effects have been contained by governments that learned the lessons of the 1930s. Stimulus programs funded by deficit spending in countries from the United States to China have sought to compensate in part for the collapse of private consumer and business demand. Systems of social insurance like unemployment insurance have ameliorated the effects of unemployment. And from the failures of the 1930s, governments in the 2000s learned the importance of the state as a lender of last resort during an economic collapse.

However, by ameliorating the effects of the Great Recession, the policies and institutions put into place after the 1930s may have disguised the severity of the present crisis from political classes, if not members of the public, in the United States and other nations. That, along with a mistaken understanding of the crisis as a severe but normal recession rather than a near-depression, may explain why in the United States and Europe the focus of elites turned almost immediately, in the years after 2008, to the long-term problem of deficit reduction, away from the short-term crises of mass unemployment and the household-debt overhang.

In the United States, the unwillingness of federal leaders to engage in much greater stimulus spending and much more energetic restructuring of home-mortgage debt resulted from an irrational fear of "big government," stoked by a Republican Party that had abandoned its northern Hamiltonian roots for the right-wing Jeffersonianism of its new regional base, the former Confederacy. It is difficult for the United States to have a rational response to the Great Recession when the opinion leaders of one of the two national parties believe that Herbert Hoover was too progressive. All too many of America's leaders have learned nothing from the mistakes of Hoover and Franklin D. Roosevelt in their premature attempts to balance the budget during the Great Depression, which backfired by contracting demand and plunging the economy back into crisis. In Europe, the misguided attachment to austerity policies on the part of Germany, the largest economy, has harmed both Europe and the world.

It can take years or decades for countries to recover from the aftermath of asset bubbles in housing or stocks that burst, leaving financial systems burdened with worthless debts that will never be repaid.[4] The long stagnation of the Japanese economy shows that policies that are too timid or too favorable to creditors who refuse to write off worthless debt can cause a nation to keep sliding back into the hole before it manages to crawl out. Moreover, previous financial crises since the Depression have been national, like late-twentieth-century crises in Japan and Sweden, or regional, like the Asian financial crisis. Those countries and regions recovered, but it is not clear that they provide precedents when the crisis is global and all countries are trying to recover at the same time, using the same methods, such as expanding exports while moving toward budgetary balance. The historians of the future will probably render a judgment on today's policymakers similar to that rendered on those of the 1930s: excessive fears of deficits and national debt, along with excessive optimism about the self-healing powers of the market, led governments to do too little, not too much.

GLOBAL REBALANCING

Whatever lies beyond the Great Recession, it will not resemble the bubble economy that caused the crisis. It is doubtful that chastened American consumers would engage in another multidecade spending spree, and even if they did the public debt overhang built up during the Great Recession would severely limit the ability of the federal government to respond to another, perhaps even greater, crisis.

Both the Great Depression and the Great Recession were preceded by periods characterized by global imbalances in trade and finance and by the maldistribution of wealth. During the Golden Age that followed World War II, both of these problems were corrected. After World War II the United States, which had worsened global imbalances by becoming the world's lender while refusing to import goods from its debtors, abandoned protectionism for reciprocal trade (which, because of Cold War considerations, mutated into a quite different system of unilateral free trade). At home, the extreme inequality of the 1920s was replaced by a compression of incomes, with incomes at the top limited by customary norms and taxation and with minimum-wage laws, unionization, and restricted immigration putting a floor on wages at the bottom. A similar combination of global rebalancing and a more equitable distribution of the gains from economic growth will be required, if America and the world are to move beyond the bubble-economy pattern of asset bubbles followed by collapses and rising inequality of income and wealth.

As we have seen, the fable that following the Cold War the world repudiated statism and embraced free-market capitalism and moved toward a borderless global market bears little resemblance to reality. What really happened is that, following the fall of the Berlin Wall, the United States sought to extend the Pax Americana system beyond its allies to incorporate formerly hostile and neutral powers, including giants like China and India. During the Cold War, the United States had offered to provide the public goods of security, the dollar as a reserve currency, and one-way access to American consumer markets to its former enemies Japan and Germany, on the condition that they accept the military leadership of the United States and concentrate on civilian industrial production. The United States turned a blind eye to their mercantilist export-promotion policies, sacrificing its own industries in the interest of alliance unity and specializing in military spending and finance.

Already by the 1970s, with the recovery of Japan and Germany, this bargain no longer benefited the United States. As it wound down the Vietnam War, the Nixon administration engaged in a policy of strategic retrenchment, while retaliating against Japanese mercantilism and abandoning the Bretton Woods fixed-exchange-rate system in an effort to help American industry. But first Jimmy Carter and then Ronald Reagan denounced Nixonian Realpolitik in favor of a vision of American foreign policy based on human-rights idealism or crusading anticommunism. The abandonment of the Bretton Woods system allowed the United States to borrow vast sums from abroad, even as its merchandise trade deficit swelled. Public borrowing enabled Reagan and George W. Bush to build up the military while cutting taxes, while private borrowing allowed Americans to live better even though their wages stagnated for a generation.

Having been strained by Japanese and German export-oriented mercantilism, the economic order of the Pax Americana was finally shattered by the attempt to admit post-Communist China to the system on terms similar to those that had been offered to the defeated Axis powers. The form that globalization took severed the link within the United States and other nation-states between domestic mass consumption, domestic investment, and domestic economic growth. On both sides of the Pacific Ocean, wages failed to rise to track productivity growth. Wage-led growth in the United States was sacrificed to debt-led growth, while in China, wage-led growth was sacrificed to investment-led growth. When debt and investment dramatically outstripped wage-based aggregate demand, a painful readjustment became inevitable.

BEYOND THE PAX AMERICANA: POSTHEGEMONIC AMERICA IN A MULTIPOLAR WORLD

By the early twenty-first century, the American consumer market, even though it was still the world's largest, was not big enough to serve as the engine of growth for the rest of the world. And even before the crash of 2008, the American public had wearied of the wars in Iraq and Afghanistan and the costs of commitments to protect the interests of other countries, allowing them to focus on economic growth instead of military spending.

Predictions that China will replace the United States as the hegemonic global power, based on straight-line extrapolations, may prove to be as premature as predictions in the 1980s that Japan would soon be "number one." By shoveling state-controlled credit at its export-manufacturing sector on the basis of political rather than economic logic, China has saddled its banks with bad debts, while by hoarding surpluses in order to keep its currency undervalued, it has set off a domestic real-estate bubble and inflation. The deflation of China's investment-led bubble economy, the corollary of America's debt-led bubble economy, may condemn China to Japanese-style stagnation, or worse. On the other hand, the sheer scale of China, along with the vast numbers of rural Chinese yet to be brought into the modern economy as workers and consumers, may allow China to transition successfully to domestic demand-led growth, an option not available for Japan, with its aging population, low fertility, and low immigration.

Whatever happens, at some point in the next few decades, the size of the Chinese economy is likely to surpass that of the US economy, which has been the world's largest since the 1870s. The average Chinese will continue to be poorer than the average American for generations. But a world economy in which America is number two will require a radical rethinking of American economic engagement with the rest of the world.

To begin with, the Pax Americana strategy will no longer serve American interests. It was one thing for the United States, as the largest economy and the greatest military power in the global system, to provide its dependent allies with military protection, unreciprocated access to American markets, and the use of the dollar as the global reserve currency. But why should the number two economy sacrifice its taxes and the blood of its soldiers to protect the overseas interests of the number one economy? China, which borders on Afghanistan and Pakistan, has far more vital interests in the region than does the United States. Likewise, China, Japan, and Europe are far more dependent on Middle Eastern oil than the United States. Should American soldiers continue to protect their interests in the Middle East, when the United States is merely one of several great powers in a multipolar world?

The use of the dollar as a reserve currency has allowed the United States to operate without the budgetary constraints imposed on other countries. It has used that privilege unwisely. The eventual replacement of the dollar's reserve currency status by several currencies or a synthetic global currency would bring some painful but perhaps necessary discipline to the posthegemonic United States.

A posthegemonic America can no longer serve as the sole engine of the world's growth. The China-centered model that preceded the Great Recession, in which industrial countries like Japan and Germany and South Korea sent components, while developing countries like Brazil sent resources, to China to be assembled into manufactured goods for American consumers is shattered beyond repair. Along with China and India, which will soon surpass China in population, the United States will be one of the three most populous countries in the world. All three continental states, along with Europe and second-tier countries like Brazil, must consume as well as produce and import as well as export.

The vision of a rule-governed global economy with free flows of goods, labor, and capital across borders will remain a fantasy in a world of sovereign states with conflicting national interests. However, the tradition of developmental capitalism, in which the government promotes growth in strategic industries, can take forms other than zero-sum trade wars. Just as countries can coordinate their exchange rate and stimulus policies, so in theory they could coordinate their industrial policies, by means such as market-share agreements or mutually agreed upon domestic content rules. In contrast, beggar-thy-neighbor mercantilist policies on the part of every country can only result in mutual impoverishment.

TOWARD THE NEXT AMERICAN SYSTEM

While particular economic interests have used the rhetoric of free markets when it served their purposes, laissez-faire economic policy has never been the American tradition. As we have seen, once the southern planter class was crushed in the Civil War, the United States successfully carried out a version of Henry Clay's American System, which built on Alexander Hamilton's vision of national economic development. On becoming the global economic hegemon, the United States shifted toward opening foreign markets for its exports and investments, as Britain had done when it briefly enjoyed industrial supremacy in the mid-nineteenth century. Today, as a former hegemon in relative decline, the United States is no longer served well by a simple-minded strategy of liberalizing trade and deregulating the economy. It needs a sophisticated, long-term national economic strategy—a new American System.

What would a twenty-first-century American System look like? Clay's American System rested on three elements: infant-industry protection for American manufacturing; federal funding of internal improvements, or infrastructure; and a sound national financial system anchored by the Bank of the United States. At the time, the United States was catching up to Britain and Western Europe by borrowing or stealing science and technology. During World War II and the Cold War, the United States created its own government-funded research-industrial complex along the lines pioneered earlier by Imperial Germany. A twenty-first-century American System needs to have four elements: innovation policy; manu-facturing policy; infrastructure policy; and financial policy.

THE NEXT AMERICAN SYSTEM: INNOVATION

In terms of real per capita income, Americans today are seven times richer than they were a century ago.[5] However, this measure understates progress, because it does not factor in revolutionary inventions. While a middle-class American household spent 4 percent of its income on illu-mination in 1800, today it spends less than 1 percent of its income and enjoys one hundred times as much light—not from candles that are one hundred times larger than candles, but from electric lightbulbs.[6]

Economic growth is a miracle—but it is not a mystery. The obser-vation of Adam Smith in the eighteenth century remains valid in the twenty-first: "The annual produce of the land and labour of any nation can be increased in its value by no other means, but by increasing either the number of its productive labourers, or the productive powers of those labourers who had before been employed."[7] Economic growth has two sources: increases in the quantity of inputs (resources and labor) or in-novation, which may take the form of new technologies or new processes and techniques. According to the Office of Technology Assessment, from the Great Depression to the present between 60 and 80 percent of produc-tivity growth has resulted from innovation.[8]

Between 1870 and 1992, the average US rate of growth in productivity was 1.8 percent a year.[9] Since the middle of the twentieth century, in the United States per capita GDP rose the most during two periods of high productivity growth, 1949 to 1973 and 1996 to 1999, and the least dur-ing two periods of slower productivity growth, 1974 to 1979 and 1980 to 1995.[10] In the early 1970s, US productivity growth, which had averaged 2.88 percent per year from 1949 to 1973, dropped to a mere 1.3 percent a year from 1973 to 1975. As a result, Americans in 1995 were only 70 percent as productive as they would have been if US productivity had continued to grow as rapidly as it had during the 1950s and 1960s. In the second half of the 1990s, however, US productivity growth returned to its earlier levels, growing at an annual rate of 2.8 percent from 1995 to March 2001 and remaining high.[11] Some economists, however, argue that the federal government has overstated productivity growth, by counting the low prices of ingredients from China and elsewhere as improvements in productivity in the United States.[12]

Productivity growth is driven by innovation. Beginning in World War II under Vannevar Bush and his colleagues, the United States has assembled the world's most successful system of innovation, based on federal funding, university-based research, and development of new technologies by entrepreneurs with the help of private and public venture capital. But the system that produced nuclear energy, computers, satellites, and the Internet depended heavily on military spending, which is likely to decline as the United States shifts from a role as global hegemon to a new role as one of several great powers. Federal civilian spending on research is inadequate and heavily skewed toward attempts to cure particular diseases like cancer. Like other discretionary spending, federal spending on R&D is likely to be among the first programs to be sacrificed during attempts to reduce deficits and the debt.

Most state and local governments use taxation to finance ordinary expenditures, while borrowing money to pay for capital investments like roads and school buildings with large up-front costs but benefits spread over many decades, and there is no reason why the federal government should not do the same. R&D is exactly the kind of productivity-enhancing investment that should be financed by borrowing. As I have proposed elsewhere, the United States should consider creating a federal R&D bank, which issues bonds in order to raise funding for basic R&D that individual companies will not fund because they cannot monopolize the benefits of breakthroughs.[13] Some of the projects could be self-financing, by means of royalties on patented discoveries or inventions, but others need not be. Because breakthroughs in science and technology benefit the economy as a whole, it is legitimate for bondholders to be repaid out of general revenues. The R&D bank could partly replace the historic role of the military in funding American innovation.

THE NEXT AMERICAN SYSTEM: MANUFACTURING

The United States should not adopt across-the-board protectionism or pursue a mercantilist trade policy except in retaliation. But a posthegemonic America needs to rebuild some of the manufacturing capability that it allowed to be lost to East Asian and European mercantilism during the latter decades of the Pax Americana. Even if, as a result of automation, domestic manufacturing in the future were to directly employ as few people as are employed today in industrialized agriculture, the United States needs to preserve its domestic manufacturing base. If the dollar ceases to be the reserve currency, the United States will have to pay for imports with exports, rather than with low-cost debt.

The most important reason for maintaining a world-class industrial base is national security. Even Adam Smith admitted the need to protect militarily relevant industries, on the grounds that "defense, however, is much more important than opulence."[14] When the United States was by far the dominant military-industrial power, it could afford to cede some of its industries to its allies as bribes, in the interest of maintaining the Cold War alliance against the Soviet bloc. But in a multipolar world with other independent centers of power, the United States must resume the concern with military and industrial independence that dates back to George Washington and Alexander Hamilton and Henry Clay. While enjoying the benefits of trade with other great powers, it must ensure that it does not become overly dependent on them for essential manufactured goods or raw materials. In the decades ahead, American defense strategists should devote more attention to ensuring that the United States has adequate manufacturing capacity in the event that one or more other great powers becomes a military rival.

Since the industrial revolution began, no empire or nation has been able to be a major military power without being a major manufacturing power. That will be as true in the twenty-first century as it was in the nineteenth and twentieth. If the United States allows itself to be deindustrialized, as a result of the mercantilist policies of other countries or the offshoring decisions of its own corporations, it will cease to be a military power of the first rank. The architects of the Confederate States of America were content to project a future in which their country would forever be a second-rank military power, specializing in the export of cotton, food, and other commodities to industrial countries—a sort of large, English-speaking Brazil or Argentina. The majority in the United States rejected that option in the 1860s, and should always reject it. Americans should look for guidance in trade policy not to Jefferson Davis but to George Washington, who, in his first annual address to Congress in January 1790, declared that "a free people ought not only to be armed but disciplined" and that "their safety and interest required that they should promote such manufactories as tend to render them independent of others for essential, particularly military, supplies."

GOVERNMENT AND BUSINESS: PARTNERS, NOT ADVERSARIES

Rethinking American manufacturing policy means rethinking the relationship between the American nation-state and the multinational corporation. There are two possible options. The United States can select certain US-based multinationals as "national champions" and favor them over foreign corporations. Or it can treat all multinational enterprises, no matter where they are chartered, as American to the extent that they carry out production and employ people in the United States, and foreign to the extent that they have activities elsewhere. In a multipolar world, America's decisions about how to treat corporations must be influenced by the policies of other countries. If other nations rely on state-owned enterprises or national champions, the United States may have no choice but to compete by using similar methods.

In promoting American manufacturing, the United States, in the future as in the past, within the limits of trade treaties that can always be amended or ended, will have a variety of methods to choose from, ranging from public ownership and tax incentives to regulations such as tariffs, quotas, and domestic-content rules. Clay's American System used tariffs to protect American infant industries, but Hamilton preferred bounties, or subsidies, on the grounds that their cost was spread over the tax-paying population as a whole, instead of falling solely on consumers. Either method may be appropriate in particular cases and either method may be abused by special interests. Abuse, though, is not an argument against a manufacturing policy, any more than it is against any other government policy, including defense, which depends on the national manufacturing base.

From the foundation of the republic, American industry has been supported by government at every stage, from federally funded invention to early adoption with the help of military procurement and protection from foreign competition during development. The federal government subsidized early American aviation and performed aeronautic research to support it, while atomic energy, jet propulsion, computers, rockets, and satellites were invented and developed in government laboratories. Early steamships and radio networks benefited from initial government-granted monopolies, while automobiles benefited from tax-funded roads and highways. The government has built and turned over telegraph lines and factories built during wartime to private owners and has set standards of best practice for private enterprise, as the nineteenth-century federal arsenals did when they taught American businesses to use the arsenal system of interchangeable parts. The American states, and the colonies before them, have been even more involved than the federal government in American enterprise, in some cases wholly or partly owning their own banks, canals, and railroads.[15]

Government in America has never been limited to enforcing property rights, educating workers, and acting as an impartial umpire in competitive markets. Industrial policy is not alien to the American tradition. It is the American tradition.

THE NEXT AMERICAN SYSTEM:
INFRASTRUCTURE

In the decades ahead, the United States needs to spend more money on infrastructure, merely to maintain the roads, railroads, airports, power lines, and water systems that have already been built. Unlike in earlier generations, when it was clear that a particular kind of infrastructure needed to be built out—canals, railroads, interstate highways, and rural electric grids—today there is no national consensus about the next American infrastructure.

In recent years many urban intellectuals and politicians in the dwindling downtowns of America have favored mass transit, high-speed rail, and renewable energy, out of a mixture of self-interest and idealism. But fewer than 4 percent of Americans commute using mass transit each day. It is wishful thinking to hope that the automobile-centered society that took shape in the twentieth century will somehow give way to pedestrian villages connected by mass transit in the twenty-first. High-speed rail might be justified in a few dense regions like the East Coast, but in most of the country it is not a plausible alternative to intercity travel by airplane or bus. The unexpected abundance of natural gas made possible by fracking means that natural gas pipelines are more likely to be in demand that high-voltage lines carrying energy from solar panels that carpet the southwestern desert or vast arrays of windmills.

A more likely scenario is the automation of otherwise conventional automobiles and airplanes. The Defense Advanced Research Projects Agency (DARPA), which in previous generations contributed to the development of the computer and the Internet, has done pioneering research in "robocars," which has been built on by Google and companies and universities around the world. The chief barriers to the automation of transportation will be legal and psychological, not technological. Another possibility is telecommuting, which may finally live up to its long-prophesied potential.

Both a transition to automated vehicles and a partial shift from commuting to telecommuting would require infrastructure investment on a grand scale. Like other capital projects, infrastructure should be paid for by borrowing—for example, by means of a federal infrastructure bank. The present federal system of funding infrastructure chiefly through the highway trust fund, which has become a slush fund allowing members of Congress to "earmark" pet projects, needs to be rethought and replaced.

THE NEXT AMERICAN SYSTEM: FINANCE

The fourth element of a new American System, financial policy, should support the previous three. One component should be an expanded system of public purpose banks, like an R&D bank and an infrastructure bank, which can tap large amounts of private capital for public investment to increase the productivity of the American economy.[16]

Successful public purpose banks have a long and successful history in the United States. They include not only the Reconstruction Finance Corporation, which was abolished after World War II, but also the Farm Credit System and the Home Loan Bank System. The worst failures were Fannie Mae and Freddie Mae. But those two government-sponsored enterprises (GSEs) failed not because they were public but because they were compelled to act like profit-maximizing corporations instead of public utilities. Free-market ideology was responsible for the privatization of Fannie Mae and the creation of Freddie Mac as a would-be competitor. Ginnie Mae, which remained a government corporation, did not engage in similar profit-driven risk taking. Nor did the Federal Home Loan Bank system, which, like the Farm Credit System, is a nonprofit cooperative, owned by risk-averse member banks. The lesson of the Fannie/Freddie debacle during the housing bubble and subsequent crash is not that public financial institutions are a bad idea, but rather that they work only when they are organized as nonprofit government corporations or public-private cooperatives.

In addition to creating new public-investment banks, Americans need to create a replacement for the dysfunctional American financial system, in which "too big to fail" financial institutions reap huge profits from highly leveraged gambling when they succeed, while their losses are socialized by the taxpayers when they lose their bets.

Because the system of financial regulation created by the New Deal created several decades of financial stability before it was dismantled in the late twentieth century, many seek to turn back the clock to the mid-twentieth century. But that would be a mistake. The purpose of New Deal financial reform was not simply to stabilize the financial system, but also to preserve small local banks from interstate and even intrastate branch banking. In other nations during the same decades, like Canada and Australia, major financial crises were also rare or absent, even though their banking systems were organized as national oligopolies with a handful of big banks.

What matters is not the size of the banks but the absence of a toxic mixture of competition for market share with explicit or implicit government insurance. Problems arose in the United States when deregulation gave banks, savings and loans, and other financial institutions opportunities to compete for market share and high profits, while pressure from shareholders compelled them to do so. In other words, banking is an industry, like railroads, airlines, and telecommunications, in which "ruinous competition" can be the problem and in which restraints on competition can be the cure.

In the first few years of the Great Recession, however, the most popular proposed reforms were inspired by ideas that assumed that the solution involved more competition, not less. On the right, libertarians failed to recognize the utility-like nature of massive, interconnected financial institutions such as megabanks by arguing that they should be allowed simply to go bankrupt periodically, as though they were corner umbrella stands. On the left, many progressives naively called for breaking up big banks into little banks, without understanding that the small-bank system of the New Deal era worked only because of the anticompetitive limits on branch banking. If big banks were broken up but mergers and branch banking were still allowed, then a few megabanks would soon grow by devouring their rivals, defeating the intent of the reform. And if megabanks were allowed to engage in risky behavior, as long as the government did not bail them out when they failed, then their periodic collapses could bring the economy down with them.

A better approach would be to focus on functions, walling off casino banking from utility banking and redefining investment banking. Proposals to revive the Glass-Steagall separation of commercial and investment banking make sense, even if other elements of the New Deal system are anachronistic. In addition, a modest financial transaction tax, or Tobin tax, which would hardly be noticed by most individuals and businesses, could raise large amounts of revenue, while discouraging the diversion of capital to unproductive, high-frequency speculation.

As in the past, merchant banks or investment banks could specialize in connecting capital with promising investment opportunities. The utility functions of banks, such as small savings accounts, deposits, and payments, might be assigned to banks that are designed as boring, low-profit utilities, whether they are publicly owned or privately owned, but highly regulated. Utility banks would resemble other utilities, like water and electricity, and other than tradition there is no reason why they should not be regional or national monopolies, with fees set by utility-regulatory commissions in the interest of the public. In other countries, public postal savings banks provide basic financial services, and the United States had its own postal savings system from 1910 to 1967. The American postal savings bank could be revived, as a low-cost national public bank for small savers and ordinary transactions.[17]

In the words of Alexander Hamilton: "Public utility is more truly the object of public banks than private profit."[18]

HOW MALDISTRIBUTION OF INCOME AND WEALTH THREATENS THE ECONOMY

A new American system, if it is successful, can increase the productivity of the US economy in the generations ahead. But productivity-driven economic growth by itself is not enough. The gains from growth must be widely shared among the citizens of the American republic.

The maldistribution of income and wealth that has occurred in the United States since the 1980s should not have come as a surprise. What else could one expect to happen, once unions were crushed, the minimum wage was reduced by inflation, labor markets were flooded with low-wage immigrants, taxes on the rich were dramatically lowered, and salaries and stock options for corporate executives were raised to obscene levels?

Apart from their tendency to fray the social fabric of a democratic republic by diminishing the middle class, extreme concentrations of income and wealth are undesirable for purely economic reasons. Modern technology-based industries benefit from increasing returns to scale, which in turn are made possible by mass markets of middle-income consumers. Even the most profligate rich people tend to spend less of their incomes on consumption than the thriftiest poor do out of necessity. As Keynes observed, the poor have a greater "marginal propensity to consume."

When too much of the wealth of a nation or the world is channeled to too few people, industries are starved of the mass demand they need to keep running or to expand. At the same time, the economy can be destabilized, when the rich try to become even richer by speculating with the money they do not consume or save. The series of asset bubbles the world economy has experienced in recent years—in housing, in stocks, and in commodities such as gold and energy—is a telltale sign that too much money is going to the rich, who use it to gamble on assets, rather than the middle class and the poor, who would have spent the money on goods and services generated in the productive economy.

The maldistribution of income is a global problem, not just an American one. While debt-led growth replaced wage-led growth in the United States in the 1990s and 2000s, on the other side of the Pacific investment-led growth replaced wage-led growth in China and other East Asian mercantilist nations. If every country tries to minimize wage costs, then global aggregate demand will be artificially suppressed, to the detriment of most of the world's people.

THE NEXT AMERICAN MIDDLE CLASS

In a Fourth Republic of the United States that emerges from the wreckage of the Great Recession and its aftermath, a new American System should be complemented by a strategy for building the next American middle class.

The middle class in America, outside of the South, has always been in part a creation of economic engineering by means of laws and public policies. The first American middle class consisted of white yeoman farmers, who benefited from land reforms like fee-simple land sales and the abolition of primogeniture and entail, the banning of slavery from the northern states and territories, the Homestead Act that allowed farm families to purchase farms with their labor, and infrastructure projects sponsored by local, state, and federal governments that connected farmers with national and global markets.

The second American middle class was based on white male factory workers. Among the measures that sought to ensure married men would earn a breadwinner's wage so they could support a homemaker wife and children were wages-and-hours regulations, government support for labor unions, and policies to create tighter labor markets by limiting immigration and removing convicts, children, and women from the labor force.

The third middle class was based in the service sector after World War II. Its members were office workers, a group that increasingly included women. Access to this new, suburban, service-sector middle class was enlarged first by compulsory public high schools and then by expansion of public colleges and universities and financial aid for higher education, including the G.I. Bill, student loans, and Pell Grants.

The fact that middle classes are made in part by enlightened public policy is illustrated by the contrast between the South and the rest of the nation. While independent yeoman farmers formed a majority in the North in the first half of the nineteenth century, in the South poor white farmers were squeezed between a tiny oligarchy of rich planters and the slaves they exploited. In northern factories, despite employer resistance, unions made gains, particularly during the New Deal and World War II. But the one-party South used law and intimidation to prevent unions from taking root in a region whose elites viewed themselves as employers or brokers of poor black, white, and Latino workers deprived of bargaining power. As a result, in the twenty-first century, many southern states have levels of inequality, poverty, and illiteracy similar to those of developing countries.

SERVICE-SECTOR FORDISM

The combination of automation and offshoring has destroyed many routine clerical and lower-level managerial jobs. With the disappearance of middle-skill jobs, the American job market has become polarized between highly paid managerial and professional jobs and poorly paid jobs in the service sector. Most of the job growth in the early 2000s has occurred in three areas: health, education, and government. According to the Bureau of Labor Statistics, health care accounts for seven out of the twenty fastest-growing occupations, more than any other category. Home health aides and personal and home-care aides are found both among the fastest-growing job categories and among the occupations with the largest overall job openings in the years ahead.

What is driving this growth? The US health-care industry is plagued by inefficiency and rent seeking by private insurers, pharmaceutical companies, hospitals, physicians, and lawyers. But even when costs are brought into line with those of other countries, the US health-care system is likely to increase its share of the economy. One reason is the aging of the population. Another is the fact that societies, like individuals, choose to purchase more health care as they grow more affluent. Health is a good that makes possible the enjoyment of all other goods.

Far from being a problem, then, the steady and sustainable growth of employment in the health-care sector, along with jobs providing care for the elderly and children, education, and the provision of public goods, may be the next stage in the evolution of advanced economies. As technology made possible greater production with fewer workers, first agriculture and then manufacturing shed labor to other sectors. Today, information technology, by eliminating much routine office work, is shifting labor into "proximity" services such as health care that cannot be offshored and cannot be automated. A high-tech economy leads to more "high-touch" jobs that only human beings can perform.

Will the health aide be the typical worker of the twenty-first century, the successor to the farmer, the factory worker, and the office worker? The German poet Johann Wolfgang von Goethe would not have been surprised. In 1787, he sardonically commented: "Speaking for myself, I too believe that humanity will win in the long run; I am only afraid that at the same time the world will have turned into one huge hospital where everyone is everybody else's humane nurse."[19]

The high-wage, high-consumption economy established in the United States and similar nations during the Glorious Thirty Years after World War II was easier to create than its equivalent would be today. In the mid-twentieth century, factory workers were a large enough proportion of the workforce that simply raising their wages stimulated the whole economy when they left the factory and spent money on rent, groceries, clothes, and haircuts. But gains in productivity in the highly robotic domestic manufacturing of the 2030s or 2050s may not translate into gains for the rest of society, even if the few remaining workers are very well paid. Higher pay for robot supervisors will not necessarily translate into higher incomes for home health aides.

It is not enough to say that everyone in society benefits from the cheaper goods and services made possible by productivity. This is true, to be sure. But if an ever-greater share of the gains from national economic growth goes to a small oligarchy of capitalists and well-paid managers, then the distance between them and the rest of society will continue to increase. In the United States, the growing share of the rich of national income and wealth has already translated into much greater political dominance than existed in the days of strong unions and local political machines. If America's rich continue to get relatively richer than the rest, they will be even more socially dominant and even more politically powerful.

As Henry Ford recognized, workers are also consumers, who need to be paid well if they are to be able to afford the products that they make. What is required is nothing less than "service-sector Fordism"— the equivalent, in the service sector, of the Fordist system in the mid-twentieth-century industrial sector. Industrial Fordism meant that factory workers made enough money to be able to buy the products they made. Service-sector Fordism means that service-sector workers should be able to obtain the kind of services they provide. Whether from the private market or public services, health-care aides should be able to afford health care, nannies should be able to afford child care, and restaurant workers should be able to afford restaurant meals. The alternative—a return to a society in which most Americans, directly or indirectly, are "in service" to the affluent few, like the butlers, valets, and maids lined up in the driveway of an Edwardian British country house—would mark the abandonment of the American Dream.

If the United States is to avoid turning into a high-tech version of stratified societies like Brazil and Mexico, with which it shares the Western Hemisphere, mechanisms must be found to allow most of American citizens to share in the gains from productivity growth, in addition to falling prices for particular services and goods. Higher taxes on the rich could finance greater redistribution of income—for example, by means of an earned-income tax credit (EITC) that goes to middle-class as well as poor Americans. Yet another possibility could be greatly expanded direct or indirect public employment, paid for out of taxes on the rents that go to the rich. One beneficial side effect of greater public employment could be tight labor markets that raise the pretax incomes of private-sector workers.

Other methods would rely less on taxation and redistribution and more on structural changes in the labor and capital markets. Tighter labor markets, produced by the combination of the restriction of unskilled immigration and the growing ratio of retirees to workers, could raise market wages at the bottom, forcing affluent Americans to pay higher wages for service workers. Another alternative to redistributive taxation would be increasing the number of Americans who own shares in highly automated industries—either directly, through some form of universal shareholding, or indirectly, through the nationalization of some industries and the public provision of goods or the use of profits from government sales to reduce tax burdens on the majority. These and other methods to enlarge the middle class are radical but may be worth considering, if the goal is to prevent the good of productivity growth from generating the evil of plutocracy.

THE NEXT SOCIAL CONTRACT

In addition to devising new forms of stakeholder capitalism and utility finance, Americans need to construct a new social contract that is suited to the workforce and economy of the twenty-first century.

The social contract that crystallized after World War II combined four different, rival approaches. The social-insurance programs, such as Social Security, Medicare, and Medicaid, were administered by government and paid for chiefly by payroll taxes. Coexisting with this system of social insurance was another system of tax-favored employer-based benefits, of which the most important were employer-provided health care and employer-provided pensions. To complicate matters further, beginning in the 1970s, two other approaches were added: tax-favored private accounts—for retirement savings and other purposes, including health care—and tax credits for welfare purposes—of which the most important were the EITC, a subsidy to low-wage workers, and the child tax credit.

Changes in the economy and society have undermined all the elements of the American social contract other than simple, straightforward social-insurance programs. The employer-based health-care system is crumbling, because the rising costs of health-care provision in the United States have caused fewer and fewer employers to offer health care. Employer-based pensions are even further along the road to extinction, having been replaced either by nothing at all or by tax-favored individual retirement accounts like 40l(k)s or IRAs. Tax credits are popular among politicians, because they allow transfers to be hidden in the tax system rather than visible among direct appropriations, but a tax code riddled with tax credits must raise revenue with higher nominal rates, which generate political opposition.

If the system of employer-based benefits collapses entirely, the alternatives, if the safety net is not simply to be reduced, are an expansion of social insurance or an expansion of tax-favored private accounts or tax credits. Most conservatives and libertarians favor replacing Social Security with private savings accounts invested in the stock market and replacing Medicare and Medicaid either with vouchers in the form of tax credits or tax-favored health savings accounts.

These are bad ideas. After two stock market crashes in the first decade of the twenty-first century and the prolonged bear market of the Great Recession, it makes no sense to argue that Americans should be more rather than less dependent on the state of the stock market at the time of their retirement. Even worse, retirement-fund managers routinely and quite legally rob American investors in private plans by charging hidden fees, while the administrative costs of Social Security are much lower. Social Security provides a more stable source of retirement income in bad times as well as good. Its long-term solvency could be assured without significant cuts either by lifting the cap on payroll taxes paid by the affluent or by adding new revenue from other sources, such as general revenues or a new dedicated tax such as a value-added tax (VAT).

The idea of using competition based on individual health-care vouchers to reduce medical costs is a naive fantasy of right-wing ideologues; no modern society does that, because no modern medical sector functions as a free market. Indeed, the combination of vouchers with uncompetitive markets is a recipe for disaster. Unlike Social Security, Medicare can be thought of as a voucher system for health care, and student loans can be thought of as vouchers for higher education. As the cancerous growth of health-care prices and tuition prices in the United States demonstrates, vouchers without price controls encourage unchecked price-gouging by the providers of subsidized goods and services, such as American health-care providers and American universities. For practical and political reasons, it is impossible to turn health care and higher education into truly competitive markets with vast numbers of small providers. Like other natural monopolies or oligopolies, health care and higher education need to be turned into publicly regulated utilities, in order to prevent their providers from extracting excessive rents from a victimized public.

Of the mechanisms that other countries use to contain health-cost increases, the most important is "all-payer regulation"—in effect, price controls, set by the government in consultation with health-care providers and renegotiated every few years. This kind of regulation of rates is taken for granted in the United States in the case of electric utilities and local water systems. Americans need to treat the health-care sector as a public utility, with publicly regulated rates. If health costs are brought under control, then the aging of the US population by itself is predicted to add only a few percent of GDP in increased spending on Medicare and Medicaid in the next half century, something that can easily be managed.[20]

Notwithstanding the enthusiasm for pseudomarket solutions that have dominated Democratic as well as Republican thinking for decades, the conclusion must be that the best way to rebuild the American social contract would be to reduce or eliminate the rickety Rube Goldberg schemes of employer-provided benefits, private savings accounts, and tax credits, and replace most or all of them with a simple, streamlined system of universal social insurance paid for out of current taxation (not necessarily payroll taxation alone). Inasmuch as employer-based benefits, private accounts, and tax credits are all government programs, replacing them with social insurance would not replace "the market" with "big government"; it would simply replace inefficient, overcomplicated, and frequently unfair government programs with government programs that are more efficient, simpler, and difficult for special interests to manipulate.

AMERICAN IMMIGRATION: FROM
NEPOTISM TO SKILLS

With the exception of the American Indians and descendants of American slaves, all Americans are the descendants of voluntary immigrants. In the past two centuries, the American population has been expanded and transformed by immigration, which will continue to reshape the nation in the generations ahead.

The major trend in the United States, as in other developed countries, has been a long-term trend toward falling birth rates, which are below replacement level for native-born white and black Americans. Only the above-replacement fertility of immigrants and their children keeps the US population growing.

During the bubble economy of the late twentieth and early twenty-first centuries, straight-line projections based on the high immigration and high immigrant fertility of the last generation led to estimates of anywhere between 400 million and a billion Americans by 2100. All such projections should be treated with caution, because even minor changes in immigration or fertility can produce major long-run differences.

Nevertheless, it is safe to predict that the United States will continue to choose to admit significant numbers of immigrants, as an alternative to allowing the population to shrink because of low native fertility. What criteria are used to select foreign nationals to work in the United States and become citizens has always been a matter of contention.

The goal of US immigration reform during the civil rights era in the 1960s was to replace a low-immigration, racist national quota regime that minimized non-European immigration with another low-immigration regime based on nonracist national quotas. It did not work out that way. Immigration based on family ties, which was expected to be minor, now accounts for the majority of legal immigration to the United States. By a sort of compound-interest effect, this has resulted in an ever-growing Latin American share of US legal immigrant flows, as the largest groups already in the United States can bring in ever-growing numbers of their relatives, in what is called "chain migration." Because of the proximity of Mexico and Central America, illegal immigrants are also overwhelmingly Latin American in origin.

Nativists to the contrary, the assimilation and intermarriage rates of Latinos in the United States are comparable to those of European immigrants in earlier generations. The problem is that most of them, through no fault of their own, are poor and poorly educated. So were many of the European immigrants of the past. But they came to a country in need of farm labor or unskilled factory labor. Today's unskilled immigrants enter a labor market that, even before the Great Recession, was producing mostly poorly paid jobs in the menial service and construction sectors.

In addition to lowering wages for native and naturalized competitors, unskilled immigration tends to retard productivity growth in an advanced industrial nation like the United States. By enlarging the pool and reducing the costs of unskilled labor, a high level of unskilled immigration warps the incentives of American employers, making it more rational for them to add unskilled workers rather than invest in innovative labor-saving equipment or innovative labor-saving techniques. As a result of Japan's restrictive immigration policies, Japan is far more advanced in robotics than the United States, while Australian agribusiness relies far more on machinery than American agribusiness, with its never-ending supply of serflike labor from south of the border.

Meanwhile, the United States is competing with other low-fertility societies for talented immigrant scientists, engineers, scholars, and entrepreneurs. From Alexander Graham Bell to Albert Einstein, skilled immigrants have always benefited the US economy. While skilled immigrants may displace Americans or reduce their wages, the economy gains as a whole from the intelligence and enterprise of the best minds from other countries. The United States can always benefit from foreign-born talent.

Britain, Canada, and Australia have created point systems that award immigrants points if they speak English and are highly educated. As a result, most immigrants to those nations are highly skilled, while the majority of immigrants to the United States are unskilled immigrants, most of them family members of Americans. The United States should encourage skilled immigration, by creating a point system for permanent immigrants based on skills. The quota should not be so large that skilled American workers are displaced in great numbers.

At the same time that the quota for skilled permanent immigrants is moderately increased, temporary worker programs, such as the H1-B visa, that tie immigrants to particular employers, in a modern version of indentured servitude, should be scaled back or eliminated. The idea of granting legal permanent resident status to all graduates of US universities— "stapling a green card to every diploma"—should be rejected. That would only encourage the creation of diploma mills with no purpose other than allowing foreign nationals to purchase American residency and citizenship with their tuition fees. And existing programs that provide privileges to prospective immigrants who promise to invest in the United States should be abolished, not expanded. American citizenship should not be for sale.

While it can always be enlarged in the future if necessary to maintain an adequate population, in the near future the numbers of unskilled immigrants legally admitted to the United States each year should be reduced. Family-based immigration should be limited to immediate family members. The illegal immigrant workforce, which is largely unskilled, should be reduced by a combination of strict sanctions on employers with the help of a national ID card, tough border enforcement and, if necessary, a one-time amnesty for some illegal immigrants coupled with symbolic penalties for their violations of law. No immigration policy is possible unless immigration laws are enforced.

From the eighteenth century to the twenty-first, America's immigration system has always been based on some form of nepotism—racial nepotism ("free white persons") from the 1790s until the 1920s, then ethnic nepotism (the national quota system) from the 1920s to the 1960s, and finally family nepotism from the 1960s to the present. The American immigration system needs to be reformed, so that the main criterion for immigration is not race, or nationality, or kinship to particular American citizens, but the potential to contribute to America's economy. Immigrants should be admitted to America on the basis of their talents, not their genes. In the words of President Lyndon Johnson when he signed the 1965 immigration reform act: "This is a simple test, and it is a fair test. Those who can contribute most to this country—to its growth, to its strength, to its spirit—will be the first that are admitted to this land."[21]

STILL A LAND OF PROMISE

Every few generations, the familiar American republic falls apart and must be rebuilt in a generation-long struggle. To date, each American republic has provided more freedom and more opportunity than the one that preceded it. The First Republic abolished aristocracy and feudalism on American soil. The Second Republic abolished slavery. The Third Republic eliminated widespread destitution and sought to suppress the exploitation of wage labor. And each republic has used the technological tools of its era to create a more productive economy with gains shared by more Americans.

In the words of the stockbroker's warning, "Past performance is not a guarantee of future results." The United States could emerge from the trial of the Great Recession as a more productive nation with more widespread sharing of the gains from growth. Or it could go into relative and even absolute decline, losing its technological and industrial edge to foreign competitors and fissioning at home along the lines of caste and class. The United States could come to resemble the oligarchic countries of Latin America—or some of its own impoverished southern states. The American experiment could end in failure.

National renewal or national decline? The question will be decided by today's Americans. In meeting the challenge, they can be inspired by those who successfully met even greater challenges in the past.

They can be warned by George Washington, who observed, in his circular letter to the states in 1783, that if the United States were to fail, then it "will be a subject of regret, that so much blood and treasure have been lavished for no purpose, that so many sufferings have been encountered without a compensation, and that so many sacrifices have been made in vain."[22] They can learn from Franklin Roosevelt, in his speech accepting his second nomination as president: "There is a mysterious cycle in human events. To some generations much is given. Of other generations much is expected. This generation of Americans has a rendezvous with destiny."[23]

And Americans can find guidance in the words of Abraham Lincoln in 1862: "The dogmas of the quiet past, are inadequate to the stormy present. The occasion is piled high with difficulty, and we must rise—with the occasion. As our case is new, so we must think anew, and act anew. We must disenthrall ourselves, and then we shall save our country."[24]

ACKNOWLEDGMENTS

I would like to express my gratitude to my editors, Adam Bellow and Kathryn Whitenight, at HarperCollins; to my agent, Kristine Dahl, of International Creative Management; and to Steve Coll, president of the New America Foundation. I would like to thank Sherle R. Schwenninger, director of the Economic Growth Program at the New America Foundation, for sharing his insights into the American and global economies; my colleagues Samuel Sherraden, Lauren Damme, Jordan D'Amato, Shayne Henry, Daniel Mandel, and Samuel Ball-Brau for their help; and Ben Katcher for his indispensable assistance. And I am grateful to Bernard L. Schwartz and Leo Hindery Jr. for their generous support for our team.

NOTES

CHAPTER 1: A LAND OF PROMISE

1. George Washington to David Humphreys, 25 July 1785, in Jared Sparks, ed., *The Writings of George Washington* (Boston: Russell, Odiorne, and Metcalf, and Hilliard, Gray, 1835), 9:113.

2. Herbert Croly, *The Promise of American Life* (New York: Macmillan, 1914 [1909]), 3.

3. Marcia A. Dente, *Great Falls of Paterson* (Charleston, SC: Arcadia Publishing, 2010), 21.

4. "S.U.M.: Society for Establishing Useful Manufactures," Paterson Friends of the Great Falls, http://www.patersongreatfalls.org/sum.html (accessed November 1, 2011).

5. "Society for Establishing Useful Manufactures," in *The Encyclopedia of New Jersey*, ed. Maxine N. Lurie and Marc Mappen (New Brunswick, NJ: Rutgers University Press, 2004), 753.

6. Dente, *Great Falls of Paterson*, 37.

7. "Economic Independence Through Industry," Hamilton Partnership for Paterson, http://www.hamiltonpartnership.org/node/257 (accessed November 1, 2011).

8. Ibid.

9. Ibid.

10. Richard Knowles Morris, *John P. Holland, 1841–1914: Inventor of the Modern Submarine* (Columbia: University of South Carolina, 1966).

11. Ibid., 116.

12. Lois Palken Rudnick, *Mabel Dodge Luhan: New Woman, New Worlds* (Albuquerque: University of New Mexico Press, 1984), 87.

13. Dente, *Great Falls of Paterson*, 52.

14. Kirk W. House, *Hell-Rider to King of the Air: Glenn Curtis' Life of Innovation* (Warrendale, PA: SAE International, 2003).

15. Richard R. Nelson and Sidney G. Winter, *An Evolutionary Theory of Economic Change* (Cambridge, MA: Belknap Press of Harvard University Press, 1985); Richard R. Nelson, *Technology, Institutions, and Economic Growth* (Cambridge, MA: Harvard University Press, 2005); Carlota Perez, *Technological Revolutions and Financial Capital: The Dynamics of Bubbles and Golden Ages* (Cheltenham and Camberley, UK; Northampton, MA: Edward Elgar, 2002); Robert D. Atkinson, *The Past and Future of America's Economy: Long Waves of Innovation That Power Cycles of Growth* (Cheltenham and Camberley, UK; Northampton, MA: Edward Elgar, 2005); Wolfgang Drechsler, Rainer Kattel, and Erik S. Reinert, *Techno-Economic Paradigms: Essays in Honour of Carlota Perez* (London and New York: Anthem Press, 2009).

16. Michael Lind, *The Next American Nation: The New Nationalism and the Fourth American Revolution* (New York: Simon & Schuster, 1995). Other interpretations of US history in terms of a series of successive republics or regimes include Theodore Lowi, *The End of Liberalism: The Second Republic of the United States* (New York: W. W. Norton, 1979); Bruce Ackerman, *We the People,* vol. 1: *Foundations* (Cambridge, MA: Belknap Press of Harvard University Press, 1991); Morton Keller, *America's Three Regimes: A New Political History* (New York: Oxford University Press, 2007).

17. George Tucker, *The Life of Thomas Jefferson* (Philadelphia: Carey, Lea, & Blanchard, 1873), 503.

18. John Maynard Keynes, *The General Theory of Employment, Interest and Money* (London: Macmillan, 1936).

19. Chalmers Johnson, "The Developmental State: Odyssey of a Concept," in *The Developmental State*, ed. Meredith Woo-Cumings (Ithaca, NY: Cornell University Press, 1999). See also Eric Reinert, *How Rich Countries Got Rich . . . and Why Poor Countries Stay Poor* (New York: Carroll and Graf, 2007).

20. The identification is found in David Nasaw, "Gilded Age Gospels," in *Ruling America: A History of Wealth and Power in a Democracy,* ed. Steve Fraser and Gary Gerstle (Cambridge, MA: Harvard University Press, 2005), 324, n9.

21. Andrew Carnegie, *The "Gospel of Wealth" Essays and Other Writings*, ed. David Nasaw (New York: Penguin, 2006), 63.

22. Doron Kornbluth, "Is History Bunk?" Chabad.org, http://www.chabad .org/library/article_cdo/aid/M67039/jewish/Is-History-Bunk.htm (accessed December 8, 2011).

CHAPTER 2: NATION BUILDING

1. Henry Adams, *History of the United States of America*, vol. 9 (New York: Charles Scribner's Sons, 1911), 195–6.

2. James Hawkes, *A Retrospect of the Boston Tea-Party, with a Memoir of George R. T. Hewes, a Survivor of the Little Band of Patriots Who Drowned the Tea in Boston Harbour in 1773* (New York: S. S. Bliss, 1834), 39.

3. Thomas Mun, *England's Treasure by Foreign Trade* (New York: Macmillan, 1895), 7–8.

4. Quoted in Ha-Joon Chang, *Bad Samaritans: The Myth of Free Trade and the Secret History of Capitalism* (New York: Bloomsbury Press, 2008), 44.

5. John Locke, *Letter Concerning Toleration*, ed. James Tully (Indianapolis: Hackett, 1983), 47–48.

6. Locke MSS., Lovelace Collection, Bodleian Library, Oxford University, c. 30, fols. 8 and 19, quoted in John Locke, *Second Treatise of Government*, ed. Richard Howard Cox (Arlington Heights, IL: H. Davidson, 1982), 175–6.

7. Quoted in David Bertelson, *The Lazy South* (New York: Oxford University Press, 1967), 86.

8. Edmund Burke, *The Works of the Right Honorable Edmund Burke*, vol. 1, 371, cited in Jonathan Haslam, *No Virtue Like Necessity: Realist Thought in International Relations Since Machiavelli* (New Haven, CT: Yale University Press, 2002), 141.

9. Samuel Eliot Morison and Henry Steel Commager, *The Growth of the American Republic*, vol. 1 (New York: Oxford University Press, 1942), 102.

10. Ha-Joon Chang, *Kicking Away the Ladder: Development Strategy in Historical Perspective* (London: Anthem, 2002), 52.

11. Morison and Commager, *Growth of the American Republic*, vol. 1, 103.

12. Chang, *Kicking Away the Ladder*, 52.

13. Ibid., 54–55.

14. Ibid., 52–55.

15. Robert E. Wright and David J. Cowen, *Financial Founding Fathers: The Men Who Made America Rich* (Chicago: University of Chicago Press, 2006), 126.

16. Charles Rappleye, *Robert Morris: Financier of the American Revolution* (New York: Simon & Schuster, 2010), 304.

17. Ibid., 306.

18. Quoted in Margaret C. S. Christman, *Adventurous Pursuits* (Washington, DC: Smithsonian Institution Press, 1984), 43.

19. Rappleye, *Robert Morris*, 105–106.

20. Wright and Cowen, *Financial Founding Fathers*, 139.

21. Ibid., 137–38.

22. Charles E. Brooks, *Frontier Settlement and the Market Revolution: The Holland Land Purchase* (Ithaca, NY: Cornell University Press, 1996), 13.

23. Washington Irving, *Life of George Washington* (New York: G. P. Putnam's Sons, 1876), 2:654.

24. Hamilton to James Duane, September 3, 1780, in *The Papers of Alexander Hamilton*, ed. Harold C. Syrett et al. (New York: Columbia University Press, 1963), 2:400–418.

25. Chang, *Kicking Away the Ladder*, 21–22.

26. "Stock Marine List," *New York Gazette*, April 2, 1792, quoted in Robert E. Wright, *One Nation under Debt: Hamilton, Jefferson, and the History of What We Owe* (New York: McGraw-Hill, 2008), 159.

27. Hamilton to Morris, April 1781, quoted in Frank Bourgin, *The Great Challenge: The Myth of Laissez-Faire in the Early Republic* (New York: George Braziller, 1989), 75.

28. Leonard L. Richards, *Shays's Rebellion: The American Revolution's Final Battle* (Philadelphia: University of Pennsylvania Press, 2002), 158–59.

29. For Hamilton's bank plan, see *The Papers of Alexander Hamilton*, ed. Syrett et al., 7:305–42.

30. Ibid., 3:419, in Bourgin, *The Great Challenge*, 80.

31. David Jack Cowen, *The Origins and Economic Impact of the First Bank of the United States, 1791–1797* (New York and London: Garland, 2000).

32. Richard Sylla, "Reversing Financial Reversals," in *Government and the American Economy: A New History*, ed. Price Van Meter Fishback (Chicago and London: University of Chicago Press, 2007), 121.

33. James O. Wettereau, "The Branches of the First Bank of the United States," *Journal of Economic History* 2 (December 1942): 66–100.

34. Thomas Jefferson, "Note on the Establishment of a Money Unit, and of a Coinage for the United States," in *The Works of Thomas Jefferson*, Federal Edition, Paul Leicester Ford, ed. (New York and London: G. P. Putnam's Sons, 1904–1905), 4:297–313.

35. James E. Vance Jr., *The Continuing City: Urban Morphology in Western Civilization* (Baltimore and London: Johns Hopkins University Press, 1990), 329.

36. Lawrence A. Peskin, *Manufacturing Revolution: The Intellectual Origins of Early American Industry* (Baltimore: Johns Hopkins University Press, 2003), 94.

37. Hamilton, "Report on Manufactures" (Washington, DC: Government Printing Office, 1913 [originally published in 1791]), 18.

38. Alexander Hamilton, *Federalist* 35, in *The Federalist Papers*, ed. Charles Kesler and Clinton Rossiter (New York: Penguin, 1999), 208.

39. Alexander Hamilton, "Report on the Subject of Manufactures," in *The Papers of Alexander Hamilton*, ed. Syrett et al., 10:285–6.

40. Doron Ben-Atar, "Alexander Hamilton's Alternative: Technology Piracy and the Report on Manufactures," *The William and Mary Quarterly*, 3d ser., 52, no. 3 (July 1995): 396.

41. Ibid., 390.

42. Ibid., 390–91.

43. Jefferson to William Crawford, June 10, 1816, in *The Writings of Thomas Jefferson*, ed. Paul Leicester Ford (New York: G. P. Putnam's Sons, 1892–1899), 10:33–35.

44. Ben-Atar, "Alexander Hamilton's Alternative," 408.

45. Ibid., 396.

46. Ibid., 407.

47. Ibid., 412.

48. *The Papers of Alexander Hamilton*, ed. Syrett et al., 10:525.

49. Hamilton to James A. Bayard, January 16, 1801, in *The Papers of Alexander Hamilton*, ed. Syrett et al. (New York: Columbia University Press, 1963), 25:319–24 ("by a trick," 25:321n).

50. Ibid., 11:131.

51. David J. Cowen, "The First Bank of the United States and the Securities Market Crash of 1792," *Journal of Economic History* 60, no. 4 (December 2000): 1041–60; Cathy Matson, "Public Vices, Private Benefit: William Duer and His Circle, 1776–1792," in *New York and the Rise of American Capitalism: Economic Development and the Social and Political History of an American State: 1780–1870*, ed. William Pencak and Conrad Edick Wright (New York: New-York Historical Society, 1989), 72–123; Joseph Stancliffe Davis, Essay II, "William Duer, Entrepreneur, 1747–1799," in *Essays on the Earlier History of American Corporations* (Cambridge, MA: Harvard University Press, 1917), 278–345.

52. Albert Gallatin, "Report on Manufactures," in Alexander Hamilton et al., *State Papers and Speeches on the Tarriff* (Cambridge, MA: Harvard University Press, 1893).

53. Thomas Jefferson, *Notes on the State of Virginia with Related Documents*, ed. Donald Waldstreicher (New York: Palgrave, 2002), 197.

54. Jefferson to General Thaddeus Kosciuszko, June 28, 1812, in *The Writings of Thomas Jefferson*, ed. Andrew A. Lipscomb and Albert E. Bergh (Washington, DC: Thomas Jefferson Memorial Association, 1905), 13:170.

55. Jefferson to William Crawford, June 20, 1816, in *Writings of Thomas Jefferson*, ed. Paul Leicester Ford (New York: Cosimo, 2009), 10:34–35.

56. Jefferson to Benjamin Austin, January 9, 1816, in *The Writings of Thomas Jefferson*, ed. H. A. Washington (New York: H. W. Derby, 1861), 6:522–23.

57. Marvin Meyers, ed., *The Mind of the Founder: Sources of the Political Thought of James Madison*, rev. ed. (Hanover, NH, and London: Brandeis University Press, 1973), 380–84.

58. Jefferson to Pierre Samuel Du Pont de Nemours, 1811, quoted in Bourgin, *The Great Challenge*, 137.

59. Jefferson to Joel Barlow, 1811, quoted in Bourgin, *The Great Challenge*, 151.

CHAPTER 3: THE FIRST AMERICAN ECONOMY

1. Adam Smith, part 2, *An Inquiry into the Nature and Causes of the Wealth of Nations* (New York: P.F. Collier & Son, 1903 [originally published in 1776]), 112.

2. *Fortune*, "Almanac of American Wealth: The Richest Americans," *CNN Money*, http://money.cnn.com/galleries/2007/fortune/0702/gallery .richestamericans.fortune/2.html (accessed September 27, 2011).

3. Angus Maddison, *The World Economy: A Millenial Perspective* (Paris: OECD Publishing, 2001), 28.

4. Gregory Clark, "Human Capital, Fertility and the Industrial Revolution," *Journal of the European Economic Association* 3, nos. 2/3 (April–May 2005): 505–15.

5. Smith, *The Wealth of Nations*, 172.

6. David Hosack, *Memoir of De Witt Clinton* (New York: J. Seymour, 1829), 347, quoted in Susan Dunn, *Dominion of Memories: Jefferson, Madison, and the Decline of Virginia* (New York: Basic Books, 2007), 91.

7. Dunn, *Dominion of Memories*, 90.

8. Jonathan Hughes and Louis P. Cain, *American Economic History*, 5th ed. (New York: Addison-Wesley, 1998), 143.

9. Carl Carmer, *The Hudson*, 2nd ed. (New York: Fordham University Press, 1989), 162.

10. Frances Trollope, *Domestic Manners of the Americans*, ed. Donald Smalley (New York: Alfred A. Knopf, 1949 [originally published in 1832]), 369, quoted in Ronald E. Shaw, *Canals for a Nation: The Canal Era in the United States, 1790–1860* (Lexington: University Press of Kentucky, 1990), 184.

11. Harriet Martineau, *Retrospect of Western Travel*, vol. 1 (New York: Saunders & Otley, 1838), 77, quoted in Shaw, *Canals for a Nation*, 183.

12. Hughes and Cain, *American Economic History*, 143.

13. George E. Pataki and Louis R. Tomson, "The Erie Canal: A Brief History," New York State Canal Corporation, www.canals.ny.gov/cculture/history/erie-canal-history.pdf (accessed September 27, 2011).

14. "The Erie Canal: A Brief History," Web site of the state of New York, http://www.canals.ny.gov/cculture/history/ (accessed December 8, 2011).

15. Carter Goodrich, *Government Promotion of American Canals and Railroads, 1800–1890* (New York: Columbia University Press, 1960), 34–35.

16. Robert J. Kapsch, *The Potomac Canal: George Washington and the Waterway West* (Morgantown: West Virginia University Press, 2007), 229.

17. Washington to David Stuart, December 2, 1788, in *The Writings of George Washington*, ed. John C. Fitzpatrick (Washington, DC: US Government Printing Office, 1931–1944), 30:146.

18. Washington to Marquis de Lafayette, January 29, 1789, in Glenn A. Phelps, *George Washington and American Constitutionalism* (Lawrence: University Press of Kansas, 1993), 64.

19. Washington, quoted in Frank Bourgin, *The Great Challenge: The Myth of Laissez-Faire in the Early Republic* (New York: George Braziller, 1989), 149.

20. John Kaminski, ed., *A Necessary Evil: Slavery and the Debate over the Constitution* (Madison, WI: Madison House Publishers, 1995), 277.

21. Julian Ursyn Niemcewicz, *Under Their Vine and Fig Tree: Travels Through America in 1797–1799* (Elizabeth, New Jersey: Grassman, 1965 [first published in 1805]), quoted in Martin Bruegel, "Unrest: Manorial Society and the Market in the Hudson Valley, 1780–1850," *Journal of American History* 82, no. 4 (March 1996): 1410–11.

22. Bruegel, "Unrest," 1399.

23. Ibid.

24. Ibid., 1407.

25. David Maldwyn Ellis, *Landlords in the Hudson-Mohawk Region, 1790–1859* (Ithaca, NY: Cornell University Press, 1946), p. 32.

26. Eric Ford, "New York's Anti-Rent War, 1845–1846," *Contemporary Review* 280, no. 1637 (June 2002): 366–69.

27. John Jay, *The Correspondence and Public Papers of John Jay*, ed. Henry P. Johnston (New York: G. P. Putnam's Sons, 1891), 3:97.

28. Margaret C. Christman, *Adventurous Pursuits: Americans and the China Trade, 1784–1844* (Washington, DC: Smithsonian Institution Press, 1984).

29. Ibid., 18–19.

30. Alfred Tamarin and Shirley Glubok, *Voyaging to Cathay: Americans in the China Trade* (New York: Viking Press, 1976).

31. Jacques M. Downs, "American Merchants and the China Opium Trade, 1800–1840," *Business History Review* 42, no. 4 (Winter 1968): 439.

32. Quoted in Charles C. Stelle, "American Trade in Opium to China, Prior to 1820," *Pacific Historical Review*, 9, no. 4 (December 1940): 425–44.

33. Downs, "American Merchants and the China Opium Trade," 438.

34. Ibid., 442.

35. Karl E. Meyer, "The Opium War's Secret History," *New York Times*, June 28, 1997.

36. John King Fairbank, *Trade and Diplomacy on the China Coast: The Opening of the Treaty Ports, 1842–1854*, 2 vols. (Cambridge, MA: Harvard University Press, 1953).

37. Girard to Mahlon Hutchinson Jr. and Myles McLeveen, January 2, 1805, Stephen Girard Papers, Girard College Library, Philadelphia, PA, quoted in Downs, "American Merchants and the China Opium Trade," 418–42.

38. David S. Miller, "The *Polly*: A Perspective on Merchant Stephen Girard," *Pennsylvania Magazine of History and Biography* 112, no. 2 (April 1988): 201.

39. Wright and Cowen, *Financial Founding Fathers*, 150–51.

40. George Wilson, *Stephen Girard: America's First Tycoon* (Conshohocken, PA: Combined Books, 1995), 303.

41. Miller, "The *Polly*," 201.

42. "Slave Cells Exhumed," *New York Daily Tribune*, October 21, 1906.

43. John Upton Terrell, *Furs by Astor* (New York: William Morrow, 1964), 93.

44. Ibid., 130.

45. Axel Madsen, *John Jacob Astor: America's First Multimillionaire* (New York: Wiley, 2001), 196.

46. Terrell, *Furs by Astor*, 404–5.

47. Quoted in Eric Jay Dolin, *Fur, Fortune, and Empire: The Epic Story of the Fur Trade in America* (New York: W. W. Norton, 2010), 268–69.

48. Madsen, *John Jacob Astor*, 197.

49. Quoted in Madsen, *John Jacob Astor*, 200.

50. Ian Frazier, *Great Plains* (New York: Farrar, Straus and Giroux, 1989), 23.

51. Terrell, *Furs by Astor*, 299.

52. 22nd Cong., 1st sess., 1832, S. doc 90, quoted in Arthur D. Howden Smith, *John Jacob Astor: Landlord of New York* (New York: Cosimo, 2005), 222.

53. Eric Jay Dolin, *Leviathan: The History of Whaling in America* (New York: W. W. Norton, 2007), 168.

54. Quoted in Dolin, *Leviathan*, 248–49.

55. Dolin, *Leviathan*, 336.

56. Ibid., 339.

57. Ibid., 362.

58. Ibid., 335.

59. See Drew R. McCoy, *The Elusive Republic: Political Economy in Jeffersonian America* (Chapel Hill: University of North Carolina Press, 1996).

60. Joseph A. Schumpeter, *History of Economic Analysis* (New York: Oxford University Press, 1954), 571.

CHAPTER 4: "THERE IS NOTHING THAT CANNOT BE PRODUCED BY MACHINERY": THE FIRST INDUSTRIAL REVOLUTION

1. Erasmus Darwin, *The Botanic Garden* (1781), pt. 1, canto 1, ll. 289–92. *The Botanic Garden, with Philosophical Notes*, 4th ed. (London: J. Johnson, 1799).

2. Ralph Waldo Emerson, "The Young American" (1844), in *Collected Works of Ralph Waldo Emerson*, vol. 1, ed. Robert Spiller (Cambridge, MA: Harvard University Press, 1971), 230.

3. Alex Roberto Hybel, *Made by the USA: The International System* (New York: Palgrave, 2001), 15.

4. "Samuel Slater," PBS Who Made America? Series, http://www.pbs.org/wgbh/theymadeamerica/whomade/slater_hi.html (accessed December 8, 2011).

5. Douglas A. Irwin and Peter Temin, "The Antebellum Tariff on Cotton Textiles Revisited," *Journal of Economic History* 61, no. 3 (September 2001).

6. Nathan Rosenberg, *Perspectives on Technology* (Cambridge, UK: Cambridge University Press, 1976), 176.

7. "Cyrus McCormick: Mechanical Reaper," MIT Inventor of the Week Archive, http://web.mit.edu/invent/iow/mccormick.html (accessed December 8, 2011).

8. "John Deere History," *RunGreen.com*, http://www.rungreen.com/John-Deere-History_ep_38-1.html (accessed December 8, 2011).

9. Robert H. Gudmestad, "Steamboats and Southern Economic Development," in *Technology, Innovation, and Southern Industrialization: From the Antebellum Era to the Computer Age*, ed. Susanna Delfino and Michele Gillespie (Columbia and London: University of Missouri Press, 2008), 30, table 1, "Average Steamboat Freight Rates in the Louisville to New Orleans Trade."

10. T. J. Stiles, "Cornelius Vanderbilt," *New York Times Online*, http://topics.nytimes.com/top/reference/timestopics/people/v/cornelius_vanderbilt/index.html (accessed December 8, 2011).

11. Quoted in Mary Bellis, "Steam in Captivity: Oliver Evans Fights for His Patent," *About.com*, http://inventors.about.com/cs/inventorsalphabet/a/oliver_evans.htm (accessed September 27, 2011).

12. Mary Bellis, "Steam in Captivity."

13. Nathan Rosenberg, *Technology and American Economic Growth* (New York: Harper & Row, 1972), 73.

14. Mary Bellis, "John Stevens and Railroads," *About.com Inventors*, http://inventors.about.com/library/inventor/bl_john_stephens.htm (accessed December 13, 2011).

15. John F. Stover, *American Railroads*, 2nd ed. (Chicago: University of Chicago Press, 1997), 13.

16. Jonathan Hughes and Louis P. Cain, *American Economic History*, 5th ed. (New York: Addison-Wesley, 1998), 151.

17. Ibid.

18. Mary Bellis, "The History of the Electric Telegraph and Telegraphy," *About.com Inventors*, http://inventors.about.com/od/tstartinventions/a/telegraph.htm (accessed December 8, 2011).

19. Bruce L. R. Smith, *American Science Policy Since World War II* (Washington, DC: Brookings Institution, 1990), 25.

20. David A. Hounshell, *From the American System to Mass Production, 1800–1932: The Development of Manufacturing Technology in the United States* (Baltimore and London: Johns Hopkins University Press, 1984), 26.

21. Ibid., 27.

22. Ibid., 192–93.

23. Quoted in Hugo Meier, "Technology and Democracy, 1800–1860," *Mississippi Valley Historical Review* 43 (1957): 622; Nathan Rosenberg, *Technology and American Economic Growth*, pt. 2 (New York: Harper & Row, 1972), 33.

24. Rosenberg, *Technology and American Economic Growth*, 35.

25. John M. Murrin et al., *Liberty, Equality, Power*, 4th ed. (Boston: Wadsworth, 2008), 370.

CHAPTER 5: AMERICAN SYSTEMS

1. Adam Smith, *An Inquiry into the Nature and Causes of the Wealth of Nations* (New York: Random House, 1937 [originally published in 1776]), 309.

2. Simon Patten, *The Economic Basis of Protection* (Philadelphia: J. B. Lippincott, 1890), 87.

3. John Gallagher and Ronald Robinson, "The Imperialism of Free Trade," *Economic History Review* 6, no. 1 (1953): 1–15.

4. Ha-Joon Chang, *Bad Samaritans: The Myth of Free Trade and the Secret History of Capitalism* (New York: Bloomsbury Press, 2008), 53.

5. Cobden, *Political Writings*, 1:150; cited in Reinert, "Raw Materials in the History of Economic Policy," 292, and Chang, *Bad Samaritans*, 23, 165n45.

6. Quoted in Robert Gilpin, *War and Change in World Politics* (Cambridge, UK: Cambridge University Press, 1981), 137.

7. John Adams, *Works of John Adams*, ed. Charles F. Adams (Boston: Little, Brown, 1850–1856), 10:384; cited in Alfred E. Eckes Jr., *Opening America's Market: U.S. Foreign Trade Policy Since 1776* (Chapel Hill: University of North Carolina Press, 1995), 19.

8. Victor S. Clark, *History of Manufactures in the United States, 1607–1860* (Washington, DC: Carnegie Institute, 1916), 240.

9. Smith, *The Wealth of Nations*, 347–48.

10. Alexander Hamilton, "The Report on the Subject of Manufactures," December 5, 1791, in *The Papers of Alexander Hamilton*, ed. Syrett et al. (New York: Columbia University Press, 1966), 10:263.

11. Heather Cox Richardson, *The Greatest Nation on Earth: Republican Economic Policies During the Civil War* (Cambridge, MA: Harvard University Press, 1997), 19.

12. Henry C. Carey, "How Can Slavery Be Extinguished?" in *The Slave Trade, Domestic and Foreign: Why It Exists and How It Might Be Extinguished* (Philadelphia: A. Hart, Late Carey & Hart, 1853), 294–307.

13. Henry C. Carey to Henry Wilson, August 26, 1867, in Henry C. Carey, *Reconstruction: Industrial, Financial, and Political* (Washington, DC: United Press Association, 1868), 16.

14. Edward G. Parker, *The Golden Age of American Oratory* (Boston: Whittemore, Niles and Hall, 1857), 36; quoted in Edgar DeWitt Jones, *The Influence of Henry Clay upon Abraham Lincoln* (Lexington, KY: Henry Clay Foundation, 1952), 13.

15. Henry Clay, speech of December 31, 1811, in Clay, *The Works of Henry*

Clay Comprising His Life, Correspondence, and Speeches, ed. Calvin Colton, 6 vols. (New York: Bannes and Burr, 1863), 6:284.

16. Ibid., 6:341.

17. Quoted in Michael Lind, *Hamilton's Republic: Readings in the American Democratic Nationalist Tradition* (New York: Free Press, 1997), 248–52.

18. Paul Bairoch, *Economics and World History: Myths and Paradoxes* (Chicago: University of Chicago Press, 1993), 34.

19. John Joseph Wallis, "The National Era," in *Government and the American Economy: A New History,* ed. Price Fishback et al. (Chicago and London: University of Chicago Press, 2007), 169.

20. Bairoch, *Economics and World History*, 34.

21. Ibid.

22. John C. Calhoun, letter, September 11, 1830, quoted in Gaillard Hunt, *John C. Calhoun* (Philadelphia: George W. Jacobs, 1907), 73.

23. Quoted in Edward Channing, *History of the United States* (New York: Macmillan, 1921), 5:397; cited in Daniel Walker Howe, *What Hath God Wrought: The Transformation of America, 1815–1848* (New York and London: Oxford University Press, 2007), 358.

24. Alfred D. Chandler Jr., *The Visible Hand: The Managerial Revolution in American Business* (Cambridge, MA, and London: Belknap Press of Harvard University Press, 1977), 30–31.

25. Nicholas Biddle, *An Ode to Bogle* (Philadelphia: Privately printed for Ferdinand J. Dreer, 1865), quoted in Hammond, *Banks and Politics in America*, 292.

26. Thomas Cooper, *Lectures on the Elements of Political Economy*, 2nd ed. (Columbia, SC: D. E. Sweeney, 1830), 246; quoted in Herbert Hovenkamp, *Enterprise and American Law, 1836–1937* (Cambridge, MA: Harvard University Press, 1991), 36.

27. Hamilton papers, quoted in Bray Hammond, *Banks and Politics in America: From the Revolution to the Civil War* (Princeton, NJ: Princeton University Press, 1985 [originally published in 1957]), 127.

28. House of Representatives Resolution 460, 2nd Cong., 1st sess., 1832, 379–80, quoted in Hammond, *Banks and Politics in America*, 355.

29. Hammond, *Banks and Politics in America*, 353.

30. Nicholas Biddle, *Correspondence*, 306; quoted in Hammond, *Banks and Politics in America*, 356.

31. James Alexander Hamilton, *Reminiscences* (New York: Charles Scribner, 1869), 69; quoted in Hammond, *Banks and Politics in America*, 345.

32. Hammond, *Banks and Politics in America*, 375.

33. Ibid., 374.

34. Albert Gallatin, *Considerations on the Currency and Banking System of the United States* (1830); Gallatin, "Suggestions on the Banks and Currency of the Several United States, in Reference Principally to the Suspension of Specie Payments" (1841).

35. *Washington Globe*, December 13, 1832, quoted in Arthur Meyer Schlesinger, *The Age of Jackson* (Boston: Little, Brown, 1945), 97.

36. US Congress, *Register of Debates* 13 (1837), pt. 1:690; quoted in Hammond, *Banks and Politics in America*, 365.

37. Robert Sobel, *The Big Board: A History of the New York Stock Market* (New York: Free Press, 1965), 87.

38. Quoted in Ronald E. Shaw, *Canals for a Nation: The Canal Era in the United States, 1790–1860* (Lexington: University Press of Kentucky, 1990), 98.

39. Table 1.2, "Government and the Economy," "Government Debt by Level of Government, Selected Years," in *Government and the American Economy*, ed. Fishback et al., 27.

40. Quoted in Ha-Joon Chang, *Kicking Away the Ladder: Development Strategy in Historical Perspective* (London: Anthem, 2002), 100.

41. *Sangamon Journal* (Springfield, IL), June 13, 1836, quoted in Kenneth J. Winkle, *The Young Eagle: The Rise of Abraham Lincoln* (Dallas: Taylor, 2001), 118.

42. William Henry Herndon and Jesse William Weik, *Herndon's Life of Lincoln*, ed. Paul M. Angle (Cleveland: World, 1942), 161.

43. J. Van Fenstermaker and John E. Filer, "Impact of the First and Second Banks of the United States and the Suffolk System on New England Bank Money, 1791–1837," *Journal of Money, Credit, and Banking* 18, no. 1 (February 1986): 28–40; Naomi R. Lamoreaux, *Insider Lending: Banks,*

Personal Connections, and Economic Development in Industrial New England (Cambridge, UK: Cambridge University Press, 1994); see also J. Van Fenstermaker, *The Development of American Commercial Banking, 1782–1837* (Kent, OH: Kent State University Press, 1965); Howard Bodenhorn, *A History of Banking in Antebellum America: Financial Markets and Economic Development in an Era of Nation-Building* (Cambridge, UK, and New York: Cambridge University Press, 2000).

44. Gary Cross and Rick Szostak, *Technology and American Society: A History* (Englewood Cliffs, NJ: Prentice-Hall, 1995), 77.

45. Ibid., 26.

46. Harold G. Vatter, *The Drive to Industrial Maturity: The U.S. Economy, 1860–1914* (Westport, CT: Greenwood Press, 1975), 13.

47. Allen Guelzo, *Abraham Lincoln: Redeemer President* (Grand Rapids, MI: Wm. B. Eerdmans, 1999), 41.

48. Recollections of George Borrett, in *Conversations with Lincoln*, ed. Charles M. Segal (New York: G. P. Putnam's Sons, 1961), cited in Olivier Fraysee, *Lincoln, Land, and Labor, 1809–60*, trans. Sylvia Neely (Chicago: University of Chicago Press, 1994), 13.

49. Sean Patrick Adams, *Old Dominion, Industrial Commonwealth: Coal, Politics, and Economy in Antebellum America* (Baltimore: Johns Hopkins University Press, 2004).

50. Peter Karsten, "'Bottomed on Justice': A Reappraisal of Critical Legal Studies Scholarship Concerning Breaches of Labor Contracts by Quitting or Firing in the U.S., 1630–1880," *American Journal of Legal History* 34, no. 3 (July 1990): 213–61; James D. Schmidt, *Free to Work: Labor Law, Emancipation, and Reconstruction, 1815–1880* (Athens: University of Georgia Press, 1998).

51. Jonathan Hughes and Louis P. Cain, *American Economic History*, 5th ed. (New York: Addison-Wesley, 1998), 112.

52. Brian Schoen, *The Fragile Fabric of Union: Cotton, Federal Politics, and the Global Origins of the Civil War* (Baltimore: Johns Hopkins University Press, 2009).

53. Guelzo, *Abraham Lincoln*, 134.

54. Angela Lakwete, *Inventing the Cotton Gin: Machine and Myth in Antebellum America* (Baltimore: Johns Hopkins University Press, 2003).

55. Gene Dattel, *Cotton and Race in the Making of America: The Human Costs of Economic Power* (Chicago: Ivan R. Dee, 2009), 98.

56. Guelzo, *Abraham Lincoln*, 134.

57. Dattel, *Cotton and Race in the Making of America*, 82.

58. Quoted in Ibid.

59. Jeffrey Rogers Hummel, "The Civil War and Reconstruction," in *Government and the American Economy: A New History*, ed. Fishback et al., 192.

60. R. Douglas Hurt, *American Agriculture: A Brief History*, rev. ed. (West Lafayette, IN: Purdue University Press, 2002), 124.

61. Adam Rothman, "The 'Slave Power' in the United States, 1783–1865," in *Ruling America: A History of Wealth and Power in a Democracy*, ed. Steve Fraser and Gary Gerstle (Cambridge, MA.: Harvard University Press, 2005), 72–73.

62. Gavin Wright, *Slavery and American Economic Development* (Baton Rouge: Louisiana State University Press, 2006), 61.

63. William Kauffman Scarborough, *Master of the Big House: Elite Slaveholders of the Mid-Nineteenth-Century South* (Baton Rouge: Louisiana State University Press, 2006), 12, 241; Rothman, "The 'Slave Power,'" 72.

64. Lawrence S. Roland, Alexander Moore, and George C. Rogers Jr., *The History of Beaufort County, South Carolina,* vol. 1, *1514–1861* (Columbia: University of South Carolina Press, 1996), 379–80.

65. "1,648 Slaves in the Estate of Nathaniel Heyward, Charlotte, SC, 1851," www.fold3.com (accessed December 12, 2011).

66. J. S. Buckingham, *The Slave States of America* (London: Fisher Son, 1842), 113; quoted in Gavin Wright, "Cheap Labor and Southern Textiles before 1880," in *Industrialization in North America*, ed. Peter Temin (Cambridge, MA: Basil Blackwell, 1994), 405.

67. Vatter, *The Drive to Industrial Maturity*, 5.

68. Friedrich Ratzel, *Sketches of Urban and Cultural Life in North America*, trans. and ed. Stewart A. Sehlin (New Brunswick, NJ: Rutgers Univer-

sity Press, 1988 [1876]), 147–48; cited in D. W. Meinig, *The Shaping of America,* vol. 3, *Transcontinental America, 1850–1915* (New Haven, CT: Yale University Press, 1999), 225.

69. *Niles Weekly Register,* xxxv, January 17, 1829, 333; quoted in James R. Gibson Jr., *Americans Versus Malthus: The Population Debate in the Early Republic, 1790–1840* (New York: Garland, 1989), 169.

70. David Christy, *Cotton Is King: or, Slavery in the Light of Political Economy,* 3rd ed., in *Cotton Is King, and Pro-Slavery Arguments,* ed. E. N. Elliott (Augusta, GA: Pritchard, Abbot & Loomis, 1860), 71; quoted in Michael Hudson, *America's Protectionist Takeoff, 1815–1914: The Neglected American School of Political Economy* (Dresden, Germany: Michael Hudson/ISLET-Verlag, 2010), 47.

71. Dattel, *Cotton and Race in the Making of America,* 82.

72. Ronald Bailey, "The Slave(ry) Trade and the Development of Capitalism in the United States: The Textile Industry in New England," *Social Science History* 14, no. 3 (Autumn 1990): 373–414.

73. Quoted in Dattel, *Cotton and Race in the Making of America,* 88.

74. Ibid., 95–96.

CHAPTER 6: PLAIN MECHANIC POWER: THE CIVIL WAR AND THE SECOND REPUBLIC

1. Herman Melville, "A Utilitarian View of the Monitor's Fight," in *Battle Pieces and Aspects of the War* (New York: Harper Brothers, 1866).

2. William Faulkner, in *The Portable Faulkner,* ed. Malcolm Cowley (New York: Random House, 1985), 255.

3. *Southern Historical Society Papers,* new no. ser. 4, whole no. 44 (1923), 171; quoted in Rose Razaghian, "Financing the Civil War: The Confederacy's Financial Strategy" (working paper, Yale ICF No. 04–45 (New Haven, MA: Yale University, January 2005).

4. James Hammond, "On the Admission of Kansas, under the LeCompton Constitution" (speech, United States Senate, March 4, 1858), http://www.sewanee.edu/faculty/Willis/Civil_War/documents/HammondCotton.html (accessed December 8, 2011).

5. Harold G. Vatter, *The Drive to Industrial Maturity: The U.S. Economy, 1860–1914* (Westport, CT: Greenwood Press, 1975), 29.

6. Table 9.4, "Structure of Commodity Trade, 1851–1860," in Jonathan Hughes and Louis P. Cain, *American Economic History*, 5th ed. (New York: Addison-Wesley, 1998), 169.

7. Quoted in Gene Dattel, *Cotton and Race in the Making of America: The Human Costs of Economic Power* (Chicago: Ivan R. Dee, 2009), 169–75.

8. Alvy L. King and Louis T. Wigfall, *Southern Fire-Eater* (Baton Rouge: Louisiana State University Press, 1970), 126; cited in Gavin Wright, *Slavery and American Economic Development* (Baton Rouge: Louisiana State University Press, 2006), 82.

9. Quoted in Thomas B. Allen and Roger MacBride Allen, *Mr. Lincoln's High-Tech War: How the North Used the Telegraph, Railroads, Surveillance Balloons, Iron-Clads, High-Powered Weapons, and More to Win the Civil War* (Washington, DC: National Geographic, 2009), 69.

10. Jeffrey Rogers Hummel, "The Civil War and Reconstruction," in *Government and the American Economy: A New History*, ed. Price Fishback et al. (Chicago and London: University of Chicago Press, 2007), 200.

11. Barbara Freese, *Coal: A Human History* (New York: Penguin, 2003), 126.

12. Raimondo Luraghi, *The Rise and Fall of the Plantation South* (New York: New Viewpoints, 1978), 123–32.

13. Ibid., 138.

14. Hummel, "The Civil War and Reconstruction," 195.

15. Luraghi, *The Rise and Fall of the Plantation South*, 118–19.

16. Quoted in Robert V. Bruce, *Lincoln and the Tools of War* (Indianapolis: Bobbs-Merrill, 1956), 140.

17. David Herbert Donald, *Lincoln* (New York: Simon & Schuster, 1995), 432.

18. Ibid., 431.

19. William Henry Herndon and Jesse William Weik, *Herndon's Life of Lincoln*, ed. Paul M. Angle (Cleveland: World, 1942), 478.

20. Abraham Lincoln, "Address before the Wisconsin State Agricultural Society" (speech, Milwaukee, September 30, 1859), http://showcase.netins.net/web/creative/lincoln/speeches/fair.htm (accessed December 6, 2011).

21. Kevin Phillips, *The Cousins Wars* (New York: Basic Books, 1999), 458.

22. Herndon and Weik, *Herndon's Life of Lincoln*, 413.

23. Quoted in Lord Charnwood (Godfrey Rathbone Benson), *Abraham Lincoln* (Garden City, NY: Henry Holt and Company, 1917), p. 65–66.

24. Quoted in Allen Guelzo, *Abraham Lincoln: Redeemer President* (Grand Rapids, MI: Wm. B. Eerdmans, 1999), 384.

25. *Recollected Words of Abraham Lincoln*, ed. Don Fehrenbacher and Virginia Fehrenbacher (Stanford, CA: Stanford University Press, 1996), 37.

26. Edgar DeWitt Jones, *The Influence of Henry Clay upon Abraham Lincoln* (Lexington, KY: Henry Clay Memorial Foundation, 1952), 33–34.

27. Ibid., 36.

28. The *New York Times* is cited in Heather Cox Richardson, *The Greatest Nation on Earth: Republican Economic Policies during the Civil War* (Cambridge, MA: Harvard University Press, 1997), 94; the Indiana Democratic state committee is quoted in Allen C. Guelzo, "Mr. Lincoln's Economics Primer," National Review Online, February 12, 2011 (accessed December 15, 2011).

29. Guelzo, *Abraham Lincoln: Redeemer President*, 170.

30. Leonard P. Curry, *Blueprint for Modern America: Nonmilitary Legislation of the First Civil War Congress* (Nashville: Vanderbilt University Press, 1968), 116.

31. Ibid., 246–247.

32. Phillips, *The Cousins Wars*, 449.

33. Richard Franklin Bensel, *Yankee Leviathan: The Origins of Central State Authority in America, 1859–1877* (Cambridge, UK: Cambridge University Press, 1990), 252.

34. Abraham Lincoln, *The Writings of Abraham Lincoln* (Charleston, SC: Forgotten Books, 2008), 5:84.

35. M. R. Eiselen, *The Rise of Pennsylvania Protectionism* (Philadelphia: University of Pennsylvania Press, 1932), 7; cited in Paul Bairoch, *Economics and World History: Myths and Paradoxes* (Chicago: University of Chicago Press, 1993), 33.

36. Basler, *Lincoln*, vol. 1, 313.

37. Gabor Borit, "Old Wine into New Bottles: Abraham Lincoln and the Tariff Reconsidered," *The Historian* 28, no. 2 (1966): 309.

38. Reinhard H. Luthin, "Abraham Lincoln and the Tariff," *American Historical Review* 49, no. 4 (July 1944): 617.

39. Letter to Noah Swayne, enclosed as copy in Swayne to Carey, February 4, 1865, Carey Papers, box 78; cited in Luthin, "Abraham Lincoln and the Tariff," 629.

40. Luthin, "Abraham Lincoln and the Tariff," 619.

41. Bairoch, *Economics and World History*, 35.

42. Quoted in Ha-Joon Chang, "Kicking Away the Ladder: Infant Industry Protection in Historical Perspective," *Oxford Development Studies* 31, no. 1 (2003): 205–26.

43. Alfred E. Eckes, *Opening America's Market: U.S. Foreign Trade Policy Since 1776* (Chapel Hill: University of North Carolina Press, 1995), 30.

44. Frank W. Taussig, *Some Aspects of the Tariff Question* (Cambridge, MA: Harvard University Press, 1918), 118.

45. Steven A. Sass, "Community and Academic Economists at the University of Pennsylvania," in *Economists and Higher Learning in the Nineteenth Century*, ed. William J. Barber (New Brunswick, NJ: Transaction, 1993), 227.

46. Steven A. Sass and Barbara Copperman, "Joseph Wharton's Argument for Protection," http://www.h-net.org (accessed November 1, 2011).

47. Sass, "Community and Academic Economists," 227.

48. Ibid., 227–28.

49. Ibid., 230–31.

50. Quoted in Robert P. Sharkey, *Money, Class, and Party: An Economic Study of Civil War and Reconstruction* (Baltimore: Johns Hopkins University Press, 1959), 289.

51. Sharkey, *Money, Class, and Party*, 122–23.

52. Bensel, *Yankee Leviathan*, 311–12.

53. Sharkey, *Money, Class, and Party*, 149–52. See also David A. Wells, *The Recent Financial, Industrial, and Commercial Experiences of the United*

States: A Curious Chapter in Politico-Economic History (New York: J. H. and C. M. Goodsell, 1872), 25.

CHAPTER 7: THE IRON HORSE AND THE LIGHTNING

1. Abraham Lincoln, "Second Lecture on Discoveries and Inventions," in *The Collected Works of Abraham Lincoln*, ed. Roy P. Basler (New Brunswick, NJ: Rutgers University Press, 1953), 3:356–63.

2. Richard Franklin Bensel, *The Political Economy of American Industrialization, 1877–1900* (Cambridge, UK: Cambridge University Press, 2000), 295.

3. Alfred D. Chandler Jr., *The Visible Hand: The Managerial Revolution in American Business* (Cambridge, MA: Harvard University Press, 1977), 90.

4. Robert D. Atkinson, *The Past and Future of America's Economy: Long Waves of Innovation That Power Cycles of Growth* (Cheltenham, UK: Edward Elgar, 2004), 23.

5. Frank Dobbin, *Forging Industrial Policy: The United States, Britain, and France in the Railroad Age* (Cambridge, UK: Cambridge University Press, 1994), 91.

6. Alasdair Nairn, *Engines That Move Markets: Technology Investing from Railroads to the Internet and Beyond* (New York: John Wiley, 2002), 63.

7. Herbert Hovenkamp, *Enterprise and American Law, 1836–1937* (Cambridge, MA: Harvard University Press, 1991), 148.

8. Dobbin, *Forging Industrial Policy*, 86.

9. Joan Robinson, *The Economics of Imperfect Competition* (London: Macmillan, 1933); Edward Chamberlain, *The Theory of Monopolistic Competition* (Cambridge, MA: Harvard University Press, 1933).

10. James Buchanan, Second Annual Message to Congress on the State of the Union, December 6, 1858, quoted in Dobbin, *Forging Industrial Policy*, 51.

11. Dobbin, *Forging Industrial Policy*, 51.

12. Ibid., 54.

13. Ibid., 55.

14. Bill Frezza, "Infrastructure Follies: Railroads, Cleantech, and Crony Capitalism," *Forbes*, September 13, 2011.

15. Michael P. Malone, *James J. Hill: Empire Builder of the Northwest* (Norman: University of Oklahoma Press, 1996), 33.

16. Charles F. Adams Jr. et al., *Chapters of Erie, and Other Essays* (Boston: James R. Osgood, 1871), 10.

17. Bouck White, *The Book of Daniel Drew* (Garden City, NY: Doubleday, 1937), 309–10; Irvin G. Wyllie, "Social Darwinism and the Businessman," *Proceedings of the American Philosophical Society* 103, no. 5 (October 1959): 633.

18. John F. Stover, *American Railroads*, 2nd ed. (Chicago: University of Chicago Press, 1997), 103–104.

19. Ronald Campbell, "Jim Fisk, or He Never Went Back on the Poor," *The Hand That Holds the Bread: Progress and Protest in the Gilded Age. Songs from the Civil War to the Columbian Exposition,* Anthology of Recorded Music, Inc., 1997.

20. Nairn, *Engines That Move Markets*, 69–73.

21. Matthew Josephson, *The Robber Barons: The Great American Capitalists, 1861–1901* (New Brunswick, NJ: Transaction, 2011), 284.

22. Ron Chernow, *Titan: The Life of John D. Rockefeller, Sr.* (New York: Random House, 1998), 132.

23. Andrew Carnegie, *The Autobiography of Andrew Carnegie* (FQ Classics, 2007), 174.

24. Peter Temin, *Iron and Steel in the Nineteenth Century* (Cambridge, MA: MIT Press, 1964), 113.

25. Quoted in Samuel E. Morison and Henry S. Commager, *The Growth of the American Republic* (New York: Oxford University Press, 1950), 2:133.

26. David Lewis Cohn, *The Good Old Days: A History of American Morals and Manners as Seen through the Sears Roebuck Catalog* (New York: Simon & Schuster, 1940).

27. Ellis Paxson Oberholtzer, *Jay Cooke: Financier of the Civil War* (Philadelphia: George W. Jacobs, 1907), 2:448–449.

28. Charles W. Calomiris, *U.S. Bank Deregulation in Historical Perspective* (New York: Cambridge University Press, 2000), 3–4.

29. Ibid., 291.

30. Gary Gorton and Lixin Huang, "Panics, Bank Coalitions, and the Origin of Central Banking" (working paper, University of Pennsylvania, May 11, 2011): 7.

31. Calomiris, *U.S. Bank Deregulation in Historical Perspective*, 18.

32. Ibid.

33. Ibid., 39–40.

34. Angus Maddison, *Monitoring the World Economy, 1820–1992* (Paris: Organization for Economic Cooperation and Development, 1995).

35. "Part Two: The Industrial City: Introduction," in *The Making of Urban America*, ed. Raymond A. Mohl (Wilmington, DE: Scholarly Resources, 1997), 94.

36. Quoted in *American Immigration*, vol. 2, *Ellis Island: Gateway to America* (Danbury, CT: Grolier Educational, 1999), 89.

37. Werner Sollors, "From the Bottom Up: Foreword by Werner Sollors," in *The Life Stories of Undistinguished Americans, As Told by Themselves*, ed. Hamilton Holt (New York: Routledge, 1990), xxi.

38. Leo Wolff, *Lockout: The Story of the Homestead Strike of 1892: A Study of Violence, Unionism, and the Carnegie Steel Empire* (London: Longmans, 1965), 18.

39. Quoted in *American Immigration*, vol. 2, *Ellis Island*, 37.

40. Sollors, *The Life Stories of Undistinguished Americans*, 37.

41. Ibid., 86.

42. Ibid., 45.

43. Ibid., 50.

44. Ibid., 50 and 54.

45. Kevin O'Rourke, Jeffrey Williamson, and Timothy Hamilton, "Mass Migration, Commodity Market Integration, and Real Wage Convergence," in *Migration and the International Labor Market, 1850–1939*, ed. Tim Hatton and Jeffrey Williamson (New York: Routledge, 1994).

46. United States Immigration Commission, *Abstracts of Reports of the Immigration Commission*, (Washington, DC: US Government Printing Office, 1911), 1:531; cited in David M. Gordon, Richard Edwards, and Michael Reich, *Segmented Work, Divided Workers: The Historical Transformation of Labor in*

the United States (Cambridge, UK: Cambridge University Press, 1982), 141; Michael Perelman, *Railroading Economics: The Creation of the Free Market Mythology* (New York: Monthly Review Press, 2006), 134.

47. James Howard Bridge, *The Inside History of the Carnegie Steel Company: A Romance of Millions* (New York: Arno Press, 1972), 81.

48. Lawrence B. Glickman, *A Living Wage* (Ithaca, NY: Cornell University Press, 1997), 87.

49. Ibid.

50. Colleen A. Dunlavy and Thomas Welskopp, "Myths and Peculiarities: Comparing U.S. and German Capitalism," *GHI Bulletin*, no. 41 (Fall 2007): 40.

51. Wolff, *Lockout*, 14.

52. Quoted in Ronald Shillingford, *The History of the World's Greatest Entrepreneurs* (The History of the World's Greatest, 2010), 141.

53. "Eugene Victor Debs: Political Activist," Debs Foundation Web site, http://debsfoundation.org/politicalactivist.html (accessed December 8, 2011).

54. Because the Judiciary Committee rejected Sherman's and other amendments, some scholars have argued that Congress indeed considered and rejected the exemption of labor unions from the provisions of the act. But it is doubtful that this was the understanding of the members of the Senate. See *Loewe v. Lawlor*, 208 US 274, 301 (1908); Edward Berman, *Labor and the Sherman Act* (New York: Russell & Russell, 1930), 11–51; James A. Emery, "Labor Organization and the Sherman Law," *Journal of Political Economy* 20, no. 6 (June 1912): 599, 604–6; Hovenkamp, *Enterprise and American Law, 1836–1937*, 229.

55. Hovenkamp, *Enterprise and American Law, 1836–1937*, 238.

56. Richard Franklin Bensel, *Yankee Leviathan: The Origins of Central State Authority in America, 1859–1877* (Cambridge, UK: Cambridge University Press, 1991); Bensel, *The Political Economy of American Industrialization, 1877–1900*.

57. Kevin Phillips, *The Cousins Wars* (New York: Basic Books, 1999), 458.

58. Ibid.

59. Henry Grady, "Address to the Bay State Club of Boston" (speech, Boston, MA, 1889), http://historymatters.gmu.edu/d/5745/ (accessed December 8, 2011).

60. Douglas A. Blackmon, *Slavery by Another Name* (New York: Random House, 2008), 358.

61. Sollors, *The Life Stories of Undistinguished Americans*, 118.

62. Ibid., 120–21.

63. Blackmon, *Slavery by Another Name*, 375.

64. "First Biennial Report of the Board of Inspectors of Convicts, September 1, 1894, to August 31, 1896" (Montgomery, AL: Roemer Printing, 1896), Alabama Department of Archives and History, quoted in Blackmon, *Slavery by Another Name*, 57.

65. R. Douglas Hurt, *American Agriculture: A Brief History*, rev. ed. (West Lafayette, IN: Purdue University Press, 2002), 188–89.

66. C. F. Emerick, "An Analysis of Agricultural Discontent in the United States, Part 1," *Political Science Quarterly* 11, no. 3 (September 1896): 456; quoted in Jack Beatty, *Age of Betrayal: The Triumph of Money in America, 1865–1900* (New York: Random House, 2008), 105.

67. "People's Party Platform," *Omaha Morning World-Herald*, July 5, 1892, http://www.wwnorton.com/college/history/eamerica/media/ch22/resources/documents/populist.htm (accessed November 1, 2011).

68. The *Atlanta Constitution*, July 10, 1896; quoted in Richard Franklin Bensel, *Passion and Preferences: William Jennings Bryan and the 1896 Democratic Convention* (Cambridge, UK: Cambridge University Press, 2008), 1.

69. Henry Adams, *The Education of Henry Adams* (Boston and New York: Houghton Mifflin, 1905), 344.

70. Vachel Lindsay, "Bryan, Bryan, Bryan, Bryan," in *The Golden Whales of California, and Other Rhymes in the American Lang*uage (New York: Macmillan, 1920), 28.

71. John Milton Cooper Jr., *Woodrow Wilson: A Biography* (New York: Alfred A. Knopf, 2009), 87.

72. Kevin Phillips, *William McKinley* (New York: Henry Holt, 2003), 126.

73. Edmund Morris, *The Rise of Theodore Roosevelt* (New York: Modern Library, 1979), 568.

74. Quoted in Bensel, *Passion and Preferences*, 227–28.

75. *The Annals of America,* vol. 12, *1895–1904: Populism, Imperialism, and Reform* (Chicago: Encyclopedia Britannica, 1968), 100–105.

76. Canton Repository, April 14, 1892; quoted in William H. Armstrong, *Major McKinley: William McKinley and the Civil War* (Kent, OH: Kent State University Press, 2000), 119.

77. Armstrong, *Major McKinley*, 133.

78. Franklin Delano Roosevelt, "Commonwealth Club Campaign Speech," in Peter Augustine Lawler and Robert Martin Schaefer, eds., *American Political Rhetoric*, 6th ed. (Lanham, MD: Rowman & Littlefield, 2010), 169–176.

CHAPTER 8: FRANKLIN'S BABY: ELECTRICITY, AUTOMOBILES, AND THE SECOND INDUSTRIAL REVOLUTION

1. Alfred North Whitehead, *Science and the Modern World* (Cambridge, UK: Cambridge University Press, 1926), 120.

2. Quoted in H. W. Brands, *The First American: The Life and Times of Benjamin Franklin* (New York: Doubleday, 2000), 202.

3. Jill Jonnes, *Empires of Light: Edison, Tesla, Westinghouse, and the Race to Electrify the World* (New York: Random House, 2003), 27–28.

4. This account follows Richard G. Lipsey, Kenneth I. Carlaw, and Clifford T. Bekar, *Economic Transformations: General Purpose Technologies and Long Term Economic Growth* (New York: Oxford University Press, 2005), 254–55.

5. Henry Adams, *The Education of Henry Adams* (Boston and New York: Houghton Mifflin, 2000), 380.

6. Seymour L. Chapin, "A Legendary Bon Mot? Franklin's 'What Is the Good of a Newborn Baby?'" *Proceedings of the American Philosophical Society* 129, no. 3 (1985): 278–90.

7. Quoted in Bence Jones, *Life and Letters of Michael Faraday*, vol. 1 (London: Spottiswoode, 1879), 218; Bernard Cohen, "Faraday and Franklin's

'Newborn Baby,'" *Proceedings of the American Philosophical Society* 131, no. 2 (June 1987): 35.

8. Joel Mokyr, "The Second Industrial Revolution, 1870–1914" (working paper, Northwestern University, August 1998), 1.

9. Gary Cross and Rick Szostak, *Technology and American Society: A History* (Englewood Cliffs, NJ: Prentice-Hall, 1995), 164.

10. John T. Ratzlaff, ed., *Tesla Said* (Millbrae, CA: Tesla Book Company, 1984), 280; Jonnes, *Empires of Light*, 105.

11. Cross and Szostak, *Technology and American Society*, 166.

12. Mary Bellis, "The History of Fluorescent Lights," About.com, "Inventors," inventors.about.com, accessed December 30, 2011.

13. Quoted in Jonnes, *Empires of Light*, 178.

14. Vaclav Smil, *Energies: An Illustrated Guide to the Biosphere and Civilization* (Cambridge, MA: MIT Press, 2000), 157.

15. R. F. Hirsh, *Technology and Transformation in the American Electric Utility Industry* (Cambridge, UK: Cambridge University Press, 1989), 20–21.

16. Smil, *Energies*, 151.

17. Barbara Freese, *Coal: A Human History* (New York: Penguin, 2003), 137.

18. Smil, *Energies*, 140.

19. Holland Thompson, *The Age of Invention: A Chronicle of Mechanical Conquest* (New Haven, CT: Yale University Press, 1921), 59 and 61.

20. Mokyr, "The Second Industrial Revolution, 1870–1914," 5.

21. Ibid., 4–5.

22. Ibid., 11.

23. Louis Ferleger and William Lazonick, "The Managerial Revolution and the Developmental State: The Case of U.S. Agriculture," *Business and Economic History* 22, no. 2 (Winter 1993): 78.

24. Ibid., 73.

25. Table 3.1, "Estimated Government Expenditures on Aviation, 1908–1913," in Vernon W. Ruttan, *Is War Necessary for Economic Growth? Military Procurement and Technology Development* (New York: Oxford University Press, 2006), 39.

26. Ibid., 33.

27. Ibid., 38.

28. Ibid., 42–43.

29. Peter J. Hugill, *Global Communications Since 1844: Geopolitics and Technology* (Baltimore: Johns Hopkins University Press, 1999), 226.

30. Cross and Szostak, *Technology and American Society*, 266.

31. James E. Vance, *The Continuing City* (Baltimore: Johns Hopkins University Press, 1990), 384.

32. Ibid., 386–87.

33. Ibid., 469.

34. Ibid., 374–76.

35. Ibid., 473.

36. Bruce Bliven Jr., *The Wonderful Writing Machine* (New York: Random House, 1954), 62.

CHAPTER 9: THE DAY OF COMBINATION

1. Henry Adams, *The Education of Henry Adams* (Boston and New York: Houghton Mifflin, 2000), 344.

2. Allan Nevins, *John D. Rockefeller* (New York: Charles Scribner's Sons, 1959), 1:622.

3. John Bates Clark, *The Control of Trusts* (New York: Macmillan, 1901), 17; quoted in Walter Adams and James W. Brock, *The Bigness Complex: Industry, Labor, and Government in the American Economy* (New York: Pantheon Books, 1986), 25.

4. Adolf A. Berle and Gardner C. Means, *The Modern Corporation and Private Property*, rev. ed. (New York: Harcourt, Brace & World, 1932), 34.

5. Nevins, *John D. Rockefeller*, 1:622nii.

6. Jean Strouse, *Morgan: American Financier* (New York: HarperCollins, 1999), 310.

7. Sanford Gordon, "The Significance of Public Opinion in the Passage of the Sherman Act" (PhD diss., New York University, 1953).

8. Richard T. Ely, "The Nature and Significance of Corporations," *Harper's Magazine* 75 (June/November 1887): 71 and 75; quoted in William L.

Letwin, "Congress and the Sherman Antitrust Law: 1887–1890," *University of Chicago Law Review* 23, no. 2 (Winter 1956): 238.

9. David Ames Wells, *Recent Economic Changes* (New York: D. Appleton, 1889), 74; quoted in Letwin, "Congress and the Sherman Antitrust Law: 1887–1890," 237.

10. Wells, *Recent Economic Changes*, 74–75.

11. John Bates Clark, "The Limits of Competition," reprinted in John Bates Clark and Franklin H. Giddings, *The Modern Distributive Process* (Boston: Ginn, 1888), 11; quoted in Letwin, "Congress and the Sherman Antitrust Law: 1887–1890," 238.

12. Naomi R. Lamoreaux, *The Great Merger Movement in American Business, 1895–1904* (Cambridge, UK: Cambridge University Press, 1985), 1.

13. Ibid., 2.

14. Table 1.2, "Market Shares of Consolidations," in ibid., 3–4.

15. Adams and Brock, *The Bigness Complex*, 25–27.

16. Moody is quoted in Louis D. Brandeis, *Other People's Money and How the Bankers Use It*, ed. Richard Abrams (New York: Frederick A. Stokes, 1914), vii–xvi.

17. Alfred D. Chandler Jr., *Scale and Scope: The Dynamics of Industrial Capitalism* (Cambridge, MA: Belknap Press of Harvard University Press, 1990), 128–29.

18. John F. Stover, *American Railroads*, 2nd ed. (Chicago: University of Chicago Press, 1997), 93; David Mark Chalmers, *Neither Socialism nor Monopoly: Theodore Roosevelt and the Decision to Regulate the Railroads* (New York: Lippencott, 1976), 1.; Frank Dobbin, *Forging Industrial Policy: The United States, Britain, and France in the Railroad Age* (Cambridge, UK: Cambridge University Press, 1994), 90.

19. Charles W. Calomiris, *U.S. Bank Deregulation in Historical Perspective* (New York: Cambridge University Press, 2000), 244–45.

20. Charles W. Calomiris, "Universal Banking and the Financing of Industrial Development" (policy research working paper 1533, World Bank, Washington, DC, 1995), 7.

21. Miguel Cantillo Simon, "The Rise and Fall of Bank Control in the United States: 1890–1939," *American Economic Review* 88, no. 5 (December 1998): 1081–82.

22. John Steel Gordon, "The Magnitude of J. P. Morgan," *American Heritage* (July–August 1989).

23. J. Bradford De Long, "What Morgan Wrought," *Wilson Quarterly* 16, no. 4 (August 1992): 22.

24. Chandler, *Scale and Scope*, 21–23; Thomas K. McCraw, "Rethinking the Trust Question," in *Regulation in Perspective*, ed. Thomas K. McCraw (Cambridge, MA: Harvard University Press, 1981), 1–55; cited in Strouse, *Morgan*, 315–16, footnote.

25. De Long, "What Morgan Wrought," 24.

26. Henry George, *A Perplexed Philosopher* (New York: Charles Webster, 1892), 164; quoted in Sidney Fine, *Laissez Faire and the General-Welfare State: A Study of Conflict in American Thought, 1865–1901* (Ann Arbor: University of Michigan Press, 1978), 44.

27. See Chapter 1, note 15, supra.

28. Henry Carter Adams, "Relation of the State to Industrial Action," *Publications of the American Economic Association* 1, no. 6 (January 1887): 64; quoted in Letwin, "Congress and the Sherman Antitrust Law: 1887–1890," 239.

29. Herbert Croly, *The Promise of American Life* (New York: Macmillan, 1914), 362.

30. Quoted in Doug Henwood, "Old Livernose and the Plungers: J. Pierpont Morgan and T. Boone Pickens," *Grand Street* 7, no. 1: 183.

31. Matthew Josephson, *The Robber Barons: The Great American Capitalists, 1861–1901* (New York: Harcourt, Brace, 1934), 448.

32. Theodore Roosevelt, "Second Annual Message to Congress," speech, Washington, DC, 1902, http://millercenter.org/president/speeches/detail/3774 (accessed November 2, 2011).

33. Theodore Roosevelt, "The New Nationalism" (speech, Osawatomie, Kansas, August 13, 1910), http://teachingamericanhistory.org/library/index.asp?document=501 (accessed December 8, 2011).

34. Quoted in Strouse, *Morgan*, 439–40.

35. Bob Batchelor, *The 1900s* (Westport, CT: Greenwood, 2002), 18.

36. *Congressional Record* 43 (1909), pt. 2, 1395; quoted in Lamoreaux, *The Great Merger Movement*, 173.

37. Woodrow Wilson, "The Puritan" (December 22, 1900), in *The Papers of Woodrow Wilson*, ed. Arthur S. Link (Princeton, NJ: Princeton University Press, 1966–1994), 1:365.

38. Woodrow Wilson, "Law or Personal Power" (address delivered before the National Democratic Club, New York, April 13, 1908), in *The Papers of Woodrow Wilson*, 2:30–31.

39. Woodrow Wilson, "What Jefferson Would Do," in *The Papers of Woodrow Wilson*, 2:424.

40. Woodrow Wilson, "The Tariff and the Trusts" (February 24, 1912), *The Papers of Woodrow Wilson*, 2:410–11.

41. Woodrow Wilson, "Acceptance Address" (Seagirt, NJ, April 7, 1912, Official Report of the Democratic National Committee), 407; quoted in Martin J. Sklar, *The Corporate Reconstruction of American Capitalism, 1890–1916: The Market, the Law, and Politics* (Cambridge, UK: Cambridge University Press, 1988), 419.

42. Quoted in Thomas McCraw, *Prophets of Regulation: Charles Francis Adams, Louis D. Brandeis, James M. Landis, Alfred Kahn* (Cambridge, MA: Harvard University Press, 1984), 108.

43. Brandeis, *Other People's Money*, 4–5.

44. Charles Francis Adams, Statement of December 15, 1884, 4 *Ry & Corp. L.J.* 579 (1888); quoted in Letwin, "Congress and the Sherman Antitrust Law: 1887–1890," 223.

45. Ida Tarbell, *All in the Day's Work* (New York: Macmillan, 1939), 364; quoted in Strouse, *Morgan*, 622.

46. Brandeis, *Other People's Money*, 51.

47. Quoted in Ron Chernow, *Titan: The Life of John D. Rockefeller, Sr.* (New York: Random House, 1998), 541.

CHAPTER 10: THE NEW ERA

1. Herbert Hoover, *Nation's Business*, June 5, 1924, 7–8; quoted in Butler Shaffer, *In Restraint of Trade: The Business Campaign Against Competition, 1918–1938* (Cranbury, NJ: Associated University Presses, 1997), 52.

2. Gary Cross and Rick Szostak, *Technology and American Society: A History* (Englewood Cliffs, NJ: Prentice-Hall, 1995), 194.

3. Marc Allen Eisner, *From Warfare State to Welfare State: World War I, Compensatory State Building, and the Limits of the Modern Order* (University Park: Pennsylvania State University Press, 2000), 60.

4. Ibid.

5. Paul A. C. Koistinen, *Mobilizing for Modern War: The Political Economy of American Warfare, 1865–1919* (Lawrence: University Press of Kansas, 1997), 116.

6. Eisner, *From Warfare State to Welfare State*, 52.

7. Koistinen, *Mobilizing for Modern War*, 121.

8. Jeff Frieden, "Sectoral Conflict and Foreign Economic Policy, 1914–1940," *International Organization* 42, no. 1 (Winter 1988): 71.

9. F. Carrington Weems, *America and Munitions: The Works of Messrs. J. P. Morgan & Co. in the World War* (New York: Privately printed, 1923), 268; quoted in Koistinen, *Mobilizing for Modern War*, 115.

10. Table 6.2, "The Financing of World War I, World War II, and the Korean War (Billions of Dollars)," in Michael Edelstein, "War and the American Economy in the Twentieth Century," in *The Cambridge Economic History of the United States*, ed. Stanley L. Engermann and Robert E. Gallman (Cambridge, UK: Cambridge University Press), 3:351.

11. Koistinen, *Mobilizing for Modern War*, 264.

12. Ibid., 265.

13. Eisner, *From Warfare State to Welfare State*, 55.

14. Edmund M. Coffman, *The War to End All Wars: The American Military Experience in World War I* (Lexington: University Press of Kentucky, 1967), 15.

15. Koistinen, *Mobilizing for Modern War*, 211.

16. Eisner, *From Warfare State to Welfare State*, 65.

17. Koistinen, *Mobilizing for Modern War*, 212.

18. Eisner, *From Warfare State to Welfare State*, 73.

19. Koistinen, *Mobilizing for Modern War*, 262.

20. Eisner, *From Warfare State to Welfare State*, 68.

21. "Herbert Hoover," The White House, www.whitehouse.gov (accessed November 1, 2011).

22. Koistinen, *Mobilizing for Modern War*, 281–85.

23. Eisner, *From Warfare State to Welfare State*, 81.

24. Bernard Baruch, *American Industry in the War* (New York: Prentice-Hall, 1941), 104.

25. Koistinen, *Mobilizing for Modern War*, 279.

26. Eric F. Goldman, *Rendezvous with Destiny: A History of Modern American Reform* (New York: Alfred A. Knopf, 1958), 307–308, quoted in Eisner, *From Warfare State to Welfare State*, 90.

27. Daniel Yergin, *The Quest: Energy, Security, and the Remaking of the Modern World* (New York: Penguin, 2011), 675.

28. Cross and Szostak, *Technology and American Society*, 234.

29. Ton Korver, *The Fictitious Commodity: A Study of the U.S. Labor Market, 1880–1940* (New York: Greenwood Press, 1990), 108.

30. Edward J. Taaffe, Howard L. Gauthier, and Morton E. O'Kelley, *Geography of Transportation* (Upper Saddle River, NJ: Prentice-Hall, 1973), 176.

31. Cross and Szostak, *Technology and American Society*, 235.

32. Yergin, *The Quest*, 674.

33. Quoted in David A. Hounshell, *From the American System to Mass Production, 1800–1932: The Development of Manufacturing Technology in the United States* (Baltimore and London: Johns Hopkins University Press, 1984), 1.

34. Henry Ford, "Mass Production," *Encyclopaedia Britannica* (1926).

35. Yergin, *The Quest*, 234.

36. Ibid., 345.

37. Thomas Parke Hughes, *American Genesis: A Century of Invention and Technological Evolution, 1870–1970* (Chicago: University of Chicago Press, 2004), 230.

38. Bob Ortega, *In Sam We Trust: The Untold Story of Sam Walton and How Wal-Mart Is Devouring the World* (New York: Random House, 1998), 39.

39. Peter Fearon, *The Origins and Nature of the Great Slump, 1929–1932* (London and Basingstoke, UK: Macmillan, 1979), 29.

40. R. I. Nelson, *Merger Movements in American History, 1895–1956* (Princeton, NJ: Princeton University Press, 1959), 94.

41. Adolf A. Berle and Gardiner C. Means, *The Modern Corporation and Private Property* (New York: Harcourt, Brace & World, 1932), 56; William Lazonick and Mary O'Sullivan, "Finance and Industrial Development, Part I: The United States and the United Kingdom," *Financial History Review* 4 (1997): 7–29.

42. Ellis W. Hawley, "Herbert Hoover, the Commerce Secretariat, and the Vision of an 'Associative State,' 1921–28," *Journal of American History* 61, no. 1 (June 1974): 128.

43. Ibid., 129.

44. Oswald Garrison Villard, "Presidential Possibilities: Herbert C. Hoover," *The Nation*, February 29, 1928, 235.

45. William Edward Leuchtenberg, *Herbert Hoover* (New York: Henry Holt, 2009), 148.

46. Ibid., 82.

47. Herbert Hoover, *American Individualism* (New York: Doubleday, Page, 1923), 11.

48. Herbert Clark Hoover, *The Memoirs of Herbert Hoover: The Cabinet and the Presidency, 1920–1933* (New York: Macmillan, 1952), 2:108.

49. Hawley, "Herbert Hoover," 132.

50. Eugene Lyons, *Our Unknown Ex-President: A Portrait of Herbert Hoover* (Garden City, NY: Doubleday, 1948), 231.

51. Hawley, "Herbert Hoover," 118n7.

52. Frederic M. Scherer, "International Competition Policy and Economic Development," Discussion Paper no. 96–26, Zentrum für Europäische Wirtschaftsforschung, Industrial Economics and International Management Series, 9. See also Frederic M. Scherer, *Competition Policies for*

an Integrated World Economy (Washington, DC: Brookings Institution, 1994).

53. Andrew R. Dick, "When Are Cartels Stable Contracts?" *Journal of Law Economics* 39, no. 1 (April 1996): 246–47.

54. Ibid., 246.

55. Ibid., 249.

56. Wyatt Wells, *Antitrust and the Formation of the Postwar World* (New York: Columbia University Press, 2002), 20–21.

57. Vernon M. Briggs, *Immigration and American Unionism* (Ithaca, NY: Cornell University Press, 2001), 97.

58. Harry A. Millis and Royal E. Montgomery, *Labor's Progress and Some Basic Labor Problems* (New York: McGraw-Hill, 1938), 31.

59. Stanley Lebergott, *Manpower in Economic Growth: The American Record Since 1800* (New York: McGraw-Hill, 1964), 27.

60. Frank Stricker, "Affluence for Whom? Another Look at Prosperity and the Working Class in the 1920s," in *The Labor History Reader*, ed. Daniel J. Leab (Urbana and Chicago: University of Illinois, 1985), 76.

61. William E. Leuchtenberg, *The Perils of Prosperity: 1914–1932* (Chicago and London: University of Chicago Press, 1958), 179ff.

62. Cross and Szostak, *Technology and American Society*, 230.

63. Ibid., 230.

64. Gene Smiley, "The U.S. Economy in the 1920s," Economic History Services, http://eh.net/encyclopedia/article/smiley.1920s.final (accessed November 2, 2011).

65. Leuchtenberg, *The Perils of Prosperity*; Korver, *The Fictitious Commodity*, 96.

66. Robert P. Keller, "Factor Income Distribution in the United States during the 1920's: A Re-examination of Fact and Theory," *Journal of Economic History* 33, no. 1, *The Tasks of Economic History* (March 1973): 252–73.

67. Leuchtenberg, *The Perils of Prosperity*, 193.

68. Stricker, "Affluence for Whom?," 296, graph 1; Korver, *The Fictitious Commodity*, 125.

69. Charles F. Holt, "Who Benefited from the Prosperity of the Twenties?" *Explorations in Economic History* 14, no. 3 (Summer 1977): 277–89.

70. Fearon, *The Origins and Nature of the Great Slump*, 34.

71. Table 13, "Percent Distribution of the World's Manufacturing Production, 1913–38," in A. G. Kenwood and A. L. Lougheed, *The Growth of the International Economy, 1820–1980* (London: Allen & Unwin, 1983), 183.

72. James D. Richardson, ed., *Messages and Papers of the Presidents* (Washington, DC: US Government Printing Office, 1896–99), 6403; quoted in Alfred E. Eckes Jr., *Opening America's Market* (Chapel Hill: University of North Carolina Press, 1995), 77–78.

73. *Congressional Record* 35, pts. 3–5, 57th Cong., 1st Sess. (27 February 1902), 2201–2202.

74. Paul Bairoch, "International Industrialization Levels, 1750–1980," *Journal of European Economic History* 11 (1982): 292, 299.

75. Herman Schwartz, "Hegemony, International Debt, and International Economic Instability," in Chronis Polychroniu, ed., *Perspectives and Issues in International Political Economy* (New York: Praeger, 1992).

76. Jeff Frieden, "Sectoral Conflict and Foreign Economic Policy, 1914–1940," *International Organization* 42, no. 1, *The State and American Foreign Policy* (Winter 1998): 63–64.

77. Quoted in Mary Jane Maltz, *The Many Lives of Otto Kahn* (New York: Macmillan, 1963), 204; cited in Frieden, "Sectoral Conflict and Foreign Economic Policy."

78. Quoted in David Burner, *Herbert Hoover: A Public Life* (New York: Alfred A. Knopf, 1979), 186; cited in Frieden, "Sectoral Conflict and Foreign Economic Policy," 80.

79. Quoted in Dan P. Silverman, *Reconstructing Europe after the Great War* (Cambridge, MA: Harvard University Press, 1982), 239; Frieden, "Sectoral Conflict and Foreign Economic Policy, 1914–1940," 59–90.

80. Fred L. Israel, ed., *The State of the Union Messages of the Presidents* (New York: Chelsea House, 1967), 3:2693; quoted in Alfred E. Eckes Jr., *Opening America's Market* (Chapel Hill: University of North Carolina Press, 1995), 301n56.

81. Norman H. Davis, "Trade Barriers and Customs Duties," *Proceedings of the Academy of Political Science* 12, no. 4 (January 1928): 69–76; quoted in Jeffrey A. Frieden, *Banking on the World: The Politics of American International Finance* (New York: Harper & Row, 1987), 50.

CHAPTER 11: A NEW DEAL FOR AMERICA

1. Franklin Delano Roosevelt, Address at the Democratic State Convention, Syracuse, New York, September 29, 1936.

2. William E. Leuchtenberg, *Herbert Hoover* (New York: Henry Holt, 2009), 129. On the 1929 crash and what led up to it, see John Kenneth Galbraith, *The Great Crash 1929*, 50th anniversary edition (New York: Houghton Mifflin, 1988); Liaquat Ahamed, *Lords of Finance: The Bankers Who Broke the World* (New York: Penguin, 2009).

3. Jude Wanniski, *The Way the World Works* (New York: Basic Books, 1978), 125.

4. Richard N. Cooper, "Trade Policy as Foreign Policy," in *U.S. Trade Policies in a Changing World Economy,* ed. Robert M. Stern (Cambridge, MA: MIT Press, 1987), 291–92.

5. Alfred E. Eckes Jr., *Opening America's Market* (Chapel Hill: University of North Carolina Press, 1995), 108.

6. Peter Temin, *Lessons from the Great Depression* (Cambridge, MA: MIT Press, 1989), 46.

7. See Gertrud M. Fremling, "Did the United States Transmit the Great Depression to the Rest of the World?" *American Economic Review* 75, no. 5 (December 1985): 1181–85; Ian Fletcher, "Protectionism Didn't Cause the Great Depression," *Huffington Post*, April 6, 2010.

8. Barry Eichengreen, "The Political Economy of the Smoot-Hawley Tariff," in *Research in Economic History*, ed. Roger L. Ransom (Greenwich, CT: JAI Press, 1989), 12:25–29.

9. Milton Friedman and Anna Jacobson Schwartz, *A Monetary History of the United States, 1867–1960* (Princeton, NJ: Princeton University Press, 1963).

10. For different interpretations of the Great Depression, see John Kenneth Galbraith, *The Great Crash: 1929* (Boston: Houghton Mifflin, 1954); Fried-

man and Schwartz, *A Monetary History of the United States*; Milton Friedman and Anna Jacobson Schwartz, *The Great Contraction 1929–1933* (Princeton: Princeton University Press, 1965); Peter Temin, *Did Monetary Forces Cause the Great Depression?* (New York: Norton, 1976); Barry J. Eichengreen, *Golden Feathers: The Gold Standard and the Great Depression* (New York: Oxford University Press, 1996); Liaquat Ahamed, *Lords of Finance: The Bankers Who Broke the World* (New York: Penguin Press, 2009).

11. William Trufant Foster and Waddill Catchings, *Profits* (Boston and New York: Houghton Mifflin, 1925); *Business Without a Buyer* (Boston: Houghton Mifflin, 1927); *The Road to Plenty* (Boston and New York: Houghton Mifflin, 1928); *Progress and Plenty* (Pollack Foundation for Economic Research, 1929); *Money* (Boston and New York: Houghton Mifflin, 1932).

12. Edward A. Filene, *Successful Living in This Machine Age* (New York: Simon & Schuster, 1932), 45.

13. Marriner Stoddard Eccles, *Beckoning Frontiers* (New York: Alfred A. Knopf, 1951), 77.

14. Donald J. Beaudreaux, *Globalization* (Westport, CT: Greenwood Press, 2008), 112.

15. Herbert Hoover, "Address Accepting the Republican Presidential Nomination" (speech, Washington, DC, August 11, 1932), http://americanhistory.about.com/library/docs/blhooverspeech1932.htm (accessed November 2, 2011).

16. Walter Lippmann, "The Permanent New Deal," *Yale Review* 24 (1935): 649–67.

17. Marc Allen Eisner, *From Warfare State to Welfare State: World War I, Compensatory State Building, and the Limits of the Modern Order* (University Park: Pennsylvania State University Press, 2000), 276.

18. Ibid.

19. Murray Newton Rothbard, *America's Great Depression* (Kansas City, KS: Sheed & Ward, 1975), 217; J. M. Clark, "Public Works and Unemployment," *American Economic Review*, Papers and Proceedings (May 1930), 15ff.

20. Eisner, *From Warfare State to Welfare State*, 278.

21. Rothbard, *America's Great Depression*, 243.

22. Ibid., 44.

23. Eisner, *From Warfare State to Welfare State*, 284; Gerald D. Nash, "Herbert Hoover and the Origins of the Reconstruction Finance Corporation," *Mississippi Valley Historical Review* 46, no. 3 (December 1959): 455–68.

24. William John Shultz and M. R. Caine, *Financial Development of the United States* (New York: Prentice-Hall, 1937), 656; Eisner, *From Warfare State to Welfare State*, 290.

25. Eisner, *From Warfare State to Welfare State*, 296.

26. Hoover memorandum quoted in William Starr Myers and Walter Hughes Newton, *The Hoover Administration: A Documented Narrative* (London: Charles Scribner's Sons, 1936), 119.

27. Quoted in Myers and Newton, *The Hoover Administration*, 249–50.

28. Roy F. Harrod, *The Life of John Maynard Keynes* (New York: Harcourt Brace, 1951), 437–48.

29. Paul Krugman, *The Return of Depression Economics and the Crisis of 2008* (New York: W. W. Norton, 2008).

30. Herbert Hoover, *The Memoirs of Herbert Hoover: The Great Depression, 1929–1941* (New York: Macmillan, 1952).

31. Quoted in Edward Angly, *Oh Yeah?* (New York: Viking, 1931), 22; Rothbard, *America's Great Depression*, 268.

32. Quoted in Paul Johnson, *A History of the American People* (New York: HarperCollins, 1998), 741.

33. Quoted in Diego Pizano, *Conversations with Great Economists: Friedrich A. Hayek, John Hicks, Nicholas Kaldor, Leonid V. Kantorovich, Joan Robinson, Paul A. Samuelson, Jan Tinbergen* (Mexico City: Jorge Pinto Books, 2008).

34. Rothbard, *America's Great Depression*, 308.

35. Henry C. Simons, *Economic Policy for a Free Society* (Chicago: University of Chicago Press, 1948), 75.

36. Quoted in Johnson, *A History of the American People*, 741; John Hoff Wilson, *Herbert Hoover: Forgotten Progressive* (Boston: Little Brown, 1974).

37. Daniel R. Fusfeld, *The Economic Thought of Franklin D. Roosevelt and the Origins of the New Deal* (New York: Columbia University Press, 1956), 267.

38. Herbert Hoover, "Address Accepting the Republican Presidential Nomination," http://americanhistory.about.com/library/docs/blhooverspeech1932 .htm (accessed November 2, 2011).

39. Leuchtenberg, *Herbert Hoover*, 134.

40. Quoted in Jordan A. Schwarz, *The Interregnum of Despair: Hoover, Congress, and the Depression* (Urbana: University of Illinois Press, 1970), 174.

41. Hoover, *The Memoirs of Herbert Hoover, 1929–1941*, vol. 3.

42. Thomas Ferguson, "From Normalcy to New Deal: Industrial Structure, Party Competition and American Public Policy During the Great Depression," *International Organization* 38, no. 1 (Winter 1984): 41–94; Thomas Ferguson, "Industrial Conflict and the Coming of the New Deal: The Triumph of Multinational Liberalism in America," in *The Rise and Fall of the New Deal Order, 1930–1980*, ed. Steve Fraser and Gary Gerstle (New York: Oxford University Press, 2007), 3–31.

43. Franklin Delano Roosevelt, First Inaugural Address, March 4, 1933, in Davis W. Houck, *FDR and Fear Itself: The First Inaugural Address* (College Station: Texas A&M University Press, 2002), 3–8.

44. William L. Silber, "Why Did FDR's Bank Holiday Succeed?" Federal Reserve Bank of New York, *Economic Policy Review* 15, no. 1 (July 2009): 19–30.

45. Charles W. Calomiris, *U.S. Bank Deregulation in Historical Perspective* (New York: Cambridge University Press, 2000), 175.

46. Franklin Delano Roosevelt, *Public Papers and Addresses of Franklin D. Roosevelt*, vol. 1, *The Genesis of the New Deal, 1928–32* (New York: Random House, 1938); quoted in Ronald Edsforth, *The New Deal: America's Response to the Great Depression* (Malden, MA: Blackwell, 2000), 57.

47. Arthur M. Schlesinger Jr., *The Age of Roosevelt*, vol. 2, *The Coming of the New Deal* (Boston: Houghton Mifflin, 1958), 96–98.

48. John Patrick Diggins, *Mussolini and Fascism: The View from America* (Princeton, NJ: Princeton University Press, 1972), 280.

49. Ibid., 279.

50. "Churchill Extols Fascismo for Italy," *New York Times*, January 21, 1927.

51. Ludwig von Mises, *Liberalism in the Classical Tradition*, 3rd ed. (Irvington-on-Hudson, NY, and San Francisco: Foundation for Economic Education and Cobden Press, 1985), 51.

52. Franklin D. Roosevelt, "The Forgotten Man" (speech, Albany, New York, April 7, 1932), in *Public Papers and Addresses of Franklin D. Roosevelt*, vol. 1, *The Year of Crisis 1933* (New York: Random House, 1938), 625.

53. Harold Laski, "The Roosevelt Experiment," *Atlantic*, February 1934.

54. Franklin D. Roosevelt: "Statement on Signing the National Industrial Recovery Act," June 16, 1933, American Presidency Project, http://www.presidency.ucsb.edu/ws/?pid=14669 (accessed October 5, 2011).

55. Harriman, quoted in the *New York Times*, July 25, 1933, 2.

56. *New York Times*, July 25, 1933, 2.

57. John Maynard Keynes, "An Open Letter to President Roosevelt," *New York Times*, December 31, 1933.

58. Arthur M. Schlesinger, *The Age of Roosevelt*, vol. 3, *The Politics of Upheaval* (Boston: Houghton Mifflin, 1958), 96–98, 404–406; quoted in Michael Janeway, *The Fall of the House of Roosevelt: Brokers of Ideas and Power from FDR to LBJ* (New York: Columbia University Press, 2004), 37.

59. Roosevelt, "The Forgotten Man," 625.

60. Quoted in Jordan A. Schwarz, *The Speculator: Bernard M. Baruch in Washington, 1917–1965* (Chapel Hill: University of North Carolina Press, 1981), 288.

61. Butler Shaffer, *In Restraint of Trade: The Business Campaign Against Competition, 1918–1938* (Cranbury, NJ: Associated University Presses, 1997), 234.

62. R. Alan Lawson, *A Commonwealth of Hope: The New Deal Response to Crisis* (Baltimore: Johns Hopkins University Press, 2006), 89.

63. Thomas G. Corcoran, "Rendezvous with Destiny," unpublished memoir, draft for "Law of Unintended Consequences" chapter, 9–10, Corcoran Papers, box 589, Library of Congress; quoted in Janeway, *The Fall of the House of Roosevelt*, 5. See also Schlesinger, *The Age of Roosevelt*, vol. 3, *The Politics of Upheaval*, 280.

64. Amity Shlaes, *The Forgotten Man: A New History of the Great Depression* (New York: HarperCollins, 2007).

65. "Arch Foes of NRA Vote for New Deal; All 16 Ballots in the Schechter Family Went to President Poultry Man Reveals," *New York Times*, November 4, 1936; quoted in Eric Rauchway, "Big Gonif, Redux," December 2, 2008, *The Edge of the American West* (blog), http://edgeofthewest .wordpress.com/2008/12/02/big-gonif-redux/ (accessed October 5, 2011).

66. Gerald Starr, *Minimum Wage Fixing* (Geneva: International Labor Organization, 1981), 4–5.

67. *Social Security Online*, Research Note # 23, "Luther Gulick Memorandum," www.socialsecurity.gov (accessed December 12, 2011).

68. Dale Russakoff, "In Second Coal Rush, New Mind-Set in the Mines," *Washington Post*, November 16, 2006.

69. Irving Bernstein, *The New Deal Collective Bargaining Policy* (Berkeley: University of California Press, 1950), 25–26.

70. Winifred D. Wandersee, "'I'd Rather Pass a Law Than Organize a Union': Frances Perkins and the Reformist Approach to Organized Labor." *Labor History*, 34.1 (1993): 5–32.

71. Eisner, *From Warfare State to Welfare State*, 333.

72. Quoted in Richard O. Boyer and Herbert Morais, *Labor's Untold Story*, 3rd ed. (New York: United Electrical, Radio, and Machine Workers of America [UE], 1980), 295.

73. Roosevelt to Edward Mandell House (November 21, 1933), quoted in *F.D.R.: His Personal Letters, 1928–1945,* ed. Elliott Roosevelt (New York: Duell, Sloan and Pearce, 1950), 373.

74. Frankin Delano Roosevelt, "Message to Congress on Curbing Monopolies" (speech, Washington, DC, April 29, 1938), http://www.presidency.ucsb.edu /ws/index.php?pid=15637#axzz1dirYhSso (accessed November 14, 2011).

75. Marc Allen Eisner, *Antitrust and the Triumph of Economics: Institutions, Expertise, and Policy Change* (Chapel Hill: University of North Carolina Press, 1991), 77–83.

76. Wyatt Wells, *Antitrust and the Formation of the Postwar World* (New York: Columbia University Press, 2002), 41–42.

77. Thurman Arnold, *Democracy and Free Enterprise* (Norman: University of Oklahoma Press, 1941), 37; quoted in Jordan A. Schwarz, *The New Dealers: Power Politics in the Age of Roosevelt* (New York: Knopf, 1993), xi; Janeway, *The Fall of the House of Roosevelt*, 37.

78. Quoted in Gaudi B. Eggertsson et al., *The Mistake of 1937: A General Equilibrium Analysis* (Institute of Monetary and Economic Studies, Bank of Japan, 2006), 25.

79. Douglas A. Irwin, "Gold Sterilization and the Recession of 1937–38" (working paper, Dartmouth College and NBER, September 9, 2011).

80. William O. Douglas, *Go East, Young Man* (New York: Random House, 1974), 284; quoted in Janeway, *The Fall of the House of Roosevelt*, 37.

81. Jordan A. Schwarz, *Liberal: Adolf A. Berle and the Vision of an American Era* (New York: The Free Press, 1987), 111–13.

82. Michael Keaney, ed., *John Kenneth Galbraith: Economist with a Public Purpose* (New York: Routledge, 2004), 224.

83. Lauchlin Currie, *Memoirs* (1952), unpublished, p. 85; quoted in Roger J. Sandilands, *The Life and Political Economy of Lauchlin Currie: New Dealer, Political Advisor, and Development Expert* (Durham, NC: Duke University Press, 1990), 94.

84. Christina Romer, "What Ended the Great Depression?" *Journal of Economic History* 52, no. 4 (December 1992): 757.

85. Eggertsson et al., *The Mistake of 1937*.

86. US Bureau of the Census, *Historical Statistics of the United States: Colonial Times to 1957* (Washington, DC: US Government Printing Office, 1969); Michael Darby, "Three and a Half Million U.S. Employees Have Been Mislaid: Or an Explanation of Unemployment 1934–1941," *Journal of Political Economy* 84, no. 1 (February 1976): 1–16.

87. Edsforth, *The New Deal*, 287.

88. Figure 10.1, "WPA's Contribution to Infrastructure, 1935–43, Based on U.S. Federal Works Agency, Final Report on the WPA Program 1935–43 (Washington: Government Printing Office, 1947)," in Edsforth, *The New Deal*, 226.

89. Ronald W. Reagan, *Ronald Reagan: An American Life* (New York: Simon & Schuster, 1990), 69.

90. John Kenneth Galbraith, *The Economic Effects of the Federal Public Works Expenditures 1933–1938* (New York: Da Capo Press, 1975 [originally published in 1940]), 109.

91. E. Cary Brown, "Fiscal Policy in the 'Thirties: A Reappraisal," *American Economic Review* 46, no. 5 (December 1956): 867.

92. Ibid., 868–69.

93. Ibid., 866.

94. Robert Emmet Sherwood, *Roosevelt and Hopkins: An Intimate History* (New York: Bantam Books, 1950), 1:90.

95. John Easton, in "You're Gonna Have Lace Curtains," in WPA Federal Writers Project, *These Are Our Lives* (New York: W. W. Norton, 1975), 15–16; quoted in Bruce J. Schulman, *From Cotton Belt to Sunbelt: Federal Policy, Economic Development, and the Transformation of the South, 1938–1980* (Durham, NC: Duke University Press, 1994), 35.

96. Quoted in Edsforth, *The New Deal*, 216.

97. Schlesinger, *The Age of Roosevelt*, vol. 3, *The Politics of Upheaval*, 424.

98. Lyndon B. Johnson, "Remarks at the Municipal Park, South Gate, California, October 11, 1964," *Public Papers of the Presidents* (Washington, DC: United States Government Printing Office, 1966), 1963–1964, 2:1296; quoted in William E. Leuchtenberg, *In the Shadow of FDR: From Harry Truman to George W. Bush* (Ithaca, NY: Cornell University Press, 1983).

CHAPTER 12: ARSENAL OF DEMOCRACY

1. Quoted in Francis Walton, *Miracle of World War II: How American Industry Made Victory Possible* (New York: Macmillan, 1956), 42.

2. Quoted in *Look* Magazine Editors, *Oil for Victory: The Story of Petroleum in War and Peace* (New York: McGraw-Hill, 1946), 15.

3. Quoted in William E. Leuchtenberg, *Franklin D. Roosevelt and the New Deal: 1932–1940* (New York: Harper & Row, 1963), 74.

4. Franklin Delano Roosevelt, "Arsenal of Democracy" (speech, Washington, DC, December 29, 1940, http://teachingamericanhistory.org/library/index.asp?documentprint=657 (accessed November 15, 2011).

5. Harold G. Vatter, *The U.S. Economy in World War II* (New York: Columbia University Press, 1985), 3. See also Gerald T. White, *Billions for Defense: Government Financing by the Defense Plant Corporation During World War II* (University, AL: University of Alabama Press, 1980).

6. Wyatt Wells, *Antitrust and the Formation of the Postwar World* (New York: Columbia University Press, 2002), 70.

7. Vatter, *The U.S. Economy in World War II*, 14.

8. Jerome G. Poppers, *History of United States Military Logistics, 1935–1985* (Huntsville, AL: Logistics Education Foundation, 1988), 6.

9. J. M. Scammell, "History of the Industrial College of the Armed Forces 1924–1946" (unpublished manuscript, National Defense University Library, 1946), 5; quoted in Alan L. Gropman, *Mobilizing U.S. Industry in World War II: Myth and Reality* (Honolulu, HI: University Press of the Pacific, 2005), 12.

10. Donald M. Nelson, *Arsenal of Democracy* (New York: Harcourt, Brace, 1946), 87–88.

11. David M. Kennedy, *Freedom from Fear: The American People in World War II* (New York: Oxford University Press, 1999), 229.

12. Jim Lacey, *Keep from All Thoughtful Men: How U.S. Economists Won World War II* (Annapolis, MD: Naval Institute Press, 2011).

13. Vatter, *The U.S. Economy in World War II*, 29.

14. Wells, *Antitrust and the Formation of the Postwar World*, 74.

15. Vatter, *The U.S. Economy in World War II*, 147.

16. David Mowery and Nathan Rosenberg, "Twentieth-Century Technological Change," in *The Cambridge Economic History of the United States*, ed. Stanley L. Engerman and Robert E. Gallman, vol. 3, *The Twentieth Century* (Cambridge, UK: Cambridge University Press, 2000), 861.

17. Walton, *Miracle of World War II*, 340.

18. Daniel Yergin, *The Quest: Energy, Security, and the Remaking of the Modern World* (New York: Penguin Press, 2011), 229.

19. Fred M. Shelley et al., *Political Geography of the United States* (New York: Guilford Press, 1996), 88, 258.

20. Bruce J. Schulman, *From Cotton Belt to Sunbelt: Federal Policy, Economic*

Development, and the Transformation of the South, 1938–1980 (Durham, NC: Duke University Press, 1994), 63.

21. GlobalSecurity.org, "Michoud Assembly Facility," www.globalsecurity .org/facility/michoud.htm (accessed December 12, 2011).

22. Gropman, *Mobilizing U.S. Industry in World War II*, 3 and 28, note 12.

23. Steven R. Waddell, *United States Army Logistics: From the American Revolution to 9/11* (Santa Barbara, CA: ABC-CLIO, 2010), 129.

24. Vatter, *The U.S. Economy in World War II*, 17.

25. Ibid., 114.

26. Ibid., 120.

27. Ibid., 122.

28. Ibid., 124.

29. Redd Evans and John Jacob Loeb, "Rosie the Riveter" (1942): Paramount Music Corporation, NY.

30. "Women in Transportation: Changing America's History," United States Department of Transportation Web site, http://www.fhwa.dot.gov/wit/ rosie.htm (accessed December 8, 2011).

31. Maureen Honey, *Creating Rosie the Riveter: Class, Gender, and Propaganda During World War II* (Amherst: University of Massachusetts Press, 1984), 21.

32. Walton, *Miracle of World War II*, 380.

33. Vatter, *The U.S. Economy in World War II*, 20.

34. Quoted in Richard Polenberg, *War and Society: The United States, 1941– 1945* (Philadelphia: J. B. Lippincott, 1972), 124.

35. Lyn Crost, *Honor by Fire: Japanese Americans at War in Europe and the Pacific* (Novato, CA: Presidio Press, 1994), xiii.

36. Vatter, *The U.S. Economy in World War II*, 106.

37. Walton, *Miracle of World War II*, 540–41.

38. Mark Harrison, "The Economics of World War II: An Overview," in *The Economics of World War II: Six Great Powers in International Competition*, ed. Mark Harrison (Cambridge, UK: Cambridge University Press, 1998), 10.

39. Louis Galambos and Joseph Pratt, *The Rise of the Corporate Commonwealth: U.S. Business and Public Policy in the Twentieth Century* (New York: Basic Books, 1988), 157.

40. Gropman, *Mobilizing U.S. Industry in World War II*, 2.

41. Ibid.

42. Tables 185–86, in Wladimir S. Woytinsky and Emma Shadkhan Woytinsky, *World Population and Production: Trends and Outlook* (New York: Twentieth Century Fund, 1953); cited in Giovanni Arrighi, *The Long Twentieth Century* (New York: Verso, 1994), 275.

43. Waddell, *United States Army Logistics*, 129.

44. Gropman, *Mobilizing U.S. Industry in World War II*, 53n38.

45. Waddell, *United States Army Logistics*, 129.

46. Ibid.

47. Michael Lind, *The American Way of Strategy* (New York: Oxford University Press, 2006), 225.

48. Alan Milward, *War, Economy, and Society: 1939–1945* (Los Angeles: University of California Press, 1979), 75.

49. Quoted in "The Power Years: World War II and Texas Oil," *Hazardous Business: Industry, Regulation, and the Railroad Commission* (online exhibit; Austin: Texas State Library and Archives Commission), 2.

CHAPTER 13: THE GLORIOUS THIRTY YEARS

1. Adolf A. Berle, *The American Economic Republic* (New York: Harcourt, Brace & World, 1965 [originally published in 1963]), 91.

2. John Kenneth Galbraith, *The Affluent Society*, 40th anniversary edition, updated and with a new introduction by the author (New York: Houghton Mifflin, 1998).

3. Michael Lind, *The American Way of Strategy* (New York: Oxford University Press, 2006), 225.

4. Wyatt Wells, *Antitrust and the Formation of the Postwar World* (New York: Columbia University Press, 2002), 188–89.

5. Daniel Yergin, *The Quest: Energy, Security, and the Remaking of the Modern World* (New York: Penguin, 2011), 281–82. See also Daniel Yergin, *The Prize: The Epic Quest for Oil, Money, and Power* (New York: Free Press, 1991).

6. Wyatt Wells, *Antitrust and the Formation of the Postwar World* (New York: Columbia University Press, 2002), 193–94.

7. Ibid., 253n14.

8. Ibid., 196.

9. Vaclav Smil, *Oil: A Beginner's Guide* (Oxford: Oneworld Publications, 2008), 26.

10. Wells, *Antitrust and the Formation of the Postwar World*, 198–99.

11. Forrest McDonald, *Insull: The Rise and Fall of a Billionaire Utility Tycoon* (Washington, DC: Beard Books, 2004).

12. Twentieth Century Fund Power Committee, *Electric Power and Government Policy: A Summary of Relations Between the Government and Electric Power Industry* (New York: Twentieth Century Fund, 1948); Ronald C. Tobey, *Technology as Freedom: The New Deal and the Electrical Modernization of the American Home* (Berkeley: University of California Press, 1996).

13. Steven Solomon, *Water: The Epic Struggle for Wealth, Power, and Civilization* (New York: HarperCollins, 2010), 343.

14. Ibid., 343.

15. Ibid., 338 and 340.

16. Alexander J. Field, "The Origins of U.S. Total Factor Productivity Growth in the Golden Age," *Cliometrica* 1 (April 2007): 74n2.

17. Alan Lawson, *A Commonwealth of Hope: The New Deal Response to Crisis* (Baltimore: Johns Hopkins University Press, 2006), 102.

18. Quoted in David Lanier Lewis, *The Public Image of Henry Ford: An American Folk Hero and His Company* (Detroit, MI: Wayne State University Press, 1976), 163.

19. John P. Ferris, "Statement of the Present Attitude of TVA Concerning Industrial Development," memorandum to H. A. Morgan, September 5, 1933, Records of the Tennessee Valley Authority, RG 142, TVA Board File Curtis-Morgan-Morgan, FARC; quoted in Bruce J. Schulman, *From Cotton Belt to Sunbelt: Federal Policy, Economic Development, and the Transformation of the South, 1938–1980* (Durham, NC: Duke University Press, 1994), 35.

20. Lawson, *A Commonwealth of Hope*, 122–23.

21. Ray Kroc, *Grinding It Out: The Making of McDonald's* (Chicago: Contemporary Books, 1977), 10.

22. Martha Bianco, *Scott L. Bottles, Los Angeles, and the Automobile: The Making of the Modern City* (Berkeley: University of California Press, 1987).

23. Ibid., 18.

24. Wendell Cox, "Transit: The 4 Percent Solution," *New Geography.com*, May 26, 2011.

25. Quoted in Schulman, *From Cotton Belt to Sunbelt*, 220.

26. Quoted in ibid., 63.

27. Charles S. Aiken, *The Cotton Plantation South Since the Civil War* (Baltimore: Johns Hopkins University Press, 1998), 228.

28. Raymond A. Mohl, ed., *The Making of Urban America* (Wilmington, DE: Scholarly Resources, 1997), "Part Two: The Industrial City: Introduction," 221.

29. Table 2.5, "Income Per Worker as a Percentage of U.S. Average, by Sector, 1869–1955," in Peter George, *The Emergence of Industrial America: Strategic Factors in American Economic Growth Since 1870* (Albany: State University of New York Press, 1982), 18.

30. Table 2.6, "Per Capita Personal Income as a Percentage of U.S. Average, by Region, 1860–1960," in ibid., 191.

31. Stanley Lebergott, *Pursuing Happiness: American Consumers in the Twentieth Century* (Princeton, NJ: Princeton University Press, 1993), 101.

32. Table 8.1, "Housework, 1900–1975, by Weekly Hours," in ibid., 51.

33. Ibid., 58.

34. Ibid., 106–107.

35. Ibid., 109.

36. Ibid., 98.

37. Ibid., 67.

38. Robert Reich, *Supercapitalism: The Transformation of Business, Democracy, and Everyday Life* (New York: Alfred A. Knopf, 2007), 24.

39. Alfred D. Chandler, *The Visible Hand: The Managerial Revolution in American Business* (Cambridge, MA, and London: Harvard University Press, 1977), 482–83.

40. John Kenneth Galbraith, *The New Industrial State*, 4th ed. (Princeton, NJ: Princeton University Press, 2007), 93.

41. Ibid., 93.

42. Berle, *The American Economic Republic*.

43. Hugh Rockoff, "The United States: From Ploughshares to Swords," in *The Economics of World War II: Six Great Powers in International Competition*, ed. Mark Harrison (Cambridge, UK: Cambridge University Press, 1998), 104–105; Robert J. Gordon, "45 Billion of U.S. Private Investment Has Been Mislaid," *American Economic Review* 59, no. 3 (June 1969): 221–38.

44. Gerald T. White, "Financing Industrial Expansion for War: The Origin of the Defense Plan Corporation Leases," *Journal of Economic History* 9, no. 2 (November 1949): 156–83.

45. M. Morton, "History of Synthetic Rubber," in *History of Polymer Science and Technology*, ed. Raymond B. Seymour (New York: Marcel Dekker, 1982), 231, 235; David Mowery and Nathan Rosenberg, "Twentieth-Century Technological Change," in *The Cambridge Economic History of the United States*, ed. Stanley L. Engermann and Robert E. Gallman, vol. 3, *The Twentieth Century* (Cambridge, UK: Cambridge University Press, 2000), 857.

46. Galbraith, *The New Industrial State*, 103.

47. "Research and Development in Industry, 1974," National Science Foundation, September 1976; cited in Galbraith, *The New Industrial State*, 38–39n10.

48. William H. Becker, "Managerial Capitalism and Public Policy," *Business and Economic History*, 2nd ser., 21 (1992): 251.

49. Joint Economic Committee, US 87th Congress, 1st Session (1962), 40–41; quoted in Carlota Perez, *Technological Revolutions and Financial Capital: The Dynamics of Bubbles and Golden Ages* (Northampton, MA: Edward Elgar, 2002), 128.

50. Galbraith, *The New Industrial State*, 118.

51. Berle, *The American Economic Republic*, 75.

52. Galbraith, *The New Industrial State*.

53. John Berleau, "What's Good for GM Is Now Terrible for America," *The American Spectator Online*, http://spectator.org/archives/2010/11/18/whats-good-for-gm-is-now-terri (accessed December 8, 2011).

54. Quoted in *Fortune*, October 1951, 98–99; Reich, *Supercapitalism*, 45.

55. Quoted in Richard B. Freedman and James L. Medoff, *What Do Unions Do?* (New York: Basic Books, 1984), 4; Greg Hannsgen and Dimitri B. Papadimitriou, "Lessons from the New Deal: Did the New Deal Prolong or Worsen the Great Depression?" (working paper no. 581, The Levy Economics Institute of Bard College, October 2009), 11.

56. William Benton, speech to CED trustees, 1949, box 1518, OF 638-A, Truman MSS; quoted in Robert M. Collins, "American Corporatism: The Committee for Economic Development, 1942–1964," *The Historian* 44, no. 2 (February 1982): 171.

57. John Chamberlain, *The American Stakes* (New York: Carrick and Evans, 1940), 31–32; quoted in Daniel T. Rodgers, *Contested Truths: Keywords in American Politics Since Independence* (New York: Basic Books, 1987), 208.

58. Roger Lowenstein, "Siphoning GM's Future," *New York Times*, July 10, 2008.

59. R. Alton Gilbert, "Requiem for Regulation Q: What It Did and Why It Passed Away," *Federal Reserve Bank of St. Louis Review*, February 1986: 22–37.

60. Michael R. Haines and Richard H. Steckel, *A Population History of North America* (Cambridge, UK: Cambridge University Press, 2000), 643.

61. Table 14.5, "Occupational Distribution of Whites and Blacks, 1950 (Percentages)," in Ibid.

62. Ibid., 645.

63. Ibid., 644.

64. Ibid., 648.

65. Ibid., 649.

66. Ibid., 642.

67. Table 14.1, "Race-Nativity Distribution of U.S. Population, 1900 and 1950 (Percentages)" in ibid., 633.

68. Paul A. Samuelson, *Economics*, sixth edition (New York: McGraw-Hill, 1964), quoted in George J. Borjas, "The Labor Demand Curve Is Downward Sloping: Reexamining the Impact of Immigration on the Labor

Market" (Cambridge, MA: National Bureau of Economic Research), working paper 9755, 2.

69. See Vernon M. Briggs, *Immigration and American Unionism*, Cornell Studies in Industrial and Labor Relations (Ithaca, NY: Cornell University Press, 2001).

70. Haines and Steckel, *A Population History of North America*, 633.

71. California Rural Legal Assistance, "Major Victories: Highlights from CRLA's Proud History of Landmark Victories for the Poor," www.crla .org/major-victories (accessed December 13, 2011).

72. Quoted in *American Immigration*, vol. 6, *Home Sweatshops–Italians* (Danbury, CT: Grolier Educational, 1999), 41.

73. Quoted in Brian D. Behnken, *Fighting Their Own Battles: Mexican Americans, African Americans, and the Struggle for Civil Rights in Texas* (Chapel Hill: University of North Carolina Press, 2011), 105.

74. Quoted in Susan Ferriss and Ricardo Sandoval, *The Fight in the Fields: Cesar Chavez and the Farmworkers Movement* (New York: Harcourt Brace, 1997), 56.

75. Quoted in Richard Jay Jensen and and John C. Hammerback, eds., *The Words of Cesar Chavez* (College Station: Texas A&M University Press, 2002), 47.

76. Census.

77. Robert J. Samuelson, "Importing Poverty," *Washington Post*, September 5, 2007.

78. Martin Anderson quoted in Mike Feinsilber, "The Transition: Reagan Aide Claims Poverty in America Is Virtually Extinct," Associated Press, December 26, 1980.

79. Gareth Davies, *From Opportunity to Entitlement: The Transformation and Decline of Great Society Liberalism* (Lawrence: University Press of Kansas, 1996), 34.

80. Dwight D. Eisenhower, letter to Edgar Newton Eisenhower, November 8, 1954, in Eisenhower, *The Papers of Dwight D. Eisenhower* (Baltimore: Johns Hopkins University Press, 1996), Document 1147. World Wide Web facsimile by the Dwight D. Eisenhower Memorial Commis-

sion of the print edition http://www.eisenhowermemorial.org/presidential
-papers/first-term/documents/1147.cfm (accessed December 8, 2011).

81. Jonathan Hughes and Louis P. Cain, *American Economic History*, 5th ed. (New York: Addison-Wesley, 1998), 437.

82. Marc Allen Eisner, *From Warfare State to Welfare State: World War I, Compensatory State Building, and the Limits of the Modern Order* (University Park: Pennsylvania State University Press, 2000).

CHAPTER 14: THE GREAT DISMANTLING

1. Ronald Reagan, First Inaugural Address (speech, Washington, DC, January 20, 1981), http://www.bartleby.com/124/pres61.html (accessed November 14, 2011).

2. Suzanne McGee, *Chasing Goldman Sachs: How the Masters of the Universe Melted Wall Street Down . . . and Why They'll Take Us to the Brink Again* (New York: Crown Business, 2010), 257.

3. D. Ravenscraft and F. M. Scherer, *Mergers, Sell-Offs, and Economic Efficiency* (Washington, DC: Brookings Institution, 1987), 39; cited in William Lazonick and Mary O'Sullivan, "Finance and Industrial Development, part I: The United States and the United Kingdom," *Financial History Review* 4 (1997): 17.

4. W. R. Grace Web site, http://www.grace.com/Products/ (accessed December 8, 2011).

5. Lazonick and O'Sullivan, "Finance and Industrial Development," 17.

6. US Bureau of the Census, *Historical Statistics of the United States: Colonial Times to 1957* (Washington, DC: US Government Printing Office, 1969), 928; Lazonick and O'Sullivan, "Finance and Industrial Development," 17.

7. Alfred E. Eckes Jr., *Opening America's Market* (Chapel Hill: University of North Carolina Press, 1995), 154.

8. Ibid., 157.

9. Ibid., 158.

10. Unpublished pages from memoirs of Harry S. Truman, quoted in ibid., 158 and 324n69.

11. Memo to American diplomatic and counselor offices, "Promotion of United States Import Trade," September 11, 1946, ITF, RG43, US National Archives; cited in Eckes, *Opening America's Market*, 165 and 326n96.

12. US Public Advisory Board for Mutual Security, "A Trade and Tariff Policy in the National Interest" (the Bell Report), 1, 3, 66, quoted in Eckes, *Opening America's Market*, 166, and 326n101.

13. Eckes, *Opening America's Market*, 328n135; discussion of 409 meeting of the National Security Council, June 4, 1959, vol. 16 (1990), document 971, DDC.

14. Eckes, *Opening America's Market*, 179.

15. Eckes, *Opening America's Market*, 186 and 330n28; Public Papers ... Kennedy, 1961, 790–91.

16. "Task Force on Foreign Economic Policy," March 25, 1964, quoted in Eckes, *Opening America's Market*, 191–92 and 331n51.

17. "Clarence Randall Diary," Randall Papers, June 25, July 7, 15, 1954, DDE; quoted in Eckes, *Opening America's Market*, 168 and 326n106.

18. Walter Adams and James W. Brock, *The Bigness Complex: Industry, Labor, and Government in the American Economy* (New York: Pantheon, 1986), 384n27.

19. A. G. Kenwood and A. L. Lougheed, *The Growth of the International Economy, 1820–1980* (London: Allen & Unwin, 1983), 306.

20. Ibid.

21. K. Otabe, quoted in minutes of Japanese–United States negotiations, February 22–April 18, 1955, ITF, RG43, National Archives; cited in Eckes, *Opening America's Market*, 171 and 327n119.

22. Eckes, *Opening America's Market*, 173–74.

23. Ibid., 169.

24. Komiya, Okuno, Suzumura, Japanese Industrial Policy (1984/985); see also Chalmers Johnson (1984).

25. Yoko Sazanami, Shujiro Urata, and Hiroki Kawai, *Measuring the Costs of Protection in Japan* (Washington, DC: Institute for International Economics, 1995).

26. Vernon W. Ruttan, *Technology, Growth, and Development: An Induced Innovation Perspective* (New York: Oxford University Press, 2001), 344–45; M. Anchordoguy, *Computers Inc.: Japan's Challenge to IBM* (Cambridge, MA: Harvard University Press, 1989), 20.

27. Herman Schwartz, "Hegemony, International Debt and International Economic Instability," in Chronis Polychroniou, ed., *Perspectives and Issues in International Political Economy* (New York: Praeger, 1992).

28. Ibid.

29. Quoted in R. Taggart Murphy, *The Weight of the Yen: How Denial Imperils America's Fate and Ruins an Alliance* (New York: W. W. Norton, 1996), 201.

30. Box 8.1, "Transfer of Petrochemical Technology to Korea," in Ruttan, *Technology, Growth, and Development*, 305–307. See also J. L. Enos and W. H. Park, *The Adoption and Diffusion of Imported Technology: The Case of Korea* (London: Croom Helm, 1988); J. J. Stern, J. Kim, D. H. Perkins, and J.-H. Yoo, *Industrialization and the State: The Korean Heavy and Chemical Industry Drive* (Cambridge, MA: Harvard University Press, 1995).

31. Ha-Joon Chang, *Bad Samaritans: The Myth of Free Trade and the Secret History of Capitalism* (New York: Bloomsbury Press, 2008).

32. John F. Kennedy, "Inaugural Address" (speech, Washington, DC, January 20, 1961), http://www.bartleby.com/124/pres56.html (accessed November 2, 2011).

33. Richard Reeves, *President Nixon: Alone in the White House* (New York: Simon & Schuster, 2001), 341.

34. Leonard Silk and David Vogel, *Ethics and Profits: The Crisis of Confidence in American Business* (New York: Simon & Schuster, 1976), 21.

35. Ibid., 59.

36. Ibid., 57.

37. Ibid., 189.

38. Quoted in ibid., 72–73.

39. Ruttan, *Technology, Growth, and Development*, 330.

40. Ronald Reagan, "First Inaugural Address" (speech, Washington, DC,

January 20, 1981), http://www.freerepublic.com/focus/news/2178758/posts (accessed November 2, 2011).

41. "January 1965 Economic Report of the President," Joint Economic Committee, 89th Cong., 1st sess. (Washington, DC: US Government Printing Office, 1965), 13.

42. Stephen Wallace Taylor, "Technocracy on the March? The Tennessee Valley Authority and the Uses of Technology," in *Technology, Innovation, and Southern Industrialization: From the Antebellum Era to the Computer Age*, ed. Susanna Delfino and Michele Gillespie (Columbia and London: University of Missouri Press, 2008), 177–78.

43. Robert M. Collins, *More: The Politics of Growth in Postwar America* (Oxford: Oxford University Press, 2000), 173.

44. Allan H. Meltzer, *A History of the Federal Reserve*, vol. 2, bk. 2, *1970–1986* (Chicago: University of Chicago Press, 2010), 925.

45. US Bureau of the Census (1980), table 679.

46. Peter Temin, *Free Land and Federalism: American Economic Exceptionalism* (Cambridge, MA: MIT Press, 1988), 386; Peter Temin, *The Fall of the Bell System: A Study in Prices and Politics* (New York: Cambridge University Press, 1987).

47. Steven A. Morrison and Clifford Winston, "The Remaining Role for Government Policy in the Deregulated Airline Industry," in *Deregulation of Network Industries: What's Next?*, ed. Sam Peltzman and Clifford Winston (Washington, DC: Brookings Institution, 2000), 9.

48. Jose A. Gomez Ibanez, *Regulating Infrastructure: Monopoly, Contracts and Discretion* (Cambridge, MA: Harvard University Press, 2003), 206–207.

49. US General Accounting Office, "Airline Competition: High Fares and Reduced Competition at Concentrated Airports," report GAO/RCED 90–102, July 1990.

50. Paul Stephen Dempsey, "The Experience of Deregulation: Erosion of the Common Carrier System," *Transportation Law Institute* 13 (1981): 121, 172–75; Paul Stephen Dempsey, *Airline Deregulation and Laissez-Faire Mythology* (Westport, CT: Quorum Books, 1992), 8–9n11.

51. "The California Crisis: California Timeline," PBS Frontline Web site, http://www.pbs.org/wgbh/pages/frontline/shows/blackout/california/timeline.html (accessed December 8, 2011).

52. S. David Freeman testimony, in "Examining Enron: Developments Regarding Electricity Price Manipulation in California," Hearing Before the Subcommittee on Consumer Affairs, Foreign Commerce, and Tourism of the Committee on Commerce, Science, and Transportation, United States Senate, One Hundred Seventh Congress, Second Session, May 15, 2002 (Washington, DC: US Government Printing Office, 2004).

53. Michael French, *U.S. Economic History Since 1945* (New York: Manchester University Press, 1997), 138.

54. Gerald F. Davis, *Managed by the Markets: How Finance Reshaped America* (New York: Oxford University Press, 2009), 114.

55. Ibid., 119.

56. Michal Kalecki, "Political Aspects of Full Employment," *Political Science Quarterly* 14 (1943), in Michal Kalecki, *Selected Essays on the Dynamics of the Capitalist Economy* (Cambridge, UK: Cambridge University Press, 1971).

57. Quoted in Nick Cohen, "Gambling with Our Future," *New Statesman*, January 13, 2003; Robert Wade, "The Economy Has Not Solved Its Problems," *Challenge* (March/April 2011): 34.

58. E. Ray Canterberry, *Wall Street Capitalism: The Theory of the Bondholding Class* (Singapore: World Scientific Publishing, 2000), 89.

59. Quoted in William Greider, *Secrets of the Temple: How the Federal Reserve Runs the Country* (New York: Simon & Schuster, 1987), 648.

60. Murphy, *The Weight of the Yen*, 192.

61. David Hale, "The Japanese Ministry of Finance and Dollar Diplomacy During the Late 1980's or How the University of Tokyo Law School Saved America from the University of Chicago Economics Department" (unpublished paper, Kemper Financial Services, Chicago, July 1989), 1; quoted in Murphy, *The Weight of the Yen*, 219.

62. Bruce Bartlett, "Supply-Side Economics: Voodoo Economics or Lasting Contribution?" Laeffer Associates Supply Side Investment Research, Nov-

ember 11, 2003, http://web2.uconn.edu/cunningham/econ309/lafferpdf .pdf (accessed November 2, 2011).

63. "Rosen Distorted Defense Spending During Carter Presidency," Colorado Media Matters, January 23, 2007, http://colorado.mediamatters.org/ items/200701240002 (accessed November 2, 2011).

CHAPTER 15: AS WE MAY THINK: THE THIRD INDUSTRIAL REVOLUTION

1. Vannevar Bush, *Science: The Endless Frontier* (Washington, DC: National Science Foundation, 1960 [originally published in 1945]), 10.

2. *The Book of the Record of the Time Capsule* (New York: Westinghouse Electric & Manufacturing Company, 1938); *Official Guide, New York World's Fair 1964/1965* (New York: Time-Life Books, 1964); "1939 Westinghouse Time Capsule Complete List Contents," *New York Times*, "Looking Forward, Looking Back," www.nytimes.com/ specials/magazine3/items.html (accessed December 12, 2011).

3. Quoted in Charles Thorpe, *Oppenheimer: The Tragic Intellect* (Chicago: University of Chicago Press, 2006), 161.

4. Vannevar Bush, "As We May Think," *Atlantic*, July 1945.

5. James M. Nyce and Paul Kahn, *From Memex to Hypertext: Vannevar Bush and the Mind's Machine* (New York: Harcourt Brace Jovanovich, 1991), 261.

6. Quoted in G. Pascal Zachary, *Endless Frontier: Vannevar Bush, Engineer of the American Century* (New York: Free Press, 1997), 356.

7. Vannevar Bush, *Pieces of the Action* (New York: Morrow, 1970), 31–32.

8. Franklin Delano Roosevelt, *Whither Bound?* (Boston and New York: Houghton Mifflin, 1926).

9. Zachary, *Endless Frontier*, 218.

10. Vannevar Bush, *Science, the Endless Frontier: A Report to the President by Vannevar Bush, Director of the Office of Scientific Research and Development, July 1945* (Washington, DC: US Government Printing Office, 1945).

11. Zachary, *Endless Frontier*, 201.

12. Edward W. Constant II, *The Origins of the Turbojet Revolution* (Baltimore: Johns Hopkins University Press, 1980), 188.

13. Ibid., 207.

14. Richard A. Leyes II and William A. Fleming, *The History of North American Small Gas Turbine Aircraft Engines* (Washington, DC: Smithsonian Institution, 1999), 236–37.

15. John E. Steiner, "Jet Aviation Development: A Company Perspective," in *The Jet Age: Forty Years of Jet Aviation*, ed. Walter J. Boyne and Donald S. Lopez (Washington, DC: National Air and Space Museum/Smithsonian, 1979), 142; Peter J. Hugill, *Global Communications Since 1844* (Baltimore: Johns Hopkins University Press, 1999), 290.

16. Vaclav Smil, *Oil: A Beginner's Guide* (Oxford: Oneworld Publications, 2008), 12.

17. Gerard J. DeGroot, *Dark Side of the Moon: The Magnificent Madness of the American Lunar Quest* (New York: New York University Press, 2006), 34.

18. *Scientific American*, June 1960.

19. Hugill, *Global Communications Since 1844*, 233.

20. Larry Owen, "Vannevar Bush and the Differential Analyzer: The Text and Context of an Early Computer," in Nyce and Kahn, *From Memex to Hypertext*, 3–5.

21. Ibid.

22. Vernon W. Ruttan, *Technology, Growth, and Development: An Induced Innovation Perspective* (New York: Oxford University Press, 2001), 316–17.

23. Ibid., 320.

24. Richard S. Tedlow, *The Watson Dynasty: The Fiery Reign and Troubled Legacy of IBM's Founding Father and Son* (New York: HarperBusiness, 2003), 103.

25. "World's Most Admired Companies," *CNN Money*, 2011.

26. "THINK: The Story of IBM," *Atari Archives*, http://www.atariarchives .org/deli/think.php (accessed November 2, 2011).

27. Martin Campbell-Kelly and William Aspray, *Computer: A History of the Information Machine* (New York: Basic Books, 1996), 127.

28. J. Carlton Gallawa, *The Complete Microwave Oven Service Handbook* (New York: Prentice-Hall, 2007).

29. Aron Clark, "The First PC," *Wired*, December 2000.

30. Richard N. Langlois, "External Economies and Economic Progress: The Case of the Microcomputer Industry," *Business History Review* 66 (1992), 14.

31. Daniel Yergin, *The Quest: Energy, Security, and the Remaking of the Modern World* (New York: Penguin, 2011), 553–54.

32. Nyce and Kahn, *From Memex to Hypertext*, 235.

33. Dylan Tweney, "Dec. 9, 1968: The Mother of All Demos," *Wired.com*, http://www.wired.com/science/discoveries/news/2008/12/dayintech_1209 (accessed November 2, 2011).

34. Theodore H. Nelson, "As We Will Think," in Nyce and Kahn, *From Memex to Hypertext*.

35. J. C. R. Licklider, *Libraries of the Future* (Cambridge, MA: MIT Press, 1965), xii.

CHAPTER 16: THE BUBBLE ECONOMY

1. James Foreman-Peck, *A History of the World Economy: International Economic Relations Since 1850* (Totowa, NJ: Barnes & Noble Books, 1983), 383.

2. Peter J. Hugill, *World Trade Since 1431* (Baltimore: Johns Hopkins University Press, 1993), 283.

3. Vaclav Smil, *Two Prime Movers of Globalization* (Cambridge, MA: MIT Press, 2000), 392.

4. Ibid., 382–83.

5. Ibid., 382.

6. Ibid., 389.

7. Ibid., 390.

8. Nelson Lichtenstein, "Wal-Mart: A Template for Twenty-first Century Capitalism," in Nelson Lichtenstein, ed., *Wal-Mart: The Face of Twenty-First Century Capitalism* (New York: New Press, 2005).

9. Smil, *Two Prime Movers of Globalization*, 391.

10. Thomas I. Palley, "The Rise and Fall of Export-Led Growth," working paper no. 6575 (Annandale-on-Hudson: Levy Institute of Bard College, July 2011).

11. Table 1, "Globalization Waves in the 19th and 20th Century," in *World Trade Report 2008: Trade in a Globalizing World* (Geneva, Switzerland: World Trade Organization, 2008), 15.

12. Peter Nolan and Jin Zhang, "Global Competition After the Financial Crisis," *New Left Review* 64 (July–August 2010): 99.

13. Vaclav Smil, *Global Catastrophes and Trends: The Next 50 Years* (Cambridge, MA: MIT Press, 2008), 164.

14. Nolan and Zhang, "Global Competition After the Financial Crisis," 102.

15. Michael Dooley, David Folkerts-Landau, and Peter Garber, *International Financial Stability: Asia, Interest Rates, and the Dollar* (New York: Deutsche Bank AG, 2005); Richard N. Cooper, "Living with Global Imbalances," *Brookings Papers on Economic Activity* 2 (2007): 91–107.

16. Smil, *Two Prime Movers of Globalization*, 389.

17. David O. Beim, "The Future of Chinese Growth," January 24, 2011, 4, http://ssrn.com/abstract=1635400 (accessed October 6, 2011).

18. Philip Lagerkranser, "China Banks Surge to World's Biggest May Be Too Good to Be True," *Bloomberg.com*, April 29, 2009.

19. Doug Palmer, "U.S. Raises Concerns About China's State-Owned Firms," Reuters, May 3, 2011, http://www.bloomberg.com/apps/news?pid=newsarchive&sid=aYQg0d5NANkM (accessed November 14, 2011).

20. Janet Ong, "China Tells Telecom Companies to Merge in Overhaul (Update 1)," *Bloomberg.com*, May 25, 2008.

21. Maurice Obstfeld and Kenneth Rogoff, "Global Imbalances and the Financial Crisis: Products of Common Causes," Paper Prepared for the Federal Reserve Bank of San Francisco Asia Economic Policy Conference, Santa Barbara, CA, October 18–20 (November 2009): 18–19.

22. Ibid., 5.

23. Stephen S. Cohen and J. Bradford DeLong, *The End of Influence* (New York: Basic Books, 2010), 93.

24. Alan Tonelson, "Obama's Trade Fantasyland: Lack of Exports to Mer-

cantilist East Asia Is America's Fault," *AmericanEconomicAlert.org*, November 26, 2009, http://www.americaneconomicalert.org/view_art .asp?Prod_ID=3354 (accessed October 6, 2011).

25. Eric Janszen, *The Post-Catastrophe Economy: Rebuilding America and Avoiding the Next Bubble* (New York: Penguin, 2010), 35.

26. Andrew Glyn, *Capitalism Unleashed: Finance Globalization and Welfare* (Oxford: Oxford University Press, 2006), 83.

27. Cohen and DeLong, *The End of Influence*, 110.

28. "Manufacturing share of employment (1970–2009," http://stats.oecd.org/ index.aspx (accessed January 6, 2012).

29. Robert Wade, "The Economy Has Not Solved Its Problems," *Challenge* 54, no. 2 (March–April 2011): 17.

30. Simon Johnson and James Kwak, *13 Bankers: The Wall Street Takeover and the Next Financial Meltdown* (New York: Pantheon, 2010), 12.

31. Gerald Frederick Davis, *Managed by the Markets: How Finance Reshaped America* (New York: Oxford University Press, 2009), 105–106.

32. Johnson and Kwak, *13 Bankers*, 85.

33. Yves Smith, *ECONned* (New York: Palgrave, 2010), 140.

34. John Arlidge, "I'm Doing 'God's Work,' Meet Mr. Goldman Sachs," London *Sunday Times*, November 8, 2009.

35. Amar Bhide, *A Call for Judgment: Sensible Finance for a Dynamic Economy* (New York: Oxford University Press, 2010), 286–87.

36. Alan Greenspan, "Government Regulation and Derivative Contracts" (speech, Financial Markets Conference of the Federal Reserve Bank of Atlanta, Coral Gables, FL, February 21, 1997).

37. Gordon Fairclough, "As Barriers Fall in Auto Business, China Jumps In," *Wall Street Journal*, November 7, 2006; cited in Gerald F. Davis, *Managed by the Markets: How Finance Reshaped America* (New York: Oxford University Press, 2009), 200.

38. Table 3.1, "Ten Largest US-Based Corporate Employers, 1960–2007," in Davis, *Managed by the Markets*, 89.

39. US Congress, Economic Report of the President, 1996 (Washington, DC: US Government Printing Office, 1996), 343 and 360; cited in Wil-

liam Lazonick and Mary O'Sullivan, "Finance and Industrial Development, Part I: The United States and the United Kingdom," *Financial History Review* 4 (1997): 20.

40. William Lazonick, *Sustainable Prosperity in the New Economy?* (Kalamazoo, MI: W. E. Upjohn Institute for Employment Research, 2009), 12.

41. Ibid.

42. Gerald F. Davis, "A New Finance Capitalism? Mutual Funds and Ownership Re-concentration in the United States," *European Management Review* 5, no. 1 (Spring 2008): 17.

43. Davis, *Managed by the Markets*, 213.

44. Matteo Tonnello, *Revisiting Stock Market Short Termism* (New York: Conference Board, 2006), 3, citing John R. Graham, R. Harvey Campbell, and Rajgopal Shivaram, "The Economic Implications of Corporate Financial Reporting," *Journal of Accounting and Economics* 4 (December 2005): 3–73; cited in Lawrence E. Mitchell, *The Speculation Economy: How Finance Triumphed over Industry* (San Francisco: Berrett-Koehler, 2008), 278.

45. Mitchell, *The Speculation Economy*, 277.

46. Ibid.

47. Quoted in Mark Maremont and Charles Forelle, "Bosses' Pay: How Stock Options Became Part of the Problem," *Wall Street Journal*, December 27, 2006.

48. Davis, *Managed by the Markets*, 243.

49. Stephen S. Cohen and J. Bradford DeLong, *The End of Influence: What Happens When Other Countries Have the Money?* (New York: Basic Books, 2010), 112; Thomas Philippon and Ariell Reshef, "Wages and Human Capital in the U.S. Financial Industry: 1909–2006" (Cambridge, MA: The National Bureau of Economic Research, 2009), working paper no. 14644.

50. Figure 4-1, "Real Average Annual Compensation, Banking vs. Private Sector Overall," in Johnson and Kwak, *13 Bankers*, 115.

51. Greg Ip, "Income-Inequality Gap Widens," *Wall Street Journal*, October 12, 2007; Davis, *Managed by the Markets*, 207.

52. Peter Drucker, "The New Society I: Revolution by Mass Production," *Harper's*, September 1949, 27.

53. Quoted in Eric J. Weiner, *What Goes Up: The Uncensored History of Wall Street as Told by the Bankers, Brokers, CEOs, and Scoundrels Who Made It Happen* (New York: Little, Brown, 2005), 31.

54. Claudia Goldin and L. Katz, "Transitions: Career and Family Life Cycles of the Educational Elite," *American Economic Review* 98, no. 2 (2008): 363–69.

55. Gar Mudmundsson, "How Might the Current Financial Crisis Shape Financial Sector Regulation and Structure?" (keynote address, Financial Technology Conference, Boston, September 23, 2008), http://www.bis.org/speeches/sp081119.htm (accessed October 6, 2011).

56. James K. Galbraith and Travis Hale, "The Evolution of Economic Inequality in the United States, 1969–2007: Evidence from Data on Inter-industrial Earnings and Inter-Regional Income," University of Texas Inequality Project Working Paper no. 57 (Austin: Lyndon B. Johnson School of Public Affairs, February 2, 2009).

57. Steven M. Yoder, "Airline, Auto Industries: Pension Protection Act Leaves Door Open to Bankruptcies, Mass Payouts," *Bankruptcy Strategist*, February 2007.

58. Phyllis C. Borzi, "Retiree Health VEBAs: A New Twist on an Old Paradigm; Implications for Retirees, Unions and Employers," Henry J. Kaiser Family Foundation, March 2009.

59. Davis, *Managed by the Markets*, 204.

60. Christopher Howard, *The Hidden Welfare State: Tax Expenditures and Social Policy in the United States* (Princeton, NJ: Princeton University Press, 2007).

61. Lawrence Mishel, "Where Has All the Income Gone? Look Up," Economic Policy Institute, March 3, 2010, http://www.epi.org/publication/where_has_all_the_income_gone_look_up/ (accessed October 6, 2011).

62. Andrea Orr, "At the Top: Soaring Incomes, Falling Tax Rates," Economic Policy Institute, April 7, 2010, http://www.epi.org/publication/for_americas_top_earners_growing_incomes_falling_tax_rates/ (accessed October 6, 2011).

63. Ibid.

64. Andrea Orr and Anna Turner, "Small Group Takes Large Slice of Capital Income," Economic Policy Institute, April 14, 2010, http://www.epi.org/publication/small_group_takes_large_slice_of_capital_income/ (accessed October 6, 2011).

65. Robert Wade, "The Economy Has Not Solved Its Problems," *Challenge* 54, no. 2 (March/April 2011): 25–26.

66. Ajay Kapur, Niall MacLeod, and Narendra Singh, "Plutonomy: Buying Luxury, Explaining Global Imbalances," Citigroup Global Markets, October 16, 2005, 1–2.

67. Rick Newman, "Why Rich Consumers Matter More," *U.S. News Online*, December 3, 2009, http://money.usnews.com/money/blogs/flowchart/2009/12/03/why-rich-consumers-matter-more (accessed October 6, 2011).

68. Menzie D. Chinn and Jeffrey A. Frieden, *Lost Decades: The Making of America's Debt Crisis and the Long Recovery* (New York: W. W. Norton, 2011), 103–104.

69. WSJ Staff, "Barney Frank Celebrates Free Market Day," *Wall Street Journal*, September 17, 2008.

70. Dean Baker, *The End of Loser Liberalism: Making Markets Progressive* (Washington, DC: Center for Economic and Policy Research, 2011), 18–19.

71. Alan Blinder and Mark Zandi, "How the Great Recession Was Brought to an End," www.economy.com/mark-zandi/documents/End-of-Great-Recession.pdf (accessed July 27, 2010).

72. Jeffrey Sachs, "Two Parties, No Solutions to Jobs," *Huffington Post*, September 16, 2011.

73. Chinn and Frieden, *Lost Decades*, 148.

74. Ibid., 155.

75. Lawrence Michel, "Huge Disparity in Share of Total Wealth Gain Since 1983," Economic Snapshot, Economic Policy Institute, September 15, 2011, http://www.epi.org/publication/large-disparity-share-total-wealth-gain/ (accessed October 6, 2011).

CHAPTER 17: THE NEXT AMERICAN ECONOMY

1. Joseph Schumpeter, *Capitalism, Socialism, and Democracy* (New York and London: Harper and Brothers, 1942), 82–83.

2. Theodore Roosevelt, "Who Is a Progressive?" (speech delivered in April 1912 in Louisville, KY), www.teachingamericanhistory.org (accessed November 1, 2011).

3. "FTZ Facts and Features," Port Authority of New York and New Jersey, www.panynj.gov (accessed November 1, 2011).

4. Carmen M. Reinhart and Kenneth Rogoff, *This Time Is Different: Eight Centuries of Financial Folly* (Princeton, NJ: Princeton University Press, 2009).

5. Ronald Bailey, "Post-Scarcity Prophet," *Reason*, December 2001.

6. The figures are from Jesse Ausubel, quoted in Ronald Bailey, "The Kyoto Protocol Launches! But Will It Matter?" *Reason.com*, February 16, 2005.

7. Adam Smith, *The Wealth of Nations* (Indianapolis: Liberty Classics, 1976), 1:343.

8. Congress of the United States, Office of Technology Assessment, "Innovation and Commercialization of Emerging Technologies," September 1995, OTA-BP-ITC-165 (Washington, DC: U.S. Government Printing Office, September 1995), 4.

9. Ronald Bailey, "Post-Scarcity Prophet," *Reason*, December 2001.

10. Chart 1 from Evan Koening, "U.S. Economy Productivity Growth," www.dallasfed.org.

11. J. Bradford DeLong, "Productivity Growth in the 2000s," Draft 1.2, www.j-bradford-delong.net, March 2002.

12. Susan N. Houseman, "Offshoring and Import Price Measurement," *Survey of Current Business* (February 2011): 7–11l; Susan N. Houseman, Christopher Kurz, Paul Lengermann, and Benjamin Mandel, "Offshoring Bias in U.S. Manufacturing," *Journal of Economic Perspectives* 25, no. 2 (2011): 111–32; Michael Mandel and Susan Houseman, "Not All Productivity Gains Are the Same. Here's Why," What Matters/McKinsey&Company, June 1, 2011.

13. Michael Lind, "Public Purpose Finance: Investing in America's Future Through Regional Economic Development Banks" (Washington, DC: New America Foundation, September 9, 2010).

14. Adam Smith, *The Wealth of Nations*, 334.

15. Jesse Jenkins, Devon Swezey, and Yael Borofsky, "Where Good Technologies Come From," Case Studies in Innovation, Breakthrough Institute, December 2010.

16. Lind, "Public Purpose Finance."

17. Michael Lind, "Mailing Our Way to Solvency," *New York Times*, October 5, 2008.

18. *The Papers of Alexander Hamilton*, ed. Harold C. Syrett et al. (New York: Columbia University Press, 1963), 3:419, quoted in Frank Bourgin, *The Great Challenge: The Myth of Laissez-Faire in the Early Republic* (New York: George Braziller, 1989), 80.

19. Quoted in Michael Lind, "Healthcare Can Get America Working," *Financial Times*, September 24, 2009.

20. Congressional Budget Office (CBO), Figure 2-1, "Total Spending for Health Care Under CBO's Extended-Baseline Scenario," in "The Long-Term Budget Outlook," June 2009; Michael Lind and David McNamee, *The American Social Contract: A Promise to Fulfill* (Washington, DC: New America Foundation, 2008), 46–47.

21. Lyndon Baines Johnson, "Remarks at the Signing of the Immigration Bill" (speech, Liberty Island, New York, October 3, 1965), http://www.lbjlib.utexas.edu/johnson/archives.hom/speeches.hom/651003.asp (accessed December 8, 2011).

22. George Washington, "Circular to the States," June 8, 1783, in *The Writings of George Washington from the Original Manuscript Sources, 1745–1799*, 39 vols., ed. John C. Fitzpatrick (Washington, DC: US Government Printing Office, 1931), 44.

23. Franklin Delano Roosevelt, "Acceptance Speech for the Re-Nomination of the Presidency," June 27, 1936, in *Great Speeches*, ed. John Grafton (Mineola, NY: Dover, 1999), 47–51.

24. Roy P. Basler, ed., *The Collected Works of Abraham Lincoln*, 8 vols. (New Brunswick, NJ: Rutgers University Press, 1953), 5: 357.

INDEX